Be prepared...
Master the test...
Score high...

Get **REA**dy. It all starts here.
REA's test prep helps get you into
the Catholic high school of your choice.

We'd like to hear from you!

*Visit **www.rea.com** to send us your comments
or email us at **info@rea.com**.*

REA: THE TEST PREP TEACHERS RECOMMEND

2ND Edition

CATHOLIC HIGH SCHOOL ENTRANCE EXAMS

COOP • HSPT • TACHS

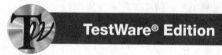

TestWare® Edition

Shannon Grey, Ed.D.
Faculty Lecturer
Princeton University
Princeton, NJ

Pauline Alexander-Travis, Ph.D.
Assistant Professor of Reading
Southwestern Oklahoma State University
Weatherford, OK

David Bell, Ed.D.
Professor of Education
Arkansas Technical University
Russellville, AR

Research & Education Association
Visit our website: www.rea.com

Planet Friendly Publishing
✔ Made in the United States
✔ Printed on Recycled Paper
Text: 30%   Cover: 10%
Learn more: www.greenedition.org

GREEN EDITION

At REA we're committed to producing books in an Earth-friendly manner and to helping our customers make greener choices.

Manufacturing books in the United States ensures compliance with strict environmental laws and eliminates the need for international freight shipping, a major contributor to global air pollution.

And printing on recycled paper helps minimize our consumption of trees, water and fossil fuels. This book was printed on paper made with **30% post-consumer waste** and the cover was printed on paper made with **10% post-consumer waste**. According to Environmental Defense's Paper Calculator, by using this innovative paper instead of conventional papers, we achieved the following environmental benefits:

Trees Saved: 33 • **Air Emissions Eliminated: 7,619 pounds**
Water Saved: 6,251 gallons • **Solid Waste Eliminated: 2,249 pounds**

For more information on our environmental practices, please visit us online at **www.rea.com/green**

Research & Education Association
61 Ethel Road West
Piscataway, New Jersey 08854
E-mail: info@rea.com

Catholic High School Entrance Exams:
COOP • HSPT • TACHS
with TestWare® on CD-ROM

Printed in the United States of America

Library of Congress Control Number 2009940931

ISBN-13: 978-0-7386-0667-5
ISBN-10: 0-7386-0667-7

Windows® is a registered trademark of Microsoft Corporation.

REA® and TestWare® are registered trademarks of Research & Education Association, Inc.

Contents

About the Author

Shannon Grey, Ed.D., earned her Bachelor of Science degree in early childhood development from New York University; her Master of Education, Elementary/Language Arts from Rutgers, The State University; and her Doctorate of Education, Sociology and Philosophical Foundations of Education Specialization in Curriculum Theory and Development from Rutgers, The State University. Dr. Grey has been an elementary school teacher, a curriculum developer, and staff trainer for kindergarten through 12th grade faculty members, staff, and administrators. She holds a permanent Supervisor Certificate, Teacher Pre-K to Grade 6 in New Jersey and New York. She currently is a faculty lecturer at Princeton University.

About Research & Education Association

Founded in 1959, Research & Education Association is dedicated to publishing the finest and most effective educational materials—including software, study guides, and test preps—for students in middle school, high school, college, graduate school, and beyond.

REA's Test Preparation series includes books and software for all academic levels in almost all disciplines. Research & Education Association publishes test preps for students who have not yet completed high school, as well as high school students preparing to enter college. Students from countries around the world seeking to attend college in the United States will find the assistance they need in REA's publications. For college students seeking advanced degrees, REA publishes test preps for many major graduate school admission examinations in a wide variety of diciplines, including engineering, law, and medicine. Students at every level, in every field, with every ambition can find what they are looking for among REA's publications.

REA's practice tests are always based upon the most recently administered exams and include every type of question that you can expect on the actual exams.

REA's publications and educational materials are highly regarded and continually receive an unprecedented amount of praise from professionals, instructors, librarians, parents, and students. Our authors are as diverse as the fields represented in the books we publish. They are well-known in their respective disciplines and serve on the faculties of prestigious high schools, colleges, and universities throughout the United States and Canada.

Today, REA's wide-ranging catalog is a leading resource for teachers, students, and professionals.

We invite you to visit us at *www.rea.com* to find out how "REA is making the world smarter."

Contributors

Anita P. Davis of Converse College, Spartanburg, SC; Mitchel G. Fedak of Community College of Allegheny County, Monroeville, PA; Mel Friedman of Delaware Valley College, Doylestown, PA; Robert F. Herrmann of Elmhurst College, Elmhurst, IL; Rev. Mr. Scott E. McCue of University of St. Mary of the Lake, Mundelein Seminary, Mundelein, IL; Michael Modugno of Piscataway High School, Piscataway, NJ; George C. Oluikpe of Friends of Crown Heights Educational Center #2, Brooklyn, NY; Mark Shapiro of University of Hartford, West Hartford, CT; Donna Stelluto of New Brunswick Public Schools Adult Learning Center, New Brunswick, NJ; C. Laurie Walsh of Round Valley Middle School, Lebanon, NJ; Brian Walsh of Rutgers University, New Brunswick, NJ; and Christine Zardecki of Rutgers University, New Brunswick, NJ; Linda Flint, Regina Gelinas, Robert Gelinas, Lorraine Ghignone, Joyce Kirchin, Joe Mancini, Melissa Pellerano, Dana Petrie, Christopher Pizzino, Peter Sharma, Erin Spanier, and James Quinlan.

Acknowledgments

In addition to our author, we would like to thank Larry B. Kling, Vice President, Editorial, for his overall direction; Pam Weston, Vice President, Publishing, for setting the quality standards for production integrity and managing the publication to completion; John Cording, Vice President, Technology, for coordinating the design and development of REA's TestWare® software; Michael Reynolds, Managing Editor, for project management; Heena Patel, Technology Project Manager, for software testing; Christine Saul, Senior Graphic Artist, for designing our cover; and S4Carlisle Publishing Services, for designing and typesetting this edition.

Introductory Letter to Students

Dear Student,

It is terrific that you have decided to prepare for your upcoming test with REA's *The Best Test Preparation for the Catholic High School Entrance Exams* book. Starting high school is a big moment in your life! Success always requires <u>focus</u>, <u>hard work</u>, and <u>preparation.</u> This book has been carefully developed to assist you in reaching your goal of obtaining a high score on the Cooperative Admissions Exam (COOP), High School Placement Test (HSPT), and the Test for Admission into Catholic High Schools (TACHS). With the support of this book, studying for your exam will help you to develop good habits that will serve you well throughout your high school years.

One important feature that the three tests represented in this book have in common is that they require you to *apply* your skills and knowledge. The questions are aimed at determining your ability to solve problems; make comparisons and inferences; comprehend text; and compute, recognize, and estimate. That's a challenge for anyone! Since you will not know exactly what's on the test, you will need to be prepared to face a variety of questions and formats. Taking the practice tests provided in REA's COOP/HSPT/TACHS preparation guide will give you the much needed experience of test taking. The practice tests mirror the actual exams, and the detailed answer explanations will clarify your understanding of concepts. You will find the foundation you need to enrich or complete your knowledge base in the thorough review sections. These chapters are designed to address concepts and skills required by the three exams. Sometimes topics overlap between two exams, some are found in only one exam, while others are included in all three. This provides you with a more comprehensive study experience. No matter which test(s) you take, in this book you will find the support you need to achieve great success.

There is enjoyment found in every challenge. Take this opportunity to learn, take pleasure in your work—and reap the rewards!

Best of luck,
Shannon Grey, Ed.D.

Our journey begins. . . .

A Look at the Three Exams

As mentioned in the opening, there are similarities and differences among the three tests addressed by this book. For instance, the HSPT, COOP, and TACHS all assess literacy skills, mathematical skills, and logical-analytical skills. You will be required to demonstrate your ability to comprehend passages and recognize vocabulary for the exams. However, some of the specific areas such as spelling, punctuation, and word categorization are represented only in the HSPT and TACHS.

For the HSPT, COOP, and TACHS you will also need to problem-solve, compute, and make comparisons in their Mathematics sections. Additionally, the COOP includes a subtest of Quantitative Reasoning, while the TACHS has a subtest titled Ability, which addresses spatial and visual understandings. Both of these sections are quite different than the more traditional computation-based aspects of the three mathematics subtests.

Please consider that the HSPT, COOP, and TACHS do differ in some important ways. Questions are posed differently, the tests are organized differently, and the timing and number of questions vary as well. The chart below should help to clarify how the exams compare.

Organization and Topics for the HSPT, COOP, and TACHS

The HSPT—approximately 298 questions during 3½ hours of allotted time, including breaks

Section	Questions	Time Length
Verbal	60	16 minutes
Quantitative	52	30 minutes
Reading	62	25 minutes
Mathematics	64	45 minutes
Language	60	25 minutes

The COOP—approximately 180 questions during 4½ hours of allotted time, including breaks

Section	Questions	Time Length
Sequences	20	15 minutes
Analogies	20	7 minutes
Quantitative Reasoning	20	15 minutes
Verbal Reasoning—Words	20	15 minutes
Verbal Reasoning—Context	20	15 minutes
Reading and Language Arts	40	40 minutes
Mathematics	40	35 minutes

The TACHS—approximately 140 questions during 3½ hours of allotted time, including breaks

Section	Questions	Time Length
Reading	Not available	N/A
Language	Not available	N/A
Mathematics Skills	40	40 minutes
Ability	10	5 minutes

HSPT/COOP/TACHS

CHAPTER 1
ABOUT THIS BOOK

CHAPTER 1

About This Book

This book will provide you with an accurate and complete representation of the Scholastic Testing Service's (STS) High School Placement Test (HSPT), CTB/McGraw-Hill's Cooperative Admissions Examination (COOP), and the Test for Admission into Catholic High Schools (TACHS). Inside you will find reviews which are designed to provide you with the information and strategies needed to do well on these tests. Two practice tests each, based on the official HSPT, COOP, and TACHS exams, are provided in the book and on TestWare®. The practice tests contain every type of question that you can expect to encounter on test day. Following each of our practice tests, you will find an answer key with detailed explanations designed to help you master the test material.

How to Use This Book and TestWare®

To thoroughly prepare for the actual tests, it's best to first read over the subject reviews and suggestions for test-taking. On our CD we provide review and drills for the HSPT optional subtests. Studying the reviews will reinforce the basic skills you need to do well on the test. Be sure to take the practice tests on CD to become familiar with the format and procedures involved with taking the actual HSPT, COOP, or TACHS examinations. Our TestWare will provide instant scoring so you can work on your areas of weakness.

To best utilize your study time, follow our Independent Study Schedule located in the front of this book. Brushing up on areas you did well on wouldn't hurt either.

When Should I Start Studying?

It is never too early to start studying for these exams. The earlier you begin, the more time you will have to sharpen your skills. Do not procrastinate! Cramming is not an effective way to study since it does not allow you the time needed to learn the test material. The sooner you learn the format of the exam you are taking, the more time you will have to familiarize yourself with its content.

The Review Sections

The reviews in this book are designed to help you sharpen the basic skills needed to approach the HSPT, COOP, and the TACHS as well as to provide strategies for attacking each type of question. You will also find drills to reinforce what you have learned. By using the reviews in conjunction with the practice tests, you will better prepare yourself for the actual exams themselves.

Tips for Taking the HSPT, COOP, and TACHS

Don't be intimidated
Fear will ruin your chances of doing the best that you can on the test. Studying this book will help you to approach the HSPT, COOP, or TACHS with confidence and poise.

Get to know the test format
Our practice tests have been specially designed to reflect the way the actual HSPT, COOP, and TACHS will look. Take some time to get familiar with the different tests that you will be taking. There shouldn't be any surprises for you on test day.

Use the process of elimination
This is possibly the easiest and quickest way to increase your score. Eliminating answer choices will lead you to the right answer almost every time. Neither CTB McGraw-Hill nor STS will deduct points for incorrect answers. This means that even if you can't seem to get an answer, just pick one letter. If you blindly guess, you'll get 1 answer in 5 right. If you can eliminate just 1 answer choice, you'll get 1 answer in 4 right. Either way, you'll raise your score because you don't lose points for leaving an answer blank.

Pay attention
Be sure that the answer oval that you are marking corresponds to the question number in the test booklet. Otherwise, you run the risk of filling in all of the wrong ovals.

Independent Study Schedule

Week	Activity
1	If you are taking the HSPT, read the "About the HSPT" chapter. Then, take the HSPT Practice Test 1 on CD and use the answer key chart and TestWare scoring feedback to determine where your weak areas are. If you are taking the COOP, do the same with COOP-related material. If you are taking the TACHS, do the same with TACHS-related material. Make sure that you study the detailed explanations to gain some initial insight into the problems that you have trouble completing.
2 & 3	Keep in mind the problems that you got wrong. Read and study the Verbal Skills and the Language Skills reviews. Make sure that you answer all of the drill questions. Learn the difference between the correct and incorrect examples. Then, review any material that you answered incorrectly in your practice test.
4 & 5	Keep in mind the problems that you got wrong in the practice tests. Now study the Reading review. Answer the drill questions and review any material that you answered incorrectly in your practice test.

6 & 7	Keep in mind the problems that you got wrong. Read and study the Mathematics and Quantitative Skills reviews. Make sure that you answer the drill questions. Pay close attention to the examples given. Now, review any material that you answered incorrectly in your practice test.
8	It's time to see how much you have improved! Take the HSPT, COOP, or TACHS Practice Test 2. Once again, study the detailed explanations to try and gain some insight into the problems that you got wrong. Go back and reread any reviews which pertain to answers that are still unclear.
9	Allow a week for review and taking the optional tests. Review the Mechanical Aptitude Section and take the test. Make sure that you examine all detailed answers.
10	Review the Science Section and take the test. Make sure that you examine all detailed answers.
11	Review the Catholic Religion Section and take the test. Make sure that you examine all detailed answers.

About the High School Placement Test (HSPT)

About the Test

Who takes the test and what is it used for?
The HSPT examination is taken by junior high students who plan on applying for admittance to private or Catholic high schools. This examination is used to evaluate a student's knowledge and determine if the student has adequate knowledge and understanding in specified subject areas.

Who administers the test?
The HSPT is developed and administered by STS and is updated each year to ensure test security. The test development process is designed and implemented to also ensure that the content and difficulty level of the test are appropriate.

When is the HSPT taken?
Students are required to take the HSPT in the fall of eighth grade so that they will have another opportunity to take it if they do not pass. Taking our practice tests will familiarize you with the types of questions on and the format of the HSPT exam to eliminate the anxiety of only being able to become familiar with the test as you take it.

When and where is the test given?
The HSPT is administered in the fall and once more in the spring, but you should check with the school you are applying to for the exact date. Also, since the test is used in different ways (again, specific to the school), you will need to take the exam at the school to which you are applying (contact the admissions office of the school for more details).

To receive information on the exam or upcoming administrations of the HSPT, contact STS.

Scholastic Testing Service, Inc.
480 Meyer Road
Bensenville, IL 60106-1617
Phone: (800) 642-6STS (6787)
Website: *www.ststesting.com*
email: sts@email.ststesting.com

Is there a registration fee?

Not exactly. Schools do not actually purchase the HSPT exams; rather, they "rent" them. To ensure test security, all materials provided to a school are returned to STS when the exams are completed. Therefore, your registration costs will most likely be added to the school's admission fees. Since each school is different, you should contact the school(s) in which you are interested to find the exact cost.

Format of the HSPT

Section	Questions	Time Length
Verbal	60	16 minutes
Quantitative	52	30 minutes
Reading	62	25 minutes
Mathematics	64	45 minutes
Language	60	25 minutes

Optional HSPT Sections (on CD)

Science	40	30 minutes
Mechanical Aptitude	40	30 minutes
Catholic Religion	40	30 minutes

Here is a quick breakdown of the test sections on the HSPT and their subjects.

Verbal Skills—This section tests synonyms, logic, verbal classification, antonyms, and analogies.

Quantitative Skills—This section tests geometric comparisons, non-geometric comparisons, number series, and number manipulations.

Reading Skills—This section tests the ability to recall information from reading material, vocabulary, intuitive thinking (what would happen next), and locating main ideas.

Mathematic Skills—This section tests mathematical concepts and problem-solving ability dealing with arithmetic, basic geometry, and elementary algebra.

Language Skills—This section tests an examinee's ability in capitalization, punctuation, word usage, spelling, and composition.

Scoring the HSPT

Since the HSPT is taken for admittance to private high schools, the score required for admittance varies from institution to institution. HSPT scores are reported on a 200 to 800 scale. Before assigning you a score from the scale, STS first calculates a raw score. The raw score is figured by adding up all of your correct answers. Since STS does not deduct for incorrect answers, it is in your best interest to answer all the questions you can. Your raw scores are scaled to compensate for the slight variations that may arise between different exams.

After you take the actual HSPT examination, the test results you receive will include five different types of scores.

1. **The Composite Score**—This is the sum of the raw scores you receive on the five parts of the HSPT, which is then converted into a standard score (standard scores are a cumulative average of the nation's test-takers per grade).
2. **National Percentile Rank (NP)**—Your score is ranked on a range from 1 to 99, which compares your HSPT results with that of other students at the same grade level. If a student scored an 81 on the Verbal Section, that student scored above 81% of the students from the national norm sample.
3. **Local Percentile Rank (LP)**—This evaluates scores much in the same manner as the National Ranking, yet it is focused on a student's comparison with a local group. Local groups are comprised of students who tested at the same school or from the same district.
4. **Grade Equivalents**—This percentile ranking compares a student's performance with that of other students at different grade levels.
5. **Cognitive Skills Quotient**—Used to replace the common IQ score, the CSQ serves also to gauge the future academic performance of a student. The CSQ is figured by combining the Verbal and Quantitative Skills scores and comparing them to the test-taker's age when he/she took the test.

How do I score my practice test?

Scoring worksheet

Use the scoring worksheet below to score each of our two practice tests. The score you earn on each of the test sections is the percentage that you scored correctly. This will help you gauge which sections of the exam on which you need to concentrate more time. Your scores, after you take the actual HSPT, will be prepared by STS according to the five divisions mentioned. It would seem logical, however, to realize that the better you score on our sample tests, the better your actual score will be.

Verbal skills

_____ ÷ 60 × 100 = _____
Questions answered   Total Questions   Percentage
correctly   in Section   Score

Quantitative skills

_____ ÷ 52 × 100 = _____
Questions answered   Total Questions   Percentage
correctly   in Section   Score

Reading skills

_____ ÷ 62 × 100 = _____
Questions answered   Total Questions   Percentage
correctly   in Section   Score

Mathematics skills

_____ ÷ 64 × 100 = _____
Questions answered   Total Questions   Percentage
correctly   in Section   Score

Language skills

_____ ÷ 60 × 100 = _____
Questions answered   Total Questions   Percentage
correctly   in Section   Score

Optional: Science

_____ ÷ 40 × 100 = _____
Questions answered   Total Questions   Percentage
correctly   in Section   Score

Optional: Mechanical aptitude

_____ ÷ 40 × 100 = _____
Questions answered   Total Questions   Percentage
correctly   in Section   Score

Optional: Catholic religion

_____ ÷ 40 × 100 = _____
Questions answered   Total Questions   Percentage
correctly   in Section   Score

About the Cooperative Admissions Examination (COOP)

About the test

Who takes the test and what is it used for?

The COOP examination is taken by junior high students who plan on applying for admittance to Catholic high schools. This examination is used to evaluate a student's knowledge and determine if he/she has adequate knowledge and understanding in specified subject areas. The test is also used as a means of course placement. Very often, your performance on the COOP will dictate the level of courses that you are assigned upon entrance to the Catholic school (if you are accepted). A very important point about the COOP is that it may only be taken once. It is imperative that you take the time to prepare for this exam and study.

Who administers the test?

The COOP is developed by CTB/McGraw-Hill Publishers of Monterey, California, and administered by Master Computer Systems. For further questions concerning the COOP exam, contact:

Cooperative Admissions Examination Office
CTB/McGraw-Hill
20 Ryan Ranch Road
Monterey, CA 93940
Phone: (800) 538-9547
Website: *www.ctb.com*

When is the COOP taken?

The COOP examination is usually administered in the fall of each year (in September, October, or November), although the exact date is different each year. Taking our practice tests will familiarize you with the types of questions and format of the COOP exam. This eliminates the anxiety of having to become familiar with the test as you take it.

Where is the test given?

The COOP is offered at most Catholic schools. To find out which schools offer the COOP in your area, check the back of the Student Handbook/Registration bulletin for a prospective school's diocese (to receive a Student Handbook, contact the school to which you are interested in applying). Students may take the test at most Catholic schools.

To receive specific information about upcoming administrations of the COOP or general information about the exam, contact your local diocese or Catholic school.

Is there a registration fee?

Yes. The COOP requires a $40.00 nonrefundable registration fee which includes reporting scores to three high schools of your choice. Check your COOP Student Handbook for more information on payment.

Format of the COOP

Section	Questions	Time Length
Sequences	20	15 minutes
Analogies	20	7 minutes
Quantitative Reasoning	20	15 minutes
Verbal Reasoning–Words	20	15 minutes
Verbal Reasoning–Context	20	15 minutes
Reading and Language Arts	40	40 minutes
Mathematics	40	35 minutes

Here is a brief breakdown of the test sections on the COOP exam and their subjects.

Sequences—This section tests the ability to distinguish various patterns in a series of numbers, figures, or similar arrangements. The examinee is responsible to select the part that will continue the pattern.

Analogies—This section tests the ability to associate a concrete or abstract relationship between two pictures, then select an image to maintain that relationship with another set of words, objects, or phrases.

Quantitative Reasoning—This section tests the examinee's ability to use reason to solve mathematical problems. The examinee is tested on number relationships, visual problems, and symbol relationships.

Verbal Reasoning: Words—This section tests the examinee's ability to reason with word relations, classifications, and patterns. The examinee is tested on the ability to infer relationships, recognize categories, and determine essential elements.

Verbal Reasoning: Context—This section tests the examinee's ability to analyze short passages and draw reasonable conclusions regarding presented concepts.

Reading and Language Arts—This section tests the examinee's ability to comprehend text, vocabulary, and language expression. The examinee is tested on language usage and conventions; word, sentence, and paragraph construction and meaning; as well as aspects of the writing process.

Mathematics—This section tests the examinee's ability in basic geometry, arithmetic, elementary algebra, and word problem solving.

Calculator use
Calculators will not be permitted during the test.

How do I score my practice test?

Use the scoring worksheet below to score each of our two practice tests. Though the COOP is scored differently from the method below, the score you earn on our practice tests should approximate how well you will perform on the COOP.

Scoring worksheet

Sequences

_____ ÷ 20 × 100 = _____

Questions answered correctly | Total Questions in Section | | Percentage Score

Analogies

_____ ÷ 20 × 100 = _____

Questions answered correctly | Total Questions in Section | | Percentage Score

Quantitative reasoning

_____ ÷ 20 × 100 = _____

Questions answered correctly | Total Questions in Section | | Percentage Score

Verbal reasoning: Words

_____ ÷ 20 × 100 = _____

Questions answered correctly | Total Questions in Section | | Percentage Score

Verbal reasoning: Context

_____ ÷ 20 × 100 = _____

Questions answered correctly | Total Questions in Section | | Percentage Score

Reading and language arts

_____ ÷ 40 × 100 = _____
Questions answered   Total Questions   Percentage
correctly   in Section   Score

Mathematics

_____ ÷ 40 × 100 = _____
Questions answered   Total Questions   Percentage
correctly   in Section   Score

About the Test for Admission into Catholic High Schools (TACHS)

About the test

Who takes the test and what is it used for?

The TACHS is taken by eighth grade students who plan on applying for admittance to a Catholic high school. This examination is used to evaluate a student's abilities in the specified areas.

Who administers the test?

The TACHS is developed by Riverside Publishing, a subsidiary of Houghton Mifflin Harcourt, in collaboration with the Archdiocese of New York and the Diocese of Brooklyn/Queens.

> TACHS Examination Office
> PO Box 64675
> Eagan, MN 55164-9522
> Phone: (866)618-2247
> Website: *tachsinfo.com*

When is the TACHS taken?

The TACHS examination is usually administered in the fall of each year; however, the exact date changes yearly.

Where is the test given?

The TACHS is offered at Catholic schools within the Archdiocese of New York and the Diocese of Brooklyn/Queens. Please refer to your TACHS Student Handbook for specific information regarding the location that best suits your needs.

Is there a registration fee?

Yes. The TACHS requires a $49.00 nonrefundable registration/examination fee. Online registration is recommended. A cashier's check or money order made payable to TACHS is required for paper registration. Check your TACHS Student Handbook for further information on payment.

Format of the TACHS

Section	Questions	Time Length
Reading	Not available	N/A
Language	Not available	N/A
Mathematics Skills	40	40 minutes
Ability	10	5 minutes

Here is a quick breakdown of the test sections on the TACHS and their subjects.

Reading—This section consists of two subtests: Vocabulary and Reading Comprehension. The **Vocabulary** section tests the ability to recognize words with similar meanings. The **Reading Comprehension** section tests the ability to comprehend passages and construct inferential meaning.

Language—This section consists of five subtests: Spelling, Capitalization, Punctuation, Usage, and Expression. The **Spelling** section tests the ability to recognize misspelled words. The **Capitalization** section tests the ability to recognize errors in the use of capital and lower case letters. The **Punctuation** section tests the ability to identify errors in the use of commas, quotation marks, apostrophes, question marks, and other forms of punctuation. The **Usage** section tests the ability to recognize errors in the use of verbs, personal pronouns, modifiers, or word choice. The **Expression** section tests the ability to determine the clearness, appropriateness, organization, and succinctness of sentences and paragraphs.

Math—This section tests a variety of skills and conceptions in the areas of computation, problem solving, and data interpretation. A subsection of problems which require **Estimation** is included in this portion of the test.

Ability—This section tests the ability to reason and think logically using abstract problems.

How do I score my practice test?

Use the scoring worksheet provided to score each of the two practice tests. Although the TACHS may be scored in a different manner from the method below, the score you earn on the practice tests should approximate how well you will perform on the TACHS exam.

Scoring worksheet

Reading

_____ ÷   50   × 100 = _____

Questions answered   Total Questions   Percentage
correctly   in Section   Score

Language

_____ ÷   40   × 100 = _____

Questions answered   Total Questions   Percentage
correctly   in Section   Score

Mathematics

_____ ÷   40   × 100 = _____

Questions answered   Total Questions   Percentage
correctly   in Section   Score

Ability

_____ ÷   10   × 100 = _____

Questions answered   Total Questions   Percentage
correctly   in Section   Score

HSPT
PRACTICE TEST 1

Verbal Skills

Time: 16 Minutes
60 Questions

DIRECTIONS: Select the best answer choice.

1. Sunrise is to morning as sunset is to
   _____C_____

   (A) horizon.
   (B) afternoon.
   (C) evening.
   (D) moon.

2. Country is to continent as county is to
   _____C_____

   (A) city.
   (B) capital.
   (C) state.
   (D) town.

3. Mumps is to swollen glands as measles is to
   _____

   (A) disease.
   (B) symptom.
   (C) fever.
   (D) rash.

4. Scissors is to cut as ruler is to _____D_____

   (A) straight.
   (B) wood.
   (C) inches.
   (D) measure.

5. She is to her as they is to _____A_____

   (A) their.
   (B) theirs.
   (C) them.
   (D) themselves.

6. Ten is to decade as one hundred is to
   _____A_____

   (A) century.
   (B) millennium.
   (C) dollars.
   (D) era.

GO TO NEXT PAGE ➡

7. Moat is to surround as canopy is to

_____ B

  (A) top.

  (B) cover.

  (C) around.

  (D) building.

8. Doctor is to hospital as teacher is to

_____ C

  (A) history.

  (B) classroom.

  (C) school.

  (D) student.

9. Play is to act as book is to _____ A

  (A) chapter.

  (B) author.

  (C) character.

  (D) title.

10. Sidewalk is to concrete as floor is to

_____ D

  (A) kitchen.

  (B) room.

  (C) table.

  (D) tile.

11. Endure means to

  (A) perish.

  (B) reject.

  (C) tolerate.

  (D) fail.

12. Pessimism most nearly means

  (A) idealism.

  (B) visionary.

  (C) cynicism.

  (D) optimism.

13. Skeptical most nearly means

  (A) doubtful.

  (B) confident.

  (C) certain.

  (D) convinced.

14. Rectify most nearly means

  (A) correct.

  (B) destroy.

  (C) dilapidate.

  (D) demolish.

15. To retract is to

  (A) uphold.

  (B) declare.

  (C) admit.

  (D) deny.

16. Protagonist most nearly means

  (A) villain.

  (B) antagonist.

  (C) professor.

  (D) hero.

GO TO NEXT PAGE ➡

17. Revenge most nearly means
   (A) repay.
   (B) clerical.
   (C) advocate.
   (D) danger.

18. Paranoid most nearly means
   (A) trusting.
   (B) angry.
   (C) suspicious.
   (D) confident.

19. A martyr is a
   (A) manager.
   (B) victim.
   (C) victor.
   (D) delinquent.

20. Regime most nearly means
   (A) reign.
   (B) generation.
   (C) luxurious.
   (D) regimen.

21. Detest most nearly means
   (A) like.
   (B) loathe.
   (C) cherish.
   (D) idolize.

22. Rational most nearly means
   (A) logical.
   (B) insane.
   (C) unreasonable.
   (D) foolish.

23. Obscure most nearly means
   (A) unclear.
   (B) distinct.
   (C) known.
   (D) evident.

24. To dissuade is to
   (A) disapprove.
   (B) camouflage.
   (C) encourage.
   (D) thwart.

25. Terminate means to
   (A) start.
   (B) originate.
   (C) conclude.
   (D) initiate.

26. Peter works harder than Patrick. Patrick works harder than Paul. Paul works harder than Victor. If the first two statements are true, the third is
   (A) true.
   (B) false.
   (C) uncertain.

27. Ashley dances better than Diane. Diane dances better than Pamela. Pamela dances better than Alison. If the first two statements are true, the third is
   (A) true.
   (B) false.
   (C) uncertain.

GO TO NEXT PAGE ➡

28. Jefferson High School has more students than Roosevelt High School. Roosevelt High School has more students than Lincoln High School. Lincoln High School has more students than Jefferson High School. If the first two statements are true, the third is
    (A) true.
    (B) false.
    (C) uncertain.

29. Mrs. Perez has more children than Mrs. Martin. Mrs. Martin has more children than Mrs. Lee. Mrs. Lee has more children than Mrs. Perez. If the first two statements are true, the third is
    (A) true.
    (B) false.
    (C) uncertain.

30. Every family in Sunrise Village has a car. The Palmers do not have a car. The Palmers do not live in Sunrise Village. If the first two statements are true, the third is
    (A) true.
    (B) false.
    (C) uncertain.

31. Every adult in Beechwood voted in the last presidential election. Mr. Turner did not vote in the last presidential election. Mr. Turner does not live in Beechwood. If the first two statements are true, the third is
    (A) true.
    (B) false.
    (C) uncertain.

32. Wednesday was warmer than Tuesday. Monday was cooler than Tuesday. Monday was cooler than Wednesday. If the first two statements are true, the third is
    (A) true.
    (B) false.
    (C) uncertain.

33. Bill's house is larger than Fred's. Lucille's house is smaller than Fred's. Lucille's house is smaller than Bill's. If the first two statements are true, the third is
    (A) true.
    (B) false.
    (C) uncertain.

34. It's farther to walk from the tennis courts to the beach than from the beach to the swimming pool. It's farther to walk from the beach to the swimming pool than from the swimming pool to the ice cream parlor. It's farther to walk from the swimming pool to the ice cream parlor than from the tennis courts to the beach. If the first two statements are true, the third is
    (A) true.
    (B) false.
    (C) uncertain.

35. It's closer to drive from the supermarket to the library than from the library to the train station. It's closer to drive from the library to the train station than from the train station to the bank. It's closer to drive from the train station to the bank than from the supermarket to the library. If the first two statements are true, the third is
    (A) true.
    (B) false.
    (C) uncertain.

GO TO NEXT PAGE ➡

36. Which word does <u>not</u> belong with the others?

(A) Program
(B) Monitor
(C) Printer
(D) Keyboard

37. Which word does <u>not</u> belong with the others?

(A) Rice
(B) Cereal
(C) Wheat
(D) Corn

38. Which word does <u>not</u> belong with the others?

(A) Alleviate
(B) Reduce
(C) Lessen
(D) Increase

39. Which word does <u>not</u> belong with the others?

(A) Gold
(B) Diamond
(C) Emerald
(D) Sapphire

40. Which word does <u>not</u> belong with the others?

(A) Reptile
(B) Snake
(C) Turtle
(D) Crocodile

41. Which word does <u>not</u> belong with the others?

(A) Piano
(B) Drums
(C) Cymbals
(D) Guitar

42. Which word does <u>not</u> belong with the others?

(A) Ounce
(B) Pound
(C) Gallon
(D) Quart

43. Which word does <u>not</u> belong with the others?

(A) Nitrogen
(B) Oxygen
(C) Helium
(D) Sodium

44. Which word does <u>not</u> belong with the others?

(A) Tin
(B) Marble
(C) Copper
(D) Nickel

45. Which word does <u>not</u> belong with the others?

(A) Tense
(B) Anxious
(C) Relaxed
(D) Nervous

GO TO NEXT PAGE ➡

46. Which word does <u>not</u> belong with the others?
    (A) Odor
    (B) Smell
    (C) Stench
    (D) Scent

47. Which word does <u>not</u> belong with the others?
    (A) Mother
    (B) Cousin
    (C) Niece
    (D) Sister

48. Which word does <u>not</u> belong with the others?
    (A) Undecided
    (B) Uncertain
    (C) Unsure
    (D) Uncomfortable

49. Which word does <u>not</u> belong with the others?
    (A) Media
    (B) Cactus
    (C) Alumni
    (D) Data

50. Which word does <u>not</u> belong with the others?
    (A) Classroom
    (B) Blackberry
    (C) Lighthouse
    (D) Dreamer

51. Which word does <u>not</u> belong with the others?
    (A) Fraction
    (B) Addition
    (C) Subtraction
    (D) Division

52. Metropolitan does not mean
    (A) urban.
    (B) cosmopolitan.
    (C) antiquated.
    (D) city-like.

53. Miserly does not mean
    (A) generous.
    (B) cheap.
    (C) avaricious.
    (D) stingy.

54. Malign does not mean
    (A) unfavorable.
    (B) malicious.
    (C) benign.
    (D) evil.

55. Impenetrable does not mean
    (A) opaque.
    (B) translucent.
    (C) obscure.
    (D) thick.

56. Courtly means the opposite of
    (A) dignified.
    (B) frivolous.
    (C) cultured.
    (D) stately.

57. Melancholy means the opposite of
    (A) sad.
    (B) depressed.
    (C) despondent.
    (D) ecstatic.

GO TO NEXT PAGE ➡

58. Occasional means the opposite of
    (A) alternate.
    (B) periodic.
    (C) rhythmical.
    (D) incessant.

59. Stalwart means the opposite of
    (A) gallant.
    (B) valorous.
    (C) timid.
    (D) dauntless.

60. Glowing means the opposite of
    (A) ruddy.
    (B) vivid.
    (C) incandescent.
    (D) doleful.

STOP

HSPT
SUBTEST 2

Quantitative Skills

Time: 30 Minutes
52 Questions

DIRECTIONS: Select the best answer choice.

61. Examine (a), (b), and (c) and find the best answer.

(a)   (b)   (c)

(A) (a) is greater than (b) and less than (c).
(B) (b) and (c) are equal.
(C) (a) and (c) are equal.
(D) (c) is less than (a) and more than (b).

62. Look at this series: 90, 77, 64, 51, ... What numeral should come next?

(A) 42
(B) 38
(C) 36
(D) 40

63. Look at this series: 86, 78, 75, 67, 64, ... What numeral should come next?

(A) 56
(B) 57
(C) 58
(D) 61

64. Examine (a), (b), and (c) and find the best answer.

(a) $(3 + 4) \times 5$
(b) $3 + (4 \times 5)$
(c) $(5 + 3) \times 4$

(A) (a) is greater than (b) and less than (c).
(B) (a) is greater than (b) and greater than (c).
(C) (a) is less than (b) and greater than (c).
(D) (a) is less than (b) and less than (c).

GO TO NEXT PAGE ➡

65. What number is 7 more than $\frac{1}{2}$ of 16?

   (A) 8
   (B) 10
   (C) 15
   (D) 23

66. Examine the equal rectangles (a), (b), and (c) and find the best answer regarding their shaded parts.

   (a)   (b)   (c)

   (A) (a), (b), and (c) are equal.
   (B) (a) is greater than (b) and equal to (c).
   (C) (b) is greater than (c).
   (D) (a) and (b) are equal and both are less than (c).

67. Examine (a), (b), and (c) and find the best answer.

   (a) $\frac{1}{2}$ of 24 12

   (b) $\frac{1}{3}$ of 48 16

   (c) $\frac{1}{4}$ of 60 15

   (A) (a), (b), and (c) are all equal.
   (B) (a) is greater than (b) and less than (c).
   (C) (c) is greater than (a) and less than (b).
   (D) (b) is greater than (c) and less than (a).

68. Look at this series: 20, 24, 30, 35, 42, ... What numeral should come next?

   (A) 49
   (B) 48
   (C) 45
   (D) 50

69. What number is 4 less than $\frac{2}{3}$ of 21?

   (A) 10
   (B) 18
   (C) 14
   (D) 3

70. What number is 10 more than $\frac{1}{5}$ of 35?

   (A) 15
   (B) 17
   (C) 10
   (D) 21

71. Examine the equal rectangles (a), (b), and (c) and find the best answer regarding their shaded parts.

   (a)   (b)   (c)

   (A) (a) is greater than (b) and greater than (c).
   (B) (a) is greater than (b) and less than (c).
   (C) (a) is less than (b) and greater than (c).
   (D) (a), (b), and (c) are equal.

72. Look at this series: 200, 180, 164, 152, 144, ... What numeral should come next?

   (A) 144
   (B) 140
   (C) 136
   (D) 132

GO TO NEXT PAGE ➡

73. What number subtracted from 22 leaves $\frac{1}{10}$ of 90?
   (A) 9
   (B) 13
   (C) 16
   (D) 20

74. What number squared is half of 72?
   (A) 3
   (B) 6
   (C) 9
   (D) 12

75. Look at this series: 35, 44, 48, 57, 61, ... What numeral should come next?
   (A) 68
   (B) 69
   (C) 70
   (D) 72

76. Look at this series: 2008, 1995, 1982, 1969, ... What numeral should come next?
   (A) 1960
   (B) 1958
   (C) 1957
   (D) 1956

77. What number multiplied by 7 is 3 more than 95?
   (A) 14
   (B) 18
   (C) 21
   (D) 28

78. Look at this series: 8, 17, 26, ___ , 44, 53, ... What numeral should fill in the blank?
   (A) 32
   (B) 33
   (C) 34
   (D) 35

79. Examine (a), (b), and (c) and find the best answer.
   (a) $\frac{11}{20}$ 55%
   (b) 60%
   (c) .5   50%
   (A) (a) is greater than (b) and greater than (c).
   (B) (b) is greater than (a) and greater than (c).
   (C) (c) is greater than (a) and greater than (b).
   (D) (c) is greater than (b) and less than (a).

80. What number divided by 3 leaves 5 less than 18?
   (A) 13
   (B) 33
   (C) 39
   (D) 42

81. Examine the equilateral (equal-sided) triangle and find the best answer.

   (A) AD is equal to AB.
   (B) AD is less than AC.
   (C) AD is greater than BC.
   (D) AD is less than CD.

82. What number multiplied by itself is 20 less than 45?
   (A) 5
   (B) 10
   (C) 6
   (D) 3

GO TO NEXT PAGE ➡

HSPT

83. Examine (a), (b), and (c) and find the best answer.

(a) $\frac{7}{16}$ $\frac{14}{32}$

(b) $\frac{3}{8}$ $\frac{12}{32}$

(c) $\frac{13}{32}$

(A) (c) is greater than (a) and greater than (b).
(B) (b) is greater than (a) and greater than (c).
(C) (a) is greater than (b) and greater than (c).
(D) (a), (b), and (c) are equal.

84. Examine the circle with center E and find the best answer.

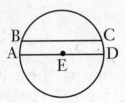

(A) BC is equal to AB.
(B) AE is equal to DE.
(C) AD is equal to BC.
(D) BC is equal to CD.

85. What number divided by 20 leaves 20 less than 30?

(A) 100
(B) 200
(C) 300
(D) 400

86. Look at this series: 512, 128, 32, 8, … What numeral should come next?

(A) 6
(B) 4
(C) 2
(D) 1

87. Look at this series: 90, 30, 27, 9, 6, … What numeral should come next?

(A) 1
(B) 2
(C) 3
(D) 4

88. Three-fourths of what number is $\frac{1}{3}$ of 36?

(A) 12
(B) 15
(C) 16
(D) 18

89. Look at this series: XX, XXV, XXX, XXXV, … What numeral should come next?

(A) XXVX
(B) XXXVI
(C) LX
(D) XL

90. Look at this series: 53, 45, 41, 33, 29, 21, … What numeral should come next?

(A) 17
(B) 15
(C) 13
(D) 11

91. One-sixth of what number is 4 multiplied by itself?

(A) 18
(B) 60
(C) 144
(D) 96

GO TO NEXT PAGE ➡

92. Examine (a), (b), and (c) and find the best answer.

  (a) $(16 \div 8) \times 2$ 4

  (b) $(16 \div 2) \times 8$ 64

  (c) $16 \div (8 \times 2)$ 1

  (A) (a), (b), and (c) are all equal.

  (B) (a) is less than (b) and less than (c).

  (C) (b) is less than (a) and less than (c).

  (D) (c) is less than (a) and less than (b).

93. Look at this series: 61, 63, 70, __ , 79, 81, 88, ... What numeral should fill in the blank?

  (A) 90

  (B) 95

  (C) 72

  (D) 59

94. What number divided by 6 is $\frac{1}{8}$ of 32?

  (A) 12

  (B) 24

  (C) 18

  (D) 36

95. Look at this series: 13, 9, 18, 14, 28, 24, ... What number should come next?

  (A) 32

  (B) 20

  (C) 56

  (D) 48

96. Examine (a), (b), and (c) and find the best answer.

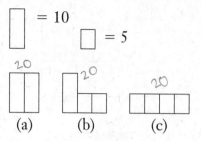

  (A) (a) is greater than (b) and greater than (c).

  (B) (b) is greater than (a) and greater than (c).

  (C) (c) is greater than (a) and greater than (b).

  (D) (a), (b), and (c) are all equal.

97. What number subtracted from 30 leaves 4 more than $\frac{5}{6}$ of 30?

  (A) 26

  (B) 1

  (C) 5

  (D) 6

98. Examine (a), (b), and (c) and find the best answer.

  (a) $2x + 3y$

  (b) $6xy$

  (c) $3x + 2y$

  (A) (a) = (b) = (c)

  (B) (a) = (b), (b) ≠ (c)

  (C) (a) ≠ (b), (b) ≠ (c), (a) ≠ (c)

  (D) (a) ≠ (b), (b) = (c)

99. Look at this series: 53, 49, 60, 56, 67, 63, ... What two numerals should come next?

  (A) 69, 65

  (B) 74, 70

  (C) 70, 66

  (D) 71, 67

GO TO NEXT PAGE ➡

100. Examine (a), (b), and (c) and find the best answer.

(a)   (b)   (c)

(A) (a) is equal to (b).

(B) (a) is equal to (c).

(C) (b) is equal to (c).

(D) (a) is equal to (b) and equal to (c).

101. What number added to 10 is twice the product of 5 and $\frac{1}{2}$ of 8?

(A) 10

(B) 20

(C) 25

(D) 30

102. Look at this series: 68, 109, 72, 101, 76, ... What numeral should come next?

(A) 105

(B) 80

(C) 103

(D) 93

103. Examine (a), (b), and (c) and find the best answer.

(a) 2^4 16

(b) 3^3 27

(c) 4^2 16

(A) (a) is equal to (b).

(B) (a) is equal to (c).

(C) (b) is equal to (c)

(D) (a) is equal to (b) is equal to (c).

104. Examine the graph and find the best answer.

(A) (a) minus (b) equals (c) minus (d).

(B) (a) minus (c) equals (b) minus (d).

(C) (a) minus (d) equals (b) plus (d).

(D) (b) plus (c) equals (a) plus (d).

105. Look at this series: 84, 81, 27, 24, 8, ... What numeral should come next?

(A) 5

(B) 7

(C) 6

(D) 3

106. What number multiplied by 2 is 3 times $\frac{1}{2}$ of 16?

(A) 4

(B) 12

(C) 15

(D) 20

107. What number added to $\frac{5}{9}$ of 36 is $\frac{2}{3}$ of 42?

(A) 8

(B) 12

(C) 14

(D) 20

GO TO NEXT PAGE ➡

108. Examine (a), (b), and (c) and find the best answer.

(a) .3 × .4   .12

(b) .6 × .2   .12

(c) 1 × 1.2   1.2

(A) (a) is equal to (b) is equal to (c).

(B) (a) is equal to (b) which is greater than (c).

(C) (a) is equal to (b) which is less than (c).

(D) (a) is greater than (b) and greater than (c).

109. Examine the parallelogram and find the best answer.

(A) The perimeter of the parallelogram is 12.

(B) The area of the parallelogram is 12.

(C) The perimeter of triangle ABD is 13.

(D) The area of triangle ABD is 5.

110. Look at this series: 42, 47, 46, 52, 49, 56, 51, ... What three numerals should come next?

(A) 59, 52, 61

(B) 60, 54, 62

(C) 57, 53, 61

(D) 62, 60, 68

111. One-third of what number subtracted from 10 is 2 times $\frac{1}{4}$ of 12?

(A) 6

(B) 12

(C) 15

(D) 18

112. Look at this series: 51, 57, 63, 60, 66, 72, ... What numeral should come next?

(A) 76

(B) 74

(C) 70

(D) 69

STOP

HSPT
SUBTEST 3

Reading

Time: 25 Minutes
62 Questions

Comprehension

> **DIRECTIONS:** Read the following passages and then select the best answer choice.

Questions 113–117 are based on the following passage.

In medieval times, an almanac was a chart showing the movements of the stars over a period of several years. Eventually, almanacs were printed in book form and included information which was especially useful to farmers. In the sixteenth century, almanacs began to be <u>issued</u> every year and included predictions of the weather based on previous weather patterns. At about the same time, almanacs included elaborate calendars that listed church feast days. In the seventeenth century, almanacs included jokes and short accounts of humorous incidents. Benjamin Franklin continued this tradition with *Poor Richard's Almanac*, which was published from 1732–1758. In Germany, almanacs of the eighteenth century included sophisticated, contemporary poetry by serious authors. The almanacs printed in the United States from 1835–1856 were called "Davy Crockett" almanacs because they included many frontier tall tales based mainly on oral tradition.

GO TO NEXT PAGE ➡

113. What appeared in almanacs a century after church holidays were included?
    (A) Weather predictions
    (B) Star movements
    (C) Jokes and humor
    (D) Elaborate calendars

114. Based on the passage, which of the following is TRUE?
    (A) The almanac included extra days for farmers.
    (B) Benjamin Franklin invented the almanac.
    (C) Almanacs are now printed every ten years.
    (D) *Poor Richard's Almanac* was published from 1732–1758.

115. The word <u>issued</u> as underlined and used in the passage most nearly means
    (A) dated.
    (B) given.
    (C) available.
    (D) numbered.

116. The poetry included in eighteenth century German almanacs was
    (A) written by farmers.
    (B) placed next to frontier tall tales.
    (C) sophisticated.
    (D) humorous.

117. In the sixteenth century, almanacs began to include
    (A) weather predictions.
    (B) "Davy Crockett."
    (C) jokes.
    (D) church feast days.

Questions 118–121 are based on the following passage.

Six members of a local university basketball team walked off the court during practice last week. They later said they were protesting unfair treatment by the head coach. The day after walking off the court, the players held a meeting with the university president to discuss their complaints. They met the Director of Athletics two days later and expressed their <u>concerns</u>. They also met with the assistant coach. After refusing to practice for four days, the team apologized to the fans, returned to practice, and promised to play the next scheduled game that season. The players also stated that their opinion of the head coach had not changed, but that they thought the assistant coach was fair.

118. According to the passage, how did the head coach feel about the protest?
    (A) Angry
    (B) Confused
    (C) Unjustly accused
    (D) Not enough information is given to answer this question.

119. The next game the team will play will be
    (A) when a new head coach is found.
    (B) the next scheduled game in the season.
    (C) when the assistant coach is promoted.
    (D) next season.

GO TO NEXT PAGE ➡

120. The word <u>concerns</u> as underlined and used in the passage most nearly means
(A) problems.
(B) caring.
(C) anxiety.
(D) playing.

121. Based on the passage, which of the following is TRUE?
(A) The five members will play the next game.
(B) The players apologized to the head coach.
(C) The players apologized to the assistant coach.
(D) The players continued to practice despite their concerns.

Questions 122–126 are based on the following passage.

The issue of adult literacy has finally received recognition as a major social problem. Unfortunately, the issue is usually presented in the media as a "women's interest issue." <u>Numerous governors' wives</u> and even Barbara Bush have publicly expressed concern about literacy. As well-meaning as the politicians' wives may be, it is more important that the politicians themselves recognize the seriousness of the problem and support increased funding for literacy programs.

Literacy education programs need to be directed at two different groups of people with very different needs. The first group is composed of people who have very limited reading and writing skills. These people are complete illiterates. A second group is composed of people who can read and write but whose skills are not sufficient to meet their needs. This second group is called functionally illiterate. Successful literacy programs must meet the needs of both groups.

Instructors in literacy programs have three main responsibilities. First, the educational needs of the illiterates and functional illiterates must be met. Second, the instructors must approach the participants in the program with empathy, not sympathy. Third, all participants must experience success in the program and must perceive their efforts as worthwhile.

122. According to the passage, some politicians
(A) have expressed great concern over adult literacy.
(B) are more concerned with complete illiterates than with functional illiterates.
(C) need to recognize the problem's seriousness and support it with increased funding.
(D) know the correct elements of literacy programs.

123. The goal of adult literacy programs is
(A) to help the functionally illiterate only.
(B) to teach people to be able to read and write for their needs.
(C) to be empathetic.
(D) to be sympathetic.

GO TO NEXT PAGE ➡

124. By stating that politicians' wives, rather than the politicians themselves, are discussing adult literacy, the author is concerned that
(A) more women than men will be literate.
(B) it is a social, not real, problem.
(C) politicians aren't women.
(D) it is not viewed as a serious problem.

125. The responsibilities of literacy programs as mentioned in this passage emphasize
(A) the self-esteem of the participants.
(B) political support.
(C) books.
(D) magazines.

126. The functional illiterate may
(A) not be able to meet his or her needs.
(B) be helped by a literacy program.
(C) have trouble writing.
(D) All of the above.

Questions 127–131 are based on the following passage.

The price of cleaning up the environment after oil spills is on the increase. After the massive Alaskan spill that created miles of sludge-covered beach, numerous smaller spills have occurred along the Gulf Coast and off the coast of California. Tides and prevailing winds carried much of this oil to shore in a matter of days. Workers tried to contain the oil with weighted, barrel-shaped plastic tubes stretched along the sand near the water. They hoped to minimize the damage. Generally, the barriers were successful, but there remained many miles of oil-covered sand. Cleanup crews shoveled the oil-covered sand into plastic bags for removal.

Coastal states are responding to the problem in several ways. California is considering the formation of a department of oceans to oversee protection programs and future cleanups. Some states have suggested training the National Guard in cleanup procedures. Other states are calling for the creation of an oil spill trust fund large enough to cover the costs of a major spill. Still other states are demanding federal action and funding. Regardless of the specific programs that may be enacted by the various states or the federal government, continued offshore drilling and the shipping of oil in huge tankers create a constant threat to the nation's shoreline.

127. Which of the following would not pose a problem for cleaning the environment?
(A) Offshore drilling
(B) Weighted, barrel-shaped plastic tubes
(C) Coastal winds
(D) Tides

128. The cost of oil spill cleanups is paid for by
(A) the oil companies.
(B) the coastal states.
(C) the National Guard.
(D) Not enough information is given.

GO TO NEXT PAGE

129. Some states want
    (A) the creation of an oil spill trust fund.
    (B) an end to offshore drilling.
    (C) plastic barrels.
    (D) oil companies.

130. After several recent oil spills, workers
    (A) tried to minimize the damage.
    (B) removed sand.
    (C) A and B.
    (D) None of the above.

131. The price of cleaning up the environment after oil spills
    (A) is decreasing.
    (B) is increasing as the number of spills increases.
    (C) is staying the same as workers clean up.
    (D) doesn't cost anything.

Questions 132–136 are based on the following passage.

It is estimated that over six million Americans suffer from diabetes. This disease, which often runs in families, is the result of insufficient amounts of insulin made by the body to meet its needs. Insulin is produced by the pancreas and is used by the body to take glucose from the blood for use as fuel. A deficiency results in high blood levels and low tissue levels of glucose.

There are two types of diabetes. The first type appears early in life and is the result of abnormal cells in the pancreas so that little or no insulin is made. This is juvenile diabetes. The standard treatment for juvenile diabetes is insulin replacement therapy. The second type of diabetes occurs later in life, usually during a person's fifties or sixties. In this type of diabetes the pancreatic beta cells are normal and produce normal amounts of insulin. However, for some unexplained reason, the tissues in the body have become resistant to the action of insulin. This second type of diabetes is more common in obese people than lean people.

Diet is very important in the treatment of both forms of diabetes. High levels of fat in the blood, which interfere with the absorption of insulin, are often associated with diabetes. A person who has either form of diabetes should reduce the total amount of fat to 20–25 percent of the total calories consumed and increase the amount of carbohydrates to approximately 40 percent. Simple sugars should be kept to 10–15 percent of all calories, and protein should not exceed 24 percent.

132. A person with diabetes should have a total diet of approximately
    (A) 80% fat; 40% carbohydrates; 10–15% sugar; and 24% protein.
    (B) 40% fat; 40% carbohydrates; 10–15% sugar; and 20% protein.
    (C) 30–35% fat; 10% carbohydrates; 50% sugar; and 14% protein.
    (D) 20–25% fat; 40% carbohydrates; 10–15% sugar; and 24% protein.

133. Insulin replacement therapy is standard treatment for
    (A) adult diabetes.
    (B) juvenile diabetes.
    (C) both.
    (D) neither.

GO TO NEXT PAGE ➡

HSPT

134. A deficiency of insulin results in
  (A) high blood levels and low tissue levels of glucose.
  (B) abnormal pancreatic cells.
  (C) obesity in adults.
  (D) obesity in juveniles.

135. High levels of fat in the blood
  (A) cause adult diabetes.
  (B) are a sign of high glucose levels.
  (C) are found in six million Americans.
  (D) interfere with insulin absorption.

136. Diabetes is usually detected or develops
  (A) when the person is a juvenile.
  (B) when a person is 50–70 years old.
  (C) when a person is 60–80 years old.
  (D) A and B.

Questions 137–141 are based on the following passage.

There's no room on the football field for "dumb jocks." Athletes who cannot consistently maintain a 2.0 grade-point average should not be permitted to participate in any sports. Athletes must realize that the purpose of school is to produce scholars, not professional ball players. If, by chance, an athlete is able to acquire a place in the professional ranks of sports, good! But the primary objective of school is the manufacturing and nurturing of productive citizens who can make worthwhile contributions to society. It is irritating to observe <u>star</u> quarterbacks who can't read, to observe star infielders who can't write, to observe star point guards who can't speak, and to observe outstanding pitchers who can't add, subtract, or multiply.

137. The word <u>star</u>, as used in this passage, most nearly means
  (A) constellation.
  (B) pointed.
  (C) successful.
  (D) athletic.

138. According to the author, what should the minimum requirement be for people who want to play sports in school?
  (A) They should be able to read and write.
  (B) They should be able to speak.
  (C) They should maintain a 2.0 grade-point average.
  (D) They should be able to subtract and multiply.

139. Which of the following sports is NOT alluded to in the passage?
  (A) Football
  (B) Basketball
  (C) Baseball
  (D) Hockey

140. Based on the passage, the author values
  (A) professional teachers over professional athletes.
  (B) professional students over professional athletes.
  (C) productive citizens over scholars.
  (D) educated athletes over uneducated athletes.

GO TO NEXT PAGE

141. The author views athletics as
- **(A)** an important part of school.
- **(B)** important in training to be a professional.
- **(C)** a part of adolescence.
- **(D)** None of the above.

Questions 142–147 are based on the following passage.

A big <u>toxic</u> spill took place on the upper Sacramento River in California on July 13, 1991, at about 10 p.m. when a slow-moving Southern Pacific train derailed north of the town of Dansmuir. A tank car containing 19,500 gallons of pesticide broke open and spilled into the river. This pesticide is used to kill soil pests. Since the spill, thousands of trout and other fish were poisoned along a 45-mile stretch of river. In addition, 190 people were treated at a local hospital for respiratory and related illnesses. Residents along the river have been warned to stay away from the tainted water. Once this water reaches Lake Shasta, a source of water for millions of Californians, samples will be taken to assess the quality of the water.

142. The pesticide was intended to
- **(A)** be diluted and entered into the river.
- **(B)** treat land pests.
- **(C)** be taken to a dump for disposal.
- **(D)** be banned by the government.

143. The water in Lake Shasta
- **(A)** is undrinkable.
- **(B)** sent 190 people to the hospital.
- **(C)** will be tested.
- **(D)** is fine for drinking.

144. The spill definitely affected
- **(A)** 45 miles of river.
- **(B)** Lake Shasta.
- **(C)** A and B.
- **(D)** None of the above.

145. The word <u>toxic</u>, as underlined and used in this passage, most nearly means
- **(A)** poisonous.
- **(B)** plastic.
- **(C)** beneficial.
- **(D)** huge.

146. How much pesticide was contained in the tank car?
- **(A)** 190 gallons
- **(B)** 45 thousand gallons
- **(C)** 10 thousand gallons
- **(D)** 19,500 gallons

147. Residents of the area have
- **(A)** been warned to avoid the river.
- **(B)** killed thousands of fish.
- **(C)** been drinking poisoned lake water.
- **(D)** None of the above.

GO TO NEXT PAGE ➡

Questions 148–152 are based on the following passage.

Lead poisoning is considered by health authorities to be the most common and devastating environmental disease of young children. According to studies made, it affects 15% to 20% of urban children and from 50% to 75% of inner-city, poor children. As a result of a legal settlement in July 1991, all of California's Medicaid-eligible children, ages one through five, will now be routinely screened annually for lead poisoning. Experts estimate that more than 50,000 cases will be detected in California because of the newly mandated tests. This will halt, at an early stage, a disease that leads to learning disabilities and life-threatening <u>disorders</u>.

148. The best title for this passage is
  (A) "Lead Poisoning and How to Stop It."
  (B) "Lead Poisoning and California."
  (C) "The History of Lead Poisoning."
  (D) "World Wide Lead Poisoning."

149. The word <u>disorders</u>, as used in this passage, most nearly means
  (A) chaos.
  (B) toxicity.
  (C) ailments.
  (D) confusion.

150. How many cases of lead poisoning are predicted to be found due to annual screening in California?
  (A) 75%
  (B) 50,000
  (C) 19,000
  (D) 20,000

151. How often will California's Medicaid-eligible children from the ages of 1–5 be tested for lead poisoning?
  (A) Every five years
  (B) 15%
  (C) Every other year
  (D) Every year

152. Lead poisoning is
  (A) the most common environmental disease of young children.
  (B) a disease that leads to life-threatening disorders.
  (C) A and B.
  (D) None of the above.

Vocabulary

DIRECTIONS: Choose the word that means the same or about the same as the underlined word.

153. a <u>vigilant</u> guard
  (A) watchful
  (B) reckless
  (C) lazy
  (D) powerful

154. a known <u>parable</u>
  (A) teacher
  (B) tale
  (C) stronghold
  (D) strength

GO TO NEXT PAGE

155. a <u>buoyant</u> spirit
   (A) scary
   (B) depressed
   (C) supernatural
   (D) light-hearted

156. a <u>gracious</u> host
   (A) elegant
   (B) beautiful
   (C) courteous
   (D) extravagant

157. pay <u>homage</u> to the winner
   (A) prizes
   (B) honor
   (C) insult
   (D) wages

158. a <u>grievous</u> burden
   (A) joyous
   (B) grave
   (C) disturbing
   (D) serious

159. the <u>incessant</u> noise
   (A) brief
   (B) loud
   (C) pleasant
   (D) constant

160. the <u>invincible</u> army
   (A) unconquerable
   (B) invisible
   (C) feeble
   (D) minute

161. a <u>portly</u> figure
   (A) sloppy
   (B) well-groomed
   (C) heavy
   (D) slim

162. the <u>ornate</u> furnishings
   (A) simple
   (B) expensive
   (C) cheap
   (D) elaborate

163. <u>encumbered</u> his movements
   (A) restricted
   (B) encouraged
   (C) lightened
   (D) watched

164. an <u>avid</u> fan
   (A) uncontrollable
   (B) ardent
   (C) lifeless
   (D) gloomy

165. to <u>vie</u> for a championship
   (A) wait
   (B) compete
   (C) advertise
   (D) survive

166. an <u>ample</u> supply
   (A) inexpensive
   (B) insufficient
   (C) equal
   (D) abundant

167. to <u>devise</u> a formula
   (A) eliminate
   (B) create
   (C) choose
   (D) delineate

168. a <u>chronic</u> ailment
   (A) small
   (B) perpetual
   (C) brief
   (D) unknown

GO TO NEXT PAGE ➡

169. a <u>haggard</u> expression
   (A) scrawny
   (B) dirty
   (C) cautious
   (D) haggle

170. to creep <u>stealthily</u>
   (A) openly
   (B) quickly
   (C) randomly
   (D) secretly

171. a <u>pathetic</u> sight
   (A) miserable
   (B) undesirable
   (C) ruthless
   (D) frustrating

172. a <u>verbose</u> speech
   (A) resignation
   (B) short
   (C) persuasive
   (D) wordy

173. <u>savor</u> a meal
   (A) enjoy
   (B) save
   (C) prepare
   (D) serve

174. a <u>rigid</u> person
   (A) warm-hearted
   (B) unyielding
   (C) tedious
   (D) loud

STOP

HSPT
SUBTEST 4

Mathematics

Time: 45 Minutes
64 Questions

Concepts

DIRECTIONS: Select the best answer choice.

175. Round off 3.47 to the nearest tenth
(A) 3.4
(B) 3.5
(C) 3.47
(D) 34.7

176. Add together: $3n + 4m - 6$ and $3m - 4n + 6$
(A) $7m - n$
(B) $7m + n$
(C) $6m$
(D) $6n$

177. Which of the following pairs of numbers is represented by the point, P, in the graph?

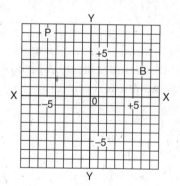

(A) $(6, 7)$
(B) $(-5, 7)$
(C) $(7, 6)$
(D) $(-7, 6)$

GO TO NEXT PAGE ➡

178. The sum of two consecutive whole numbers is 55. What are the two numbers?

(A) 25, 30

(B) 26, 29

(C) 27, 28

(D) 28, 29

179. If $x = 2$, $y = -5$ and $z = 0$, then $3x - 2y + 5z =$

(A) -4

(B) 1

(C) 16

(D) 21

180. Simplify: $12\frac{3}{4} + 5\frac{1}{3}$.

(A) $8\frac{1}{12}$

(B) $17\frac{1}{12}$

(C) $17\frac{4}{7}$

(D) $18\frac{1}{12}$

181. A prime number has no factors other than 1 and the number itself. Which of the following numbers is prime?

(A) 36

(B) 37

(C) 38

(D) 39

182. To compute the area of any rectangle, Rose applied the formula:

Area = length × width.

After computing the areas of four rectangles, including one square, Rose lost the paper from which she copied the figures. Remember that the length and width of a square are equal. Which of the following numbers represents the area of the square?

(A) 42

(B) 45

(C) 49

(D) 51

183. Simplify: $3(2 + 5) - 12$

(A) -9

(B) -1

(C) 1

(D) 9

184. Simplify: $5\frac{1}{4} \times 2\frac{1}{3}$

(A) $12\frac{1}{4}$

(B) $2\frac{1}{4}$

(C) $1\frac{1}{2}$

(D) $\frac{4}{9}$

185. What mixed number is the same as $5.\overline{3}$?

(A) $5\frac{1}{3}$

(B) $5\frac{3}{10}$

(C) $5\frac{3}{100}$

(D) $5\frac{3}{30}$

186. What percent of 60 is 75?

(A) 1.25%

(B) 15%

(C) 80%

(D) 125%

GO TO NEXT PAGE ➡

187. Rewrite $2\frac{1}{2}$ as a percent.

   (A) 250%
   (B) 50%
   (C) 25%
   (D) 2.5%

188. $q(r - s) =$

   (A) $q + r - s$
   (B) $qr - s$
   (C) $r - qs$
   (D) $qr - qs$

189. The sum of the measures of any two sides of a triangle is always greater than the measure of the third side of that triangle. Which of the following sets of sticks can be joined together, end-to-end, to form a triangle?

   (A)   3
         4
         5

   (B)   2
         5
         7

   (C)   5
         5
         12

   (D)   5
         6
         12

190. The sum of the measures of the three interior angles of a triangle is always 180 degrees. Which of the following sets of numbers represents the measures of interior angles of a triangle?

   (A) 60, 60, 90
   (B) 55, 65, 75
   (C) 60, 70, 80
   (D) 30, 75, 75

191. The following table shows the areas of the four classrooms and the number of students in each room in one small school.

Classroom	Area (in square feet)	Number of students
A	770	22
B	960	24
C	540	18
D	627	19

Judging by the figures in this table, which of the four classrooms is the least crowded?

   (A) A
   (B) B
   (C) C
   (D) D

The graph below shows the average rainfall (in inches) in a small town for a 5-month period. Use the information in the graph to answer questions 192 and 193.

GO TO NEXT PAGE ➡

192. How much more rain fell in the wettest month than during the driest month for this period?

(A) 5 in.
(B) 30 in.
(C) 50 in.
(D) 60 in.

193. What was the average rainfall for the five months?

(A) 30 in.
(B) 46 in.
(C) 50 in.
(D) 60 in.

The graph below shows Matthew's mathematic performance scores for 12 months in a year-round school. Use the information in this graph to answer questions 194 and 195 that follow. Please note that each point on the graph represents the average exam score for each month.

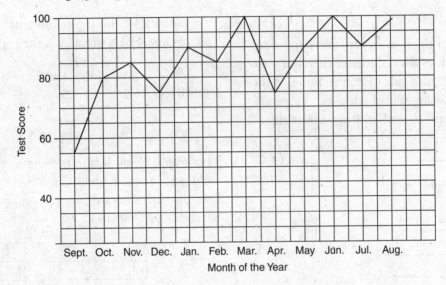

194. Which month's average shows the greatest gain compared to the prior month's average?

(A) October
(B) March
(C) June
(D) August

195. By how many points did Matthew's score improve between January and March?

(A) 5
(B) 20
(C) 15
(D) 10

196. The "3" in 54,362 is in the hundreds place. In what place is the "3" in 29.536?

(A) hundredths
(B) tenths
(C) singles
(D) hundreds

GO TO NEXT PAGE ➡

197. Which of the following is an acute triangle?

(A)

(B)

(C)

(D)

198. In this right triangle, find the value of x:

(A) 90°
(B) 74°
(C) 26°
(D) 16°

Problem-Solving

199. Carol earns $9.50 per hour as a teller in a neighborhood bank. How much does she earn in 8 hours at this rate?

(A) $17.50
(B) $76.00
(C) $175.00
(D) $760.00

200. The population of a small town increased from 360 to 468 in 9 years. What was the percent increase?

(A) 12%
(B) 30%
(C) 77%
(D) 108%

201. The formula for the area of a rectangle is:
Area = length × width.
The cost of carpeting a floor is $1.50 per square foot. What is the cost of carpeting a floor measuring 18 feet by 15 feet?

(A) $27.00
(B) $40.50
(C) $270.00
(D) $405.00

202. A bee flies 45 m in 10 seconds. At this rate, how far would this bee fly in 2 minutes?

(A) 90 m
(B) 450 m
(C) 540 m
(D) 900 m

203. Rhonda, Paula, and Brenda jointly own a small business. Rhonda owns $\frac{1}{2}$ of the business, while Paula owns $\frac{2}{5}$ of it. What fraction of the business does Brenda own?

(A) $\frac{1}{10}$

(B) $\frac{1}{2}$

(C) $\frac{3}{5}$

(D) $\frac{9}{10}$

204. The value of a car decreases at the rate of 14% per year. If a new car cost $15,000.00, how much would it be worth at the end of the first year?

(A) $12,900.00
(B) $14,914.00
(C) $14,986.00
(D) $17,100.00

GO TO NEXT PAGE

205. The marked price for a sofa is $460. If Alice buys this sofa with a 25% discount, how much does she pay for it?

(A) $345.00

(B) $435.00

(C) $485.00

(D) $575.00

206. Mrs. Smith left Starttown at 6:00 p.m. and drove non-stop to Endcity, 81 miles away. If Mrs. Smith arrived at Endcity at 7:30 p.m., what was her average speed per hour?

(A) 50

(B) 54

(C) 60

(D) 65

207. Jack cut one long strip of wood into 4 pieces and then joined these pieces end-to-end, as shown, to make a rectangle. What was the length of the original strip before Jack cut it up?

25 ft

35 ft

(A) 60 ft

(B) 120 ft

(C) 437.5 ft

(D) 875 ft

208. A rabbit may weigh up to 7 kg, while an adult harvest mouse weighs only 7 g. How many harvest mice would together weigh as much as one rabbit?

(A) 1

(B) 10

(C) 100

(D) 1,000

209. The Goliath beetle is 5 in. long and the fairy fly is only 1/100 in. long. What is the ratio of the length of a fairy fly to the length of a Goliath beetle?

(A) 500:1

(B) 1:100

(C) 100:500

(D) 1:500

210. A full grown ostrich weighs up to 156 kg. If the bee hummingbird weighs only 2 g, what fraction of an ostrich's weight is the bee hummingbird's weight?

(A) $\dfrac{1}{78,000}$

(B) $\dfrac{1}{7800}$

(C) $\dfrac{1}{780}$

(D) $\dfrac{1}{78}$

211. An adult elephant may weigh up to 6,600 kg. If the blue whale weighs 200,000 kg, by how many kilograms is the blue whale heavier than the elephant?

(A) 294,400

(B) 293,400

(C) 19,340

(D) 193,400

GO TO NEXT PAGE ➡

212. Mrs. Knight cut a loaf of bread into 16 equal slices. Her children ate $\frac{5}{8}$ of the whole bread. How many slices of bread did they eat?

(A) 5

(B) 6

(C) 8

(D) 10

213. A book dealer sold a book for $30, making a profit of 20%. How much did the book dealer pay for the book?

(A) $10

(B) $24

(C) $25

(D) $50

214. A farmer has 3,000 acres of farm land. If he cultivates 18% of this land each year, how many acres are left uncultivated?

(A) 540

(B) 2,460

(C) 2,912

(D) 2,982

215. The flea is only $\frac{1}{8}$ in. long and can jump 13 in. The Goliath beetle is 5 in. long. If jumping strength is directly proportional to its height, how far can a Goliath beetle jump?

(A) 40 in.

(B) 65 in.

(C) 104 in.

(D) 520 in.

Use the diagram below to answer questions 216 and 217.

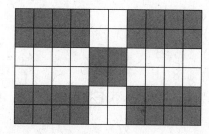

216. What fraction of this rectangle is <u>not</u> shaded?

(A) $\frac{3}{5}$

(B) $\frac{2}{5}$

(C) $\frac{5}{9}$

(D) $\frac{4}{9}$

217. What percent of the rectangle is shaded?

(A) 76%

(B) 60%

(C) 40%

(D) 24%

218. Alice scored 82, 79, 91, and 85 points on the first 4 science tests during one year. If her total score on 5 tests was 425, what was her score on the fifth test?

(A) 88

(B) 80

(C) 337

(D) 90

219. The clear portions in this picture are quarter-circles. Find the area of the shaded region in the picture.

The area of a circle may be calculated from the formula:

Area = $3.14 \times r^2$, where r = measure of radius of circle.

(A) 400 cm^2

(B) 243 cm^2

(C) 157 cm^2

(D) 86 cm^2

10 cm

10 cm

10 cm   10 cm

GO TO NEXT PAGE ➡

220. The picture shows a wire bent into the shape of a semi-circle. What is the length of this wire?
You may compute the circumference of a circle from the formula:
Circumference $= 3.14 \times d$, where $d =$ measure of diameter of circle.

14 in.

(A) 21.98 in.

(B) 47.96 in.

(C) 17.14 in.

(D) 10.14 in.

221. Find the area of the parallelogram below.

12 cm

25 cm

(A) 300 cm^2

(B) 150 cm^2

(C) 74 cm^2

(D) 37 cm^2

Sue receives $20.00 a week as pocket money. The circle graph shows how Sue spent her pocket money in one week. Use this information to answer questions 222 and 223 which follow.

Soda $2.25

Chips $3.50

Charity

Warm Food $5.00

222. How much money did Sue donate to charity that week?

(A) $10.75

(B) $9.25

(C) $5.75

(D) $6.00

223. What percent of Sue's pocket money did she spend on chips?

(A) 3.5%

(B) 46.25%

(C) 35%

(D) 17.5%

224. Rhonda made "cool aid" with 1.2 liters of iced tea and 300 milliliters of lemon juice. What percent of the drink is tea?

(A) 80%

(B) 40%

(C) 25%

(D) 2.5%

225. The ratio of boys to girls in a school is 52 to 48. If there are 500 students in the school, how many are boys?

(A) 260

(B) 240

(C) 52

(D) 480

226. Mike Smith earned $899.60 during one week by working overtime. Assume that he earned a basic hourly rate for the first 40 hours and an overtime rate for each hour after 40 hours. If he worked a total of 48 hours, what was his overtime rate? Assume overtime rate = (1.5) (basic rate).

(A) $17.30

(B) $18.74

(C) $25.95

(D) $28.11

GO TO NEXT PAGE

227. Laura Brown decides to invest $6,000 into an account which pays 13% per year simple interest. How much money should she invest into a second account paying 16.25% per year simple interest, so that the total interest for the year is $1,348.75?

(A) $3,500.00

(B) $3,883.75

(C) $4,267.50

(D) $4,651.25

228. How many ounces of pure water should be added to 50 ounces of a water-based solution which is 12% salt in order to produce a solution which is 4% salt?

(A) 50

(B) 100

(C) 150

(D) 200

229. In 31 years, Alice will be three times as old as she was last year. How old is she now?

(A) 18

(B) 17

(C) 16

(D) 15

230. Working together, Dave and Wendy can complete an assignment in 4 hours. Working alone, Dave would require 6 hours. How many hours would Wendy require if she worked alone?

(A) 6

(B) 8

(C) 10

(D) 12

231. What is the measure of the angle formed by the minute and hour hands of a clock at 3:20?

(A) 5°

(B) 10°

(C) 20°

(D) 30°

232. The length of a rectangle is 6 times its width. If its area is 37.5, what is its perimeter?

(A) 40

(B) 35

(C) 30

(D) 25

233. What is the area of a sector in a circle of radius 4 for which the central angle is 72°?

(A) 1.6 π

(B) 2.4 π

(C) 3.2 π

(D) 4.0 π

234. In the figure below, $\overline{AB}$ and $\overline{AC}$ are radii of a circle and are perpendicular to each other. $\overparen{BC}$ is an arc of that circle. If $\overparen{AB}$ is an arc of a circle for which $\overline{AB}$ is a diameter, what is the ratio of the shaded area to the unshaded area?

(A) $\dfrac{4}{\pi}$

(B) $\dfrac{1}{1}$

(C) $\dfrac{3}{\pi}$

(D) $\dfrac{1}{\pi}$

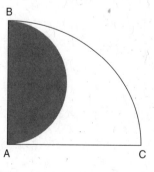

GO TO NEXT PAGE ➡

235. A gum-ball dispenser is filled with exactly 900 pieces of gum. The gum balls are always dispensed in the following order: 2 red, 3 yellow, 4 green, and 5 white. What is the color of the last gum ball to be dispensed?
    (A) green
    (B) red
    (C) white
    (D) yellow

236. Maria Jones earned a score of 75% on a calculus exam. If she had gotten 3 more correct answers, her score would have been 80%. Assuming each problem counted equally, how many actual problems did Maria answer correctly?
    (A) 54
    (B) 51
    (C) 48
    (D) 45

237. If 70% of the workers in an office are non-smokers, what is the ratio of smokers to non-smokers?
    (A) 3:7
    (B) 7:10
    (C) 10:7
    (D) 7:3

238. The marked price on a sofa is $520. After the first week, the price is marked down 20%. After the second week, the price is marked down an additional 30% and sold. What is the selling price?
    (A) $124.80
    (B) $260.00
    (C) $291.20
    (D) $426.40

STOP

HSPT
SUBTEST 5

Language Skills

Time: 25 Minutes
60 Questions

Punctuation, capitalization, and usage

DIRECTIONS: Look for errors of punctuation, capitalization, or usage in the following sentences. If there are no mistakes, mark "D."

239. **(A)** Tony walked across the lawn.
(B) John eats dinner last night.
(C) Traci danced with her friends.
(D) No mistakes.

240. **(A)** Luis is looking for martha.
(B) Please check your work.
(C) Dan is playing football.
(D) No mistakes.

241. **(A)** George wants to watch television.
(B) The book is on the table next to the lamp.
(C) Cindy is looking for my watch.
(D) No mistakes.

242. **(A)** My family went to Pittsburgh last summer.
(B) "What can I do for you?" she asked.
(C) I bought notebooks pens and a pencil for school.
(D) No mistakes.

243. **(A)** Laura went to visit her friend at the hospital.
(B) The black car drove past us.
(C) My uncle baked a lot of food for the Holidays.
(D) No mistakes.

244. **(A)** I feed our fishes every day.
(B) His birthday is January 12, 1965.
(C) April is my favorite month.
(D) No mistakes.

245. **(A)** Lou finished the assignment on time.
(B) Jason walked into the room with a smile on his face.
(C) Bob a good friend is famous.
(D) No mistakes.

GO TO NEXT PAGE

246. (A) Jennifer do a good job on this painting.
(B) Mike will be in the concert on Saturday.
(C) We are going to the movies tomorrow night.
(D) No mistakes.

247. (A) They walked over to the store.
(B) Are you going to the library after school.
(C) We are playing soccer later.
(D) No mistakes.

248. (A) I need to by some milk later.
(B) Sal is playing tennis with us later.
(C) We are going on vacation next month.
(D) No mistakes.

249. (A) My mother wants to have lunch with me.
(B) I didn't have time to finish reading the book.
(C) Our cat's name is Max.
(D) No mistakes.

250. (A) Tanya moved to Wisconsin.
(B) What time is it? "Joy asked."
(C) My sister has a splinter in her hand.
(D) No mistakes.

251. (A) Paul is a very good photographer.
(B) We usually get something to drink after school.
(C) Everything is all right.
(D) No mistakes.

252. (A) I would like some cookies to.
(B) My father wants me to come home now.
(C) Let's go to the dance later.
(D) No mistakes.

253. (A) The phone is ringing.
(B) I checked to see if the mail arrived yet.
(C) Their going to meet us later for dinner.
(D) No mistakes.

254. (A) We wanted to see the museum later.
(B) Her close were all over the floor.
(C) Mike will go away next year.
(D) No mistakes.

255. (A) I looked for a new skateboard yesterday.
(B) All he thinks about is basketball.
(C) She is going to Florida to visit her grandparents.
(D) No mistakes.

256. (A) I like that song alot.
(B) We have band practice after school tomorrow.
(C) Something is going to happen.
(D) No mistakes.

257. (A) Nancy is going to call me later.
(B) John likes to watch shows about penguins.
(C) I left your wallet in the table.
(D) No mistakes.

258. (A) If you find out what time we should meet, let me know.
(B) We took a lot of pictures at the show.
(C) How many money do you have?
(D) No mistakes.

259. (A) If we were in class, I'd be home sleeping.
(B) Yesterday, my brother went to the park.
(C) They talked loudly before the movie began.
(D) No mistakes.

GO TO NEXT PAGE ➡

260. **(A)** Shelly's little sister broked the vase.
     (B) Ian wrote a really good story.
     (C) Sam wants to use the computer.
     (D) No mistakes.

261. **(A)** She has done many strange things.
     (B) We went on a boat on lake erie.
     (C) Did you ever think about talking to her?
     (D) No mistakes.

262. **(A)** My aunt sent us some magazines to read.
     (B) We saw the following people at the park Marie, John, and his aunt.
     (C) Tomorrow we are going to the beach.
     (D) No mistakes.

263. **(A)** Please bring that newspaper article tomorrow.
     (B) We watched the sun set.
     (C) Mrs. Dodson came over to visit my mother.
     (D) No mistakes.

264. **(A)** After we brought home the dog my dad started to smile.
     (B) My cousins live at the beach.
     (C) Evan started to sing.
     (D) No mistakes.

265. **(A)** My baseball team has practice on Tuesdays.
     (B) The bottles of milk, and not the cereal, goes in the refrigerator.
     (C) She asked a very important question.
     (D) No mistakes.

266. **(A)** They painted the house a strange blue color.
     (B) We walked around the lake and played on the swings.
     (C) I wanted to borrow Judys bike.
     (D) No mistakes.

267. **(A)** I wanted to get that roll in the school play.
     (B) We watched the news on television last night.
     (C) The store sells different kinds of bread.
     (D) No mistakes.

268. **(A)** Saturday we are going to the dance.
     (B) The home team won the game.
     (C) My teacher really likes me writing.
     (D) No mistakes.

269. **(A)** What time are you going to the fair?
     (B) I paints a good picture.
     (C) We walked all the way to the park yesterday.
     (D) No mistakes.

270. **(A)** Phil likes to play video games.
     (B) There are thirty-nine students in my math class.
     (C) Marc watched the fireworks at the river.
     (D) No mistakes.

271. **(A)** Karen wants to go to England.
     (B) Joanna was on the phone all night long.
     (C) after I talked to Dana, I went to sleep.
     (D) No mistakes.

GO TO NEXT PAGE ➡

272. **(A)** After last nights performance, he was a little embarrassed.
     (B) The letter arrived in yesterday's mail.
     (C) Of course, I forgot my homework.
     (D) No mistakes.

273. **(A)** I broke my leg skiing last winter.
     (B) Four feet of snow fell last night.
     (C) Who's book is this?
     (D) No mistakes.

274. **(A)** My aunt was born on a leap day.
     (B) Afterwards, she lead us to the farm.
     (C) The clouds started to get darker.
     (D) No mistakes.

275. **(A)** She gave me some very important advice.
     (B) The dentist told me that I have three cavities.
     (C) Basically, he want me to go camping with him.
     (D) No mistakes.

276. **(A)** We went to a very good restaurant last night.
     (B) Why are you always late?
     (C) Its time for us to go home.
     (D) No mistakes.

277. **(A)** Can we see a menu?
     (B) He lie the book on the counter.
     (C) I tried to find it, but the library was closed.
     (D) No mistakes.

278. **(A)** He dances good.
     (B) The rain leaked through the roof.
     (C) I went to the doctor for an eye exam.
     (D) No mistakes.

Spelling

DIRECTIONS: Choose the sentence that contains a spelling error. If there are no errors, choose "D."

279. **(A)** The weather forecaster predicted rain for tomorow.
     (B) The musician played the piccolo in the orchestra.
     (C) The students were permitted to use calculators on the mathematics examination.
     (D) No mistakes.

280. **(A)** The sailors were stranded on a dessert island.
     (B) Several mourners gathered at the cemetery.
     (C) His fatigue may be caused by a vitamin deficiency.
     (D) No mistakes.

GO TO NEXT PAGE

281. (A) The retired English professor volunteers at the library on Wednesdays.
     (B) He canceled his dental appointment.
     (C) Max's guidance counseler advised him to take Spanish.
     (D) No mistakes.

282. (A) There are alot of vehicles in line at the inspection station.
     (B) My niece Jennifer performed in a dance recital yesterday.
     (C) The elderly gentleman preferred to travel by train.
     (D) No mistakes.

283. (A) A committee meeting was scheduled for 7:30 on February 1st.
     (B) His secretary's habitual tardiness cost her a promotion.
     (C) The investigator figured out the criminal's elaborate scheme.
     (D) No mistakes.

284. (A) Self-confidence is a valuable asset.
     (B) The reporter's constant interruptions were unnecessary.
     (C) The sophmore class assembled in the cafeteria.
     (D) No mistakes.

285. (A) The personnel manager interviewed the candidate.
     (B) The accomodations at the new waterfront hotel are luxurious.
     (C) We viewed the French countryside from a hot air balloon.
     (D) No mistakes.

286. (A) The politician delivered a lengthy campaign speech.
     (B) The optimistic job seeker submitted an application.
     (C) The high school principle addressed the student body.
     (D) No mistakes.

287. (A) Ann handed the police officer her license, registration, and insurance card.
     (B) Her patient exhibited signs of depression.
     (C) The signature on the perscription is illegible.
     (D) No mistakes.

288. (A) All roads in the vicinity of the accident were closed.
     (B) Eight planets revolve around the sun in our solar system.
     (C) Gossip is truly a waste of time and energy.
     (D) No mistakes.

GO TO NEXT PAGE ➡

HSPT

Composition

DIRECTIONS: Select the best answer choice.

289. Choose the correct word to join the thoughts together.

Tony's car registration had expired, _____ the police officer didn't give him a ticket.

(A) but
(B) and
(C) so
(D) None of these.

290. Choose the correct word to join the thoughts together.

I needed my friend's address at summer camp, _____ I called his parents.

(A) but
(B) so
(C) for
(D) None of these.

291. Choose the correct word to join the thoughts together.

Adriana set her alarm clock for one hour earlier than usual last night _____ she had to study for a science test.

(A) although
(B) if
(C) because
(D) None of these.

292. Choose the correct word to join the thoughts together.

Mary put on the sunscreen she bought _____ she had been at the beach for three hours.

(A) while
(B) before
(C) after
(D) None of these.

293. Choose the group of words that best completes the sentence.

Alyssa's bus was late; however, _____.

(A) she was late for school.
(B) she was on time for school.
(C) she was never on time for school.
(D) she had band practice before school.

294. Choose the group of words that best completes the sentence.

John wants to do well on the math test; therefore, _____.

(A) math is his favorite subject.
(B) he has not studied.
(C) he has been studying all week.
(D) it is the last test before the final exam.

GO TO NEXT PAGE

HSPT

295. Which of these expresses the idea most clearly?

(A) Jim went to Florida on vacation several people told me.

(B) To Florida on vacation, several people told me Jim went.

(C) Several people told me Jim went to Florida on vacation.

(D) Several people told me to Florida Jim went on vacation.

296. Which of these expresses the idea most clearly?

(A) Phyllis decided to invite some friends over on Saturday to celebrate her birthday.

(B) On Saturday to celebrate her birthday, Phyllis decided to invite some friends over.

(C) To celebrate her birthday, to invite some friends over Phyllis decided on Saturday.

(D) Phyllis decided on Saturday to celebrate her birthday to invite some friends over.

297. Which of these expresses the idea most clearly?

(A) I asked my friend to return my new baseball bat in time for the game.

(B) To return my new baseball bat I asked my friend in time for the game.

(C) In time for the game, I asked my friend to return my new baseball bat.

(D) I asked my friend in time for the game to return my new baseball bat.

298. Which of these expresses the idea most clearly?

(A) On the table, our parents were surprised to find dinner when they came home.

(B) Our parents were surprised to find dinner when they came home on the table.

(C) To find dinner on the table our parents were surprised when they came home.

(D) When they came home, our parents were surprised to find dinner on the table.

STOP

HSPT

Practice Test 1—Answer Key

Question Number	Correct Answer	If You Answered this Question Incorrectly, Refer to . . .
SUBTEST 1: VERBAL SKILLS		
1.	(C)	P. 231
2.	(C)	P. 228
3.	(D)	P. 231
4.	(D)	P. 231
5.	(A)	P. 227
6.	(A)	P. 228
7.	(B)	P. 231
8.	(C)	P. 228
9.	(A)	P. 229
10.	(D)	P. 229
11.	(C)	P. 233
12.	(C)	P. 233
13.	(A)	P. 233
14.	(A)	P. 233
15.	(D)	P. 233
16.	(D)	P. 233
17.	(A)	P. 233
18.	(C)	P. 233
19.	(B)	P. 233
20.	(A)	P. 233
21.	(B)	P. 233
22.	(A)	P. 233
23.	(A)	P. 233
24.	(D)	P. 233
25.	(C)	P. 233
26.	(C)	P. 224
27.	(C)	P. 224

HSPT

Question Number	Correct Answer	If You Answered this Question Incorrectly, Refer to . . .
28.	(B)	P. 224
29.	(B)	P. 224
30.	(A)	P. 224
31.	(A)	P. 224
32.	(A)	P. 224
33.	(A)	P. 224
34.	(B)	P. 226
35.	(B)	P. 226
36.	(A)	P. 231
37.	(B)	P. 231
38.	(D)	P. 231
39.	(A)	P. 231
40.	(A)	P. 231
41.	(D)	P. 231
42.	(B)	P. 231
43.	(D)	P. 231
44.	(B)	P. 231
45.	(C)	P. 231
46.	(C)	P. 231
47.	(B)	P. 231
48.	(D)	P. 231
49.	(B)	P. 231
50.	(D)	P. 231
51.	(A)	P. 231
52.	(C)	P. 232
53.	(A)	P. 232
54.	(C)	P. 232
55.	(B)	P. 232
56.	(B)	P. 232
57.	(D)	P. 232
58.	(D)	P. 232
59.	(C)	P. 232
60.	(D)	P. 232

SUBTEST 2: QUANTITATIVE SKILLS

61.	(D)	P. 424
62.	(B)	P. 422
63.	(A)	P. 422
64.	(B)	P. 424
65.	(C)	P. 350, 428
66.	(A)	P. 424
67.	(C)	P. 350, 428
68.	(B)	P. 422
69.	(A)	P. 350, 428
70.	(B)	P. 350, 428
71.	(C)	P. 424
72.	(B)	P. 422
73.	(B)	P. 350, 428
74.	(B)	P. 350, 392, 428
75.	(C)	P. 422
76.	(D)	P. 422
77.	(A)	P. 428
78.	(D)	P. 422
79.	(B)	P. 350, 373, 399, 427
80.	(C)	P. 350, 428
81.	(B)	P. 424
82.	(A)	P. 428
83.	(C)	P. 350, 427
84.	(B)	P. 424
85.	(B)	P. 428
86.	(C)	P. 422
87.	(B)	P. 422
88.	(C)	P. 350, 428
89.	(D)	P. 422
90.	(A)	P. 422
91.	(D)	P. 350, 428
92.	(D)	P. 388, 424
93.	(C)	P. 422
94.	(B)	P. 350, 428
95.	(D)	P. 422

Question Number	Correct Answer	If You Answered this Question Incorrectly, Refer to . . .
96.	(D)	P. 424
97.	(B)	P. 350, 428
98.	(C)	P. 427
99.	(B)	P. 422
100.	(A)	P. 424
101.	(D)	P. 350, 428
102.	(D)	P. 422
103.	(B)	P. 388, 427
104.	(C)	P. 424
105.	(A)	P. 422
106.	(B)	P. 350, 428
107.	(A)	P. 350, 428
108.	(C)	P. 379, 427
109.	(B)	P. 395, 424
110.	(A)	P. 422
111.	(B)	P. 350, 428
112.	(D)	P. 422
SUBTEST 3: READING COMPREHENSION		
113.	(C)	P. 302
114.	(D)	P. 302
115.	(C)	P. 302
116.	(C)	P. 302
117.	(A)	P. 302
118.	(D)	P. 302
119.	(B)	P. 302
120.	(A)	P. 310
121.	(D)	P. 302
122.	(C)	P. 302
123.	(B)	P. 302
124.	(D)	P. 302
125.	(A)	P. 302
126.	(D)	P. 302
127.	(B)	P. 302
128.	(D)	P. 302

129.	(A)	P. 302
130.	(C)	P. 302
131.	(B)	P. 302
132.	(D)	P. 302
133.	(B)	P. 302
134.	(A)	P. 302
135.	(D)	P. 302
136.	(D)	P. 302
137.	(C)	P. 310
138.	(C)	P. 302
139.	(D)	P. 305
140.	(D)	P. 302
141.	(D)	P. 302
142.	(B)	P. 302
143.	(C)	P. 302
144.	(A)	P. 302
145.	(A)	P. 310
146.	(D)	P. 302
147.	(A)	P. 302
148.	(B)	P. 300
149.	(C)	P. 310
150.	(B)	P. 302
151.	(D)	P. 302
152.	(C)	P. 302
VOCABULARY		
153.	(A)	P. 233, 313
154.	(B)	P. 233, 313
155.	(D)	P. 233, 313
156.	(C)	P. 233, 313
157.	(B)	P. 233, 313
158.	(C)	P. 233, 313
159.	(D)	P. 233, 313
160.	(A)	P. 233, 313
161.	(C)	P. 233, 313
162.	(D)	P. 233, 313
163.	(A)	P. 233, 313
164.	(B)	P. 233, 313

HSPT

Question Number	Correct Answer	If You Answered this Question Incorrectly, Refer to . . .
165.	(B)	P. 233, 313
166.	(D)	P. 233, 313
167.	(B)	P. 233, 313
168.	(B)	P. 233, 313
169.	(A)	P. 233, 313
170.	(D)	P. 233, 313
171.	(A)	P. 233, 313
172.	(D)	P. 233, 313
173.	(A)	P. 233, 313
174.	(B)	P. 233, 313
SUBTEST 4: MATHEMATICS CONCEPTS		
175.	(B)	P. 373
176.	(A)	P. 428
177.	(B)	P. 424
178.	(C)	P. 337, 428
179.	(C)	P. 428
180.	(D)	P. 350, 352
181.	(B)	P. 356
182.	(C)	P. 395
183.	(D)	P. 388
184.	(A)	P. 352, 365
185.	(A)	P. 352
186.	(D)	P. 399
187.	(A)	P. 399
188.	(D)	P. 388
189.	(A)	P. 407
190.	(D)	P. 407
191.	(B)	P. 395
192.	(B)	P. 424
193.	(B)	P. 390, 424
194.	(A)	P. 424
195.	(D)	P. 424
196.	(A)	P. 373
197.	(C)	P. 407
198.	(D)	P. 407

PROBLEM-SOLVING		
199.	**(B)**	P. 379
200.	**(B)**	P. 399, 410
201.	**(D)**	P. 378, 395
202.	**(C)**	P. 341, 345
203.	**(A)**	P. 355
204.	**(A)**	P. 410
205.	**(A)**	P. 402
206.	**(B)**	P. 390
207.	**(B)**	P. 395
208.	**(D)**	P. 341, 345
209.	**(D)**	P. 341, 345
210.	**(A)**	P. 341, 345
211.	**(D)**	P. 339
212.	**(D)**	P. 350
213.	**(C)**	P. 399
214.	**(B)**	P. 402
215.	**(D)**	P. 341, 365, 370
216.	**(B)**	P. 351
217.	**(B)**	P. 399
218.	**(A)**	P. 337, 339
219.	**(B)**	P. 408
220.	**(A)**	P. 408
221.	**(A)**	P. 396
222.	**(B)**	P. 375, 377
223.	**(D)**	P. 400
224.	**(A)**	P. 400
225.	**(A)**	P. 402
226.	**(C)**	P. 379, 427
227.	**(A)**	P. 399, 427
228.	**(B)**	P. 399
229.	**(B)**	P. 427
230.	**(D)**	P. 427
231.	**(C)**	P. 408
232.	**(B)**	P. 395
233.	**(C)**	P. 407
234.	**(B)**	P. 407

Question Number	Correct Answer	If You Answered this Question Incorrectly, Refer to . . .
235.	(D)	P. 337, 345
236.	(D)	P. 399, 427
237.	(A)	P. 399
238.	(C)	P. 410
SUBTEST 5: LANGUAGE SKILLS PUNCTUATION, CAPITALIZATION, AND USAGE		
239.	(B)	P. 245
240.	(A)	P. 275
241.	(D)	P. 247, 275
242.	(C)	P. 261
243.	(C)	P. 275
244.	(A)	P. 279
245.	(C)	P. 264
246.	(A)	P. 246
247.	(B)	P. 261
248.	(A)	P. 279
249.	(D)	P. 269
250.	(B)	P. 270
251.	(C)	P. 281
252.	(A)	P. 279
253.	(C)	P. 251
254.	(B)	P. 279
255.	(D)	P. 247
256.	(A)	P. 279
257.	(C)	P. 246
258.	(C)	P. 257
259.	(A)	P. 239
260.	(A)	P. 246
261.	(B)	P. 276
262.	(B)	P. 268
263.	(D)	P. 275, 283
264.	(A)	P. 262
265.	(B)	P. 247
266.	(C)	P. 269

267.	(A)	P. 279
268.	(C)	P. 254
269.	(B)	P. 247
270.	(D)	P. 247
271.	(C)	P. 275
272.	(A)	P. 269
273.	(C)	P. 254
274.	(B)	P. 279
275.	(C)	P. 247
276.	(C)	P. 269
277.	(B)	P. 245
278.	(A)	P. 258

SPELLING

279.	(A)	P. 283
280.	(A)	P. 281
281.	(C)	P. 280
282.	(A)	P. 279
283.	(D)	P. 279
284.	(C)	P. 283
285.	(B)	P. 279
286.	(C)	P. 283
287.	(C)	P. 283
288.	(D)	P. 279

COMPOSITION

289.	(A)	P. 242
290.	(B)	P. 242
291.	(C)	P. 242
292.	(C)	P. 242
293.	(B)	P. 242
294.	(C)	P. 242
295.	(C)	P. 239
296.	(A)	P. 239
297.	(A)	P. 239
298.	(D)	P. 239

HSPT

Verbal Skills—Detailed Explanations of Answers

1. **(C)** A *sunset* occurs in the *evening* as a *sunrise* occurs in the *morning*.

2. **(C)** A *county* is part of a *state* as a *country* is part of a *continent*.

3. **(D)** A *rash* is a visible symptom of *measles* as *swollen glands* are visible symptoms of *mumps*. Although an elevated body temperature, or *fever* **(C)**, is a symptom of an infection, it is not the correct answer because it is not a visible symptom like a *rash*.

4. **(D)** A *ruler* is used to *measure* as *scissors* are used to *cut*.

5. **(A)** *Her* is the possessive form of the third person singular pronoun *she*; *their* is the possessive form of the third person plural pronoun *they*. *Theirs* **(B)** is also a possessive form of the pronoun *they*; however, it is not the correct answer. Unlike *her* and *their*, which must be followed by nouns (*her* blanket; *their* children), *theirs* stands alone. (The new black car is *theirs*.)

6. **(A)** A *century* is one hundred years as a *decade* is ten years. A *millennium* **(B)** is 1,000 years.

7. **(B)** A *canopy covers* as a *moat surrounds*.

8. **(C)** A *teacher* works in a *school* as a *doctor* works in a *hospital*. Although a *teacher* does teach in a *classroom* **(B)**, the *school*, or the building, is analogous to a *hospital*, not a single room.

9. **(A)** A *book* is divided into *chapters* as a *play* is divided into *acts*.

10. **(D)** A *floor* can be made of *tile* as a *sidewalk* can be made of *concrete*.

11. **(C)** *Endure* means to *tolerate* **(C)**. The two words are similar and are synonyms. The word *perish* **(A)** means to *pass away*. The word *reject* **(B)** means to *discard* or *lay aside*, and the word *fail* **(D)** means to *fall short*. Neither **(A)**, **(B)**, nor **(D)** is a synonym of the word *endure*. Since *tolerate* **(C)** means the same as *endure*, it is the best answer.

12. **(C)** *Pessimism* most nearly means *distrust* or *cynicism* **(C)**. *Pessimism* does not mean *idealism* **(A)**, *visionary* **(B)**, or *optimism* **(D)**; these words suggest a positive outlook and hope. They are opposites of *pessimism*. The best choice for a synonym of *pessimism* is *suspicion* **(C)**.

13. **(A)** *Skeptical* most nearly means *unbelieving* or *doubtful* **(A)**. The words *confident* **(B)** and *convinced* **(D)** imply that something is believed. They are not synonymous with the word *skeptical*. The word *certain* **(C)** is the opposite of *skeptical*. The best answer for a synonym of *skeptical* is *doubtful* **(A)**.

14. **(A)** *Rectify* most nearly means to *right*, to *correct* **(A)**, to *make better*, or to *ameliorate*. The best answer is **(A)**. The word *rectify* does not mean to *destroy* **(B)**, to *dilapidate* **(C)**, or to *demolish* **(D)**—words which imply ruination. The word most nearly like *rectify* is the synonym *correct* **(A)**.

15. **(D)** To *retract* is to *take back*, to *reconsider*, to *deny* **(D)**. *Retract* is the opposite of *uphold* **(A)**, *declare* **(B)**, or *admit* **(C)**. To *admit* **(C)** is to *clear up*, to *make clear*, to *explain*; this term is not synonymous with *retract*. The best answer for a synonym of *retract* is **(D)**—*deny*.

16. **(D)** *Protagonist* most nearly means *hero* **(D)**. The *protagonist* is the opposite of the *villain* **(A)**, the *antagonist* **(B)**, or the "bad guy." Although the *protagonist* might be a *professor* **(C)**, the word *professor* **(C)** is not necessarily a synonym of the word *protagonist*. *Hero* **(D)** is the synonym the test is seeking.

17. **(A)** *Revenge* means to *get even*, to *repay* **(A)**. The word *revenge* may suggest the word *rector* and *clerical* **(B)** to some test-takers, but the religious rector or cleric is not synonymous with *revenge*. To *advocate* **(C)** or to *suggest* is not the same as to *repay* or to *retaliate*. Neither **(B)** nor **(C)** is the correct answer. *Danger* **(D)** does not necessarily mean *revenge*; **(D)** is not the best synonym. The best choice as a synonym of *revenge* is *repay* **(A)**.

18. **(C)** *Paranoid* most nearly means *suspicious* **(C)**, *uneasy*, *mistrustful*. *Paranoid* is the opposite of *trusting* **(A)**; the test-taker, however, is seeking a synonym, not an antonym. The word *angry* **(B)** is not a word which means the same as *paranoid*. The word *confident* **(D)** is also an antonym of *paranoid*. The best choice is *suspicious* **(C)**.

19. **(B)** A *martyr* is a *victim* **(B)**. In fact, the martyr often loses his life. A *martyr* is not a *victor* **(C)**, or one who wins. A *martyr* is not necessarily a *manager* **(A)** or an *overseer*. A *delinquent* **(D)** is the antonym of *martyr*. The best choice for a synonym of *martyr* is clearly *victim* **(B)**.

20. **(A)** *Regime* most nearly means the *reign* **(A)** or the *rule* of a particular period or person. The *regime* may last a *generation* **(B)** or longer—or shorter; the time span of a *generation* is not necessarily a component of *regime* and is not a synonym of the term. *Luxurious* **(C)** means *elegant*; **(C)** is not the best choice as a word meaning the same as *regime*. The test-taker who selected *regimen* **(D)** as the synonym of *regime* probably confused the shape of the words. The best word to express a similar meaning to a *regime* is *reign* **(A)**.

21. **(B)** *Detest* most nearly means *loathe* **(B)**. The words *like* **(A)**, *cherish* **(C)**, and *idolize* **(D)** are antonyms of the word *detest*. These words suggest *love* or *appreciation*. The best answer for a synonym of *detest* is *loathe* **(B)**.

22. **(A)** *Rational* most nearly means *logical* **(A)** or *sensible*. The words *insane* **(B)**, *unreasonable* **(C)**, and *foolish* **(D)** are opposite from the word *rational*. The best answer is **(A)**.

23. **(A)** *Obscure* means *unclear* **(A)**. The two words are synonyms. The words *distinct* **(B)** and *evident* **(D)** imply *clarity* and *clearness*. The word *known* **(C)** means the opposite of *obscure*. The best answer for a synonym of *obscure* is *unclear* **(A)**.

24. **(D)** To *dissuade* is to *deter, hinder, obstruct,* or *thwart* **(D)**. The best synonym for *dissuade* is choice **(D)**—*thwart. Disapprove* **(A)** is similar in shape—not meaning—to *dissuade. Camouflage* **(B)** means to *mask,* to *cover,* or to *hide.* Choice **(B)** is not a similar word to *dissuade* and is not a good choice. *Encourage* **(C)** is an antonym or an opposite word from *dissuade.* Again, **(A)**, **(B)**, and **(C)** are not acceptable answers. The best synonym is **(D)**.

25. **(C)** *Terminate* is to *finish* or *conclude* **(C)**. These are synonyms. The words *start* **(A)**, *originate* **(B)**, and *initiate* **(D)** are antonyms of the word *terminate.* They refer to a beginning, while *terminate* refers to an end. The best answer is **(C)**.

26. **(C)** **Uncertain** is correct. The truth of the third statement is uncertain because the first two statements, which we know are true, give us no information about Victor.

27. **(C)** **Uncertain** is correct. The truth of the third statement is uncertain because the first two statements, which we know are true, give us no information about Alison.

28. **(B)** **False** is correct. If Jefferson High School has more students than Roosevelt High School, and Roosevelt has more students than Lincoln High School, then Lincoln cannot have more than Jefferson.

29. **(B)** **False** is correct. If Mrs. Perez has more children than Mrs. Martin, and Mrs. Martin has more children than Mrs. Lee, then Mrs. Lee cannot have more children than Mrs. Perez.

30. **(A)** **True** is correct. If every family in Sunrise Village has a car, and the Palmers do not have a car, then the Palmers cannot live in Sunrise Village.

31. **(A)** **True** is correct. If every adult in Beechwood voted in the last presidential election, and Mr. Turner didn't vote, then Mr. Turner cannot live in Beechwood.

32. **(A)** **True** is correct. If Wednesday was warmer than Tuesday, and Monday was cooler than Tuesday, then Monday also must have been cooler than Wednesday.

33. **(A)** **True** is correct. If Bill's house is larger than Fred's, and Lucille's house is smaller than Fred's, then Lucille's house also must be smaller than Bill's.

34. **(B)** **False** is correct. If the first two statements are true, then the opposite of the third statement is true: The swimming pool is *closer* to the ice cream parlor than the tennis courts are to the beach.

35. **(B)** **False** is correct. If the first two statements are true, then the opposite of the third statement is true: The train station is *farther* from the bank than the supermarket is from the library.

36. **(A)** A *program* is computer software, while a *monitor,* a *printer,* and a *keyboard* are computer hardware.

37. **(B)** *Rice, wheat,* and *corn* are all kinds of *cereals,* or grains, that can be eaten.

38. **(D)** *Alleviate, reduce,* and *lessen* have nearly the same meaning, while *increase* has the opposite meaning.

39. **(A)** *Gold* is a precious metal, while *diamonds, emeralds,* and *sapphires* are precious gemstones.

40. **(A)** *Snakes*, *turtles*, and *crocodiles* are all kinds of *reptiles*.

41. **(D)** A *guitar* is classified as a stringed instrument, while the *piano*, *drums*, and *cymbals* are classified as percussion instruments.

42. **(B)** A *pound* is a unit of dry measurement, while an *ounce*, a *gallon*, and a *quart* are units of liquid measurement. Although an *ounce* can also be used in dry measurement, *pound* is the correct answer because it is never used for liquid measurement.

43. **(D)** *Sodium* is solid, while *nitrogen*, *oxygen*, and *helium* are gases.

44. **(B)** *Marble* is a kind of stone, while *tin*, *copper*, and *nickel* are metals.

45. **(C)** *Tense*, *anxious*, and *nervous* have nearly the same meaning, while *relaxed* has the opposite meaning.

46. **(C)** *Odor*, *smell*, and *scent* have nearly the same meaning. *Stench* is also a smell, but it is only an unpleasant smell; the other words can be either pleasant or unpleasant.

47. **(B)** A *mother*, a *niece*, and a *sister* are female relatives; a *cousin* can be either male or female.

48. **(D)** All of the words begin with the prefix *un-*, which means *not*. However, *uncomfortable* has a different meaning from *undecided*, *uncertain*, and *unsure*, which are synonyms.

49. **(B)** *Cactus* is a singular form of a word, while *media*, *alumni*, and *data* are plural forms.

50. **(D)** *Classroom*, *blackberry*, and *lighthouse* are all compound words, that is, words that are formed by joining two words. *Dreamer* is not a compound word.

51. **(A)** *Addition*, *subtraction*, and *division* are all mathematical operations; however, a *fraction* is a way to express a number.

52. **(C)** *Metropolitan* means *urban* **(A)**, *cosmopolitan* **(B)**, *city-like* **(D)**, and *current* or *up-to-date*. The word does NOT mean *old* or *antiquated* **(C)**. Because *antiquated* is the opposite of *current*, it is an antonym. The best answer for an opposite word is *antiquated* **(C)**.

53. **(A)** *Miserly* means *saving*, *cheap* **(B)**, *avaricious* **(C)**, or *stingy* **(D)**. It does not mean *generous* **(A)** or *open-handed*. The best of the choices for a word opposite of *miserly* is *generous* **(A)**.

54. **(C)** *Malign* means *unfavorable* **(A)**, *malicious* **(B)**, or *evil* **(D)**. *Malign* does not mean *good*, *gracious*, *kind*, *harmless*, or *benign* **(C)**. The opposite word, then, is **(C)**.

55. **(B)** *Impenetrable* means *not penetrable*, *not pervious*, *not transparent*. An impenetrable paint is *thick* **(D)**, heavy; because one cannot see through impenetrable paint, it is *opaque* **(A)**, or *nontransparent*. Something that is difficult to understand or to see through easily is *obscure* **(C)**. *Impenetrable*, then, is opposite of *translucent*, which means thin or almost transparent. The best choice for an antonym of *impenetrable* is *translucent* **(B)**.

56. **(B)** *Courtly* means *sophisticated*, *dignified* **(A)**, *cultured* **(C)**, and *stately* **(D)**. It is the opposite (the antonym) of *frivolous* **(B)**, which means *unimportant* or *trivial*. The word *frivolous* **(B)** is the best answer as an antonym to *courtly*.

57. **(D)** *Melancholy* means *sad* **(A)** or *depressed* **(B)**; it can also be a synonym of *dejected*, *gloomy*, or *despondent* **(C)**. It is the opposite of *happy* or *ecstatic* **(D)**. The antonym of *melancholy* is **(D)**.

58. **(D)** *Occasional* means *alternate* **(A)**, *periodic* **(B)**, or *rhythmical* **(C)**. *Incessant* **(D)** means *nonstopping*. It is the opposite of *occasional*. The antonym of *occasional* is **(D)**.

59. **(C)** *Stalwart* means *gallant* **(A)**, *valorous* **(B)**, or *dauntless* **(D)**. It does not mean *cowardly*, *fearful*, or *timid* **(C)**. The opposite of the word *stalwart* is **(C)**.

60. **(D)** *Glowing* means *ruddy* **(A)**, *vivid* **(B)**, or *incandescent* **(C)**. It does not mean *doleful* **(D)**, *sad*, or *dismal*. The right choice for the antonym of *glowing* is *doleful* **(D)**.

HSPT

HSPT

Quantitative Skills—Detailed Explanations of Answers

For each problem, the answer will be given first. Then we will name the type of question—Series, Comparison, or Pre-algebra.

For Series questions, we will show the pattern on the list of numbers, state the rule, and get the answer.

For Comparison questions, we will give the quantities associated with (a), (b), and (c) or the picture, and, if necessary, explain how to get them. The correct choice of (A), (B), (C), or (D) will then be obvious.

For Pre-algebra questions, we will use the word method to arrive at the correct answer. Remember: You may want to use trial-and-error for some or all of the Pre-algebra questions.

61. **(D)** (c) is less than (a) and more than (b). Comparison. (a) = 11, (b) = 9, and (c) = 10. Count items.

62. **(B)** 38. Series.

$$
\begin{array}{ccccccccc}
& -13 & & -13 & & -13 & & -13 = \underline{38} \\
& \diagup \;\diagdown & & \diagup \;\diagdown & & \diagup \;\diagdown & & \diagup \\
90 & & 77 & & 64 & & 51 &
\end{array}
$$

Rule: Subtract 13. Answer: $51 - 13 = 38$.

63. **(A)** 56. Series.

$$
\begin{array}{ccccccccccc}
& -8 & & -3 & & -8 & & -3 & & -8 = 56 \\
& \diagup \;\diagdown & & \diagup \;\diagdown & & \diagup \;\diagdown & & \diagup \;\diagdown & & \diagup \\
86 & & 78 & & 75 & & 67 & & 64 &
\end{array}
$$

Rule: Subtract 8, then subtract 3. Answer: $64 - 8 = 56$.

64. **(B)** (a) is greater than (b) and greater than (c). Comparison. (a) = $7 \times 5 = 35$, (b) = $3 + 20 = 23$, and (c) = $8 \times 4 = 32$.

65. (C)   15. Pre-algebra. $\frac{1}{2}$ of 16 = $\frac{1}{2}$ × 16 = 8; 7 more than 8 = 8 + 7 = 15.

66. (A)   (a), (b), and (c) are equal. Comparison. Each shaded area represents $\frac{1}{2}$ of the rectangle.

67. (C)   (c) is greater than (a) and less than (b). Comparison. (a) = 12, (b) = 16, and (c) = 15. Multiplication of fractions.

68. (B)   48. Series.

$$
\begin{array}{ccccccccc}
& +4 & & +6 & & +5 & & +7 & & +6 = \underline{48} \\
\diagup & \diagdown & \diagup & \diagdown & \diagup & \diagdown & \diagup & \diagdown & \diagup \\
20 & & 24 & & 30 & & 35 & & 42
\end{array}
$$

Rule: Add a number, add 2 more than the previous number, add 1 less than the previous, add 2 more than the previous, etc. 42 + 6 = 48.

69. (A)   10. Pre-algebra. $\frac{2}{3}$ of 21 = $\frac{2}{3}$ × 21 = 14. 4 less than 14 = 14 − 4 = 10.

70. (B)   17. Pre-algebra. $\frac{1}{5}$ of 35 = $\frac{1}{5}$ × 35 = 7. 10 more than 7 = 7 + 10 = 17.

71. (C)   (a) is less than (b) and greater than (c). Comparison. (a) = $\frac{5}{9}$ = $\frac{10}{18}$, (b) = $\frac{2}{3}$ = $\frac{12}{18}$, and (c) = $\frac{1}{2}$ = $\frac{9}{18}$. Find a common denominator: 18.

72. (B)   140. Series.

$$
\begin{array}{ccccccccc}
& -20 & & -16 & & -12 & & -8 & & -4 = \underline{140} \\
\diagup & \diagdown & \diagup & \diagdown & \diagup & \diagdown & \diagup & \diagdown & \diagup \\
200 & & 180 & & 164 & & 152 & & 144
\end{array}
$$

Rule: Subtract 20, then amounts that drop by 4 each time. 144 − 4 = $\underline{140}$.

73. (B)   13. Pre-algebra. $\frac{1}{10}$ of 90 = $\frac{1}{10}$ × 90 = 9. The number subtracted from 22 to give 9 is 22 − 9, or 13.

74. (B)   6. Pre-algebra. Half of 72 = $\frac{1}{2}$ × 72 = 36. The number which multiplied by itself gives 36 is 6.

75. (C)   70. Series.

$$
\begin{array}{ccccccccc}
& +9 & & +4 & & +9 & & +4 & & +9 = \underline{70} \\
\diagup & \diagdown & \diagup & \diagdown & \diagup & \diagdown & \diagup & \diagdown & \diagup \\
35 & & 44 & & 48 & & 57 & & 61
\end{array}
$$

Rule: Add 9, then add 4. 61 + 9 = 70.

76. **(D)** 1956. Series.

$$\underset{2008\qquad 1995\qquad 1982\qquad 1969}{\overset{-13\qquad -13\qquad -13\qquad -13 = \underline{1956}}{\diagup\diagdown\diagup\diagdown\diagup\diagdown\diagup}}$$

Rule: Subtract 13. 1969 − 13 = 1956.

77. **(A)** 14. Pre-algebra. 3 more than 95 = 95 + 3 = 98. The number multiplied by 7 to give 98 is 98 ÷ 7, or 14.

78. **(D)** 35. Series.

$$\underset{8\qquad 17\qquad 26\qquad \underline{35}\qquad 44\qquad 53}{\overset{+9\qquad +9\qquad +9\qquad +9\qquad +9}{\diagup\diagdown\diagup\diagdown\diagup\diagdown\diagup\diagdown}}$$

Rule: Add 9. 26 + 9 = 35.

79. **(B)** (b) is greater than (a) and greater than (c). Comparison. (a) = .55, (b) = .60, and (c) = .50. Convert to the same form of fraction. You could also use ratios or percents.

80. **(C)** 39. Pre-algebra. 5 less than 18 = 18 − 5 = 13. The number divided by 3 to yield 13 is 3 times 13, or 39.

81. **(B)** *AD* is less than *AC*. Comparison. Since the triangle is equilateral, all sides are equal in length. The altitude or height (*AD*) in an equilateral triangle is shorter than the sides, but greater than half a side.

82. **(A)** 5. Pre-algebra. 20 less than 45 = 45 − 20 = 25. The number multiplied by itself to give 25 is 5.

83. **(C)** (a) is greater than (b) and greater than (c). Comparison. (a) $= \frac{7}{16} = \frac{14}{32}$, (b) $= \frac{3}{8} = \frac{12}{32}$, and (c) $= \frac{13}{32}$. Find a common denominator: 32.

84. **(B)** *AE* is equal to *DE*. Comparison. As the circle is drawn, the only thing we can be sure of is that the radii, *AE* and *DE*, are equal in length. As shown in the picture, the other relationships do not appear to be true.

85. **(B)** 200. Pre-algebra. 20 less than 30 = 30 − 20 = 10. The number divided by 20 that gives 10 is 20 × 10, or 200.

86. **(C)** 2. Series.

$$\underset{512\qquad 128\qquad 32\qquad 8}{\overset{\div 4\qquad \div 4\qquad \div 4\qquad \div 4 = \underline{2}}{\diagup\diagdown\diagup\diagdown\diagup\diagdown\diagup}}$$

Rule: Divide by 4. 8 ÷ 4 = 2.

87. (B) 2. Series.

$$\overset{\div 3}{\underset{90 \qquad 30}{\diagup \diagdown}} \quad \overset{-3}{\underset{27}{\diagup \diagdown}} \quad \overset{\div 3}{\underset{9}{\diagup \diagdown}} \quad \overset{-3}{\underset{6}{\diagup \diagdown}} \quad \overset{\div 3 = \underline{2}}{\diagup}$$

Rule: Divide by 3, then subtract 3. $6 \div 3 = 2$.

88. (C) 16. Pre-algebra. $\frac{1}{3}$ of $36 = \frac{1}{3} \times 36 = 12$. If $\frac{3}{4}$ of a number is 12, the number must be $\frac{4}{3}$ of 12. $\frac{4}{3}$ of $12 = \frac{4}{3} \times 12 = 16$.

89. (D) XL. Series.

$$\overset{+5}{\underset{XX \qquad XXV}{\diagup \diagdown}} \quad \overset{+5}{\underset{XXX}{\diagup \diagdown}} \quad \overset{+5}{\underset{XXXV}{\diagup \diagdown}} \quad \overset{+5 = \underline{40} \text{ or } \underline{XL}}{\diagup}$$

Rule: Add 5. $35 + 5 = 40$, which is written XL in Roman numerals.

90. (A) 17. Series.

$$\overset{-8}{\underset{53 \qquad 45}{\diagup \diagdown}} \quad \overset{-4}{\underset{41}{\diagup \diagdown}} \quad \overset{-8}{\underset{33}{\diagup \diagdown}} \quad \overset{-4}{\underset{29}{\diagup \diagdown}} \quad \overset{-8}{\underset{21}{\diagup \diagdown}} \quad \overset{-4 = \underline{17}}{\diagup}$$

Rule: Subtract 8, subtract 4. $21 - 4 = 17$.

91. (D) 96. Pre-algebra. 4 multiplied by itself $= 4 \times 4 = 16$. If $\frac{1}{6}$ of a number is 16, the number must be 6×16, or 96.

92. (D) (c) is less than (a) and less than (b). Comparison. (a) $16 \div 8 = 2$, and $2 \times 2 = 4$, (b) $16 \div 2 = 8$, and $8 \times 8 = 64$, and (c) $8 \times 2 = 16$, and $16 \div 16 = 1$.

93. (C) 72. Series.

$$\overset{+2}{\underset{61 \qquad 63}{\diagup \diagdown}} \quad \overset{+7}{\underset{70}{\diagup \diagdown}} \quad \overset{+2}{\underset{\underline{72}}{\diagup \diagdown}} \quad \overset{+7}{\underset{79}{\diagup \diagdown}} \quad \overset{+2}{\underset{81}{\diagup \diagdown}} \quad \overset{+7}{\underset{88}{\diagup \diagdown}}$$

Rule: Add 2, then add 7. $70 + 2 = 72$.

94. (B) 24. Pre-algebra. $\frac{1}{8}$ of $32 = \frac{1}{8} \times 32 = 4$. The number divided by 6 to get 4 is 6 times 4, or 24.

95. (D)   48. Series.

Rule: Subtract 4, then multiply by 2. $24 \times 2 = 48$.

96. (D)   (a), (b), and (c) are all equal. Comparison. Each part of the picture graph represents 20. (a) = $2 \times 10 = 20$, (b) = $10 + 5 + 5 = 20$, and (c) = $4 \times 5 = 20$.

97. (B)   1. Pre-algebra. $\frac{5}{6}$ of $30 = \frac{5}{6} \times 30 = 25$. 4 more than $25 = 25 + 4 = 29$. The number subtracted from 30 to give 29 must be $30 - 29$, or 1.

98. (C)   (a) $\neq$ (b), (b) $\neq$ (c), (a) $\neq$ (c). Comparison. None of the three algebraic expressions are equal.

99. (B)   74, 70. Series.

Rule: Subtract 4, then add 11. $63 + 11 = 74$, $74 - 4 = 70$.

100. (A)   (a) is equal to (b). Comparison. (a) = 24 ounces, or $1\frac{1}{2}$ pounds, (b) = 24 ounces or $1\frac{1}{2}$ pounds, and (c) = 2 pounds, or 32 ounces. We must know that 1 pound is equal to 16 ounces.

101. (D)   30. Pre-algebra. $\frac{1}{2}$ of $8 = \frac{1}{2} \times 8 = 4$, the product of 5 and $4 = 5 \times 4 = 20$, twice $20 = 2 \times 20 = 40$. The number added to 10 to get 40 is $40 - 10$, or 30.

102. (D)   93. Series.

68   109   72   101   76   93

Rule: Use every other number. For 68, 72, 76, add 4. For 109, 101, subtract 8. $101 - 8 = 93$. It is possible to do this using one number after the other, but the rule is more complicated: the number you subtract is 4 less than the previous number that you added, and the number you add is 8 less than the previous number that you subtracted.

103. (B) (a) is equal to (c). Comparison. (a) = 2^4 = $2 \times 2 \times 2 \times 2$ = 16, (b) = 3^3 = $3 \times 3 \times 3$ = 27, and (c) = 4^2 = 4×4 = 16. The exponent tells the number of times the base number must be written before it is multiplied.

104. (C) (a) minus (d) equals (b) plus (d). Comparison. Here, the length of the bar on the bar graph gives the size. (a) = 50, (b) = 30, (c) = 20, and (d) = 10.

105. (A) 5. Series.

Rule: Subtract 3, then divide by 3. $8 - 3 = 5$.

106. (B) 12. Pre-algebra. $\frac{1}{2}$ of 16 = $\frac{1}{2} \times 16$ = 8. 3 times 8 = 3×8 = 24. The number multiplied by 2 to give 24 is $24 \div 2$, or 12.

107. (A) 8. Pre-algebra. $\frac{2}{3}$ of 42 = $\frac{2}{3} \times 42$ = 28, $\frac{5}{9}$ of 36 = $\frac{5}{9} \times 36$ = 20. The number added to 20 to get 28 is $28 - 20$, or 8.

108. (C) (a) is equal to (b) which is less than (c). Comparison. (a) = $.3 \times .4$ = .12, (b) = $.6 \times .2$ = .12, and (c) = 1×1.2 = 1.2. When numbers are multiplied, add the number of decimal places in the factors to get the number of decimal places in the answer.

109. (B) The area of the parallelogram is 12. Comparison. This is more of a geometry question. The area of a parallelogram is given by multiplying the base times the height, in this case 3×4, which equals 12. We can figure out the lengths of the slanting sides in the parallelogram using the Pythagorean Theorem: $a^2 + b^2 = c^2$. $3^2 + 4^2 = 9 + 16 = 25$, and $5^2 = 25$, so the other side is 5. Because b is the correct answer, we don't actually need to know this length for this problem.

110. (A) 59, 52, 61. Series.

Rule: Add, then subtract, then add, etc. The amount we add increases by 1. The amount we subtract increases by 2. $51 + 8 = 59$, $59 - 7 = 52$, and $52 + 9 = 61$.

111. (B) 12. Pre-algebra. $\frac{1}{4}$ of 12 = $\frac{1}{4} \times 12$ = 3. 2 times 3 = 2×3 = 6. The number subtracted from 10 to give 6 is $10 - 6$, or 4. $\frac{1}{4}$ of a number equals 4, so the number must be 3×4, or 12.

112. (D)   69. Series.

$$
\begin{array}{ccccccccccc}
 & +6 & & +6 & & -3 & & +6 & & +6 & & -3 = \underline{69}\\
 & \diagup & \diagdown & \diagup & \diagdown & \diagup & \diagdown & \diagup & \diagdown & \diagup & \diagdown & \diagup\\
51 & & 57 & & 63 & & 60 & & 66 & & 72 &
\end{array}
$$

Rule: Add 6, add 6, subtract 3. $72 - 3 = 69$.

Reading—Detailed Explanations of Answers

Comprehension

113. (C) According to the passage, star movements **(B)** appeared in the medieval almanac. Church feast days and elaborate calendars **(D)** were added in the sixteenth century, as were weather predictions **(A)**. Jokes and humor **(C)** appeared in the seventeenth century.

114. (D) The almanac did not include extra days **(A)**. Contemporary almanacs are not discussed in this passage **(C)**. The passage discusses almanacs from medieval times, so Franklin could not have invented the almanac **(C)**; however, Franklin published his *Poor Richard's Almanac* from 1732–1758 **(B)**.

115. (C) Choices **(A)**, **(B)**, and **(D)** are not supported by the passage.

116. (C) The passage states that almanacs in Germany included "sophisticated, contemporary poetry by serious authors."

117. (A) The passage describes how almanacs in the sixteenth century began to be issued every year and included weather predictions.

118. (D) The passage does not describe how the coach felt about the protest.

119. (B) The passage describes how the players promised to play the next scheduled game that season.

120. (A) The players met with the Director of Athletics to discuss their reasons for walking off of the court. The word *problems* best expresses this.

121. (D) The passage does state that the members of the team will play again; however, there were six members who walked off and not five **(A)**. It did not mention any apologies **(B, C)**. But it did state that the six members would practice despite their concerns.

122. (C) This passage does not support choices **(A)**, **(B)**, or **(D)**.

123. **(B)** While it is expressed that a literacy program needs to be empathetic towards its participants **(C)**, the overall goal is to teach its participants to read and write **(B)**. The program should not be sympathetic **(D)** but should meet the needs of both functional **(A)** and complete illiterates.

124. **(D)** The author is concerned that the issue of adult literacy is not viewed as a serious problem **(D)** since politicians do not seem to be addressing it. Calling adult literacy a "women's interest issue" does not mean that more women are affected by it **(A)**. Being a social problem does not make it less real **(B)**. Many women are politicians **(C)**.

125. **(A)** The emphasis placed on empathy and on ensuring that the participants experience success shows how the self-esteem of the participants is an important responsibility for literacy programs **(A)**. Political support is not the responsibility of the program **(B)**. Books and magazines **(C, D)** are not mentioned as part of a literacy program's responsibilities.

126. **(D)** The passage describes how a functionally illiterate person can read and write a little **(A and C)** and can be helped by a literacy program **(B)**. The correct answer is **(D)**, all of the above.

127. **(B)** Weighted, plastic barrel-shaped tubes were used to help clean up the environment **(B)**. Offshore drilling can result in oil spills **(A)** and coastal winds and tides **(C, and D)**, carry the oil to the shore quickly.

128. **(D)** The passage does not describe who pays the cost of oil spill cleanups **(D)**.

129. **(A)** The passage says some states want to help cover the cost of cleaning up oil spills.

130. **(C)** The passage describes how the workers tried to minimize the damage caused by the oil spill by using the weighted, barrel-shaped tubes **(A)** and by shoveling oil-covered sand into plastic bags for removal **(B)**. The correct answer is **(C)**.

131. **(B)** The opening sentence states that the price of cleaning up after oil spills is increasing, and the passage continues to describe how numerous spills have occurred

132. **(D)** The last paragraph of the passage states the breakdown of a proper diet for a person with diabetes **(D)**.

133. **(B)** The second paragraph states that the standard treatment for juvenile diabetics is insulin replacement therapy **(B)**.

134. **(A)** The first paragraph of the passage describes how diabetes is the result of insufficient amounts of insulin made by the body. Insulin is used by the body to take glucose from the blood for fuel; a deficiency in insulin results in high blood levels and low tissue levels of glucose **(A)**. The presence of abnormal pancreatic cells causes juvenile diabetes **(B)**. Adult diabetes is more common in obese adults **(C)**. Obese juveniles **(D)** are not discussed in the passage.

135. **(D)** The third paragraph details how high levels of fat in the blood interfere with insulin absorption **(D)**.

136. **(D)** Diabetes is usually detected when the person is a juvenile **(A)** or when the person is 50−70 years old **(B)**. The correct answer is **(D)**.

137. (C) *Successful* **(C)** is the best choice to mean *star* as in "star quarterback."

138. (C) The author states in the second paragraph that students who cannot maintain a 2.0 grade-point average should not be permitted to participate in any sports **(C)**. The other choices describe the opposite of what the author finds irritating in athletes.

139. (D) Hockey is the only sport not described; football ("quarterbacks") **(A)**, basketball ("point guard") **(B)**, and baseball ("infielders") **(C)** are described.

140. (D) The passage describes how the author does not like to see uneducated athletes; it does not describe how the author prefers teachers or students over athletes **(A and B)**, or how the author prefers citizens over scholars **(C)**.

141. (D) The author does not describe athletics as any of the mentioned choices.

142. (B) The passage describes how the pesticide is used to kill soil pests **(B)**.

143. (C) The passage describes how once the river water reaches Lake Shasta, the lake will have to be tested for poison **(C)**. We do not know the safety status of the water from this passage.

144. (A) The passage states how thousands of trout and other fish were poisoned along a 45-mile stretch of river after the oil spill.

145. (A) *Poisonous* is the best choice.

146. (D) The passage states how the train was carrying 19,500 gallons **(D)** of the pesticide.

147. (A) The passage states how residents around the Sacramento River in California were warned to stay away from the tainted water **(A)**.

148. (B) The passage describes lead poisoning and legislation in California to test for it **(B)**. It does not describe how to stop it entirely **(A)**, its history **(C)**, or its effects around the world **(D)**.

149. (C) The word *disorders* refers to the life-threatening ailments **(C)** that result from lead poisoning.

150. (B) The passage states that 50,000 cases will be detected in California as a result of the newly mandated tests **(B)**.

151. (D) Children from the ages of 1–5 will be tested annually, which means every year **(D)**.

152. (C) The beginning of the passage describes how health authorities consider lead poisoning to be the most common and devastating environmental disease of young children. The end of the passage describes how lead poisoning, if undetected, can result in life-threatening disorders. The correct answer is **(C)**.

Vocabulary

153. (A) The word *vigilant* means *watchful* **(A)** or observant. *Reckless* **(B)** means *rash* and *careless* and would be incorrect since it is closer to being an antonym of *vigilant*. *Lazy* **(C)** means *inactive* or *slothful* and would also be the wrong answer. *Powerful* **(D)** means *strong* and does not imply watchfulness.

154. (B) The word *parable* is a kind of *tale* **(B)** or morality story. A *teacher* **(A)** might be the sort of person who would tell a *parable* to instruct others, but this answer choice is incorrect since a teacher is not a parable. A *stronghold* **(C)** is a domain in which a person may have security or safety; this choice is also incorrect. Choice **(D)**, *strength*, means *power* and is not a synonym of the word *parable*.

155. (D) A *buoyant* spirit is one that is joyful or *light-hearted* **(D)**. A *scary* **(A)** spirit is one that inflicts fear or dread—which is incorrect. Choice **(B)**, *depressed*, means *gloomy* or *sad* and is an antonym of *buoyant*. *Supernatural* **(D)** means *abnormal* and would not be a synonym for *buoyant*.

156. (C) The word *gracious* describes someone who is thoughtful or *courteous* **(C)**. This word does not mean *elegant* **(A)**, since elegant describes a person's refinement. It does not mean *beautiful* **(B)**, since beauty refers to a person's attractiveness. Nor does it mean *extravagant* **(D)**, which describes something's luxury.

157. (B) When you pay *homage* to someone, you bestow *honor* **(B)** upon them. *Prizes* **(A)** or gifts may accompany *homage*, but *homage* is the act of reverence. An *insult* **(C)** or slander would be incorrect since they are antonyms of *homage*. *Wages* **(D)** are a person's salary or pay and are not related in giving honor to someone.

158. (C) A *grievous* burden is *disturbing* **(C)** or sad. Answer choice **(A)**, *joyous*, which means *bright* or *happy*, is an antonym of *grievous* and is incorrect. If something were *grave* **(B)** or *serious* **(D)**, it would be important and would not necessarily be *grievous* which makes both answer selections incorrect.

159. (D) An *incessant* noise is *constant* **(D)**. It is not *brief* **(A)** or periodic; those selections would be the word's antonyms. Though an *incessant* noise could be *loud* **(B)**, loudness measures the noise's intensity, whereas an *incessant* noise describes its duration. Likewise, answer choice **(C)** is incorrect since *pleasant*, which means *good* or *favorable*, does not even relate to the word *incessant*.

160. (A) When an *invincible* army is not able to be defeated, it is *unconquerable* **(A)**. Answer choice **(B)**, *invisible*, may relate to why the army was so powerful, but it does not relate to whether it is *invincible* or not. Answer choice **(C)**, *feeble*, is incorrect since *feeble* is an antonym of *invincible*. *Minute* **(D)** means *small* or *insignificant* and does not relate to *invincible*.

161. (C) The word *portly* means *heavy* **(C)** or *stocky*. Answer choice **(A)**, *sloppy*, means *messy* or *careless* and **(B)**, *well-groomed*, means *clean* and *ordered*; these words are opposites and would not be correct choices. The last answer choice, *slim* **(D)**, which means *thin* or *lean*, is the antonym of *portly* and would also be incorrect.

162. (D) *Ornate* furnishings are *elaborate* **(D)** and lavish. They are not *simple* **(A)**, which means *easy* or *basic*, the antonym of *ornate*. Answer choice **(B)**, *expensive*, which means *costly* or *valuable*, and **(C)**, *cheap*, which means *budget* or *flimsy*, could only describe the cost of the furnishings and would not be correct answer choices.

163. (A) Movements that are *encumbered* are not able to move freely, they are *restricted* **(A)**. Answer choice **(B)** would not be correct since *encourage* means to *assure* or *advocate*. *Lighten* **(C)**

means to *ease* or *unburden* and is incorrect. Choice **(D)**, *watched*, means *viewed* or *examined* and is also incorrect.

164. (B)   An *avid* fan is someone who is *enthusiastic, excited,* or *ardent* **(B)** about his/her interest. Though a fan may become *uncontrollable* **(A)**, to be enthusiastic about something is much different than being *uncontrollable*. A *lifeless* **(C)** fan would be the antonym of the *avid* fan—dull and lifeless. Answer choice **(D)**, *gloomy*, which means *sad* or *depressed*, would be incorrect also.

165. (B)   When you *vie* for something, you need to *contend* or *compete* **(B)** for it. You might be required to *wait* **(A)**, which means to *anticipate*, but this answer choice is incorrect. Answer choice **(C)**, *advertise*, means to *publicize* or *broadcast* and is not a synonym for *vie*. You might choose the last answer choice, *survive* **(D)**, which means to *endure* or *persevere*, since a connection might be made to the word—in that you hope to *survive* the competition—but it is not correct.

166. (D)   When you have an *ample* supply of something, you have more than you need; the amount is *abundant* **(D)**. Answer choice **(A)**, *inexpensive*, means *reasonable* or *low-priced*, and is not the correct answer choice. *Insufficient* **(B)**, which means *lacking* or *scanty*, would be the antonym of *ample*. Lastly, *equal* **(C)**, which means *even* or *uniform*, would also be an incorrect answer choice.

167. (B)   The word *devise* means to *create* **(B)**. Answer choice **(A)**, *eliminate*, which means to *exterminate* (an antonym of *devise*) is an incorrect answer choice. Choice **(C)**, which means to *select*, is also incorrect as is choice **(D)**, *delineate*, which means to *depict* or *portray*.

168. (B)   A *chronic* ailment is *unceasing* or *perpetual* **(B)** throughout a person's life. Answer choice **(A)**, *small*, meaning *little* or *tiny* is an incorrect choice. *Brief* **(C)**, which means *temporary*, would be incorrect since it is the antonym of *chronic*. Choice **(D)**, *unknown*, is also incorrect since it means *strange* or *hidden*.

169. (A)   The word *haggard* means *starved* or *scrawny* **(A)**. It does not mean *dirty* **(B)**, which means *filthy* or *unclean*, *cautious* **(C)**, which means *careful*, or *haggle* **(D)** which means to *bargain* or *argue*.

170. (D)   The word *stealthily* means *slyly* or *secretly* **(D)**. *Openly* **(A)**, which means *candidly* or *out in the open*, would be incorrect because it is an antonym of *stealthily*. Answer choice **(B)**, *quickly*, means *quick* or *immediate* and **(C)**, *randomly*, means *by chance*, and are both incorrect answer choices.

171. (A)   The word *pathetic* means *miserable* **(A)** or *pitiful*. If something is *miserable*, it might be *undesirable* **(B)**, which means *unwanted*, but this is not a correct answer choice in this context. Answer choice **(C)**, *ruthless*, which means *merciless*, and choice **(D)**, *frustrating*, are also wrong answer choices.

172. (D)   A speech is *verbose* if it is *wordy* **(D)** or *long-winded*. Answer choice **(A)**, *resignation*, would be a wrong answer choice. *Short* **(B)**, which means *little* or *small*, would be incorrect since it is an antonym of verbose. *Persuasive* **(C)**, which means *convincing* or *compelling*, would also be a wrong answer choice.

173. **(A)** The word *savor* means to *appreciate* or *enjoy* **(A)**. It does not mean *save* **(B)**, which means to *preserve* or *maintain*, *prepare* **(C)**, which means to *arrange* or *make*, or *serve* **(D)**, which means to *aid* or *help*.

174. **(B)** The word *rigid* means *unyielding* **(B)**. It does not mean *loud* **(D)**, which means *noisy*, or *tedious* **(C)**, which means *dull*. It is the opposite of *warm-hearted* **(A)**.

Mathematics—Detailed Explanations of Answers

Concepts

175. (B) The digit that comes immediately after the tenths place is 7, which is greater than 5. So we add 1 to the digit in the tenths place: $3.47 \cong 3.5$.

176. (A) Arrange like terms vertically and add:

$$
\begin{array}{r}
3n + 4m - 6 \\
-4n + 3m + 6 \\
\hline
-n + 7m + 0
\end{array}
$$

Rearrange terms: $7m - n$

177. (B) P is 5 spaces to the left of the Y-axis, so the first number in the pair is -5. P is also 7 spaces above the X-axis, so the second number is 7. Therefore, the position of P is represented by $(-5, 7)$.

178. (C) Let x represent the smaller number, so the larger number must be $(x + 1)$. Then the sum of the two numbers must be: $x + (x + 1) = 2x + 1 = 55$. To solve this equation,

add -1 to both sides:
$$
\begin{array}{r}
2x + 1 = 55 \\
-1 \quad -1 \\
\hline
\end{array}
$$

divide both sides by 2: $\quad 2x = 54 \quad x = 27$.

The smaller number is $x = 27$ and the larger number is $x + 1 = 27 + 1 = 28$.

179. (C) Replace x with 2, y with $=5$, and z with 0: $\quad 3x - 2y + 5z$
$$= 3(2) - 2(-5) + 5(0)$$
Simplify: $= 6 + 10 + 0 = 16$

180. (D) $12\dfrac{3}{4} + 5\dfrac{1}{3} = (12+5) + \dfrac{3}{4} + \dfrac{1}{3} = 17 + \dfrac{9+4}{12} = 17 + \dfrac{13}{12} = 8\dfrac{1}{12}$

181. (B) All the numbers listed have factors, except 37. So 37 is a prime number.

182. (C) Since width of square = length of square, the number representing the area of a square must be a perfect square number. That is, the number must have two identical factors. Here is one way to test for identical factors:

$42 = 2 \times 21 = 3 \times 14 = 6 \times 7$. (no pair of identical factors)
$45 = 3 \times 15 = 5 \times 9$. (no pair of identical factors)
$49 = 7 \times 7$. (one pair of identical factors)
$51 = 3 \times 17$. (no pair of identical factors)
The answer must be 49.

183. (D) $3(2 + 5) - 12 = (3 \times 7) - 12 = 21 - 12 = 9.$

184. (A) $5\frac{1}{4} \times 2\frac{1}{3} = \frac{21}{4} \times \frac{7}{3} = \frac{49}{4} = 12\frac{1}{4}.$

185. (A) $5.\overline{3} = 5.333\ldots$ To change this number to a mixed number, let $n = 5.\overline{3}$ ....(1)

Append the repeating digit (3) once to obtain a modified equation, $n = 5.3\overline{3}$ ....(2)

Since there is only one repeating digit, multiply both sides of the equation by 10: $10n = 53.\overline{3}$ ....(3)

Subtract equation (2) from equation (3):
$$\begin{array}{r} 10n = 53.3 \\ \underline{n = 5.3} \\ 9n = 48 \end{array}$$

Divide both sides by 9: $\frac{48}{9} = 5\frac{3}{9} = 5\frac{1}{3}.$

186. (D) To express 75 as a percent of 60, write: $\frac{75}{60} \times \frac{100}{1} = 125\%.$

187. (A) $2\frac{1}{2} = 2.5.$ So $2\frac{1}{2} = 2.5 \times 100 = 250\%$

188. (D) $q(r - s) = qr - qs.$

189. (A) One of the most efficient methods is to add only the measures of the shortest sticks: (a) $(3 + 4) = 7$ and $7 > 5$.

It would be possible to join sticks measuring 3 units, 4 units, and 5 units, end-to-end to form a triangle. This must be the right set. [Just to verify, we may try the sticks in sets (b), (c), and (d). For example, for set (b), $(2 + 5) = 7$ and $7 = 7$. There is no way to join these three sticks end-to-end to form a triangle.]

190. (D) If we add the three numbers in each set, we find that the only set that adds to exactly 180 is set (d).

191. (B) To determine which is the least crowded classroom, we must first find out how many square feet of space each child has in each classroom:

In classroom A, each child has $770 \div 22 = 35$ ft^2 of space.

In classroom B, each child has $960 \div 24 = 40$ ft^2 of space.

In classroom C, each child has $540 \div 18 = 30$ ft^2 of space.

In classroom D, each child has $627 \div 19 = 33$ ft^2 of space.

Classroom B has the most space per student; so it is the <u>least</u> crowded.

192. (B)   The wettest month was April, with 60 in. of rain. The driest month was March, with only 30 in. of rainfall. The difference is (60 − 30) = 30 in. of rainfall.

193. (B)   The total rainfall for the five months was (40 + 50 + 30 + 60 + 50) = 230 in. The average rainfall for the 5 months was 230 ÷ 5 = 46 in.

194. (A)   Notice that each space on the test scale represents 5 points. Matthew scored 55 points in September and 80 points in October. So his score rose by 25 points in October. If we check the months of November, January, March, May, June, and August, his score rose by fewer points in each of these months than in October.

195. (D)   Matthew scored 90 in January and 100 in March, so his score improved by (100 − 90) = 10 points.

196. (A)   The "3" in 29.536 is in the hundredths position.

197. (C)   An acute triangle is one that has exactly three acute triangles. The triangle in (c) is the only one that has exactly 3 acute angles.

198. (D)   The small box signifies that angle ACB is a right angle (90°), so the sum of angles ACD and BCD is 90°. Then the measure of angle ACD must be (90° − 74°) = 16°.

Problem-Solving

199. (B)   To determine Carol's earnings for 8 hours, multiply the hourly earning by 8: $9.50 × 8 = $76.00

200. (B)   The increase in population is (468 − 360) = 108. Express 108 to a percent of 360:

$$\frac{108}{360} \times \frac{100}{1} = 30\%.$$

201. (D)   First, find the area of the floor, using the given formula: Area = 18 × 15 = 270 ft². To find the cost of carpeting the floor, multiply the cost of carpeting 1 square foot by the area of the floor: $1.50 × 270 = $405.

202. (C)   First, convert 2 minutes to seconds, to make computation easy: 2 min. = 2 × 60 = 120 seconds. If in 10 seconds the bee travels 45 m, then in 1 second it must travel 45 ÷ 10 = $\frac{45}{10}$ meters. In 120 seconds, it must travel $\frac{45}{10} \times \frac{120}{1}$ = 540 meters.

203. (A)   Rhonda and Paula together own $\frac{1}{2} + \frac{2}{5} = \frac{5+4}{10} = \frac{9}{10}$. Then Brenda owns $1 - \frac{9}{10} = \frac{1}{10}$.

204. (A)   At the end of the year, the value of the car decreases to 100 − 14 = 86%. Find 86% of the value of a new car:

$$\frac{86}{100} \times \frac{15,000}{1} = \$12,900.$$

205. (A)   With a discount of 25%, Alice would have to pay only (100 − 25) = 75% of the marked price. 75% of $460 = $\frac{75}{100} \times \frac{460}{1}$ = $345.

206. (B)   From 6:00 p.m. to 7:30 p.m. is 1 hour 30 minutes = $1\frac{1}{2}$ hours. Since, in $1\frac{1}{2}$ hours, Mrs. Smith traveled 81 miles, in 1 hour she must have traveled $81 \div 1\frac{1}{2} = \frac{81}{1} \div \frac{3}{2} = \frac{81}{1} \times \frac{2}{3} = 54$ miles.

207. (B)   In a rectangle, the opposite sides are equal in measure. So there are two sides each measuring 35 ft and two sides each measuring 25 ft. So the four pieces that make up the given rectangle must add up to (35 + 35) + (25 + 25) = 120 ft.

208. (D)   Convert 7 kg to grams: 7 kg = 7 × 1,000 = 7,000 g. To find the number of harvest mice that would weigh as much as 1 rabbit, divide: 7,000 ÷ 7 = 1,000.

209. (D)   1/100 in. = 1 hundredth of an inch. So the fairy fly is 1 hundredth of an inch long. The Goliath beetle is 5 in. long. Convert 5 in. to hundredths of an inch, so we can deal with only hundredths of an inch: 5 in. = 5 × 100 = 500 hundredths of an inch. The ratio of the length of a fairy fly to the length of a Goliath beetle is 1 to 500, that is, 1:500.

210. (A)   Convert 156 kg to grams, so we can work with grams only: 156 kg = 156 × 1,000 = 156,000 g. The required fraction is $\frac{2}{156,000} = \frac{1}{78,000}$.

211. (D)   The blue whale is heavier than an elephant by (200,000 − 6,600) = 193,400 kg.

212. (D)   There are 16 slices of bread. $\frac{5}{8}$ of 16 = $\frac{5}{8} \times \frac{16}{1}$ = 10 slices.

213. (C) $30 represents (100 + 20) = 120% of the cost price. The cost price must be $\frac{30}{120} \times \frac{100}{1}$ = $25.

214. (B)   Since the farmer cultivates 18% of the land, then (100 − 18) = 82% must lie uncultivated. 82% of 3,000 = $\frac{82}{100} \times \frac{3,000}{1}$ = 2,460 acres.

215. (D)   For every $\frac{1}{8}$ in. of body length, an insect jumps 13 in. For every full inch, the insect must jump $13 \div \frac{1}{8} = \frac{13}{1} \times \frac{8}{1}$ in. For 5 in. of body length, the insect would jump $\frac{13}{1} \times \frac{8}{1} \times 5 = 520$ in.

216. (B)   The rectangle has a total of 60 small squares, of which 24 are not shaded. The fraction of the rectangle that is not shaded is $\frac{24}{60} = \frac{2}{5}$.

217. (B)   36 of the 60 small squares are shaded. This represents $\frac{36}{60} \times \frac{100}{1}$ = 60%.

218. (A)   Alice's total score on the first 4 tests must be (82 + 79 + 91 + 85) = 337. Her total score on the first five tests was 425; this included her score on the fifth test. So her score on the fifth test must be (425 − 337) = 88.

219. (B)   The rectangle in the picture is a square, since each side measures (10 + 10) = 20 cm. The area of the square must be 20 × 20 = 400 cm². The area of each clear region is one-quarter of a full circle with the same radius. The area of such circle is (3.14 × 10²) = 314 cm².

The area of each clear region must be $314 \div 4 = 78.5$ cm². The combined areas of the two quarter circles must be $78.5 \times 2 = 157$ cm². The area of the unshaded region must be $(400 - 157) = 243$ cm².

220. (A)   The wire is shaped like a half-circle. The circumference of a full circle with the same diameter would be $(3.14 \times 14) = 43.96$ in. Since the wire is only a half-circle, its length must be $43.96 \div 2 = 21.98$ in.

221. (A)   The area of the parallelogram would be the same as that of a rectangle with the same length and height. That is, $12 \times 25 = 300$ cm².

222. (B)   The total amount that Sue spent on food and drink is ($2.25 + $3.50 + $5.00) = $10.75. The remainder from $20.00 must be ($20.00 − $10.75) = $9.25. This is the amount she donated to charity.

223. (D)   Sue spent $3.50 on chips. Express this as a percent of $20.00: $\dfrac{3.50}{20.00} \times \dfrac{100}{1} = 17.5\%$.

224. (A)   It would be most convenient to work with similar units, so convert 1.2 liters to milliliters: 1.2 liters $= (1.2 \times 1,000) = 1,200$ milliliters. The "cool aid" consisted of (1,200 milliliters + 300 milliliters) = 1,500 milliliters. Now express 1,200 as a percent of 1,500:

$\dfrac{1,200}{1,500} \times = 80\%$.

225. (A)   The ratio of boys to girls may be written as 52:48 and the sum of the terms is $(52 + 48) = 100$. What per 500 is equivalent to 52 per 100? Let n represent the unknown number.

Then we can write: $52{:}100 = n{:}500$ or $\dfrac{52}{100} = \dfrac{n}{500}$. So $100 \times n = 52 \times 500 = 26,000$ and $n = 260$.

226. (C)   Let $x =$ basic rate and $1.5x =$ overtime rate. The 48 hours total consists of 40 hours at the basic rate and 8 hours at the overtime rate. Then $40x + (8)(1.5x) = \$899.60$. Simplifying, $52x = 899.60$, so $x = \$17.30$. The overtime rate, denoted by $1.5x = (1.5)(\$17.30) = \$25.95$.

227. (A)   Let $x =$ amount to be invested into a second account. To determine the simple interest for one year, multiply the amount invested by the corresponding percent. Then ($6,000)(.13) + (x)(.1625) = \$1,348.75$. Simplifying, $\$780.00 + .1625x = \$1,348.75$. Solving, $x = \$3,500.00$.

228. (B)   Let $x =$ number of ounces of pure water. The amount of salt in each of the 3 solutions becomes $0x$, $(.12)(50)$, and $(.04)(x + 50)$. Then $0x + (.12)(50) = .04(x + 50)$. This becomes $0 + 6 = .04x + 2$. So, $4 = .04x$ and thus $x = 100$.

229. (B)   Let $x =$ her present age. Then $x - 1 =$ last year's age and $x + 31$ is her age in 31 years. So, $x + 31 = 3(x - 1)$; then $2x = 34$, and $x = 17$.

230. (D)   Let $x =$ Wendy's time alone. In 1 hour, Wendy does $\dfrac{1}{x}$ of the work, Dave does $\dfrac{1}{6}$ of the work, and $\dfrac{1}{4}$ of the work is finished. Then $\dfrac{1}{x} + \dfrac{1}{6} = \dfrac{1}{4}$. Simplifying, $\dfrac{1}{x} = \dfrac{1}{4} - \dfrac{1}{6} = \dfrac{1}{12}$. Solving, $x = 1 \Big/ \dfrac{1}{12} = 12$.

231. (C) At 3:20, the minute hand faces the 4, and the hour hand has moved $\frac{20}{60} = \frac{1}{3}$ of the distance between the 3 and the 4. Now, the two hands lie $\frac{2}{3}\left(1-\frac{1}{3}\right)$ of the distance between the numbers 3 and 4. In angular measure, the distance between these two numbers $\frac{1}{12} = (360°) = 30°$. Now, the angular measure between the two hands $= \left(\frac{2}{3}\right)(30°) = 20°$.

232. (B) Let $x =$ width, $6x =$ length. The area is given by $(6x)(x) = 6x^2 = 37.5$, so $x^2 = 6.25$ and $x = \sqrt{6.25} = 2.5$. The width $= 2.5$ and the length $= (6)(2.5) = 15$. The perimeter $= (2)(15) + (2)(2.5) = 35$.

233. (C) The area of the entire circle $= (\pi)(4^2) = 16\pi$. The area of a sector with a 72° central angle $= \left(\frac{72}{360}\right)(16\pi) = 3.2\pi$.

234. (B) Let $1 =$ length of $\overline{AC} = \overline{AB}$. The quarter-circle for which $\overline{AC}$ is the radius has an area of $\left(\frac{1}{4}\right)(\pi)(1^2) = \frac{1}{4}\pi$. For the shaded area, the half-circle for which is the diameter has an area of $\left(\frac{1}{2}\right)(\pi)(.5^2) = \frac{1}{8}\pi$. Then the unshaded area $= \frac{1}{4}\pi - \frac{1}{8}\pi = \frac{1}{8}\pi$. Finally, $\frac{1}{8}\pi / \frac{1}{8}\pi = \frac{1}{1}$.

235. (D) A complete cycle of dispensed gum balls is 2 red, 3 yellow, 4 green, 5 white, which is 14 gum balls. Now $900 \div 14 = 64$ and a remainder of 4. This means that 64 cycles could be completed with $(64)(14) = 896$ gum balls. The last 4 gum balls are red, red, yellow, and yellow.

236. (D) Let $x =$ actual number of questions on the exam. Then $.75x =$ number of correct answers. By getting 3 more right, $.75x + 3$ is equivalent to $.80x$. Solving, $.75x + 3 = .80x$, we get $x = 60$. Thus, the number of questions answered correctly $= (.75)(60) = 45$.

237. (A) Since 70% are non-smokers, $100\% - 70\% = 30\%$ are smokers. The required ratio is 30:70 or 3:7.

238. (C) After the first week, the price is $\$520 - (.20)(\$520) = \$416$. After the second week, the price becomes $\$416 - (\$416)(.30) = \$291.20$.

Language Skills—Detailed Explanations of Answers

Punctuation, Capitalization, and Usage

239. (B) The sentence should read "John ate dinner last night" to match the tense of "to eat" with "last night."

240. (A) The proper noun *Martha* needs to be capitalized.

241. (D) There are no mistakes.

242. (C) The list of objects in this example needs to be separated by commas: "I bought notebooks, pens, and a pencil for school."

243. (C) *Holidays* should not be capitalized.

244. (A) The plural of *fish* is *fish* or *fishes*, not *fishs*.

245. (C) The phrase *a good friend* should be separated by commas: "Bob, a good friend, is famous."

246. (A) The phrase *Jennifer do* should be *Jennifer did* for proper agreement.

247. (B) Since "Are you going to the library after school?" is a question, it should end in a question mark.

248. (A) The correct word should be the verb *buy* rather than its homonym *by*.

249. (D) There are no mistakes.

250. (B) The quotation marks are incorrectly placed. The sentence should read, "What time is it?" Joy asked.

251. (C) The word *alright* should be spelled as two words, *all right*.

252. (A) The word *too*, meaning *also*, should be used.

253. (C) The word *they're*, which is the contraction for *they are*, should be used rather than the possessive pronoun *their*.

254. (B) *Close* is a verb; the noun *clothes* is needed.

255. (D) There are no mistakes.

256. (A) *A lot* should be written as two words.

257. (C) The correct preposition should be *on* rather than *in* the table.

258. (C) *Much*, which generally refers to an amount or quantity, is the proper adjective for this example.

259. (A) The speaker could not be in class and be home sleeping at the same time. The sentence should read "If I weren't in class, I'd be home sleeping."

260. (A) The correct form of the irregular verb *to break* in this example is *broke*.

261. (B) *Lake Erie* is a proper noun and should be capitalized.

262. (B) A colon should be placed before the list begins. The sentence should read "We saw the following people at the park: Marie, John, and his aunt."

263. (D) There are no mistakes.

264. (A) Introductory clauses should be separated with a comma: "After we brought home the dog, my dad started to smile."

265. (B) The verb *to go* needs to agree with the plural subject bottles. The sentence should read: "The bottles of milk, and not the cereal, go in the refrigerator."

266. (C) An apostrophe should be added to show possession: "Judy's bike."

267. (A) A *role*, rather than a *roll*, is a character in a play.

268. (C) Should be "my" writing.

269. (B) The verb *paint* needs to agree with the subject *I*.

270. (D) There are no mistakes.

271. (C) A sentence must start with a capital letter.

272. (A) The possessive form of *night* is needed.

273. (C) The possessive form of *who* is needed: "Whose book is this?" *Who's* is a contraction of *who is*.

274. (B) This sentence requires the past tense of the verb: "Afterwards, she led us to the farm."

275. (C) The verb in this sentence should be *wants* or *wanted*.

276. (C) This sentence requires the contraction *It's* or the phrase *It is*.

277. (B) The verb in this sentence should be *lays*, which means to put something down, rather than *lie*, which means to rest or to recline.

278. (A) The adverb *well* is needed to describe the verb *dances*. *Good* is an adjective used to describe nouns.

Spelling

279. (A) *The weather forecaster predicted rain for **tomorow**.* The correct spelling is ***tomorrow***.

280. (A) *The sailors were stranded on a **dessert** island.* The correct spelling is ***desert***.

281. (C) *Max's guidance **counseler** advised him to take Spanish.* The correct spelling is ***counselor***.

282. (A) *There were **alot** of vehicles in line at the inspection station.* The correct spelling is ***a lot***. "A lot" is two words.

283. (D) There are no misspelled words.

284. (C) *The **sophmore** class assembled in the cafeteria.* The correct spelling is ***sophomore***.

285. (B) *The **accomodations** at the new waterfront hotel are luxurious.* The correct spelling is ***accommodations***.

286. (C) *The high school **principle** addressed the student body.* The correct spelling is ***principal***.

287. (C) *The signature on the **perscription** is illegible.* The correct spelling is ***prescription***.

288. (D) There are no misspelled words.

Composition

289. (A)   All of the answer choices are coordinating conjunctions, which are used to connect independent clauses. The two independent clauses in the sentence express contrasting ideas. *But* is the correct choice because it is the only word of the three choices that is used to join contrasting ideas.

290. (B)   All of the answer choices are coordinating conjunctions, which are used to connect independent clauses. The two independent clauses in the sentence express a cause and effect relationship. *So* is the correct choice because it is the only word of the three choices that is used to join a cause to an effect.

291. (C)   All of the answer choices are subordinating conjunctions, which are used to connect independent and dependent clauses. The clauses express a cause and effect relationship. *Because* is the correct choice since it is the only word of the three choices used to join a cause to an effect.

292. (C)   All of the answer choices are subordinating conjunctions, which are used to connect independent and dependent clauses. In addition, all three of the choices are used to show a time relationship. *After* is the only answer choice that makes sense.

293. (B)   **However** is a conjunctive adverb used to connect contrasting ideas. Of the four answer choices, *she was on time for school*, is the only choice that contrasts the first independent clause, *Alyssa's bus was late*.

294. (C)   **Therefore** is a conjunctive adverb used to show a cause and effect relationship. Of the four answer choices, *he has been studying all week* is the only choice that expresses the effect, or result, of the first independent clause, *John wants to do well on the math test*. The first clause expresses the cause or reason; the second clause expresses the effect, or result.

295. (C)   Sentence (C) expresses the idea most clearly.

296. (A)   Sentence (A) expresses the idea most clearly.

297. (A)   Sentence (A) expresses the idea most clearly.

298. (D)   Sentence (D) expresses the idea most clearly.

COOP
PRACTICE TEST 1

COOP
SUBTEST 1

Sequences

Time: 15 Minutes
20 Questions

DIRECTIONS: Study the sequences and then choose the best answer from the choices given.

1. ○○□□|○□○□|○□□○| ___
   - (A) □□□○
   - (B) □○○□
   - (C) □○□○
   - (D) ○□○□

2. TY↑|Y↑|↑↑|↑↑ ↑___
   - (F) ↑T
   - (G) ↑↑
   - (H) ↑Y
   - (J) ↑Y

3. ▪▪▫|▪▫▪|▫▪▪|▫▪▫|
   - (A) ▪▪
   - (B) ▫▪
   - (C) □▫
   - (D) ▪▫

4. △○□◇|○△□◇|○□△◇| ___
   - (F) □△○◇
   - (G) ○□◇△
   - (H) ○◇□△
   - (J) ○△◇⊏

5. ⊠⊠⊠⊠|⊠⊠⊠⊠|⊠⊠⊠⊠| ___
   - (A) ⊠⊠⊠⊠
   - (B) ⊠⊠⊠⊠
   - (C) ⊠⊠⊠⊠
   - (D) ⊠⊠⊠⊠

6. □□□□|△□□□|___|△△△□
   - (F) △□△□
   - (G) △△□□
   - (H) □□□△
   - (J) □△□□

GO TO NEXT PAGE ➡

107

7. $\bigcirc\triangle\triangle\square \mid \bigcirc\square\triangle\triangle \mid \bigcirc\triangle\triangle\square \mid \square\bigcirc\triangle\triangle \mid$ ____
  - (A) $\bigcirc\square\triangle\triangle$
  - (B) $\triangle\triangle\bigcirc\square$
  - (C) $\bigcirc\triangle\triangle\square$
  - (D) $\bigcirc\triangle\square\triangle$

8. WVU | SRQ | ONM | _____ | GFE
  - (F) DCB
  - (G) LKJ
  - (H) JIH
  - (J) KJI

9. PQR | QRS | RST | _____ | TUV
  - (A) STU
  - (B) SUT
  - (C) TVU
  - (D) STV

10. ABEF | EFIJ | IJMN | _____
  - (F) MNOP
  - (G) MNQR
  - (H) OPQR
  - (J) OPST

11. PEAL | LEAN | _____ | TEAL
  - (A) DEAL
  - (B) NEAT
  - (C) NEAL
  - (D) LEAP

12. $Y_3 X_2 T_1$ | $Y_3 X_2 T_2$ | $Y_3 X_3 T_2$ | _____ | $Y_4 X_3 T_3$
  - (F) $Y_3 X_3 T_3$
  - (G) $Y_3 X_3 T_1$
  - (H) $Y_4 X_3 T_1$
  - (J) $Y_4 X_3 T_2$

13. $R\,S_3\,T_3$ | $R\,S_3\,T_2$ | $R\,S_2\,T_2$ | _____ | $R\,S_1\,T_1$
  - (A) $R\,S_2\,T_1$
  - (B) $R\,S_3\,T_1$
  - (C) $R\,S_3\,T_2$
  - (D) $R\,S_1\,T_2$

14. $A_1 B_2 C$ | $A_2 B_2 C$ | $A_2 B_3 C$ | _____ | $A_3 B_4 C$
  - (F) $A_2 B_4 C$
  - (G) $A_3 B_2 C$
  - (H) $A_3 B_3 C$
  - (J) $A_4 B_3 C$

15. 4 2 12 | 8 6 36 | 10 __ 48
  - (A) 4
  - (B) 12
  - (C) 8
  - (D) 6

16. 88 90 30 | 28 30 10 | 58 60 __
  - (F) 10
  - (G) 20
  - (H) 40
  - (J) 30

17. 81 9 27 | $\frac{1}{3}$ __ __
  - (A) $\frac{1}{27}$ $\frac{1}{9}$
  - (B) $\frac{1}{12}$ $\frac{1}{6}$
  - (C) $\frac{1}{27}$ $\frac{1}{8}$
  - (D) $\frac{1}{21}$ $\frac{1}{7}$

GO TO NEXT PAGE ➡

18. 33 27 24 | 28 27 19 | 21 27 12 | 18 __ __

(F) 24 9

(G) 24 10

(H) 27 10

(J) 27 9

19. 2 3 5 8 | 3 5 8 13 | 5 8 13 21 | __ __ __ __

(A) 13 21 34 55

(B) 8 13 21 33

(C) 13 21 43 64

(D) 8 13 21 34

20. 8 32 20 | 15 60 48 | 32 128 116 | 24 __ __

(F) 48 36

(G) 96 84

(H) 72 60

(J) 106 94

COOP

STOP

COOP
SUBTEST 2

Analogies

Time: 7 Minutes
20 Questions

DIRECTIONS: For numbers 1–20, choose the picture that would go in the empty box so that the bottom two pictures are related in the same way the top two are related.

GO TO NEXT PAGE ➡

4.   (F)   (G)   (H)   (J)

5.   (A)   (B)   (C)   (D)

6.   (F)   (G)   (H)   (J)

7.   (A)   (B)   (C)   (D)

8.   (F)   (G)   (H)   (J)

9.   (A)   (B)   (C)   (D)

GO TO NEXT PAGE ➡

10.

(F)   (G)   (H)   (J)

11.

(A)   (B)   (C)   (D)

12.

(F)   (G)   (H)   (J)

13.

(A)   (B)   (C)   (D)

14.

(F)   (G)   (H)   (J)

15.

(A)   (B)   (C)   (D)

COOP

GO TO NEXT PAGE ➡

COOP

16.

(F) (G) (H) (J)

17.

(A) (B) (C) (D)

18.

(F) (G) (H) (J)

19.

(A) (B) (C) (D)

20.

(F) (G) (H) (J)

STOP

COOP
SUBTEST 3

Quantitative Reasoning

Time: 15 Minutes
20 Questions

DIRECTIONS: For numbers 1–7, find the relationship of the numbers in one column to the numbers in the other column. Find the missing number.

1.

2 ➡ ☐ ➡ 4   (A) 6   (C) 2

5 ➡ ☐ ➡ 7   (B) 10   (D) 12

   ☐

8 ➡ ➡ ?

2.

7 ➡ ☐ ➡ 11   (F) 5   (H) 9

4 ➡ ☐ ➡ 8   (G) 4   (J) 6

1 ➡ ➡ ?

3.

3 ➡ ☐ ➡ 9   (A) 3   (C) 5

6 ➡ ☐ ➡ 18   (B) 12   (D) 10

4 ➡ ➡ ?

4.

1 ➡ ☐ ➡ 5   (F) 15   (H) 30

7 ➡ ☐ ➡ 35   (G) 20   (J) 25

5 ➡ ➡ ?

5.

8 ➡ ☐ ➡ 5   (A) 3   (C) 13

3 ➡ ☐ ➡ 0   (B) 2   (D) 9

6 ➡ ➡ ?

6.

12 ➡ ☐ ➡ 4   (F) 16   (H) 2

9 ➡ ☐ ➡ 1   (G) 5   (J) 11

10 ➡ ➡ ?

7.

24 ➡ ☐ ➡ 3   (A) 8   (C) 6

40 ➡ ☐ ➡ 5   (B) 2   (D) 12

16 ➡ ➡ ?

GO TO NEXT PAGE ➡

DIRECTIONS: For numbers 8–14, find the fraction of the grid that is shaded black.

8.

(A) $\frac{1}{3}$ (B) $\frac{1}{6}$ (C) $\frac{1}{12}$ (D) $\frac{1}{4}$

9.

(F) $\frac{1}{6}$ (G) $\frac{1}{3}$ (H) $\frac{1}{3}$ (J) $\frac{1}{12}$

10.

(A) $\frac{1}{2}$ (B) $\frac{1}{4}$ (C) $\frac{1}{3}$ (D) $\frac{1}{12}$

11.

(F) $\frac{2}{3}$ (G) $\frac{1}{6}$ (H) $\frac{1}{2}$ (J) $\frac{1}{4}$

12.

(A) $\frac{1}{2}$ (B) $\frac{5}{8}$ (C) $\frac{3}{8}$ (D) $\frac{3}{4}$

13.

(F) $\frac{2}{3}$ (G) $\frac{1}{5}$ (H) $\frac{1}{6}$ (J) $\frac{2}{6}$

14.

(A) $\frac{5}{9}$ (B) $\frac{5}{8}$ (C) $\frac{4}{9}$ (D) $\frac{1}{2}$

DIRECTIONS: For numbers 15–20, the scale shows sets of shapes with equal weight. Find an equivalent pair of sets that would balance the scale as well.

15.

(A)

(B)

(C)

(D)

GO TO NEXT PAGE ➡

COOP

STOP

COOP
SUBTEST 4

Verbal Reasoning–Words

Time: 15 Minutes
20 Questions

DIRECTIONS: For numbers 1–6, find the word that names a necessary part of the underlined word.

1. egg

 (A) bacon
 (B) breakfast
 (C) shell
 (D) hatch

2. car

 (F) driver's license
 (G) passenger
 (H) map
 (J) engine

3. highway

 (A) cars
 (B) pavement
 (C) toll
 (D) bridge

4. fireplace

 (F) fire
 (G) logs
 (H) chimney
 (J) matches

5. language

 (A) voice
 (B) speak
 (C) Spanish
 (D) vocabulary

6. dinner

 (F) fork
 (G) table
 (H) food
 (J) napkin

GO TO NEXT PAGE

DIRECTIONS: For numbers 7–12, the words in the top row are related in some way. The words in the bottom row are related in the same way. For each item, find the word that completes the bottom row of words.

7. peas   lettuce   cucumbers

    cherry   strawberry

    (A) apple   **(C)** banana
    (B) orange   **(D)** peach

8. transportation   car   Mustang

    food   vegetable

    (F) fruit   **(H)** corn
    (G) dinner   **(J)** garden

9. London   Paris   Munich

    New York   San Francisco

    (A) Montreal   **(C)** California
    (B) Texas   **(D)** England

10. paint   canvas   brushes

    nails   wood

    (F) hammer   **(H)** carpenter
    (G) furniture   **(J)** hardware store

11. walk   jog   sprint

    giggle   laugh

    (A) chuckle   **(C)** shout
    (B) guffaw   **(D)** cry

12. sand   glass   window

    tree   lumber

    (F) plank   **(H)** deck
    (G) oak   **(J)** knot

GO TO NEXT PAGE

DIRECTIONS: For numbers 13–20, the underlined words are related in some way. Find the word that is most like the underlined words.

13. horse   sheep   dog

    (A) mouse   **(C)** elephant
    (B) turtle   **(D)** snake

14. colander   funnel   grate

    (F) bucket   **(H)** cup
    (G) strainer   **(J)** bowl

15. rollerblades   ice skates   tap shoes

    (A) cleats   **(C)** ballet slippers
    (B) boots   **(D)** sneakers

16. lever   pulley   wheel

    (F) saw   **(H)** hammer
    (G) inclined plane **(J)** drill

17. elevator   staircase   ramp

    (A) escalator   **(C)** basement
    (B) floor   **(D)** story

18. coffee   tea   soup

    (F) lemonade   **(H)** punch
    (G) juice   **(J)** cocoa

19. court   hoop   center

    (A) baseball   **(C)** soccer
    (B) basketball   **(D)** hockey

20. binding   jacket   title page

    (F) pencil   **(H)** pages
    (G) computer   **(J)** printer

COOP

STOP

COOP
SUBTEST 5

Verbal Reasoning–Context

Time: 15 Minutes
20 Questions

DIRECTIONS: For numbers 1–20, find the statement that is true according to the given information.

1. Alfred couldn't wait to go to the zoo. When he got there, he raced straight to the reptile house and went inside. There, he began to describe each reptile to his mom in great detail. His mom was impressed.
   - (A) Alfred's mom was afraid of reptiles.
   - (B) Alfred was afraid of reptiles.
   - (C) Alfred goes to the zoo every week.
   - (D) Alfred knew quite a bit about reptiles.

2. As she was leaving for school one morning, Jesse stepped outside and then quickly ran back inside again, dripping wet. She ran upstairs and grabbed an umbrella from her closet and then went to catch the bus.
   - (F) It looked like it might rain.
   - (G) Jesse forgot her homework and ran back inside to get it.
   - (H) It was raining outside.
   - (J) Jesse doesn't like school.

3. Max got home from work late one night. He didn't feel like eating spaghetti since that was what he had had the night before, and there weren't any hamburgers. So, even though he doesn't really like hot dogs, he cooked some for dinner.
   - (A) Max doesn't like hamburgers.
   - (B) Max is a good cook.
   - (C) There was nothing else in the house to eat except hot dogs.
   - (D) Max had hot dogs for dinner.

4. On the way home, Jill stopped and picked tulips, pansies, and daisies from her friend's garden. She did not pick any roses.
   - (F) Jill doesn't like roses.
   - (G) Jill's friend doesn't grow roses.
   - (H) Jill is allergic to roses.
   - (J) Jill picked three kinds of flowers.

GO TO NEXT PAGE

COOP

5. Jane currently has two pets. She used to have a dog named Rover. She now has a cat named Mittens.

(A) Rover ran away.

(B) Jane now has two cats.

(C) Jane has never had a rabbit.

(D) Jane now has at least one cat.

6. The Eiffel Tower is a building in France. On a family vacation, Michael visited the Eiffel Tower.

(F) There are many buildings in France.

(G) The Eiffel Tower is a popular place to visit.

(H) Michael has been to France.

(J) Many people visit France each year.

7. Amber wanted to make a fruit salad for her family. She cut up bananas, apples, oranges, and pineapple, and mixed them in a big bowl. Her family ate it all.

(A) Amber does not like pears.

(B) Amber's favorite snack is fruit salad.

(C) Fruit salad is a healthy snack.

(D) Amber's family likes fruit salad.

8. Willem took out his model car collection. He lined up convertibles, police cars, and race cars. He did not take out his buses.

(F) Willem has a small collection of cars.

(G) Willem has at least three kinds of cars.

(H) Willem does not like buses.

(J) Willem likes his race cars the best.

9. Claire went to the state fair. She only rode the merry-go-round and the Ferris wheel. She did not ride the bumper cars.

(A) Claire did not spend much time at the fair.

(B) The bumper cars were too expensive.

(C) Claire's afraid of the bumper cars.

(D) Claire went on two rides.

10. Nathaniel was excited to see a movie at the theater. When he got there he bought two tickets and then got on the snack line. He bought two small sodas, two medium bags of popcorn, and a bag of fruit chews.

(F) Nathaniel watched the movie with a friend.

(G) Nathaniel did not eat breakfast.

(H) There was a sale at the snack counter.

(J) Nathaniel missed the beginning of the movie.

11. Beatrice was looking forward to her school's art show. She wanted her parents to see her drawings. Once they arrived Beatrice told her parents all about how she used special pencils and shading techniques to create her picture. Her parents were proud.

(A) Beatrice's parents are artists.

(B) Beatrice does not like to paint.

(C) Beatrice knows how to draw well.

(D) Beatrice loves her art teacher.

12. Jeffrey headed out to meet his friends at the park. He walked outside and quickly came back in shivering. Before going back outside, he put on a hat, scarf, and gloves.

(F) It was cold outside.

(G) Jeffrey did not want to go to the park.

(H) Jeffrey forgot his football.

(J) It was snowing outside.

13. Kendra spent the afternoon at a playground. She went down the slides and the ladders. Then she went on the monkey bars. Kendra went on the swings right before she went home.

(A) Kendra goes to the playground a lot.

(B) Kendra went down a tunnel slide first.

(C) Kendra did not want to go home.

(D) The last thing Kendra went on was the swings.

GO TO NEXT PAGE

14. Jamal has 2 hamsters. He also has 6 gold fish, but he does not have a dog.

   (F) Jamal has at least 8 pets.

   (G) Jamal is allergic to dogs.

   (H) Jamal does not like cats.

   (J) Jamal wants a dog.

15. Maria was invited to a special party. She took out her favorite dress and the white shoes that matched. When she got dressed for the party, Maria was disappointed to find that the shoes were too tight to wear.

   (A) Maria had to miss the party.

   (B) Maria's feet had grown.

   (C) Maria wore a different dress.

   (D) Maria has lots of shoes.

16. Dominic had hockey practice in the evening. His mother told him that he had to finish his science project or he would not get to go to practice. Dominic shot 2 goals at practice.

   (F) Dominic's favorite sport is hockey.

   (G) Dominic's mother was proud of him.

   (H) Dominic finished his science project.

   (J) Dominic likes science.

17. In third grade Carla learned how to play the violin. Then in middle school she learned how to play the trumpet and saxophone. Now she wants to play the drums.

   (A) Carla did not like playing the violin.

   (B) The school band needs drummers.

   (C) The saxophone is hard to play.

   (D) Carla plays different instruments.

18. Mount Rushmore is in South Dakota. April's aunt and uncle live in South Dakota. April visited her aunt and uncle last summer.

   (F) April has been to Mount Rushmore.

   (G) April's aunt and uncle go to Mount Rushmore often.

   (H) April has been to South Dakota.

   (J) April wants to visit Mount Rushmore.

19. Jay went to a family barbeque. He had 2 hot dogs, some salad, and chips. He had lemonade to drink. After playing softball, Jay had 2 pieces of chicken and more chips.

   (A) Playing softball made Jay hungry.

   (B) Jay won his softball game.

   (C) Jay is a picky eater.

   (D) Playing softball made Jay tired.

20. It was the Fourth of July. Sophia saw several marching bands. One with baton twirlers was her favorite. She also saw some girl scout and boy scout troops. She saw many fire trucks and people waving.

   (F) Sophia is a girl scout.

   (G) Sophia wants to learn how to twirl a baton.

   (H) Sophia loves marching bands.

   (J) Sophia went to a Fourth of July parade.

COOP

STOP

COOP
SUBTEST 6
Reading and Language Arts

Time: 40 Minutes
40 Questions

DIRECTIONS: Each passage is followed by questions based on its content. After reading the passage, choose the best answer to each question. Answer all questions based on what is indicated or implied in that passage.

Questions 1–4 are based on the following passage.

Spa water quality is maintained through a filter to ensure cleanliness and clarity. Wastes such as perspiration, hairspray, and lotions which cannot be removed by the spa filter can be controlled by shock treatment or super chlorination every other week. Although the filter traps most of the solid material to control bacteria and algae and to oxidize any organic material, the addition of disinfectants such as bromine or chlorine is necessary.

As all water solutions have a pH which controls corrosion, proper pH balance is also necessary. A pH measurement determines if the water is acid or alkaline. Based on a 14-point scale, a pH reading of 7.0 is considered neutral while a lower reading is considered acidic, and a higher reading indicates alkalinity or basic. High pH (above 7.6) reduces sanitizer efficiency, clouds water, promotes scale formation on surfaces and equipment, and interferes with filter operation. When pH is high, add a pH decreaser such as sodium bisulphate (e.g., Spa Down). Because the spa water is hot, scale is deposited more rapidly. A weekly dose of a stain and scale fighter will also help to control this problem. Low pH (below 7.2) is equally damaging, causing equipment corrosion, water which is irritating, and rapid sanitizer dissipation. To increase pH add sodium bicarbonate (e.g., Spa Up).

The recommended operating temperature of a spa (98°–104°) is a fertile environment for the growth of bacteria and viruses. This growth is prevented when appropriate sanitizer

GO TO NEXT PAGE

levels are continuously monitored. Bacteria can also be controlled by maintaining a proper bromine level of 3.0 to 5.0 parts per million (ppm) or a chlorine level of 1.0–2.0 ppm. As bromine tablets should not be added directly to the water, a bromine floater will properly dispense the tablets. Should chlorine be the chosen sanitizer, a granular form is recommended, as liquid chlorine or tablets are too harsh for the spa.

1. Who is the intended audience for this passage?

(A) scientists

(B) home-spa owners

(C) spa manufacturers

(D) spa salespeople

2. The main purpose of the passage is

(F) to convince shoppers to buy a spa.

(G) to convince shoppers not to buy a spa.

(H) to explain why spas are dangerous.

(J) to instruct spa owners on how to care for their spa.

3. According to the passage, why is the use of sanitizer important?

(A) Sanitizer keeps the pH balanced.

(B) Sanitizer can be used instead of a filter.

(C) Sanitizer keeps the spa from developing bacteria and viruses in the warm water.

(D) Sanitizer helps maintain the right temperature.

4. Why is the use of a spa filter important?

(F) The filter maintains the water quality by trapping most solid material.

(G) The filter keeps the pH balanced.

(H) The filter maintains the right temperature.

(J) The filter removes perspiration, hairspray, and other lotions from the water.

Questions 5–8 are based on the following passage.

The relationship of story elements found in children's generated stories to reading achievement was analyzed. Correlations ranged from .61101 ($p = .64$) at the beginning of first grade to .83546 ($p = .24$) at the end of first grade, to .85126 ($p = .21$) at the end of second grade, and to .82588 ($p = .26$) for fifth/sixth grades. Overall, the correlation of the story elements to reading achievement appeared to indicate a high positive correlation trend even though it was not statistically significant.

Multiple regression equation analyses dealt with the relative contribution of the story elements to reading achievement. The contribution of certain story elements was substantial. At the beginning of first grade, story conventions added 40 percent to the total variance while the other increments were not significant. At the end of first grade, story plot contributed 44 percent to the total variance, story conventions contributed 20 percent, and story sources contributed 17 percent. At the end of second grade, the story elements contributed more equal percentages to the total partial correlation of .8513. Although none of the percentages were substantial, story plot (.2200), clausal connectors (.1858), and T-units (.1590) contributed the most to the total partial correlation. By the fifth and sixth grades three other story elements—T-units (.2241), story characters (.3214), and clausal connectors (.1212)—contributed most to the total partial correlation. None of these percentages were substantial.

GO TO NEXT PAGE

5. This passage is most likely intended for
- **(A)** young readers.
- **(B)** first through fifth graders.
- **(C)** researchers or scientists.
- **(D)** parents.

6. The main idea of this passage is that
- **(F)** there is a direct relationship between the sophistication level of the stories children make up and their reading level.
- **(G)** there is a direct relationship between children's IQs and their reading levels.
- **(H)** children who want to improve their reading should watch less TV.
- **(J)** children who watch more TV tend to be better storytellers.

7. Which elements were used to analyze the children's stories?
- **(A)** story conventions and T-units
- **(B)** story plot and story characters
- **(C)** story sources and causal connectors
- **(D)** All of the above.

8. The study focused on
- **(F)** pre-school and kindergarten-aged children.
- **(G)** children in grades K-8.
- **(H)** children in public school.
- **(J)** children in grades 1-6.

COOP

Questions 9–13 are based on the following passage.

Mark Twain has been characterized as "an authentic American author" and as "a representative American author." These descriptions seem to suit the man and his writings. He was born Samuel Clemens in 1835, when Missouri and Louisiana were the only states west of the Mississippi River. His birthplace was less than fifty miles from the river. His father, John Clemens, a lawyer and merchant, was rarely far from financial disaster. When Samuel Clemens was four, the family settled in Hannibal, Missouri, and it was there beside the great river that Samuel lived out the adventurous life he describes in his best-loved novels. Samuel traveled extensively and tasted life as no other author had done. He said of his life, "Now then: as the most valuable capital, or culture, or education usable in the building of novels is personal experience, I ought to be well equipped for that trade." He acquired a wealth of personal experiences for his novels. As a boy of twelve he was apprenticed to the printer of his brother's newspaper in Hannibal. Six years later, in 1853, he set out to see the world as a printer in St. Louis, then in Chicago, Philadelphia, Keokuk, and Cincinnati. In 1857 he impulsively apprenticed himself to Horace Bixby, a riverboat pilot, and traveled all 1,200 miles of the Mississippi River. He said of his years on the river, "I got personally and familiarly acquainted with all the different types of human nature that are to be found in fiction, biography, or history."

The Civil War ended his steamboating and he served briefly in a Confederate militia company. Following his stint in the military, he set out with his brother, Orion, by stagecoach over the Rockies. While in the West he tried prospecting and speculating, but found his true calling in journalism. He was greatly influenced by the literary comedians and local colorists of the period, Bret Harte and Artemus Ward. He became more skillful than his

GO TO NEXT PAGE

teachers in developing his rich characterizations. In 1865 he attained national fame using his pseudonym, Mark Twain, with his story "The Celebrated Jumping Frog of Calaveras County." He also discovered a new vocation as a popular lecturer in San Francisco, keeping his audiences convulsed with tales of his adventures. Full public recognition came with the publishing of *Innocents Abroad* (1869), a wild and rollicking account of his invasion of the Old World, much of which would seem quite languid by today's standards. Some of his finest writings were three works filled with lively adventures on the Mississippi River and based on his boyhood: *Tom Sawyer* (1876), *Old Times on the Mississippi* (1883), and *Huckleberry Finn* (1884). Throughout his career Twain preferred to display his flair for journalistic improvisation rather than maintain the artist's concern for form. In his artfully told stories, Mark Twain conveyed his keen powers of observation and perception, his broad understanding of human nature, and his refreshing sense of humor.

9. The author of the passage considers Samuel Clemens to be an authentic and representative American author because

(A) he traveled throughout the United States.

(B) he set all of his stories in the United States.

(C) his style was humorous and informal.

(D) Both (A) and (C).

10. The passage describes Twain's novel *Innocents Abroad* as an "account of his invasion of the Old World." By "invasion of the Old World," the author means

(F) Twain's visit to a museum.

(G) Twain's journey on the Mississippi.

(H) Twain's travels in Europe.

(J) Twain's travels in the United States.

11. Mark Twain was at some time in his life all of the following EXCEPT

(A) a newspaper editor.

(B) a militiaman.

(C) a printer.

(D) a lecturer.

12. The author's attitude toward Mark Twain is

(F) negative.

(G) admiring.

(H) confused.

(J) sentimental.

13. Mark Twain stopped working on the steamboat because

(A) he became a popular writer.

(B) he joined the Confederate militia company.

(C) he became editor of his brother's newspaper.

(D) he decided to travel by land throughout the United States.

Questions 14–17 are based on the following passage.

As noted by Favat in 1977, the study of children's stories has been an ongoing concern of linguists, anthropologists, and psychologists. The past decade has witnessed a surge of interest in children's stories from researchers in these and other disciplines. The use of narratives for reading and reading instruction has been commonly accepted by the educational

GO TO NEXT PAGE

community. The notion that narrative is highly structured and that children's sense of narrative structure is more highly developed than expository structure has been proposed by some researchers.

Early studies of children's stories followed two approaches for story analysis: the analysis of story content or the analysis of story structure. Story content analysis has centered primarily on examining motivational and psychodynamic aspects of story characters as noted in the works of Erikson and Pitcher and Prelinger in 1963 and Ames in 1966. These studies have noted that themes or topics predominate and that themes change with age.

Early research on story structure focused on formal models of structure such as story grammar and story schemata. These models specified basic story elements and formed sets of rules similar to sentence grammar for ordering the elements.

The importance or centrality of narrative in a child's development of communicative ability has been proposed by Halliday (1976) and Hymes (1975). Thus, the importance of narrative for language communicative ability and for reading and reading instruction has been well documented. However, the question still remains about how these literacy abilities interact and lead to conventional reading.

14. What was the main purpose of the author in writing this passage?
   (F) to suggest that existing research on children's literature is incorrect
   (G) to suggest that more research be done on whether stories are important to children's communication
   (H) to give a brief overview of existing research on children's stories
   (J) to explain why researchers are interested in children's stories

15. The word *narrative* as used in this passage means
   (A) content.
   (B) analysis.
   (C) structure.
   (D) story.

16. The studies of children's stories the author discusses analyzed which two elements?
   (F) story content and story structure
   (G) literacy abilities and conventional reading
   (H) communicative ability and conventional reading
   (J) reading and reading instruction

17. Why does the author say that "the question still remains about how these literacy abilities interact and lead to conventional reading"?
   (A) The author failed in his/her research about this point.
   (B) The author suggests that this could be a question for future research.
   (C) The author believes the past research was wrong.
   (D) The author believes the past research was not important.

COOP

GO TO NEXT PAGE ➡

Questions 18–21 are based on the following passage.

Seldom has the American school system not been the target of demands for change to meet the social priorities of the times. This theme has been traced through the following significant occurrences in education: Benjamin Franklin's advocacy in 1749 for a more useful type of education; Horace Mann's zealous proposals in the 1830s espousing the tax-supported public school; John Dewey's early twentieth century attack on traditional schools for not developing the child effectively for his or her role in society; the post-Sputnik pressure for academic rigor; the prolific criticism and accountability pressures of the 1970s, and the ensuing disillusionment and continued criticism of schools until this last decade of the twentieth century. Indeed, the waves of criticism about American education have reflected currents of social dissatisfaction for any given period of this country's history.

As dynamics for change in the social order result in demands for change in the American educational system, so in turn has insistence developed for revision of teacher education (witness the more recent Holmes report (1986)). Historically, the education of American teachers has reflected evolving attitudes about public education. With slight modifications the teacher education pattern established following the demise of the normal school during the early 1900s has persisted in most teacher preparation programs. The pattern has been one requiring certain academic and professional (educational) courses often resulting in teachers teaching as they had been taught.

18. The main purpose of this passage is to
   (F) argue for further changes to the school system.
   (G) argue against further changes to the school system.
   (H) show that changes in the school system and teacher education are linked to popular concerns of American society.
   (J) show that changes in the school system and teacher education occur independently of the concerns of American society.

19. The passage describes all of the following reforms EXCEPT
   (A) increasing academic rigor.
   (B) paying for public schools with tax money.
   (C) increasing the "usefulness" of education.
   (D) creating normal school programs.

20. According to the passage, why is the education of teachers revised?
   (F) Changes in society lead to the revision of teacher education.
   (G) Teachers tend to teach as they have been taught.
   (H) Teachers need to learn new methods of teaching to compete with television.
   (J) Public- and private-school teachers are dissatisfied with the way they have been taught and demand revisions to teacher education.

21. According to the passage, teachers are prone to teaching as they have been taught because
   (A) the normal schools were replaced.
   (B) other teachers take the same educational courses.
   (C) the education of teachers reflects public opinion.
   (D) teachers try to keep pace with other teachers.

GO TO NEXT PAGE

DIRECTIONS: For numbers 22–27, choose the word or words that best complete the sentence.

22. I really don't know where Ms. Jasper's coat has gone. She _____ it when we left the museum.
    (A) is carrying
    (B) will be carrying
    (C) will have been carrying
    (D) was carrying

23. The pumpkin on the right is the _____ of the two being judged.
    (F) heavier
    (G) heaviest
    (H) most heavy
    (J) heavy

24. Because they want to go fishing on Saturday, Maggie and her sister Cassie _____ to finish all their schoolwork on Friday night.
    (A) plans
    (B) plan
    (C) is planning
    (D) was planning

25. The movie we watched last night was the _____ of all those we watched over the vacation.
    (F) scarier
    (G) scariest
    (H) more scary
    (J) scary

26. By the time we get to Aunt Harriet's, you _____ all of the chocolates in that box.
    (A) ate
    (B) have eaten
    (C) will have eaten
    (D) will have been eating

27. Beth set the table for dinner in the dining room. _____, her brother made the mashed potatoes in the kitchen.
    (F) Anyway
    (G) Regardless
    (H) Meanwhile
    (J) In spite of this

DIRECTIONS: Choose the sentence that is complete and that is written correctly.

28. (A) Janice brushed her hair she was going to a party.
    (B) Going to the party while Janice brushed her hair.
    (C) As she was brushing her hair for the party.
    (D) Janice brushed her hair because she was going to a party.

29. (F) While he went to the store and bought soup and bread.
    (G) Going to the store, the bread and soup were bought.
    (H) He bought the soup and bread when he went to the store.
    (J) He went to the store he bought soup and bread.

GO TO NEXT PAGE

30. **(A)** Before the accident when he saw the lights of the oncoming car.

    (B) When he saw the lights of the oncoming car before the accident.

    (C) He saw the lights of the oncoming car before the accident.

    (D) He saw the lights of the oncoming car then he had the accident.

31. **(F)** Mom took Dad's car when she went to work.

    (G) Mom went to work she took Dad's car.

    (H) When Mom took Dad's car as she went to work.

    (J) Taking Dad's car to work this morning.

32. **(A)** Playing the trombone in the marching band, the football game was played.

    (B) Allen played the trombone in the band he marched at the football game.

    (C) Marching in the band and playing the trombone at the football game.

    (D) Allen played the trombone in the marching band at the football game.

33. **(F)** Dotty and Kim are on the phone all the time they are best friends.

    (G) Because they are best friends and are talking on the phone all the time.

    (H) Dotty and Kim, who are best friends, are on the phone all the time.

    (J) Talking on the phone all the time and being best friends.

DIRECTIONS: For numbers 34–37, choose the sentence that uses verbs correctly.

34. **(A)** The snow was really deep in Rachel's neighborhood, so we brang our sleds to her house and played all afternoon.

    (B) The school bus pulled up in front of my house, and we race for the front door to get warm.

    (C) Whenever Michael comes to my house for dinner, he ate more food than anyone else.

    (D) These last few weeks have been very stressful, so I'm looking forward to our spring vacation.

35. **(F)** They came to the party on time, but they wasn't supposed to leave so early.

    (G) Next summer we are going camping in Virginia, so my brother is saving his money for a new tent.

    (H) New Jersey, my home state, and Pennsylvania, the state to our west, is part of the Mid-Atlantic states.

    (J) Not wearing his helmet could of been the reason that Jake didn't survive the crash.

GO TO NEXT PAGE

36. **(A)** For three days we waited for the rafts to rescue us; then we took our chances and swam for the island in the distance.

   (B) When he turned the corner onto 14th Street, Andy sees a man breaking into the drug store.

   (C) Mannie lifts weights for three years before he became the champion at our high school.

   (D) The snow had been falling for hours when he finally calls to me he's running late.

37. **(F)** Swimming and ballroom dancing is a good way to keep fit.

   (G) When I get back from the grocery store, I will expect you to have started making dinner.

   (H) My snow board was buried in the garage somewhere because it hasn't yet snowed this winter.

   (J) Jackie and Neil left my house at 6:00, so they should be home soon.

DIRECTIONS: In numbers 38–40, choose the topic sentence that best fits the paragraph.

38. _____. Most people recognize the names Siamese, Persian, Burmese, and Manx as popular breeds of cats. There are actually nearly 40 distinctive breeds of cats grouped into two categories: the Persian and the domestic shorthair. What many people do not realize is that until 100 years ago, cats interbred freely all over the world, and few distinctive breeds were recognized. As cat fanciers came to value certain qualities or features in their pets, they interbred similar cats until all litters all had similar offspring. When this occurred, they were said to have "bred true," and a new breed was established.

   (A) Purebred cats make wonderful pets.

   (B) Cats have been companions for centuries and now are becoming more popular.

   (C) Some breeds of cats are more valuable than others because of their distinctive qualities.

   (D) Although cat fanciers may take pride in their purebred pets, the idea of distinctive breeds of cats is a relatively new one.

39. _____. Many common beetles from our woodlands are black or brown with patterns or markings that help them blend in with the wood or soil around them. Others from rain forests and jungles may be orange, red, yellow, or even metallic green or blue. This helps them blend in with the brilliant flowers in their surroundings. Beetles may have huge ornate antennae, large hooked jaws or mandibles, or even horns protruding from their foreheads.

   (F) Beetles come in many colors and can be fascinating to study.

   (G) Beetles come in a variety of colors and shapes that may help them blend in with their environment.

   (H) Beetles can easily be identified by their many shapes and sizes.

   (J) Beetles are identified by their colors and shapes and are designed to do various important jobs in the world.

COOP

GO TO NEXT PAGE

40. _____. It is the largest and most populated of all the world's continents. It has the highest mountains, most of the longest rivers, and the largest deserts in the world. The countries of Asia include some of the poorest and some of the richest in the world, and while several of the world's largest cities are in Asia, most of its people are rural farmers working with simple tools. Birthplace of some of the world's oldest cultures, Asian nations compete on the cutting edge of modern technology.

(A) Asia contains many contrasts in geography, economy, and technology.

(B) Asia has many interesting geographical qualities.

(C) Asia is different from the other continents of the world.

(D) Asia combines the old and the new in its many nations.

STOP

COOP
SUBTEST 7

Mathematics

Time: 35 Minutes
40 Questions

DIRECTIONS: Select the best answer choice.

1. What is the value of *x* in the equation:
   $3x - 6 = 15$?
   - **(A)** 21
   - **(B)** 9
   - **(C)** 7
   - **(D)** 3

2. Albert bought a jacket for $50 from pocket money he had collected from five of his relatives. He received $12.00 from his aunt, $8.25 from his uncle, $12.50 from his mother, and $7.50 from his father. His grandfather made up the rest. How much did Albert's grandfather give him?
   - **(F)** $50.00
   - **(G)** $10.75
   - **(H)** $10.25
   - **(J)** $9.75

3. Sara drank 7 oz. of milk on Monday, 6 oz. on Tuesday, 5 oz. on Wednesday, an unknown amount on Thursday, and 5 oz. on Friday. If Sara drank an average of 6 oz. per day for the five days, how much did she drink that Thursday?
   - **(A)** 3 oz.
   - **(B)** 4 oz.
   - **(C)** 5 oz.
   - **(D)** 7 oz.

4. In the number 534.0024, what is the value of the 2?
   - **(F)** 2
   - **(G)** 2 tenths
   - **(H)** 2 hundredths
   - **(J)** 2 thousandths

GO TO NEXT PAGE ➡

5. Instead of multiplying a certain number by 100, Tina divided it by 100. If her answer was 37625.45, what should be the correct answer?
   (A) 376254500
   (B) 3762545
   (C) 376.2545
   (D) 3.762545

6. One day, when Janet was trying to use a new calculator to add 54 to a certain number, she pressed the minus button (−) instead of the plus (+) button. The calculator showed −13. If Janet had pressed the correct button, what should have been the answer?
   (F) 108
   (G) 95
   (H) 67
   (J) 41

7. Arrange the following quantities in order, from smallest to greatest: 83%, 0.78, $\frac{13}{16}$

   (A) $0.78, \frac{13}{16}, 83\%$

   (B) $0.78, 83\%, \frac{13}{16}$

   (C) $\frac{13}{16}, 0.78, 83\%$

   (D) $\frac{13}{16}, 83\%, 0.78$

8. Mrs. Fraser took her class of 18 students to lunch at a restaurant. If she spent $4.93 on each student, how much did the students' lunches cost her?
   (F) $936.70
   (G) $887.40
   (H) $93.67
   (J) $88.74

9. If $x = 3$ and $y = -2$, what is the value of $2x + 3y$?
   (A) −12
   (B) −1
   (C) 0
   (D) 12

10. If $y = 6$ and $z = -2$, find the value of $\frac{3y}{z}$.
    (F) −9
    (G) −3
    (H) 3
    (J) 9

11. Alice can arrange all her cards in exactly 5 sets of 7, with 4 left over. How many cards does Alice have?
    (A) 39
    (B) 35
    (C) 28
    (D) 20

12. Cathy packs 357 videocassettes in boxes designed to hold 15 cassettes. How many additional cassettes does she need in order to fill the last box?
    (F) 345
    (G) 23
    (H) 12
    (J) 3

13. The sum of two consecutive multiples of 4 is 12 less than the product of 8 and 9. Find the smaller of the two multiples of 4.
    (A) 44
    (B) 40
    (C) 32
    (D) 28

GO TO NEXT PAGE ➡

14. In the picture, $\overline{OD} \perp \overline{AB}$. Find the value of x.

(F) 110

(G) 60

(H) 65

(J) 55

15. Find the value of y in the figure.

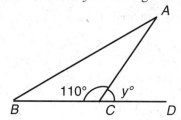

(A) 110

(B) 80

(C) 70

(D) 60

16. In the figure, ABC is a right triangle. What is the value of x?

(F) 43

(G) 45

(H) 47

(J) 57

17. Two sets of straws are shown, with the measures of their lengths. Which straw in set 2 would you combine with the three straws in set 1 so they can be joined end-to-end to form a rectangle?

20 in.

12 in.   Set 1

20 in.

(A) —————————— 20 in.

(B) ———————— 16 in.   Set 2

(C) ————— 12 in.

(D) ————————— 22 in.

18. Two sets of rods are shown, with the measures of their lengths. Which rod in set 2 would you combine with the two rods in set 1 so they can be joined end-to-end to form a scalene triangle?

15 in.

6 in.   Set 1

(F) ————— 10 in.

(G) ———— 9 in.   Set 2

(H) ——— 6 in.

(J) ————— 15 in.

19. Xena is 2 years older than her sister, Yvonne, who is 5 years younger than their elder brother Steve. Let x stand for Xena's age. Which one of the following expressions best represents Steve's age?

(A) $2x + 3$

(B) $x - 2$

(C) $x + 5$

(D) $x + 3$

GO TO NEXT PAGE ➡

COOP

20. Edith earned the same amount of money for each of her first 9 months on the job. For the next 3 months, she earned $15 less per month due to frequent absences. Let d represent Edith's earnings per month for each of the first 9 months. Which one of the following expressions accurately describes her total earnings for the 12 months?

    (F) $12d + 45$

    (G) $12d - 45$

    (H) $9d - 15$

    (J) $3d - 15$

21. Find the product of $(3n + 4)$ and $(n - 2)$.

    (A) $3n^2 + 10n - 8$

    (B) $3n^2 - 2n - 8$

    (C) $3n^2 + 2n - 8$

    (D) $3n^2 - 10n - 8$

22. Simplify $24 \div 6 + 2 \times 8$.

    (F) 20

    (G) 24

    (H) 48

    (J) 50

23. Divide 20% of 90 by 25% of 36.

    (A) 2

    (B) 9

    (C) 18

    (D) 36

24. Find 210% of 420.

    (F) 882

    (G) 840

    (H) 630

    (J) 88.2

25. Plywood is sold in sheets of 4 ft by 8 ft What is the smallest number of sheets that a carpenter must buy in order to build a temporary fence 40 ft by 7 ft?

    (A) 8

    (B) 9

    (C) 10

    (D) 12

Information for questions 26 to 29

Seven of Mr. Lee's students did poorly on their final examination. Mr. Lee decided to give them a chance to improve their test scores. Here are the students' scores on the two tests. Someone misplaced Tamara's score on Test 2.

Student's name	Test 1	Test 2
Nancy	64	70
Rhoda	71	69
Clara	58	65
Gregory	49	58
Jerome	56	67
Bill	60	58
Tamara	65	x

GO TO NEXT PAGE ➡

26. Which one of the students improved the most, from the first to the second test?

(F) Gregory

(G) Nancy

(H) Rhoda

(J) Jerome

27. If the two tests are combined, which student did the worst?

(A) Bill

(B) Clara

(C) Gregory

(D) Rhoda

28. What was the average score for the seven students on the first test?

(F) 64

(G) 61

(H) 58

(J) 56

29. If the average score for the 7 students on the second test was 66, what was Tamara's score on this test?

(A) 64

(B) 66

(C) 69

(D) 75

30. Wong drove from Alphatown to Betatown in 4 hours at an average of 45 mph, then from Betatown to Chetatown in 5 hours at an average of 54 mph. What was Wong's average speed for the entire journey?

(F) 49 mph

(G) 49.5 mph

(H) 50 mph

(J) 50.5 mph

31. A certain printer makes the dot over the letter "i" approximately 0.0012 inch in diameter. A magnifying glass enlarges this dot by a factor of 10,000. What is the diameter of the dot in the magnifying glass?

(A) 0.000012

(B) 0.00012

(C) 12

(D) 120

32. Solve for x: $3x - 6 = 42$.

(F) 48

(G) 36

(H) 16

(J) 12

33. Find the slope of the line in the graph.

(A) $-\dfrac{4}{5}$

(B) $\dfrac{4}{5}$

(C) $-\dfrac{5}{4}$

(D) $\dfrac{5}{4}$

GO TO NEXT PAGE ➡

34. The sum of the 5 interior angles of a penta-gon is 540°. If angles *A* and *E* are right angles, find the sum of the remaining angles.

(F) 90

(G) 120

(H) 240

(J) 360

35. Find the total area of the 3 visible faces of the box shown in the figure.

(A) 284 in²

(B) 420 in²

(C) 568 in²

(D) 840 in²

36. The formula for the area of a circle is πr^2, where *r* stands for the radius of the circle. Find the area of the shaded portion of the figure below, if $\pi = 3.14$.

(F) 252 cm²

(G) 175 cm²

(H) 154 cm²

(J) 98 cm²

37. If one kilogram is equal to 2.2 pounds, how many pounds is equal to 150 kilograms?

(A) 33

(B) 68

(C) 330

(D) 3,300

38. The finance charge for a $25,000 car is $3,000. At the same rate, what is the finance charge for a $30,000 car?

(F) $3,800

(G) $3,600

(H) $4,200

(J) $4,400

GO TO NEXT PAGE ➡

COOP

Information for questions 39 and 40

The graph shows the average temperature, in degrees Fahrenheit, in a certain city, from January to August of the same year.

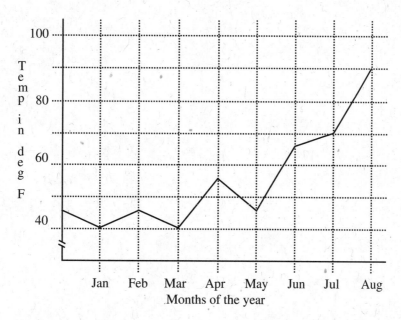

39. Between which two-month interval did the temperature rise the most steeply?

(A) February–April

(B) March–May

(C) April–June

(D) May–July

40. What was the average temperature rise between March and August?

(F) 40°

(G) 35°

(H) 10°

(J) 7°

COOP

STOP

COOP

Practice Test 1—Answer Key

Question Number	Correct Answer	If You Answered this Question Incorrectly, Refer to . . .
SUBTEST 1: SEQUENCES		
1.	(C)	P. 422
2.	(F)	P. 422
3.	(A)	P. 422
4.	(G)	P. 422
5.	(D)	P. 422
6.	(G)	P. 422
7.	(C)	P. 422
8.	(J)	P. 422
9.	(A)	P. 422
10.	(G)	P. 422
11.	(B)	P. 422
12.	(J)	P. 422
13.	(A)	P. 422
14.	(H)	P. 422
15.	(C)	P. 422
16.	(G)	P. 422
17.	(A)	P. 422
18.	(J)	P. 422
19.	(D)	P. 422
20.	(G)	P. 422

COOP

Question Number	Correct Answer	If You Answered this Question Incorrectly, Refer to . . .
SUBTEST 2: ANALOGIES		
1.	(B)	P. 227
2.	(J)	P. 227
3.	(B)	P. 227
4.	(F)	P. 227
5.	(D)	P. 227
6.	(H)	P. 227
7.	(A)	P. 227
8.	(G)	P. 227
9.	(A)	P. 227
10.	(H)	P. 227
11.	(B)	P. 227
12.	(F)	P. 227
13.	(A)	P. 227
14.	(H)	P. 227
15.	(C)	P. 227
16.	(G)	P. 227
17.	(D)	P. 227
18.	(H)	P. 227
19.	(A)	P. 227
20.	(H)	P. 227
SUBTEST 3: QUANTITATIVE REASONING		
1.	(B)	P. 417
2.	(F)	P. 417
3.	(B)	P. 417
4.	(J)	P. 417
5.	(A)	P. 417
6.	(H)	P. 417
7.	(B)	P. 417
8.	(D)	P. 418
9.	(G)	P. 418
10.	(A)	P. 418

11.	(J)	P. 418
12.	(B)	P. 418
13.	(H)	P. 418
14.	(C)	P. 418
15.	(D)	P. 421
16.	(F)	P. 421
17.	(B)	P. 421
18.	(J)	P. 421
19.	(C)	P. 421
20.	(H)	P. 421

SUBTEST 4: VERBAL REASONING—WORDS

1.	(C)	P. 228
2.	(J)	P. 228
3.	(B)	P. 228
4.	(H)	P. 228
5.	(D)	P. 228
6.	(H)	P. 228
7.	(A)	P. 228
8.	(H)	P. 228
9.	(A)	P. 228
10.	(F)	P. 228
11.	(B)	P. 228
12.	(H)	P. 228
13.	(C)	P. 227
14.	(G)	P. 227
15.	(A)	P. 227
16.	(G)	P. 227
17.	(A)	P. 227
18.	(J)	P. 227
19.	(B)	P. 227
20.	(H)	P. 227

COOP

COOP

Question Number	Correct Answer	If You Answered this Question Incorrectly, Refer to . . .
SUBTEST 5: VERBAL REASONING—CONTEXT		
1.	(D)	P. 302
2.	(H)	P. 302
3.	(D)	P. 302
4.	(J)	P. 302
5.	(D)	P. 302
6.	(H)	P. 302
7.	(D)	P. 302
8.	(G)	P. 302
9.	(D)	P. 302
10.	(F)	P. 302
11.	(C)	P. 302
12.	(F)	P. 302
13.	(D)	P. 302
14.	(F)	P. 302
15.	(B)	P. 302
16.	(H)	P. 302
17.	(D)	P. 302
18.	(H)	P. 302
19.	(A)	P. 302
20.	(J)	P. 302
SUBTEST 6: READING AND LANGUAGE ARTS		
1.	(B)	P. 302
2.	(J)	P. 300
3.	(C)	P. 302
4.	(F)	P. 302
5.	(C)	P. 302
6.	(F)	P. 300
7.	(D)	P. 302
8.	(J)	P. 302
9.	(D)	P. 302
10.	(H)	P. 310
11.	(A)	P. 303
12.	(G)	P. 308

13.	(B)	P. 302
14.	(H)	P. 300
15.	(D)	P. 310
16.	(F)	P. 302
17.	(B)	P. 304
18.	(H)	P. 300
19.	(D)	P. 303
20.	(F)	P. 302
21.	(B)	P. 302
22.	(D)	P. 246
23.	(F)	P. 257
24.	(B)	P. 247
25.	(G)	P. 259
26.	(C)	P. 246
27.	(H)	P. 246
28.	(D)	P. 239
29.	(H)	P. 239
30.	(C)	P. 239
31.	(F)	P. 239
32.	(D)	P. 239
33.	(H)	P. 239
34.	(D)	P. 245
35.	(G)	P. 245
36.	(G)	P. 245
37.	(A)	P. 245
38.	(G)	P. 300
39.	(D)	P. 300
40.	(G)	P. 300
41.	(A)	P. 300

SUBTEST 7: MATHEMATICS

1.	(C)	P. 427
2.	(J)	P. 375
3.	(D)	P. 390
4.	(J)	P. 373
5.	(A)	P. 379, 381
6.	(G)	P. 337, 339
7.	(A)	P. 350, 373, 391
8.	(J)	P. 379

COOP

Question Number	Correct Answer	If You Answered this Question Incorrectly, Refer to . . .
9.	(C)	P. 337, 427
10.	(F)	P. 345, 427
11.	(A)	P. 341
12.	(J)	P. 345
13.	(D)	P. 341
14.	(J)	P. 408
15.	(C)	P. 408
16.	(H)	P. 408
17.	(C)	P. 395
18.	(F)	P. 395, 407
19.	(D)	P. 427
20.	(G)	P. 427
21.	(B)	P. 427
22.	(F)	P. 388
23.	(A)	P. 402
24.	(F)	P. 402
25.	(B)	P. 395
26.	(J)	P. 339
27.	(C)	P. 337
28.	(G)	P. 390
29.	(D)	P. 390
30.	(H)	P. 390
31.	(C)	P. 379
32.	(H)	P. 427
33.	(B)	P. 424
34.	(J)	P. 407
35.	(A)	P. 395
36.	(G)	P. 407
37.	(C)	P. 379
38.	(G)	P. 345, 379
39.	(D)	P. 424
40.	(H)	P. 390, 424

Sequences—Detailed Explanations of Answers

1. **(C)** The squares move right to left, one at a time.

2. **(F)** The first figure in each set is removed; the second becomes the first; the third becomes the second; a new figure becomes the third.

3. **(A)** The dots move above the squares, then move back into the squares.

4. **(G)** The triangle switches with the figure to its right.

5. **(D)** The last figure becomes the first; the other figures move one position to the right.

6. **(G)** The number of triangles increases from the left in each set.

7. **(C)** The first and third sets are the same; the second and fourth sets are the same; the fifth must be the same as the first and third since they alternate.

8. **(J)** This is a section of the alphabet in reverse order with one letter missing between each set of three letters.

9. **(A)** The first letter in each set is removed; the next two letters in each set move one position to the left; the next letter in the alphabet becomes the third letter.

10. **(G)** Each set is missing in the middle two letters in alphabetical order. The last two letters of each set become the first two in the next set.

11. **(B)** The two middle letters are always EA; the last letter of each set becomes the first letter of the next set.

12. **(J)** The subscripts increase by one, from right to left, one at a time.

13. **(A)** The subscripts decrease by one, from right to left, one at a time.

14. **(H)** The subscripts increase by one, from left to right, one at a time.

15. **(C)** The second number in each set is 2 less than the first number; the third number is six times the second number.

16. **(G)** The second number in each set is 2 more than the first number; the third number is the second number divided by three.

17. **(A)** The second number in each set is the first number divided by 9; the third number is 3 times the second.

18. **(J)** The second number in each set is always 27; the third number is 9 less than the first number.

19. **(D)** The third number in each set is the sum of the first and second numbers; the fourth is the sum of the second and third numbers; the first three numbers of a set are the last three numbers of the previous set.

20. **(G)** The second number in each set is 4 times the first number; the third number is 12 less than the second number.

COOP
SUBTEST 2

Analogies—Detailed Explanations of Answers

1. **(B)** A finger is part of the hand, just as an eye is part of the face, choice **(B)**. Choice **(A)**, mouth, is another part of the face, but the relationship is part to whole. Thumb, choice **(C)**, is another part of the hand, but does not belong listed in the second relationship. Foot, choice **(D)**, is another body part, but does not complete the relationship with eye.

2. **(J)** In the same way that an ocean liner can transport more people by sea than a canoe, so can a bus, choice **(J)**, transport more people by land than a buggy. **(F)** and **(G)**, an airplane and a hot air balloon, are similar to a buggy because they are used for travel, but these two choices travel in the air and not the ground as a buggy does. **(H)**, a boat, is another mode of transportation, like the bus, but boats travel by water.

3. **(B)** A house is a home for humans and a nest is a home for birds, just as a hamburger is a meal for humans and a worm **(B)** is a meal for birds. A bird, choice **(A)**, uses the nest, but the relationship is that of SYNONYMS. An apple, choice **(C)**, could be food for birds; however, worm is a better choice. A tree, choice **(D)**, does not complete the relationship and would be incorrect.

4. **(F)** A baby primarily drinks from a bottle, just as a child usually drinks from a cup. Choice **(G)**, pacifier, **(H)**, rattle, and **(J)**, highchair, are all items used by a baby. In addition, these words do not have any relation to bottle in their usage. The word needed to complete the analogy would have to be an object used by a child. The cup, answer choice **(F)**, can be used by a child for drinking (just like a bottle).

5. **(D)** A part of a bird is its beak, and the corresponding part of a person is his/her mouth, choice **(D)**. Choice **(A)**, bird legs, would be incorrect since the missing word would have to be a body part of a human and relate to beak. Choice **(B)**, eye, is incorrect for the same reason; it is a body part, but it does not relate to the bird's beak. Hand, choice **(C)**, is part of a person, but it also does not relate to a bird's beak.

6. **(H)** Just as milk is produced by a cow, honey is produced by a bee, choice **(H)**. Choice **(F)**, butter, and **(G)**, tea cup are incorrect because the missing word would need to be the

producer of honey. Butter and tea cups are not even animate objects! Choice (J), child, may be thought to be correct, but a child does not produce honey.

7. (A) A button is part of a shirt that keeps it closed, just as shoe laces are the part of shoes that keep them closed. A coat, choice (B), hat, choice (C), and dress, choice (D), are not kept closed with shoe laces.

8. (G) A hot air balloon is an old-fashioned mode of traveling by air, and an airplane is a modern mode of air travel, just as a horse and buggy is an old-fashioned mode of ground travel, and a car is a modern way of traveling by ground. Choice (F), boat, is incorrect since it is a mode of traveling by water. Choice (H), horse, is a method of ground transportation, but it is not one that is contemporary. A tire, choice (J), is part of a car, and alone is not a method of travel.

9. (A) A weak or damaged leg can be assisted by a crutch, just as weak or damaged eyes can be assisted by glasses. Choice (B), face, is related to the word eye, but it is not an aiding device that would relate to crutch. Eye might relate to choice (C), book, since most people use their eyes to read, but the relationship would be completed with glasses (which relates to crutch much better). Choice (D), shoe, is related to a foot, not an eye—and would be incorrect.

10. (H) A hand is found at the end of an arm, just as a foot is found at the end of a leg (H). Choice (F), finger, and choice (G), toes, are related to this analogy since they are further extremities of a hand and foot. However, the word that is necessary to complete this relationship would need to compare with arm, and choices (F) and (G) are the incorrect body parts. Choice (J), shoe, would go on a foot, but the missing word would need to show what the foot is at the end of (not what goes on the end of a foot).

11. (B) A young flower emerges from a seed, just as a young bird (B) emerges from an egg. If the observation is made that a flower emerges from a seed, then answer choices (A) tree, (C) nest, and (D) leaf are incorrect since the answer choices do not emerge from eggs. The only answer choice that emerges from an egg is choice (B), the bird.

12. (F) A glove is placed over a hand, just as a sock is put on over a foot (F). Though you might think answer choices (G) and (J) are relevant, socks are not put on over shoes or boots. Answer choice (H), mitten, would not complete the analogy since socks are not normally placed over mittens.

13. (A) The United States is where the Statue of Liberty is located, just as Italy is where the Roman Colosseum (A) is located. (A) is correct since the completed analogy required a monument/landmark that was within Italy. Answer choice (B), Mount Rushmore, is located in the United States, and would be incorrect. Choice (C), castle, is too broad. There are many castles located in many different countries, so it is not the best choice. Lastly, choice (D), Eiffel Tower, is located in France.

14. (H) A fish and a sea horse are found in the water, just as a horse and a lion (H) are found on land. Answer choices (F) and (J), starfish and octopus, are incorrect since they are primarily found in water, not land. Choice (G), bird, can be found on land, but is generally associated with the sky.

15. (C) A school bus is used to take people to school, just as an ambulance is used to take people to a hospital **(C)**. Choice **(A)**, doctor, is one of the reasons why people are brought to the hospital, but choice **(B)**, police car, is incorrect since it is another mode of transportation and not the destination of ambulances. Person, choice **(D)**, is too vague, but would be incorrect for the same reason as choice **(A)**.

16. (G) A tire is part of a car that aids in its movement, just as the propeller of a ship **(G)** aids its movement. This analogy deals with propulsion and answer choice **(F)**, anchor, helps a ship stop or remain stationary. Answer choice **(H)**, would be incorrect since a crew boat does not have a propeller—it is moved by oars. Person, choice **(J)**, would also be incorrect since people do not have propellers attached to them to move around—just ships.

17. (D) A basketball is thrown in the air through a basketball hoop to score points, just as a football is kicked in the air through the uprights to score points. Answer choice (A), umpire, officiates sports games and is not involved in scoring points. Soccer ball, answer choice **(B)**, is not used in the game of football or basketball and would not be the correct answer in this analogy. Choice **(C)**, football helmet could be a good match with a football for a component relationship. However, the word that is needed serves as the goal through which the first word must pass in order for a team to score points.

18. (H) Halloween is closely associated with trick-or-treating and candy, just as the Christmas holiday is associated with gift-giving and presents. Answer choice **(F)**, diploma, is connected to graduations and not to the aforementioned holidays. While turkey, choice **(G)**, is a common meal during many holidays, it is most closely associated with Thanksgiving. Shamrocks **(J)** are symbols of Ireland and the holiday of St. Patrick's Day. Answer choice **(H)**, stockings/presents, is the best answer choice to relate with Christmas.

19. (A) An automobile drives with the use of the tire as a person walks with the use of his/her feet. A shirt **(C)** and a hat **(D)** are connected with accessories and are not essential to moving. The hand **(B)** is not essential to walking unless one has a handicap.

20. (H) A teacher works at a school, just as a doctor works at a hospital **(H)**. Since the analogy requires a location to complete itself, answer choice **(F)**, school bus, would be incorrect. The same is true for answer choice **(G)**, desk. Though it is associated with the teacher and school, it is incorrect. Though an ambulance, choice **(J)**, is associated with doctors, it is also (with the same reasoning as choice **(F)**) incorrect. Hospital, choice **(H)**, is the appropriate answer selection since it is the place where most doctors work.

COOP

Quantitative Reasoning— Detailed Explanations of Answers

1. **(B)** Here 2 is added to each number. 8 plus 2 equals 10, which is the correct answer.

2. **(F)** Here 4 is added to each number. 1 plus 4 equals 5, which is the correct answer.

3. **(B)** Here each number is multiplied by 3. 4 times 3 equals 12, which is the correct answer.

4. **(J)** Here each number is multiplied by 5. 5 times 5 equals 25, which is the correct answer.

5. **(A)** Here 3 is subtracted from each number. 6 minus 3 equals 3, which is the correct answer.

6. **(H)** Here 8 is subtracted from each number. 10 minus 8 equals 2, which is the correct answer.

7. **(B)** Here each number is divided by 8. 16 divided by 8 equals 2, which is the correct answer.

8. **(D)** In this example, 1 out of 4 boxes is shaded. The correct answer is 1/4.

9. **(G)** In this example, 2 out of 6 boxes are shaded. The fraction 2/6 can be reduced to 1/3, which is the correct answer.

10. **(A)** In this example, 1 full box and 2 half boxes are shaded. Since 2 halves equal 1 whole, there are a total of 2 out of 4 boxes shaded. The fraction 2/4 can be reduced to ½, which is the correct answer.

11. **(J)** In this example, 2 out of 8 boxes are shaded. The fraction 2/8 can be reduced to ¼, which is the correct answer.

12. **(B)** In this example, 5 out of 8 boxes are shaded. The correct answer is 5/8.

13. **(H)** In this example, 2 half boxes are shaded out of 6 boxes. Since 2 halves equal 1 whole, there are a total of 1 out of 6 boxes shaded. The correct answer is 1/6.

14. **(C)** In this example, 3 whole and 2 half boxes out of 9 are shaded. Since 2 halves equal 1 whole and 1 plus 3 equals 2, 4 boxes are shaded. The correct answer is 4/9.

15. **(D)** 2 cones are equal to 4 cubes. In this example, the scale is balanced with 2 cubes on one side and 1 cone on the other. 2 cubes are equal to 1 cone.

16. **(F)** 3 cones and 2 cubes are equal to 3 cubes. In this example, the scale is balanced with 1 cube on one side and 3 cones on the other. 1 cube is equal to 3 cones.

17. **(B)** 3 cones are equal to 3 cubes. In this example, the scale is balanced with 2 cones and 1 cube on one side and 3 cubes on the other. 1 cone is equal to 1 cube.

18. **(J)** 4 cones are equal to 2 cubes. In this example, the scale is balanced with 2 cubes and 1 cone on one side and 5 cones on the other. 2 cones equal 1 cube.

19. **(C)** 3 cubes are equal to 4 cones and 1 cube. In this example, the scale is balanced with 2 cones and 3 cubes on one side and 2 cubes and 4 cones on the other. 1 cube equals 2 cones.

20. **(H)** 1 cube and 2 cones are equal to 6 cones. In this example, the scale is balanced with 5 cones on one side and 1 cube and 1 cone on the other. 4 cones are equal to 1 cube.

COOP
SUBTEST 4

Verbal Reasoning–Words— Detailed Explanations of Answers

1. **(C)** Shell. Every egg has a shell **(C)**; it is the part that holds an egg in its form. The shell is a necessary part of an egg. Bacon is often eaten with eggs for breakfast. Bacon **(A)** and breakfast **(B)** are associated with an egg, not parts of a whole. Hatch **(D)** is what some eggs do. However, not all eggs hatch, so that is not a necessary part of an egg.

2. **(J)** Engine. Without an engine, a car will go nowhere. A car must have an engine in order to be useful; an engine is a necessary part of a car. One needs a driver's license **(F)** to operate a car, but it is not considered a part of a car. A person can be a passenger and consider a car quite useful, even without a license. A passenger **(G)** uses a car but is not a part of a car. A car sitting in a driveway is without passengers, but it is still a perfectly functioning car. A map **(H)** can be helpful when in a car. However, it is only a tool to help one who is using a car; it is not a necessary part of a car. A person can certainly use a car without a map.

3. **(B)** Pavement. Highways are paved; it is this pavement that creates the highway. Without it, there would be no highway, just a dirt road, so pavement is a necessary part of a highway. Cars **(A)** utilize a highway, but if you take away the cars, the highway still exists. Cars are not a necessary part of a highway. Some highways have bridges **(D)** and some have tolls **(C)**. They are sometimes part of a highway, but if you took away the tolls or the bridges, you could still have a highway; they are not a necessary part of all highways.

4. **(H)** Chimney. In order to be able to use a fireplace, there must be a chimney for ventilation. In order for it to function properly, a chimney is a necessary part of a fireplace. Sometimes there is a fire **(F)** in a fireplace, and sometimes there is not. A fire might be considered a part of a fireplace, but it is not a necessary part. The fireplace still exists in the same form, even when there is no fire. In order to create a fire in the fireplace, one must use some sort of fuel (like logs **(G)**) and something to start the fire (like matches **(J)**). However, like the fire, these things might be commonly associated with a fireplace, but they are not necessary parts. Again, the fireplace still exists in the same form, even when there is no fire (or logs or matches).

5. **(D)** Vocabulary. To use a language, one must know the vocabulary or words. Vocabulary is a necessary part of language. Voice **(A)** is used to speak **(B)** a language, but language is also written. There can also be language without voice, such as sign language. Spanish **(C)** is one example of language; it is not a part of language.

6. **(H)** Food. An essential component of dinner is food. While dinner may be eaten at a table **(G)**, with a fork **(F)**, or accompanied by a napkin **(J)**, the necessary part is food **(H)**.

7. **(A)** Apple. The relationship between peas/lettuce/cucumbers is that they are all green vegetables. Cherry/strawberry/apple are all red fruits. All of the items are connected based on their color and type. The other choices **(B)**, **(C)**, and **(D)** are all fruits, but none is red.

8. **(H)** Corn. The relationship between transportation/car/Mustang is that each word is more specific than the previous word. Car is more specific than transportation—it is a mode of transportation. Mustang is more specific than car—it is a type of car. Vegetable is more specific than food, and corn is more specific than vegetable. All of the items are connected by going from general to specific. Fruit **(F)** is another food group like vegetables. It is not a specific type of vegetable. Dinner **(G)** may be associated with food and vegetables, but it is not a specific type of vegetable. A garden **(J)** may be associated with vegetables because it is a place where vegetables grow, but it is not a specific type of vegetable.

9. **(A)** Montreal. The relationship between London/Paris/Munich is that they are cities in Europe. New York/San Francisco/Montreal are all cities in North America. All of the cities are connected based on their location. Answers **(B)**, **(C)**, and **(D)** are states or countries, not cities.

10. **(F)** Hammer. The relationship between paint/canvas/brushes is that they are tools used by a painter. Nails/wood/hammer are all tools used by a carpenter. All of the items are connected based on who uses them. A carpenter makes furniture **(G)**, like an artist makes a painting, but this does not convey the same relationship as brush and hammer. There is not enough information given about carpenter **(H)** and the hardware store **(J)** to establish a relationship.

11. **(B)** Guffaw. The relationship between walk/jog/sprint is that they show an increase in intensity. Jog is faster than walk, and sprint is stronger than jog. Giggle/laugh/guffaw also show an increase in intensity. Laugh is stronger than giggle, and guffaw is stronger than laugh. All of the items are connected based on an increase in intensity. Chuckle **(A)** is softer than laugh, not stronger. That would show a decreased intensity. Shout **(C)** and cry **(D)** are other actions a person can do, but they are not the same type of action as giggle and laugh.

12. **(H)** Deck. The relationship between sand/glass/window is that glass is made from sand, and windows are made from glass. Tree/wood/deck shows the same relationship. Wood is made from a tree, and a deck is made from wood. All of these items are connected based on material and use. A plank **(F)** is a specific size piece of lumber, not what one would create out of the lumber. Oak **(G)** is just a type of tree. It has nothing to do with the use of lumber. A knot **(J)** is part of a tree or lumber. The connection needs to be based on use, not the relation of a part to a whole.

13. **(C)** Elephant. The relationship between horse/sheep/dog is that they are all animals that are mammals. The other choices were animals that were are not mammals.

14. **(G)** Strainer. The relationship between colander/funnel/grate is that they all allow liquid to run through them. The other choices hold liquid, without allow it to run through.

15. **(A)** Cleats. The relationship between rollerblades/ice skates/tap shoes is that they are all footwear that has something attached to the bottom. The other choices are footwear with no attachments.

16. **(G)** Inclined plane. The relationship between lever/pulley/wheel is that they are all examples of simple machines.

17. **(A)** Escalator. The relationship between elevator/staircase/ramp is that they all allow access to upper and/or lower levels.

18. **(J)** Cocoa. The relationship between coffee/tea/soup is that they all are consumed warm or hot. The other choices are usually served cool or cold.

19. **(B)** Basketball. The relationship between court/hoop/center is that they are all associated with the sport basketball.

20. **(H)** Pages. The relationship between binding/jacket/title page is that they are all parts of a hardcover book. The other choices are associated with writing, but not necessarily books.

COOP
SUBTEST 5

Verbal Reasoning–Context—Detailed Explanations of Answers

1. **(D)** Alfred knew quite a bit about reptiles. If Alfred or his mom were afraid **(A)** and **(B)**, they probably would not go to the reptile house to begin with. Also, there is nothing indicating that they were afraid. There is nothing indicating whether Alfred goes to the zoo every week **(C)**. He might, but we can't know for sure, so it is not the best answer.

2. **(H)** It was raining outside. Jesse was dripping wet when she came back for the umbrella. Most likely she got wet from the rain **(H)**, so **(H)** is the best choice for this question. Since Jesse got wet, it is safe to assume it is already raining **(F)**, not that it might in the future. There is no mention of homework. Also, since she grabbed an umbrella (not her homework **(G)**), it seems that she probably came back for that. There is also nothing indicating whether Jesse likes school **(J)**. She may or may not.

3. **(D)** Max had hot dogs for dinner. Since it states that Max cooked hot dogs for dinner, we can guess that that's what he ate. Max looked for hamburgers so we can guess he probably likes them; even if we don't guess that, there isn't anything indicating that he doesn't like them **(A)**. Although he is able to make hamburgers, spaghetti, and hot dogs, there is nothing indicating whether he is actually a good cook **(B)**. He may or may not be. This is not likely to be the best answer. We know that there weren't any hamburgers, but there was spaghetti, and there may or may not have been anything else **(C)**.

4. **(J)** Jill picked three kinds of flowers. Count up the types of flowers, and you can see that Jill picked at least three types of flowers, making **(J)** the best answer. All we know for sure is that Jill did not pick any roses, but we have no idea why. Whether she doesn't like them **(F)**, her friend doesn't grow them **(G)**, or whether she is allergic to them **(H)** are all possibilities, but we do not know for sure. There is nothing indicating whether any of these things is true.

5. **(D)** Jane now has at least one cat. Jane has two pets, and one is definitely a cat. The other pet may or may not be a cat. We're not sure, but we know she has at least one cat (Mittens). We have no idea whether she has a rabbit **(C)** or whether Rover ran away **(A)**. Neither rabbits nor what happened to Rover is mentioned, so we cannot make guesses. We only

know Jane has two pets **(B)**, and one of them is a cat. We do not know anything about the second pet; it may or may not be another cat.

6. **(H)** Michael has been to France. Since it states that the Eiffel Tower is in France and that Michael visited the Eiffel Tower, we know that he has then been to France. It may or may not be true that many people visit the Eiffel Tower **(C)**, that it is a popular place to visit **(B)** and that there are many buildings in France **(A)**.

7. **(D)** Amber's family likes fruit salad. We do not know for sure if Amber does or does not like pears just because she did not put them in this salad. It does not state that Amber's favorite snack is fruit salad **(G)**. While fruit salad is generally considered to be a healthy snack **(J)**, it is not the best choice in this scenario.

8. **(G)** Willem has at least three kinds of cars. Since it states that he lined up convertibles, police cars, and race cars, we know he has 3 or more types of cars. Even though it states that he did not take out his buses **(C)**, it does not mean he does not like buses. There is no information on the size of the collection **(A)** or which types of cars Willem likes best **(D)**.

9. **(D)** Claire went on two rides. It directly states that she only rode the merry-go-round and the Ferris wheel. Claire may or may not have spent much time at the fair **(F)**. It states that she did not ride the bumper cars, but not the reason why **(G & H)**.

10. **(F)** Nathaniel watched the movie with a friend. Since it states that he bought two tickets, two small sodas, and two medium bags of popcorn we can figure that these items are for two people. Although there is no statement about a friend, it is the best answer since there is no mention of breakfast **(B)**, a sale **(C)**, or missing the movie **(D)**.

11. **(C)** Beatrice knows how to draw well. We know that Beatrice used special pencils and shading techniques to create her picture. It indicates that her parents were proud, which implies that she draws well. This is the best answer. Her parents may or may not be artists **(A)**. It states that Beatrice used pencils not paint **(B)**. There is no mention that Beatrice loves her art teacher **(D)**.

12. **(F)** It was cold outside. It states that he was shivering and he came back with a hat, scarf, and gloves, which makes this the best answer. There is no information that tells us that Jeffrey did not want to go to the park **(G)**. If Jeffrey forgot his football, he would have come back out with it **(H)**. It might have been snowing outside, but this was not mentioned.

13. **(D)** The last thing Kendra went on was the swings. It states that Kendra went on the swings right before she went home. There is no information on whether Kendra goes to the playground a lot **(A)** or if Kendra did not want to go home **(C)**. It does not mention what Kendra went on first **(B)**.

14. **(F)** Jamal has at least 8 pets. Since it states that Jamal has 2 hamsters and 6 gold fish, we know he has at least 8 pets. We know that Jamal does not have a dog, but that does not necessarily mean that he is allergic to dogs **(G)** or that he wants a dog **(J)**. There is no mention of cats **(H)**.

15. **(B)** Maria's feet had grown. This is the best answer since it states that she was disappointed to find that the shoes were too tight to wear. There is no information that implies that

Maria had to miss the party **(A)**. Maria may or may not have worn a different dress; however it does state that she planned to wear her favorite dress **(C)**. We do not know how many shoes Maria has **(D)**.

16. **(H)** Dominic finished his science project. It states that his mother told him that he had to finish his science project or he would not get to go to practice. Since it also states that he shot 2 goals at practice, we know that Dominic went to practice so he must have finished his project. Dominic's favorite sport may or may not be hockey **(F)**. Dominic's mother may have been proud of him, but this is not the best choice **(G)**. We do not know if Dominic likes science **(J)**.

17. **(D)** Carla plays different instruments. This is the best answer since it states that Carla plays the violin, trumpet, and saxophone. We know that she wants to play the drums, but this does not necessarily mean that **(A)** Carla did not like playing the violin or that **(B)** the school band needs drummers. There is no information to tell us if the saxophone is hard to play **(C)**.

18. **(H)** April has been to South Dakota. It states that April's aunt and uncle live in South Dakota and that she visited her aunt and uncle last summer. Just because Mount Rushmore is in South Dakota does not mean that April has been to Mount Rushmore **(F)** or that **(J)** April wants to visit Mount Rushmore. April's aunt and uncle may or may not go to Mount Rushmore often **(G)**.

19. **(A)** Playing softball made Jay hungry. Since Jay ate food before he played softball and then he had more food after playing, this is the best answer. There is no information regarding who won the softball game **(B)** or if playing made Jay tired **(D)**. Because he ate several different items it is unlikely that **(C)** Jay is a picky eater.

20. **(J)** Sophia went to a Fourth of July parade. Since it states that Sophia saw several marching bands, girl scout and boy scout troops, many fire trucks, and people waving, it seems that she has been to a parade. It does not mention if **(F)** Sophia is a girl scout. Although we know that her favorite marching band had baton twirlers it does not necessarily mean that **(G)** Sophia wants to learn how to twirl a baton. Sophia may or may not love marching bands.

COOP

Reading and Language Arts— Detailed Explanations of Answers

1. **(B)** The passage gives directions on how to use a spa and explains how to take care of a spa; therefore, we can tell that the passage is directed toward spa owners **(B)**, not scientists **(A)**, spa manufacturers **(C)**, or spa salespeople **(D)**.

2. **(J)** The passage focuses on giving directions for spa care, thereby assuming that the reader already owns one, making **(F)** and **(G)** false. The passage does not say spas are dangerous **(H)**.

3. **(C)** The third paragraph of the passage says that the growth of bacteria and viruses is prevented with sanitizer. Sanitizer doesn't control the pH **(A)**, doesn't affect water temperature **(D)**, and cannot be used instead of a filter **(B)**.

4. **(F)** The first paragraph of the passage describes the work of the filter. The filter does not control the pH **(G)** or temperature **(H)**, and the passage explicitly states that it cannot remove the items listed in **(J)**.

5. **(C)** The technical language and statistics show that this passage is intended for researchers. The passage is too technical to be intended for children **(A)** and **(B)** or parents **(D)**.

6. **(F)** The entire passage reports the findings of a study on the relationship between children's reading levels and the stories they make up. The passage does not mention IQ levels **(G)** or television **(H)** and **(J)**.

7. **(D)** All of the elements were used in the study according to the passage.

8. **(J)** The passage only discusses the findings about children in grades 1-6. The passage does not mention any other grades **(F)** and **(G)**. The passage says nothing about public or private school **(H)**.

9. **(D)** Twain's travels in the United States and his writing style are reasons the author gives for Twain's Americanness. Twain did not set all of his stories in the United States **(B)**, as *Innocents Abroad* is set in Europe.

10. **(H)** Europe is sometimes called "the Old World" and by Twain's account of his invasion of the Old World, the author means Twain's travels in Europe as an American. A museum **(F)**, the Mississippi **(G)**, and the United States **(J)** are not known as "the Old World."

11. **(A)** Twain did not work as a newspaper editor, although he did work as a printer's apprentice **(C)**, a lecturer **(D)**, and was in the Confederate militia **(B)**.

12. **(G)** From the very beginning of the passage, an admiring tone is used to describe Twain's life. The author is definitely not negative **(F)** and is neither confused **(H)** nor sentimental **(J)** about the details of Twain's life.

13. **(B)** The first sentence of the second paragraph tells us that the Civil War ended Twain's steamboating and that he served in a Confederate militia company. Twain was never a newspaper editor **(C)**, and although he did travel in the U.S. **(D)** and did become a popular writer **(A)**, these elements had nothing to do with ending his steamboating career.

14. **(H)** This passage gives a brief overview of research on children's stories. The author does not disagree with the findings **(F)** or explain why researchers are interested in this topic **(J)**. Although the last sentence of the passage suggests a possible area for more research, there is nothing in the paragraph about children's communication **(G)**.

15. **(D)** The word *narrative* means *story*. Content **(A)**, analysis **(B)**, and structure **(C)** are all parts of a story, but they do not mean narrative.

16. **(F)** The first sentence of the second paragraph lists the two approaches to analyzing children's stories. Although the elements listed in **(G)**, **(H)**, and **(J)** are discussed in the passage, they are not described as approaches.

17. **(B)** In the last sentence of the passage, the author suggests a direction for future research. The author does not conduct any research **(A)**, he/she is only summarizing past research, which he/she does not believe is wrong **(C)** or unimportant **(D)**.

18. **(H)** From the very first sentence this passage asserts that demands for changes in the school system are a result of the changing concerns of American society, not the opposite **(J)**. The passage does not argue for **(F)** or against **(G)** more changes.

19. **(D)** The passage mentions the end of the normal school during the early 1900s but does not discuss its creation. The passage does discuss the reforms listed in **(A)**, **(B)**, and **(C)**.

20. **(F)** The second paragraph of the passage is about the revision of teacher education and how it reflects changes in society. Although the paragraph states that teachers tend to teach as they have been taught **(G)**, this is an effect, rather than a cause, of change. The passage does not discuss television **(H)** or teacher dissatisfaction **(J)**.

21. **(B)** The last sentence of the passage explains that teachers tend to teach as they have been taught because they take the same educational courses. **(A)** and **(C)** are both true in and of themselves, but they are not causes of teachers teaching as they have been taught. The passage does not mention teachers trying to keep pace with other teachers **(D)**.

22. **(D)** It is the only choice that is in the past tense.

23. **(F)** When comparing two items, heavier is the correct adjective.

24. **(B)** Together, Maggie and Carrie are "they" and this requires the word *plan*.

25. **(G)** When comparing three or more items, the superlative *scariest* is used.

26. **(C)** Because it relates to an action that will be completed in the future, *will have eaten*, which is future perfect, is used.

27. **(H)** Because it refers to an action that is taking place at the same time as another, *meanwhile* is the correct choice.

28. **(D)** **(A)** is two sentences without punctuation, and **(B)** and **(C)** are dependent clauses.

29. **(H)** **(F)** is a dependent clause; **(G)** contains a dangling participle, and **(J)** is two sentences.

30. **(C)** **(A)** and **(B)** are dependent clauses, and **(D)** is two sentences.

31. **(F)** **(G)** is two sentences, and **(H)** and **(J)** are dependent clauses.

32. **(D)** **(A)** has a dangling participle; **(B)** is two sentences, and **(C)** is only participial phrases.

33. **(H)** **(F)** is two sentences; **(G)** is a dependent clause, and **(J)** is a participial phrase.

34. **(D)** **(A)** uses *brang*, and **(B)** has inconsistent tenses, as does **(C)**.

35. **(G)** **(F)** uses *wasn't* for *weren't*; **(H)** has a compound subject and needs *are*; and **(J)** uses *could of* for *could have*.

36. **(A)** **(B)**, **(C)**, and **(D)** have inconsistent tenses.

37. **(G)** **(F)** has a compound subject and requires *are*, and **(H)** and **(J)** have inconsistent tenses.

38. **(D)** The main idea of the paragraph is not related to cats as good pets, cats being popular, or the value of certain breeds.

39. **(G)** There is no mention of beetles being fascinating to study or of ways of identifying them. There is also no mention of the jobs that they do.

40. **(A)** The paragraph discusses more than geography; no other continents are described, and the last option does not cover geography.

COOP

Mathematics—Detailed Explanations of Answers

1. **(C)** Add 6 to both sides of the equation: $3x - 6 + 6 = 15 + 6$, $3x = 21$. Divide both sides by 3: $\dfrac{3x}{3} = \dfrac{21}{3}$; so $x = 7$.

2. **(J)** The total amount Albert collected from his aunt, uncle, mother, and father was ($12.00 + $8.25 + $12.50 + $7.50) = $40.25. So the amount he received from his grandfather must be $50.00 − $40.25 = $9.75.

3. **(D)** The total amount of milk that Sara drank is (7 + 6 + 5 + 5) = 23 oz. The total amount of milk she drank for the 5 days is (6 × 5) = 30 oz. The missing amount of milk (for Thursday) must be 30 − 23 = 7 oz.

4. **(J)** The "2" is the third digit to the right of the decimal point. So it must be 2 thousandths.

5. **(A)** To multiply a number by 100 results in shifting the decimal point 2 places to the right. Dividing by 100 results in shifting the decimal point 2 places to the left. When the decimal point is shifted 2 places to the left instead of 2 places to the right, it results in the decimal point being 4 places to the left of where it should have been. To correct this, we shift the decimal point 4 places to the right:

$$3\,7\,6\,2\,5\,.\,4\,5\,0\,0$$

6. **(G)** If Janet had pressed the plus button, the original number would have increased by 54. By pressing the minus button, she caused the number to decrease by 54. So she lost 54 twice. To make up for this double loss, we must add (54 + 54) = 108 to the result. Janet should have obtained −13 + 108 = 95.

7. **(A)** We begin by converting the given numbers to similar expressions. Here it is best to convert to decimal fractions: $83\% = 0.83$, $\dfrac{13}{16} = 0.8125$, and 0.78 is already a decimal fraction.

   Now we see that the correct order is 0.78, 0.8125, 0.83. This is the same as $0.78, \dfrac{13}{16}, 83\%$.

8. **(J)** The total cost of the students' lunches must be $4.93 \times 18 = \$88.74$.

9. **(C)** If we replace x with 3 and y with -2, we obtain $2x + 3y = 2(3) + 3(-2) = 6 - 6 = 0$.

10. **(F)** If we replace y with 6 and z with -2, we obtain $\dfrac{3y}{z} = \dfrac{3(6)}{-2} = -9$.

11. **(A)** 5 sets of 7 result in $5 \times 7 = 35$. If we include the 4 that were left over, we obtain $35 + 4 = 39$.

12. **(J)** Divide 357 by 15: $357 \div 15 = 23$, remainder 12. So there are already 23 full boxes, and the 24th box would need $15 - 12 = 3$ cassettes to fill it.

13. **(D)** Let m represent the smaller multiple of 4. Then the next higher multiple of 4 must be $m + 4$. The sum of these two multiples of 4 must be $m + (m + 4) = 2m + 4$. The product of 8 and 9 is $8 \times 9 = 72$. The number that is 12 less than the product of 8 and 9 is $72 - 12 = 60$. So, to rephrase the original story, we may say $2m + 4 = 60$. Now, add -4 to both sides: $2m + 4 - 4 = 60 - 4$, so $2m = 56$. Divide both sides by 2: $\dfrac{2m}{2} = \dfrac{56}{2}$, so $m = 28$.

14. **(J)** Since $\overline{OD} \perp \overline{AB}$ the measure of angle DOB must be $90°$. So $x° + (x° - 20°) = 90°$. Now combine like terms (ignoring the degree sign): $2x - 20 = 90$. Add 20 to both sides: $2x - 20 + 20 = 90 + 20$, so $2x = 110$. Divide both sides by 2: $\dfrac{2x}{2} = \dfrac{110}{2}$, so $x = 55$.

15. **(C)** [In the figure, we do not need to pay attention to the triangle.] $\overline{AC}$ meets straight line $\overline{BC}$ at C, making angles BCA and ACD supplementary (their sum is $180°$). That is: $y + 110 = 180$ (ignoring the degree sign). Subtract 110 from both sides: $y + 110 - 110 = 180 - 110$, so $y = 70$.

16. **(H)** Recall that the sum of the two acute angles of a right triangle is $90°$. That is: $x + 43 = 90$ (again ignoring the degree sign). Add -43 to both sides: $x + 43 - 43 = 90 - 43$, so $x = 47$.

17. **(C)** A rectangle must contain two pairs of congruent sides. In set 1, we already have two straws, measuring 20 in. each. We needed to find a match for the 12-in. side.

18. **(F)** A scalene triangle has 3 unequal sides. So we cannot choose **(H)** or **(J)**. We must also bear in mind that the sum of the measures of any two sides of a triangle must be greater than the measure of the third side. So we cannot choose **(G)**, since $9 + 6 = 15$. The correct choice is **(F)**. [Check: (1) 15, 6, and 10 are mutually unequal, and (2) $6 + 10 > 15$.]

19. **(D)** If we let x represent Xena's age, then Yvonne's age must be $x - 2$. Since Yvonne is 5 years younger than Steve, his age must be $(x - 2) + 5$, that is, $x + 3$.

20. **(G)** At d dollars per month for 9 months, Edith would earn $9d$. For the next 3 months, she earned $d - \$15$ per month. So for the last 3 months, she earned $3(d - 15)$ (we can safely ignore the dollar sign). For the 12 months, she would earn a total of $9d + 3(d - 15)$. Clear brackets: $9d + 3(d - 15) = 9d + 3d - 45 = 12d - 45$.

21. **(B)** Multiply each term in $(3n + 4)$ by each term in $(n - 2)$ and simplify: $(3n + 4)(n - 2) = 3n^2 - 2n - 8$.

22. **(F)** Although it is not absolutely necessary, it would help to group the numbers, as a reminder of the operations that must be performed first: $24 \div 6 + 2 \times 8 = (24 \div 6) + (2 \times 8) = 4 + 16 = 20$.

23. (A) First, find 20% of 90: $\dfrac{20 \times 90}{100} = 18$. Next, find 25% of 36: $\dfrac{25 \times 36}{100} = 9$. Finally, divide 18 by 9: $18 \div 9 = 2$.

24. (F) 210% of 420 is $\dfrac{210 \times 420}{100} = 882$.

25. (B) First, compute the area of 1 sheet of plywood $4 \times 8 = 32$ ft². Next, compute the area of the fence: $40 \times 7 = 280$ ft². Then, divide the area of the fence by the area of 1 sheet of plywood: $280 \div 32 = 8.75$. Since plywood is sold only in whole sheets, the carpenter must buy 9 sheets.

26. (J) Gregory improved his score by $58 - 49 = 9$; Nancy improved hers by $70 - 64 = 6$; Jerome improved his by $67 - 56 = 11$; and Rhoda actually decreased. Jerome showed the most improvement.

27. (C) First, compute the total score for each of these four students: Bill: $60 + 58 = 118$, Clara: $58 + 65 = 123$, Gregory: $49 + 58 = 107$, and Rhoda: $71 + 69 = 140$. We see that Gregory did the worst.

28. (G) The average score for the 7 students on the first test was $(64 + 71 + 58 + 49 + 56 + 60 + 65) \div 7 = 423 \div 7 = 60.43$. The nearest number given is 61.

29. (D) If the average score for the 7 students on the second test was 66, then the total score must be $66 \times 7 = 462$. The subtotal from the first 6 students is $(70 + 69 + 65 + 58 + 67 + 58) = 387$. So the missing score must be $462 - 387 = 75$.

30. (H) First, compute the distance between Alphatown and Betatown: $45 \times 4 = 180$ miles. Next, calculate the distance between Betatown and Chetatown: $54 \times 5 = 270$ miles. So Wong's total driving time was $4 + 5 = 9$ hours, for a total distance of $180 + 270 = 450$ miles. His average speed must be $450 \div 9 = 50$ mph.

31. (C) Multiply 0.0012 by 10,000: $0.0012 \times 10,000 = 12$.

32. (H) Add 6 to both sides of the equation: $3x - 6 + 6 = 42 + 6$, so $3x = 48$. Divide both sides by 3: $\dfrac{3x}{3} = \dfrac{48}{3}$; so $x = 16$.

33. (B) The line intersects the y-axis at 4 units from 0 and intersects the x-axis 5 units from 0. So the slope of the line is $\dfrac{4}{5}$. Since we can clearly see that the line is right-inclined (runs from lower left to upper right), the slope is positive. (This is why we could safely ignore the signs of the x- and y-intercepts.)

34. (J) The sum of angles A and E is $90° + 90° = 180°$. The sum of the three remaining angles must be $540° - 180° = 360°$. These three angles may may have different values, but they must equal 360°.

35. (A) Compute the area of the front face: $6 \times 10 = 60$ in². Compute the area of the top face: $10 \times 14 = 140$ in². Compute the area of the side face: $6 \times 14 = 84$ in². Add these three areas together: $60 \text{ in}^2 + 140 \text{ in}^2 + 84 \text{ in}^2 = 284 \text{ in}^2$.

36. **(G)** The width of the rectangle containing a semicircle is (7 cm + 7 cm) = 14 cm. The area of the complete rectangle is $18 \times 14 = 252$ cm^2. The area of the semicircle is half the area of a complete circle with the same radius; the radius of the circle is 7, so its area is $3.14 \times 7^2 = 3.14 \times 7 \times 7 = 153.86$ cm^2. The area of the semicircle must be 153.86 cm^2 ÷ 2 = 76.93 cm^2. The area of the shaded region of the rectangle must be 252 cm^2 − 76.93 cm^2 = 175.07 cm^2, which is close to 175 cm^2.

37. **(C)** If 1 kg = 2.2 lbs, then 150 kg = $2.2 \times 150 = 330$ lbs.

38. **(G)** One way to answer this question is to begin by expressing $3,000 as a fraction of $25,000: $\frac{3000}{25000} = 0.12$. Then multiply $30,000 by 0.12: $30,000 × 0.12 = $3,600.

39. **(D)** Here we are interested in the <u>net rise</u>, that is, temperature at the end of a period minus temperature at the beginning of that period. So the temperature rises are: February − April = 10°, March − May = 5°, April − June = 10°, and May − July = 25°.

40. **(H)** We need the <u>net rise</u>. The easiest way to compute the average temperature rise between March and August is as follows: find the difference between the temperature readings for the two months. The temperature in August was 90°, while in March it was 40°. So the net rise was 90° − 40° = 50°. This is a 5-month interval; hence, the average temperature rise must be 50° ÷ 5 = 10°.

TACHS

PRACTICE TEST 1

TACHS
SUBTEST 1

Reading

Time: Unspecified
50 Questions

DIRECTIONS: Questions 1–20 comprise the Vocabulary portion of the Reading test. Read each phrase or sentence to determine the word choice that most nearly means the same as that word.

1. <u>Eradicate</u> that waste
   (A) increase
   (B) debate
   (C) eliminate
   (D) humiliate

2. A <u>suspicious</u> feeling
   (J) apprehensive
   (K) thoughtful
   (L) trusting
   (M) annoyed

3. He felt <u>indifferent</u>
   (A) uninterested
   (B) similar
   (C) concerned
   (D) responsive

4. <u>Alleviate</u> the pain
   (J) lessen
   (K) include
   (L) aggravate
   (M) endure

5. <u>Luxurious</u> furnishings
   (A) meager
   (B) rough
   (C) lavish
   (D) slippery

6. <u>Repel</u> the bugs
   (J) attract
   (K) collect
   (L) resist
   (M) explore

7. <u>Incriminate</u> the robber
   (A) contradict
   (B) excuse
   (C) reduce
   (D) accuse

GO TO NEXT PAGE

TACHS

8. <u>Opaque</u> paint
   (J) transparent
   (K) liquid
   (L) clear
   (M) not clear

9. <u>Defy</u> his fear
   (A) resist
   (B) remove
   (C) obey
   (D) destroy

10. To <u>sustain</u> the project
    (J) continue
    (K) ignore
    (L) substitute
    (M) quit

11. A <u>momentary</u> rain shower
    (A) constant
    (B) sudden
    (C) fleeting
    (D) drenching

12. A <u>speculative</u> answer
    (J) definite
    (K) approximate
    (L) incorrect
    (M) fruitful

13. <u>Reprimand</u> the dog
    (A) praise
    (B) scold
    (C) discuss
    (D) include

14. A <u>gradual</u> increase
    (J) speedy
    (K) finite
    (L) declining
    (M) ongoing

15. <u>Persuade</u> your parents
    (A) insult
    (B) sadden
    (C) convince
    (D) accuse

16. A <u>woeful</u> song
    (J) cheerful
    (K) sorrowful
    (L) brave
    (M) energetic

17. She felt <u>empathy</u>
    (A) understanding
    (B) trustworthy
    (C) indifference
    (D) cruelty

18. A <u>crucial</u> assignment
    (J) hidden
    (K) explosive
    (L) critical
    (M) mundane

19. He will <u>scrutinize</u> the work
    (A) revolutionize
    (B) examine
    (C) terminate
    (D) ignore

20. A <u>nonchalant</u> feeling
    (J) worried
    (K) sincere
    (L) sophisticated
    (M) unconcerned

GO TO NEXT PAGE ➡

TACHS

DIRECTIONS: Questions 21–50 comprise the Reading Comprehension portion of the Reading test. Each passage is followed by questions based on its content. After reading the passage, choose the best answer for each question.

Questions 21–24 are based on the following passage.

Frederick Douglass was born Frederick Augustus Washington Bailey in 1817 to a white father and a slave mother. Frederick was raised by his grandmother on a Maryland plantation until he was eight. It was then that he was sent to Baltimore by his owner to be a servant to the Auld family. Mrs. Auld recognized Frederick's intellectual acumen and defied the law of the state by teaching him to read and write. When Mr. Auld warned that education would make the boy unfit for slavery, Frederick sought to continue his education in the streets. When his master died, Frederick was returned to the plantation to work in the fields at age sixteen. Later, he was hired out to work in the shipyards in Baltimore as a ship caulker. He plotted an escape but was discovered before he could get away. It took five years before he made his way to New York City and then to New Bedford, Massachusetts, eluding slave hunters by changing his name to Douglass.

At an 1841 anti-slavery meeting in Massachusetts, Douglass was invited to give a talk about his experiences under slavery. His impromptu speech was so powerful and so eloquent that it thrust him into a career as an agent for the Massachusetts Anti-Slavery Society.

Douglass wrote his autobiography in 1845 primarily to counter those who doubted his authenticity as a former slave. This work became a classic in American literature and a primary source about slavery from the point of view of a slave. Douglass went on a two-year speaking tour abroad to avoid recapture by his former owner and to win new friends for the abolition movement. He returned with funds to purchase his freedom and to start his own anti-slavery newspaper. He became a consultant to Abraham Lincoln and throughout Reconstruction fought doggedly for full civil rights for freedmen; he also supported the women's rights movement.

21. Why, most probably, did some people doubt that Frederick Douglass was a former slave?
   (A) He was inexperienced at plantation work.
   (B) He was such a powerful and eloquent speaker and writer.
   (C) He knew several trades.
   (D) He wrote his own autobiography.

22. Which of the following jobs did Frederick Douglass NOT have?
   (J) Agent for an anti-slavery society
   (K) Consultant to the President of the United States
   (L) Lawyer for anti-slavery causes
   (M) Publisher of an anti-slavery newspaper

GO TO NEXT PAGE ➡

23. It can be inferred from the passage that Frederick Douglass sought to continue his education in the streets because
    (A) Mr. Auld probably forbade Mrs. Auld to teach Douglass further.
    (B) Mrs. Auld had taught him all she knew.
    (C) Douglass needed to find a teacher with more experience in writing books.
    (D) Douglass began to work in the ship-yards and no longer lived with the Aulds.

24. According to the passage, which of the following did Douglas support?
    (J) Civil rights
    (K) The women's rights movement
    (L) Both (J) and (K)
    (M) Neither (K) nor (J)

Questions 25–29 are based on the following passage.

Passive-aggressive personality disorder has as its essential characteristic covert noncompliance to ordinary performance demands made in social and occupational situations. To a greater extent than in other personality disorders, this pattern may be context dependent, appearing only in certain situations.

Aggressive impulses and motives are expressed by passivity. These represent its primary dynamic and may take the form of inaction, inefficiency, procrastination, or obstructionism. It is an interpersonal disorder, the recognition of which depends on the seemingly unjustified frustration and hostility others feel toward such individuals. By the use of verbal expressions indicating compliance or agreement, the passive-aggressive person conceals his/her actual noncompliance and the secret sadistic satisfaction he/she derives from the frustration he/she thereby causes. This dynamic is distinguished from that associated with masochism, in which self-punitive actions are used to control others or to evoke protective responses from them. It is also distinguished from the ambivalence and indecision of obsessive-compulsive persons, who may appear passive and obstructionistic, but are not motivated by a wish to evoke frustration in others.

25. What was the main purpose of the author in writing this passage?
    (A) To describe passive-aggressive personality disorder
    (B) To discuss treatments for passive-aggressive personality disorder
    (C) To list situations that may cause passive-aggressive behavior
    (D) To list clinics where patients can be treated for passive-aggressive behavior

26. Which of the following statements is supported by the passage?
    (J) Passive-aggressive personality disorder is probably a genetic disorder.
    (K) Passive-aggressive behavior is more common in men than women.
    (L) Passive-aggressive behavior may be triggered by certain situations and not by others.
    (M) Passive-aggressive behavior is more common in children than in adults.

GO TO NEXT PAGE

27. According to the passage, one can recognize that a person has a passive-aggressive personality disorder by

(A) taking a blood sample.

(B) the frustrated reactions of others around that person.

(C) giving the person a personality test.

(D) having a psychologist evaluate the person.

28. How is passive-aggressive personality disorder defined in the passage?

(J) The person often gets in fights with others.

(K) The person can't make decisions and constantly changes his/her mind.

(L) The person says he/she agrees with others, but then acts contrary to that agreement, thereby frustrating other people.

(M) By punishing him/herself, the person controls others.

29. As used in the first sentence of the passage, the word *covert* most nearly means

(A) aggressive.

(B) secretive.

(C) open.

(D) evoke.

Questions 30–34 are based on the following passage.

Instructions for Absentee Voting

These instructions describe conditions under which voters may register for or request absentee ballots to vote in the November 5 election.

(1) If you moved on or prior to October 7 and did not register to vote at your new address, you are not eligible to vote in this election.

(2) If you move after this date, you may vote via absentee ballot or at your polling place, using your previous address as your address of registration for this election.

(3) You must register at your new address to vote in future elections.

(4) The last day to request an absentee ballot is October 29.

(5) You must be a registered voter in the county.

(6) You must sign your request in your own handwriting.

(7) You must make a separate request for each election.

(8) The absentee ballot shall be issued to the requesting voter in person or by mail.

GO TO NEXT PAGE

TACHS

30. What is the main purpose of this passage?
    (J) to instruct voters at the polls
    (K) to instruct vote-counters on how to count absentee ballots
    (L) to instruct people interested in using an absentee ballot
    (M) to explain how to work a voting machine

31. According to the passage, when is the deadline for getting an absentee ballot?
    (A) November 5
    (B) October 7
    (C) October 28
    (D) October 29

32. This passage was most likely written by
    (J) an organization that encourages people to vote.
    (K) the United States government.
    (L) voters who have used absentee ballots before.
    (M) the League of Women Voters.

33. In number two of this passage, the word *via* most nearly means
    (A) without.
    (B) over.
    (C) by.
    (D) not.

34. If a person moved on October 8, and did not register to vote at the new address, how could he/she vote?
    (J) at his/her old polling place
    (K) with an absentee ballot
    (L) at the nearest polling place in his/her new county
    (M) Either (A) or (B), but not (C).

Questions 35–39 are based on the following passage.

One of the many tragedies of the Civil War was the housing and care of prisoners. The Andersonville prison, built by the Confederates in 1864 to accommodate 10,000 Union prisoners, was not completed when prisoners started arriving. Five months later the total number of men incarcerated there had risen to 31,678.

The sounds of death and dying were not diminished by surrender of weapons to a captor. Chances of survival for prisoners in Andersonville were not much better than in the throes of combat. Next to overcrowding, inadequate shelter caused unimaginable suffering. The Confederates were not equipped with the manpower, tools, or supplies necessary to house such a population of captives; prisoners themselves gathered lumber, logs, anything they could find to construct some sort of protection from the elements. Some prisoners dug holes in the ground, risking suffocation from cave-ins, but many hundreds were left exposed to the wind, rain, cold, and heat.

Daily food rations were exhausted by the sheer numbers they had to serve, resulting in severe dietary deficiencies. The overcrowding, meager rations, and deplorable unsanitary conditions resulted in rampant disease and a high mortality rate. The consequences

GO TO NEXT PAGE

of a small scratch or wound could result in death in Andersonville. During the prison's thirteen-month existence, more than 12,000 prisoners died and were buried in the Andersonville cemetery. Most of the deaths were caused by diarrhea, dysentery, gangrene, and scurvy that could not be treated due to inadequate staff and supplies.

35. What is the main idea of this passage?
    (A) The Union prisons were better than the Confederate prisons.
    (B) The chances of survival for prisoners were about the same as for soldiers in combat.
    (C) Many Union prisoners suffered and died at Andersonville prison because the Confederates could not provide enough shelter and supplies.
    (D) The food in prisons is very unhealthy.

36. According to the passage, which of the following problems did Andersonville prison have?
    (J) Prison doctors couldn't handle emergencies.
    (K) Prisoners did not get enough exercise.
    (L) Prisoners did not have enough food.
    (M) All of the above.

37. According to the passage, how long did the prison stay open?
    (A) five months
    (B) one year
    (C) thirteen months
    (D) two years

38. According to the passage, prisoners died from all the following EXCEPT
    (J) gangrene.
    (K) scurvy.
    (L) dermatitis.
    (M) dysentery.

39. This passage was most likely taken from
    (A) a textbook.
    (B) a government report.
    (C) prison records.
    (D) journals kept by prisoners.

Questions 40–44 are based on the following passage.

Beginning readers, and those who are experiencing difficulty with reading, benefit from assisted reading. During assisted reading the teacher orally reads a passage with a student or students. The teacher fades in and out of the reading act. For example, the teacher lets his or her voice drop to a whisper when students are reading on their own at an acceptable rate and lets his or her voice rise to say the words clearly when the students are having difficulty.

Students who are threatened by print, read word-by-word, or rely on grapho-phonemic cues will be helped by assisted reading. These students are stuck on individual language units which can be as small as a single letter or as large as phrases or sentences. As Frank Smith (1977) and other reading educators have noted, speeding up reading, not slowing it down, helps the reader make sense of a passage. This strategy allows students to concentrate on meaning as the short-term memory is not overloaded by focusing on small language units. As the name implies, assisted reading lets the reader move along without being responsible for every language unit; the pressure is taken off the student. Consequently, when the reading act is sped up, it sounds more like language, and students can begin to integrate the cuing systems of semantics and syntax along with grapho-phonemics.

GO TO NEXT PAGE ➡

TACHS

40. According to the passage, assisted reading

(J) hurts slow readers because they don't get to figure it out on their own.

(K) helps slow readers understand what they are reading.

(L) hurts slow readers because it doesn't give them time to understand what they are reading.

(M) helps slow readers by putting more pressure on them.

41. Assisted reading is

(A) when the reader gives out definitions of hard words in the passage.

(B) when the teacher reads out loud with the students, getting louder or quieter depending on the students' abilities.

(C) when the passage has pictures to help students understand it.

(D) when the teacher reads to the student.

42. The passage says all of the following about assisted reading EXCEPT that

(J) it speeds up reading.

(K) it takes pressure off of the students.

(L) it lets the students concentrate on what the passage means.

(M) it makes the students responsible for every language unit.

43. According to the passage, a beginning reader can most easily make sense of a reading by

(A) reading slowly.

(B) concentrating on every word.

(C) speeding up and concentrating on the meaning.

(D) focusing on small language units.

44. As used in the passage, "individual language units" means

(J) small parts of language such as letters, phrases, or sentences.

(K) big pieces of language like paragraphs.

(L) a unit in a language textbook.

(M) an entire story or book.

Questions 45–50 are based on the following passage.

The First Amendment to the Constitution of the United States guarantees that Congress shall not make a law prohibiting the free exercise of religion or respecting an establishment of religion. Many voices in the country offer conflicting ideas. A Chief Justice of the Supreme Court of the United States described the separation of church and state as a wall based on bad history, a guide which is useless to judging, and a metaphor which should be discarded. A contemporary, prominent church pastor viewed this enforced separation of civil and religious authority as the result of the work of an infidel. A religious leader of the colonial period reaffirmed this amendment by asking that government continue to let people speak as they please and worship freely whether it be none, one, or 20 gods. In the modern context, then, it seems that threats to religious freedom still exist. Separation of church and state is not universally accepted.

GO TO NEXT PAGE ➡

TACHS

45. The First Amendment prohibits

   (A) the free exercise or establishment of religion.

   (B) laws which prohibit freedom of religion.

   (C) free speech.

   (D) the free exercise or establishment of organizations.

46. According to the passage, critics of the First Amendment

   (J) believe the Constitution is useless.

   (K) believe it is the work of an infidel.

   (L) believe that religious leaders should rewrite the Constitution.

   (M) believe that churches have the final authority over the United States government.

47. In the passage, the word *reaffirmed* means

   (A) agreed with.

   (B) disagreed with.

   (C) ignored.

   (D) celebrated.

48. According to the passage, a Supreme Court Justice believes the First Amendment is all of the following EXCEPT

   (J) a useless guide.

   (K) a barrier based on a misinterpretation of history.

   (L) a clear guide.

   (M) a metaphor.

49. The main purpose of this passage is

   (A) to show that the separation of church and state is under attack.

   (B) to show that everyone believes in the separation of church and state.

   (C) to show that no one pays attention to the separation of church and state anymore.

   (D) to prove that the government should control religion.

50. According to the tone and content of the passage, which of the following is most likely the intended audience?

   (J) religous leaders

   (K) teachers

   (L) judges

   (M) students

STOP

TACHS

TACHS
SUBTEST 2

Language

Time: Unspecified
40 Questions

DIRECTIONS: Questions 1–10 comprise the Spelling portion of the Language Test. Look at the four words carefully to determine if there are any errors in <u>spelling</u>. Choose the word that is misspelled or choose "no mistakes."

1. **(A)** surprise
   (B) atention
   (C) crunch
   (D) along
   (E) No mistakes

2. **(J)** reverse
   (K) together
   (L) mention
   (M) allways
   (N) No mistakes

3. **(A)** tapping
   (B) pretend
   (C) laughing
   (D) search
   (E) No mistakes

4. **(J)** cancil
   (K) beautiful
   (L) extreme
   (M) transit
   (N) No mistakes

5. **(A)** offer
   (B) explain
   (C) comment
   (D) travel
   (E) No mistakes

6. **(J)** trash
   (K) wonderfull
   (L) balance
   (M) offer
   (N) No mistakes

GO TO NEXT PAGE ➡

7. (A) rectangle
   (B) purpose
   (C) include
   (D) creat
   (E) No mistakes

8. (J) apologe
   (K) friendship
   (L) consider
   (M) caution
   (N) No mistakes

9. (A) answer
   (B) uniform
   (C) computer
   (D) explood
   (E) No mistakes

10. (J) responsible
    (K) carefree
    (L) purhaps
    (M) harmful
    (N) No mistakes

DIRECTIONS: Questions 11–20 comprise the Capitalization portion of the Language Test. Look at the sentences carefully to determine if there are any errors in <u>capitalization</u>. Choose the section that contains the error or choose "no mistakes."

11. (A) Our friend tammy
    (B) likes to order the chocolate
    (C) ice cream every time we go out.
    (D) No mistakes

12. (J) This Saturday my brother
    (K) and i will go to our
    (L) grandparents' house.
    (M) No mistakes

13. (A) Last halloween my friends
    (B) came over my house for
    (C) a special party.
    (D) No mistakes

14. (J) Walter went to story time
    (K) at the library, where he
    (L) heard *where the wild things are*.
    (M) No mistakes

15. (A) Connor was excited to see
    (B) his favorite band, *the fray* was
    (C) playing his local arena.
    (D) No mistakes

16. (J) The steady rain that
    (K) fell this week will help
    (L) the Carrots to grow.
    (M) No mistakes

17. (A) Kelsey's favorite season
    (B) is spring, with its warm weather
    (C) and colorful flowers.
    (D) No mistakes

18. (J) The play, *Death of a salesman* made
    (K) a return to Broadway earlier
    (L) this year.
    (M) No mistakes

GO TO NEXT PAGE ➡

19. **(A)** Do you think that we
    (B) will take a trip to france
    (C) when we are seniors?
    (D) No mistakes

20. **(J)** Mondays and wednesdays
    (K) are the days I work out
    (L) at the gym.
    (M) No mistakes

DIRECTIONS: Questions 21–30 comprise the Punctuation portion of the Language Test. Look at the sentences carefully to determine if there are any errors in <u>punctuation</u>. Choose the section that contains the error or choose "no mistakes."

21. **(A)** When Matt got home
    (B) from school, he made a
    (C) peanut butter, and jelly sandwich.
    (D) No mistakes

22. **(J)** Since her birthday is tomorrow:
    (K) we should bake the
    (L) cake later today.
    (M) No mistakes

23. **(A)** That's Kims book, so
    (B) you shouldn't touch it
    (C) without asking her.
    (D) No mistakes

24. **(J)** Billy was so hungry that
    (K) he ordered eggs pancakes and
    (L) bacon for breakfast.
    (M) No mistakes

25. **(A)** Since you are really good
    (B) at playing the piano, you
    (C) should do well at your recital.
    (D) No mistakes

26. **(J)** Kelly asked, "Do you know what"
    (K) the homework was
    (L) last night?
    (M) No mistakes

27. **(A)** Make sure to be polite when
    (B) you eat dinner at your
    (C) friends house.
    (D) No mistakes

28. **(J)** Its only natural to be
    (K) nervous before your first
    (L) solo performance.
    (M) No mistakes

29. **(A)** He doesn't always
    (B) answer his cell phone
    (C) when I call.
    (D) No mistakes

30. **(J)** When it's time to do a
    (K) fire drill it's important to
    (L) listen for it's announcements.
    (M) No mistakes

GO TO NEXT PAGE ➡

TACHS

DIRECTIONS: Questions 31–40 comprise the Usage and Expression portion of the Language Test. Look at the sentences carefully to determine if there are any errors in word <u>usage and expression</u>. Choose the section that contains the error or choose "no mistakes."

31. **(A)** The library was open.
    (B) I goed straight to the non-fiction section.
    (C) I found a book that was perfect for my report.
    (D) No mistakes

32. **(J)** The dog barked and barked.
    (K) It seemed to be afraid of the truck.
    (L) When the truck drived away the dog calmed down.
    (M) No mistakes

33. **(A)** Keith don't have his homework again.
    (B) The teacher said he must do it today.
    (C) Keith had to complete it after class.
    (D) No mistakes

34. **(J)** The basketball game was exciting.
    (K) Both teams played their absolute best.
    (L) The crowd went wild.
    (M) No mistakes

35. **(A)** Tara had went home early.
    (B) The nurse said she had a fever.
    (C) Now Tara needed to stay home and rest.
    (D) No mistakes

36. **(J)** It was pouring outside.
    (K) The rain fall all day.
    (L) Streets flooded across the town.
    (M) No mistakes

For Questions 37 and 38, choose the best way of <u>expressing</u> an idea.

37. **(A)** Before you bake, the correct temperature preheat the oven to you need to.
    (B) The oven you need to preheat to the correct temperature before you bake.
    (C) You need to preheat the oven to the correct temperature before you bake.
    (D) Before you bake to the correct temperature you need to preheat the oven.

38. **(J)** With a gauge to make sure you add the right amount of air check the tire pressure.
    (K) Check the tire pressure to make sure with a gauge you add the right amount of air.
    (L) You add the right amount of air check the tire pressure with a gauge to make sure.
    (M) Check the tire pressure with a gauge to make sure you add the right amount of air.

GO TO NEXT PAGE ➡

For Questions 39 and 40, choose the best answers based on the following passage.

[1] When you are cooking a meal, it is important to read the recipe carefully. [2] First, you must determine what ingredients are necessary. [3] Then you should write a shopping list, which includes all of the items you need. [4] When you are at the store, be sure to check your list to ensure that you have found everything noted in the recipe. [5] Some supermarkets are more expensive than others. [6] Once you are home and ready to cook, arrange all the ingredients on the counter. [7] Last, follow the recipe step by step <u>because</u> you will be successful.

39. Which sentence should be left out of this paragraph?

(A) Sentence 2

(B) Sentence 4

(C) Sentence 5

(D) Sentence 7

40. What is the <u>best</u> way to write the underlined part of sentence 7?

(J) and

(K) or

(L) than

(M) (*No change*)

TACHS

STOP

TACHS
SUBTEST 3

Mathematics

Time: 40 Minutes
40 Questions

DIRECTIONS: Select the best answer choice.

1. What is the value of *x* if $64 \div x = 8$ is a true statement?
   - (A) 3
   - (B) 5
   - (C) 7
   - (D) 8

2. Which of the following is not a factor of 36?
   - (J) 3
   - (K) 5
   - (L) 6
   - (M) 9

3. Sarah earns money by babysitting. She charges $15 an hour. If she works 2 hours a week for 3 weeks, what will be her total earnings?
   - (A) $45
   - (B) $60
   - (C) $90
   - (D) $120

4. Jeff wants to buy a new bicycle. It costs $350. He has saved $185 from his job. How much more money does Jeff need to save in order to purchase the bike?
   - (J) $165
   - (K) $135
   - (L) $235
   - (M) $350

5. What is the value of *x*, if $24 \div x = 8$ is a true statement?
   - (A) 6
   - (B) 2
   - (C) 3
   - (D) 7

6. Which of the following is **not** a factor of 40?
   - (J) 4
   - (K) 5
   - (L) 8
   - (M) 9

GO TO NEXT PAGE ➡

7. Tess set a goal to read 20 books before the summer ends. She has read 9 so far. If she reads 2 books a week, what is the fewest number of weeks Tess will need to read to reach her goal?

    (A) 3

    (B) 6

    (C) 8

    (D) 11

8. What is the difference of 5.38 and 3.91?

    (J) 1.47

    (K) 2.67

    (L) 4.29

    (M) 9.29

9. Find the sum of $2\frac{1}{3}$, $3\frac{1}{2}$, and $3\frac{3}{4}$.

    (A) $8\frac{5}{9}$

    (B) $8\frac{4}{6}$

    (C) $9\frac{7}{12}$

    (D) $9\frac{2}{6}$

10. Which of the following is a prime number?

    (J) 4

    (K) 6

    (L) 9

    (M) 11

11. Sal took weekly quizzes in math class. Over a period of 5 weeks he got the following scores: 87, 92, 84, 89, 92. What was the average test score Sal earned? Round to the nearest whole number.

    (A) 92

    (B) 88

    (C) 89

    (D) 90

DIRECTIONS: Use the graph below to answer questions 12 and 13.

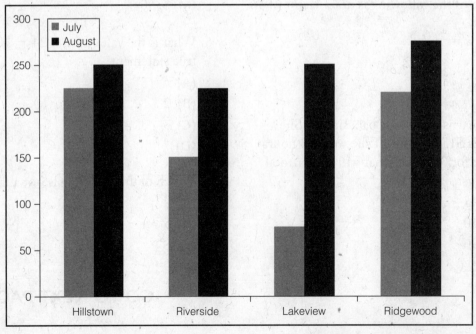

Valley County Summer Recycling Challenge

GO TO NEXT PAGE ➡

TACHS

12. Which of the following towns had the largest increase in recycling collections from July to August?

(J) Hillstown

(K) Riverside

(L) Lakeview

(M) Ridgewood

13. Which two towns, when combined, had the greatest number of collections in August?

(A) Hillstown and Riverside

(B) Lakeview and Ridgewood

(C) Hillstown and Lakeview

(D) Riverside and Lakeview

14. Find the quotient of 1,924 and 37.

(J) 58

(K) 62

(L) 52

(M) 49

15. Convert 5.20 to a mixed numeral and reduce it to the lowest terms.

(A) $5\frac{1}{5}$

(B) $5\frac{20}{100}$

(C) $5\frac{2}{10}$

(D) $5\frac{1}{2}$

16. A group of students had a car wash to help pay for their end of the trip. They collected a total of $700, which they shared equally. How many students were in the group?

(J) 12

(K) 17

(L) 15

(M) 14

17. Find the product of $\frac{2}{3}$ and $\frac{3}{4}$. Reduce the fraction to the lowest terms.

(A) $\frac{5}{6}$

(B) $\frac{1}{2}$

(C) $\frac{5}{12}$

(D) $\frac{6}{12}$

18. Kelly went shopping for a new coat. She has $150 to spend. The coat she wants is $180. It is on sale for 10% off. How much more money does Kelly need in order to buy this coat?

(J) $20

(K) $30

(L) $12

(M) $18

19. Change $6\frac{5}{8}$ to a decimal.

(A) 6.490

(B) 7.600

(C) 6.250

(D) 6. 625

20. What is the equivalent of $(+2) - (-1) + (+4)$?

(J) 5

(K) 3

(L) 7

(M) 4

21. Carlos went on a road trip to visit a friend who had moved 275 miles away. He left his house at 7 a.m. and arrived at 12 p.m. He made no stops along the way. What was his average rate of speed?

(A) 55 mph

(B) 52 mph

(C) 57 mph

(D) 60 mph

GO TO NEXT PAGE ➡

TACHS

DIRECTIONS: Use the pie chart below to answer questions 22 and 23.

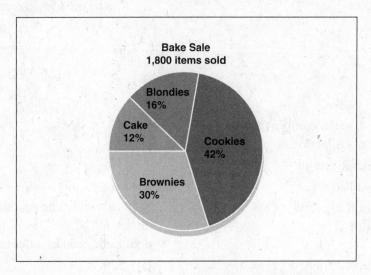

Bake Sale
1,800 items sold

Blondies 16%

Cake 12%

Cookies 42%

Brownies 30%

22. According to the pie chart, how many brownies were sold?

(J) 498

(K) 512

(L) 600

(M) 540

23. How many more cookies were sold than blondies?

(A) 756

(B) 468

(C) 634

(D) 288

24. Which of the following is equal to 7^3?

(J) 621

(K) 490

(L) 343

(M) 147

25. Round off 4.892 to the nearest hundredth.

(A) 489

(B) 4.90

(C) 500

(D) 4.89

26. Multiply 15% of 60 by 20% of 75.

(J) 140

(K) 135

(L) 128

(M) 138

27. In this right triangle, find the value of x.

24

x

7

(A) 25

(B) 27

(C) 29

(D) 31

28. The sum of the angles of figure A B C D E is 540°. If angles A and B are each 105°, what is the sum of angles C, D, and E?

A B

E C

D

(J) 210°

(K) 225°

(L) 330°

(M) 435°

GO TO NEXT PAGE ➡

DIRECTIONS: Use the chart below to answer questions 29 and 30.

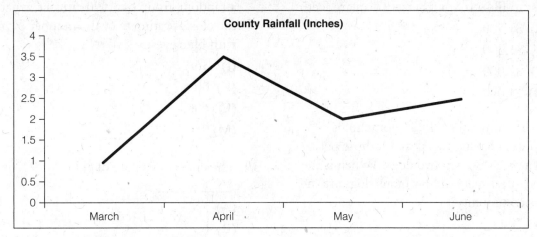

29. What is the approximate difference in the amount of rainfall in March and April?

(A) 4.5 inches

(B) 2.5 inches

(C) 1 inch

(D) 3.5 inches

30. What was the average amount of rainfall in this county over the months shown?

(J) 2.05 inches

(K) 1.55 inches

(L) 2.25 inches

(M) 1.75 inches

Estimation

DIRECTIONS: For questions 31–40, <u>estimate</u> the answer in your head. No scratch work is allowed. Do <u>not</u> to try to compute the exact answers. Choose the best answer.

31. The closest estimate of 143×97 is _____.

(A) 1,300

(B) 1,400

(C) 1,500

(D) 1,600

32. The closest estimate of $482 \div 8$ is _____.

(J) 70

(K) 80

(L) 50

(M) 60

33. The closest estimate of $5{,}691 - 2{,}038$ is _____.

(A) 4,000

(B) 5,000

(C) 3,000

(D) 7,000

34. The closest estimate of

$3\,\dfrac{1}{2} + 5\,\dfrac{3}{4} + 3\,\dfrac{1}{16}$ is _____.

(J) $11\,\dfrac{1}{2}$

(K) $12\,\dfrac{5}{12}$

(L) $12\,\dfrac{1}{4}$

(M) 13

GO TO NEXT PAGE

TACHS

35. Floor tiles cost $3.95 per square foot. At this price, which is the closest estimate of the cost to tile a room that is 487 square feet?

(A) $3,500

(B) $1,200

(C) $2,000

(D) $4,000

36. In one community 1,225 households reported having two pets. Of those pet owners, 30% own two dogs. Which is the closest estimate of how many dogs are in this community?

(J) 700

(K) 300

(L) 400

(M) 900

37. The closest estimate of $(2.9)^3$ is _____.

(A) 9

(B) 18

(C) 21

(D) 27

38. Surveys show that 1 out of every 6 children born in the United States has blue eyes. In a random group of 3,690 citizens, what is the closest estimate of the number of people with blue eyes?

(J) 36

(K) 60

(L) 600

(M) 850

39. The closest estimate of $7,243 \div 927$ is _____.

(A) 5

(B) 6

(C) 7

(D) 8

40. A family of four spends about $155 a week food shopping. In an average four-week month what is the closest estimate of their total food shopping bill?

(J) $200

(K) $400

(L) $600

(M) $800

TACHS
SUBTEST 4

Ability

Time: 5 Minutes
10 Questions

1

2

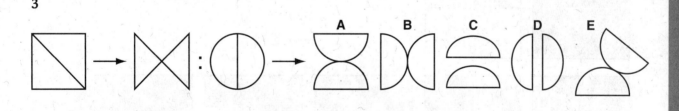

3

4

5

E → E : U → ∪ ∪ ∩ ∪ ∪

A   B   C   D   E

6

J   K   L   M   N

7

A   B   C   D   E

For question 8, a square piece of paper is given in Figure 1, along with how the paper will be folded. In Figure 2, a hole is punched. Which answer choice shows how the paper will look when it is completely unfolded?

8

Figure 1   Figure 2

A   B   C   D   E

GO TO NEXT PAGE ➡

For question 9, a square piece of paper is given in Figure 1, along with how the paper will be folded. In Figure 2, two holes are punched. Which answer choice shows how the paper will look when it is completely unfolded?

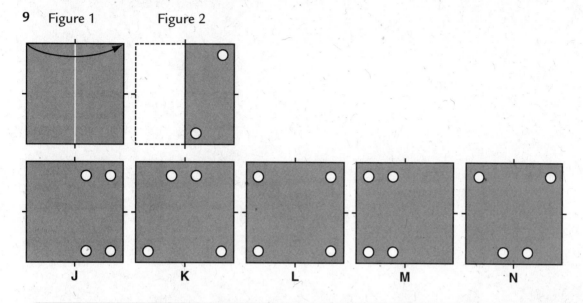

For question 10, a square piece of paper is given in Figure 1, along with how the paper will be folded. In Figure 2, the paper will be folded again, as indicated by the arrow. In Figure 3, a hole is punched. Which answer choice shows how the paper will look when it is completely unfolded?

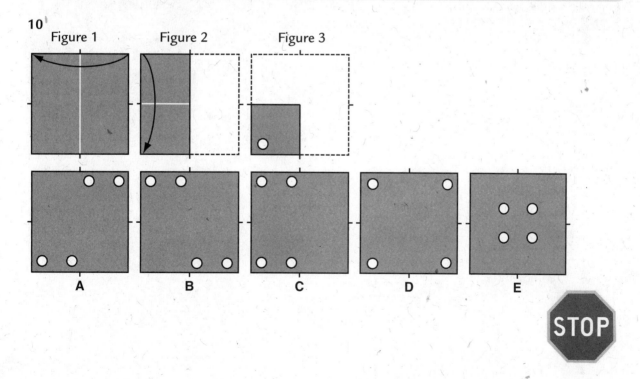

TACHS

STOP

TACHS

Practice Test 1—Answer Key

Question Number	Correct Answer	If You Answered this Question Incorrectly, Refer to . . .
SUBTEST 1: READING		
1.	(C)	P. 313
2.	(J)	P. 313
3.	(A)	P. 313
4.	(J)	P. 313
5.	(C)	P. 313
6.	(L)	P. 313
7.	(D)	P. 313
8.	(M)	P. 313
9.	(A)	P. 313
10.	(J)	P. 313
11.	(C)	P. 313
12.	(K)	P. 313
13.	(B)	P. 313
14.	(M)	P. 313
15.	(C)	P. 313
16.	(K)	P. 313
17.	(A)	P. 313
18.	(L)	P. 313
19.	(B)	P. 313
20.	(M)	P. 313

Question Number	Correct Answer	If You Answered this Question Incorrectly, Refer to . . .
21.	(B)	P. 297
22.	(L)	P. 297
23.	(A)	P. 297
24.	(L)	P. 297
25.	(A)	P. 297
26.	(L)	P. 297
27.	(B)	P. 297
28.	(L)	P. 297
29.	(B)	P. 297
30.	(L)	P. 297
31.	(D)	P. 297
32.	(K)	P. 297
33.	(C)	P. 297
34.	(M)	P. 297
35.	(C)	P. 297
36.	(L)	P. 297
37.	(C)	P. 297
38.	(L)	P. 297
39.	(A)	P. 297
40.	(K)	P. 297
41.	(B)	P. 297
42.	(M)	P. 297
43.	(C)	P. 297
44.	(J)	P. 297
45.	(B)	P. 297
46.	(K)	P. 297
47.	(A)	P. 297
48.	(L)	P. 297
49.	(A)	P. 297
50.	(M)	P. 297

TACHS

SUBTEST 2: LANGUAGE		
1.	(B)	P. 280
2.	(M)	P. 280
3.	(E)	P. 279
4.	(J)	P. 280
5.	(E)	P. 279
6.	(K)	P. 284
7.	(D)	P. 281
8.	(J)	P. 280
9.	(D)	P. 281
10.	(L)	P. 282
11.	(A)	P. 275
12.	(K)	P. 275
13.	(A)	P. 275
14.	(L)	P. 275
15.	(B)	P. 275
16.	(L)	P. 275
17.	(D)	P. 275
18.	(J)	P. 275
19.	(B)	P. 275
20.	(J)	P. 275
21.	(C)	P. 261
22.	(J)	P. 261
23.	(A)	P. 269
24.	(K)	P. 261
25.	(D)	P. 261
26.	(L)	P. 270
27.	(C)	P. 269
28.	(J)	P. 269
29.	(D)	P. 261
30.	(L)	P. 269
31.	(B)	P. 245
32.	(L)	P. 245
33.	(A)	P. 245
34.	(M)	P. 245
35.	(A)	P. 245
36.	(K)	P. 245

Question Number	Correct Answer	If You Answered this Question Incorrectly, Refer to . . .
37.	(C)	P. 239
38.	(M)	P. 239
39.	(C)	P. 239
40.	(J)	P. 239
SUBTEST 3: MATHEMATICS		
1.	(D)	P. 345
2.	(K)	P. 356
3.	(C)	P. 341
4.	(J)	P. 339
5.	(C)	P. 345
6.	(M)	P. 356
7.	(B)	P. 337, 339
8.	(J)	P. 377
9.	(C)	P. 350
10.	(M)	P. 356
11.	(C)	P. 390
12.	(L)	P. 339
13.	(B)	P. 339
14.	(L)	P. 345
15.	(A)	P. 350
16.	(M)	P. 345
17.	(B)	P. 365
18.	(L)	P. 399
19.	(D)	P. 350, 373
20.	(L)	P. 339
21.	(A)	P. 339, 345
22.	(M)	P. 379
23.	(B)	P. 339, 379
24.	(L)	P. 392
25.	(D)	P. 373
26.	(K)	P. 402
27.	(A)	P. 407
28.	(L)	P. 407
29.	(B)	P. 377

30.	(L)	P. 390
31.	(B)	P. 341
32.	(M)	P. 345
33.	(A)	P. 339
34.	(L)	P. 337, 355
35.	(C)	P. 341
36.	(J)	P. 341
37.	(D)	P. 341
38.	(L)	P. 345
39.	(D)	P. 345
40.	(L)	P. 337, 341

SUBTEST 4: ABILITY

1.	(C)	P. 422
2.	(J)	P. 422
3.	(E)	P. 422
4.	(J)	P. 422
5.	(D)	P. 422
6.	(L)	P. 422
7.	(D)	P. 422
8.	(B)	P. 419
9.	(N)	P. 419
10.	(D)	P. 419

TACHS

TACHS
SUBTEST 1

Reading—Detailed Explanations of Answers

Vocabulary 1–20

1. **(C)** **Eliminate.** *Eradicate* means to *get rid of, remove,* or *eliminate.*

2. **(J)** **Apprehensive.** *Suspicious* means *doubtful, mistrustful,* or *apprehensive.*

3. **(A)** **Uninterested.** *Indifferent* means to be *uncaring* or *uninterested.* The opposite would be *concerned* or *interested.*

4. **(J)** **Lessen.** *Alleviate* means to *ease, lighten, improve,* or *lessen.*

5. **(C)** **Lavish.** *Luxurious* means *opulent, deluxe, grand,* or *lavish.* The opposite would be *meager.*

6. **(L)** **Resist.** *Repel* means to *fend off, prevent, keep away,* or *resist.*

7. **(D)** **Accuse.** *Incriminate* means to *lay the blame on, implicate,* or *accuse.*

8. **(M)** **Not clear.** *Opaque* means *solid, dense,* or *not clear.* The opposite would be *transparent.*

9. **(A)** **Resist.** *Defy,* similar to *repel,* means to *resist, challenge,* or *rebel against.*

10. **(J)** **Continue.** *Sustain* means to *maintain, keep going,* or *continue.* The opposite would be *quit.*

11. **(C)** **Fleeting.** *Momentary* means *brief, short-lived, passing,* or *fleeting.*

12. **(K)** **Approximate.** *Speculative* means *rough, tentative,* or *approximate.* The opposite would be *definite.*

13. **(B)** **Scold.** *Reprimand* means to *warn, tell off,* or *scold.*

14. **(M)** **Ongoing.** *Gradual* means *steady, continuing, regular,* or *ongoing.*

15. **(C)** **Convince.** *Persuade* means to *influence, plead, sway,* or *convince.*

16. **(K)** **Sorrowful.** *Woeful* means *unhappy, sad,* or *sorrowful.*

17. **(A)** **Understanding.** *Empathy* means *compassion, sympathy,* or *understanding.*

18. **(L)** **Critical.** *Crucial* means *important, necessary,* or *critical.* The opposite would be *trivial.*

19. **(B)** **Examine.** *Scrutinize* means to *inspect, study, analyze,* or *examine.*

20. **(M)** **Unconcerned.** *Nonchalant* means *cool, relaxed, indifferent,* or *unconcerned.*

Reading Comprehension 21–50

21. **(B)** Douglass was such a good speaker that some people didn't believe that he could have been a slave. He wrote his autobiography after they doubted him, in order to prove them wrong **(D)**. His plantation **(A)** and work experience **(C)** did not cause people to doubt that he was a former slave.

22. **(L)** According to the passage, Douglass worked against slavery as an agent **(J)**, a consultant to the president **(K)**, and as a publisher **(M)**, but the passage does not say he was a lawyer **(L)**.

23. **(A)** The passage states that Douglass had to continue his education in the streets because Mr. Auld warned Mrs. Auld that education would make Douglass unfit for being a slave. We can assume that Mr. Auld was in control of everyone in the household and was able to keep Mrs. Auld from continuing to teach Douglass. **(B)** and **(C)** are false because Douglass could certainly have continued to learn from Mrs. Auld. Mrs. Auld was forced to stop teaching Douglass before Douglass moved and began working in a shipyard **(D)**.

24. **(L)** The passage states that Douglass worked to get both civil rights for freed men **(J)** and rights for women **(K)**.

25. **(A)** This passage describes passive-aggressive personality disorder but does not list the situations that cause it **(B)**, discuss treatments **(C)**, or list clinics **(D)**.

26. **(L)** The first paragraph of the passage says that this disorder "may be context dependent, appearing only in certain situations." The passage does not discuss causes of the disorder **(J)**, nor does it discuss the distribution of the disease **(K)** and **(M)**.

27. **(B)** The second paragraph of the passage says that the disorder is recognized by the "seemingly unjustified frustration and hostility others feel toward such individuals." The passage does not mention a blood sample **(A)**, a personality test **(C)**, or a psychiatrist **(D)**.

28. **(L)** The first sentence of the passage defines the disorder. Choice **(J)** is the exact opposite of passive-aggressive behavior, as fighting is open aggression. The passage does not mention indecision **(K)**. Choice **(M)** describes masochism, not passive-aggressive disorder.

29. **(B)** *Covert* means *hidden* or *secretive. Open* **(C)** is the opposite of covert. *Aggressive* **(A)** and *evoke* **(D)** are unrelated to covert.

30. **(L)** This passage tells the reader how to use an absentee ballot and when it can be used. If a voter were at the poll, he/she would have no use for these instructions **(J)**. The passage does not explain how to work a voting machine **(M)** or how to count ballots **(K)**.

31. **(D)** Condition four explains that the last day to request an absentee ballot is October 29. The passage gives the dates of choices **(A)** and **(B)** for other deadlines. The date of choice **(C)** is not in the passage at all.

32. **(K)** "Instructions for Absentee Voting" is probably a government publication because the government controls voting. The instructions are not by previous absentee voters **(L)** because the instructions are formal in tone and seem official. There is no evidence in the passage to support the idea that the passage was authored by the League of Women Voters **(M)** or any other organization **(J)**.

33. **(C)** *Via* means *by way of*. Choices **(A)**, **(B)**, and **(D)** are unrelated to via.

34. **(M)** According to condition two, the person could vote at his/her old polling place **(J)** or with an absentee ballot **(K)**. The person could not vote somewhere where he/she isn't registered **(L)**.

35. **(C)** The passage describes the suffering and death of the Union prisoners at Andersonville prison due to the lack of shelter and supplies. The passage doesn't discuss Union prisons **(A)**. The passage mentions the chances of survival **(B)** and the lack of food **(D)**, but neither of these is the main idea of the passage.

36. **(L)** The first sentence of the last paragraph states that the prisoners didn't get enough food. The passage does not mention doctors **(J)** or lack of exercise **(K)**; in fact, the passage discusses the physical work done by the prisoners.

37. **(C)** The last paragraph states that the prison was open thirteen months.

38. **(L)** The last sentence of the passage lists the causes from which the prisoners died; the list includes the diseases of choices **(J)**, **(K)**, and **(M)**.

39. **(A)** This passage was probably taken from a textbook because it is a formal overview. This indicates that there is some distance between the event and the writers of the passage. A government report **(B)** would probably have been more technical and given more statistics. Prison records would not have given a detached summary of the conditions of the prison. Journals kept by prisoners **(D)** would have been personal stories full of details about their lives.

40. **(K)** The second paragraph explains that assisted reading makes slow readers read faster and lets them concentrate on figuring out the meaning of the reading and does not hurt slow readers **(J)**. It does give them time to understand what they are reading **(L)**. Assisted reading eases slow readers and does not put pressure on them **(M)**.

41. **(B)** Assisted reading is defined in the first paragraph. The teacher does not give definitions **(A)** or read to the students **(D)**. Readings with illustrations **(C)** are not called assisted readings.

42. **(M)** The second paragraph says that "assisted reading lets the reader move along without being responsible for every language unit." Assisted reading does speed up reading **(J)**, take pressure off the students **(K)**, and let the students concentrate on meaning **(L)**.

43. **(C)** The passage says that beginning readers can make sense of a reading by speeding up the reading so that it sounds more like language. Reading slowly **(A)**, concentrating on every word **(B)**, and focusing on small language units **(D)** are all problems for the beginning reader.

44. **(J)** The second sentence of the second paragraph gives the definition of "individual language units." Paragraphs **(K)** and stories and books **(M)** are the opposite of individual language units. A unit in a language textbook **(L)** is unrelated to the topic.

45. (B) The answer to this question is found in the very first sentence of the passage: the First Amendment outlaws any laws which prohibit freedom of religion. Outlawing freedom of religion is the opposite **(A)**. Choices **(C)** and **(D)** are wrong because they are about free speech, not freedom of religion.

46. (K) The passage states that one critic of the First Amendment has called it the work of an infidel. The statements in choices **(J)**, **(L)**, and **(M)** are not included in the passage.

47. (A) *Reaffirmed* most nearly means *agreed with*. *Disagreed with* **(B)** is the opposite and *ignored* **(C)** and *celebrated* **(D)** are unrelated.

48. (L) The statement by the Supreme Court Justice calls the First Amendment a metaphor **(M)**, a barrier **(K)**, and a useless guide **(J)**, which is the opposite of a clear guide **(L)**.

49. (A) The second to last sentence states that threats to religious freedom still exist **(A)**. Choice **(B)** is disproved in the last sentence, which says that not everyone accepts the separation of church and state. This passage shows that there is still interest in the separation of church and state **(C)** and it is against government control of religion **(D)**.

50. (M) The tone of the passage is neutral and explanatory. The passage is most likely aimed at students **(M)**, who are learning about the Constitution. Religious leaders **(J)**, teachers **(K)**, and judges **(L)** are less likely audiences.

TACHS
SUBTEST 2

Language–Detailed Explanations of Answers

1. **(B)** *Atention to detail is always important.* The correct spelling is **attention**.

2. **(M)** *He allways picks chocolate ice cream.* The correct spelling is **always**.

3. **(E)** There are no misspelled words.

4. **(J)** *They had to cancil picnic due to heavy rain.* The correct spelling is **cancel**.

5. **(E)** There are no misspelled words.

6. **(K)** *You did a wonderful job at the concert.* The correct spelling is **wonderful**.

7. **(D)** *Each group will need to creat a poster for the project.* The correct spelling is **create**.

8. **(J)** *Please say an apologe for your rude comment.* The correct spelling is **apology**.

9. **(D)** Careful or it will **explood**! The correct spelling is **explode**.

10. **(L)** *Purhaps you would like a turn.* The correct spelling is *perhaps*.

11. **(A)** The proper noun *Tammy* needs to be capitalized.

12. **(K)** The pronoun *I* needs to be capitalized.

13. **(A)** Since holidays are proper nouns, *Halloween* needs to be capitalized.

14. **(L)** The title of the book *Where the Wild Things Are* needs to be capitalized as such.

15. **(B)** Since the names of bands are proper nouns, "The Fray" needs to be capitalized.

16. **(L)** Since *carrots* is a common noun, it should not be capitalized.

17. **(D)** There are no errors in capitalization.

18. **(J)** The title of the play *Death of a Salesman* needs to be capitalized as such.

19. **(B)** Since the names of countries are proper nouns, *France* needs to be capitalized.

20. **(J)** The proper noun *Wednesday* needs to be capitalized.

21. **(C)** A comma is not needed before "and." It should read "peanut butter and jelly."

22. **(J)** Introductory clauses should be separated with a comma instead of a colon: "Since her birthday is tomorrow, we should bake the cake later today."

23. **(A)** An apostrophe should be added to show possession: "Kim's book."

24. **(K)** The list of breakfast items in this example needs to be separated by commas: "Billy was so hungry that he ordered eggs, pancakes and bacon for breakfast."

25. **(D)** There are no errors in punctuation.

26. **(L)** The closing quotation mark is missing. The sentence should read, Kelly asked, "Do you know what the homework was last night?"

27. **(C)** An apostrophe should be added to show possession: "friend's house" or if referring to more than one friend: "friends' house."

28. **(J)** In this example *its* is the shortened form of *it is*. The contraction should be written as *it's*.

29. **(D)** There are no errors in punctuation.

30. **(L)** In this example *its* is used as a pronoun, referring to the announcements that accompany the drill. The word should be written without an apostrophe before the *s*.

31. **(B)** The phrase *I goed* should be *I went* for proper verb usage.

32. **(L)** The correct form of the verb *drive* in this example is *drove*.

33. **(A)** The phrase *Keith don't* should be *Keith went* for proper verb usage.

34. **(M)** There are no errors in this sentence.

35. **(A)** Instead of *went*, the correct form of the verb *go* in this example should be *gone*.

36. **(K)** The sentence should read: "The rain fell all day" to reflect the past tense.

37. **(C)** The sentence is best written: "You need to preheat the oven to the correct temperature before you bake."

38. **(M)** The sentence is best written: "Check the tire pressure with a gauge to make sure you add the right amount of air."

39. **(C)** Sentence 5: "Some supermarkets are more expensive than others" is unnecessary to the passage.

40. **(J)** The correct conjunction should be *and* rather than *because*.

Mathematics—Detailed Explanations of Answers

1. **(D)** To find the value of x, divide 64 by 8. $64 \div 8 = 8$. $x = 8$.

2. **(K)** Factors of 36 include 3, 6, and 9. 5 does not divide 36 into equal groups with no remainder.

3. **(C)** First multiply $15 by 2 (hours) to get $30 a week. Next multiply $30 by 3 weeks for a total of $90.

4. **(J)** Find the difference between what Jeff needs ($350) and what he has ($185).

$$350 - 185 = 165$$

5. **(C)** To find the value of x, divide 24 by 8. $24 \div 8 = 3$. $x = 3$.

6. **(M)** Factors of 40 include 4, 5, and 8. 9 does not divide 40 into equal groups with no remainder.

7. **(B)** First find the difference between the number of books Tess wants to read (20) and the number she has read (9). $20 - 9 = 11$ books. Next, since Tess reads 2 books a week, one way to solve this is to count up by 2s. 1 week = 2 books, 2 weeks = 4 books, 3 weeks = 6 books, 4 weeks = 8 books, 5 weeks = 10 books, and 6 weeks = 12 books.

8. **(J)** To find the difference, line up the numbers and then subtract.

$$5.38 - 3.91 = 1.47$$

9. **(C)** To find the sum, find the least common denominator and then add.

$$2\frac{1}{3} = 2\frac{4}{12}$$
$$+ \quad 3\frac{1}{2} = 3\frac{6}{12} = \quad 8\frac{19}{12} = 9\frac{7}{12}$$
$$3\frac{3}{4} = 3\frac{9}{12}$$

10. **(M)** Prime numbers are only divisible by one and themselves. 11 is the only prime number among the choices.

11. **(C)** First add the math scores to find the sum

    $87 + 92 + 84 + 89 + 92 = 444$. Then divide 444 by the number of tests (5)

    $\frac{444}{5} = 88.8$. Next round 88.8 to the nearest whole number, which is 89.

12. **(L)** Find the difference between each town's July collection and August collection. Lakeview's collections increase from about 75 to 250. $250 - 75 = 175$. This is the greatest increase.

13. **(B)** Find the sum of August collections for each pair of towns. Lakeview (250) and Ridgewood (275) had the most. $250 + 275 = 525$.

14. **(L)** To find the quotient you must divide 1,924 by 37.

    $\frac{1,924}{37} = 52$.

15. **(A)** First write 5.20 as a mixed number. Then reduce this fraction to its lowest term.

    $5.20 = 5\frac{20}{100} = 5\frac{2}{10}$ (Divide the numerator and denominator by 10, then reduce further by dividing by 2) $= 5\frac{1}{5}$.

16. **(M)** In order to find out how many students were in the group, divide each of the answer choices into 700 (the amount of dollars collected). The number that divides evenly with no remainders is the correct answer. $\frac{700}{14} = 50$.

17. **(B)** First multiply the numerators and denominators. Then reduce the fraction to lowest terms. $\frac{2}{3} \times \frac{3}{4} = \frac{6}{12} = \frac{1}{2}$

18. **(L)** First calculate 10% of $180. Divide 180 by 10 = 18. Subtract 18 from 180 to find the sale price of the coat. $180 - 18 = 162$. Now find the difference between what Kelly needs ($162) and what she has ($150). $162 - 150 = 12$.

19. **(D)** To change a fraction to a decimal, divide the denominator by the numerator and include remainders. Since $\frac{5}{8} = .625$, $6\frac{5}{8} = 6.625$.

20. **(L)** Change the signs in the parentheses. $(+2) - (-1) + (+4) = 2 + 1 + 4 = 7$

21. **(A)** First find how much time elapsed between 7 a.m. and 12 p.m. Then divide the distance traveled (275 miles) by the time passed (5 hours). $275 \div 5 = 55$ miles per hour.

22. **(M)** Find 30% of the total $1,800. Change 30% to 0.30 and multiply by 1,800. Thus, $0.30 \times 1,800 = 540$.

23. (B) Find the number of cookies (42% of 1,800) and blondies (16% of 1,800) sold. Then find the difference. 42% is equivalent to 0.42, and 0.42 × 1,800 = 756. 16% is equivalent to 0.16, and 0.16 × 1,800 = 288. Thus, 756 − 288 = 468.

24. (L) To find 7^3 multiply 7 × 7 = 49 × 7 = 343.

25. (D) First, to round to the nearest hundredth you need to look at the thousandths place 4.89<u>2</u>. Since 2 is less than five, the 9 remains unchanged. 4.89 is the nearest hundredth.

26. (K) Find 15% of 60 (9) and 20% of 75 (15). Then multiply those numbers to find the product. 9 × 15 = 135.

27. (A) Use the Pythagorean theorem. $7^2 + 24^2 = X^2$, which becomes $49 + 576 = X^2$. Then, $X^2 = 625$, so $X = \sqrt{625} = 25$.

28. (L) The sum of angles A and B is 2 × 105° = 210°. Therefore, the sum of the remaining three angles is 540° − 210° = 330°

29. (B) First read the chart to determine the inches of rainfall in March (1) and in April (3.5), then subtract. 3.5 − 1.0 = 2.5 inches.

30. (L) To find the average add the inches of rainfall in each month, then divide by the number of months (4).

$$1.0 + 3.5 + 2.0 + 2.5 = \frac{9.0}{4} = 2.25$$

31. (B) In order to estimate the answer, round each number and then multiply.

$$143 \times 97 \quad 140 \times 100 = 1,400$$

32. (M) In order to divide in your head, round 482 to 480, and then drop the zero. 48 ÷ 8 = 6. Then put the zero back to make 60.

33. (A) Round the numbers to easier terms, then find the difference.

$$5,691 − 2,038 \quad 6,000 − 2,000 = 4,000$$

34. (L) To estimate the sum of $3\frac{1}{2}$, $5\frac{3}{4}$, and $3\frac{1}{16}$, first add the whole numbers, then the larger fractions. You can drop $\frac{1}{16}$ because it is so small.

$$3 + 5 + 3 = 11 \quad \frac{1}{2} = \frac{2}{4} \quad \frac{2}{4} + \frac{3}{4} = \frac{5}{4} \text{ or } 1\frac{1}{4} \quad 11 + 1\frac{1}{4} = 12\frac{1}{4}$$

35. (C) Round $3.95 to $4.00. Then round 487 square feet to 500 square feet.

$$\$4.00 \times 500 = \$2000$$

36. (J) Round 1,225 to 1,200. 10% of 1,200 = 120. 120 × 3 = 360. Since the problem states that these households have two dogs, multiply by 2. 360 × 2 ≈ 700

37. **(D)** To estimate $(2.9)^3$, round 2.9 to 3, then multiply as follows:

$3 \times 3 = 9 \times 3 = 27$

38. **(L)** Round 3,690 to 3,600. Since $36 \div 6 = 6$, then $3,600 \div 6 = 600$.

39. **(D)** Round the numbers, then divide the simpler terms.

$7,243 \div 927$ $\qquad$ $72 \div 9 = 8$

40. **(L)** To estimate the average, first round 155 to 150. $150 + 150 = 300 \times 2 = 600$

TACHS
SUBTEST 4

Ability—Detailed Explanations of Answers

Time: 5 Minutes
10 Questions

1. **(C)** In the example, an inner square is removed and a small solid square remains. Choice **C** shows this same change for the circle shown.

2. **(J)** In the example, a large "v" becomes a small "v" with diagonal stripes. Choice **J** shows this same change for the large "h" shown.

3. **(E)** In this example, the square is split into two tilted triangles that touch at a point. This same change for the circle is shown in choice **E**.

4. **(J)** In this example, the square is divided by four inside lines and then by three. Choice **J** shows this same change for the circle shown.

5. **(D)** In this example, a small shaded "E" becomes a large spotted "E." This same change is made to the small shaded "u" in choice **D**.

6. **(L)** In this progression, the inner triangle is striped, then just the outer square; next just the lower half of the square. Choice **L** shows the remaining part of the sequence.

7. **(D)** In this progression, only the left section of the plus is shaded, then the left and top sections are shaded; next the left, top and right sections are shaded. The remaining part of the sequence is shown in choice **D**.

8. **(B)** The paper is folded upward so that the 2nd hole will appear just below the crease line.

9. **(N)** The paper is folded from left to right so that two more holes will appear in places that are mirror images over the crease line.

10. **(D)** On the first unfold, there will be a hole in the upper left corner and in the lower left corner. On the second unfold, there will be four holes, one in each corner.

HSPT/COOP/TACHS

CHAPTER 2
VERBAL SKILLS REVIEW

CHAPTER 2
Verbal Skills Review

I. Analytical Reasoning Questions

II. Analogy Questions

III. Verbal Reasoning Questions

IV. Antonym Questions

V. Synonym Questions

VI. Other Test-Taking Tips

As you probably noticed on the practice tests, there are several types of problems on the HSPT, COOP, and the TACHS that require a solid command of verbal skills. Furthermore, as you get ready to take the actual *Verbal Skills* subtest of the HSPT or the *Analogies* test on the COOP or Language subtest of the TACHS, you'll need to be aware of the following question types:

- Analogies
- Synonyms
- Antonyms
- Verbal Classification
- Verbal Reasoning
- Analytical Reasoning

A prospective test-taker should carefully consider each type of problem.

I. Analytical Reasoning Questions
Types of Questions in the Verbal Skills Section of the HSPT

An analytical reasoning question requires the test-taker to break a passage into parts and to study or analyze carefully **the parts** of the passage. **The arrangement problem** and **the spatial relationship problem** are two distinct types of analytical reasoning questions on the verbal skills section of the HSPT.

The arrangement or ordering problems

Arrangement problems involve ordering persons, places, or things into a set position. Test-takers must rank, sort chronologically, or assign a physical position on these questions. The arrangements may be linear—as on a time line—or even nonlinear—as around a banquet table. These arrangement problems may involve attributes, conditional statements, ordering and spatial relations, or time assignments.

Some of the ordering or arrangement questions may include a set of conditions. In answering some of the questions, it may be useful to draw a rough diagram before choosing the response that most accurately and completely answers the question and blackening the corresponding space on the answer sheet.

Below are tips on answering the arrangement or ordering questions:

Tip 1: Determine the problem type. Because there are several types of problems on the HSPT, the test-taker must, first of all, determine the kind of problem.

Tip 2: If you decide the problem is an analytical (ordering or arrangement) type of problem, you must look carefully at the parts and determine what you have to do with the information.

Tip 3: Read the question and as you read,

a) summarize,

b) take notes, and/or

c) diagram.

Tip 4: Make any deductions you can.

Tip 5: Compare your answer to the answer choices on the HSPT to find the best selection. Let's see how these tips work with an actual problem.

First, you must determine the problem type. Consider the following question:

1. Bernice weighs more than Winneka. Winneka weighs more than Nicole. Nicole weighs more than Bernice. If the first two statements are true, then the third statement is

(A) true.

(B) false.

(C) uncertain.

Is the question an **analogy question**—which means does it ask for a relationship such as, "Big is to little as fat is to_____."? Is it an **antonym question** requiring the reader to select words that are opposite? Is the question a **synonym question** requiring the reader to select words that are similar in meaning? Does the problem involve **verbal reasoning**, which requires one to choose a word that does not belong? Is it an **analytical reasoning** question—which means does it ask the test-taker to look carefully at the individual parts of a passage?

Question 1 above requires the reader to study each part of the passage carefully and to analyze the parts. This means that the question is an analytical reasoning question. The reader must determine if the response is 1) to draw a map (spatial relationship) or 2) to arrange the parts in a specific order. (The question above seems to be an ordering or arrangement question.)

Second, once you decide the question is an arrangement or ordering question, you may wish to try reading the question at the end of the passage and the answers before you read the first part of the passage. Some test-takers find this preview helpful to determine what they have to do with the information. For instance, consider question number 1 above.

1. Bernice weighs more than Winneka. Winneka weighs more than Nicole. Nicole weighs more than Bernice. If the first two statements are true, then the third statement is

(A) true.

(B) false.

(C) uncertain.

The question asks the status of the third sentence if the first two sentences are true. This tells you that the third sentence may or may not be true. If you are making a diagram of this question, you may not want to enter the third sentence into your diagram as permanent or true information at this time.

Third, you should summarize, take notes, and diagram as you read. The following guides will save you time on the test and help you to improve your score on the HSPT.

1. Summarize and take notes as you read.

a) Abbreviate. It is helpful if you use a single letter to record the facts. If the characters in the paragraph are Bob, Charles, Dedo, and Elbert, abbreviate the facts by using B, C, D, and E. If their names are Barnard, Beld, and Bill, use BA, BE, and BI. With the previous question you can use B, N, and W.

b) Relationship. You might find it helpful to use some of the symbols you used in math classes to speed your diagramming and to prevent your having to re-read the passage. You might diagram "Chief weighs less than Ace" as C < A. You might consider drawing a continuum with the largest size, number, age, etc. at the right-hand side and the smallest number at the left-hand side.

        −   +

    Chief........ < ....Ace

c) The equal sign. To show that two persons must stand next to each other, you might use the equal sign. You might represent "Ace must always stand next to Anita" by AC = AN.

2. Diagram as you read.

Some diagrams are simple to construct. Consider the arrangement problem you saw earlier:

Bernice weighs more than Winneka. Winneka weighs more than Nicole. Nicole weighs more than Bernice. If the first two statements are true, then the third statement is

(A) true.

(B) false.

(C) uncertain.

Your diagram might look like this:
B ......> .... W .... > .... N

Fourth, make your deductions after you read. Ask yourself what the question asks you about the remaining information. (Can Nicole weigh more than Bernice?)

You have a key deduction: Nicole cannot simultaneously weigh both more than Bernice and less than Winneka.

Fifth, look at the question that you must answer. In this case the question asks if the third sentence is

(A) true.

(B) false.

(C) uncertain.

Sixth, make your final deduction.

Notice how in this case all the statements are helpful to you in determining that the answer is false. You cannot say Nicole weighs less than Winneka and weighs more than Bernice. Choice (B) is the best answer.

Spatial relationship problems

In spatial relationship problems, you will have to determine the position of objects. The following is an example of such a question. Carefully read through the passage, the conditions/clues, and the questions.

PASSAGE: I must walk east from my house on Elm Street to the mall, the grocery store, and the church; all three are on Elm Street. 1) It is farther to walk from my house to the mall than to walk from my house to the grocery store. 2) It is farther to walk west from the mall to the church than to walk west from the grocery store to the church. 3) It is closer to walk west from the mall to the church than to walk east from the house to the mall. If the first two statements are true, the third is

(A) true.

(B) false.

(C) uncertain.

After you have read through the passage and conditions or clues, you can more easily determine if you are dealing with a spatial relationship question. If so, the next step you should take is to indicate, on paper, the relationships expressed in the conditions/clues. You may want to draw a diagram that expresses the spatial relationship expressed in the conditions/clues.

In the question on the previous page, the first condition concerns the walk from my house to the mall and the walk from my house to the grocery store.

House————————————Grocery————————————Mall

The second condition states it is farther to walk west from the mall to the church than to walk west from the grocery store to the church. You can add that information to the map you are making. The diagram for these conditions follows.

House—————Church—————Grocery——————Mall

The third condition states that it is closer to walk west from the mall to the church than to walk east from the house to the mall. (Observe your diagram above.)

The question the reader must answer is if the first two sentences are true, is the third sentence true, false, or uncertain? The third sentence reads that it is closer to walk west from the mall to the church than to walk east from the house to the mall.

It is easy after the quick diagramming to determine that the final sentence is true.
Tips on the spatial relationship questions:

Tip 1: Read through each condition.
Tip 2: Do one part of the diagram at a time.
Tip 3: Do not impose your own assumptions or beliefs on the conditions or clues.

II. Analogy Questions

Analogies are an important part of the Verbal Review for the HSPT. An analogy is a comparison between items that are basically different but that have some similarities. An analogy is similar to a math proportion. In math you might say that "4 to 1 is the same as 8 to _____." A **verbal analogy question** asks for a relationship. An example might be, "Big is to little as fat is to _____."

Both accuracy and speed are important parts of the HSPT. The key to completing analogies is to identify the pattern in a timely manner. There are several types of analogies which one often sees on the HSPT.

Analogy Question Type One: Word to Definition, Synonym, or Antonym

The HSPT may ask the test-taker to identify patterns. These patterns might include the word and its definition, the word and its synonym, or the word and its antonym. Consider the examples below:

A. Pattern one: *Word-Definition*
Example: Regurgitate is to disgorge as incorporate is to _____.

(A) merge
(B) dissuade
(C) separate
(D) segregate

Because *regurgitate* means to throw up or to disgorge, the analogy or pattern is word to definition. *Incorporate* means to combine; the correct answer is *merge*, which also means to meld or combine.

B. Pattern two: *Word-Antonym*
Example: Meld is to separate as dissuade is to _____.

(A) withhold
(B) preclude
(C) prevent
(D) encourage

Because the opposite of *meld* (join) is to *separate*, the test-taker must choose the opposite of *dissuade* (hinder). The word *encourage* is the best choice as an antonym.

C. Pattern three: *Word-Synonym*
   Example: Captivate is to entice as overestimate is to _____.
   (A) exaggerate
   (B) understate
   (C) postpone
   (D) alliterate

Captivate is similar to *entice*; the pattern seems to be similarity, or synonym. The word *overestimate* means to *exaggerate*. Choice (A) is the best choice because the relationship between the two is the same as that in the first part of the analogy: synonym.

Analogy Question Type Two: Part-To-Whole Analogy

With part-to-whole analogy, the part comes first and the whole comes second. The reader should try to express the relationship in the first example in a sentence. (See Tips below.)

   An example of a part-to-whole analogy is the following:

   Notes are to music as chapters are to _____.
   (A) sentences
   (B) words
   (C) books
   (D) letters

   Tip 1: First try to find the type of relationship.
   Notes are to music as chapters are to _____.
   (A) sentences
   (B) words
   (C) books
   (D) letters

   In the example above, the sequence is from part (notes) to whole (music).
   Tip 2: Use sentences to help you express the relationship.
   For instance, you might simply say, "Notes make up music as chapters make up _____."
   Tip 3: Watch out for mirror relationships.
   Often the answers will include a choice that is the opposite pattern from the example; this opposite, a reverse, or "mirror," answer should not mislead you. Watch out for it!
   In the example above, for instance, *chapter* to *sentences* or *chapter* to *words* or *chapter* to *letters* is the opposite from part to whole. The pattern, if the test-taker falls for the incorrect pattern, is a whole-to-part—not part-to-whole—relationship. It is the opposite (a mirror image) of the example that the reader should choose.

Analogy Question Type Three: Whole-To-Part Analogy

Consider the following: Seam is to stitch as paragraph is to sentences. The pattern of the analogy above is whole to part. Some simple tips will help you with this type of analogy.

Tip 1: First, try to find the type of relationship.

Libraries are to books as skeletons are to _____.

(A) muscles

(B) tendons

(C) bones

Tip 2: Use sentences to help you express the relationship.

In the example above, the sequence is from whole to part. For instance, you might make up a sentence which says, "Libraries are made up of books as skeletons are made up of _____."

Tip 3: Watch out for mirror relationships.

As with part-to-whole analogies, the answers will often include a choice that is the opposite pattern from the example; this opposite, reverse, or "mirror" answer should not mislead you. Watch out for it!

Analogy Question Type Four: User-To-Tool Analogy

Consider the following: Carpenter is to hammer as cook is to pot.

Just as a carpenter uses a hammer as a primary tool, a cook uses a pot as a primary tool; the preceding example illustrates a user-to-tool analogy. Below are some tools and the person who often uses the implement:

Tool	User	Tool	User
awl	leather-maker	anvil	blacksmith
pliers	electrician	screwdriver	mechanic
knife	surgeon	ball	ballplayer
chalk	teacher	helmet	race car driver

Some of the previous tips hold true with tool-to-user analogy questions.

Tip 1: First try to find the type of relationship.

Consider the following example:

Telephones are to operators as salad bowls are to _____.

(A) tongs

(B) lettuce

(C) chef

In the example above, the sequence is from an object to a person. The category is tool to user.

Tip 2: Use sentences to help you express the relationship.

You might make up a sentence which says, "Telephones are used by operators; salad bowls are used by _____."

Tip 3: Watch out for incorrect relationships.

Often the answers will include a choice that is closely related but is not the same pattern as the example.

For example, in the problem above, *lettuce* does go in a salad bowl but the pattern sought is tool-to-user pattern. Again, tongs are often associated with salad bowls, but the analogy is tool-to-user.

Analogy Question Type Five: Group-To-Member

Flock is to sheep as school is to _____.

(A) teacher

(B) fish

(C) learn

Just as a flock is a group of sheep, a school is a group of fish; the preceding is an example of a group-to-member analogy. Because the HSPT uses some of the group-to-member analogies regularly, you might want to look over the following list:

Group	Animal	Group	Animal
covey	quail	pride	lions
flock	geese	group	people
herd	cattle	school	fish
swarm	bees	sleuth	bears
hover	trout	knot	toads
army	caterpillars	exaltation	larks
bed	clams	pod	whales
smack	jellyfish	litter	kittens

Tip 1: First try to find the type of relationship.

Consider the following example:

Flock is to geese as school is to _____.

(A) teacher

(B) fish

(C) learn

In the example above, the sequence is from group to animal.

Tip 2: Use sentences to help you express the relationship.

You might make up a sentence which says, "A flock is a group of geese; a school is a group of _____."

Tip 3: Watch out for incorrect relationships.

A school does have a teacher and over a period of time one can get a complete education in a school. The relationship with the first part of the analogy, however, is group to individual animal.

Analogy Question Type Six: Cause-And-Effect

Drought is to famine as school is to _____.

(A) teacher

(B) education

(C) learning

The preceding example illustrates cause and effect.

Just as a *drought* causes or results in *famine*, *school* has the effect (usually) of causing one to *learn*. Choice (B) is a better choice than (C) for several reasons. Notice the form of the words: *education* and *learning*. Notice that one ends in *-ing* and the other does not. Because the pattern the test-taker must replicate ("Drought is to famine") does not have any *-ing* words, the comparative analogy will normally follow the same form. Choice (C) is a gerund ending in *-ing*; (B) is the best answer.

Because there are numerous types of possible analogies, the following tips may help the test-taker.

Tip 1: Make up a sentence that shows the connection between the first two words in the analogy. Establishing this sentence is often the difference between a low and a high score on the analogy section on the HSPT.

Tip 2: The parts of speech must match. If the first pair is NOUN to NOUN, the correct answer must also be NOUN to NOUN; if the first pair is NOUN to VERB, the correct answer must also be NOUN to VERB. For example, consider the following analogy: SWIM is to FISH as WADDLE is to _____. The pattern is VERB to NOUN. If one's answer choices were DUCK, WALK, AWKWARD, and FEET, one could immediately see that the correct answer should be a noun. The only correct noun choice is DUCK.

Tip 3: The answer must be in the same order as the example. For instance, in the analogy ARTIST is to PAINTING, the test-taker might make a sentence like, "An artist makes a painting." Possible answers might read:

(A) skyscraper is to blueprint

(B) music is to composer

(C) novel is to writer

(D) carpenter is to house

It is clear to the test-taker that (A) is incorrect because it is not a pattern of "one who makes" to "what is made." The three remaining answer choices (music is to composer, novel is to writer, carpenter is to house) all include the names of "producers" and the "products" they make. The order varies. Only choice (D) has the same pattern as the example analogy: producer-product. (D) is the best answer.

III. Verbal Reasoning Questions

The verbal reasoning questions on the exams require the student taking the test to choose the word in a list which does not belong with the others. The test-taker must look at the words and choose the pattern of the choices. For example, a test-taker might find the following list of words:

(A) paper
(B) pencil
(C) eraser
(D) teacher

The item that is different is (D) teacher. The other items are inanimate and are all connected with school; the teacher also is connected with school, but a teacher is a person while the others are objects. The test-taker must try to figure out the relationship of three of the four things. The remaining item is the answer.

Consider the following list of words:

(A) Sahara
(B) Nile
(C) Congo
(D) Mississippi
(E) Missouri

Items (B), (C), (D), and (E) are all the names of rivers. Item (A) is a desert and does not belong. A student may have selected (D) Mississippi since the first three choices are outside the United States. However, places within the United States and outside the United States cannot be used as the criteria since both (D) and (E) are within the United States.

Look at the following:

(A) cat
(B) catfish
(C) dog
(D) whale
(E) elephant

The difference is not size because both the elephant and whale are huge. The difference is not land-dwellers and water-dwellers because both (B) and (D) are water dwellers. The classification of mammals and fish is the difference; only item (B) is a fish. The rest are mammals.

IV. Antonym Questions

Antonym questions are those which require the test-taker to identify an answer choice that is most nearly opposite in meaning to the word in the question *stem*, or statement of the question. Some test-taking tips will help you to score high on this section.

Tip 1: Read the question stem carefully.

Tip 2: Note the qualifier in the question stem. (A *qualifier* is a word that tells you to find the *opposite* of the word in the stem. With the synonym questions in the next section of this review, you will be asked to find words that are the *same*.) You should **circle** the qualifying word; this heavy black circle will remind you what you are looking for in the question. Circling the qualifier will remind you that your task is to find the opposite meaning and ensure that you distinguish antonym questions from synonym questions.

Tip 3: Watch out for incorrect relationships.

Often the answers will include a choice that is related closely but is not the same pattern as the example. For example, a synonym or synonyms might be in the answer choices. If the test-taker has not read the question stem correctly and noted the qualifying word(s), the first instinct might be to circle the word that is similar in meaning.

Now try the following:

1. Chasm does not mean _____.
   (A) ravine
   (B) abyss
   (C) canyon
   (D) mount

The word *chasm* means *a gully, a gorge, a ravine* (A), *an abyss* (B), or *a canyon* (C). The word *mount* (D) is the opposite or the antonym of a *chasm*. The word *mount* implies a peak—the opposite of *chasm*. The antonym of *chasm* is *mount* (D).

2. The opposite of procrastinate is _____.
   (A) prolong
   (B) stall
   (C) delay
   (D) hasten

The word *procrastinate* means *to prolong* (A), *to stall* (B), *to delay* (C). The opposite of *to procrastinate, to prolong* (A), *to stall* (B), or *to delay* (C) is *to speed up* or *to hasten* (D). Choice (D) is the best selection of an antonym for procrastinate.

V. Synonym Questions

Synonym questions are those that require the test-taker to identify a word in the choices that is similar in meaning to the word in the question *stem*, or statement of the question. Some test-taking tips will help you to score high on this section.

Tip 1: Read the question stem carefully. Reasoning questions, analogies, synonyms, antonyms, and analytical questions are "mixed in" together. In other words, the questions are not separated according to type. Again, you must read the directions for each question carefully to make certain you answer the question appropriately.

Tip 2: Note any qualifier in the question stem. (A *qualifier* is a word that tells you in a synonym question to find *the word that means the same, the word that most nearly means the same,* etc. With the antonym questions in the previous section of this review, for example, you were asked to find words that are the *opposite*.) With the synonym section, you will be finding similar words or words that mean almost the same. You should **circle** the qualifying word(s); this heavy black circle will remind you what you are looking for in the question. If the previous question was an antonym question, for example, it is easy to answer the following question in the same way.

If you have to come back to this question, it is easy to forget what you are to do. The heavy circle will be an instant reminder to you! You will not have to use precious time re-reading the question.

Tip 3: Watch out for incorrect relationships.

Often the answers will include a choice that is closely related but is not the same pattern as the example. For example, an antonym or antonyms might be in the choices. If the test-taker has not read the question stem correctly and noted the qualifying word(s), the first instinct might be to circle the word that is similar in meaning.

Try these questions:

1. Frantic means most nearly _____.
   (A) calm
   (B) ignorant
   (C) excited
   (D) frisk

Frantic means (C) *excited*, *wild*, or *distraught*. *Frantic* does not mean *calm* (A), *ignorant* (B), or *frisk* (D). The best choice is (C).

2. Construct most nearly means _____.
   (A) erect
   (B) wreck
   (C) destroy
   (D) raze

To construct means most nearly *to erect* (A), *to form*, *to build*, or *to assemble*. The antonym or opposite of *construct* or to build is *to wreck* (B), *to destroy* (C), or *to raze* (D).

3. Coddle most nearly means to _____.
   (A) pamper
   (B) reject
   (C) tolerate
   (D) fail

The word *coddle* means *to pamper* (A), *to baby*, *to humor*, or *to spoil*. The opposite of *coddle* is *reject* (B); choice (B) is not the best answer for a synonym. *To tolerate* (C) implies *to endure*, *to accept*, or *to abide*; choice (C) is not a synonym for *coddle*. *To fail* (D), *to displease* is not the same as *to coddle*; choice (D) is not an appropriate synonym.

VI. Other Test-Taking Tips

Some general test-taking pointers are helpful for anyone attempting a standardized test.

Tip 1: Spend some time taking practice tests. Make the environment as much like a real testing situation as you can when you try the test. Take the phone off the hook. Time yourself. Do not peek at the answers until you finish. Work your way through the entire test.

Tip 2: Take several number 2 pencils with you to the test. There is nothing more frustrating than to have a pencil point break and to have to waste valuable test time in securing another pencil. Lay several sharpened pencils on the desk in front of you to save time.

Tip 3: Mark in your test booklet. If you have a question about one of the questions, put a large "?" in the margin of the book. If you have time, you can come back to that question.

Tip 4: Be sure that you are clear on whether wrong answers will count against your score on the test administration you are attending. In other words, be sure you know if the scorer will count off a full point or a portion of a point for each incorrect answer you have. This will certainly make a difference in how you answer the questions. Be certain you are clear on the procedure for the test administration **you are attending** because the procedure may vary from test to test. For instance:

a) If incorrect answers count against you on the test administration, your method of answering the questions will differ from your method if wrong answers do not count against you.

    If wrong answers count against you,

     i) do not guess if you have no idea what the right answer is. Instead, put a "?" in the margin. Come back to that question if you have time.

    ii) guess if you can narrow your choice down from three choices to two choices. You have a better chance of getting the answer correct (1 out of 2—not 1 out of 3). Put a "?" in the margin, but mark out the choice you know is wrong on the test booklet. If you have time to review the section, you will not have to read all the choices.

b) If wrong answers do not count against you,

     i) Guess!

    ii) you will want to indicate in the margin by a "?" any item you may want to review again if time permits.

    iii) do not leave any question blank.

Tip 5: Take a watch with you to the test. Continue to watch your time and pace yourself accordingly. Do not trust the test center to have a clock available for you. Take your own watch.

Tip 6: Review, review, review. Looking over the sample tests ahead of time and reviewing the form of the test will make you feel more confident and will prevent surprises. Remember the best surprise on any exam is to find no surprise at all when you go to take the test.

Study hard and best wishes! As those in show business say, "Break a leg!"

HSPT/COOP/TACHS

CHAPTER 3
LANGUAGE SKILLS REVIEW

CHAPTER 3
Language Skills Review

I. Sentence Structure Skills
II. Verbs
III. Pronouns
IV. Adjectives and Adverbs
V. Punctuation
VI. Capitalization
VII. Spelling

The HSPT's *Language Skills*, COOP's Verbal Reasoning, and the TACHS's Reading and Language Sections cover a variety of topics in language. To succeed on these tests, you will need knowledge in the following areas:

- Punctuation
- Capitalization
- Usage
- Spelling
- Composition

I. Sentence Structure Skills

Parallelism

Parallel sentences contain a series of words or phrases that have the same grammatical structure. Parallel words or phrases can be structured like any of the following:

Phrases:

The squirrel ran *along the fence, up the tree, and into his burrow* with a mouthful of acorns.

Adjectives:

The job market is flooded with *very talented, highly motivated, and well-educated* young people.

Nouns:

You will need a *notebook, pencil,* and *dictionary* for the test.

Clauses:

The children were told to decide *which toy they would keep* and *which toy they would give away.*

Verbs:

The farmer *plowed, planted,* and *harvested* his corn in record time.

Verbals:

Reading, writing, and *calculating* are fundamental skills that all of us should possess.

Correlative conjunctions:

Either you will do your homework *or* you will fail.

Structural signals:

(such as articles, auxiliaries, prepositions, and conjunctions)

INCORRECT: I have quit my job, enrolled in school, and looking for a reliable babysitter.

CORRECT: I *have quit* my job, *have enrolled* in school, and *am looking* for a reliable babysitter.

Note: Repetition of prepositions is considered formal and is not necessary.

You can travel *by car, by plane, or by train*; it's all up to you.

OR

You can travel *by car, plane, or train*; it's all up to you.

When a sentence contains items in a series, check for both punctuation and sentence balance. When you check for punctuation, make sure the commas are used correctly. When you check for parallelism, make sure that each item in the series has the same grammatical structure.

Misplaced and Dangling Modifiers

A misplaced modifier is one that is in the wrong place in the sentence. Misplaced modifiers come in all forms—words, phrases, and clauses. Sentences containing misplaced modifiers are often very comical: *Mom made me eat the spinach instead of my brother.* Misplaced modifiers, like the one in this sentence, are usually too far away from the word or words they modify. This sentence should read: *Mom made me, instead of my brother, eat the spinach.*

Modifiers like *only, nearly,* and *almost* should be placed next to the word they modify and not in front of some other word, especially a verb, that they are not intended to modify.

A modifier is misplaced if it appears to modify the wrong part of the sentence or if we cannot be certain what part of the sentence the writer intended it to modify. To correct a misplaced modifier, move the modifier next to the word it describes.

INCORRECT: She served hamburgers to the men on paper plates.

CORRECT: She served hamburgers on paper plates to the men.

Split infinitives also result in misplaced modifiers. Infinitives consist of the marker *to* plus the plain form of the verb. The two parts of the infinitive make up a grammatical unit that should not be split. Splitting an infinitive is placing an adverb between *to* and the verb.

INCORRECT: The weather service expects temperatures to not rise.

CORRECT: The weather service expects temperatures not to rise.

Sometimes a split infinitive may be natural and preferable, though it may still bother some readers.

es expect to more than *triple* their use of robots within the next

hat may refer to either a preceding or a following word, leav-
at it is intended to modify. Correct a squinting modifier by
ended to modify.

ho fired on the soldiers often escaped capture.

ho often fired on the soldiers escaped capture.

ho fired on the soldiers escaped capture often.

odifier or verb in search of a subject: the modifying phrase
d or *-en* word group, or a *to* + *a verb* word group—participle
tively) either appears to modify the wrong word or has nothing at the beginning or the end of a sentence. The sentences
be a student government officer, your grades must be above average.
nothing to describe. Who is *to be a student government officer*?
ype require you to determine whether a modifier has a head-
the beginning or the end of the sentence.
ier, reword the sentence by either: 1) changing the modifying
, or 2) changing the subject of the sentence to the word that
g are examples of a dangling gerund, a dangling infinitive, and

fter leaving home, the accident occurred.

eaving home, the accident?

fter we left home, the accident occurred.

p on time, a great effort was needed.

To get up needs a subject.

CORRECT: To get up on time, I made a great effort.

Fragments

A fragment is an incomplete construction which may or may not have a subject and a verb. Not all fragments appear as separate sentences. Often, fragments are separated by semicolons.

INCORRECT: Traffic was stalled for ten miles on the freeway. Because repairs were being made on potholes.

CORRECT: Traffic was stalled for ten miles on the freeway because repairs were being made on potholes.

INCORRECT: It was a funny story; one that I had never heard before.

CORRECT: It was a funny story, one that I had never heard before.

Run-On/Fused Sentences

A run-on or fused sentence is not necessarily a long sentence or a sentence that the reader considers too long. Often it may be two short sentences: *Dry ice does not melt it evaporates.* A run-on results when the writer fuses or runs together two separate sentences without any correct mark of punctuation separating them.

INCORRECT: Knowing how to use a dictionary is no problem each dictionary has a section in the front of the book telling how to use it.

CORRECT: Knowing how to use a dictionary is no problem. Each dictionary has a section in the front of the book telling how to use it.

Even if one or both of the fused sentences contains internal punctuation, the sentence is still a run-on.

INCORRECT: Bob bought dress shoes, a suit, and a nice shirt he needed them for his sister's wedding.

CORRECT: Bob bought dress shoes, a suit, and a nice shirt. He needed them for his sister's wedding.

Comma Splices

A comma splice is the incorrect use of a comma to combine what really is two separate sentences.

INCORRECT: One common error in writing is incorrect spelling, the other is the occasional use of faulty diction.

CORRECT: One common error in writing is incorrect spelling; the other is the occasional use of faulty diction.

Both run-on sentences and comma splices may be corrected in one of the following ways:

RUN-ON: Neal won the award he had the highest score.

COMMA SPLICE: Neal won the award, he had the highest score.

Separate the sentences with a period:

Neal won the award. He had the highest score.

Separate the sentences with a comma and a coordinating conjunction (*and, but, or, nor, for, yet, so*):

Neal won the award, for he had the highest score.

Separate the sentences with a semicolon:

Neal won the award; he had the highest score.

Separate the sentences with a subordinating conjunction such as *although, because, since, if*:

Neal won the award because he had the highest score.

Subordination, Coordination, and Predication

Suppose, for the sake of clarity, you wanted to combine the information in these two sentences to create one statement:

I studied a foreign language. I found English quite easy.

How you decide to combine this information should be determined by the relationship you'd like to show between the two facts. *I studied a foreign language, and I found English quite easy* seems rather illogical. The **coordination** of the two ideas (connecting them with the coordinating conjunction *and*) is ineffective. Using **subordination** instead (connecting the sentences with a subordinating conjunction) clearly shows the degree of relative importance between the expressed ideas:

After I studied a foreign language, I found English quite easy.

When using a conjunction, be sure that the sentence parts you are joining are in agreement.

INCORRECT: She loved him dearly but not his dog.

CORRECT: She loved him dearly but she did not love his dog.

A common mistake that is made is to forget that each member of the pair must be followed by the same kind of construction.

INCORRECT: They complimented them both for their bravery and they thanked them for their kindness.

CORRECT: They both complimented them for their bravery and thanked them for their kindness.

While refers to time and should not be used as a substitute for *although*, *and*, or *but*.

INCORRECT: While I'm usually interested in Fellini movies, I'd rather not go tonight.

CORRECT: Although I'm usually interested in Fellini movies, I'd rather not go tonight.

Where refers to location and should not be used as a substitute for *that*.

INCORRECT: We read in the paper where they are making great strides in DNA research.

CORRECT: We read in the paper that they are making great strides in DNA research.

After words like reason and explanation, use *that*, not *because*.

INCORRECT: His explanation for his tardiness was because his alarm did not go off.

CORRECT: His explanation for his tardiness was that his alarm did not go off.

Drill: Sentence structure skills

DIRECTIONS: Choose the sentence that expresses the thought most clearly and that has no error in structure.

1. (A) Many gases are invisible, odorless, and they have no taste.
   (B) Many gases are invisible, odorless, and have no taste.
   (C) Many gases are invisible, odorless, and tasteless.
   (D) Many gases are invisible and odorless and have no taste.

2. (A) Everyone agreed that she had neither the voice or the skill to be a speaker.
   (B) Everyone agreed that she had neither the voice nor the skill to be a speaker.
   (C) Everyone agreed that she had either the voice nor the skill to be a speaker.
   (D) Everyone agreed that she had not the voice nor the skill to be a speaker.

3. (A) The mayor will be remembered because he kept his campaign promises and because of his refusal to accept political favors.

   (B) The mayor will be remembered because he kept his campaign promises and because he refused to accept political favors.

   (C) The mayor will be remembered because of his refusal to accept political favors and because he kept his campaign promises.

   (D) The mayor will be remembered because of his refusal to accept political favors and that he kept his campaign promises.

4. (A) While taking a shower, the doorbell rang.

   (B) While I was taking a shower, the doorbell rang.

   (C) While taking a shower, someone rang the doorbell.

   (D) The doorbell rang, while taking a shower.

5. (A) He swung the bat, while the runner stole second base.

   (B) The runner stole second base while he swung the bat.

   (C) While he was swinging the bat, the runner stole second base.

   (D) The runner was stealing second base while he was swinging the bat.

DIRECTIONS: Choose the correct option.

6. Nothing grows as well in Mississippi as cotton. <u>Cotton being</u> the state's principal crop.

   (A) cotton, cotton
   (B) cotton; cotton
   (C) cotton cotton
   (D) No change is necessary.

7. It was a heartwrenching <u>movie; one</u> that I had never seen before.

   (A) movie and
   (B) movie, one
   (C) movie. One
   (D) No change is necessary.

8. Traffic was stalled for three miles on the <u>bridge. Because</u> repairs were being made.

   (A) bridge because
   (B) bridge; because
   (C) bridge, because
   (D) No change is necessary.

9. The ability to write complete sentences comes with <u>practice writing</u> run-on sentences seems to occur naturally.

   (A) practice, writing
   (B) practice. Writing
   (C) practice and
   (D) No change is necessary.

10. Even though she had taken French classes, she could not understand native French <u>speakers they</u> all spoke too fast.

    (A) speakers, they
    (B) speakers. They
    (C) speaking
    (D) No change is necessary.

II. Verbs
Verb Forms

This section covers the principal parts of some irregular verbs including troublesome verbs like *lie* and *lay*. The use of regular verbs like *look* and *receive* poses no real problem to most writers because the past and past participle forms end in *-ed*; it is the irregular forms that pose the most serious problems—for example, *seen*, *written*, and *begun*.

Irregular verbs

Irregular verbs are words that have past tense and past participle forms that do not end in -ed or -d. Although a standard pattern does not exist, most irregular verbs are commonly known.

The lightning almost struck the tree by my house.
He had run all the way to the store.

In reviewing the table below, remember that the action being described in the past tense has occurred entirely in the past; it does not take a helping verb. Past participles take a helping verb.

Yesterday, Alex drew a picture of my mother. (past tense)
If you look on the table, you will see the portrait drawn by my friend. (past participle)

Frequently Used Irregular Verbs

Infinity	Past Tense	Past Participle
to be	was/were	been
to begin	began	begun
to break	broke	broken
to buy	bought	bought
to come	came	come
to do	did	done
to eat	ate	eaten
to fly	flew	flown
to give	gave	given
to get	got	gotten
to go	went	gone
to lay	laid	laid
to lie	lay	lain
to see	saw	seen
to seek	sought	sought
to sit	sat	sat

Infinity	Past Tense	Past Participle
to swim	swam	swum
to throw	threw	thrown
to use	used	used
to wear	wore	worn
to write	wrote	written

Verb tenses

In grammar, the word *tense* refers to the time an action takes place.

Use present tense

in statements of universal truth:

In I learned that the sun is *ninety-million* miles from the earth.

in statements about the contents of literature; other published works; or art work:

In this book, Sandy *becomes* a nun and *writes* a book on psychology.

Use past tense

for action that occurred in some past time:

He *wrote* his first book in 1949, and it *was published* in 1952.

Use present perfect tense

for an action that began in the past but continues into the future:

I *have lived* here all my life.

Use past perfect tense

for an earlier action that is mentioned in a later action:

Cindy ate the apple that she *had picked*.

(First she picked it, then she ate it.)

Use future perfect tense

for an action that will have been completed at a specific future time:

By May, I *shall have graduated*.

Use a present participle

for action that occurs at the same time as the verb:

As Ray and I *were speeding* down the interstate, I saw a cop's flashing lights.

Use a perfect participle

for action that occurred before the main verb:

Having read the directions, I started the test.

Use the subjunctive mood

to express a wish or state a condition contrary to fact:

If it were not raining, we could have a picnic.

in *that* clauses after verbs like *request, recommend, suggest, ask, require,* and *insist*; and after such expressions like *it is important* and *it is necessary*:

It is necessary that all papers *be* submitted on time.

Subject-verb agreement

Agreement is the grammatical correspondence between the subject and the verb of a sentence: All verbs must agree with their subjects in person and number. If the subject is first person singular (I) the verb must also be first person singular: *I do, I say, I walk*. If the subject is third person singular, the verb form must agree: *he does, he says, he walks.*

Study these rules governing subject-verb agreement:

A verb must agree with its subject not with any other phrase in the sentence such as a prepositional or verbal phrase. Ignore such phrases.

> Your *copy* of the rules *is* on the desk.
>
> Ms. Craig's *record* of community service and outstanding teaching *qualifies* her for promotion.

In an inverted sentence, which begins with a prepositional phrase, the verb still agrees with its subject.

> At the end of the summer *come* the best *sales.*
>
> Under the house are some old Mason jars.

Prepositional phrases beginning with compound prepositions such as *along with, together with, in addition to,* and *as well as* should be ignored. They do not affect subject-verb agreement.

> *Gladys Knight,* as well as the Pips, *is* riding the midnight train to Georgia.

A verb must agree with its subject and not its subject complement. A subject complement is a word or phrase that follows a linking verb and describes the subject of a sentence.

> *Taxes are* a problem.
>
> A *problem is* taxes.
>
> His main *source* of pleasure is cycling and tennis.
>
> *Tennis and cycling are* his main source of pleasure.

The words *there, here,* or *it* are considered expletives when they are used at the beginning of a clause and the subject is not in its usual position before the verb. In such sentences, the verb should still agree with the subject and not the expletive.

> Surely, there *are* several *alumni* who would be interested in forming a group.
>
> There are 50 *students* in my English class.
>
> There is a horrifying *study* on child abuse in *Psychology Today.*

Indefinite pronouns, which refer to a non-specific person or thing, include *each, either, one, everyone, everybody,* and *everything* and are singular.

> *Somebody* in Detroit loves me.
>
> Does either [one] of you have a pencil?
>
> Neither of my brothers has a car.

Indefinite pronouns such as *several, few, both,* and *many* are plural.

> Both of my sorority sisters have decided to live off-campus.
>
> Few seek the enlightenment of transcendental meditation.

Indefinite pronouns such as *all, some, most,* and *none* may be singular or plural depending on their referents.

> *Some* of the food *is* cold.
>
> *Some* of the vegetables *are* cold.
>
> I can think of some retorts, but *none seem* appropriate.
>
> *None* of the children *is* as sweet as Sally.

Fractions such as *one-half* and *one-third* may be singular or plural depending on what is being described.

> *Half* of the mail *has* been delivered.
>
> *Half* of the letters *have* been read.

Subjects joined by *and* take a plural verb unless the subjects are thought to be one item or unit.

> *Jim and Tammy were* televangelists.
>
> *The Cure is* my favorite group.

In cases when the subjects are joined by *or, nor, either . . . or,* or *neither . . . nor,* the verb must agree with the subject closer to it.

> Either the teacher or the *students are* responsible.
>
> Neither the students nor the *teacher is* responsible.

Relative pronouns, such as *who, which,* or *that,* introduce adjective clauses within a sentence. When the relative pronoun describes a plural subject, the verb should be plural. Relative pronouns describing singular subjects should take singular verbs.

> She is one of the girls *who cheer* on Friday nights.
>
> She is the only cheerleader *who has* a broken leg.

Subjects preceded by *every, each,* and *many a* are singular.

> *Every* man, woman, and child *was* given a life preserver.
>
> *Each* undergraduate *is* required to pass a proficiency exam.
>
> *Many a* tear *has* to fall before one matures.

Nouns that name a group of persons or objects, such as *audience, faculty, jury,* etc., are collective nouns. Collective nouns require a singular verb when the group is regarded as a whole, and a plural verb when the members of the group are regarded as individuals.

> The *jury has made its decision.*
>
> The *faculty are* preparing their grade rosters.

Subjects preceded by *the number of* or *the percentage of* are singular, whereas subjects preceded by *a number of* or *a percentage of* are plural.

> *The number of* vacationers in Florida *increases* every year.
>
> *A number of* vacationers *are* young couples.

Titles of books, companies, name brands, and groups are singular or plural depending on their meaning.

> *Great Expectations is* my favorite novel.
>
> The *Rolling Stones are* performing in the Super Dome.

Certain nouns of Latin and Greek origin have unusual singular and plural forms.

Singular	Plural
criterion	criteria
alumnus	alumni
datum	data
medium	media

The *data are* available for inspection.

The only *criterion* for membership *is* a high GPA.

Some nouns such as *deer*, *shrimp*, and *sheep* have the same spellings for both their singular and plural forms. In these cases, the meaning of the sentence will determine whether they are singular or plural.

Deer are beautiful animals.

The spotted *deer is* licking the sugar cube.

Some nouns like *scissors* and *jeans* have plural forms but no singular counterparts. These nouns almost always take plural verbs.

The *scissors are* on the table.

My new *jeans fit* me like a glove.

Words used as examples, not as grammatical parts of the sentence, require singular verbs.

Can't is the contraction for "cannot."

Cats is the plural form of "cat."

Mathematical expressions of subtraction and division require singular verbs, while expressions of addition and multiplication take either singular or plural verbs.

Ten *divided* by two *equals* five.

Five *times* two *equals* ten.

OR: Five *times* two *equal* ten.

Nouns expressing time, distance, weight, and measurement are singular when they refer to a unit and plural when they refer to separate items.

Fifty yards is a short distance.

Ten years have passed since I finished college.

Expressions of quantity are usually plural.

Nine out of ten dentists *recommend* that their patients floss.

Some nouns ending in *-ics*, such as *economics* and *ethics*, take singular verbs when they refer to principles or a field of study; however, when they refer to individual practices, they usually take plural verbs.

Ethics is being taught in the spring.

His unusual business *ethics are* what got him into trouble.

Some nouns like *measles*, *news*, and *calculus* appear to be plural but are actually singular in number. These nouns require singular verbs.

Measles is a very contagious disease.

Calculus requires great skill in algebra.

Gerund and infinitive verbs can be used as nouns. A gerund is a verb ending in *-ing*, such as *running, sitting, reading*. An infinitive is the word *to* plus a verb, such as *to be*. Gerunds and infinitives are considered verbal nouns and are treated as singular even if the object of the verbal phrase is plural.

> *Hiding* your mistakes *does* not make them go away.

> To *run* five miles *is* my goal.

A noun phrase or clause acting as the subject of a sentence requires a singular verb.

> What I need is to be loved.

> Whether there is any connection between them is unknown.

Clauses beginning with *what* may be singular or plural depending on the meaning, that is, whether *what* means "the thing" or "the things."

> What I want for Christmas is a new motorcycle.

> What matters are Clinton's ideas.

Appositives are nouns or pronoun phrases that rename the nouns or pronouns and have the same function as the words they describe.

> When the girls throw a party, *they* each bring a *gift*.

> The *board*, all ten members, *is* meeting today.

Drill: Verbs

DIRECTIONS: Choose the correct option.

1. If you <u>had been concerned</u> about Marilyn, you <u>would have went</u> to greater lengths to ensure her safety.
   - **(A)** had been concern . . . would have gone
   - **(B)** was concerned . . . would have gone
   - **(C)** had been concerned . . . would have gone
   - **(D)** No change is necessary.

2. Susan <u>laid</u> in bed too long and missed her class.
   - **(A)** lays
   - **(B)** lay
   - **(C)** lied
   - **(D)** No change is necessary.

3. The Great Wall of China <u>is</u> fifteen hundred miles long; it <u>was built</u> in the third century B.C.
   - **(A)** was . . . was built
   - **(B)** is . . . is built
   - **(C)** has been . . . was built
   - **(D)** No change is necessary.

4. Joe stated that the class <u>began</u> at 10:30 a.m.
   - **(A)** begins
   - **(B)** had begun
   - **(C)** was beginning
   - **(D)** No change is necessary.

5. The ceiling of the Sistine Chapel <u>was</u> paint-
   ed by Michelangelo; it <u>depicted</u> scenes from
   the Creation in the Old Testament.
   - **(A)** was . . . depicts
   - **(B)** is . . . depicts
   - **(C)** has been . . . depicting
   - **(D)** No change is necessary.

6. After Christmas <u>comes</u> the best sales.
   - **(A)** has come
   - **(B)** come
   - **(C)** is coming
   - **(D)** No change is necessary.

7. The bakery's specialty <u>are</u> wedding cakes.
   - **(A)** is
   - **(B)** were
   - **(C)** be
   - **(D)** No change is necessary.

8. Every man, woman, and child <u>were given</u> a
   life preserver.
   - **(A)** have been given
   - **(B)** had gave
   - **(C)** was given
   - **(D)** No change is necessary.

9. Hiding your mistakes <u>don't</u> make them go
   away.
   - **(A)** doesn't
   - **(B)** do not
   - **(C)** have not
   - **(D)** No change is necessary.

10. The Board of Regents <u>has recommended</u> a
    tuition increase.
    - **(A)** have recommended
    - **(B)** has recommend
    - **(C)** had recommended
    - **(D)** No change is necessary.

III. Pronouns

Pronoun Case

Nominative case (also called subjective) pronouns function as subjects or subject complements in a sentence. Objective case pronouns function as objects in a sentence.

Nominative Case	Objective Case
I	me
he	him
she	her
we	us
they	them
who	whom

This review section answers the most frequently asked grammar questions: when to use *I* and when to use *me*; when to use *who* and when to use *whom*. Some writers avoid *whom* altogether, and instead of distinguishing between *I* and *me*, many writers incorrectly use *myself*.

Use the nominative case (subject pronouns)

for the subject of a sentence:

We students studied until early morning for the final.

Alan and *I* "burned the midnight oil," too.

for pronouns that rename nouns or pronouns and have the same meaning or function as the words they rename (also called in apposition).

Only two students, Alex and *I*, were asked to report on the meeting.

for words that follow a linking verb and describe the subject of a sentence (subject complement):

The actors nominated for the award were *she* and *I*.

for the subject in a comparison (Note: think of the words missing from the sentence: Molly is more experienced than *he* is.):

Molly is more experienced than *he*.

for the subject of a clause that cannot stand on its own (subordinate clause):

Robert is the driver *who* reported the accident.

as part of a direct object comprised of a infinitive verb and a pronoun.

I would not want to be *he*.

Use the objective case (object pronouns)

for the direct object of a sentence:

Mary invited *us* to her party.

for the object of a preposition:

The books that were torn belonged to *her*.

Just between you and *me,* I'm bored.

for the indirect object of a sentence:

Walter gave a dozen red roses to *her*.

for the appositive of a direct object:

The committee elected two delegates, Barbara and *me*.

for the object of an infinitive:

The young boy wanted to help *us* paint the fence.

for the object of a gerund:

Enlisting *him* was surprisingly easy.

for the object of a past participle:

Having called the other students and *us*, the secretary went home for the day.

for a pronoun that precedes an infinitive (the subject of an infinitive):

The supervisor told *him* to work late.

for the complement of an infinitive with an expressed subject:

The fans thought the best player to be *him*.

for an object of a comparison (Note: think of the words missing from the sentence. Bill tackled Joe harder than he tackled me.)

> Bill tackled Joe harder than *me*.

for the object of a verb in apposition:

> Charles invited two extra people, Carmen and *me*, to the party.

When a conjunction connects two pronouns or a pronoun and a noun, remove the "and" and the other pronoun or noun to determine what the correct pronoun form should be:

> Mom gave ~~Tom and~~ myself a piece of cake.
>
> Mom gave ~~Tom and~~ I a piece of cake.
>
> Mom gave ~~Tom and~~ me a piece of cake.

Removal of these words reveals what the correct pronoun should be:

> Mom gave *me* a piece of cake.

The only pronouns that are acceptable after *between* and other prepositions are: *me, her, him, them,* and *whom*.

When deciding between *who* and *whom*, try substituting *he* for *who* and *him* for *whom*; then follow these easy transformation steps:

1. Isolate the *who* clause or the *whom* clause:

   > whom we can trust

2. Invert the word order, if necessary. Place the words in the clause in the natural order of an English sentence, subject followed by the verb:

   > we can trust whom

3. Read the final form with the *he* or *him* inserted:

   > We can trust ~~whom~~ him.

When a pronoun follows a comparative conjunction like *than* or *as*, complete the elliptical construction to help you determine which pronoun is correct.

> EX: She has more credit hours than me [do].
>
> She has more credit hours than I [do].

Pronoun-Antecedent Agreement

An antecedent is a noun or pronoun to which another noun or pronoun refers. Questions on pronoun-antecedent agreement test your knowledge of using an appropriate pronoun to agree with its antecedent in number (singular or plural form) and gender (masculine, feminine, or neuter).

Here are the two basic rules for pronoun reference-antecedent agreement:

1. Every pronoun must agree with its antecedent in number, gender, and person.
2. Every pronoun must have a conspicuous antecedent.

When an antecedent is one of dual gender like *student, singer, artist, person, citizen,* etc., use his or her. Some careful writers change the antecedent to a plural noun to avoid using the sexist, singular masculine pronoun his:

> INCORRECT: Everyone hopes that he will win the lottery.
>
> CORRECT: Most people hope that they will win the lottery.

Ordinarily, the relative pronoun *who* is used to refer to people, *which* to refer to things and places, *where* to refer to places, and *that* to refer to places or things. The distinction between *that* and *which* is a grammatical distinction (see the section on Word Choice Skills).

Many writers prefer to use *that* to refer to collective nouns.

EX: A family *that* traces its lineage is usually proud of its roots.

Many writers, especially students, are not sure when to use the reflexive case pronoun and when to use the possessive case pronoun. The rules governing the usage of the reflexive case and the possessive case are quite simple.

Use the possessive case

before a noun in a sentence:

Our friend moved during the semester break.

My dog has fleas, but *her* dog doesn't.

before a gerund in a sentence:

Her running helps to relieve stress.

His driving terrified her.

as a noun in a sentence:

Mine was the last test graded that day.

to indicate possession:

Karen never allows anyone else to drive *her* car.

Brad thought the book was *his,* but it was someone else's.

Use the reflexive case

as a direct object to rename the subject:

I kicked *myself.*

as an indirect object to rename the subject:

Henry bought *himself* a tie.

as an object of a prepositional phrase:

Tom and Lillie baked the pie for *themselves.*

as a predicate pronoun:

She hasn't been *herself* lately.

Do not use the reflexive in place of the nominative pronoun:

INCORRECT: Both Randy and *myself* plan to go.

CORRECT: Both Randy and *I* plan to go.

INCORRECT: *Yourself* will take on the challenges of college.

CORRECT: *You* will take on the challenges of college.

INCORRECT: Either James or *yourself* will paint the mural.

CORRECT: Either James or *you* will paint the mural.

Watch out for careless use of the pronoun form:

INCORRECT: George *hisself* told me it was true.

CORRECT: George *himself* told me it was true.

INCORRECT: They washed the car *theirselves*.

CORRECT: They washed the car *themselves*.

Notice that reflexive pronouns are not set off by commas:

INCORRECT: Mary, *herself*, gave him the diploma.

CORRECT: Mary *herself* gave him the diploma.

INCORRECT: I will do it, *myself*.

CORRECT: I will do it *myself*.

Pronoun Reference

Writing without pronouns would sound dull. For example: "Jack finished Jack's homework before Jack went to bed" is a very repetitive sentence. Using pronouns to replace some of those nouns makes the sentence flow better: "Jack finished his homework before he went to bed." The pronoun "his" and "he" are used to replace "Jack." In grammatical terms, "Jack" is known as the antecedent, the word to which the pronouns refer. It is important to make sure that the antecedent to which the pronoun refers is conspicuously clear or obvious to the reader. It is also important to be sure that pronouns refer only to another noun or pronoun and not to an idea or a sentence.

Pronoun reference problems occur

when a pronoun refers to either of two antecedents:

INCORRECT: Joanna told Julie that *she* was getting fat.

CORRECT: Joanna told Julie, "I'm getting fat."

when a pronoun refers to a remote antecedent:

INCORRECT: A strange car followed us closely, and *he* kept blinking his lights at us.

CORRECT: A strange car followed us closely, and its driver kept blinking his lights at us.

when *this*, *that*, and *which* refer to the general idea of the preceding clause or sentence rather than the preceding word:

INCORRECT: The students could not understand the pronoun reference handout, which annoyed them very much.

CORRECT: The students could not understand the pronoun reference handout, a fact that annoyed them very much.

OR: The students were annoyed because they could not understand the pronoun reference handout.

when a pronoun refers to an unexpressed but implied noun:

INCORRECT: My husband wants me to knit a blanket, but I'm not interested in it.

CORRECT: My husband wants me to knit a blanket, but I'm not interested in knitting.

when *it* is used at the beginning of a clause and the subject of the sentence is not before the verb.

INCORRECT: It says in today's paper that the newest shipment of cars from Detroit, Michigan, seems to include outright imitations of European models.

CORRECT: Today's paper says that the newest shipment of cars from Detroit, Michigan, seems to include outright imitations of European models.

INCORRECT: The football game was canceled because it was bad weather.

CORRECT: The football game was canceled because the weather was bad.

when *they* or *it* is used to refer to something or someone nonspecific:

INCORRECT: At the job placement office, they told me to stop wearing ripped jeans to my interviews.

CORRECT: At the job placement office, I was told to stop wearing ripped jeans to my interviews.

when the pronoun does not agree with its antecedent in number, gender, or person:

INCORRECT: Any graduate student, if they are interested, may attend the lecture.

CORRECT: Any graduate student, if he or she is interested, may attend the lecture.

OR: All graduate students, if they are interested, may attend the lecture.

INCORRECT: Many Americans are concerned that the overuse of slang and colloquialisms is corrupting the language.

CORRECT: Many Americans are concerned that the overuse of slang and colloquialisms is corrupting their language.

INCORRECT: The Board of Regents will not make a decision about a tuition increase until their March meeting.

CORRECT: The Board of Regents will not make a decision about a tuition increase until its March meeting.

when a noun or pronoun has no clear antecedent:

INCORRECT: In the President's address to the union, he promised no more taxes.

CORRECT: In his address to the union, the President promised no more taxes.

Drill: Pronouns

DIRECTIONS: Choose the correct option.

1. My friend and <u>myself</u> bought tickets for *Cats*.
   - **(A)** I
   - **(B)** me
   - **(C)** us
   - **(D)** No change is necessary.

2. Alcohol and tobacco are harmful to <u>whomever</u> consumes them.
   - **(A)** whom
   - **(B)** who
   - **(C)** whoever
   - **(D)** No change is necessary.

3. Everyone is wondering <u>whom</u> her successor will be.
   - **(A)** who
   - **(B)** whose
   - **(C)** who'll
   - **(D)** No change is necessary.

4. Rosa Lee's parents discovered that it was <u>her who</u> wrecked the family car.
   - **(A)** she who
   - **(B)** she whom
   - **(C)** her whom
   - **(D)** No change is necessary.

5. A student <u>who</u> wishes to protest <u>his or her</u> grades must file a formal grievance in the Dean's office.
   - **(A)** that . . . their
   - **(B)** which . . . his
   - **(C)** whom . . . their
   - **(D)** No change is necessary.

6. One of the best things about working for this company is that <u>they pay</u> big bonuses.
   - **(A)** it pays
   - **(B)** they always pay
   - **(C)** they paid
   - **(D)** No change is necessary.

7. Every car owner should be sure that <u>their</u> automobile insurance is adequate.
   - **(A)** your
   - **(B)** his or her
   - **(C)** its
   - **(D)** No change is necessary.

8. My mother wants me to become a teacher, but I'm not interested in <u>it</u>.
   - **(A)** this
   - **(B)** teaching
   - **(C)** that
   - **(D)** No change is necessary.

9. Since I had not paid my electric bill, <u>they</u> sent me a delinquent notice.
   - **(A)** the power company
   - **(B)** he
   - **(C)** it
   - **(D)** No change is necessary.

10. Margaret seldom wrote to her sister when <u>she</u> was away at college.
    - **(A)** who
    - **(C)** her
    - **(B)** her sister
    - **(D)** No change is necessary.

IV. Adjectives and Adverbs

Correct Usage

Adjectives are words that modify nouns or pronouns by defining, describing, limiting, or qualifying those nouns or pronouns.

Adverbs are words that modify verbs, adjectives, or other adverbs and that express ideas such as time, place, manner, cause, and degree.

EX: The old man's speech was eloquent.	ADJECTIVE
Mr. Brown speaks eloquently.	ADVERB
Please be careful.	ADJECTIVE
Please drive carefully.	ADVERB

Good or well

Good should be used as an adjective; not as an adverb.

    INCORRECT: He plays *good*.

    CORRECT: He looks *good* to be an eighty-year-old.

               The quiche tastes very *good*.

Well may be either an adverb or an adjective.
As an adjective, *well* means "in good health."

    CORRECT: He plays *well*.   ADVERB

               My mother is not *well*.   ADJECTIVE

Bad or badly

Bad is an adjective used after sense verbs such as *look, smell, taste, feel,* or *sound,* or after linking verbs (*is, am, are, was, were*).

    INCORRECT: I feel *badly* about the delay.

    CORRECT: I feel *bad* about the delay.

Badly is an adverb used after all other verbs.

    INCORRECT: It doesn't hurt very *bad*.

    CORRECT: It doesn't hurt very *badly*.

Real or really

Real is an adjective meaning "genuine." *Really* is an adverb meaning "very."

    INCORRECT: He writes *real* well.

    CORRECT: This is *real* leather.

    INCORRECT: This is *really* diamond.

    CORRECT: Have a *really* nice day.

    EX: This is a *real* amethyst.   ADJECTIVE

        This is *really* difficult.   ADVERB

        This is a *real* crisis.   ADJECTIVE

        This is *really* important.   ADVERB

Sort of and kind of

Sort of and *kind of* are often misused in written English by writers who actually mean *rather* or *somewhat*.

    INCORRECT: Jan was *kind of* saddened by the results of the test.

    CORRECT: Jan was *somewhat* saddened by the results of the test.

Faulty Comparisons

Sentences containing a faulty comparison often sound correct because their problem is not one of grammar but of logic. Read these sentences closely to make sure that like things are being compared, that the comparisons are complete, and that the comparisons are logical.

When comparing two persons or things, use the comparative (better, older), not the superlative (best, oldest), form of an adjective or an adverb. The superlative form is used only for comparison of more than two persons or things. Use *any*, *other*, or *else* when comparing one thing or person with a group of which it, he, or she is a part.

Most one- and two-syllable words form their comparative and superlative degrees with -er and -est suffixes. Adjectives and adverbs of more than two syllables form their comparative and superlative degrees with the addition of *more* and *most*.

Positive	Comparative	Superlative
good	better	best
old	older	oldest
friendly	friendlier	friendliest
lonely	lonelier	loneliest
talented	more talented	most talented
beautiful	more beautiful	most beautiful

A double comparison occurs when the writer incorrectly adds both -er and *more* or -est and *most* to the adjective or adverb.

INCORRECT: He is the *most nicest* brother.

CORRECT: He is the *nicest* brother.

INCORRECT: She is the *more meaner* of the sisters.

CORRECT: She is the *meaner* sister.

Illogical comparisons occur when there is an implied comparison between two things that are not actually being compared or that cannot be logically compared.

INCORRECT: The interest at a loan company is higher *than* a bank.

CORRECT: The interest at a loan company is higher *than* that *at* a bank.

OR: The interest at a loan company is higher *than at* a bank.

Ambiguous comparisons occur when elliptical words (those omitted) create for the reader more than one interpretation of the sentence.

INCORRECT: I like Mary better than you. (than you *what*?)

CORRECT: I like Mary better than I like you.

OR: I like Mary better than you do.

Incomplete comparisons occur when the basis of the comparison (the two categories being compared) is not clearly stated.

INCORRECT: Skywriting is *more* spectacular.

CORRECT: Skywriting is *more* spectacular *than* billboard advertising.

Do not omit the words *other*, *any*, or *else* when comparing one thing or person with a group of which it, he, or she is a part.

INCORRECT: Joan writes better *than any* student in her class.

CORRECT: Joan writes better *than any other* student in her class.

Do not omit the second *as* of *as . . . as* when making a point of equal or superior comparison.

INCORRECT: The University of West Florida is *as large* or larger than the University of North Florida.

CORRECT: The University of West Florida is *as large as* or larger than the University of North Florida.

Do not omit the first category of the comparison, even if the two categories are the same.

INCORRECT: This is one of the best, if not the best, college in the country.

CORRECT: This is one of the best colleges in the country, if not the best.

The problem with the incorrect sentence is that *one of the best* requires the plural word *colleges*, not *college*.

Drill: Adjectives and Adverbs

DIRECTIONS: Choose the correct option.

1. Although the band performed <u>badly</u>, I feel <u>real bad</u> about missing the concert.
   - **(A)** badly . . . real badly
   - **(B)** bad . . . badly
   - **(C)** badly . . . very bad
   - **(D)** No change is necessary.

2. These reports are <u>relative simple</u> to prepare.
   - **(A)** relatively simple
   - **(B)** relative simply
   - **(C)** relatively simply
   - **(D)** No change is necessary.

3. He did <u>very well</u> on the test although his writing skills are not <u>good</u>.
   - **(A)** real well . . . good
   - **(B)** very good . . . good
   - **(C)** good . . . great
   - **(D)** No change is necessary.

4. Shake the medicine bottle <u>good</u> before you open it.
   - **(A)** very good
   - **(B)** real good
   - **(C)** well
   - **(D)** No change is necessary.

5. Though she speaks <u>fluently</u>, she writes <u>poorly</u> because she doesn't observe <u>closely</u> or think <u>clear</u>.
   - **(A)** fluently, poorly, closely, clearly
   - **(B)** fluent, poor, close, clear
   - **(C)** fluently, poor, closely, clear
   - **(D)** No change is necessary.

DIRECTIONS: Select the sentence that clearly and effectively states the idea and has no structural errors.

6. **(A)** Los Angeles is larger than any city in California.
   (B) Los Angeles is larger than all the cities in California.
   (C) Los Angeles is larger than any other city in California.
   (D) Los Angeles is larger than the cities in California.

7. **(A)** Art history is as interesting as, if not more interesting than, music appreciation.
   (B) Art history is as interesting, if not more interesting than, music appreciation.
   (C) Art history is as interesting as, if not more interesting, music appreciation.
   (D) Art history is as interesting as, if not more interesting as, music appreciation.

8. **(A)** The baseball team here is as good as any other university.
   (B) The baseball team here is as good as all the other universities.
   (C) The baseball team here is as good as any other university's.
   (D) The baseball team here is as good as the other universities.

9. **(A)** I like him better than you.
   (B) I like him better than I like you.
   (C) I like him better.
   (D) I like him more than you.

10. **(A)** You are the most stingiest person I know.
    (B) You are the most stingier person I know.
    (C) You are the stingiest person I know.
    (D) You are the more stingiest person I know.

V. Punctuation

Commas

Commas should be placed according to standard rules of punctuation for purpose, clarity, and effect. The proper use of commas is explained in the following rules and examples.

In a series

When more than one adjective describes a noun, use a comma to separate and emphasize each adjective. The comma takes the place of the word *and* in the series.

> the long, dark passageway
>
> another confusing, sleepless night
>
> an elaborate, complex, brilliant plan
>
> the old, gray, crumpled hat

Some adjective-noun combinations are thought of as one word. In these cases, the adjective in front of the adjective-noun combination needs no comma. If you inserted *and* between the adjective-noun combination, it would not make sense.

> a stately oak tree
>
> an exceptional wine glass
>
> my worst report card
>
> a china dinner plate

The comma is also used to separate words, phrases, and whole ideas (clauses); it still takes the place of *and* when used this way.

> an apple, a pear, a fig, and a banana
>
> a lovely lady, an elegant dress, and many admirers
>
> She lowered the shade, closed the curtain, turned off the light, and went to bed.

The only question that exists about the use of commas in a series is whether or not one should be used before the final item. It is standard to do so, although many newspapers and magazines have stopped using the final comma. Occasionally, the omission of the comma can be confusing.

> CORRECT: She ate lunch with Susan, saw a movie with Harold and Joan, and had coffee with Gregory.

With a long introductory phrase

Usually if a phrase of more than five or six words or a clause that cannot stand alone as a sentence (a dependent clause) precedes the subject at the beginning of a sentence, a comma is used to set it off.

> After last night's fiasco at the party, she couldn't bear the thought of looking at him again.
>
> Whenever I try to talk about politics, my wife leaves the room.
>
> Provided you have said nothing, they will never guess who you are.

It is not necessary to use a comma with a short sentence.

> In January she will go to Switzerland.
>
> After I rest I'll feel better.
>
> During the day no one is home.

If an introductory phrase includes a verb form that is being used as another part of speech (a *verbal*), it must be followed by a comma.

> INCORRECT: When eating Mary never looked up from her plate.
>
> CORRECT: When eating, Mary never looked up from her plate.

> INCORRECT: Because of her desire to believe her faith in James wavered.
>
> CORRECT: Because of her desire to believe, her faith in James wavered.

> INCORRECT: Having decided to leave Mary James wrote her a letter.
>
> CORRECT: Having decided to leave Mary, James wrote her a letter.

To separate sentences with two main ideas

To understand this use of the comma, you need to be able to recognize compound sentences. When a sentence contains more than two subjects and verbs (clauses), and the two clauses are joined by a conjunction (*and, but, or, nor, for, yet*), use a comma before the conjunction to show that another clause is coming.

> I thought I knew the poem by heart, but he showed me three lines I had forgotten.
>
> Are we really interested in helping the children, or are we more concerned with protecting our good names?
>
> He is supposed to leave tomorrow, but he is not ready to go.
>
> Jim knows you are disappointed, and he has known it for a long time.

If the two parts of the sentence are short and closely related, it is not necessary to use a comma.

> He threw the ball and the dog ran after it.
>
> Jane played the piano and Michael danced.

Be careful not to confuse a sentence that has a compound verb and a single subject with a compound sentence. If the subject is the same for both verbs, there is no need for a comma.

> INCORRECT: Charles sent some flowers, and
> wrote a long letter explaining
> why he had not been able to attend.
>
> CORRECT: Charles sent some flowers and
> wrote a long letter explaining why
> he had not been able to attend.
>
> INCORRECT: Last Thursday we went to the concert with Julia,
> and afterwards dined at an old Italian restaurant.
>
> CORRECT: Last Thursday we went to the concert with Julia and afterwards dined at an old
> Italian restaurant.
>
> INCORRECT: For the third time, the teacher explained that the literacy level for high school
> students was much lower than it had been in previous years, and, this time,
> wrote the statistics on the board for everyone to see.
>
> CORRECT: For the third time, the teacher explained that the literacy level for high school
> students was much lower than it had been in previous years and this time wrote
> the statistics on the board for everyone to see.

In general, words and phrases that stop the flow of the sentence or are unnecessary for the main idea are set off by commas.

Abbreviations after names

> Did you invite John Paul, Jr., and his sister?
>
> Martha Harris, Ph.D., will be the speaker tonight.

Interjections (an exclamation without added grammatical connection)

> Oh, I'm so glad to see you.
>
> I tried so hard, alas, to do it.
>
> Hey, let me out of here.

Direct address

Roy, won't you open the door for the dog?

I can't understand, Mother, what you are trying to say.

May I ask, Mr. President, why you called us together?

Hey, lady, watch out for that car!

Tag questions

I'm really hungry, aren't you?

Jerry looks like his father, doesn't he?

Geographical names and addresses

The concert will be held in Chicago, Illinois, on August 12.

The letter was addressed to Mrs. Marion Heartwell, 1881 Pine Lane, Palo Alto, California 95824.

(Note: No comma is needed before the zip code, because it is already clearly set off from the state name.)

Transitional words and phrases

Transitional words and phrases serve as a bridge between sentence parts and complete sentences, such as *"as a matter of fact, for example, however."*

On the other hand, I hope he gets better.

In addition, the phone rang constantly this afternoon.

I'm, nevertheless, going to the beach on Sunday.

You'll find, therefore, that no one is more loyal than I am.

Parenthetical words and phrases

Parenthetical words and phrases are expressions that interrupt the flow of a sentence with extra information.

You will become, I believe, a great statesman.

We know, of course, that this is the only thing to do.

In fact, I planted corn last summer.

The Mannes affair was, to put it mildly, a surprise.

Unusual word order

The dress, new and crisp, hung in the closet.

Intently, she stared out the window.

With nonrestrictive elements

Parts of a sentence that modify other parts are sometimes essential to the meaning of the sentence and sometimes not. When a modifying word or group of words is not vital to the meaning of the sentence, it is set off by commas. Since it does not restrict the meaning of the words it modifies, it is called "nonrestrictive." Modifiers that are essential to the meaning of the sentence are called "restrictive" and are not set off by commas.

ESSENTIAL: The girl *who wrote the story* is my sister.

NONESSENTIAL: My sister, *the girl who wrote the story,* has always loved to write.

ESSENTIAL: The cup *that is on the piano* is the one I want.

NONESSENTIAL: The cup, *which my brother gave me last year,* is on the piano.

ESSENTIAL: The people *who arrived late* were not seated.

NONESSENTIAL: George, *who arrived late,* was not seated.

To set off direct quotations

Most direct quotes or quoted materials are set off from the rest of the sentence by commas.

"Please read your part more loudly," the director insisted.

"I won't know what to do," said Michael, "if you leave me."

The teacher said sternly, "I will not dismiss this class until I have silence."

Who was it who said "Do not ask for whom the bell tolls; it tolls for thee"?

Note: Commas always go inside the closing quotation mark, even if the comma is not part of the material being quoted.

Be careful not to set off indirect quotes or quotes that are used as subjects or complements.

"To be or not to be" is the famous beginning of a soliloquy in Shakespeare's *Hamlet*. (subject)

She said she would never come back. (indirect quote)

Back then my favorite poem was "Evangeline." (complement)

To set off contrasting elements

Her intelligence, not her beauty, got her the job.

Your plan will take you a little further from, rather than closer to, your destination.

It was a reasonable, though not appealing, idea.

He wanted glory, but found happiness instead.

In dates

Both forms of the date are acceptable.

She will arrive on April 6, 1998.

He left on 5 December 1980.

In January 1967, he handed in his resignation.

On October 22, 1992, Frank and Julie were married.

After Subordinate Clauses

Subordinate clauses are comprised of a subject and a verb that cannot stand alone as a sentence. When these clauses appear at the beginning of a sentence, they should be separated with a comma.

If we hurry, we can still make the early movie.

Unless my mom changes her mind, I won't be able to go to the concert.

Listed below are several subordinate conjunctions, which are words that are used to join subordinate clauses to independent clauses in a sentence. If one of these words begins a clause that is an incomplete thought and it begins the sentence, the clause should be followed by a comma.

after	since
although	so that
as	though
as if	till
because	unless
before	until
even though	when
if	whenever
inasmuch as	while

Semicolons

Questions testing semicolon usage require you to be able to distinguish between the semicolon and the comma, and the semicolon and the colon. This review section covers the basic uses of the semicolon: (1) to separate independent clauses not joined by a coordinating conjunction, (2) to separate independent clauses separated by a conjunctive adverb, and (3) to separate items in a series with internal commas. It is important to be consistent; if you use a semicolon between *any* of the items in the series, you must use semicolons to separate *all* of the items in the series.

Usually, a comma follows the conjunctive adverb. A conjunctive adverb is an adverb that connects independent clauses in a sentence or group of sentences.

My teeth were chattering and feet were freezing. Nonetheless, I still wanted to continue skiing.

Note also that a period can be used to separate two sentences joined by a conjunctive adverb. The following are some common conjunctive adverbs:

accordingly	nevertheless
besides	next
consequently	nonetheless
finally	now
furthermore	on the other hand
however	otherwise
indeed	perhaps
in fact	still
moreover	therefore

Note: *Then* is also used as a conjunctive adverb, but it is not usually followed by a comma.

Use the Semicolon

to separate independent clauses that are not joined by a coordinating conjunction:

I understand how to use commas; the semicolon I have not yet mastered.

to separate two independent clauses connected by a conjunctive adverb:

He took great care with his work; *therefore*, he was very successful.

to combine two independent clauses connected by a coordinating conjunction if either or both of the clauses contain other internal punctuation:

> Success in college, some maintain, requires intelligence, industry, and perseverance; *but* others, fewer in number, assert that only personality is important.

to separate items in a series when each item has internal punctuation:

> I bought an old, dilapidated chair; an antique table that was in beautiful condition; and a new, ugly, blue and white rug.

> Call our customer service line for assistance: Arizona, 1-800-555-6020; New Mexico, 1-800-555-5050; California, 1-800-555-3140; or Nevada, 1-800-555-3214.

Do Not Use the Semicolon

to separate a dependent and an independent clause:

> INCORRECT: You should not make such statements; even though they are correct.

> CORRECT: You should not make such statements even though they are correct.

to separate an appositive phrase or clause from a sentence:

> INCORRECT: His immediate aim in life is centered around two things; becoming an engineer and learning to fly an airplane.

> CORRECT: His immediate aim in life is centered around two things: becoming an engineer and learning to fly an airplane.

to precede an explanation or summary of the first clause:

Note: Although the sentence below is punctuated correctly, the use of the semicolon provides a miscue, suggesting that the second clause is merely an extension, not an explanation, of the first clause. The colon provides a better clue.

> WEAK: The first week of camping was wonderful; we lived in cabins instead of tents.

> BETTER: The first week of camping was wonderful: we lived in cabins instead of tents.

to substitute for a comma:

> INCORRECT: My roommate also likes sports; particularly football, basketball, and baseball.

> CORRECT: My roommate also likes sports, particularly football, basketball, and baseball.

to set off other types of phrases or clauses from a sentence:

> INCORRECT: Being of a cynical mind; I should ask for a recount of the ballots.

> CORRECT: Being of a cynical mind, I should ask for a recount of the ballots.

> INCORRECT: The next meeting of the club has been postponed two weeks; inasmuch as both the president and vice-president are out of town.

> CORRECT: The next meeting of the club has been postponed two weeks, inasmuch as both the president and vice-president are out of town.

Note: The semicolon is not a terminal mark of punctuation; therefore, it should not be followed by a capital letter unless the first word in the second clause ordinarily requires capitalization.

Colons

Although it is true that a colon is used to precede a list, one must also make sure that a complete sentence precedes the colon. The colon signals the reader that a list, explanation, or restatement of the preceding will follow. It is like an arrow, indicating that something is to follow. The difference between the colon and the semicolon and between the colon and the period is that the colon is an introductory mark, not a terminal mark. Look at the following examples:

The Constitution provides for a separation of powers among the three branches of government.

government. The period signals a new sentence.

government; The semicolon signals an interrelated sentence.

government, The comma signals a coordinating conjunction followed by another independent clause.

government: The colon signals a list.

The Constitution provides for a separation of powers among the three branches of *government:* executive, legislative, and judicial.

Use the Colon

to introduce a list:

I hate this one course: English.

Note: One item may constitute a list:

Three plays by William Shakespeare will be presented in repertory this summer at the University of Michigan: *Hamlet, Macbeth,* and *Othello.*

to introduce a list preceded by *as follows* or *the following*:

The reasons he cited for his success are as follows: integrity, honesty, industry, and a pleasant disposition.

to separate two independent clauses, when the second clause is a restatement or explanation of the first:

All of my high school teachers said one thing in particular: college is going to be difficult.

to introduce a word or word group that is a restatement, explanation, or summary of the first sentence:

These two things he loved: an honest man and a beautiful woman.

to introduce a formal appositive:

I am positive there is one appeal that you can't overlook: money.

to separate the introductory words from a long or formal quotation:

The actor then stated: "I would rather be able to adequately play the part of Hamlet than to perform a miraculous operation, deliver a great lecture, or build a magnificent skyscraper."

The colon should only be used after statements that are grammatically complete.

Do *Not* Use the Colon

after a verb:

INCORRECT: My favorite holidays are: Christmas, New Year's Eve, and Halloween.

CORRECT: My favorite holidays are Christmas, New Year's Eve, and Halloween.

after a preposition:

INCORRECT: I enjoy different ethnic foods such as: Greek, Chinese, and Italian.

CORRECT: I enjoy different ethnic foods such as Greek, Chinese, and Italian.

interchangeably with the dash:

INCORRECT: Mathematics, German, English: these gave me the greatest difficulty of all my studies.

CORRECT: Mathematics, German, English—these gave me the greatest difficulty of all my studies.

Information preceding the colon should be a complete sentence regardless of the explanatory information following the clause.

before the words *for example, namely, that is,* or *for instance* even though these words may be introducing a list.

INCORRECT: We agreed to it: namely, to give him a surprise party.

CORRECT: There are a number of well-known American women writers, for example, Nikki Giovanni, Phyllis Wheatley, Emily Dickinson, and Maya Angelou.

Apostrophes

Apostrophe questions require you to know when an apostrophe has been used appropriately to make a noun possessive, not plural. Remember the following rules when considering how to show possession.

Add *'s* to singular nouns and indefinite pronouns:

Tiffany's flowers

a dog's bark

everybody's computer

at the owner's expense

today's paper

Add *'s* to singular nouns ending in *s*, unless this distorts the pronunciation:

Delores's paper

the boss's pen

Dr. Yots' class

for righteousness' sake

Dr. Evans's office OR Dr. Evans' office

Add *an apostrophe* to plural nouns ending in *s* or *es*:

two cents' worth

ladies' night

thirteen years' experience

two weeks' pay

Add *'s* to plural nouns not ending in *s*:

men's room

children's toys

Add *'s* to the last word in compound words or groups:

> brother-in-law's car
>
> someone else's paper

Add *'s* to the last name when indicating joint ownership:

> Joe and Edna's home
>
> Julie and Kathy's party
>
> women and children's clinic

Add *'s* to both names if you intend to show individual ownership:

> Joe's and Edna's trucks
>
> Julie's and Kathy's pies
>
> Ted's and Jane's marriage vows

Possessive pronouns do not require the addition of an apostrophe:

> her, his, hers
>
> your, yours
>
> their, theirs
>
> it, its

Use the possessive form of a noun when it precedes a gerund:

> His driving annoys me.
>
> My bowling a strike irritated him.
>
> Do you mind our stopping by?
>
> We appreciate your coming.

Add *'s* to words and initials to show that they are plural:

> no if's, and's, or but's
>
> the do's and don't's of dating
>
> three A's

Add *s* to numbers, symbols, and letters to show that they are plural:

> TVs
>
> VCRs
>
> the 1800s
>
> the returning POWs

Quotation Marks and Italics

These kinds of questions test your knowledge of the proper use of quotation marks with other marks of punctuation, with titles, and with dialogue. These kinds of questions also test your knowledge of the correct use of italics and underlining with titles and words used as sample words (for example, *the word is is a common verb*).

The most common use of double quotation marks (", ") is to set off quoted words, phrases, and sentences.

"If everybody minded their own business," said the Duchess in a hoarse growl, "the world would go round a great deal faster than it does."

"Then you would say what you mean," the March Hare went on.

"I do," Alice hastily replied: "at least—at least I mean what I say—that's the same thing, you know."

—from Lewis Carroll's *Alice in Wonderland*

Single quotation marks are used to set off quoted material when it appears within another set of quotes.

"Shall I bring 'Rime of the Ancient Mariner' along with us?" she asked her brother.

Mrs. Green said, "The doctor told me, 'Go immediately to bed when you get home!'"

"If she said that to me," Katherine insisted, "I would tell her, 'I never intend to speak to you again! Goodbye, Susan!'"

When writing dialogue, begin a new paragraph each time the speaker changes.

"Do you know what time it is?" asked Jane.

"Can't you see I'm busy?" snapped Mary.

"It's easy to see that you're in a bad mood today!" replied Jane.

Use quotation marks to enclose words used as words (sometimes italics are used for this purpose).

"Judgment" has always been a difficult word for me to spell.

Do you know what "abstruse" means?

"Horse and buggy" and "bread and butter" can be used either as adjectives or as nouns.

If slang is used within more formal writing, the slang words or phrases should be set off with quotation marks.

Harrison's decision to leave the conference and to "stick his neck out" by flying to Jamaica was applauded by the rest of the conference attendees.

When words are meant to have an unusual or specific significance to the reader, for instance irony or humor, they are sometimes placed in quotation marks.

For years, women were not allowed to buy real estate in order to "protect" them from unscrupulous dealers.

The "conversation" resulted in one black eye and a broken nose.

To set off titles of TV shows, poems, stories, and book chapters, use quotation marks. (Book, motion picture, newspaper, and magazine titles are underlined when handwritten and italicized when printed.)

The article "Moving South in the Southern Rain," by Jergen Smith in the *Southern News*, attracted the attention of our editor.

The assignment is "Childhood Development," Chapter 18 of *Human Behavior*.

My favorite essay by Montaigne is "On Silence."

"Happy Days" led the TV ratings for years, didn't it?

You will find Keats' "Ode on a Grecian Urn" in Chapter 3, "The Romantic Era," in Lastly's *Selections from Great English Poets*.

Errors to Avoid

Be sure to remember that quotation marks always come in pairs. Do not make the mistake of using only one set.

INCORRECT: "You'll never convince me to move to the city, said Thurman. I consider it an insane asylum."

CORRECT: "You'll never convince me to move to the city," said Thurman. "I consider it an insane asylum."

INCORRECT: "Idleness and pride tax with a heavier hand than kings and parliaments," Benjamin Franklin is supposed to have said. If we can get rid of the former, we may easily bear the latter."

CORRECT: "Idleness and pride tax with a heavier hand than kings and parliaments," Benjamin Franklin is supposed to have said. "If we can get rid of the former, we may easily bear the latter."

When a quote consists of several sentences, do not put the quotation marks at the beginning and end of each sentence; put them at the beginning and end of the entire quotation.

INCORRECT: "It was during his student days in Bonn that Beethoven fastened upon Schiller's poem." "The heady sense of liberation in the verses must have appealed to him." "They appealed to every German." —John Burke

CORRECT: "It was during his student days in Bonn that Beethoven fastened upon Schiller's poem. The heady sense of liberation in the verses must have appealed to him. They appealed to every German." —John Burke

Instead of setting off a long quote with quotation marks, if it is longer than four lines you may want to indent and single space it. If you do indent, do not use quotation marks.

In his *First Inaugural Address,* Abraham Lincoln appeals to the war-torn American people:
We are not enemies, but friends. We must not be enemies. Though passion may have strained, it must not break, our bonds of affection. The mystic chords of memory, stretching from every battlefield and patriot grave to every living heart and hearthstone all over this broad land, will yet swell the chorus of the Union when again touched, as surely they will be, by the better angels of our nature.

Be careful not to use quotation marks with indirect quotations.

INCORRECT: Mary wondered "if she would get over it."

CORRECT: Mary wondered if she would get over it.

INCORRECT: The nurse asked "how long it had been since we had visited the doctor's office."

CORRECT: The nurse asked how long it had been since we had visited the doctor's office.

When you quote several paragraphs, it is not sufficient to place quotation marks at the beginning and end of the entire quote. Place quotation marks at the *beginning of each paragraph,* but only at the *end of the last paragraph.* Here is an abbreviated quotation for an example:

"Here begins an odyssey through the world of classical mythology, starting with the creation of the world . . .

"It is true that themes similar to the classical may be found in any corpus of mythology . . . Even technology is not immune to the influence of Greece and Rome . . .

"We need hardly mention the extent to which painters and sculptors . . . have used and adapted classical mythology to illustrate the past, to reveal the human body, to express romantic or antiromantic ideals, or to symbolize any particular point of view."

Remember that commas and periods are *always* placed inside the quotation marks even if they are not actually part of the quote.

INCORRECT: "Life always gets colder near the summit", Nietzsche is purported to have said, "—the cold increases, responsibility grows".

CORRECT: "Life always gets colder near the summit," Nietzsche is purported to have said, "—the cold increases, responsibility grows."

INCORRECT: "Get down here right away", John cried. "You'll miss the sunset if you don't."

CORRECT: "Get down here right away," John cried. "You'll miss the sunset if you don't."

INCORRECT: "If my dog could talk", Mary mused, "I'll bet he would say, 'Take me for a walk right this minute'".

CORRECT: "If my dog could talk," Mary mused, "I'll bet he would say, 'Take me for a walk right this minute'."

Other marks of punctuation, such as question marks, exclamation points, colons, and semicolons, go inside the quotation marks only if they are part of the quoted material. If they are not part of the quotation, they go outside the quotation marks. Be careful to distinguish between the guidelines for the comma and period, which always go inside the quotation marks, and those for other marks of punctuation.

INCORRECT: "I'll always love you"! he exclaimed happily.
CORRECT: "I'll always love you!" he exclaimed happily.

INCORRECT: Did you hear her say, "He'll be there early?"
CORRECT: Did you hear her say, "He'll be there early"?

INCORRECT: She called down the stairs, "When are you going"?
CORRECT: She called down the stairs, "When are you going?"

INCORRECT: "Let me out"! he cried. "Don't you have any pity"?
CORRECT: "Let me out!" he cried. "Don't you have any pity?"

Remember to use only one mark of punctuation at the end of a sentence ending with a quotation mark.

INCORRECT: She thought out loud, "Will I ever finish this paper in time for that class?".
CORRECT: She thought out loud, "Will I ever finish this paper in time for that class?"

INCORRECT: "Not the same thing a bit!", said the Hatter. "Why, you might just as well say that 'I see what I eat' is the same thing as 'I eat what I see'!".
CORRECT: "Not the same thing a bit!" said the Hatter. "Why, you might just as well say that 'I see what I eat' is the same thing as 'I eat what I see'!"

Drill: Punctuation

DIRECTIONS: Choose the correct option.

1. Indianola, <u>Mississippi, where B.B. King and my father grew up,</u> has a population of less than 50,000 people.
   (A) Mississippi where, B.B. King and my father grew up,
   (B) Mississippi where B.B. King and my father grew up,
   (C) Mississippi; where B.B. King and my father grew up,
   (D) No change is necessary.

2. John Steinbeck's best known novel *The Grapes of Wrath* is the story of the <u>Joads an Oklahoma family</u> who were driven from their dustbowl farm and forced to become migrant workers in California.
   (A) Joads, an Oklahoma family
   (B) Joads, an Oklahoma family,
   (C) Joads; an Oklahoma family
   (D) No change is necessary.

3. All students who are interested in student teaching next <u>semester, must submit an application to the Teacher Education Office.</u>
   (A) semester must submit an application to the Teacher Education Office.
   (B) semester, must submit an application, to the Teacher Education Office.
   (C) semester: must submit an application to the Teacher Education Office.
   (D) No change is necessary.

4. Whenever you travel by <u>car, or plane, you</u> must wear a seatbelt.
   (A) car or plane you
   (B) car, or plane you
   (C) car or plane, you
   (D) No change is necessary.

5. Wearing a seatbelt is not just a good <u>idea, it's</u> the law.
   (A) idea; it's
   (B) idea it's
   (C) idea. It's
   (D) No change is necessary.

6. Senators and representatives can be reelected <u>indefinitely; a</u> president can serve only two terms.
   (A) indefinitely but a
   (B) indefinitely, a
   (C) indefinitely a
   (D) No change is necessary.

7. Students must pay a penalty for overdue library <u>books, however, there</u> is a grace period.
   (A) books; however, there
   (B) books however, there
   (C) books: however, there
   (D) No change is necessary.

8. Among the states that seceded from the Union to join the Confederacy in 1860–1861 <u>were:</u> Mississippi, Florida, and Alabama.
   (A) were
   (B) were;
   (C) were.
   (D) No change is necessary.

9. The art exhibit displayed works by many famous <u>artists such as:</u> Dali, Picasso, and Michelangelo.
   (A) artists such as;
   (B) artists such as
   (C) artists. Such as
   (D) No change is necessary.

10. The National Shakespeare Company will
perform <u>the following plays:</u> *Othello,*
Macbeth, Hamlet, and *As You Like It.*

    (A) the following plays,

    (B) the following plays;

    (C) the following plays

    (D) No change is necessary.

VI. Capitalization

When a word is capitalized, it calls attention to itself. This attention should be for a good reason.
There are standard uses for capital letters. In general, capitalize (1) all proper nouns, (2) the first
word of a sentence, and (3) the first word of a direct quotation.

Words You Should Also Capitalize

Names of ships, aircraft, spacecraft, and trains:

Apollo 13	*Mariner IV*
DC-10	S.S. *United States*
Sputnik 11	Boeing 707

Names of deities:

God	Jupiter
Allah	Holy Ghost
Buddha	Venus
Jehovah	Shiva

Geological periods:

Neolithic age	Cenozoic era
late Pleistocene times	

Names of astronomical bodies:

Mercury	Big Dipper
the Milky Way	Halley's comet
Ursa Major	North Star

Personifications:

Reliable Nature brought her promised Spring.

Bring on Melancholy in his sad might.

She believed that Love was the answer to all her problems.

Historical periods:

the Middle Ages	World War I
Reign of Terror	Great Depression
Christian Era	Roaring Twenties
Age of Louis XIV	Renaissance

Organizations, associations, and institutions:

Girl Scouts	North Atlantic Treaty Organization
Kiwanis Club	League of Women Voters
New York Yankees	Unitarian Church
Smithsonian Institution	Common Market
Library of Congress	Franklin Glen High School
New York Philharmonic	Harvard University

Government and judicial groups:

United States Court of Appeals	Senate
Committee on Foreign Affairs	Parliament
Newark City Council	Peace Corps
Arkansas Supreme Court	Census Bureau
House of Representatives	Department of State

A general term that accompanies a specific name is capitalized only if it follows the specific name. If it stands alone or comes before the specific name, it is put in lowercase:

Washington State	the state of Washington
Senator Dixon	the senator from Illinois
Central Park	the park
Golden Gate Bridge	the bridge
President Clinton	the president
Pope John XXIII	the pope
Queen Elizabeth I	the queen of England
Tropic of Capricorn	the tropics
Monroe Doctrine	the doctrine of expansion
the Mississippi River	the river
Easter Day	the day
Treaty of Versailles	the treaty
Webster's Dictionary	the dictionary
Equatorial Current	the equator

Use a capital to start a sentence:

Our car would not start.

When will you leave? I need to know right away.

Never!

Let me in! Please!

When a sentence appears within a sentence, start it with a capital letter:

We had only one concern: When would we eat?

My sister said, "I'll find the Monopoly game."

He answered, "We can only stay a few minutes."

The most important words of titles are capitalized. Those words not capitalized are conjunctions (*and, or, but*) and short prepositions (*of, on, by, for*). The first and last word of a title must always be capitalized:

A Man for All Seasons	*Crime and Punishment*
Of Mice and Men	*Rise of the West*

Strange Life of Ivan Osokin	"Sonata in G Minor"
"Let Me In"	"Ode to Billy Joe"
"Rubaiyat of Omar Khayyam"	"All in the Family"

Capitalize newspaper and magazine titles:

U.S. News & World Report
National Geographic
The New York Times
Sports Illustrated

Capitalize radio and TV station call letters:

ABC	NBC
WNEW	WBOP
CNN	HBO

Do not capitalize compass directions or seasons:

west	north
east	south
spring	winter
autumn	summer

Capitalize regions:

the South	the Northeast
the West	Eastern Europe
BUT:	the south of France
	the east part of town

Capitalize specific military units:

the U.S. Army
the 7th Fleet
the German Navy
the 1st Infantry Division

Capitalize political groups and philosophies:

Democrat	Communist
Marxist	Nazism
Whig	Federalist
Existentialism	Transcendentalism

BUT: do not capitalize systems of government or individual adherents to a philosophy:

democracy	communism
fascist	agnostic

Drill: Capitalization

DIRECTIONS: Choose the correct option.

1. Mexico is the southernmost country in <u>North America</u>. It borders the United States on the north; it is bordered on the <u>south</u> by Belize and Guatemala.
   - **(A)** north America . . . South
   - **(B)** North America . . . South
   - **(C)** North america . . . south
   - **(D)** No change is necessary.

2. **(A)** Until 1989, Tom Landry was the only Coach the Dallas cowboys ever had.
   - **(B)** Until 1989, Tom Landry was the only coach the Dallas Cowboys ever had.
   - **(C)** Until 1989, Tom Landry was the only Coach the Dallas Cowboys ever had.
   - **(D)** Until 1989, Tom Landry was the only Coach The Dallas Cowboys ever had.

3. The <u>Northern Hemisphere</u> is the half of the <u>earth</u> that lies north of the <u>Equator</u>.
   - **(A)** Northern hemisphere . . . earth . . . equator.
   - **(B)** Northern hemisphere . . . Earth . . . Equator.
   - **(C)** Northern Hemisphere . . . earth . . . equator.
   - **(D)** No change is necessary.

4. **(A)** My favorite works by Ernest Hemingway are "The Snows of Kilamanjaro," *The Sun Also Rises*, and *For Whom the Bell Tolls*.
   - **(B)** My favorite works by Ernest Hemingway are "The Snows Of Kilamanjaro," *The Sun Also Rises*, and *For Whom The Bell Tolls*.
   - **(C)** My favorite works by Ernest Hemingway are "The Snows of Kilamanjaro," *The Sun also Rises*, and *For whom the Bell Tolls*.
   - **(D)** My favorite works by Ernest Hemingway are "The Snows of Kilamanjaro," *The Sun also Rises*, and *For Whom the Bell Tolls*.

5. Aphrodite (<u>Venus in Roman Mythology</u>) was the Greek goddess of love.
   - **(A)** Venus in Roman mythology . . . greek
   - **(B)** venus in roman mythology . . . Greek
   - **(C)** Venus in Roman mythology . . . Greek
   - **(D)** No change is necessary.

6. The <u>Koran</u> is considered by <u>Muslims</u> to be the holy word.
   - **(A)** koran . . . muslims
   - **(B)** koran . . . Muslims
   - **(C)** Koran . . . muslims
   - **(D)** No change is necessary.

7. **(A)** The freshman curriculum at the community college includes english, a foreign language, Algebra I, and history.
   - **(B)** The freshman curriculum at the community college includes English, a foreign language, Algebra I, and history.
   - **(C)** The Freshman curriculum at the Community College includes English, a foreign language, Algebra I, and History.
   - **(D)** The freshman curriculum at the community college includes english, a foreign language, algebra I, and history.

8. At the <u>spring</u> graduation ceremonies, the university awarded over 2,000 <u>bachelor's</u> degrees.
   - **(A)** Spring . . . Bachelor's
   - **(B)** spring . . . Bachelor's
   - **(C)** Spring . . . bachelor's
   - **(D)** No change is necessary.

9. The fall of the <u>Berlin wall</u> was an important symbol of the collapse of <u>Communism</u>.

   (A) berlin Wall . . . communism.

   (B) Berlin Wall . . . communism.

   (C) berlin wall . . . Communism.

   (D) No change is necessary.

10. A photograph of <u>mars</u> was printed in the *New York Times*.

    (A) Mars . . . *The New York Times*.

    (B) mars . . . *The New York times*.

    (C) mars . . . *The New York Time*s.

    (D) No change is necessary.

VII. Spelling

Spelling questions test your ability to recognize misspelled words. This section reviews spelling tips and rules to help you spot incorrect spellings. Problems such as the distinction between *to* and *too* and *lead* and *led* are covered under the Word Choice Skills section of this review.

- Remember, *i* before *e* except after *c*, or when sounded as "a" as in *neighbor* and *weigh*.
- There are only three words in the English language that end in -*ceed*:

    proceed, succeed, exceed

- There are several words that end in -*cede*:

    secede, recede, concede, precede

- There is only one word in the English language that ends in -*sede*:

    supersede

   Many people learn to read English phonetically; that is, by sounding out the letters of the words. However, many English words are not pronounced the way they are spelled, and those who try to spell English words phonetically often make spelling *errors*. It is better to memorize the correct spelling of English words rather than relying on phonetics to spell correctly.

Frequently Misspelled Words

The following is a list of words that are frequently misspelled. Study the spelling of each word by having a friend or teacher drill you on the words. Then mark down the words that you misspelled and study those select ones again. (The words appear in their most popular spellings.)

a lot	accomplish	acquire	advice
ability	accumulation	across	advisable
absence	accuse	address	advise
absent	accustomed	addressed	advisor
abundance	ache	adequate	aerial
accept	achieve	advantage	affect
acceptable	achievement	advantageous	affectionate
accident	acknowledge	adventure	again
accommodate	acquaintance	advertise	against
accompanied	acquainted	advertisement	aggravate

aggressive	artificial	breadth	comedy
agree	ascend	breath	comfortable
aisle	assistance	breathe	commitment
all right	assistant	brilliant	committed
almost	associate	building	committee
already	association	bulletin	communicate
although	athletes	bureau	company
altogether	attempt	burial	comparative
always	attendance	buried	compel
amateur	attention	bury	competent
American	audience	bushes	competition
among	August	business	compliment
amount	author	cafeteria	conceal
analysis	automobile	calculator	conceit
analyze	autumn	calendar	conceivable
angel	auxiliary	campaign	conceive
angle	available	capital	concentration
annual	avenue	capitol	conception
another	awful	captain	condition
answer	awkward	career	conference
antiseptic	bachelor	careful	confident
anxious	balance	careless	congratulate
apologize	balloon	carriage	conquer
apology	bargain	carrying	conscience
apparatus	basic	category	conscientious
apparent	basically	ceiling	conscious
appear	beautiful	cemetery	consequence
appearance	beauties	cereal	consequently
appetite	because	certain	considerable
application	become	changeable	consistency
apply	before	characteristic	consistent
appreciate	beginning	charity	continual
appreciation	being	chief	continuous
approach	believe	choose	controlled
appropriate	benefit	chose	controversy
approval	benefited	cigarette	convenience
approve	between	circumstance	convenient
approximate	bicycle	citizen	conversation
argue	board	clothes	corporal
arguing	bored	clothing	corroborate
argument	borrow	coarse	council
arouse	bottle	coffee	counsel
arrange	bottom	collect	counselor
arrangement	boundary	college	courage
article	brake	column	courageous

course	direction	enough	fourteen
courteous	disappear	entrance	fourth
courtesy	disappoint	envelope	frequent
create	disappointment	environment	friend
criticism	disapproval	equipment	frightening
criticize	disapprove	equipped	fundamental
crystal	disastrous	especially	further
curiosity	discipline	essential	gallon
cylinder	discover	evening	garden
daily	discriminate	evident	gardener
daughter	disease	exaggerate	general
daybreak	dissatisfied	exaggeration	genius
death	dissection	examine	government
deceive	dissipate	exceed	governor
December	distance	excellent	grammar
deception	distinction	except	grateful
decide	division	exceptional	great
decision	doctor	exercise	grievance
decisive	dollar	exhausted	grievous
deed	doubt	exhaustion	grocery
definite	dozen	exhilaration	guarantee
delicious	earnest	existence	guess
dependent	easy	exorbitant	guidance
deposit	ecstasy	expense	half
derelict	ecstatic	experience	hammer
descend	education	experiment	handkerchief
descent	effect	explanation	happiness
describe	efficiency	explode	healthy
description	efficient	extreme	heard
desert	eight	facility	heavy
desirable	either	factory	height
despair	eligibility	familiar	heroes
desperate	eligible	fascinate	heroine
dessert	eliminate	fascinating	hideous
destruction	embarrass	fatigue	himself
determine	embarrassment	February	hoarse
develop	emergency	financial	holiday
development	emphasis	financier	hopeful
device	emphasize	flourish	hopeless
dictator	enclosure	forcibly	hospital
died	encouraging	forehead	humorous
difference	endeavor	foreign	hurried
different	engineer	formal	hurrying
dilemma	English	former	ignorance
dinner	enormous	fortunate	imaginary

imbecile	knowledge	misspelled	original
imitation	labor	mistake	oscillate
immediately	laboratory	momentous	ought
immigrant	laid	monkey	ounce
incidental	language	monotonous	outside
increase	later	moral	overcoat
independence	latter	morale	paid
independent	laugh	mortgage	pamphlet
indispensable	leisure	mountain	panicky
inevitable	length	mournful	parallel
influence	lesson	muscle	parallelism
influential	library	mysterious	particular
initiate	license	mystery	partner
innocence	light	narrative	pastime
inoculate	lightning	natural	patience
inquiry	likelihood	necessary	peace
insistent	likely	needle	peaceable
instead	literal	negligence	pear
instinct	literature	neighbor	peculiar
integrity	livelihood	neither	pencil
intellectual	loaf	newspaper	people
intelligence	loneliness	newsstand	perceive
intercede	loose	niece	perception
interest	lose	noticeable	perfect
interfere	losing	o'clock	perform
interference	loyal	obedient	performance
interpreted	loyalty	obstacle	perhaps
interrupt	magazine	occasion	period
invitation	maintenance	occasional	permanence
irrelevant	maneuver	occur	permanent
irresistible	marriage	occurred	perpendicular
irritable	married	occurrence	perseverance
island	marry	ocean	persevere
its	match	offer	persistent
it's	material	often	personal
itself	mathematics	omission	personality
January	measure	omit	personnel
jealous	medicine	once	persuade
journal	million	operate	persuasion
judgment	miniature	opinion	pertain
kindergarten	minimum	opportune	picture
kitchen	miracle	opportunity	piece
knew	miscellaneous	optimist	plain
knock	mischief	optimistic	playwright
know	mischievous	origin	pleasant

please	pronounce	rhythmical	specimen
pleasure	pronunciation	ridiculous	speech
pocket	propeller	right	stationary
poison	prophet	role	stationery
policeman	prospect	roll	statue
political	psychology	roommate	stockings
population	pursue	sandwich	stomach
portrayal	pursuit	Saturday	straight
positive	quality	scarcely	strength
possess	quantity	scene	strenuous
possession	quarreling	schedule	stretch
possessive	quart	science	striking
possible	quarter	scientific	studying
post office	quiet	scissors	substantial
potatoes	quite	season	succeed
practical	raise	secretary	successful
prairie	realistic	seize	sudden
precede	realize	seminar	superintendent
preceding	reason	sense	suppress
precise	rebellion	separate	surely
predictable	recede	service	surprise
prefer	receipt	several	suspense
preference	receive	severely	sweat
preferential	recipe	shepherd	sweet
preferred	recognize	sheriff	swimming
prejudice	recommend	shining	syllable
preparation	recuperate	shoulder	symmetrical
prepare	referred	shriek	sympathy
prescription	rehearsal	siege	synonym
presence	reign	sight	technical
president	relevant	signal	telegram
prevalent	relieve	significance	telephone
primitive	remedy	significant	temperament
principal	renovate	similar	temperature
principle	repeat	similarity	tenant
privilege	repetition	sincerely	tendency
probably	representative	site	tenement
procedure	requirements	soldier	therefore
proceed	resemblance	solemn	thorough
produce	resistance	sophomore	through
professional	resource	soul	title
professor	respectability	source	together
profitable	responsibility	souvenir	tomorrow
prominent	restaurant	special	tongue
promise	rhythm	specified	toward

tragedy	unnecessary	vicious	weigh
transferred	unusual	view	weird
treasury	useful	village	whether
tremendous	usual	villain	which
tries	vacuum	visitor	while
trophy	valley	voice	whole
truly	valuable	volume	wholly
twelfth	variety	waist	whose
twelve	vegetable	weak	wonderful
tyranny	vein	wear	wretched
undoubtedly	vengeance	weather	
United States	versatile	Wednesday	
university	vicinity	week	

Drill: Spelling

> **DIRECTIONS:** Identify the misspelled word in each set.

1. **(A)** probly
   (B) accommodate
   (C) acquaintance
   (D) among

2. **(A)** auxiliary
   (B) atheletic
   (C) beginning
   (D) awkward

3. **(A)** environment
   (B) existence
   (C) Febuary
   (D) daybreak

4. **(A)** ocassion
   (B) occurrence
   (C) omitted
   (D) fundamental

5. **(A)** perspiration
   (B) referring
   (C) priviledge
   (D) kindergarten

DIRECTIONS: Choose the correct option.

6. <u>Preceding</u> the <u>business</u> session, lunch will be served in a <u>separate</u> room.
   - **(A)** preceeding . . . business . . . seperate
   - **(B)** proceeding . . . bussiness . . . seperate
   - **(C)** proceeding . . . business . . . seperite
   - **(D)** No change is necessary.

7. Monte <u>inadvertently</u> left <u>several</u> of his <u>libary</u> books in the cafeteria.
   - **(A)** inadverdently . . . serveral . . . libery
   - **(B)** inadvertently . . . several . . . library
   - **(C)** inadvertentely . . . several . . . librery
   - **(D)** No change is necessary.

8. Sam wished he had more <u>liesure</u> time so he could <u>persue</u> his favorite hobbies.
   - **(A)** leisure . . . pursue
   - **(B)** Liesure . . . pursue
   - **(C)** leisure . . . persue
   - **(D)** No change is necessary.

9. One of my <u>favrite charecters</u> in <u>litrature</u> is Bilbo from *The Hobbit*.
   - **(A)** favrite . . . characters . . . literature
   - **(B)** favorite . . . characters . . . literature
   - **(C)** favourite . . . characters . . . literature
   - **(D)** No change is necessary.

10. Even <u>tho</u> Joe was badly hurt in the <u>accidant</u>, the company said they were not <u>lible</u> for damages.
   - **(A)** though . . . accidant . . . libel
   - **(B)** though . . . accident . . . liable
   - **(C)** though . . . acident . . . liable
   - **(D)** No change is necessary.

Language Skills Review— Answer Key

Drill: Sentence structure skills

1. (C)	3. (B)	5. (A)	7. (B)	9. (B)
2. (B)	4. (B)	6. (A)	8. (C)	10. (B)

Drill: Verbs

1. (C)	3. (D)	5. (A)	7. (A)	9. (A)
2. (D)	4. (A)	6. (B)	8. (C)	10. (D)

Drill: Pronouns

1. (A)	3. (A)	5. (D)	7. (B)	9. (A)
2. (C)	4. (A)	6. (A)	8. (B)	10. (C)

Drill: Adjectives and adverbs

1. (C)	3. (D)	5. (A)	7. (A)	9. (B)
2. (A)	4. (C)	6. (C)	8. (C)	10. (C)

Drill: Punctuation

1. (D)	3. (A)	5. (A)	7. (A)	9. (B)
2. (A)	4. (C)	6. (D)	8. (A)	10. (D)

Drill: Capitalization

1. (D)	3. (C)	5. (C)	7. (B)	9. (B)
2. (B)	4. (A)	6. (D)	8. (D)	10. (A)

Drill: Spelling

1. (A)	3. (C)	5. (C)	7. (B)	9. (B)
2. (B)	4. (A)	6. (D)	8. (A)	10. (B)

Detailed Explanations of Answers

Drill: Sentence structure skills

1. (C)   Choice **(C)** is correct. Each response contains items in a series. In choices **(A)**, **(B)**, and **(D)** the word group after the conjunction is not an adjective like the first words in the series. Choice **(C)** contains three adjectives.

2. (B)   Choice **(B)** is correct. Choices **(A)** and **(C)** combine conjunctions incorrectly. Choice **(D)** incorrectly uses the adverb *not*.

3. (B)   Choice **(B)** is correct. Choices **(A)** and **(C)** appear to be parallel because the conjunction *and* connects two word groups that both begin with *because*, but the structure on each side of the conjunction is very different. Choice **(D)** has the same structural problem as both **(A)** and **(C)** and it uses the conjunction *that* unnecessarily. *Because he kept his campaign promises* is a clause; *because of his refusal to accept political favors* is a prepositional phrase. Choice **(B)** connects two dependent clauses.

4. (B)   Choice **(B)** is correct. Choices **(A)**, **(C)**, and **(D)** contain the elliptical clause *While . . . taking a shower*. It appears that the missing subject in the elliptical clause is the same as that in the independent clause—the *doorbell* in choice **(A)** and *someone* in choice **(C)**, neither of which is a logical subject for the verbal *taking a shower*. Choice **(B)** removes the elliptical clause and provides the logical subject.

5. (A)   Choice **(A)** is correct. Who swung the bat? Choices **(B)**, **(C)**, and **(D)** imply that it is the runner who swung the bat. Only choice **(A)** makes it clear that as *he* swung the bat, someone else (the *runner*) stole second base.

6. (A)   Choice **(A)** is correct. The punctuation in the original sentence and in choice **(B)** creates a fragment. *Cotton being the state's principal crop* is not an independent thought because it lacks a complete verb—*being* is not a complete verb.

7. (B)   Choice **(B)** is correct. The punctuation in the original sentence and in choice **(A)** creates a fragment. Both the semicolon and the period should be used to separate two independent clauses. The word group *one that I have never seen before* does not express a complete thought and therefore is not an independent clause.

8. (C)   Choice **(C)** is correct. The dependent clause *because repairs were being made* in choices **(B)** and **(C)** is punctuated as if it were a sentence. The result is a fragment.

9. **(B)** Choice **(B)** is correct. Choices **(A)** and **(C)** do not separate the complete thoughts in the independent clauses with the correct punctuation.

10. **(B)** Choice **(B)** is correct. Choices **(A)** and **(C)** do not separate the independent clauses with the correct punctuation.

Drill: Verbs

1. **(C)** Choice **(C)** is correct. The past participle form of each verb is required because of the auxiliaries (helping verbs) *had been* (concerned) and *would have* (gone).

2. **(D)** Choice **(D)** is correct. The forms of the irregular verb meaning *to rest* are *lie (rest), lies (rests), lay (rested),* and *has lain (has rested).* The forms of the verb meaning *to put* are *lay (put), lays (puts), laying (putting), laid (put),* and *have laid (have put).*

3. **(D)** Choice **(D)** is correct. The present tense is used for universal truths and the past tense is used for historical truths.

4. **(A)** Choice **(A)** is correct. The present tense is used for customary happenings. Choice **(B)**, *had begun,* is not a standard verb form. Choice **(C)**, *was beginning,* indicates that 10:30 a.m. is not the regular class time.

5. **(A)** Choice **(A)** is correct. The past tense is used for historical statements, and the present tense is used for statements about works of art.

6. **(B)** Choice **(B)** is correct. The subject of the sentence is the plural noun *sales,* not the singular noun *Christmas,* which is the object of the prepositional phrase.

7. **(A)** Choice **(A)** is correct. The subject *specialty* is singular.

8. **(C)** Choice **(C)** is correct. Subjects preceded by *every* are considered singular and therefore require a singular verb form.

9. **(A)** Choice **(A)** is correct. The subject of the sentence is the gerund *hiding,* not the object of the gerund phrase *mistakes. Hiding* is singular; therefore, the singular verb form *does* should be used.

10. **(D)** Choice **(D)** is correct. Though the form of the subject *Board of Regents* is plural, it is singular in meaning.

Drill: Pronouns

1. **(A)** Choice **(A)** is correct. Do not use the reflexive pronoun *myself* as a substitute for I.

2. **(C)** Choice **(C)** is correct. In the clause *whoever consumes them, whoever* is the subject. *Whomever* is the objective case pronoun and should be used only as the object of a sentence, never as the subject.

3. **(A)** Choice **(A)** is correct. Use the nominative case pronoun *who* as the subject complement after the verb *is.*

4. **(A)** Choice **(A)** is correct. In this sentence use the nominative case/subject pronouns *she who* as the subject complement after the *be* verb *was*.

5. **(D)** Choice **(D)** is correct. *Student* is an indefinite, genderless noun that requires a singular personal pronoun. While *his* is a singular personal pronoun, a genderless noun includes both the masculine and feminine forms and requires *his or her* as the singular personal pronoun.

6. **(A)** Choice **(A)** is correct. The antecedent *company* is singular, requiring the singular pronoun *it*, not the plural *they*.

7. **(B)** Choice **(B)** is correct. Choice **(A)** contains a person shift: *Your* is a second person pronoun, and *his* and *her* are third person pronouns. The original sentence uses the third person plural pronoun *their* to refer to the singular antecedent *every car owner*. Choice **(B)** correctly provides the masculine and feminine forms *his or her* required by the indefinite, genderless *every car owner*.

8. **(B)** Choice **(B)** is correct. The implied antecedent is *teaching*. Choices **(A)** and **(C)** each contain a pronoun with no antecedent. Neither *it* nor *this* are suitable substitutions for *teacher*.

9. **(A)** Choice **(A)** is correct. The pronoun *they* in the original sentence has no conspicuous antecedent. Since the doer of the action is obviously unknown (and therefore genderless), choice **(B)**, *he*, is not the correct choice.

10. **(C)** Choice **(C)** is correct. The original sentence is ambiguous: the pronoun *she* has two possible antecedents; we don't know whether it is Margaret or her sister who is away at college.

Drill: Adjectives and adverbs

1. **(C)** Choice **(C)** is correct. *Bad* is an adjective; *badly* is an adverb. *Real* is an adjective meaning *genuine* (*a real problem*, *real leather*). To qualify an adverb of degree to express how bad, how excited, how boring, etc., choose *very*.

2. **(A)** Choice **(A)** is correct. Use an adverb as a qualifier for an adjective. *How simple? Relatively simple.*

3. **(D)** Choice **(D)** is correct. *Good* is an adjective; *well* is both an adjective and an adverb. As an adjective, *well* refers to health; it means "not ill."

4. **(C)** Choice **(C)** is correct. All the other choices use *good* incorrectly as an adverb. *Shake* is an action verb that requires an adverb, not an adjective.

5. **(A)** Choice **(A)** is correct. The action verbs *speaks*, *writes*, *observe*, and *think* each require adverbs as modifiers.

6. **(C)** Choice **(C)** is correct. The comparisons in choices **(A)**, **(B)**, and **(D)** are illogical: these sentences suggest that Los Angeles is not in California because it *is larger than any city in California*.

7. (A) Choice **(A)** is correct. Do not omit the second *as* of the correlative pair *as . . . as* when making a point of equal or superior comparison, as in choice **(B)**. Choice **(C)** omits *than* from "if not more interesting [than]." Choice **(D)** incorrectly uses *as* instead of *than*.

8. (C) Choice **(C)** is correct. Choice **(A)** illogically compares *baseball team* to a *university*, and choices **(B)** and **(D)** illogically compare *baseball team* to *other universities*. Choice **(C)** logically compares the baseball team here to the one at any other university, as implied by the possessive ending on university—*university's*.

9. (B) Choice **(B)** is correct. Choices **(A)**, **(C)**, and **(D)** are ambiguous; because these sentences are too obscure, the reader does not know where to place the missing information.

10. (C) Choice **(C)** is correct. Choice **(A)** is redundant; there is no need to use *most* with *stingiest*. Choice **(B)** incorrectly combines the superlative word *most* with the comparative form *stingier*. Choice **(D)** incorrectly combines the comparative word *more* with the superlative form *stingiest*.

Drill: Punctuation

1. (D) Choice **(D)** is correct. Nonrestrictive clauses, like other nonrestrictive elements, should be set off from the rest of the sentence with commas.

2. (A) Choice **(A)** is correct. Use a comma to separate a nonrestrictive appositive from the word it modifies. "An Oklahoma family" is a nonrestrictive appositive.

3. (A) Choice **(A)** is correct. Do not use unnecessary commas to separate a subject and verb from their complement. Both choices **(B)** and **(C)** use extra punctuation.

4. (C) Choice **(C)** is correct. Do not separate two items in a compound with commas. The original sentence incorrectly separates "car or plane." Choice **(A)** omits the comma after the introductory clause.

5. (A) Choice **(A)** is correct. Use a semicolon to separate two independent clauses/sentences that are not joined by a coordinating conjunction, especially when the ideas in the sentences are interrelated.

6. (D) Choice **(D)** is correct. Use a semicolon to separate two sentences not joined by a coordinating conjunction.

7. (A) Choice **(A)** is correct. Use a semicolon to separate two sentences joined by a conjunctive adverb.

8. (A) Choice **(A)** is correct. Do not use a colon after a verb or a preposition. Remember that a complete sentence must precede a colon.

9. (B) Choice **(B)** is correct. Do not use a colon after a preposition, and do not use a colon to separate a preposition from its objects.

10. (D) Choice **(D)** is correct. Use a colon preceding a list that is introduced by words such as *the following* and *as follows*.

Drill: Capitalization

1. (D) Choice **(D)** is correct. *North America*, like other proper names, is capitalized. *North, south, east,* and *west* are only capitalized when they refer to geographic regions (*the Southwest, Eastern Europe)*; as compass directions, they are not capitalized.

2. (B) Choice **(B)** is correct. Although persons' names are capitalized, a person's title is not (*coach*, not *Coach* since it stands alone). Capitalize the complete name of a team, school, river, etc. (as in Dallas Cowboys). *The* is not part of the official title. Therefore, it is never capitalized when it appears in text.

3. (C) Choice **(C)** is correct. Capitalize all geographic units, and capitalize *earth* only when it is mentioned with other planets. *Equator* is not capitalized.

4. (A) Choice **(A)** is correct. Capitalize the first and last words in a title and all other words in a title except articles, prepositions with fewer than five letters, and conjunctions.

5. (C) Choice **(C)** is correct. Capitalize proper adjectives (proper nouns used as adjectives): *Greek* goddess, *Roman* mythology.

6. (D) Choice **(D)** is correct. Capitalize all religious groups, books, and names referring to religious deities.

7. (B) Choice **(B)** is correct. Do not capitalize courses unless they are languages (English) or course titles followed by a number (Algebra I).

8. (D) Choice **(D)** is correct. Do not capitalize seasons unless they accompany the name of an event such as *Spring Break*. Do not capitalize types of degrees (*bachelor's degrees*); capitalize only the name of the degree (*Bachelor of Arts degree*).

9. (B) Choice **(B)** is correct. As a landmark, *Berlin Wall* is capitalized; however, do not capitalize systems of government or individual adherents to a philosophy, such as *communism*.

10. (A) Choice **(A)** is correct. The names of planets, as well as the complete names of newspapers and other periodicals, are capitalized.

Drill: Spelling

1. (A) The correct spelling of choice **(A)** is *probably*.

2. (B) The correct spelling is *athletic*.

3. (C) Choice **(C)** should be spelled *February*.

4. (A) The correct spelling of this word is *occasion*.

5. (C) Choice **(C)** should be spelled *privilege*.

6. (D) Choice **(D)** is the best response. *Business* has only three *-s's*. Separate has an *-e* at the beginning and the end, not in the middle.

7. (B) Choice **(B)** is the best response. *Library* has two *r's*.

8. **(A)** Choice **(A)** is the best response. *Leisure* is one of the few English words that does not follow the *i* before *e* except after *c* rule. *Pursue* has two *u's* and only one *e*.

9. **(B)** Choice **(B)** is the best response. *Favorite*, *characters*, and *literature* are commonly mispronounced, and when someone who mispronounces them tries to spell them phonetically, he or she often misspells them.

10. **(B)** Choice **(B)** is the best response. Advertisements often misspell words to catch the consumer's eye (*lite* for light, *tho* for though, etc.), and these misspellings are becoming more common in student writing. *Accident* and *liable* are examples of words that are not pronounced the way they are spelled.

HSPT/COOP/TACHS

CHAPTER 4
READING REVIEW

CHAPTER **4**

Reading Review

I. **Reading Comprehension**
II. **Vocabulary**

The following review will give you some techniques and strategies that will increase your reading comprehension skills and help you get better scores on the *HSPT: Subtest 3*, the *COOP: Test 5*, or the TACHS: Practice Test 1.

All of these tests require a strong understanding of reading skills. You will improve your performance on the *Reading* subtest of the HSPT or *Reading Comprehension* COOP and TACHS tests if you know and prepare for three things.

- How do you read effectively?
- What are the six basic questions commonly asked?
- Do you have a good understanding of the English vocabulary?

I. Reading Comprehension

Effective Reading Tips

While the following proven strategies and techniques will improve your overall comprehension in any reading situation, they are particularly effective in helping you find the type of information needed to answer the reading questions on the HSPT, COOP, and TACHS.

Let's look at each and decide how and why it works.

Step 1: Skim the passage and the questions

Skimming is a quick technique that takes only seconds. It gives a general idea of the passage. You can understand a passage better if you know the general subject it will discuss before you read it. You can also answer questions with more success if you have a basic idea of what will be asked before you read. When you skim the questions, you read ONLY the questions and not the answer choices. You want to know the general information they will ask for. You don't need to remember them exactly; that will come later. Knowing the general subject and the general questions gives you a head start.

Skimming is a simple way to find the important ideas that will be discussed. It can also help you to identify the major idea of the passage. There are two different ways to skim a passage, depending on its structure. The reading passages have two basic structures: one long paragraph or two or more shorter paragraphs.

If the passage is constructed in *one long paragraph*, read

the first two sentences and the last sentence of the paragraph.

then skim the questions.

If the passage is constructed of *two or more paragraphs*, read

the first sentence of each paragraph.

then skim the questions.

Step 2: Read the passage

This is simple. This is where the real comprehension occurs. There are a number of techniques to improve both comprehension and test scores.

1. **Pace Yourself.** There are usually 4 to 6 passages with questions in the reading portion of the test. Try to spend no more than a few minutes to complete each passage and its questions. And remember the first passage may be easier than the second and so on. Extra time will be needed for the later passages.

2. **Read Ideas, Not Just Words.** Read sentences. Read ideas. Try to hear your own voice inside your head speaking naturally. If you don't understand a sentence, read it again. Try varying the phrasing of the sentence. Ask yourself "Who or what is this sentence about?" to find the subject. Look for action words and results. Ask yourself "What is this about?" to find main ideas. "How do I know?" to find supporting ideas. Try to see how they are organized.

3. **Use Context Clues to Understand Difficult Words.** Many times when you read a passage, you will find words whose meanings are not clear. Luckily, the sentence that the word is in and the other sentences in the passage will often provide context clues—information that helps to explain what that word means. There are many types of context clues and with them you can increase your understanding of particular words and thereby increase your general understanding of the passage.

NOTE: A full discussion of context clues is given in the Vocabulary section.

Step 3: Scan to answer questions

Once you have completed steps 1 and 2, you are ready to deal with the questions.

Scanning is a quick way of finding specific words in a passage. Those specific words mark the location in the passage where you can find the information you need to answer a question. Scanning is not reading! When you scan, your eyes move very quickly through the sentences and paragraphs. You have only one purpose: find the key word. Once you have found the key word, begin to read for the information you need to answer the question. Let's look at a passage:

There are many important resort areas in the state of New Jersey. They include popular ski areas in the northern part of the state and the river and forest wilderness of the Pinelands in the central region, but both of these areas draw a relatively small number of tourists compared to the coastal resorts which attract millions each year to their beaches for sand, sea, and sun. Probably the best known of these resorts are Long Beach Island, which provides activity for the whole family; Atlantic City, whose casinos provide the excitement of gambling and nightlife; and Cape May, a small town which has carefully preserved its rich history and architecture, and which is today home to some of the finest restaurants in the country.

Key words in the questions [we've put them in boldface] will indicate where to look for the answers!

1. The **Pinelands** is famous for what physical features?
2. A **family man** would probably choose which beach resort?
3. A **gourmet** would probably choose which beach resort?

Scan quickly through the passage to find where the key words are located. The information needed to answer each question is nearby. Repeat the key word in your mind as you scan.

Let's look at the passage again. The key words are in boldface and the essential information is <u>underlined</u>.

There are many important resort areas in the state of New Jersey. They include popular ski areas in the northern part of the state and the <u>river and forest wilderness</u> of the **Pinelands** in the central region, but both of these areas draw a relatively small number of tourists compared to the coastal resorts which attract millions each year to their beaches for sand, sea, and sun. Probably the best known of these resorts are <u>Long Beach Island</u>, which provides activity for **the whole family**; Atlantic City, whose casinos provide the excitement of gambling and nightlife; and <u>Cape May</u>, a small town which has carefully preserved its rich history and architecture, and which is today home to some of the finest **restaurants** in the country.

QUESTION #1: Once we find the key word "Pinelands," we can quickly find the answer. "Physical features?"

ANSWER: "river and forest wilderness"

QUESTION #2: A "family man" wants a resort which provides activities for the "whole family."
ANSWER: "Long Beach Island"

QUESTION #3: The first two questions were fairly easy to answer, but the last question required you to know what a "gourmet" is. The key word "gourmet" is never mentioned in the passage, but if you know that the word means "a person who is an expert in fine food and dining," then scanning still provides the answer. We see "the finest restaurants" and we know these would interest a gourmet.

ANSWER: "Cape May . . . home to some of the finest restaurants"

These three basic techniques will help you to read with greater speed and comprehension, and they will provide you with effective ways to answer the questions which the reading portion of the HSPT, COOP, and TACHS will ask. But to be fully prepared for this section of the test, you need to understand and be familiar with the types of questions you will be asked so that you can practice our reading techniques on them.

Basic Questions

Let's look at six basic questions asked on the test.

Basic question 1

What is the main idea of the passage?

Good writing is carefully organized around an important idea. This idea controls all of the other ideas within the passage. Sometimes this main idea is clearly stated in one or two sentences in the passage BUT not always. Sometimes it is not directly mentioned in the passage at all.

Let's look at an example:

Marge sure knows how to have a party. I got there at nine o'clock and the place was already jumping. People were laughing and shouting as waiters ran back and forth from the kitchen with trays loaded down with lobster and caviar. A mariachi band was performing on the patio and a long line of people was doing the "conga." I didn't see who was the first person to jump into the pool, but before long everyone at the party had joined in. People tell me it was around midnight when the circus performers showed up, but I really couldn't tell you for sure.

One main idea controls all of the facts, examples, and discussion in this passage:

Marge's party was a lot of fun.

In this passage the first sentence ("Marge sure knows how to have a party.") gives us a very clear indication of what that main idea is, but it is not exactly the main idea. Marge's general ability to plan and give parties is not the central idea. The main idea of a passage will *sometimes* be stated in the first or second sentence of the passage.

Many times the main idea is not directly stated in the passage. But even without that first sentence the main idea is clear. Look at the examples presented:

. . . the place was jumping . . . people laughing and shouting . . . trays loaded with lobster and caviar . . . a mariachi band . . . people dancing . . . people jumping into the pool . . . and circus performers too.

All of these examples point to only one central idea: The party was fun.

Let's look at another example:

Life in Colorado was changed overnight by the Gold Rush of 1859. Miners needed supplies and, at first, depended upon the foodstuffs imported from the Midwest. Flour cost as much as $50 a barrel, but hungry miners were willing to pay these inflated prices. Further, because many of these Fifty-niners had farming backgrounds, they turned to agriculture after they were unable to survive in the mines. These people found the land fertile and began to farm the land. They did not plant crops for survival but rather to sell. At this point agriculture in Colorado changed from subsistence to commercial farming.

The first sentence of this paragraph gives us important information about the central idea, but it is not the central idea. The first sentence is too general. Read the passage again and try to decide what idea controls the discussion.

Yes, "Life in Colorado was changed overnight by the gold rush," but the passage does not discuss all the ways "life" was changed. The passage discusses only one aspect of life in Colorado which changed: agriculture. The controlling idea is

Farming in Colorado was changed suddenly by the gold rush.

Let's look at the **important supporting ideas.**

Life in Colorado was changed overnight by the Gold Rush of 1859. Miners needed supplies and, at first, **depended upon the foodstuffs** imported from the Midwest. **Flour cost** as much as $50 a barrel, but **hungry miners were willing to pay** these inflated prices. Further, because many of **these Fifty-niners had farming backgrounds**, they **turned to agriculture** after they were unable to survive in the mines. These people found the **land fertile** and **began to farm** the land. They did not **plant crops** for survival but rather to sell. At this point **agriculture in Colorado changed** from subsistence to **commercial farming**.
All of these supporting ideas point in only one direction.

NOT: Life in Colorado
NOT: The Gold Rush
NOT: Farming in Colorado
BUT: . . . **How farming was changed by the Gold Rush in Colorado**

Remember: The first and last sentences of each paragraph are very important. They usually point towards the main idea.

Once we know what the main idea is, we will be able to answer many questions. The HSPT, COOP, TACHS reading comprehension section uses information connected to the main idea to ask many different types of questions.

Examples:
  1. What would be a good title for this passage?
    (A) Farming in Colorado
    (B) The Gold Rush of '59
    (C) The Real Gold Grew Out of the Ground
    (D) Go West, Young Man

All of these ideas are connected to the passage, but only one is a good title. To choose the best answer we must know that the main idea is neither farming nor the Gold Rush but the relationship between the two. The best title is (C) because it mentions both.

  2. What is the author's main purpose?
    (A) To discuss Colorado's interesting history
    (B) To show that farming is sometimes better than mining
    (C) To show that the Gold Rush was an exciting time to be alive
    (D) To show the effects of the Gold Rush upon agriculture in Colorado

All of these ideas were in the passage, but only one of them was the main purpose. The author's main purpose is always to clearly express and to support his main idea. The main purpose of this passage is (D).

Related Questions:
    What is the subject of the passage?
    What is the topic of the passage?
    What is the emphasis of the passage?
    What is the controlling idea?

The answer to all of these questions can be found in the main idea.

Basic question 2

What specific facts were stated in the passage?

Let's look at an example:

Coral reef communities are normally classified in two ways: live bottom or patch reef. The live bottom community, also known as hardground, is generally found closest to shore in tidal passes, under bridges, and short distances seaward of the intertidal zone. It usually occupies fossil reef formations, limestone, and other rocky substrates. Animal and plant life are not consistent from reef to reef but are usually visually dominated by octocorals, algae, and sponges.

This passage appears to be quite difficult. The reason it appears so difficult is because of the technical words which it uses. It is not necessary to know every word in a passage in order to understand it.

Read the passage again and see if you can answer these questions.

1. What is the general subject of the discussion?
2. How many types of reef communities are there?
3. Which type of reef community is discussed?
4. Where is this type of reef found?
5. What does it occupy?
6. What plants and animals dominate?

To read with understanding it is necessary to understand how a basic sentence in written English works.

There is a SUBJECT and there is a VERB.

The SUBJECT is		The VERB is	
	a person		an action
	a place		a state of being
	a thing		
	an idea		

To put it simply: SOMEONE OR SOMETHING **DOES** SOMETHING!

or

SOMEONE OR SOMETHING **IS** SOMETHING!

"Bob eats hamburgers."

Subject   BOB
Verb   EATS

"Bob is a policeman."

Subject   BOB
Verb   IS

Every sentence contains at least one idea. To understand that idea, you must know what the subject is and what the subject does.

Let's look at the passage again. The subjects will be shown in **boldface** and the verbs will be <u>underlined</u>.

Coral reef communities <u>are</u> normally <u>classified</u> in two ways: live bottom or patch reef. The **live bottom community,** also known as hardground, <u>is</u> generally <u>found</u> closest to shore in tidal passes, under bridges, and short distances seaward of the intertidal zone. **It**

usually <u>occupies</u> fossil reef formations, limestone, and other rocky substrates. **Animal and plant life** <u>are</u> not consistent from reef to reef, but <u>are</u> usually visually <u>dominated</u> by octocorals, algae, and sponges.

Understanding this passage is much easier now even with the technical vocabulary. Try answering these questions:

1. How are reef communities classified?
2. Where is the live bottom community found?
3. What does it usually occupy?
4. What types of plants and animals visually dominate the reefs?

If you understand the subject and the verb of each sentence, the information that follows is easier to understand even when the vocabulary is very difficult.

Let's look at the passage again. This time look for the important information which follows the verbs. The verbs will be <u>underlined</u> and the factual information will be in **boldface**.

Coral reef communities <u>are</u> normally <u>classified</u> in two ways: **live bottom or patch reef.** The live bottom community, also known as hardground, <u>is</u> generally <u>found</u> closest to shore **in tidal passes, under bridges, and short distances seaward of the intertidal zone.** It usually <u>occupies</u> **fossil reef formations, limestone, and other rocky substrates.** Animal and plant life <u>are</u> **not consistent** from reef to reef, but <u>are</u> usually visually <u>dominated</u> by **octocorals, algae, and sponges.**

1. How are reef communities classified?
  Live bottom or patch reef
2. Where is the live bottom community found?
  In tidal passes, under bridges, and seaward of the intertidal zone
3. What does it usually occupy?
  Fossil reef formations, limestone, and rocky substrates
4. What types of plants and animals visually dominate the reefs?
  Octocorals, algae, and sponges

By understanding the structure and organization of a sentence, you can understand the idea it expresses even when the meanings of many words in that sentence are unclear.

Be Careful of Reverse Questions!

Many times the questions will ask not only what was discussed but also **what wasn't discussed.** Let's look at an example:

Chicago, the windy city, as it is sometimes called, has always possessed its own unique style. Its citizens are justly proud of its long, glorious, and slightly notorious history. Its reputation, deservedly or not, is known throughout the world. Mention Al Capone, prohibition, or a mobster with a machine gun and only one city comes to mind.

A reverse question might ask:

According to the passage, Chicago's history has **NOT** been
(A) developed over many years.
(B) filled with glory.
(C) somewhat notorious.
(D) carefully recorded.

Our key word is "history." When we scan quickly for the word, we see that it is described as "long, glorious, and slightly notorious." The choices we are given have been slightly changed, but we can see **(A)**, **(B)**, and **(C)** are used in the passage to describe Chicago's history. **(D)** "Carefully recorded" has NOT been mentioned. It is the correct choice.

Here's another example:

According to the passage, Chicago quickly comes to mind to people all over the world EXCEPT when you mention

(A) windy city. **(B)** Al Capone.
(C) prohibition. **(D)** mobsters.

The key words in this question are "all over the world." Three examples are mentioned after this phrase. They are **(B)**, **(C)**, and **(D)**. **(A)** "windy city" is mentioned at the beginning of the passage, but it is not a specific example which causes people throughout the world to think of Chicago. **(A)** is correct.

Basic question 3
What new ideas can be inferred from the passage?
In question 2 we were asked to find facts, data, and other types of information which were stated in the passage. But in basic question 3 we have to take the next step. We have to develop new ideas which are based upon the facts that we have read. These new ideas are called inferences.

Let's look at an example:

FACT: Oliver Twist was having his ninth birthday.
FACT: He was pale and thin.

You know this information is correct.

When you make an inference, you have to study the facts carefully and decide what new idea can be formed.

From the facts that you know, decide which inference concerning Oliver Twist's birthday would be most reasonable.

INFERENCE 1: Oliver has not eaten properly up to his ninth birthday.
INFERENCE 2: Oliver probably has not eaten properly up to his ninth birthday.
INFERENCE 3: As Oliver has grown, he has become thin.

The only difference between 1 and 2 is the word "probably." If you chose 2, then you are correct. What's wrong with 1? Well. . . . do you know for sure that the reason Oliver was thin was that he had not eaten? NO! The problem with one is that it leaves no room for questions or possibilities, and there are both.

Inference 2 is a good inference because it uses the correct word "probably" to describe the relationship between the facts.

Inference 3, "As Oliver has grown, he has become thin," was a trick! It is not really an inference. Inference 3 does not give you any new information. It only gives you the facts that you already knew. An inference must give new information.

Now read the whole story.

In this excerpt from Dickens' *Oliver Twist*, we read the early account of Oliver's birth and the beginning of his life.

It cannot be expected that this system of farming would produce any very extraordinary or luxuriant crop. Oliver Twist's ninth birthday found him a pale thin child, somewhat diminutive in stature, and decidedly small in circumference. But nature or inheritance had implanted a good sturdy spirit in Oliver's breast. It had plenty of room to expand, thanks to the spare diet of the establishment; and perhaps to this circumstance may be attributed his having any ninth birthday at all.

When you look at a statement of fact, you can say that it is either true or false. But when you look at an inference, you have to judge it in a different way. You can say that it is:

ALMOST CERTAIN	The world will not end tomorrow.
VERY PROBABLE	It will rain in New York this summer.
PROBABLE	You will lose your car keys someday.
POSSIBLE	You will meet a movie star.
UNLIKELY	You will live to be 90 years old.
VERY UNLIKELY	You will live to be 100 years old.
ALMOST IMPOSSIBLE	You will win the lottery this week.

Let's look at several inferences connected to the passage and decide if they are weak or strong.

INFERENCE:	Oliver's guardians are not concerned with Oliver's well-being.
PROBABLE	WHY? You know from the passage that the "establishment" that he resides in provides him with a "spare diet." And you know that Oliver appears very small in size.
INFERENCE:	The fact that Oliver was able to survive for this long should be credited to the kind of food that he did eat.
UNLIKELY	WHY? The last two sentences explain that while he did have a "spare diet," Oliver was able to develop "a good sturdy spirit." His "spirit" is what enabled him to survive.

DIRECTIONS: Look at the inferences listed below and decide if they are weak or strong. Find clues from the passage to support your ideas.

1. Oliver would be a good person to have with you in a time of emergency.
2. We can be fairly sure that Oliver liked living in the conditions that he had.
3. Oliver will have a very productive life.
4. People were surprised with the way that Oliver looked.
5. Oliver got his outlook on life from his parents.

Let's discuss each inference and the information from the passage which shows it to be weak or strong.

Inferences:

1. PROBABLE: It seems clear to the reader that despite his life's hardship, he has used this misfortune to grow and become more hopeful. Perhaps, one can infer that Oliver was a very resourceful child. It can even be inferred that it was mainly because of this hardship that he got this far in life.

2. POSSIBLE: In this passage, we are given information that could point in two different directions. The opening sentence stresses that nobody can be expected to thrive in a place like this, yet we are told that he does. There is really never any specific reference to Oliver's feelings on the matter. We don't know if he thrives out of anger, spiritual fulfillment, or something else. This inference is possible, but you can't be sure.

3. PROBABLE/VERY PROBABLE: Having made it through life this far with his diet, one could logically surmise he would be productive in whatever he chooses. He will probably be able to accomplish this feat whether he likes the way his life feels or not.

4. UNLIKELY: Immediately, the reader is told that "it cannot be expected that his system of farming would be a luxuriant crop." It also states the effects of this "farming." It says that he was "small in circumference" and "diminutive in stature." It is unlikely that people were surprised by him.

5. POSSIBLE: There is only one small clue to indicate where Oliver gets his outlook from. The passage says that "nature or inheritance" had given him his spirit. We aren't sure if this was given to him by nature or his family because the passage isn't sure either. Therefore, there is no way for us to determine this.

Basic question 4
What might be discussed before or after the passage?
This is a very difficult question for most students to answer. The reason why it is so difficult is that most students never ask themselves this question. Their major problem is understanding the passage, which is difficult enough without thinking about "What might come before?" or "What might come next?" But it's not hard if you know what to look for. The secret to answering this type of question is to recognize the structure of the passage.

The purpose of writing is to express ideas. Many times those ideas are complicated. Good writers know that their ideas have to be carefully organized.

Once the pattern of the organization is understood, it is easy to know what would come before and what would come after. There are many ways to organize these ideas. Let's look at some examples:

Order of importance
PROBLEM: Imagine you have a brother whom you love very much but whom you haven't seen for many years. In the years you have been away, you have become very rich. You are flying home for his birthday party, and you have decided to buy him three presents:

(A) a beautiful watch
(B) a trip to Hawaii
(C) a brand new Mercedes-Benz 540 sport coupe

You want him to enjoy his party and you want him to appreciate each of his presents, but you can't decide which gift to give him first, which second, and which last.

There is only one **effective** way to give him the presents. Decide which present should be given first and so on.

Remember: You want him to appreciate all three gifts.

The gifts must be organized this way:

First the watch

Second the trip

Last the Mercedes

What happens if you give the trip first? Your brother will love it. But how will he feel when he gets the watch next? He will feel let down because the first gift was better than the second. The pattern has to follow from good to better to best. This pattern is called order of importance. In this example it moves from least important to most important.

Process

PROBLEM: Your Aunt Mary went to Florida to see her sister. Uncle Harry, her husband, is having his boss come over for dinner. Unfortunately, Uncle Harry is a terrible cook. He calls you for help. You know a wonderful way to make lasagna. How do you explain it to him so he can prepare it properly? How do we organize the steps?

Making lasagna is a PROCESS. There is only one way to organize a process: STEP BY STEP.

What is done first?

What is done second?

What is done next?

And so on until the process is complete.

General to Specific

PROBLEM: The year is 2345 and you are visiting a faraway planet. You have met a resident of this planet and you have become friends. You want to tell him about your hometown. His only knowledge of earth is its general location in the universe. Where do you begin your discussion?

Begin with the general and move to the specific.

1. Solar system
2. Planet
3. Continent
4. Country
5. State
6. City
7. Street
8. House
9. Room

If the passage is moving from GENERAL TO SPECIFIC, then you can determine what would be discussed before and after the passage.

A passage discussing California would probably have a discussion about the United States coming before it, and the passage would probably be followed by a discussion of cities in California.

Cause and effect

This is another common method of organization. It would follow this pattern:

General Discussion of   *Discussion*   *Discussion*   *Discussion*
Problem or Situation   *of Causes*   *of Effects*   *of Solutions*

If the subject of the passage is the "effects of drug abuse," then a discussion of its causes would have come before and possible solutions would be discussed after the effects.

Compare and contrast

Usually you don't have one without the other. When you **compare**, you examine how two things are similar or the **same**. When you **contrast**, you examine how two things are **different**.

Usual Pattern: *Discussion of*   *then*   *Discussion of*
                  similarities   *differences*

Because there are many different ways to organize information, we have only discussed the most common methods. The other methods all follow a pattern. The pattern will be logical. It will make sense. Listed below are some other common patterns.

Most to Least	Far to Near
Least to Most	Near to Far
Large to Small	Left to Right
Small to Large	Morning to Evening

Basic question 5

What is the author's attitude toward a subject?

The author, like any person, has an opinion about a subject. He or she might consider it to be right or wrong, good or bad, sad or happy, or wise or silly. Very seldom do you have an opinion of something without having some emotional feeling concerning the same subject. The emotional feeling can be strong or weak or anywhere in between.

An author's attitude is this combination: OPINION and EMOTION.

How can you recognize the author's attitude?

There are two types of clues:

1. The selection of specific facts mentioned in the passage.
2. Choice of specific words used in the passage.

Let's look at an example:

Roger and Mary were married for many years. Their children were all grown and had moved out of the house. With the children gone, Mary felt bored and lonely. Mary had been thinking about getting a job for years now, and Roger said that he thought it was a good time to get started. While Roger earned a good living, he believed that Mary's new job would add significantly to the household income. Sitting around the house all day with nothing to do but watch television, Mary began to work on her resume. Roger helped her organize all her employment history. Additionally, Mary began to look on the Internet each day before dinner for ads. While Roger spent long hours at work, he made phone calls around town for Mary every day. Eventually, Mary discovered a job online and accepted it. Now, Roger works less time and the family makes more money. Mary seems energetic and is more content with her new job. Roger half-jokingly takes all the credit for Mary's new-found employment and their renewed happiness. Mary says that it has nothing to do with him. Who should take credit?

MARY'S OPINION: Roger should not get credit.
ROGER'S OPINION: Mary should not get credit.

There are facts to support each opinion, but a writer will select certain facts to show his opinion is strong. Here are some facts. Look at them carefully and decide which opinion they support.

FACTS:

1. Mary was spending time on the Internet each day before dinner.
2. Roger prompted Mary to start looking for a job.
3. Roger helped Mary organize her employment history.
4. Mary discovered the job.
5. Mary had been thinking about getting a job for years.
6. While Roger was at work, he made phone calls for Mary.

These facts don't change but each side in the argument selects only those facts which support its opinion.

MARY'S OPINION: 1, 4, 5   ROGER'S OPINION: 2, 3, 6

Authors have many words to choose from when stating their ideas. Their attitudes toward a subject will determine which words they will select.

DIRECTIONS: Look at the following examples and decide what each author's attitude is concerning the same subject: **SNAKES**.

Peter: "Like a thin ribbon of many colors, it glides softly through the grass and calmly disappears before our eyes."

Paul: "The cold beady eyes of the deadly assassin are watchful. It lurks hidden, ready to strike and devour its prey."

George: "This limbless, scaled reptile has a long, tapering body. One of its many unusual characteristics is that it is known to exist in all types of habitat except for the polar regions."

Who hates snakes?
Who loves snakes?
Who considers them an interesting subject for study?

Read the sentences again and notice the highlighted words.

Peter: "Like a **thin ribbon** of **many colors,** it **glides softly** through the grass and **calmly disappears** before our eyes."

Paul: "The **cold beady eyes** of the **deadly assassin** are watchful. It **lurks hidden,** ready to **strike and devour** its prey."

George: "This **limbless scaled reptile** has a **long tapering body.** One of its many **unusual characteristics** is that it is known to **exist** in all types of **habitat** except for the polar regions."

Each author chose different words to refer to the snake.

Peter:	**thin ribbon**
Paul:	**deadly assassin**
George:	**limbless scaled reptile**

Each author described the snake differently.

Peter:	**many colors . . . glides softly . . . calmly disappears**
Paul:	**cold beady eyes . . . lurks hidden . . . strike and devour**
George:	**long tapering body . . . unusual characteristics . . . exists . . . habitat**

Peter chose words to show that the snake is a beautiful creature with graceful movements. "thin ribbon . . . many colors . . . glides softly . . . calmly disappears"

Attitude: Snakes are wonderful creatures.

Paul chose words to make the snake appear dangerous and evil. "cold beady eyes . . . deadly assassin . . . lurks hidden . . . strike and devour"

Attitude: Snakes are terrible creatures.

George gave scientific facts. The only opinion given is that the snake has "many unusual characteristics" which can indicate that he finds snakes interesting.

Attitude: Snakes are scientifically interesting.

Remember: By examining the author's choice of words and facts, you can determine his attutide.

Basic question 6

What is the meaning of the word or phrase?

The reading portions of the HSPT, COOP, and TACHS will ask you questions related to the meaning of specific words in the passages. The questions will ask you to choose a suitable replacement for a word or phrase.

Let's look at a passage:

Mr. Brown's odious habits were disgusting to strangers and even more so to his coworkers who, day after day, were forced to watch and listen as he scratched, belched, and spit. He was a walking collection of nasty gestures and poor manners. In addition to this, he was an insult to the olfactory sense of anyone who by bad luck happened to have a nose.

A replacement question might ask:

1. In the first sentence, the word *odious* could best be replaced by which of the following?

(A) Unpleasant

(B) Evil

(C) Hateful

(D) Foul smelling

Vocabulary questions such as the one above can be answered in two different ways:

1. Using our knowledge of vocabulary.
2. Using context clues to discover the meaning of an unknown word.

You might know simply by looking at the word *odious* that it means: deserving hatred or repugnance. But this will *not* usually be the case. The meaning of many words will be unclear to you, but there are ways to solve this problem. Context clues given in the passage can help you to understand what the word means. Context clues can come from the facts and the grammar which surround the word.

Let's look at the passage again, this time with context clues in boldface:

Mr. Brown's <u>odious</u> habits were **disgusting** to strangers and even more so to his coworkers who, day after day, were forced to watch and listen as he **scratched, belched, and spit.** He was a walking collection of **nasty gestures and poor manners.** In addition to this, he was an insult to the olfactory sense of anyone who by bad luck happened to have a nose.

The grammatical structure of the first sentence shows us that *odious* is an adjective which modifies "habits." If you know something about these "habits," you will have a good clue towards understanding *odious*.

What specifically were the habits of Mr. Brown?

1. Scratched
2. Belched
3. Spit

How would you describe these habits?
How would you feel if you had to watch someone doing this every day?

By answering these questions you begin to see that these habits are "not nice." But when you look at the answer choices, you see that all of the choices are "not nice." You need to be more specific and more exact.

In the first sentence, his habits are described as "disgusting to strangers and coworkers." The second sentence calls them "nasty gestures."

Now when you look at the answer choices, you are able to eliminate certain ones:

(D) Foul smelling. At the end of the passage there is a discussion about how Mr. Brown smells but this is not related to his habits and has nothing to do with "odious." It is incorrect.

(B) Evil. This choice is **too strong.** "Evil" causes harm or injury to others. His habits cause unhappiness to those around him but they do not cause harm or injury. It is incorrect.

Next you have to decide which word is best: unpleasant or hateful. Both are related to "odious" in meaning but one is a much better replacement. The most important context clues are "disgusting and nasty" and the examples themselves. A disgusting and nasty habit, such as spitting, is more than "unpleasant"; the correct answer is "hateful."

Try another example on your own.

In the last sentence of the passage, what does the word *olfactory* mean? There are several context clues to help you understand its meaning. Read the sentence carefully.

This is only a brief discussion of how you can use context clues to discover the meaning of words. In the Vocabulary section, we will discuss with explanations and examples all of the various context clues.

Additional Tips

It is impossible to include in any review a discussion of all the problems which a student may face during the HSPT, COOP, and TACHS but there are elements in the test that are sure to appear.

Two different ideas are often joined together in one sentence. The word that joins these two ideas expresses their relationship to one another. To increase comprehension, it is essential to understand that relationship, but that can only be done when you understand the meaning of the connecting word.

Simple Connectors: The most simple of the two types of connectors are called *coordinating conjunctions*. Most students will easily recognize and understand the meaning of these basic connectors:

AND	OR	BUT
FOR	SO	YET
NOR		

"AND" means the addition of both ideas.
Example: Bob **and** Sally went to the party. (These two people went to the party.)

"OR" means there is a choice of only one.
Example: Bob **or** Sally will go to the party. (Only one person will go. If Bob, then not Sally. If Sally, then not Bob.)

"BUT" and **"YET"** have the same basic meaning. They both are used to show the differences in the ideas being joined.
Example: Fred has a lot of money, but his car is very old. (We know that Fred has a lot of money. We expect his car to be new. His car is not new. These ideas contrast with one another. They are different ideas.)

"FOR" and **"SO"** are opposites which are used to show the correct relationship between a cause and an effect. There are two possibilities:

CAUSE	"SO"	EFFECT
EFFECT	"FOR"	CAUSE

Example: <u>Marta broke her leg</u> **so** <u>she went to the hospital</u>.
          CAUSE   EFFECT

Example: <u>Jose worked day and night</u> **for** <u>he needed money badly</u>.
          EFFECT   CAUSE

"NOR" performs the same basic function as "AND" but it is used with negative ideas.
Example: Bob will go home and Mary will too.
Example: Bob will not go home nor will Mary.

Confusing Connectors: While most students recognize and understand coordinating conjunctions, they are often confused by the connectors called *conjunctive adverbs*. An easy way to understand what they mean is to know that most of them share a common meaning with one of the seven basic conjunctions. For example, the connector "nevertheless" serves the same basic function as "but."

The lists below will group the confusing connectors which share a common meaning with one of the simple connectors.

AND	BUT/YET	SO
ALSO	HOWEVER	CONSEQUENTLY
BESIDES	NEVERTHELESS	HENCE
FURTHERMORE	NONETHELESS	THEREFORE
MOREOVER	STILL	THUS
IN ADDITION	ALTHOUGH	ACCORDINGLY

Modals: Modals are auxiliary verbs that are used with the base form of another verb to express differences in mood. Auxiliary verbs include words such as can, could, may, might, shall, should, will, would, and must. A clear understanding of how modals function to change the meaning of a sentence is essential for developing your reading comprehension.

Let's look at a basic sentence and see how it and its meaning will change with the addition of a modal.

BASIC SENTENCE: ERIC FLIES AIRPLANES.

Ability:	Eric **can** fly an airplane.
Possibility:	Eric **could** fly an airplane.
Slight Possibility:	Eric **may** fly an airplane.
Slight Possibility:	Eric **might** fly an airplane.
Permission:	**Can** Eric fly the airplane?
	Could Eric fly the airplane?
	May Eric fly the airplane?
	Might Eric fly the airplane?
Obligation:	Eric **should** fly an airplane.
	Eric **ought** to fly an airplane.
Necessity:	Eric **must** fly the airplane.
	Eric **has to** fly the airplane.
Prohibition:	Eric **must not** fly the airplane.
No Necessity:	Eric **does not have** to fly the airplane.
Inference:	Eric **must** fly an airplane since he is a pilot.
Preference:	Eric **would rather** fly an airplane than drive a bus.
Past habit:	Eric **would** fly his airplane every Saturday before the accident happened.
Advisability:	Eric **had better** fly his plane before the storm comes.

II. Vocabulary

Your knowledge of English vocabulary will be tested within the reading comprehension sections of the exams. All of the questions will deal with vocabulary to some degree. Vocabulary is the base for all reading comprehension because the reader must understand the meaning of the words before the meaning of the passage can be learned.

Sometimes, the meaning of a word will be clear to you, but many times the meaning of a word will not be clear. To solve this problem, use context clues inside the sentence. Not every sentence will provide enough clues to allow you to determine the meaning of the words, but many times they will.

Problem Situations

Following are four main problem situations, along with discussions, explanations, and strategies that can be used to manage them. The strategies presented below will help you answer those questions faster and with more accuracy.

Situation 1: *You are familiar with the word. You are familiar with the answer choices. You think you know the correct choice.*

You have to be careful. A single word can have many meanings. Often, these meanings will be very similar to one another, but only one will be correct.

Let's look at examples using the word *collect.*

Example **1:** Many animals <u>collect</u> seeds and nuts for the winter.

  (A) pick up
  (B) organize
  (C) store
  (D) need

Example **2:** She wanted to <u>collect</u> her thoughts before she spoke to her boss.

  (A) pick up
  (B) organize
  (C) store
  (D) need

The correct answer for Example 1 is (A) "pick up." It would be very easy to choose (C) "store" because animals store food after they collect it, but it is not the best replacement. They (D) "need" seeds and nuts to survive the winter, but "need" and "collect" are not synonyms. (B) "organize" makes no sense in the context of the sentence.

The correct answer for Example 2 is (B) "organize." Her thoughts need to be arranged and organized before she speaks to her boss. In this example, the word does **not** mean "pick up" as it did in the first example.

Situation 2: *You understand the meaning of the word, but you are not sure which answer choice is correct.*

When there are no context clues to help you understand the meaning of answer choices, you need to deal with them quickly and to take your chances. Follow these simple rules:

1. Eliminate the choices you know are incorrect.
2. Don't choose a word because it looks like or sounds like the word. These words are often used to confuse or trick you. They are usually not the correct choice.
3. After going through steps one and two, make your best guess. Many times, your first choice will be the best.
4. Don't waste valuable time.

Situation 3: *The meaning of the word is not clear, but you are familiar with the answer choices and their meanings.*

Use context clues in the sentence to help you discover the meaning of a word. This is probably the most common situation you will face, and there are many ways to manage it which are explained on the following pages.

Situation 4: *You don't understand the meaning of the word. You don't know the meanings of the answer choices.*

You can often discover the meaning of a word by using context clues, but if you have no idea what an answer choice means, you face an unsolvable problem. Waste no time! Take a guess and move to the next question.

Context Clues

Context clues come in many shapes and forms. They include examples, synonyms, antonyms, grammatical structures, and the general idea of a sentence or passage. What type of clues they are doesn't matter. What matters is being able to use whatever information you are given to discover the meaning.

> **DIRECTIONS:** Read the examples below and underline what you think are context clues. Then try to write a definition for the italicized word.

1. The war caused tremendous *turmoil* but, eventually, order and calm were restored to the nation.
2. The drug was widely used and was considered *innocuous*; however, recent studies indicate many harmful side effects can occur with its usage.
3. She had been *sterilized* as a young girl, so now it was impossible for her to have children even if she wanted to.
4. There was no *malice* in her heart towards the murderer, for she had forgiven him years before.

In the examples above, the connecting words give you information about the relationship between ideas. If you understand the relationship and you understand one idea, then you can often understand the other idea. Important context clues are in **boldface** below that help to define the italicized word.

1. The war caused tremendous *turmoil* **but**, eventually, **order and calm were restored** to the nation.
2. The drug was widely used and was considered *innocuous*; **however**, recent studies **indicate many harmful side effects can occur with its usage.**
3. She had been *sterilized* as a young girl, **so** now **it was impossible for her to have children** even if she wanted to.
4. There was no *malice* in her heart towards the murderer, **for** she **had forgiven** him years before.

Discussion

In sentence 1, the connector *but* indicates ideas that contrast or are different. The second idea is "order and calm." The first idea must be different or opposite. *Turmoil* means disorder, chaos, or confusion.

In sentence 2, the word *however* functions the same way as *but*, so again there are contrasting ideas. On one side are "harmful side effects," so on the other side you can assume there is no harm or danger. *Innocuous* means harmless.

In sentence 3, the connector *so* shows a relationship of cause-and-effect. The result or effect is that she can't have children. The cause is something that prevents having children. "Sterilized" is a medical procedure which prevents a woman from becoming pregnant.

In sentence 4, *for* indicates a cause-and-effect relationship, but it is the opposite of *so*. After "so" you have the result. After "for" you have the cause. What is the result of having "forgiven him"? No malice. Malice means anger, ill will, or bad intentions towards someone.

Let's look at some more sentences.

> **DIRECTIONS:** Again, look for context clues and then try to write a definition for the underlined word.

1. Vulgar habits, such as spitting, belching, or wiping your nose without a handkerchief, are considered most inappropriate in public.
2. The city's most impressive attractions, including the Empire State Building, Radio City Music Hall, and the Museum of Modern Art, are the recipients of millions of eager tourists each year.

These two sentences include examples of the underlined words.

1. Vulgar habits, **such as spitting, belching, or wiping your nose without a handkerchief,** are considered most inappropriate in public.
2. The city's most impressive attractions, **including the Empire State Building, Radio City Music Hall, and the Museum of Modern Art,** are the recipients of millions of eager tourists each year.

Discussion

By looking at the examples that follow the underlined word, you get a good idea of what that word means.

1. *Vulgar* is an adjective that modifies "habits." The specific habits that are considered "vulgar" in public are spitting, belching, or wiping your nose without a handkerchief. These are not considered to be proper actions when done in public. Someone who does them in public does not have good manners. *Vulgar* means having the qualities of being rude, unpleasant, or disgusting.
2. The examples that follow *attractions*, the Empire State Building, Radio City Music Hall, and the Museum of Modern Art, give important clues. When you put these clues together with "eager tourists," you can guess that "attractions" are famous places where tourists go.

Another important source of information can come from **adjective clauses.** An easy way to spot them is to look for the relative pronouns that introduce them: **who, whom, which, that,** and **whose.** Relative clauses provide information about the noun they modify.

Let's look at some examples.

> **DIRECTIONS:** Find the key words that introduce the clause. Underline the clause. What information does it give about the italicized noun in front of it? Try to write a definition.

1. The *gizmo*, which regulates the valves and the choke mechanism, must be carefully installed.
2. The *benefactress*, who gave huge sums of money to schools and hospitals in our city, died recently.

Discussion

1. What kind of thing "regulates the valves and the choke mechanism?"
   Answer: Some kind of mechanical device.
2. What kind of person "gave huge sums of money to schools and hospitals"?
   Answer: Someone who is very generous with her money.

There are many different types of context clues. Look at the information that surrounds the words. It can help you understand the word's meaning.

Vocabulary Word List

The following list consists of commonly used words that may help you during the reading comprehension section of the exams. Study these words and then complete the following 25 exercises.

There are a few ways to go about studying this section. Choose the one with which you feel most comfortable.

1. Study 25 words a day for three weeks.
2. Study the words in the list that you consider to be difficult words.
3. Study each word and example sentence. Make up your own sentence using the word.
4. Try to use words from the list in conversations with your friends and family every day before the day of the test.

abandon, *v.* to leave alone or to give up. *The baby wolf was abandoned in the woods when its mother was killed.*

abate, *v.* to decrease or diminish. *For three terrible days, the heat of the sun never abated.*

abet, *v.* to help or aid. *The stranger abetted the lost child by taking him to the police station.*

abhor, *v.* to hate something. *Everyone abhors war and the loss of life it causes.*

abject, *adj.* hopeless or miserable. *Many charities have been started as a result of the abject poverty existing in many countries.*

absorbent, *adj.* having the quality of holding water. *The paper towels were almost as absorbent as the sponge.*

abundance, *n.* a greater amount than needed. *There is an abundance of oil in Saudi Arabia.*

accessory, *n.* an extra or added part. *A beautiful handbag is an important accessory to a woman's wardrobe.*

accommodation, *n.* something supplied for convenience. *Temporary accommodations were provided to the refugees.*

accomplice, *n.* someone who helps another to break the law. *The bank robber claims to have acted alone, but the police believe he had an accomplice.*

accomplish, *v.* to achieve. *Everyone wishes to accomplish something important in his life.*

accost, *v.* to bother or threaten. *A person walking alone in the city can be accosted at any time.*

accrue, *v.* to build up over time. *As a result of his wise investments in stocks and bonds, he had accrued a fortune by the age of 80.*

accumulate, *v.* to build up, to collect. *If a room is not used, dust begins to accumulate.*

acrid, *adj.* having an unpleasant, irritating quality. *The acrid smoke from the chemicals burned his eyes.*

acuity, *n.* sharpness of perception. *Visual acuity is important to an airline pilot.*

adapt, *v.* to change. *Many wild animals cannot adapt to life in a zoo.*

admonish, *v.* to advise or to warn against. *Parents must admonish their children about the use of drugs.*

adroitly, *adv.* with easy skill and ability. *A great soccer player like Pele could adroitly pass the ball to a teammate.*

advantage, *n.* benefit. *One advantage of not smoking is that you save a lot of money.*

advocate, *v.* to propose or to support. *Many doctors advocate a balanced diet that includes only a small amount of red meat.*

affluent, *adj.* rich or wealthy. *From the size of our large homes, people assume we live in an affluent society.*

aggravate, *v.* to make worse. *He aggravated his sore elbow by trying to play tennis.*

agile, *adj.* able to move quickly and easily. *A deer in the woods is the most agile of runners.*

agitate, *v.* to cause trouble and upset. *The students agitated the teacher by talking during class.*

ailment, *n.* physical or mental problem. *Coughing is a common ailment for people who work in coal mines.*

akin, *adj.* like or similar to. *Although ice skating is akin to roller skating, it is often more difficult for some people.*

alleviate, *adj.* to fix or remedy a problem or condition. *Winning a million dollars in the lottery would alleviate many of his financial problems.*

allure, *n.* the ability to strongly attract. *The allure of easy money and little work attracts many to a life of crime.*

amateur, *n.* a nonprofessional. *An amateur should never try to fix a problem that concerns electrical wiring.*

ambiguous, *adj.* unclear. *The clues found by the detective were so ambiguous that he had no idea who had committed the crime.*

amicable, *adj.* friendly. *An amicable man like Joe has many friends and belongs to many clubs.*

ample, *adj.* more than enough. *We had ample time to answer all of the questions and to finish the test with ease.*

analyst, *n.* person who carefully studies data in order to reach a conclusion. *The analyst studied the decline in church attendance.*

anchor, *v.* to hold in position. *Only a steel chain with a great weight can anchor a large ship.*

anguish, *n.* great worry or concern. *Moving away from his friends caused the young man great anguish.*

angular, *adj.* to have sharp, pointed angles. *His long pointed nose and chin gave his face a very angular appearance.*

antique, *adj.* old or old-fashioned. *The antique chair had been made in 1745.*

apex, *n.* the highest point. *At the apex of his career, he had great wealth and power.*

apparatus, *n.* device or machine. *A chemistry lab is equipped with an apparatus to allow students to perform experiments.*

appreciable, *adj.* noticeable or substantial. *For weeks, there was no appreciable change in his illness until doctors began to administer antibiotics.*

approximate, *adj.* not exact but close to the amount or number. *No one knows for sure exactly how many people live in China, but the approximate number is one billion.*

arduous, *adj.* difficult. *Sailing alone across an ocean is an arduous task.*

argue, *v.* to strongly support an idea. *He argued that the money should be spent for health care and not for weapons.*

arouse, *v.* to excite. *Sharks are aroused by the smell of blood in water.*

arrogance, *n.* offensive display of superiority; overbearing pride. *The man showed his arrogance by pushing his way to the front of the line and demanding that he be served first.*

artifact, *n.* object made in the past. *Archaeologists dig through the ruins of ancient cities in order to find artifacts.*

aspire, *v.* to desire or to long for. *The young actor aspired to someday be a famous movie star.*

assert, *v.* to say that something is true or correct. *Columbus asserted that the world was round and not flat as most people believed in his time.*

assuage, *v.* to ease or to relieve. *His mother tried to assuage his fears by holding his hand and whispering that everything would be all right.*

atop, *prep.* on top of. *A radio tower was placed atop the building.*

attain, *v.* to reach a goal or position. *We can attain our dreams with hard work and dedication.*

audacious, *adj.* bold, daring, willing to risk danger. *Many believed that Lindbergh's audacious plan to cross the Atlantic alone in a single-engine plane was impossible.*

augment, *v.* to add to. *He had to take a second job at night to augment his low salary.*

authentic, *adj.* real. *The jewels in her necklace were so large that many believed they were not authentic.*

automaton, *n.* machine which performs jobs normally done by humans. *Automatons will be used in space flights to distant planets because of the many years the journeys will take.*

aversion, *n.* dislike. *She has a strong aversion to most insects, but she hates flies most of all.*

ban, *v.* to make illegal. *Many drugs have been banned after it was found that they caused dangerous side effects.*

barricade, *v.* to be surrounded with walls for protection. *The soldiers built a barricade to keep their enemies out.*

basis, *n.* the foundation, what we build upon. *A good education is the basis for a successful career.*

behavior, *n.* conduct or actions. *The student's rude and noisy behavior was unacceptable to his teacher.*

bewilder, *v.* to confuse. *He was bewildered by many of the difficult questions asked in the test.*

blame, *n.* guilt or fault. *A careless cigarette smoker was to blame for the forest fire.*

blight, *n.* disease or curse, or a run-down condition. *The blight of many of our inner cities is caused by poor economic conditions.*

blunder, *n.* a bad mistake. *Trying to cheat on the test was a blunder that caused him to fail the course.*

bribe, *n.* the illegal act of giving money to someone in order to influence his or her actions. *The man tried to give the policeman a bribe so that he wouldn't get a speeding ticket.*

brittle, *adj.* easily broken. *When we grow older, our bones may become brittle.*

callous, *adj.* having no feeling. *Her callousness kept her from making a donation to the charity.*

canal, *n.* structure designed to carry liquids. *A canal was built across the desert to provide water for the new city.*

capacious, *adj.* having a large area. *It was a huge house and the capacious dining room could seat 100 guests.*

captive, *n.* one who is held hostage or imprisoned. *The lion was held captive before it could be released in the wild.*

castigate, *v.* to strongly criticize. *The politician was castigated for having lied about his love affair.*

category, *n.* division or class within a larger group. *Snakes are usually divided into two categories: poisonous or nonpoisonous.*

cessation, *n.* an ending or completion. *With the cessation of the war, refugees returned to their homes and began to rebuild.*

chaos, *n.* total confusion. *The effects of the earthquake created chaos in the city.*

characteristic, *n.* an aspect or feature. *Most employers look for characteristics such as motivation, dedication, and a good attitude in their prospective employees.*

chasm, *n.* a deep hole. *The explosion caused a chasm in the side of the mountain.*

chore, *n.* a small job or an unpleasant task. *Washing the dishes each night after supper is a real chore if you have worked all day.*

clumsy, *adj.* awkward in actions or movements. *Everyone appears clumsy the first time they ice-skate.*

coerce, *v.* to try to force one to do or say something against his/her will. *She felt coerced by her friends who promised never to talk to her again if she didn't help them cheat on the test.*

cogent, *adj.* convincing or persuasive. *His speech was so powerful and his ideas so cogent that everyone agreed that his plan was best.*

commerce, *n.* the activity of business and trade. *Commerce between the two countries has increased because of the new trade policy.*

compassion, *n.* sympathy for the problems of others. *The nurse's compassion for her patients made them love her.*

composite, *n.* something formed by the combination of different elements or substances. *Salt is a composite of sodium and chloride.*

compulsory, *adj.* required, necessary, or mandatory. *Compulsory education in the United States requires that every child attend school until the age of 16.*

concentration, *n.* a gathering or collection. *The highest concentration of big-game animals can be found in national parks.*

concoct, *v.* to create by mixing things together. *He concocted a bad-tasting drink by mixing milk and apple juice.*

condone, *v.* to approve of or to forgive an action. *The judge condoned the woman's actions by saying she acted in self-defense.*

confidant, *n.* one to whom secrets can be told. *She was not only his wife but also his closest confidant, and therefore, knew all of his deepest secrets.*

confide, *v.* to tell someone a secret or personal information. *The boy confided to his mother that he had broken the window by accident.*

confine, *v.* to limit or restrict movement. *After the accident, he was confined to a wheelchair for many weeks.*

confiscate, *v.* to take or seize goods because of criminal activity. *The police confiscated the robber's gun once he was arrested.*

congeal, *v.* to change from liquid to solid. *The milk that was left in the glass overnight slowly began to congeal.*

congenial, *adj.* friendly and pleasant to be with. *They were such congenial people that everyone wished to attend their parties.*

conscientious, *adj.* careful to fulfill responsibilities. *Since the lives of many people are in their hands, doctors and airline pilots have to be conscientious.*

consequence, *n.* results of an action. *There is strong evidence to indicate that there are many harmful consequences of smoking cigarettes.*

consummate, *v.* to perfect or complete. *Their long romance was consummated in marriage.*

contaminate, *v.* to make dirty or impure. *Water in the bay was contaminated by oil leaking from the ship.*

contingent, *adj.* likely but not certain to happen. *Payment of the money was contingent upon delivery of the goods.*

conventional, *adj.* common or usual. *In Japan, wood is the conventional material used to build houses.*

core, *n.* the center, the heart. *We eat most of the apple, but we usually leave the core.*

corroborate, *v.* to confirm or support what someone else has said. *Mr. Brown's explanation of what caused the accident was corroborated by a policeman who saw it happen.*

create, *v.* to make for the very first time. *The Bible says that God created the world in six days and then rested on the seventh.*

credulous, *adj.* trusting or unsuspecting. *A credulous person is often the first to be robbed or cheated.*

creed, *n.* one's belief or faith. *The creed that we follow helps us to determine which actions are good and which are evil.*

cruel, *adj.* lacking human kindness, mean or vicious. *The cruel man refused to help the lost couple.*

cryptic, *adj.* difficult to understand. *The note that was found in the bottle was too cryptic to understand.*

dangle, *v.* to hang down. *The windstorm knocked over trees and utility poles; the electric wires that dangled were a real danger.*

decade, *n.* period of ten years. *The 1980s was a decade of economic prosperity.*

decency, *n.* the moral state of good behavior. *Decency demands that we do the right thing whether we want to or not.*

decrepit, *adj.* old and in poor condition. *The house was so decrepit that it would be cheaper to tear it down and start again rather than try to repair it.*

defect, *n.* a flaw or imperfection. *His job was to find any product with a defect and see that it was corrected.*

deficiency, *n.* something needed but not present. *In the past, sailors who had no fresh vegetables suffered from vitamin deficiencies and became ill.*

deliberately, *adv.* to do something on purpose with a clear understanding of the consequences. *He deliberately slammed the door in his boss's face.*

dependable, *adj.* can be relied upon. *American cars are very dependable and seldom break down.*

depict, *v.* to describe or characterize. *In the movie, he was depicted as kind and gentle.*

deprecate, *v.* to criticize or belittle. *Thomas Edison's efforts to create a light bulb were deprecated by many experts as impossible until he achieved success.*

deprive, *v.* to prevent from having. *A child whose parents have died is often deprived of the love that he needs.*

deride, *v.* to strongly criticize. *Critics derided the writer's new book as being poorly written and filled with lies.*

desire, *v.* a strong wish or want. *Everyone desires health, happiness, and sometimes, a piece of chocolate.*

destiny, *n.* fate or the future. *A fortune-teller claims to be able to know our destiny.*

detect, *v.* to notice or to find. *The doctors gave her a blood test, but they could not detect any signs of disease.*

deterioration, *n.* the state of declining or decaying. *The deterioration of the old church prompted the community to raise money to rebuild it.*

determinant, *n.* important factor that affects the result. *Exercise is a major determinant in losing weight.*

deviate, *v.* to change course. *If we never deviate from our normal activities, our lives will be boring.*

devise, *v.* to conceive, design, or create. *He devised a new method to change sea water to fresh water.*

diagnosis, *n.* the conclusion reached by a doctor as to the cause of an illness. *After a thorough examination, the doctor's diagnosis was that the patient had the flu.*

digress, *v.* to turn away from the main subject of attention. *To be an effective writer, you must organize your thoughts and never digress too far from your main idea.*

diligent, *adj.* hard-working. *The diligent way he performed his work earned him many promotions.*

diminutive, *adj.* small. *The problem was so diminutive that no one was concerned about it.*

discern, *v.* to discover or to be able to tell the difference between two things. *Only an expert could discern which painting was the original.*

discontinue, *v.* to stop. *The sale of many toys has been discontinued because of their danger to children.*

disposal, *n.* having the property to get rid of or to eliminate. *The garbage disposal unit failed to operate as the salesman promised it would.*

dissect, *v.* to cut something up in order to study it. *Sandy refused to dissect the frog, and as a result, failed the biology course.*

disseminate, *v.* to send out. *His job as a mailman is to disseminate the mail.*

dissolvable, *adj.* the ability to break down and disappear in a liquid. *Instead of swallowing them, Denise put the dissolvable tablets in her glass of water.*

divulge, *v.* to give secret or personal information. *Mrs. Haddy was angry that her sister Sylvia divulged her secrets to the neighborhood gossip.*

documentation, *n.* written evidence or proof. *Sarah's documentation showed that she was an official member of the club.*

dominant, *adj.* strongest or most powerful. *Jack's talkative nature made him the dominant member of the discussion group.*

drought, *n.* a long period of time with little or no rainfall. *Because of the long drought and dry conditions in the western states, many homes have been destroyed by fire.*

dubious, *adj.* doubtful or uncertain. *Fred was not hired for the position because of his dubious reputation.*

durable, *adj.* able to last a long time. *The label on the uniform stated that the fabric was durable and stain resistant.*

eccentric, *adj.* odd or unusual. *Jonathan was considered by the local community to be an eccentric inventor whose creations were useless.*

ecosystem, *n.* the complex of living things and their environment which functions as a single unit or a whole. *Many local scientists have warned about the effects of pollution on the fragile ecosystem of the bay.*

effects, *n.* the results or consequences. *The effects of his recent medical treatments are not yet known.*

elicit, *v.* to draw out. *The inspector was determined to elicit as much information as he could from each suspect.*

elucidate, *v.* to explain or clarify. *Marcus was always proud of his ability to elucidate the more difficult passages in the chemistry book.*

elusive, *adj.* difficult to find, catch, or see. *The Zodiac Killer had remained elusive to the New York City Police Department for months.*

emerge, *v.* to come out of. *Maria has emerged as one of the most talented female basketball players the school has ever had.*

emit, *v.* to send out. *The residents of Pleasant Park have been complaining about the foul odors being emitted by the new recycling center in town.*

emulate, *adj.* to copy or to follow. *Many children like to emulate their parents in some ways.*

energetically, *adv.* to act with vigor. *When Billy's father promised him ten dollars to rake the fall leaves, Billy energetically completed the task.*

enhance, *v.* to make better or clearer. *The attractive pink eyeglass frames enhanced the color of her eyes.*

ensnare, *v.* to trap or entangle. *As the township administrator, she had no intention of becoming ensnared in the local corruption scandal.*

ensue, *v.* to follow. *With the help of his college counselor, Carlos was determined to ensue the career path he had chosen.*

enterprise, *n.* a business venture. *The dream of launching the enterprise soon collapsed when the two businessmen realized the amount of money that would be needed.*

enticement, *n.* something which attracts or lures. *The enticement of winning a vacation in Hawaii for two weeks caused Lisa to fill out 15 entry forms for the contest.*

equivocal, *adj.* uncertain or vague. *Sharice's equivocal response did not tell me whether she liked the idea or not.*

erosion, *n.* the process of wearing away caused by wind or water. *The retired couple could not fulfill their dream of building a home near the beach because of erosion along the coast.*

essential, *adj.* necessary or most important. *It is essential that each student pass every exam in order to receive credit for the course.*

esteem, *n.* honor or respect. *General Tindal was held in high esteem by the soldiers because of his courage.*

evidence, *n.* facts or data which support an idea. *Enough evidence was gathered to indict three employees with illegally tampering with government documents.*

evolve, *v.* to change. *His ideas on life in the twentieth century evolved into one of the most complex philosophies she had ever read.*

exacting, *adj.* carefully precise. *The professor's exacting instructions made the assignment lengthy and complicated.*

examiner, *n.* one who carefully inspects. *The claims examiner rejected the customer's request for payment of medical treatment due to restrictions in the policy.*

exasperate, *v.* to annoy a person until he/she reaches a state of confusion or anger. *Manny's wife exasperated him so much that he backed into a neighbor's fence with his car.*

excessive, *adj.* more than is needed. *Eating a whole bag of candy after trick-or-treating is a bit excessive.*

exempt, *v.* to release from a commitment. *Jimmy was exempted from gym class for a week after running into the fence while playing baseball.*

exhaust, *v.* to tire out or to use up completely. *The gambler exhausted his family's savings and sold their house to pay off his debts.*

exist, *v.* to be alive. *Scholars consider William Faulkner to be one of the greatest American writers who ever existed.*

exorbitant, *adj.* extremely high priced. *They were selling hot dogs for the exorbitant price of $10 apiece.*

exotic, *adj.* unusual or uncommon. *Mary always considered her friend Susan's taste in clothing to be exotic.*

expensive, *adj.* costly or high priced. *When the Martins heard how expensive the new house was, they were shocked and decided not to buy it.*

explicit, *adj.* clear and specific. *Norma considered her instructions explicit and could not understand why her husband kept overcooking the pasta for dinner.*

explore, *v.* to investigate or to search through new territory. *He explored the passages of the cave.*

expose, *v.* to uncover or to reveal. *The political scandal was exposed on Friday, and by Saturday morning it was on the front page of every newspaper in the city.*

extensive, *adj.* covering a large area or amount. *The Pacific Ocean covers an extensive portion of Earth.*

extinct, *adj.* no longer in existence. *Dinosaurs have been extinct for millions of years.*

extravagant, *adj.* excessive or lavish. *Owning a house with 24 bedrooms is extravagant, even for a rich person.*

facile, *adj.* easy or simple. *For some complex problems, there are no facile solutions.*

facilitate, *v.* to aid or assist. *Automatic doors facilitate the movement of handicapped people who use wheelchairs.*

fail, *v.* unable to succeed. *He was sure that his plan could not fail.*

falter, *v.* to stumble or to momentarily hesitate. *At first he was winning the race, but as the pain in his leg increased, he began to falter.*

fascinate, *v.* to strongly attract someone's interest. *Children are fascinated by toys and games.*

feebleness, *n.* weakness. *With old age comes a gradual loss of hearing and a general state of feebleness.*

feud, *n.* an argument or quarrel which has lasted a long time. *The two families had a feud for so long that no one was quite sure how the argument had started.*

flee, *v.* to try to escape from some danger. *The war in Vietnam caused thousands of farmers to flee their homes.*

flimsy, *adj.* weak, easily broken. *A kite is a flimsy toy which can be easily damaged by a high wind.*

follow, *v.* to come after. *A dinner party later that afternoon will follow the wedding ceremony.*

foremost, *adj.* first or most important. *Water is of foremost importance when traveling across a desert.*

foresee, *v.* to see what will happen in the future. *Fortune tellers claim to foresee the future, but most simply want our money.*

forfeit, *v.* to lose or to surrender. *If you don't vote, then you are forfeiting your rights to participate in our democratic process of elections.*

foster, *v.* to help to grow with care and support. *Sunlight and water help to foster the growth of plants.*

fraction, *n.* a part of the whole. *The Christian population in Egypt makes up only a small fraction of the total population there.*

fraud, *n.* the attempt to cheat people with lies and deception. *If someone tries to sell you a watch on the street, be careful it isn't a fraud.*

fret, *v.* to worry. *Don't fret over how you will do on the test; study hard and hope for the best.*

fugitive, *n.* someone trying to escape the law. *Sometimes it takes years, but most fugitives are eventually caught and sent back to jail.*

futile, *adj.* useless or hopeless. *He made a futile attempt to put out the fire, but the building burned to the ground.*

genealogy, *n.* study of one's family and relatives in the past. *Many people study their genealogy to see if they are related to famous people.*

generic, *adj.* common or general. *A generic brand of aspirin is much cheaper than one with a brand name, even though they are the same product.*

genuinely, *adv.* honestly. *Even after he apologized for the insults, she didn't believe that he was genuinely sorry for his behavior.*

germinate, *v.* to begin to grow. *It takes two weeks after the seeds have been planted for them to begin to germinate.*

gist, *n.* the essential part or a summary. *He told her he didn't have time for all the details; he just wanted the gist of the story.*

glitter, *v.* to sparkle with light, to shine. *On a clear night, the stars glitter like diamonds.*

globose, *adj.* shaped like a globe or a sphere. *The shape of the fat man's stomach was globose.*

greed, *n.* the extreme desire to possess more than is needed. *The man's greed for money and power caused him to lose his friends.*

grievance, *n.* a complaint or an objection. *If a worker has a grievance, he should discuss it with his supervisor before he files a written complaint.*

group, *n.* a collection of things. *Many animals live in groups in order to survive.*

grudge, *n.* a feeling of resentment caused by an action in the past. *Even though the man had forgiven her, the girl still felt as though he was holding a grudge.*

guarantee, *n.* an assurance for the fulfillment of a condition. *The VCR came with a 12-month guarantee on all parts and service.*

hamper, *v.* to bother or hinder. *Rain and snow hampered the construction of the new building.*

handicap, *n.* problem or disability that limits actions. *Being unable to hear is a handicap that many people have to overcome.*

haphazard, *adj.* in a careless or disorganized fashion. *She was such a haphazard driver that she had four accidents in four days.*

harsh, *adj.* hard or cruel. *Without any concern for her feelings, the policeman yelled at the woman in a harsh manner.*

hectic, *adj.* confused or chaotic. *Traffic is most hectic at 5:00 p.m. when everyone is leaving work.*

hold, *v.* to argue or propose. *Many geographers held that the world was flat until Columbus proved that it was round by sailing to America.*

hilarious, *adj.* extremely funny or humorous. *The audience in the theater thought the movie was so hilarious that they couldn't stop laughing.*

hoax, *n.* a joke or deception meant to fool people. *Mary's boyfriend pretended to be a policeman, but she knew it was a hoax when she heard his voice.*

humid, *adj.* weather condition of very wet or moist air. *Summer is more humid than winter because warm air can carry more moisture than cold air.*

hypothesis, *n.* prediction or guess. *With careful experiments, scientists can usually determine if a hypothesis is correct or not.*

ignorant, *adj.* lacking knowledge. *People who do not go to school are ignorant of the many cultures and societies that exist in the world.*

illuminate, *v.* to brighten with light or to clarify. *Street lights help to illuminate dark roads.*

imaging, *n.* the process of producing a picture or image. *The powerful imaging produced by the telescope allowed the scientists to see the planet in much clearer detail.*

immature, *adj.* not yet adult or fully grown. *An immature bird can't fly.*

imminent, *adj.* approaching, near, about to happen. *The residents who remained in the city were in imminent danger from the approaching storm.*

impede, *v.* to hinder, restrict, or delay. *Doctors had to operate to remove the obstacle which impeded the flow of blood to his heart.*

impediment, *n.* obstacle or barrier. *Nervousness is often an impediment to learning to speak a new language.*

impinge, *v.* to impact, make an impression on. *The long hours he spent at work impinged upon his relationship with his family.*

inaugurate, *v.* to begin. *A ceremony took place to inaugurate the opening of the new bridge.*

inception, *n.* the beginning. *At the inception of the company there were only two employees; a year later, there were a hundred.*

incessant, *adj.* constant or continuous. *He had to leave the city to escape the incessant noise of the traffic.*

incisive, *adj.* a clear, sharp understanding. *His incisive ideas helped them to find a solution to the problems.*

inconsequential, *adj.* of no real importance. *We do a thousand inconsequential actions each day which our minds quickly forget after having done them.*

index, *v.* to put into a list or catalog. *Every magazine purchased by the library was carefully indexed.*

indict, *v.* to be brought to trial and accused. *The wife, who was found holding the gun, was indicted for the murder of her husband.*

induce, *v.* to cause to happen. *Doctors often prescribe drugs that induce sleep.*

inept, *adj.* lacking the necessary skill or ability. *She was a skillful writer, but her nervousness made her totally inept as a speaker.*

infamous, *adj.* famous for bad actions. *Hitler was an infamous dictator who caused the death of millions of people.*

inferior, *adj.* lower in degree or rank. *Shoppers prefer fresh vegetables rather than frozen ones which are inferior in taste.*

infest, *v.* to occupy or spread over in a troubling way. *The apartment was infested with bugs and had to be sprayed before the people could move in.*

inflammable, *adj.* having the ability to burn easily. *Petroleum is an inflammable substance.*

inhabit, *v.* to normally live in or occupy a particular place. *Camels inhabit the dry regions of the earth because of their ability to go long periods without water.*

injustice, *n.* a wrong action done to someone. *To purposely damage or destroy the property or goods of others is an injustice.*

inquisitive, *adj.* curious. *Children are inquisitive because they want to know why and how things happen.*

integrate, *v.* to combine with or to unite together. *In the early 1960s, schools in America were integrated so that black and white children could attend classes together.*

intentionally, *adv.* done on purpose. *The fire was no accident; it had been started intentionally.*

interactive, *adj.* acting with or in response to another. *An interactive exchange of ideas between countries is the best way to prevent wars.*

intrepid, *adj.* adventurous or fearless. *Early American pioneers had to be intrepid to face the dangers of the wilderness.*

intricate, *adj.* complex or complicated. *A wristwatch is a very intricate machine.*

intruder, *n.* a person who enters without permission. *An intruder broke the lock on their back door and entered their house while they were sleeping.*

invalid, *n.* one unable to live normally because of an illness or handicap. *The invalid had been confined to a wheelchair since the car accident.*

investment, *n.* money used for income or profit. *He bought land in Florida in hopes that it would increase in value, but his investment never paid off.*

irritation, *n.* an annoyance or problem. *A piece of sand in your eye can be a painful irritation.*

jilt, *v.* to abandon one's lover. *After waiting an hour in a restaurant for her boyfriend to appear, she knew she had been jilted.*

lack, *n.* the absence of something. *The lack of rain caused the grass to die.*

lament, *v.* to express great sorrow, to cry and moan. *For many years, the mother lamented the death of her son.*

lapses, *n.* periods of omissions or errors. *The lapses in his memory were caused by a blow to the head.*

leisure, *adj.* free time. *He likes to swim and play golf in his leisure time.*

lengthwise, *adv.* in relation to something's length (end to end). *The tree, measured lengthwise, was 100 feet long.*

license, *n.* legal document which allows an action to be performed. *To be legally married, a young couple must first apply for a marriage license.*

limb, *n.* an arm or leg on a person, or a branch on a tree. *In the storm, a limb of the tree fell down.*

litter, *v.* to dirty with trash or garbage. *People who litter our streets with trash cost the state millions of dollars each year to collect that trash.*

loathe, *v.* to hate or despise. *George loathes broccoli since he was forced to eat it as a child.*

locate, *v.* to exist in a particular spot. *Paris is located in France.*

longitudinal, *adj.* moving from top to bottom. *The ship was moving in a longitudinal direction from north to south.*

loot, *v.* to steal. *When the electricity went out, people began to loot the shops along the darkened street.*

luminous, *adj.* filled with light. *The full moon was so luminous that the night seemed like day.*

maintain, *v.* to keep in current condition. *A car has to be maintained to stay in good condition.*

malign, *v.* to injure someone by saying bad things about him or her. *His good name was maligned by the story in the newspaper which called him a liar.*

masonry, *n.* blocks or bricks jointed together with cement. *The masonry of ancient Egyptians can be seen in their pyramids.*

massive, *adj.* very large, huge. *A whale is a massive mammal.*

mature, *adj.* adult or fully grown. *Grapes are picked as soon as they are mature.*

meddle, *v.* to interfere in the business of others. *The young husband told his mother-in-law not to meddle in his affairs.*

melancholy, *adj.* sad or unhappy. *The play was so melancholy that it made the audience cry.*

menace, *n.* a threat or threatening. *Air pollution is a menace to our health.*

merge, *v.* to join or combine together. *The two small companies merged to form one large company.*

metabolism, *n.* the processes by which energy is provided for life. *Our metabolism slows when we go to sleep.*

meticulous, *adj.* precise and careful about even the smallest detail. *She was so meticulous with her house that she even scrubbed and waxed the garage floor.*

migrate, *v.* to travel from place to place. *Every year, the photography club gathers at the state park to photograph birds that migrate south for the winter.*

morbid, *adj.* psychologically unhealthy. *Sally was so morbid at times that many of her friends stopped calling her.*

mundane, *adj.* common or ordinary. *The professor always tried to persuade his students from living a mundane life.*

mutual, *adj.* in conjunction with another. *A mutual feeling of resentment and anger built up between the couple after only two years of marriage.*

nadir, *n.* the lowest point. *He considered the six months he lived in New York City without a job or a decent place to live as the nadir of his existence.*

neglect, *v.* to fail to provide what is needed. *Rita caught the flu and her doctor admonished her for neglecting to eat and rest properly during the winter months.*

negligent, *adj.* responsible for improper actions. *Dan's electricity was turned off yesterday because he was negligent in paying his monthly bill.*

negligible, *adj.* unimportant or insignificant. *At the office meetings, Debbie felt her opinions were considered negligible by her coworkers, and so she decided not to speak up any more.*

nomadic, *adj.* having the characteristic of moving from place to place without a fixed pattern. *As a child, Howard resented his family's nomadic lifestyle because he was never able to develop lasting friendships.*

notorious, *adj.* famous for wrong actions. *Luiz was notorious for borrowing money and failing to pay it back.*

objective, *n.* goal or purpose. *Her main objective was to find her own apartment to live in as soon as possible.*

obscure, *adj.* not well known. *Alex always enjoyed the obscure writings of the early philosophers.*

obsolete, *adj.* no longer of any use. *The customer knew the record player would soon become obsolete, but he bought it anyway.*

occurrence, *n.* event or happening. *The repeated occurrence of missing funds at the bank baffled the investigators.*

ominous, *adj.* menacing or threatening. *The large black clouds looked ominous, and so the baseball game was canceled.*

omit, *v.* to leave out. *Betty was hurt when she heard her name was omitted from Ana's wedding invitation list.*

orbit, *n.* circular pattern of movement around another object. *Christopher won second prize at the science fair for his detailed diagram of the orbit of the planets.*

ordeal, *n.* a painful or difficult experience. *Mr. Thompson considered his visit to the dentist such a frightening ordeal that he vowed never to go back.*

origin, *n.* the source or cause. *Cindy was determined to find the origin of the rumors circulating about her in the office.*

ostensibly, *adv.* as it appears, apparently. *Ostensibly, he was honest about his past, but she didn't trust him.*

output, *n.* what was produced. *The production manager was troubled over the recent drop in output by his employees.*

pact, *n.* an agreement. *Before Jerry moved, he made a pact with his best friend that they would meet at Hadley's Park on Jerry's eighteenth birthday.*

palatable, *adj.* eatable or good tasting. *Mike and Sara agreed that their dinner at the new restaurant was just about palatable.*

paralyze, *v.* to cause something to be unable to move. *Some predators will paralyze their prey with poison and then devour them.*

parasitic, *adj.* the quality of living off others. *This parasitic species of fish was called "bloodsucker" by local fishermen.*

patent, *n.* legal right of ownership. *Tom was advised to obtain a patent for his latest invention.*

penetrable, *adj.* can be entered. *The commander realized the fort was penetrable and ordered his troops to attack the weak point.*

penetrate, *v.* to enter into. *Since the spilled wine penetrated the upholstery, Lydia decided to purchase a new couch.*

perforated, *adj.* filled with holes. *The bucket of water was found empty since the boy hadn't noticed that it was perforated.*

perish, *v.* waste away, disappear, to die. *Abe watched Loretta's love letters perish as he placed each one of them into the fireplace.*

perpetual, *adj.* lasting forever. *Margaret hoped that her neighbor's sunrise visits would not become a perpetual problem.*

persist, *v.* to continue an action despite obstacles. *Mr. Price persisted in eating a breakfast of eggs and sausage every morning in spite of his high cholesterol readings.*

pessimist, *n.* one who expects the worst will happen. *Mary came to be known as the pessimist in her family because she always found something to worry about.*

petition, *n.* a written request. *Many angry residents circulated a petition to repeal the large tax increases in the state.*

phenomenon, *n.* an unusual event or occurrence. *Many consider the aurora borealis to be a spectacular phenomenon of nature.*

phlegmatic, *adj.* showing no feeling or energy. *Having studied for two straight days without stopping to sleep, he appeared phlegmatic as he sat at his desk with the test before him.*

placate, *v.* to make peace with an enemy. *He tried to placate his angry wife by bringing her flowers.*

plea, *n.* a request, usually with strong emotion. *The Red Cross made an urgent plea for blood donors to aid the victims of the fire.*

plethora, *n.* a large amount or variety. *She said it was just a dinner party, but when he saw the plethora of food and drink, he knew it was a real feast.*

pollute, *v.* to make dirty. *Exhaust from cars pollutes our air.*

ponder, *v.* to think carefully. *Great men often ponder the eternal questions of why we were born and why we must die.*

postpone, *v.* to delay an action until a later time. *The class picnic had to be postponed because of the heavy rain.*

precede, *v.* to come before. *Fall precedes winter.*

predator, *n.* a creature that survives by attacking and eating another creature. *The most feared of all marine predators is the great white shark.*

predetermine, *v.* to decide the outcome or result before it occurs. *She hoped to predetermine the questions she would be asked in the test so that she would be better prepared.*

prelude, *n.* what comes before. *The dark skies and the sound of distant thunder were a prelude to the storm.*

premise, *n.* an unproven idea which is the basis for research. *His theory was based on the premise that animals could be taught to speak.*

prescription, *n.* a written order of medicine given by a doctor. *The prescription stated that the antibiotics were to be taken three times a day.*

prevalent, *adj.* common in many areas. *Colds are most prevalent during the winter months.*

prior, *adj.* before or previous. *He graduated from high school three years prior to entering college.*

probe, *n.* a careful study to discover information. *The detective began to probe through the dark house with his flashlight.*

prolific, *adj.* abundant or productive. *He was such a prolific writer that he was able to complete a novel every three weeks.*

prosecute, *v.* to seek punishment for breaking the law. *The banker was prosecuted for stealing money from his own bank.*

prudent, *adj.* careful. *It is considered prudent for a married man to have life insurance.*

purify, *v.* to make pure or clean. *Charcoal filters in the air conditioner were used to purify the air coming into the house.*

quality, *n.* a feature or characteristic. *One quality common to all societies is the love and care given to children.*

random, *adj.* with no pattern or organization. *The numbers for the lottery are chosen at random.*

raze, *v.* to demolish or destroy. *It took the bulldozer only one hour to raze the old building into a pile of bricks.*

recede, *v.* to go back to a previous state. *After the high tide caused by the rain and storm, the water slowly began to recede to its normal level.*

receptive, *adj.* open to new ideas. *His father was very old-fashioned, so he was not receptive to new ideas.*

recite, *v.* to read aloud. *Most children learn the alphabet by reciting it many times.*

recluse, *n.* one who wishes to live alone. *The old recluse lived deep in the woods, ten miles from the nearest neighbor.*

reconcile, *v.* to make peace. *When a husband and wife cannot reconcile their differences, a divorce is likely to occur.*

refine, *v.* to make better by removing impurities. *Petroleum has to be refined before it can be used as fuel.*

remnant, *n.* something left behind. *The only remnant left of the ancient city is a pile of rocks.*

repel, *v.* to fight off. *Fire will repel wild animals.*

repugnant, *adj.* offensive, distasteful, repulsive. *Bad manners are quite repugnant.*

resolute, *adj.* very determined to do something. *A resolute person will endure any hardship to reach his or her goal.*

retard, *v.* to slow down. *The five car pile-up retarded the progress of the other motorists on the highway.*

revenue, *n.* money collected from taxes or by a business. *The government receives the revenue needed to operate by taxing people and companies.*

ridicule, *v.* to make fun of. *The student was ridiculed by his classmates for giving the wrong answer in class.*

ripe, *adj.* mature, fully grown, or ready to eat. *A green banana is usually not ripe enough to eat.*

rivalry, *n.* competition. *In the Olympic Games, there is a rivalry between many nations.*

sagacity, *n.* wisdom or great knowledge. *Through long years of experience and study, the old man had acquired a sagacity about the ways of men.*

savage, *n.* one who is not civilized or educated. *Savages in the jungles of the Amazon use primitive stone tools.*

scarce, *adj.* in short supply, hard to find. *Diamonds and gold have always been scarce; that is part of the reason they are so valuable.*

scatter, *v.* to throw in many directions. *The strong wind scattered the leaves across the yard.*

schedule, *v.* to assign a particular time for an event to occur. *He was scheduled to see the doctor at 10:00 a.m. and the dentist at 1:00 p.m.*

scorn, *v.* to ridicule or to express great contempt. *The man who ran away from the battle was scorned by the other soldiers who had fought.*

scrutiny, *n.* a careful investigation or examination. *The liar hoped that the story he had told the police would pass their scrutiny.*

secure, *adj.* safe. *Until army troops move over the border and away from the city, local citizens will never feel truly secure.*

seemingly, *adv.* apparently. *Seemingly, the stranger had knocked at the door to get directions into town.*

seize, *v.* to quickly grab and hold. *The policeman seized all of the drugs and money found in the apartment.*

selective, *adj.* careful when making a choice. *We have to be very selective when purchasing a used car.*

self-reliance, *n.* to depend upon oneself. *Camping in the woods is a good test of self-reliance.*

senility, *n.* mental condition of confusion caused by old age. *Everyone reaches a state of senility if they live long enough.*

shatter, *v.* to break into many pieces. *The window was shattered by a rock.*

shield, *v.* to protect from outside harm. *A mother bear will shield her young from any danger.*

shrewd, *adj.* very clever. *A shrewd man knows both his strengths and his weaknesses.*

simulate, *v.* to copy or imitate. *Pilots often practice in a machine which simulates the problems they might face when flying.*

situate, *v.* to locate. *Los Angeles is situated in California.*

skeptical, *adj.* unbelieving. *We should always be skeptical when someone tells us they know an easy way to make money.*

sleazy, *adj.* of low quality. *The hotel room was so sleazy that not even the rats wanted to be there.*

sluggish, *adj.* slow in movement. *Bob's mind and actions are very sluggish when he first wakes up in the morning.*

soluble, *adj.* able to dissolve or melt in water or liquids. *Sugar is soluble in water.*

soothe, *v.* to ease or to calm. *Cool water is soothing on a hot day.*

species, *n.* a category of biological classification. *A new species of animal was discovered by the zoologist.*

specific, *adj.* particular or designated. *The judge wanted the defendant to give a specific answer to the question: yes or no.*

spill, *v.* to overturn so that liquid escapes. *Despite his years of experience as a waiter, Walter managed to spill the wine on the customer.*

sporadic, *adj.* occurring at odd intervals. *At sporadic times, the sky was lit by flashes of lightning.*

spurn, *v.* to reject. *She would never forget how her boyfriend had spurned her for another woman.*

squash, *v.* to stop or to destroy. *He squashed the bug with his shoe.*

stable, *adj.* steady and not easily changed. *They couldn't build the skyscraper since the area was not stable enough to support the great weight.*

stagnant, *adj.* not flowing or moving. *Mosquitoes will breed in stagnant water.*

static, *adj.* not changing. *She felt her life had grown too static; she wanted to make some changes.*

stimulate, *v.* to cause action. *The ideas in the book stimulated his imagination.*

strain, *n.* tension or stress. *The worries that he faced each day on his job caused him great strain.*

stun, *v.* to daze or to shock. *He was stunned to find out that his uncle had died and left him a million dollars.*

subject, *v.* to cause to experience or to submit to. *A traveler is subjected to the laws of the country in which he is traveling.*

subordinate, *v.* to put under the control of higher power. *The employees were surprised to hear that the company subordinated Bob, a long-time employee, to Stan, the new employee.*

substance, *n.* matter or material. *Vivian was unsure of the substance in the package, so she threw the package out.*

supersede, *v.* to displace. *Judy Cameron superseded Beatrice Mills as the president of the Women's Club on campus.*

surmise, *v.* to assume. *Many students surmised that the history class would be difficult merely by the stern look on their professor's face.*

surname, *n.* family name. *By changing his surname to Walters, Albert Waltinchizsky thought he could become a famous actor.*

survive, *v.* to continue to live. *No one can survive without food or water.*

symbolize, *v.* to represent or to stand for. *Since the American flag symbolizes freedom to many, Americans are proud to display it on the Fourth of July.*

sympathy, *n.* feelings of understanding for the problems of others. *Many people in the neighborhood like to visit the elderly woman because of her great sympathy and concern for others.*

synchronize, *v.* to align or to match the movement of two. *It took great skill for the two skaters to synchronize their movements during the performance.*

taciturn, *adj.* quiet and stern. *Jean complains that her husband is so taciturn that she can't even have an argument with him.*

tactile, *adj.* related to the sense of touch. *The curators of the state museum were pleased that the tactile activities delighted the children who visited the exhibit.*

tailor, *v.* to design to fit particular needs. *Many passengers on the cruise ship had such a good time that they swore the trip was tailored especially for them.*

tangible, *adj.* touchable or real. *Marissa insisted on some tangible evidence from her friend before she would believe her husband was cheating on her.*

tentative, *adj.* temporary or uncertain. *A tentative schedule was set up for the employees until the new business was fully operational.*

tenuous, *adj.* vague or weak. *She felt her husband's tenuous grasp of their marital problems would lead them to divorce.*

terminate, *v.* to bring to an end or to stop. *Teresa was distraught when she learned her position at the company would be terminated.*

terse, *adj.* short or brief. *She abruptly hung up the phone after Kurt's terse reply.*

therapy, *n.* treatment provided to restore good health. *After the accident, Randy received three weeks of physical therapy and was soon back at his job.*

tolerant, *adj.* open to many ideas. *The class discussions were often lively and controversial due to the instructor's tolerant attitude.*

track, *v.* to follow something's movements. *The hunter's adept ability to silently track the movements of his prey brought him many awards.*

tract, *n.* an area or region. *City officials plan to turn the tract of land along the river into a park.*

tranquility, *n.* a state of complete rest and peace. *Many people spend all their lives seeking peace and tranquility.*

transact, *v.* to engage in or to accomplish. *Simon hated the daily grind of transacting with business leaders, so he quit and became a sculptor.*

transcribe, *v.* to write down what is spoken. *Fortunately, many of the poet's last words were transcribed by his wife.*

trauma, *n.* a severe injury or a state of emotional distress. *The patients in the intensive care unit had been in a car accident and suffered heavy trauma.*

traverse, *v.* to cross. *Because the bridge was traversed by so many people traveling into the city, it was finally closed for repairs.*

trivial, *adj.* unimportant. *He thought her complaints were trivial and left the room.*

tumble, *v.* to fall down or to roll. *Mrs. Benthill shrieked as she watched her new vase tumble to the floor and shatter.*

tumult, *n.* chaos or upheaval. *The sudden cancellation of the concert caused such a tumult in the crowd that extra police were called to the site.*

turmoil, *n.* confusion. *The turmoil over her daughter's upcoming wedding gave Mrs. Windman constant headaches.*

ultimate, *adj.* the highest, the best, the most important. *Bernie's ultimate goal was to become president of the company by the age of 40.*

unique, *adj.* unlike anything else. *His paintings were so unique that he was complimented on his imagination and ingenuity.*

unreliable, *adj.* cannot be trusted. *Pete's plumbing business finally went bankrupt because of his unreliable service.*

vacillate, *v.* to hesitate or to waver. *Archie impatiently drummed his fingers on the table as his wife vacillated between ordering chicken or seafood for dinner.*

vary, *v.* to change. *The teacher always varied her lesson plans in order to keep her students stimulated and motivated.*

venture, *n.* a gamble or risk. *Mr. Stanton refused to financially support his son's latest business venture.*

verify, *v.* to check that something is true or correct. *Every statement by the bank teller about the robbery was verified by witnesses standing in the lobby.*

vibrant, *adj.* full of life. *Emma had such a vibrant personality that no one could believe she was 82 years old.*

vibrate, *v.* to move in a back-and-forth motion. *Charlie's washing machine would vibrate so loudly in the spin cycle that his neighbors constantly complained to the landlord.*

vigorously, *adv.* showing great energy or life. *Shirley spent an hour vigorously scrubbing her kitchen floor before her dinner guests arrived.*

volatile, *adj.* explosive or unsteady. *After the shooting of an innocent victim, the crowds in the streets became volatile and citizens were advised to stay at home.*

vulnerable, *adj.* open to danger or damage. *A woman walking alone at night on a deserted street is vulnerable to an attack.*

warranty, *n.* a written guarantee. *Arthur searched and searched through the box but could not find the warranty that was supposed to come with his new car radio.*

wither, *v.* to die slowly because of a lack of water. *On the fifth day of no rain, Bernice's flowers began to wither and die.*

wrath, *n.* great anger. *His wrath was so great that many employees refused to go near his office.*

zone, *n.* a specific region or area. *Because of an attack by a bear on campers, the area was declared a danger zone and visitors were denied access to it.*

HSPT/COOP/TACHS

CHAPTER 5
MATHEMATICS REVIEW

CHAPTER 5

Mathematics Review

I. Whole Numbers
II. Fractions
III. Decimals
IV. Topics in Mathematics
V. Percents
VI. Advanced Topics

Take a look back at the *Mathematics* portion of the HSPT practice test 1 or *Mathematics* test of the COOP and TACHS. If you didn't do as well here, you may or may not have to do some more work in the following areas of math:

- Concepts and Computation
- Problem Solving

I. Whole Numbers

Addition of Whole Numbers

The easiest way to add whole numbers is to write the numbers in a column with the place values lined up. That is, the ones digits are lined up in one column, the tens digits are lined up in the next column, etc. Then we add the digits down each column, moving from the right to the left to calculate our overall answer. If the sum of a column is ten or more, we place the right-hand digit of the answer column in our overall answer and "carry" the tens (or possibly hundreds) position to the next column. In the following examples we will consider some problems where carrying is necessary.

Examples
Add the following numbers.

(a) Add 345, 401, and 232.

$$
\begin{array}{r}
345 \\
401 \\
+232 \\
\end{array}
\qquad \longrightarrow \qquad
\begin{array}{r}
345 \\
401 \\
+232 \\
\hline
978 \\
\end{array}
$$

By adding the ones column, we get $5 + 1 + 2 = 8$. The tens column gives $4 + 0 + 3 = 7$, and the hundreds column gives $3 + 4 + 2 = 9$. Carrying is not used in this problem. The final answer is 978.

(b) Add 3,456; 2,589; 3,764; and 4,607.

$$
\begin{array}{r}
3456 \\
2589 \\
3764 \\
+4607 \\
\end{array}
\qquad \longrightarrow \qquad
\begin{array}{r}
\overset{2\,2\,2}{3456} \\
2589 \\
3764 \\
+4607 \\
\hline
14416 \\
\end{array}
$$

By adding the ones column, we get $6 + 9 + 4 + 7 = 26$. We can place the 6 in our answer line and carry the 2 to the tens column. (This accounts for the 2 above the 5 in the rewrite.) By adding the tens column, we get $2 + 5 + 8 + 6 + 0 = 21$. We can place the 1 in the answer line and carry the 2 to the hundreds column. (This accounts for the 2 above the 4 in the rewrite.) By adding the hundreds column, we get $2 + 4 + 5 + 7 + 6 = 24$. We can place the 4 in the answer line and carry the 2 to the thousands column. (This accounts for the 2 above the 3 in the rewrite of the problem.) By adding the thousands column, we get $2 + 3 + 2 + 3 + 4 = 14$. Since we have no more columns to add, we can write the 14 in our answer line. The final answer is 14,416.

Drill: Addition of whole numbers

Add the following numbers.

1. $245 + 912 + 357$

2. $4,376 + 1,994 + 8,953$

3. $15,274 + 98,407$

4. $4,275 + 7,136 + 3,983 + 5,648$

5. $67,134 + 34,673 + 25,876$

Answers to drill questions

1. 1,514

$$
\begin{array}{r}
\overset{1\,1}{} \\
245 \\
912 \\
+\ 357 \\
\hline
1514 \\
\end{array}
$$

2. 15,323

221

4376

1994

+ 8953

15323

3. 113,681

$1\ \ 1$

15274

+ 98407

113681

4. 21,042

222

4275

7136

3983

+ 5648

21042

5. 127,683

1111

67134

34673

+ 25876

127683

Subtraction of Whole Numbers

Now that we are "experts" at adding numbers, we want to discuss the other operations that can be used with whole numbers. In this section, we will consider subtraction. As with addition, in subtraction we will write our numbers in column format with the place values lined up. We will subtract the bottom number from the top number (if possible), moving right to left. If the subtraction is not possible, we can borrow one from the next larger column. In the following examples, we will borrow where necessary.

Examples
Subtract the following pairs of numbers.

(a) $4{,}572 - 3{,}469$

$$
\begin{array}{r} 4572 \\ -\,3469 \\ \hline \end{array}
\longrightarrow
\begin{array}{r} 45\overset{6}{\cancel{7}}2 \\ -\,3469 \\ \hline 1103 \end{array}
$$

If we try to subtract the ones column, we see that we have a difficulty ($2 - 9$ cannot be done using whole numbers). In order to do this subtraction, we need to borrow 1 from the tens column. This would change the 7 to a 6 in the tens position and change 2 into 12 in the ones position. We are now able to subtract the ones column. This will give $12 - 9 = 3$. We can write this value on our answer line. By subtracting the tens column, we get $6 - 6 = 0$. We can write this value on our answer line. By subtracting the hundreds column, we get $5 - 4 = 1$. We can write this value on our answer line. By subtracting the thousands column, we get $4 - 3 = 1$. We can write this value on our answer line. The final value is 1,103.

(b) $8,737 - 4,364$

$$
\begin{array}{r}
8737 \\
-\,4364 \\
\end{array}
\qquad\longrightarrow\qquad
\begin{array}{r}
8\overset{6}{7}37 \\
-\,4364 \\
\hline
4373 \\
\end{array}
$$

By subtracting the ones column, we get $7 - 4 = 3$. We can write this value on our answer line. In order to subtract the tens column, we need to borrow 1 from the hundreds column. The 7 becomes a 6 and the 3 becomes a 13. Therefore, subtracting the tens column gives $13 - 6 = 7$. This value can be placed on our answer line. By subtracting the hundreds column, we get $6 - 3 = 3$. We can write this value on our answer line. By subtracting the thousands column, we get $8 - 4 = 4$. We can write this value on our answer line. The final answer is 4,373.

Drill: Subtraction of whole numbers
Subtract the following pairs of numbers.

1. $9,846 - 1,345$

2. $4,256 - 2,133$

3. $3,457 - 1,246$

4. $89,725 - 68,413$

5. $2,795 - 1,257$

6. $5,637 - 4,258$

7. $85,267 - 25,456$

Answers to drill questions

1. 8,501

$$
\begin{array}{r}
9846 \\
-\,1345 \\
\hline
8501 \\
\end{array}
$$

2. 2,123

$$\begin{array}{r} 4256 \\ -\ 2133 \\ \hline 2123 \end{array}$$

3. 2,211

$$\begin{array}{r} 3457 \\ -\ 1246 \\ \hline 2211 \end{array}$$

4. 21,312

$$\begin{array}{r} 89725 \\ -\ 68413 \\ \hline 21312 \end{array}$$

5. 1,538

$$\begin{array}{r} {\scriptstyle 81} \\ 2795 \\ -\ 1257 \\ \hline 1538 \end{array}$$

6. 1,379

$$\begin{array}{r} {\scriptstyle 5121} \\ 5637 \\ -\ 4258 \\ \hline 1379 \end{array}$$

7. 59,811

$$\begin{array}{r} {\scriptstyle 7141} \\ 85267 \\ -\ 25456 \\ \hline 59811 \end{array}$$

Multiplication of Whole Numbers

The next operation that we want to discuss is multiplication. As with addition and subtraction, we will write our problems in a column format. We will begin by multiplying the ones digit in the second number by each digit in the first number. Then, if it exists, we will repeat this process with the tens digit in the second number. This action will continue until we have used each digit in the second number. Remember to carry where necessary. After multiplying the next digits, we need to add in anything carried over from the preceding product. If the second number contains more than one digit, our final step is to add down each column to get our final answer. In the following examples, we will address a variety of problems.

Examples
Multiply the following pairs of numbers.

(a) 3,451 × 67

$$
\begin{array}{r}
3451 \\
\times\ 67 \\
\end{array}
\longrightarrow
\begin{array}{r}
\overset{3\ 3}{3451} \\
\times\ 67 \\
\hline
24157
\end{array}
$$

$$
\longrightarrow
\begin{array}{r}
\overset{2\ 3}{3451} \\
\times\ 67 \\
\hline
24157 \\
+\ 207060 \\
\end{array}
\longrightarrow
\begin{array}{r}
\overset{1\ 1}{24157} \\
+\ 207060 \\
\hline
231217
\end{array}
$$

We begin by multiplying the 7 and the 1 together, producing 7. We write this value on our answer line. Then we multiply the 7 and the 5 together, getting 35. We can place the 5 on our answer line and carry the 3. (This accounts for the 3 above the 4 in the second rewrite of this problem.) We can continue this process by multiplying the 7 and the 4 together. This results in 28. When we add in the 3 that was carried over, we get 31. We can write the 1 on our answer line and carry the 3. (This accounts for the 3 appearing above the 3 in the second rewrite of the example.) By multiplying the 7 and the 3 together, we get 21. When we add in the 3 that was carried over, we get a result of 24. We can write this value on our answer line. Since the second number contains two digits, we must multiply each digit by the first number. At this point, we have only multiplied the ones digit in the second number by the first number. Now we have to do the same thing with the tens digit of the second number. We have placed a 0 in the ones digit on the answer line for the second step of this problem in order to keep the proper columns. (This is the italicized zero (0) appearing in the third rewrite of this example.) We then take 6 and multiply it by 1. This results in 6, and we can place this value on our answer line. Next, we multiply the 6 and the 5. In this case we get 30. We can place the 0 on our answer line and carry the 3. (This accounts for the 3 appearing above the 4 in the third rewrite of the above problem.) Now we can multiply the 6 and the 4 to get 24. When we add in the 3 that was carried over, we get 27. We can write the 7 on our answer line and carry the 2. (This accounts for the 2 appearing above the 3 in the third rewrite of this problem.) When we multiply the 6 and the 3 together, we get 18. When we add in the 2 that was carried over, we get 20. We can place this value on our answer line. The final stage of this problem is to add the two answer lines together. Keep in mind that we also need to carry here when necessary. Our final answer is 231,217.

(b) 736 × 142

$$
\begin{array}{r}
736 \\
\times\,142 \\
\end{array}
\longrightarrow
\begin{array}{r}
\overset{1}{736} \\
\times\,142 \\
\hline
1472 \\
\end{array}
\longrightarrow
\begin{array}{r}
\overset{12}{736} \\
\times\,142 \\
\hline
1472 \\
+\,29440 \\
\end{array}
$$

$$
\longrightarrow
\begin{array}{r}
736 \\
\times\,142 \\
\hline
1472 \\
29440 \\
+\,73600 \\
\end{array}
\longrightarrow
\begin{array}{r}
\overset{111}{1472} \\
29440 \\
+\,73600 \\
\hline
104512 \\
\end{array}
$$

We begin by multiplying the ones digit in the second number by the first number. In this problem, we would get $736 \times 2 = 1{,}472$. We place this value on our first answer line. Remember to carry when necessary. We then need to take the tens digit in the second number and multiply it by the first number. In this example, we would get $736 \times 4 = 2{,}944$. We have placed a zero (0) in the ones position of our second answer line in order to keep the proper columns. Therefore, our second answer line would be 29,440. We now need to take the hundreds digit in the second number and multiply it by the first number. In this example, we would get $736 \times 1 = 736$. We have placed zeros (0) in the ones and tens positions of our third answer line in order to keep the proper columns. Therefore, our third answer line would be 73,600. To finish up this problem, we must add the three answer lines together. If we again remember to carry where needed, we will get a final answer of 104,512. Notice that in the work above we have shown all carried numbers in italics.

(c) 632 × 113

$$
\begin{array}{r}
632 \\
\times\,113 \\
\end{array}
\longrightarrow
\begin{array}{r}
632 \\
\times\,113 \\
\hline
1896 \\
\end{array}
\longrightarrow
\begin{array}{r}
632 \\
\times\,113 \\
\hline
1896 \\
+\,6320 \\
\end{array}
$$

$$
\longrightarrow
\begin{array}{r}
632 \\
\times\,113 \\
\hline
1896 \\
6320 \\
+\,63200 \\
\end{array}
\longrightarrow
\begin{array}{r}
\overset{111}{1896} \\
6320 \\
+\,63200 \\
\hline
71416 \\
\end{array}
$$

We begin by multiplying the ones digit in the second number by the first number. In this problem, we would get $632 \times 3 = 1,896$. We place this value on our first answer line. Remember to carry when necessary. We then need to take the tens digit in the second number and multiply it by the first number. In this example, we would get $632 \times 1 = 632$. We have placed a zero (0) in the ones position of our second answer line in order to keep the proper columns. Therefore, our second answer line would be $6,320$. We now need to take the hundreds digit in the second number and multiply it by the first number. In this example, we would get $632 \times 1 = 632$. We have placed (0) in the ones and tens positions of our third answer line in order to keep the proper columns. Therefore, our third answer line would be $63,200$. To finish up this problem, we must add the three answer lines together. If we again remember to carry where needed, we will get a final answer of $71,416$. Notice that in the work above we have shown all carried numbers in italics.

Drill: Multiplication of whole numbers
Multiply the following pairs of numbers.

1. $8,157 \times 46$

2. 370×51

3. 607×32

4. 816×79

5. 434×65

Answers to drill questions

1. 375,222

$$
\begin{array}{r}
8157 \\
\times\ 46 \\
\hline
48942 \\
+\ 32628 \\
\hline
375222
\end{array}
$$

2. 18,870

$$
\begin{array}{r}
370 \\
\times\ 51 \\
\hline
370 \\
+\ 1850 \\
\hline
18870
\end{array}
$$

3. 19,424

$$
\begin{array}{r}
607 \\
\times\ 32 \\
\hline
1214 \\
+\ 1821 \\
\hline
19424
\end{array}
$$

4. 64,464

$$
\begin{array}{r}
816 \\
\times\ 79 \\
\hline
7344 \\
+\ 5712 \\
\hline
64464
\end{array}
$$

5. 28,210

$$
\begin{array}{r}
434 \\
\times\ 65 \\
\hline
2170 \\
+\ 2604 \\
\hline
28210
\end{array}
$$

Division of Whole Numbers

The last operation that we want to cover is division. By writing the problems in long division format, we can compare digits. Here we are looking to see how many times a number goes into another. That is, what must a number be multiplied by to get the other? Hopefully, this can be an exact number. If not, we have a **remainder**. In this book, we will write "R" and then the value to denote a remainder. Here we want the largest value possible without exceeding the number. This is a quick overview of the method that we will use. In the examples below, we will refine this technique.

Examples
Divide the following numbers

(a) $4{,}768 \div 32$

$$
32\,\overline{)4768} \quad \longrightarrow \quad
\begin{array}{r}
1 \\
32\,\overline{)4768} \\
-\ 32 \\
\hline
156
\end{array}
$$

$$
\longrightarrow \quad
\begin{array}{r}
14 \\
32\,\overline{)4768} \\
-\ 32 \\
\hline
156 \\
-\ 128 \\
\hline
288
\end{array}
\quad \longrightarrow \quad
\begin{array}{r}
149 \\
32\,\overline{)4768} \\
-\ 32 \\
\hline
156 \\
-\ 128 \\
\hline
288 \\
-\ 288 \\
\hline
0
\end{array}
$$

Since it is not possible for 32 to go into 4, we consider how many times 32 goes into 47. Our answer here is 1. By multiplying 32 and 1 together, we get 32. We can place this value under the first number and subtract. Here we get $47 - 32 = 15$ and bring down the next digit (6). We now consider how many times 32 goes into 156. This gives 4, since 32×4 equals 128. When we place this value under the first number and subtract, we get 28. We bring down the next digit (8) and repeat this procedure. We now consider how many times 32 goes into 288. This gives 9, since $32 \times 9 = 288$. If we place this value under the first number and subtract, we get 0. There is no remainder in this problem.

(b) $16,468 \div 46$

$$
46\,\overline{)16468} \longrightarrow
\begin{array}{r}
3 \\
46\,\overline{)16468} \\
-138 \\
\hline
266
\end{array}
\longrightarrow
$$

$$
\longrightarrow
\begin{array}{r}
35 \\
46\,\overline{)16468} \\
-138 \\
\hline
266 \\
-230 \\
\hline
368
\end{array}
\longrightarrow
\begin{array}{r}
358 \\
46\,\overline{)16468} \\
-138 \\
\hline
266 \\
-230 \\
\hline
368 \\
-368 \\
\hline
0
\end{array}
$$

Since it is not possible for 46 to go into 1 or 16, we consider how many times 46 goes into 164. Our answer here is 3. By multiplying 46 and 3 together, we get 138. We can place this value under the first number and subtract. Here we get $164 - 138 = 26$ and bring down the next digit (6). We now consider how many times 46 goes into 266. This gives 5, since $46 \times 5 = 230$. When we place this value under the first number and subtract, we get 36. We bring down the next digit (8) and repeat this procedure. We now consider how many times 46 goes into 368. This gives 8, since $46 \times 8 = 368$. If we place this value under the first number and subtract, we get 0. There is no remainder in this problem.

(c) $15,799 \div 61$

$$
61\,\overline{)15799} \longrightarrow
\begin{array}{r}
2 \\
61\,\overline{)15799} \\
-122 \\
\hline
359
\end{array}
\longrightarrow
$$

$$
\longrightarrow
\begin{array}{r}
25 \\
61\,\overline{)15799} \\
-122 \\
\hline
359 \\
-305 \\
\hline
549
\end{array}
\longrightarrow
\begin{array}{r}
259 \\
61\,\overline{)15799} \\
-122 \\
\hline
359 \\
-305 \\
\hline
549 \\
-549 \\
\hline
0
\end{array}
$$

Since it is not possible for 61 to go into 1 or 15, we consider how many times 61 goes into 157. Our answer here is 2. By multiplying 61 and 2 together, we get 122. We can place this value under the first number and subtract. Here we get $157 - 122 = 35$ and bring down the next digit (9). We now consider how many times 61 goes into 359. This gives 5, since $61 \times 5 = 305$. When we place this value under the first number and subtract, we get 54. We bring down the next digit (9) and repeat this procedure. We now consider how many times 61 goes into 549. This gives 9, since $61 \times 9 = 549$. If we place this value under the first number and subtract, we get 0. There is no remainder in this problem.

(d) $9,625 \div 21$

$$
21\overline{)9625} \longrightarrow
\begin{array}{r}
4 \\
21\overline{)9625} \\
-\ 84 \\
\hline
122
\end{array}
$$

$$
\longrightarrow
\begin{array}{r}
45 \\
21\overline{)9625} \\
-\ 84 \\
\hline
122 \\
-\ 105 \\
\hline
175
\end{array}
\longrightarrow
\begin{array}{r}
458\ \text{R}\ 7 \\
21\overline{)9625} \\
-\ 84 \\
\hline
122 \\
-\ 105 \\
\hline
175 \\
-\ 168 \\
\hline
7
\end{array}
$$

We begin by considering how many times 21 goes into 96. Our answer is 4. Since $21 \times 4 = 84$, we can place this value under the first number and subtract. After subtracting and bringing down the next digit, we get 122. We now consider how many times 21 goes into 122. Our answer here is 5. Since $21 \times 5 = 105$, we can place this value under the first number and subtract. After subtracting and bringing down the next digit, we get 175. We now consider how many times 21 goes into 175. Our answer is 8. Since $21 \times 8 = 168$, we can place this value under the first number and subtract. This subtraction result is 7. Since we have no more digits in the first number, this result (7) becomes our remainder. Our overall answer is 458 R 7.

Drill: Division of whole numbers

Divide the following numbers.

1. $7,912 \div 17$

2. $7,799 \div 25$

3. $53,920 \div 43$

4. $122,444 \div 128$

Answers to drill questions

1. 465 R 7

$$
\begin{array}{r}
4 \\
17\overline{)7912} \\
-68 \\
\hline
111
\end{array}
\longrightarrow
\begin{array}{r}
46 \\
17\overline{)7912} \\
-68 \\
\hline
111 \\
-102 \\
\hline
92
\end{array}
$$

$$
\longrightarrow
\begin{array}{r}
465\ \text{R}\ 7 \\
17\overline{)7912} \\
-68 \\
\hline
111 \\
-102 \\
\hline
92 \\
-85 \\
\hline
7
\end{array}
$$

2. 311 R 24

$$
\begin{array}{r}
3 \\
25\overline{)7799} \\
-75 \\
\hline
29
\end{array}
\longrightarrow
\begin{array}{r}
31 \\
25\overline{)7799} \\
-75 \\
\hline
29 \\
-25 \\
\hline
49
\end{array}
$$

$$
\longrightarrow
\begin{array}{r}
311\ \text{R}\ 24 \\
25\overline{)7799} \\
-75 \\
\hline
29 \\
-25 \\
\hline
49 \\
-25 \\
\hline
4
\end{array}
$$

3. 1,253 R 41

$$
\begin{array}{r}
1 \\
43 \overline{\smash{)}53920} \\
-43 \\
\hline
109
\end{array}
\longrightarrow
\begin{array}{r}
12 \\
43 \overline{\smash{)}53920} \\
-43 \\
\hline
109 \\
-86 \\
\hline
232
\end{array}
$$

$$
\longrightarrow
\begin{array}{r}
125 \\
43 \overline{\smash{)}53920} \\
-43 \\
\hline
109 \\
-86 \\
\hline
232 \\
-215 \\
\hline
170
\end{array}
\longrightarrow
\begin{array}{r}
1253 \; R\, 41 \\
43 \overline{\smash{)}53920} \\
-43 \\
\hline
109 \\
-86 \\
\hline
232 \\
-215 \\
\hline
170 \\
-129 \\
\hline
41
\end{array}
$$

4. 956 R 76

$$
\begin{array}{r}
9 \\
128 \overline{\smash{)}122444} \\
-1152 \\
\hline
724
\end{array}
\longrightarrow
\begin{array}{r}
95 \\
128 \overline{\smash{)}122444} \\
-1152 \\
\hline
724 \\
-640 \\
\hline
844
\end{array}
$$

$$
\longrightarrow
\begin{array}{r}
956 \; R\, 76 \\
128 \overline{\smash{)}122444} \\
-1152 \\
\hline
724 \\
-640 \\
\hline
844 \\
-768 \\
\hline
76
\end{array}
$$

II. Fractions

Introduction to Fractions

As we saw in the last section, whole numbers are just one type of number that can be discussed. Another kind of number is called a fraction. Fractions are expressions that are the quotient of a number expressed $\frac{a}{b}$ (where b does not equal zero). An example of a fraction would be $\frac{1}{2}$. Instead of dividing out the numbers and getting a decimal, we leave it in a "fraction format." The number on the top part of the fraction (1 in this case) is referred to as the **numerator**. The bottom part of a fraction (2 in this example) is called the **denominator**. Depending on the operation that we are looking at, each of these parts of a fraction has a significant role.

Example

In the fraction below, determine whether the 5 appears in the numerator or denominator.

$\frac{3}{5}$

In this example, the 5 appears in the bottom part of the fraction. From our discussion above, we know that this is the denominator.

Any whole number can be made into a fraction by putting it over 1. We can place the whole number in the numerator of a fraction and place a 1 in the denominator. At this point, we might have a hard time seeing why this would be of any importance. But as we proceed through this section, we will come across examples where this will be needed.

Example

Write the following whole number as a fraction.

3

In order to write this number as a fraction, we can write this value (3) in the numerator and place a one in the denominator. This gives us $\frac{3}{1}$.

If we are considering a fraction where the numerator (top part of the fraction) is smaller than the denominator (bottom part of a fraction), then we have a number that is less than one. Some examples are $\frac{1}{2}$, $\frac{3}{9}$, and $\frac{7}{11}$. In each of the above cases, the numerator is less than the denominator. Some of these fractions can be **reduced**. Instead of working with $\frac{3}{9}$, we could consider $\frac{1}{3}$. Even though these fractions look different, they have the same value. If we would divide each of them out, we would get exactly the same value (0.3333). How did we do this? By looking at the top and the bottom of $\frac{3}{9}$, we see that both the numerator and denominator have a similarity. Both of them can be divided by 3. If we divide 3 by 3 and 9 by 3, we would get 1 and 3. These are the same values that we stated above.

$$\frac{3}{9} \rightarrow \begin{array}{l} 3 \div 3 = 1 \\ 9 \div 3 = 3 \end{array} \rightarrow \frac{1}{3}$$

If we have any fractions where the top and bottom have this type of similarity, we know that we can reduce them. By reducing a fraction, we are rewriting it with smaller values in the numerator and denominator.

Examples
Reduce the following fractions.

(a) $\dfrac{4}{8}$

In this example, we have a 4 in the numerator and an 8 in the denominator. We can see that they are both divisible by 4. If we divide the numerator and denominator by 4, we get $\dfrac{1}{2}$. Below are the detailed steps.

$$\dfrac{4 \to 4 \div 4 = 1 \to 1}{8 \to 8 \div 4 = 2 \to 2}$$

(b) $\dfrac{5}{20}$

In this example, we have a 5 in the numerator and a 20 in the denominator. We can see that they are both divisible by 5. If we divide the numerator and denominator by 5, we get $\dfrac{1}{4}$. Below are the steps needed for this reduction.

$$\dfrac{5 \to 5 \div 5 = 1 \to 1}{20 \to 20 \div 5 = 4 \to 4}$$

Example
Simplify the following fraction.

$$\dfrac{86}{86}$$

In this example, we have an 86 in the numerator and denominator. These values can be divided by 86. This gives us $\dfrac{1}{1}$. Since any whole number can be written as a fraction by placing it over one, we can rewrite this fraction as 1. Below are the details needed to get this answer.

$$\dfrac{86 \to 86 \div 86 = 1 \to 1}{86 \to 86 \div 86 = 1 \to 1} = 1$$

If the numerator is greater than the denominator, we have a fraction greater than one. These types of fractions are also referred to as **improper fractions** and can be rewritten as **mixed numbers**. A mixed number is a whole number combined with a fraction. Instead of writing the number $\dfrac{11}{6}$, we can also think of it as $1\dfrac{5}{6}$. At first glance this seems strange. But, as we considered above, when the numerator and denominator match, we get 1. If we subtract 6 from 11, we get 5. This accounts for the 5 appearing as the numerator of the fractional part of the mixed number. Notice that the denominator of the fractional part has the same value as the denominator of the original fraction. In the example below, we will discuss converting improper fractions into mixed numbers.

There is another way of approaching improper fractions that some students may find easier.

Take $\dfrac{11}{6}$ from the above example. What we want to do here is take the denominator of the improper fraction and divide it into the numerator. In other words, we want to see how many 6's are in 11. We see that 6 goes into 11 once, with a remainder of 5 (there is only one 6 in 11 with 5 left over). We then place the 5 over the original denominator, 6, and place the 1 (for the amount of times 6 goes into 11) in front of $\dfrac{5}{6}$, to get the mixed number $1\dfrac{5}{6}$.

Examples

Convert these fractions into mixed numbers.

(a) $\dfrac{7}{4}$

In this example, we can see that the numerator is larger than the denominator. This tells us that this fraction has a value larger than 1. By subtracting the denominator from the numerator ($7 - 4 = 3$), we will get the numerator of the fractional part of our mixed number. Therefore, another way of saying $\dfrac{7}{4}$ is $1\dfrac{3}{4}$.

If we divide, we see 7 is divisible by 4 once with 3 left over or $1\dfrac{3}{4}$.

(b) $\dfrac{9}{7}$

In this example, we can see that the numerator is larger than the denominator. This tells us that this fraction has a value larger than 1. By subtracting the denominator from the numerator ($9 - 7 = 2$), we will get the numerator of the fractional part of our mixed number. Therefore, another way of saying $\dfrac{9}{7}$ is $1\dfrac{2}{7}$.

Dividing 9 by 7 will give us 1, with 2 left over, or $1\dfrac{2}{7}$.

Since we are able to rewrite improper fractions as mixed numbers, it would make sense that we could also go the other way. Changing mixed numbers into improper fractions is very similar to the above discussion, but in reverse. The next example will demonstrate how this can be done.

Examples

Write the following mixed numbers as improper fractions.

(a) $1\dfrac{1}{2}$

Before, we subtracted the denominator from the numerator to get the fractional part of our answer. In this case, we want to do the opposite. Here we want to think of the whole number 1 as $\dfrac{2}{2}$ (It should be noted that this method only works when the whole number of the mixed number is one). We know that these values are equal. Therefore, by adding the numerator and denominator together ($1 + 2 = 3$), we will get the numerator of our improper fraction. Another way of saying $1\dfrac{1}{2}$ would be $\dfrac{3}{2}$. Notice that the denominator of the fractional part becomes the denominator of the improper fraction.

Another way to get this answer is to multiply the denominator by the whole number and add that sum to the numerator to get our new numerator. Leaving out the whole number, and keeping the original denominator, we get the improper fraction. Take $1\frac{1}{2}$ from above. We multiply 2 and 1 and get 2. We then add this number to our current numerator to get 3. Placing the 3 in the numerator and the 2 in the denominator, we have $\frac{3}{2}$.

(b) $2\frac{4}{5}$

In this case, we are dealing with a number that has a whole part larger than 1. In order to handle this problem, we can apply the above procedure twice. Each of these procedures will convert one whole number into the corresponding fractional part. First, we want to think of 2 as $\frac{10}{5}$. We know that these values are equal. Therefore, by adding the numerator and denominator together $(4 + 10 = 14)$, we will get the numerator of our improper fraction. Another way of saying $2\frac{4}{5}$ would be $1\frac{9}{5}$. We can replace the remaining one with its fraction part. We again think of 1 as $\frac{5}{5}$. By adding the numerator and denominator together $(9 + 5 = 14)$, we will get the numerator of our improper fraction. Another way of saying $1\frac{9}{5}$ would be $\frac{14}{5}$. Therefore, we can write $2\frac{4}{5}$ as $\frac{14}{5}$. Notice that the denominator of the fractional part remains the denominator in the improper fraction.

In previous sections, we discussed the ideas of a number being less than another, two numbers being equal, and a number being greater than another. In the next section we will also discuss this notion using fractions.

Drill: Introduction to fractions

In the fractions below, determine whether the even number appears in the numerator or denominator.

1. $\frac{7}{8}$

2. $\frac{10}{13}$

Write the numbers below as fractions.

3. 43
4. 152

Reduce the following fractions as much as possible.

5. $\frac{27}{49}$

6. $\frac{12}{18}$

Convert these fractions into mixed numbers.

7. $\dfrac{26}{19}$

8. $\dfrac{18}{7}$

Write the following mixed numbers as improper fractions.

9. $2\dfrac{3}{14}$

10. $3\dfrac{1}{2}$

Answers to drill questions

1. Denominator
2. Numerator
3. $\dfrac{43}{1}$
4. $\dfrac{152}{1}$
5. $\dfrac{27}{49}$ Cannot be reduced.
6. $\dfrac{2}{3}$

$$\dfrac{12\ (\div 6)}{18\ (\div 6)} = \dfrac{2}{3}$$

7. $1\dfrac{7}{19}$

$$\dfrac{26}{19} = 1\dfrac{7}{19}$$

8. $2\dfrac{4}{7}$

$$\dfrac{18}{7} = 2\dfrac{4}{7}$$

9. $\dfrac{31}{14}$

$$2\dfrac{3}{14} = \dfrac{31}{14}$$

10. $\dfrac{7}{2}$

$$3\dfrac{1}{2} = \dfrac{7}{2}$$

Addition of Fractions

Now that we understand what fractions and mixed numbers are, we want to discuss adding, subtracting, multiplying, and dividing. This section looks at addition. In the following sections, we will address the other operations. We will discover, as we have in previous sections, that working with fractions has similarities to working with whole numbers. These topics are not exactly the same, but we will see how a good understanding of whole numbers will help us here.

The first case of adding fractions that we will consider will be when the denominators are equal. In this case, we just need to add the numerators together and bring the common denominator along for the ride. As we saw in our discussion on mixed numbers, the denominator will play a very important role in addition.

Example
Add the following fractions.

$$\dfrac{5}{12} + \dfrac{1}{12}.$$

In this example, we notice that the denominators of these fractions have the same value (12). This being the case, we just need to add the numerators together ($5 + 1 = 6$) and bring the denominator (12) along. Therefore, our answer is $\dfrac{6}{12}$. Below are the detailed steps needed to complete this problem.

$$\dfrac{5}{12} + \dfrac{1}{12} = \dfrac{5+1}{12} = \dfrac{6}{12}$$

But is this our final answer? Recall our discussions in the previous section. We saw that some fractions can be reduced. In our answer above, both the numerator and denominator can be reduced by 6. When this is accomplished, our final answer will be $\dfrac{1}{2}$. Below are the detailed steps.

$$\dfrac{6}{12} \rightarrow \dfrac{6 \div 6 = 1}{12 \div 6 = 2} \rightarrow \dfrac{1}{2}$$

We now need to look at problems where the denominators are not the same. In order to add fractions, we need to transform the denominator in each fraction into a common value. One way of accomplishing this is by taking the denominators and multiplying them together. We can easily transform each denominator into this value, but in most cases this gives an extremely large value. An example of this would be $\dfrac{6}{12} + \dfrac{7}{18}$. If we multiply the denominators together (12×18), we would get 216. This value would work as a common denominator, but is there a smaller value that would also work?

The smallest value possible that could be used is referred to as the **Lowest Common Denominator** or **LCD**. Instead of using large numbers, the LCD allows us to use the smallest value possible. Sometimes this is still a large value but, in most cases, the value we are working with is much more tolerable. The big question now becomes how do we find the LCD. The traditional way to find the LCD is to form factor trees of each denominator and then compare the factors. If we stick with the above problem ($\frac{6}{12} + \frac{7}{18}$), we would break down 12 and 18 into a list of prime numbers multiplied together.

$$12 \qquad\qquad 18$$
$$2 \times 6 \qquad\quad 2 \times 9$$
$$2 \times 2 \times 3 \qquad 2 \times 3 \times 3$$

In each level of these factor trees, we still have 12 or 18, depending on which tree we are considering. Also, in each level we are breaking down parts of the original number. We began by breaking 12 into 2×6. Since 2 is already prime, we can leave it alone. The 6, on the other hand, is not prime and can be broken down into 2×3. By combining everything together, we get $2 \times 2 \times 3$. We followed similar thinking to get the above factor tree for 18.

We now need to compare the last line of each factor tree. We begin by letting the LCD equal the bottom line of the first factor tree. In this example, we would get LCD = $2 \times 2 \times 3$. We now compare each factor in the bottom line of the other factor tree to this LCD and see what is already there and what needs to be included. We first compare the 2 to the LCD that we already have (LCD = $\underline{2} \times 2 \times 3$). Since we already have a 2 in our LCD line (the under-lined 2 in our LCD statement), we do not need to include it again. Now, we compare the next factor (3) to our LCD line. Since we already have a 3 in our LCD line (LCD = $2 \times 2 \times \underline{3}$), we don't need to include it again. The last factor we need to compare to our LCD line is another 3. This time, when we compare the 3 to our LCD line, we see that we have to include another 3 in our LCD line. This is because we have already accounted for the underlined 3. Therefore, our LCD would be $2 \times 2 \times 3 \times 3$ or 36. Even though this value is a bit large, it is nowhere near the 216 that we discussed. Knowing this, we would then transform each fraction into one that has a 36 in the denominator. Once this is done, we can add the fractions.

Even though this method works, we hope that there is an easier way. Surprisingly, there is yet another method that can be used. The main point of this method is reducing a special fraction called the **test fraction**. This test fraction is made up of the denominators in the original problem. Since denominators play such an active role in adding fractions, we want to get them involved as soon as possible. If we consider the problem from above, $\frac{6}{12} + \frac{7}{18}$, our test fraction would be $\frac{12}{18}$. We just put one denominator on the top and the other on the bottom of our test fraction. Can this fraction be reduced? Our answer here is "Yes!" Both 12 and 18 can be divided by 6 evenly. This gives $\frac{2}{3}$.

$$\frac{12}{18} \begin{array}{l} \rightarrow 12 \div 6 = 2 \rightarrow \\ \rightarrow 18 \div 6 = 3 \rightarrow \end{array} \frac{2}{3}$$

We can now take this reduced test fraction to get the LCD to appear in both fractions. Since the 2 "corresponds" with the 12 (they are both in the numerator of equal fractions), we want to place this value in both the numerator **and** denominator of the fraction that does **not** have 12 in the denominator, that is $\frac{7}{18}$. Therefore,

$$\frac{6}{12} + \frac{7}{18} = \frac{6}{12} + \frac{7 \times 2}{18 \times 2}$$

Now we can continue this process by looking at the denominators of the test fraction. Since 3 "corresponds" with the 18 (they are both in the denominator of equal fractions), we want to place this value in both the numerator **and** denominator of the fraction that does **not** have 18 in the denominator, that is, $\frac{6}{12}$. Therefore,

$$\frac{6}{12} + \frac{7 \times 2}{18 \times 2} = \frac{6 \times 3}{12 \times 3} + \frac{7 \times 2}{18 \times 2}$$

At first glance, it does not seem to help in any way. But, if we simplify both of these fractions, we will get

$$\frac{6 \times 3}{12 \times 3} + \frac{7 \times 2}{18 \times 2} = \frac{18}{36} + \frac{14}{36}$$

At this point, we notice the denominators are the same. The surprising thing is that this value (36) is the LCD. Even though this method appears lengthy, all we have to do is reduce our test fraction. Here, we don't need to worry about factor trees (or anything like this). Now that the denominators are the same, we can add the numerators. If we complete this problem, we will get

$$\frac{18}{36} + \frac{14}{36} = \frac{18 + 14}{36} + \frac{32}{36}$$

Even though we have simplified these fractions, this is not our final answer. As with our test fraction, this answer can also be reduced.

$$\frac{32}{36} \rightarrow \frac{32 \div 4}{36 \div 4} \rightarrow \frac{8}{9}$$

At last, we have our answer. Thus, $\frac{6}{12} + \frac{7}{18} = \frac{8}{9}$. Both methods discussed above will always work. Since most students prefer the second one, this will be the one stressed here.

Example
Add the following fractions.

(a) $\frac{3}{10} + \frac{2}{15}$

Our test fraction in this example is $\frac{10}{15}$. This is a must here because the denominators do not match. Our test fraction can be reduced to find out what value must be used for the LCD.

$$\frac{10}{15} \rightarrow \frac{10 \div 5 = 2}{15 \div 5 = 3} \rightarrow \frac{2}{3}$$

Since the 2 corresponds with the 10, we multiply the numerator and the denominator of the fraction that does not contain the 10 in the denominator by 2.

$$\frac{3}{10} + \frac{2}{15} = \frac{3}{10} + \frac{2 \times 2}{15 \times 2}$$

Likewise, since 3 corresponds to 15, we multiply the numerator and the denominator of the fraction that does not contain the 15 in the denominator by 3.

$$\frac{3}{10} + \frac{2 \times 2}{15 \times 2} = \frac{3 \times 3}{10 \times 3} + \frac{2 \times 2}{15 \times 2}$$

We simplify both of these fractions and see that the denominators now match. This being the case, we are able to add the numerators together.

$$\frac{9}{30} + \frac{4}{30} = \frac{9 + 4}{30} = \frac{13}{30}$$

Since this answer cannot be reduced or rewritten as a mixed number, we are done with this problem.

(b) $\frac{5}{6} + \frac{3}{8}$

In order to add these fractions, the denominators must have the same value. To begin with they do not, but we can create our test fraction and use it to determine what value should be used. Here, our test fraction is $\frac{6}{8}$.

$$\frac{6}{8} \rightarrow \frac{6 \div 2 = 3}{8 \div 2 = 4} \rightarrow \frac{3}{4}$$

Since 3 "corresponds" with the 6 (they are both in the numerator of equal fractions), we want to place this value in both the numerator **and** denominator of the fraction that does **not** have 6 in the denominator. That is, the fraction that has the 8.

$$\frac{5}{6} + \frac{3}{8} = \frac{5}{6} + \frac{3 \times 3}{8 \times 3}$$

Since 4 "corresponds" with the 8 (they are both in the denominator of equal fractions), we want to place this value in both the numerator **and** denominator of the fraction that does **not** have 8 in the denominator. That is, the fraction that has the 6.

$$\frac{5}{6} + \frac{3 \times 3}{8 \times 3} = \frac{5 \times 4}{6 \times 4} + \frac{3 \times 3}{8 \times 3}$$

If we now simplify both of these fractions, we will get $\frac{20}{24} + \frac{9}{24}$. Since the denominators are finally the same, we can add the two fractions. This will give

$$\frac{20}{24} + \frac{9}{24} = \frac{20 + 9}{24} = \frac{29}{24}$$

Since our numerator is larger than the denominator, we know that this fraction is larger than one and can be written as a mixed number. By subtracting the denominator from the numerator ($29 - 24 = 5$), we will get the numerator of the fractional part of our mixed number. Therefore, another way of saying $\frac{29}{24}$ is $1\frac{5}{24}$.

Now that we are "experts" at adding fractions, we want to consider adding mixed numbers. As we saw earlier in this section, we can rewrite mixed numbers as improper fractions. With this in mind, we want to convert the mixed numbers into fractions, add the fractions as we did above, and then convert our answer back into a mixed number if needed. The examples below show this idea in more detail.

Examples
Add the following numbers.

(a) $1\frac{1}{2} + 1\frac{2}{3}$

We begin by converting both of these mixed numbers into improper fractions. This would change the problem into $\frac{3}{2} + \frac{5}{3}$. Our test fraction in this example is $\frac{2}{3}$. Since we cannot reduce this fraction, we have $\frac{2}{3} = \frac{2}{3}$. We now know that we can multiply the top and bottom of the fraction containing a 3 in the denominator by 2. Likewise, we can multiply the top and bottom of the fraction containing a 2 in the denominator by 3.

$$\frac{3}{2} + \frac{5}{3} = \frac{3 \times 3}{2 \times 3} + \frac{5 \times 2}{3 \times 2} = \frac{9}{6} + \frac{10}{6}$$

Now that we have matching denominators, we can add the numerators. This gives us the following:

$$\frac{9}{6} + \frac{10}{6} = \frac{9 + 10}{6} = \frac{19}{6}$$

Again, in this example, our answer is an improper fraction. We know this since the top of our fraction is larger than the bottom. If we subtract the denominator from the numerator ($19 - 6 = 13$), we see that $\frac{19}{6}$ equals $1\frac{13}{6}$. We can continue this process a few more times and get $3\frac{1}{6}$. Therefore, $\frac{19}{6}$ is the same as $3\frac{1}{6}$.

(b) $3\frac{3}{4} + 1\frac{5}{6}$

We can begin by converting both of these mixed numbers into improper fractions. This will change the problem into $\frac{15}{4} + \frac{11}{6}$. Our test fraction in this example is $\frac{4}{6}$. Reducing this fraction, we have $\frac{4}{6} = \frac{2}{3}$. We now know that we can multiply the top and bottom of the fraction containing a 6 in the denominator by 2. Likewise, we can multiply the top and bottom of the fraction containing a 4 in the denominator by 3.

$$\frac{15}{4} + \frac{11}{6} = \frac{15 \times 3}{4 \times 3} + \frac{11 \times 2}{6 \times 2}$$

$$= \frac{45}{12} + \frac{22}{12}$$

Now that we have matching denominators, we can add the numerators. This gives us the following:

$$\frac{45}{12} + \frac{22}{12} = \frac{45 + 22}{12} = \frac{67}{12}$$

Again, in this example, our answer is an improper fraction. We know this because the top of our fraction is larger than the bottom. If we divide 67 by 12 we get $5\frac{7}{12}$ as our answer.

We now want to consider some unusual cases. In the examples below we will look at problems involving fractions and whole numbers, as well as problems with more than two fractions. We will see that in both cases our work is very similar to what we have already done.

Examples
Add the following numbers.

(a) $\frac{1}{2} + 3$

When adding fractions, we know that the denominators must match. In this example, the second number is not a fraction. In order to overcome this situation, we can rewrite this number as a fraction by placing it over 1 (as we did in the previous section). Therefore, we get $\frac{1}{2} + \frac{3}{1}$. Now, we need to get the bottoms of these fractions to be the same value. In this case, the LCD is 2. Since the first fraction already has 2 in its denominator, we will leave it alone. In the second fraction, we have to multiply the denominator by 2 to get our LCD to appear. To keep this fraction equal, we must also multiply the numerator by the same value (2).

$$\frac{1}{2} + \frac{3}{1} = \frac{1}{2} + \frac{3 \times 2}{1 \times 2} = \frac{1}{2} + \frac{6}{2}$$

Since the denominators are both 2, we can now add the fractions.

$$\frac{1}{2} + \frac{6}{2} = \frac{1 + 6}{2} = \frac{7}{2}$$

This answer is an improper fraction and we can simplify it to get $3\frac{1}{2}$.

(b) $\frac{1}{2} + \frac{3}{4} + \frac{7}{8}$

As with adding two fractions, in order to add three fractions, we also need a common denominator throughout the problem. It is always a good idea to use the LCD whenever possible. This keeps our numbers somewhat small. Our LCD in this example is 8. In order to get an 8 in the denominator of the first fraction, we must multiply both the top and bottom of that fraction by 4. To get an 8 to appear in the denominator of the second fraction, we must multiply the top and bottom of that fraction by 2. Since the third fraction already has 8 appearing in the denominator, we do not need to do anything with this fraction. In the first and second fractions, the numerator is also multiplied by the same value we used in the denominator so that the value of the fractions stays the same. Therefore,

$$\frac{1}{2} + \frac{3}{4} + \frac{7}{8} = \frac{1 \times 4}{2 \times 4} + \frac{3 \times 2}{4 \times 2} + \frac{7}{8}$$

We can now simplify these fractions and add them together.

$$\frac{4}{8} + \frac{6}{8} + \frac{7}{8} = \frac{4+6+7}{8} = \frac{17}{8}$$

Since the top of the fraction is larger than the bottom, we know that we have an improper fraction. If we subtract the denominator from the numerator, we can see that $\frac{17}{8}$ is $2\frac{1}{8}$.

Drill: Addition of fractions

Add the following fractions.

1. $\frac{15}{31} + \frac{9}{31}$

2. $\frac{5}{7} + \frac{6}{7}$

Add the following numbers.

3. $6\frac{4}{15} + 3\frac{1}{60}$

4. $\frac{4}{7} + 6$

5. $\frac{3}{4} + \frac{1}{8} + \frac{7}{16}$

Answers to drill questions

1. $\frac{24}{31}$

   $$\frac{15}{31} + \frac{9}{31} = \frac{24}{31}$$

2. $1\frac{4}{7}$

   $$\frac{5}{7} + \frac{6}{7} = \frac{11}{7} \text{ or } 1\frac{4}{7}$$

3. $9\frac{17}{60}$

   $$6\frac{4}{15} + 3\frac{1}{60} = 6\frac{16}{60} + 3\frac{1}{60}$$
   $$= 9\frac{17}{60}$$

4. $6\frac{4}{7}$

   $$\frac{4}{7} + 6 = 6\frac{4}{7}$$

Just combine the whole number with the proper fraction.

5. $1\dfrac{5}{16}$

$$\frac{3}{4} + \frac{1}{8} + \frac{7}{16} = \frac{12}{16} + \frac{2}{16} + \frac{7}{16}$$
$$= \frac{21}{16} = 1\frac{5}{16}$$

Subtraction of Fractions

As we saw before, addition and subtraction are not that much different. In order to subtract fractions, we need to have denominators that are the same. Our test fraction idea that we used when adding fractions will also be used here.

Example
Subtract the following numbers.

$$\frac{21}{25} - \frac{16}{25}$$

We can subtract the numerators right away since the denominators are already the same value. This gives

$$\frac{21}{25} - \frac{16}{25} = \frac{21 - 16}{25} = \frac{5}{25}$$

If we look closely at our answer, we see that it can be reduced.

$$\frac{5}{25} \rightarrow \begin{array}{l} 5 \div 5 = 1 \\ 25 \div 5 = 5 \end{array} \rightarrow \frac{1}{5}$$

Therefore, our final answer is $\dfrac{1}{5}$.

Examples
Subtract the following fractions.

(a) $\dfrac{5}{6} - \dfrac{1}{8}$

The first thing we need to do here is to get the denominators to have the same value. We can create our test fraction from the denominators in the original problem. This is $\dfrac{6}{8}$ in this case. We can reduce this fraction to get $\dfrac{3}{4}$. Since 3 corresponds to 6, we multiply the top and bottom of the fraction containing the 8 in the denominator by 3. Since 4 corresponds to 8, we multiply the top and bottom of the fraction containing the 6 in the denominator by 4.

$$\frac{5}{6} - \frac{1}{8} = \frac{5 \times 4}{6 \times 4} - \frac{1 \times 3}{8 \times 3}$$

If we simplify these fractions, we can subtract the numerators.

$$\frac{20}{24} - \frac{3}{24} = \frac{20 - 3}{24} = \frac{17}{24}$$

Since this fraction cannot be reduced, our final answer is $\frac{17}{24}$.

(b) $\frac{7}{12} - \frac{5}{9}$

First we need to use our test fraction idea to change the denominators to the same value. In this case, our test fraction would be $\frac{12}{9}$ or $\frac{4}{3}$ if we reduce it. Since the 4 corresponds to the 12, we multiply the top and bottom of the fraction containing the 9 by 4. Since the 3 corresponds to the 9, we multiply the top and bottom of the fraction containing 12 by 3.

$$\frac{7}{12} - \frac{5}{9} = \frac{7 \times 3}{12 \times 3} - \frac{5 \times 4}{9 \times 4}$$

Next, we can simplify these fractions and then subtract the numerators. This gives us

$$\frac{21}{36} - \frac{20}{36} - \frac{21 - 20}{36} = \frac{1}{36}$$

Since this fraction cannot be reduced, our final answer is $\frac{1}{36}$.

Examples
Subtract the following numbers.

(a) $3\frac{1}{2} - 2\frac{3}{4}$

When dealing with mixed numbers, the first step that we want to do is convert everything into improper fractions. In this example, our problem becomes $\frac{7}{2} - \frac{11}{4}$. Now we need to get the denominators to have the same value. This can be done using our test fraction idea. Our test fraction is $\frac{2}{4}$, or $\frac{1}{2}$ if we reduce it. Since the 1 corresponds to the 2, we multiply the top and bottom of the fraction that contains 4 by 1. Since the 2 corresponds to the 4, we multiply the top and bottom of the fraction containing 2 by 2. Therefore,

$$\frac{7}{2} - \frac{11}{4} = \frac{7 \times 2}{2 \times 2} - \frac{11 \times 1}{4 \times 1}$$

If we simplify these fractions, we can then subtract the numerators. Thus,

$$\frac{14}{4} - \frac{11}{4} - \frac{14 - 11}{4} = \frac{3}{4}$$

Since this fraction cannot be reduced, our final answer is $\frac{3}{4}$.

(b) $2\frac{1}{6} - 1\frac{7}{8}$

When dealing with mixed numbers, the first step that we want to do is convert everything into improper fractions. In this example, our problem becomes $\dfrac{13}{6} - \dfrac{15}{8}$. Now we need to get the denominators to have the same value. This can be done using our test fraction idea. Our test fraction is $\dfrac{6}{8}$, or $\dfrac{3}{4}$ if we reduce it. Since the 3 corresponds to the 6, we multiply the top and bottom of the fraction that contains 8 by 3. Since the 4 corresponds to the 8, we multiply the top and bottom of the fraction containing 6 by 4. Therefore,

$$\frac{13}{6} - \frac{15}{8} = \frac{13 \times 4}{6 \times 4} - \frac{15 \times 3}{8 \times 3}$$

If we simplify these fractions, we can then subtract the numerators. Thus,

$$\frac{52}{24} - \frac{45}{24} = \frac{52 - 45}{24} = \frac{7}{24}$$

Since this fraction cannot be reduced, our final answer is $\dfrac{7}{24}$.

Drill: Subtraction of fractions

Subtract the following numbers.

1. $\dfrac{11}{36} - \dfrac{5}{24}$

2. $\dfrac{2}{3} - \dfrac{26}{51}$

3. $2\dfrac{1}{3} - 1\dfrac{7}{9}$

4. $5\dfrac{1}{2} - 2\dfrac{5}{16}$

5. $7\dfrac{19}{36} - 5\dfrac{11}{24}$

Answers to drill questions

1. $\dfrac{7}{72}$

$$\frac{11}{36} - \frac{5}{24} = \frac{22}{72} - \frac{15}{72} - \frac{7}{72}$$

Convert each fraction to a denominator of 72, which is the lowest common denominator of 24 and 36.

2. $\dfrac{8}{51}$

$$\frac{2}{3} - \frac{26}{51} = \frac{34}{51} - \frac{26}{51} = \frac{8}{51}$$

Convert $\frac{2}{3}$ to a fraction with a denominator of 51. Subtract in the numerator.

3. $\frac{5}{9}$

$$2\frac{1}{3} - 1\frac{7}{9} = 2\frac{3}{9} - 1\frac{7}{9}$$
$$= 1\frac{12}{9} - 1\frac{7}{9} = \frac{5}{9}$$

Convert first fractional part to ninths. Change $2\frac{3}{9}$ to $1\frac{12}{9}$. Subtract whole parts and fractional parts separately.

4. $3\frac{3}{16}$

$$5\frac{1}{2} - 2\frac{5}{16} = 5\frac{8}{16} - 2\frac{5}{16} = 3\frac{3}{16}$$

Convert first fractional part to sixteenths. Subtract whole parts and fractional parts separately.

5. $2\frac{5}{72}$

$$7\frac{19}{36} - 5\frac{11}{24} = 7\frac{38}{72} - 5\frac{33}{72} = 2\frac{5}{72}$$

Convert both fractional parts to a denominator of 72, which is the lowest common denominator of 24 and 36. Subtract whole parts and fractional parts separately.

Multiplication of Fractions

Now that we understand adding and subtracting fractions, we want to switch gears and discuss multiplying fractions. Even though this topic may sound more involved, it is actually easier. In multiplication, there is no need for an LCD. Multiplying fractions is one of the most intuitive operations. For the most part, we just multiply straight across. We multiply the numerators together to get the resulting "answer" numerator, and then multiply the denominators together to get the resulting "answer" denominator. We can then reduce this "answer" (if possible) to get our final answer. As we move through this section, we see a few short-cuts that can be used to make the problems more tolerable. Initially, we will just multiply straight across.

Examples
Multiply the following numbers.

(a) $\frac{1}{2} \times \frac{1}{3}$

When multiplying fractions, we just multiply straight across. We multiply the numerators and then the denominators. In this example, we get $1 \times 1 = 1$ in the numerator and $2 \times 3 = 6$ in the denominator.

$$\frac{1}{2} \times \frac{1}{3} = \frac{1 \times 1}{2 \times 3} = \frac{1}{6}$$

Since $\frac{1}{6}$ cannot be reduced, our final answer is $\frac{1}{6}$.

(b) $\frac{4}{7} \times \frac{1}{2}$

When multiplying fractions, we just multiply straight across. We multiply the numerators and then the denominators. In this example, we get $4 \times 1 = 4$ in the numerator and $7 \times 2 = 14$ in the denominator.

$$\frac{4}{7} \times \frac{1}{2} = \frac{4 \times 1}{7 \times 2} = \frac{4}{14}$$

Notice that this fraction can be reduced. Both the top and the bottom are divisible by 2.

$$\frac{4}{14} \rightarrow \begin{array}{l} 4 \div 2 = 2 \rightarrow \\ 14 \div 2 = 7 \rightarrow \end{array} \frac{2}{7}$$

Therefore, our final answer is $\frac{2}{7}$.

Even though the method described above will always work, there is a short-cut that can help us out. A good example of these special problems is example (b) above. Instead of waiting and reducing at the end of the problem, in some problems we are able to reduce in the beginning and work with smaller numbers. In order to do this, we must have a common factor appearing in both a numerator and a denominator. The difference here is that they do not have to be in the same fraction. As long as one is above the fraction bar, one is below the fraction bar, and the operation between the fractions is multiplication, we can do a type of cancellation. Let us reconsider the above problem.

$$\frac{4}{7} \times \frac{1}{2}$$

Notice that a common factor of 2 appears in the numerator of the first fraction and in the denominator of the second fraction. Two can be divided evenly into both 4 and 2. If we do this cancellation, we replace the 4 with a 2 ($\frac{4}{2}$) and replace the 2 with a 1 ($\frac{2}{2}$).

$$\frac{4}{7} \times \frac{1}{2} = \frac{\overset{2}{4}}{7} \times \frac{1}{\underset{1}{2}} = \frac{2}{7} \times \frac{1}{1}$$

After this cancellation has been done, we multiply the fractions together as we talked about earlier.

$$\frac{2}{7} \times \frac{1}{1} = \frac{2 \times 1}{7 \times 1} = \frac{2}{7}$$

Since $\frac{2}{7}$ cannot be reduced, our answer this time is $\frac{2}{7}$. Notice that in both cases (here and example (b)), we get the same value for our answer.

Examples

Multiply the following numbers. Cancel where possible.

(a) $\dfrac{4}{5} \times \dfrac{3}{8}$

Instead of multiplying straight across, we want to consider if cancellation is possible. In this example, notice the top of the first fraction and the bottom of the second fraction. Four can be divided into both 4 and 8 evenly. Therefore, we get

$$\dfrac{4}{5} \times \dfrac{3}{8} = \dfrac{\overset{1}{\cancel{4}}}{5} \times \dfrac{3}{\underset{2}{\cancel{8}}} = \dfrac{1}{5} \times \dfrac{3}{2}$$

Now that we have cancelled where possible, we can multiply the fractions straight across.

$$\dfrac{1}{5} \times \dfrac{3}{2} = \dfrac{1 \times 3}{5 \times 2} = \dfrac{3}{10}$$

Since $\dfrac{3}{10}$ cannot be reduced, our final answer is $\dfrac{3}{10}$. Notice in this example, by cancelling first, the numbers we multiply together are smaller and easier to deal with.

(b) $\dfrac{5}{6} \times \dfrac{12}{13}$

Instead of multiplying straight across, we first want to consider if cancellation is possible. In this example, notice the bottom of the first fraction and the top of the second fraction. Six can be divided into both 6 and 12 evenly. Therefore, we get

$$\dfrac{5}{6} \times \dfrac{12}{13} = \dfrac{5}{\underset{1}{\cancel{6}}} \times \dfrac{\overset{2}{\cancel{12}}}{13} = \dfrac{5}{1} \times \dfrac{2}{13}$$

Now that we have cancelled where possible, we can multiply the fractions straight across.

$$\dfrac{5}{1} \times \dfrac{2}{13} = \dfrac{5 \times 2}{1 \times 13} = \dfrac{10}{13}$$

Since $\dfrac{10}{13}$ cannot be reduced, our final answer is $\dfrac{10}{13}$.

Now that we understand how to multiply fractions, we want to move our discussion to mixed numbers. As we did in the addition and subtraction sections, we will begin by rewriting the mixed number as an improper fraction. Then we can cancel where possible and finally multiply straight across.

Examples

Multiply the following numbers.

(a) $1\dfrac{1}{2} \times 1\dfrac{1}{3}$

We begin by converting both of these mixed numbers into improper fractions. In this example, we have $\dfrac{3}{2} \times \dfrac{4}{3}$. Instead of multiplying straight across, we want to consider if cancellation is possible. In this example, notice the top of the first fraction and the bottom of the second fraction. Three can be divided into both 3 and 3 evenly. Also, consider the bottom of the first fraction and the top of the second fraction. Two can be divided into both 2 and 4 evenly. Therefore, we get

$$\frac{3}{2} \times \frac{4}{3} = \frac{1}{1} \times \frac{2}{1} = \frac{1}{1} \times \frac{2}{1}$$

Now that we have cancelled where possible, we can multiply the fractions straight across.

$$\frac{1}{1} \times \frac{2}{1} = \frac{1 \times 2}{1 \times 1} = \frac{2}{1}$$

Since we can rewrite $\frac{2}{1}$ as 2, our final answer is 2.

(b) $3\frac{3}{4} \times 2\frac{2}{5}$

We begin by converting both of these mixed numbers into improper fractions. In this example, we have $\frac{15}{4} \times \frac{12}{5}$. Instead of multiplying straight across, we want to consider if cancellation is possible. In this example, notice the top of the first fraction and the bottom of the second fraction. Five can be divided into both 15 and 5 evenly. Also, consider the bottom of the first fraction and the top of the second fraction. Four can be divided into both 4 and 12 evenly. Therefore, we get

$$\frac{15}{4} \times \frac{12}{5} = \frac{\overset{3}{\cancel{15}}}{\underset{1}{\cancel{4}}} \times \frac{\overset{3}{\cancel{12}}}{\underset{1}{\cancel{5}}} = \frac{3}{1} \times \frac{3}{1}$$

Now that we have cancelled where possible, we can multiply the fractions straight across.

$$\frac{3}{1} \times \frac{3}{1} = \frac{3 \times 3}{1 \times 1} = \frac{9}{1}$$

Since we can rewrite $\frac{9}{1}$ as 9, our final answer is 9.

Drill: Multiplication of fractions
Multiply the following numbers.

1. $\frac{7}{13} \times \frac{3}{14}$

2. $\frac{10}{27} \times \frac{3}{20}$

3. $4\frac{2}{7} \times 5\frac{1}{6}$

4. $7\frac{1}{2} \times 1\frac{1}{3}$

5. $3\frac{4}{5} \times 2\frac{9}{38}$

Answers to drill questions

1. $\dfrac{3}{26}$

$$\frac{7}{13} \times \frac{3}{14} = \frac{\overset{1}{\cancel{7}}}{13} \times \frac{3}{\underset{2}{\cancel{14}}} = \frac{3}{26}$$

Divide 7 and 14 by 7 to produce 1 and 2. Multiply the numerators, then multiply the denominators.

2. $\dfrac{1}{18}$

$$\frac{10}{27} \times \frac{3}{20} = \frac{\overset{1}{\cancel{10}}}{\underset{9}{\cancel{27}}} \times \frac{\overset{1}{\cancel{3}}}{\underset{2}{\cancel{20}}} = \frac{1}{18}$$

Divide 10 and 20 by 10 to produce 1 and 2. Divide 3 and 27 by 3 to produce 1 and 9. Multiply the numerators, then multiply the denominators.

3. $22\dfrac{1}{7}$

$$4\frac{2}{7} \times 5\frac{1}{6} = \frac{30}{7} \times \frac{31}{6}$$

$$= \frac{\overset{5}{\cancel{30}}}{7} \times \frac{31}{\underset{1}{\cancel{6}}} = \frac{155}{7} = 22\frac{1}{7}$$

Convert mixed fractions to improper fractions. Divide 6 and 30 by 6 to produce 1 and 5. Multiply the numerators, then the denominators. Convert the improper fraction to a mixed fraction.

4. 10

$$7\frac{1}{2} \times 1\frac{1}{3} = \frac{15}{2} \times \frac{4}{3}$$

$$= \frac{\overset{5}{\cancel{15}}}{\underset{1}{\cancel{2}}} \times \frac{\overset{2}{\cancel{4}}}{\underset{1}{\cancel{3}}} = \frac{10}{1} = 10$$

Convert mixed fractions to improper fractions. Divide 3 and 15 by 3 to produce 1 and 5. Divide 2 and 4 by 2 to produce 1 and 2. Multiply the numerators, then the denominators. Reduce $\dfrac{10}{1}$ to 10.

5. $8\frac{1}{2}$

$$3\frac{4}{5} \times 2\frac{9}{38} = \frac{19}{5} \times \frac{85}{38}$$

$$= \frac{\overset{1}{\cancel{19}}}{\underset{1}{\cancel{5}}} \times \frac{\overset{17}{\cancel{85}}}{\underset{2}{\cancel{38}}} = \frac{17}{2} = 8\frac{1}{2}$$

Convert mixed fractions to improper fractions. Divide 19 and 38 by 19 to produce 1 and 2. Divide 5 and 85 by 5 to produce 1 and 17. Multiply the numerators, then the denominators. Convert the improper fraction to a mixed fraction.

Division of Fractions

As with multiplication, division does not require the use of an LCD. In some ways, division is similar to multiplication. In order to divide fractions, we rewrite the first fraction, flip the second fraction, and then multiply. Mathematicians love to change problems into ones that they already know how to simplify. In this case, they change division into multiplication. Instead of "flipping" the second fraction, sometimes this will be referred to as forming the **reciprocal**. Whether we refer to it as forming the reciprocal or flipping, we are just switching the positions of the numerator and denominator.

Examples
Divide the following fractions.

(a) $\dfrac{6}{13} \div \dfrac{12}{5}$

In order to divide these fractions, we rewrite the first fraction, flip the second fraction, and then multiply. In this problem, we have

$$\frac{6}{13} \times \frac{5}{12} = \frac{\overset{1}{\cancel{6}}}{13} \times \frac{5}{\underset{2}{\cancel{12}}}$$

$$= \frac{1}{13} \times \frac{5}{2} = \frac{1 \times 5}{13 \times 2} = \frac{5}{26}$$

Since $\dfrac{5}{26}$ cannot be reduced, our final answer is $\dfrac{5}{26}$. Notice that we cancelled where possible. Remember that we want to reconstruct our problem into multiplication before any cancelling is done.

(b) $\dfrac{5}{9} \div \dfrac{10}{18}$

In order to divide these fractions, we rewrite the first fraction, flip the second fraction, and then multiply. In this problem, we have

$$\frac{5}{9} \times \frac{18}{10} = \frac{\overset{1}{\cancel{5}}}{9} \times \frac{\overset{2}{\cancel{18}}}{\cancel{10}}_{}$$

$$= \frac{1}{1} \times \frac{\overset{1}{\cancel{2}}}{\cancel{2}} = \frac{1 \times 1}{1 \times 1} = \frac{1}{1}$$

Since $\frac{1}{1}$ can be written as 1, our final answer is 1. Notice that we cancelled where possible. Remember that we want to reconstruct our problem into multiplication before any cancelling is done.

Examples

Divide the following fractions.

(a) $2\frac{1}{5} \div 1\frac{7}{15}$

As before, we begin by writing the mixed numbers as improper fractions. In this example, we get $\frac{11}{5} \div \frac{22}{15}$. We now rewrite the first fraction, flip the second fraction, and then multiply.

$$\frac{11}{5} \times \frac{15}{22} = \frac{\overset{1}{\cancel{11}}}{\cancel{5}} \times \frac{\overset{3}{\cancel{15}}}{\cancel{22}}_{}$$

$$= \frac{1}{1} \times \frac{3}{2} = \frac{1 \times 3}{1 \times 2} = \frac{3}{2}$$

Since the numerator is larger than the denominator, we know that we are dealing with a number larger than 1. By subtracting the denominator from the numerator, we see that $\frac{3}{2}$ equals $1\frac{1}{2}$. Therefore, our final answer is $1\frac{1}{2}$.

(b) $4\frac{2}{9} \div 3\frac{1}{6}$

As before, we begin by writing the mixed numbers as improper fractions. In this example, we get $\frac{38}{9} \div \frac{19}{6}$. We now rewrite the first fraction, flip the second fraction, and then multiply.

$$\frac{38}{9} \times \frac{6}{19} = \frac{\overset{2}{\cancel{38}}}{\cancel{9}} \times \frac{\overset{2}{\cancel{6}}}{\cancel{19}}_{}$$

$$= \frac{2}{3} \times \frac{2}{1} = \frac{2 \times 2}{3 \times 1} = \frac{4}{3}$$

Since the numerator is larger than the denominator, we know that we are dealing with a number larger than 1. By subtracting the denominator from the numerator, we see that $\frac{4}{3}$ equals $1\frac{1}{3}$. Therefore, our final answer is $1\frac{1}{3}$.

Drill: Division of fractions

Divide the following fractions.

1. $\dfrac{2}{3} \div \dfrac{4}{7}$

2. $\dfrac{5}{9} \div \dfrac{10}{13}$

3. $\dfrac{13}{5} \div \dfrac{26}{50}$

4. $2\dfrac{9}{13} \div 3\dfrac{23}{39}$

5. $5\dfrac{4}{9} \div 1\dfrac{3}{18}$

Answers to drill questions

1. $1\dfrac{1}{6}$

$$\frac{2}{3} \div \frac{4}{7} = \frac{2}{3} \times \frac{7}{4} = \frac{\overset{1}{\cancel{2}}}{3} \times \frac{7}{\underset{2}{\cancel{4}}} = \frac{7}{6} = 1\frac{1}{6}$$

2. $\dfrac{13}{18}$

$$\frac{5}{9} \div \frac{10}{13} = \frac{5}{9} \times \frac{13}{10} = \frac{\overset{1}{\cancel{5}}}{9} \times \frac{13}{\underset{2}{\cancel{10}}} = \frac{13}{18}$$

3. 5

$$\frac{13}{5} \div \frac{26}{50} = \frac{13}{5} \times \frac{50}{26}$$
$$= \frac{\overset{1}{\cancel{13}}}{\underset{1}{\cancel{5}}} \times \frac{\overset{10}{\cancel{50}}}{\underset{2}{\cancel{26}}} = \frac{10}{2} = 5$$

4. $\dfrac{3}{4}$

$$2\frac{9}{13} \div 3\frac{23}{39} = \frac{35}{13} \div \frac{140}{39} = \frac{35}{13} \times \frac{39}{140}$$
$$= \frac{\overset{1}{\cancel{35}}}{\underset{1}{\cancel{13}}} \times \frac{\overset{3}{\cancel{39}}}{\underset{4}{\cancel{140}}} = \frac{3}{4}$$

5. $4\frac{2}{3}$

$$5\frac{4}{9} \div 1\frac{3}{18} = \frac{49}{9} \div \frac{21}{18} = \frac{49}{9} \times \frac{18}{21}$$

$$= \frac{\overset{7}{\cancel{49}}}{\underset{1}{\cancel{9}}} \times \frac{\overset{2}{\cancel{18}}}{\underset{3}{\cancel{21}}} = \frac{14}{3} = 4\frac{2}{3}$$

III. Decimals

Introduction to Decimals

As we go through life we learn that not all numbers are whole numbers. In some cases, we have "pieces" of a whole number, for example, when we work with money. When visiting a store, we often find prices like $4.99, $10.35, and $1.79. In each of these cases, we have **decimals**. The digit or digits to the left of the decimal point (.) is the whole number part of our price and the digit or digits to the right of the decimal point is the decimal part. Working with decimals is very similar to working with whole numbers. Decimal numbers also have place values in the same way as whole numbers. The whole number part of a decimal number has the same place values as we discussed in Section I. The place values for the decimal part are very similar except that instead of the place values ending in "s," the decimal place values end in "ths." If we consider the decimal number below, we can see an example of this.

15.3864
1 is in the tens place
5 is in the ones place
3 is in the ten*ths* place
8 is in the hundred*ths* place
6 is in the thousand*ths* place
4 is in the ten thousand*ths* place

The only confusing part of this discussion is that there is no "oneths" or "onths" place. Except for that, the place values are exactly the same. If we pair the decimal point with the ones place, we can see the similarities better—tens and tenths, hundreds and hundredths, etc.

Example

Write the place value of the 7 in the following numbers.

(a) 29.<u>7</u>52

This 7 is in the <u>tenths</u> place.

(b) 6.12<u>7</u>5

This 7 is in the <u>thousandths</u> place.

(c) 5.2<u>7</u>3

This 7 is in the <u>hundredths</u> place.

(d) 0.659<u>7</u>

This 7 is in the <u>ten</u> <u>thousandths</u> place.

Rounding decimal numbers is very similar to rounding whole numbers. Sometimes an approximation can be used instead of working with the exact value. A few examples are listed below.

Examples
Round the following numbers to the appropriate position.

   (a) Round 3.467 to the hundredths position.
   3.4<u>6</u>7—Since the digit to the right is 7, we would add 1 to the marked digit and drop the remainder of the number: 3.47

   (b) Round 14.5299 to the tenths position.
   14.<u>5</u>299—Since the digit to the right is 2, we would leave the marked digit alone and drop the remainder of the number: 14.5

   (c) Round 0.245789 to the ten thousandths position.
   0.245<u>7</u>89—Since the digit to the right is 8, we would add 1 to the marked digit and drop the remainder of the number: 0.2458

   (d) Round 7.29342 to the thousandths position.
   7.29<u>3</u>42—Since the digit to the right is 4, we would leave the marked digit alone and drop the remainder of the number: 7.293

Drill: Introduction to decimals
Write the place value of the underlined digit in the following numbers.

1. 234.67<u>8</u>9 _____

2. 8.1<u>2</u>4 _____

3. 0.7640<u>2</u> _____

4. 69.34<u>6</u>56 _____

5. 49.5<u>3</u>561 _____

Round the following numbers to the underlined position.

6. 56.5<u>4</u>78 _____

7. 0.4<u>8</u>36 _____

8. 7.583<u>1</u>34 _____

9. 67.528<u>4</u>5 _____

10. 0.<u>8</u>64 _____

Answers to drill questions

1. Thousandths. The third place value to the right of the decimal point is the thousandths place.

2. Tenths. The first place value to the right of the decimal point is the tenths place.

3. Hundred thousandths. The fifth place value to the right of the decimal point is the hundred thousandths place.

4. Thousandths. The third place value to the right of the decimal point is the thousandths place.

5. Hundredths. The second place value to the right of the decimal point is the hundreths place.

6. 56.54<u>8</u>

7. 0.4<u>8</u>

8. 7.583<u>13</u>

9. 67.528<u>5</u>

10. 0.<u>9</u>

Addition of Decimals

Now that we have a better understanding of decimals, what can we do with them? The same four operations (addition, subtraction, multiplication, and division) can be used here. The following sections will deal with each of these operations in turn.

In order to add decimal numbers, we must write the numbers in a column with the decimal points lined up. To help with spacing and columns, we can use zero (0) as a place holder to block off the problem. The examples below demonstrate this method.

Examples
Add the following numbers.

(a) Add 2.467482, 1.4126, and 3.46571.

$$
\begin{array}{r}
\overset{1\ \ 111}{2.467482} \\
1.412600 \\
+\ 3.465710 \\
\hline
7.345792
\end{array}
$$

$$
\begin{array}{r}
2.467482 \\
1.4126 \\
+\ 3.46571 \\
\hline
\end{array} \quad \rightarrow
$$

(b) Add 7.5189, 5.789, 1.7826, and 2.54799.

	_2 2 2 2_
7.5189	7.51890
5.789	5.78900
1.7826	1.78260
+ 2.54799 →	+ 2.54799
	17.63849

(c) 2.45789 + 3.483

	_11_
2.45789	2.45789
+ 3.483 →	+ 3.48300
	5.94089

(d) 34.6 + 65.856 + 43.68743

	_12 11_
34.6	34.60000
65.856	65.85600
+ 43.68743 →	+ 43.68743
	144.14343

Drill: Addition of decimals
Add the following numbers.

1. 4.57457 + 3.4678

2. 3.4896 + 8.57046 + 3.489861

3. 24.589434 + 56.7257 + 6.76821

4. 8.72566 + 4.5745 + 3.463019

5. 24.5869 + 8.24567 + 452.772

Answers to drill questions
1. 8.04237

_1111_
4.57457
+ 3.4678
8.04237

2. 15.549921

$\underline{12111}$
3.4896
8.57046
+ 3.489861
15.549921

3. 88.083344

$\underline{12121}$
24.589434
56.7257
+ 6.76821
88.083344

4. 16.763179

$\underline{1111}$
8.72566
4.5745
+ 3.463019
16.763179

5. 485.60457

$\underline{11\ 211}$
24.5869
8.24567
+ 452.772
485.60457

Subtraction of Decimals

As we saw in the previous section, working with decimals is very similar to working with whole numbers. Some of the same ideas that we used in addition also apply to subtraction. We need to begin by lining up the decimal points. Using zeros as place holders can also help keep the columns and place values straight. Recall that sometimes we need to borrow in order to subtract. The examples below demonstrate these topics.

Examples
Subtract the following numbers. Borrow when necessary.

(a) 4.25734 − 3.4857

$\qquad\qquad\qquad\qquad\qquad \underline{111}$
4.25734 $\qquad\qquad$ 3.4857
− 3.4857 $\quad \longrightarrow \quad$ − 3.48570

$\qquad\qquad\qquad\qquad\qquad$ 0.77164

(b) 86.8348 − 34.5786

$$
\begin{array}{r}
86.8348 \\
-\ 34.5786 \\
\hline
\end{array}
\qquad \longrightarrow \qquad
\begin{array}{r}
{\scriptstyle 11} \\
86.7248 \\
-\ 34.5786 \\
\hline
52.2562
\end{array}
$$

Drill: Subtraction of decimals

Subtract the following numbers.

1. 9.5867 − 4.1571

2. 65.876 − 48.1323

3. 45.892459 − 2.35634

4. 12.3415 − 2.63756

5. 458.9756 − 245.86789

Answers to drill questions

1. 5.4296

$$
\begin{array}{r}
9.5867 \\
-\ 4.1571 \\
\hline
5.4296
\end{array}
$$

2. 17.7437

$$
\begin{array}{r}
65.8760 \\
-\ 48.1323 \\
\hline
17.7437
\end{array}
$$

3. 43.536119

$$
\begin{array}{r}
45.892459 \\
-\ 2.356340 \\
\hline
43.536119
\end{array}
$$

4. 9.70394

$$\overset{\overset{1}{1}}{}\quad\overset{\overset{3\,0\,4}{1\,1\,1}}{}$$

12.34150
− 2.63756
─────────
9.70394

5. 213.10771

$$\overset{6\,4\,5}{1\,1\,1}$$

458.97560
− 245.86789
──────────
213.10771

Multiplication of Decimals

Now that we are "experts" in addition and subtraction of decimals, we can switch our discussion to multiplication. Multiplying decimals is closer to working with whole numbers than either of the above topics. Here we want to write the numbers in a table format and multiply them together as if the decimal points were not present. After we get a result we must take into account that the original problem was made up of decimal numbers. Next, we must add the decimal places in all the numbers involved in the problem. In order to get the proper placement of the decimal point in the final answer, we count off the correct number of places moving right to left. The examples that follow consider most of the details that might arise.

Examples
Multiply the following numbers.

(a) 5.68×2.3

5.68	568	5.68 (2 decimal places)
× 2.3 →	× 23 →	× 2.3 (1 decimal place)
	1704	13.064 (3 decimal places)
	+ 11360	
	13064	

(b) 4.564×3.12

4.564	4564	4.564 (3 decimal places)
× 3.12 →	× 312 →	× 3.12 (2 decimal places)
	9128	14.23968 (5 decimal places)
	45640	
	+ 1369200	
	1423968	

(c) 0.258×0.6

0.258		258		0.258	(3 decimal places)
$\times\ 0.6$	$\rightarrow$	$\times\ 6$	$\rightarrow$	$\times\ 0.6$	(1 decimal place)
		1548		0.1548	(4 decimal places)

(d) 0.023×0.07

0.023		23		0.023	(3 decimal places)
$\times\ 0.07$	$\rightarrow$	$\times\ 7$	$\rightarrow$	$\times\ 0.07$	(2 decimal places)
		161		0.00161	(5 decimal places)

(e) 341.786×6.7

341.786		341786		341.786	(3 decimal places)
$\times\ 6.7$	$\rightarrow$	$\times\ 67$	$\rightarrow$	$\times\ 6.7$	(1 decimal place)
		2392502		2289.9662	(4 decimal places)
		$+\ 20507160$			
		22899662			

(f) 0.6045×3.7

0.6045		6045		0.6045	(4 decimal places)
$\times\ 3.7$	$\rightarrow$	$\times\ 37$	$\rightarrow$	$\times\ 3.7$	(1 decimal place)
		42315		2.23665	(5 decimal places)
		$+\ 181350$			
		223665			

Drill: Multiplication of decimals
Multiply the following numbers.

1. 0.9674×0.56

2. 3.1358×0.512

3. 34.7×0.68

4. 2.356×0.971

5. 134.689×2.34

Answers to drill questions

1. 0.541744

0.9674	(4 decimal places)
$\times\ 0.56$	(2 decimal places)
58044	
$+\ 48370$	
0.541744	(6 decimal places)

2. 1.6055296

        3.1358   (4 decimal places)

     × 0.512   (3 decimal places)

       62716

       31358

  +156790

   1.6055296   (7 decimal places)

3. 23.596

        34.7   (1 decimal place)

    × 0.68   (2 decimal places)

     2776

  + 2082

  23.596   (3 decimal places)

4. 2.287676

      2.356   (3 decimal places)

   × 0.971   (3 decimal places)

     2356

   16492

  + 21204

  2.287676   (6 decimal places)

5. 315.17226

    134.689   (3 decimal places)

    × 2.34   (2 decimal places)

   538756

   404067

 +269378

 315.17226   (5 decimal places)

Division of Decimals

We divide decimals in essentially the same way that we divided whole numbers. If we are dividing by a whole number, we just bring the decimal point up to our answer line and then divide as we did in the previous chapter. On the other hand, if we are dividing by a decimal number, we must first move the decimal point of this number to the right as many spaces as needed to make it a whole number. In order to keep our problem equivalent, we must move the decimal point of the number under the division bar by the same number of places. If we move the decimal point two spaces to the right in the number outside, we must also move the decimal point two spaces to the right inside the division bar. In the following examples, we will address both of these situations. Instead of leaving our answer with a remainder, we can use zeros as place holders and continue dividing until our answer works out exactly.

Examples

Divide the following numbers.

(a) $5.8956 \div 17$

$$
17 \overline{)5.8956} \longrightarrow
\begin{array}{r}
0.3 \\
17 \overline{)5.8956} \\
-51 \\
\hline
79
\end{array}
\longrightarrow
\begin{array}{r}
0.34 \\
17 \overline{)5.8956} \\
-51 \\
\hline
79 \\
-68 \\
\hline
115
\end{array}
\longrightarrow
$$

$$
\begin{array}{r}
0.346 \\
17 \overline{)5.8956} \\
-51 \\
\hline
79 \\
-68 \\
\hline
115 \\
-102 \\
\hline
136
\end{array}
\longrightarrow
\begin{array}{r}
0.3468 \\
17 \overline{)5.8956} \\
-51 \\
\hline
79 \\
-68 \\
\hline
115 \\
-102 \\
\hline
136 \\
-136 \\
\hline
0
\end{array}
$$

Since we are dividing by a whole number, we just need to move the decimal point up to our answer line and divide as we did in the last section. How many times will 17 go into 58? Our answer here would be 3. Since $17 \times 3 = 51$, we can place this value under the first number and subtract. If we subtract and bring down the next digit, we get 79. Now we need to consider how many times 17 goes into 79. Our answer is 4. Since $17 \times 4 = 68$, we can place this value under the first number and subtract. If we subtract and bring down the next digit, we get 115. Now we consider how many times 17 goes into 115. Our answer is 6. Since $17 \times 6 = 102$, we can place this value under the first number and subtract. If we subtract and bring down the next digit, we will get 136. Now we consider how many times 17 goes into 136. Our answer is 8. Since $17 \times 8 = 136$, we can place this value under the first number and subtract. Here we get $136 - 136 = 0$. We have no remainder in this problem. Our overall answer would be 0.3468.

(b) $1218.14 \div 49$

$$
\begin{array}{r}
. \\
49\,\overline{)1218.14}
\end{array}
\longrightarrow
\begin{array}{r}
2. \\
49\,\overline{)1218.14} \\
-\,98 \\
\hline
238
\end{array}
\longrightarrow
\begin{array}{r}
24. \\
49\,\overline{)1218.14} \\
-\,98 \\
\hline
238 \\
-\,196 \\
\hline
42.1
\end{array}
$$

$$
\longrightarrow
\begin{array}{r}
24.8 \\
49\,\overline{)1218.14} \\
-\,98 \\
\hline
238 \\
-\,196 \\
\hline
421 \\
-\,392 \\
\hline
294
\end{array}
\longrightarrow
\begin{array}{r}
24.86 \\
49\,\overline{)1218.14} \\
-\,98 \\
\hline
238 \\
-\,196 \\
\hline
421 \\
-\,392 \\
\hline
294 \\
-\,294 \\
\hline
0
\end{array}
$$

Since we are dividing by a whole number, we just need to move the decimal point up to our answer line and divide as we did in the last section. How many times will 49 go into 121? Our answer is 2. Since $49 \times 2 = 98$, we can place this value under the first number and subtract. If we subtract and bring down the next digit, we will get 238. Now we need to consider how many times 49 goes into 238. Our answer is 4. Since $49 \times 4 = 196$, we can place this value under the first number and subtract. If we subtract and bring down the next digit, we get 421. Now we consider how many times 49 goes into 421. Our answer is 8. Since $49 \times 8 = 392$, we can place this value under the first number and subtract. If we subtract and bring down the next digit, we will get 294. Now we consider how many times 49 goes into 294. Our answer is 6. Since $49 \times 6 = 294$, we can place this value under the first number and subtract. Here we get $294 - 294 = 0$. We have no remainder in this problem. Therefore, our overall answer is 24.86.

(c) $74.36 \div 0.2$

$$
\begin{array}{r}
. \\
0.2\,\overline{)74.36}
\end{array}
\longrightarrow
\begin{array}{r}
3. \\
2\,\overline{)743.6} \\
-\,6 \\
\hline
14
\end{array}
\longrightarrow
\begin{array}{r}
37. \\
2\,\overline{)743.6} \\
-\,6 \\
\hline
14 \\
-\,14 \\
\hline
3
\end{array}
$$

$$
\longrightarrow
\begin{array}{r}
371. \\
2\,\overline{)743.6} \\
-\,6 \\
\hline
14 \\
-\,14 \\
\hline
3 \\
-\,2 \\
\hline
16
\end{array}
\longrightarrow
\begin{array}{r}
371.8 \\
2\,\overline{)743.6} \\
-\,6 \\
\hline
14 \\
-\,14 \\
\hline
3 \\
-\,2 \\
\hline
16 \\
-\,16 \\
\hline
0
\end{array}
$$

We are familiar with dividing a number by 3 or 7, but not by 0.2. By moving the decimal point one place to the right, this value becomes 2. In order to keep this problem equivalent, we must also move the decimal inside the division bar one space to the right. This changes 74.36 into 743.6. Now we divide 2 into 743.6 as we did in the examples above. Two goes into 7 three times. Since $2 \times 3 = 6$, we can place this value under the first number and subtract. This gives 1, and by bringing down the next digit, we get 14. Two goes into 14 seven times. Since $2 \times 7 = 14$, we can place this value under the first number and subtract. This gives 0. When we bring down the next digit, we get 3. Two goes into 3 once. Since $2 \times 1 = 2$, we can place this value under the first number and subtract. This gives 1. When we bring down the next digit, we get 16. Two goes into 16 eight times. Since $2 \times 8 = 16$, we can place this value under the first number and subtract. This gives us 0. Our overall answer is 371.8.

(d) $0.876 \div 0.06$

$$
0.06\,\overline{)\,0.876} \longrightarrow
\begin{array}{r} 1. \\ 6\,\overline{)\,87.6} \\ -6 \\ \hline 27 \end{array}
\longrightarrow
\begin{array}{r} 14. \\ 6\,\overline{)\,87.6} \\ -6 \\ \hline 27 \\ -24 \\ \hline 36 \end{array}
\longrightarrow
\begin{array}{r} 14.6 \\ 6\,\overline{)\,87.6} \\ -6 \\ \hline 27 \\ -24 \\ \hline 36 \\ -36 \\ \hline 0 \end{array}
$$

Since we are dividing by 0.06, we must move the decimal point two places to the right. In order to keep this problem equivalent, we must also move the decimal point under the division bar two places to the right. This changes 0.876 into 87.6. Six goes into 8 once. Since $6 \times 1 = 6$, we can place this value under the first number and subtract. This gives 2. When we bring down the next digit, we get 27. Six goes into 27 four times. Since $6 \times 4 = 24$, we can place this value under the first number and subtract. This will give us 3. When we bring down the next digit, we get 36. Six goes into 36 six times. Since $6 \times 6 = 36$, we can place this value under the first number and subtract. This gives us 0. Therefore, our final answer is 14.6.

(e) $6.1663 \div 0.23$

$$
0.23\,\overline{)\,6.1663} \longrightarrow
\begin{array}{r} 2. \\ 23\,\overline{)\,616.63} \\ -46 \\ \hline 156 \end{array}
\longrightarrow
\begin{array}{r} 26. \\ 23\,\overline{)\,616.63} \\ -46 \\ \hline 156 \\ -138 \\ \hline 186 \end{array}
$$

$$
\longrightarrow
\begin{array}{r} 26.8 \\ 23\,\overline{)\,616.63} \\ -46 \\ \hline 156 \\ -138 \\ \hline 186 \\ -184 \\ \hline 23 \end{array}
\longrightarrow
\begin{array}{r} 26.81 \\ 23\,\overline{)\,616.63} \\ -46 \\ \hline 156 \\ -138 \\ \hline 186 \\ -184 \\ \hline 23 \\ -23 \\ \hline 0 \end{array}
$$

Since we are dividing by 0.23, we must move the decimal point two places to the right. In order to keep this problem equivalent, we must also move the decimal point under the division bar two places to the right. This changes 6.1663 into 616.63. Twenty-three goes into 61 twice. Since $23 \times 2 = 46$, we can place this value under the first number and subtract. This gives 15, and when we bring down the next digit, we get 156. Twenty-three goes into 156 six times. Since $23 \times 6 = 138$, we can place this value under the first number and subtract. This will give us 18, and when we bring down the next digit, we get 186. Twenty-three goes into 186 eight times. Since $23 \times 8 = 184$, we can place this value under the first number and subtract. This gives us 2, and when we bring down the next digit, we get 23. Twenty-three goes into 23 once. Since $23 \times 1 = 23$, we can place this value under the first number and subtract. This gives us 0. Therefore, our final answer is 26.81.

(f) $0.2235 \div 0.06$

$$
0.06 \overline{)0.2235} \quad \longrightarrow \quad
\begin{array}{r}
3. \\
6\overline{)22.35} \\
-18 \\
\hline
43
\end{array}
\quad \longrightarrow \quad
\begin{array}{r}
3.7 \\
6\overline{)22.35} \\
-18 \\
\hline
43 \\
-42 \\
\hline
15
\end{array}
$$

$$
\longrightarrow \quad
\begin{array}{r}
3.72 \\
6\overline{)22.35} \\
-18 \\
\hline
43 \\
-42 \\
\hline
15 \\
-12 \\
\hline
3
\end{array}
\quad \longrightarrow \quad
\begin{array}{r}
3.725 \\
6\overline{)22.350} \\
-18 \\
\hline
43 \\
-42 \\
\hline
15 \\
-12 \\
\hline
30 \\
-30 \\
\hline
0
\end{array}
$$

Here, we are dividing 0.2235 by 0.06. In order to do this, we must move our decimal points two places to the right. We now have 6 being divided into 22.35. Six goes into 22 three times. Since $6 \times 3 = 18$, we can place this value under the first number and subtract. This will give us 4, and when we bring down the next digit, we get 43. Six goes into 43 seven times. Since $6 \times 7 = 42$, we can place this value under the first number and subtract. This gives 1, and when we bring down the next digit, we get 15. Six goes into 15 twice. Since $6 \times 2 = 12$, we can place this value under the first number and subtract. This will give us 3. If we place a zero after the number and continue our division, we can work this problem out exactly. Six goes into 30 five times. Since $6 \times 5 = 30$, we can place this value under the first number and subtract. This gives us 0. Therefore, our final answer is 3.725.

(g) $1.8629 \div 0.25$

$$
0.25 \overline{)1.8629} \quad \longrightarrow \quad
\begin{array}{r}
7. \\
25\overline{)186.29} \\
-175 \\
\hline
112
\end{array}
\quad \longrightarrow \quad
\begin{array}{r}
7.4 \\
25\overline{)186.29} \\
-175 \\
\hline
112 \\
-100 \\
\hline
129
\end{array}
\quad \longrightarrow
$$

$$
\begin{array}{r}
7.45 \\
25\overline{\smash{)}186.29} \\
-175 \\
\hline
112 \\
-100 \\
\hline
129 \\
-125 \\
\hline
4
\end{array}
\quad\longrightarrow\quad
\begin{array}{r}
7.451 \\
25\overline{\smash{)}186.290} \\
-175 \\
\hline
112 \\
-100 \\
\hline
129 \\
-125 \\
\hline
40 \\
-25 \\
\hline
15
\end{array}
\quad\longrightarrow\quad
\begin{array}{r}
7.4516 \\
25\overline{\smash{)}186.2900} \\
-175 \\
\hline
112 \\
-100 \\
\hline
129 \\
-125 \\
\hline
40 \\
-25 \\
\hline
150 \\
-150 \\
\hline
0
\end{array}
$$

In order to divide 1.8629 by 0.25, we must move the decimal points two places to the right. Now we are dividing 186.29 by 25. Twenty-five goes into 186 seven times. Since 25 × 7 = 175, we can place this value under the first number and subtract. This gives 11, and when we bring down the next digit, we get 112. Twenty-five goes into 112 four times. Since 25 × 4 = 100, we can place this value under the first number and subtract. This gives 12, and when we bring down the next digit, we get 129. Twenty-five goes into 129 five times. Since 25 × 5 = 125, we can place this value under the first number and subtract. This gives us 4, and if we bring down the next digit (a zero used as a place holder at the end of the number), we get 40. Twenty-five goes into 40 once. Since 25 × 1 = 25, we can place this value under the first number and subtract. This gives us 15, and when we bring down the next digit (another zero used as a place holder at the end of the number), we get 150. Twenty-five goes into 150 six times. Since 25 × 6 = 150, we can place this value under the first number and subtract. This gives us 0. Our final answer is 7.4516.

Drill: Division of decimals
Divide the following numbers.

1. 1,135.52 ÷ 47

2. 59.276 ÷ 0.7

3. 35.075 ÷ 0.61

4. 163.1463 ÷ 4.3

5. 0.941196 ÷ 0.123

Answers to drill questions

1. 24.16

```
      2  .              24.                24.1               24.16
47 ⌐1135.52   →   47 ⌐1135.52   →   47 ⌐1135.52   →   47 ⌐1135.52
  − 94              − 94               − 94               − 94
   195               195                195                195
                   − 188              − 188              − 188
                     75                 75                 75
                                      − 47               − 47
                                       282                282
                                                        − 282
                                                           0
```

2. 84.68

```
                       8.                84.                84.6               84.68
0.7 ⌐59.276   →   7 ⌐592.76   →   7 ⌐592.76   →   7 ⌐592.76   →   7 ⌐592.76
                   − 56              − 56              − 56              − 56
                    32                32                32                32
                                    − 28              − 28              − 28
                                      47                47                47
                                                      − 42              − 42
                                                        56                56
                                                                        − 56
                                                                           0
```

3. 57.5

```
                         5.                57.                57.5
0.61 ⌐35.075   →   .61 ⌐3507.5   →   .61 ⌐3507.5   →   .61 ⌐3507.5
                     − 305              − 305              − 305
                      457                457                457
                                       − 427              − 427
                                         305                305
                                                          − 305
                                                             0
```

4. 37.941

```
             .                 3.                37.
4.3 ⌐163.1463   →   43 ⌐1631.463   →   43 ⌐1631.463
                     − 129              − 129
                      341                341
                                       − 301
                                         404
```

```
         37.9              37.94              37.941
    43 ⎡ 1631.463  →   43 ⎡ 1631.463  →   43 ⎡ 1631.463
       – 129             – 129              – 129
       ─────             ─────              ─────
         341               341                341
       – 301             – 301              – 301
       ─────             ─────              ─────
         404               404                404
       – 387             – 387              – 387
       ─────             ─────              ─────
         176               176                176
                         – 172              – 172
                         ─────              ─────
                           43                 43
                                            – 43
                                            ─────
                                               0
```

5. 7.652

```
                              7.                    7.6
  0.123 ⎡ 0.941196   →   123 ⎡ 941.196   →   123 ⎡ 941.196
                            – 861                 – 861
                            ─────                 ─────
                              801                   801
                                                  – 738
                                                  ─────
                                                    639
```

```
            7.65                  7.652
     123 ⎡ 941.196   →     123 ⎡ 941.196
        – 861                 – 861
        ─────                 ─────
          801                   801
        – 738                 – 738
        ─────                 ─────
          639                   639
        – 615                 – 615
        ─────                 ─────
           24                   246
                              – 246
                              ─────
                                 0
```

IV. Topics in Mathematics

Simplifying Expressions

Since we have a good understanding of natural numbers and decimals, we want to move our attention to other topics in mathematics. In this section, we will begin to see how mathematics can be used in physical situations. In order to make our work easier, we first want to discuss the "Order of Operations." These rules give us a recipe, or **algorithm**, to follow when simplifying mathematical expressions. We start at the top of the list and proceed down until all operations have been completed. The list below sets the order of operations. This order makes sure that we all get the same answer from a problem. Most of these ideas have already been discussed, but a few are new to the section. We will explain in detail those topics that have not already been explained.

Order of operations

1. Do the operations above and below the fraction bar separately.
2. Work inside the parentheses (innermost first). Note that ( ), [ ], and { } can all be used as grouping symbols and are generally referred to as parentheses.
3. Simplify exponents.
4. Multiply and divide from left to right. Note that multiplication and division are done at the same time as we move left to right.
5. Add and subtract from left to right. Note that addition and subtraction are also done at the same time as we move left to right.

Examples

Simplify the following expressions.

    (a) $4 + 2(1 + 6)$

In this example, we must begin inside the parentheses and simplify this part of the expression. Here $1 + 6$ equals 7. If we substitute this value into our expression we get

$4 + 2(7)$

According to our order of operations, the next thing to do is the multiplication (2×7). Even though the multiplication symbol does not appear in the original expression, it is implied. Anytime we have a parenthesis next to another parenthesis or number together without an operation, such as ")(" and "2(," it is understood that multiplication is the operation being indicated. In this example, 2×7 equal 14. Thus, our expression becomes

$4 + 14$

Finally, we can do the addition and get our answer. Here our final answer is 18.

    (b) $\dfrac{1 + 2(7 - 5)}{4(9 - 6) + 3}$

In this example, we must simplify the numerator and denominator of this expression separately. Keep in mind that we must follow the order of operations. In simplifying the numerator, we must work inside the parentheses first. This gives

$$\frac{1 + 2(2)}{4(9 - 6) + 3}$$

We then do the multiplication in the numerator.

$$\frac{1 + 4}{4(9 - 6) + 3}$$

We now do the addition in the numerator, getting

$$\frac{5}{4(9-6)+3}$$

Next, we follow the same ideas with the denominator.

$$\frac{5}{4(3)+3}$$

When we do the multiplication in the denominator, we get

$$\frac{5}{12+3}$$

By doing the addition in the denominator and reducing the fraction, our expression becomes

$$\frac{1}{3} = 0.\overline{3}$$

Therefore, our answer is $0.\overline{3}$ rounded to one decimal place. The short line appearing above the 3 denotes that the value repeats ($0.333333333333\ldots$).

Averages

Sometimes finding the middle value of a list of numbers is important to us. Mathematically, this is referred to as the **average**. For example, a number of people take a certain standardized test. After the group members receive their scores, they want to know the average score. Knowing this, they can compare their scores easily to see how the group did. This can be done by adding the scores together and then dividing by the number of scores (or items). This would be the score of the "typical" student.

Example
Find the average of the following
75, 81, and 99
In order to calculate this average, we must begin by adding the numbers together. In this case, we get $75 + 81 + 99 = 255$. Since we are trying to find the average of three numbers, we divide the sum of the scores by 3. Therefore, 255/3 equals 85. This shows that the "typical" student would score 85. We can also look at this as an equation.

$$\frac{75 + 81 + 99}{3} = \frac{255}{3} = 85$$

Drill: Simplifying expressions and averages
Simplify the following expressions.

1. $11 + 3(7 - 2)$
2. $4.7 + 2.1(6.5 - 3.9)$

Find the averages of the following numbers.
3. 85, 95, and 97
4. 1, 3, 5, 7, 9, and 9
5. 10, 75, 80, and 92

Answers to drill questions

1. 26

$$11 + 3(7 - 2) = 11 + 3(5)$$
$$= 11 + 15$$
$$= 26$$

2. 10.16

$$4.7 + 2.1(6.5 - 3.9) = 4.7 + 2.1(2.6)$$
$$= 4.7 + 5.46$$
$$= 10.16$$

3. $92.3\overline{3}$

```
        1
   85        92.33
   95      3 | 277
 + 97       - 27
 -----       ----
  277         07
            -  6
            ----
             10
            -  9
            ----
             10
```

4. $5.6\overline{6}$

$$1 + 3 + 5 + 7 + 9 + 9 = 34$$

```
        5.66
    6 | 34
     - 30
     ----
       40
     - 36
     ----
       40
```

5. 64.25

```
    10
    75
    80
  + 92
  -----
   257
```

$$
\begin{array}{r}
6 \\
4\overline{)257} \\
-24 \\
\hline
17
\end{array}
\qquad \longrightarrow \qquad
\begin{array}{r}
64.25 \\
4\overline{)257.00} \\
-24 \\
\hline
17 \\
-16 \\
\hline
10 \\
-8 \\
\hline
20 \\
-20 \\
\hline
0
\end{array}
$$

Cubes and Roots

This section will look at exponents and roots. Exponents can be used to denote repetitive multiplication. The following two expressions mean the same thing.

$$ 11 \times 11 \times 11 \times 11 \qquad \text{or} \qquad \mathbf{11^4} $$

The second form is the **exponential** form. Since we are multiplying 11 by itself, we use that value as a **base**. Because we are multiplying four 11's together, we place a 4 in the **exponent position**. This is the little number appearing above and to the right of the base. Using exponents condenses the expression. In the next two sets of examples, we will become familiar with switching to and from exponents.

Examples
Rewrite the following as an exponent or equation.

(a) 5×5

Rewrite this as 5^2. The base is 5, so we know that we have a line of 5's being multiplied together. Since our exponent is 2, we know that we will have two 5's multiplied; therefore, we get 5×5. The important point here is being able to convert back and forth between the multiplication form and the exponential form. If we want to or are asked to, we could also multiply this out and get 25.

(b) 2^3

The base is 2, so we know that we have a line of 2's being multiplied together. Since our exponent is 3, we know that we will have three 2's multiplied; therefore, we get $2 \times 2 \times 2$. The important point here is being able to convert back and forth between the multiplication form and the exponential form. If we want to or are asked to, we could also multiply this out and get 8.

Examples
Rewrite the following using exponents.

(a) $7 \times 7 \times 7$

In this example, we are multiplying a line of 7's together. Therefore, our base is 7. Since we have three 7's being multiplied, our exponent is 3. Thus, we get

7^3

(b) 9×9

In this example, we are multiplying a line of 9's together. Therefore, our base is 9. Since we have two 9's being multiplied, our exponent is 2. Thus, we get

9^2

Another related topic is **roots**. We will begin by discussing **square roots**. Later, we will see that **cube roots** are very similar. When asked for the square root of a number, we want to find a number that, when we square it, gives us the original number. Knowing this gives us an immediate check to see if our answer is correct. The symbol for square root is something like a check mark with an extended top ($\sqrt{}$).

Examples

Find the square root of the following numbers.

(a) $\sqrt{4}$ or the square root of 4 is _____.

When asked to find the square root of 4, we want to find a number that when squared equals 4. After some consideration, we can see that our answer is 2. This is because

$2^2 = 2 \times 2 = 4$

and this is the beginning value.

(b) $\sqrt{25}$ or the square root of 25 is _____.

When asked to find the square root of 25, we want to find a number that when squared equals 25. After some consideration, we can see that our answer is 5. This is because

$5^2 = 5 \times 5 = 25$

and this is the beginning value.

(c) $\sqrt{9}$ or the square root of 9 is _____.

When asked to find the square root of 9, we want to find a number that when squared equals 9. After some consideration, we can see that our answer is 3. This is because

$3^2 = 3 \times 3 = 9$

and this is the beginning value.

(d) $\sqrt{100}$ or the square root of 100 is _____.

When asked to find the square root of 100, we want to find a number that when squared equals 100. After some consideration, we can see that our answer is 10. This is because

$10^2 = 10 \times 10 = 100$

and this is the beginning value.

Now that we have an understanding of exponents, we want to consider what happens when we put them into problems involving order of operations. Recall that the order of operations tells us to simplify the exponents after the parentheses, but before we do the multiplying and dividing. In the following example we will show, in detail, the steps needed.

Example
Simplify the following expression.

$$2 \times 3 + 5 - 2^3$$

In this example, we need to begin with simplifying the exponent. Two cubed is the same as $2 \times 2 \times 2$ or 8. This converts our expression to

$$2 \times 3 + 5 - 8$$

Next, we need to simplify the multiplication in our problem. Since 2×3 equals 6, our expression becomes

$$6 + 5 - 8$$

We now must add and subtract, moving from left to right as they appear. Thus, we add 6 and 5 together first. This gives

$$11 - 8$$

Finally, we are able to do the subtraction and get 3 as our final answer.

Drill: Cubes and roots
Rewrite the following without using exponents.

1. 3^2

2. 2^4

Rewrite the following using exponents.

3. $5 \times 5 \times 5$

4. $2 \times 2 \times 2 \times 2 \times 2$

Find the square root of the following numbers.

5. 49

6. 81

Simplify the following expression.

7. $7 \times 2 - 6 - 2^3$

Answers to drill questions
1. 3×3

2. $2 \times 2 \times 2 \times 2$

3. 5^3

4. 2^5

5. 7

$$7 \times 7 = 49$$

6. 9

$9 \times 9 = 81$

7. 0

$$(7 \times 2) - 6 - 2^3 = (7 \times 2) - 6 - 8$$
$$= 14 - 6 - 8$$
$$= 8 - 8$$
$$= 0$$

Measurement

Working with figures is yet another important part of mathematics. Two common figures that we regularly deal with are **rectangles** and **squares**. A **square** is a rectangle with all the sides of the same length. As we move through this section, notice that in each problem the units are constant. This is very important when dealing with the units. If the measurements are not already the same, we want to convert them.

We can calculate a few measurements to learn a lot about an object. Some of these measurements are perimeter, area, and volume. We will discuss each of these in detail as we move through this section.

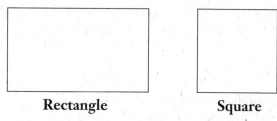

Rectangle   **Square**

The **perimeter** is the distance around the outside of the object. Imagine that we are able to walk around the object and measure the distance we travel. In a rectangle, the perimeter will be twice the length plus twice the width. Notice that if we add numbers together that have inches for units, our answer will also have inches for units. As a formula, we have

Perimeter = 2(length) + 2(width)

Example

Find the perimeter of a rectangle with the following dimensions.

length = 5 feet and width = 4 feet

Since we know the length and width of our rectangle, we can substitute these values into our formula. Notice that since our dimensions are given in feet, our answer will also have feet as a unit.

Perimeter = 2(length) + 2(width)
Perimeter = 2(5) + 2(4)

We can now do the multiplication and then the addition to get our answer.

Perimeter = 10 + 8 = 18 feet

We now want to consider what happens to our formula when we look at a square. Since all four sides have the same length, our perimeter will be determined by multiplying the measure of one side and 4 together. In the example below, you will see that our work is not much different than for a rectangle. As a formula, this would be

Perimeter = 4(side)

Example

Find the perimeter of the square with the following measurement on each side.

side = 5 inches

Since we know the measure of each side of our square, we can substitute this value into our formula. Notice that since our dimension is given in inches, our answer will also have inches as a unit.

Perimeter = 4(side)
Perimeter = 4(5)

We can now do the multiplication to get our answer.

Perimeter = 20 inches

Another useful measurement is the **area** of an object. This is the amount of space enclosed by the boundaries of the object. In a rectangle, the area is the length and width multiplied together. Notice that if we multiply two numbers together that have feet as units, our answer will have *square* feet as its unit. As a formula, we have

Area = (length) × (width)

Examples

Find the areas of rectangles with the following dimensions.

(a) length = 2 inches and width = 3 inches

Since we know the length and width of our rectangle, we can substitute these values into our formula. Notice that since our dimensions are given in inches, our answer will have square inches as a unit.

Area = (length) × (width)
Area = (2) × (3)

We can now do the multiplication to get our answer.

Area = 6 inches^2

(b) length = 5 feet and width = 2 feet

Since we know the length and width of our rectangle, we can substitute these values into our formula. Notice that since our dimensions are given in feet, our answer will have square feet as a unit.

Area = (length) × (width)
Area = (5) × (2)

We can now do the multiplication to get our answer.

Area = 10 feet^2

When dealing with a square, our area formula becomes a little bit easier. Since all sides have the same length, our formula becomes the measure of one side squared. Written as a formula, we get

Area = (side)^2

Examples

Find the areas of squares with the following measures on each side.

(a) side = 9 inches

Since we know the measure of the sides of our square, we can substitute this value into our formula. Notice that since our dimension is given in inches, our answer will have square inches as a unit.

Area = (side)^2
Area = (9)^2 = 9 × 9

We can now simplify this to get our answer.

Area = 81 inches^2

(b) side = 6 feet

Since we know the measure of the sides of our square, we can substitute this value into our formula. Notice that since our dimension is given in feet, our answer will have square feet as a unit.

Area = (side)^2
Area = (6)^2 = 6 × 6

We can now simplify this to get our answer.

Area = 36 feet^2

Now we want to consider a box. A useful measure here is the **volume**. The volume is the amount of stuff that can be placed into the object. We can find this measurement by multiplying the length, width, and height together. Notice that if we multiply three numbers together that have inches as their units, our answer will have units of *cubic* inches. As a formula, we have

Volume = (length) × (width) × (height)

Examples

Find the volumes of the following boxes.

(a) length = 6 inches, width = 4 inches, and height = 2 inches

Since we know the measure of the length, width, and height of our box, we can substitute these values into our formula. Notice that since our dimensions are given in inches, our answer will have cubic inches as a unit.

Volume = (length) × (width) × (height)
Volume = (6) × (4) × (2)

We can now do the multiplication and get our answer.

Volume = (24) × (2) = 48 inches³

(b) length = 1 foot, width = 2 feet, and height = 3 feet

Since we know the measure of the length, width, and height of our box, we can substitute these values into our formula. Notice that since our dimensions are given in feet, our answer will have cubic feet as a unit.

Volume = (length) × (width) × (height)
Volume = (1) × (2) × (3)

We can now do the multiplication and get our answer.

Volume = (2) × (3) = 6 feet³

Drill: Measurement

Find the perimeters of rectangles with the following dimensions.

1. length = 1 foot and width = 6 feet
2. length = 2 inches and width = 4 inches

Find the perimeters of squares with the following measure on each side.

3. side = 3 inches
4. side = 6 feet

Find the areas of rectangles with the following dimensions.

5. length = 9 feet and width = 12 feet
6. length = 11 inches and width = 6 inches

Find the areas of squares with the following distances on each side.

7. side = 11 inches
8. side = 2 feet

Find the volumes of the following boxes.

9. length = 4 inches, width = 7 inches, and height = 3 inches
10. length = 5 feet, width = 4 feet, and height = 6 feet.

Answers to drill questions

1. 14 feet
   Perimeter = 2(width) + 2(length)
   = 2(6) + 2(1)
   12 + 2 = 14 feet

2. 12 inches

Perimeter = 2(width) + 2(length)

= 2(4) + 2(2)

8 + 4 = 12 inches

3. 12 inches

Perimeter = 4(side)

4(3) = 12 inches

4. 24 feet

Perimeter = 4(side)

4(6) = 24 feet

5. 108 feet^2

Area = length × width

9 × 12 = 108 feet^2

6. 66 inches^2

Area = length × width

11 × 6 = 66 inches^2

7. 121 inches^2

Area = side^2

11^2 = 121 inches^2

8. 4 feet^2

Area = side^2

22 = 4 feet^2

9. 84 inches^3

Volume = length × width × height

4 × 7 × 3 = 84 inches^3

4 × 7 = 28

28 × 3 = 84

10. 120 feet^3

Volume = length × width × height

5 × 4 × 6 = 120 feet^3

5 × 4 = 20

20 × 6 = 120

V. Percents

Introduction to Percents

Percents play an important role in our lives. It is hard to pick up a newspaper or listen to the news without hearing the word percent or seeing the symbol (%). Some examples of this are: "Crime Rate Up 32%," "Car Prices Increase 10%," and "Going Out of Business Sale—75% Off of Everything."

The easiest way to understand percents is to think of them as so many out of 100. If, at a 100-person party, 15 of the people are males, then we know that 15% of the people are male. Likewise, if 57% of the city voted for a school levy, then we know that out of every 100 people, 57 voted yes. If the city's population is 200 people, then 114 people voted for the levy. As we saw in the last example, we do not always have 100 people but, when working with percents, it is just easier to think in that format.

If we are given information about a situation that does not involve exactly 100 people, we can convert it to a percent by dividing the number of people that meet some type of requirement by the total group. This "answer" will come out as a decimal. In order to write this value using the percent symbol, we must move the decimal point two places to the *right*. Therefore, for example, 0.39 would represent 39%. Thus, out of every 100 people, 39 would act in a certain way.

Examples
Write the following decimals as percents.

(a) 0.24

In order to change this into a percent, we must move the decimal point two places to the right. Therefore, 0.24 would be 24%.

(b) 0.457

In order to change this into a percent, we must move the decimal point two places to the right. Therefore, 0.457 would be 45.7%.

(c) 1.52

In order to change this into a percent, we must move the decimal point two places to the right. Therefore, 1.52 would be 152%.

It is also helpful to be able to convert percentages to decimals. In order to change a percent into its decimal value, we must move the decimal point two places to the left. Therefore, 16% is the same as 0.16. As we will see in the next section, when working with a percent, we must remember to convert to a decimal before any calculations are done.

Examples
Write the following percents as decimals.

(a) 38%

In order to convert a percent into a decimal, we must move the decimal point two places to the left. Even though the original problem does not contain a decimal point, one is assumed to be after the last digit. This can be written as 38.%. Therefore, 38% would be 0.38.

(b) 61.3%

In order to convert a percent into a decimal, we must move the decimal point two places to the left. Therefore, 61.3% would be 0.613.

(c) 7%

In order to convert a percent into a decimal, we must move the decimal point two places to the left. Since we only have one digit here, it might be a good idea to place a zero in front of the seven so that we can see two positions. This gives us 07%. Therefore, 7% would be 0.07.

(d) 378%

In order to convert a percent into a decimal, we must move the decimal point two places to the left. Therefore, 378% would be 3.78.

As we mentioned before, we can find the percent of something by dividing. Another way to look at this is in a fractional form. The numerator contains the number of people who meet a certain requirement. The denominator contains the total number of people. In the examples below, we will see how easy it is to find the percent.

Examples
Find the percents in the following situations.

(a) 6 is what percent of 8?

In order to find the percent here, we place the 6 in the numerator and the 8 in the denominator. This division gives us 6/8 or 0.75. From our discussion, we know that this is 75%.

(b) 9 is what percent of 72?

In order to find the percent here, we place the 9 in the numerator and the 72 in the denominator. This division gives us 9/72 or 0.125. From our discussion, we know that this is 12.5%.

(c) 4 is what percent of 28?

In order to find the percent here, we place the 4 in the numerator and the 28 in the denominator. This division gives us 4/28 or 0.1428571. From our discussion, we know that this is 14.29%, rounded to two decimal places.

Drill: Introduction to percents
Write the following decimals using the percent symbol.

1. 0.59

2. 7.04

3. 0.085

Write the following percents as decimals.

4. 38%

5. 17.4%

6. 5.2%

Find the percents in the following situations.

7. 5 out of 25

8. 2 out of 20

9. 45 out of 405

10. 28 out of 42

Answers to drill questions

1. 59%

Move the decimal point two places to the right to convert from a decimal to a percent.

2. 704%

Move the decimal point two places to the right to convert from a decimal to a percent.

3. 8.5%

Move the decimal point two places to the right to convert from a decimal to a percent.

4. 0.38

Move the decimal point two places to the left when converting a percent to a decimal.

5. 0.174

Move the decimal point two places to the left when converting a percent to a decimal.

6. 0.052

Move the decimal point two places to the left when converting a percent to a decimal.

7. 20%

$$5 \text{ out of } 25 = \frac{5}{25} = .2 = 20\%$$

8. 10%

$$2 \text{ out of } 20 = \frac{2}{20} = .1 = 10\%$$

9. 11.1$\overline{1}$%

$$45 \text{ out of } 405 = \frac{45}{405}$$
$$= .111\overline{1}$$
$$= 11.1\overline{1}\%$$

10. 66.66%

$$28 \text{ out of } 42 = \frac{28}{42}$$
$$= .666\overline{6}$$
$$= 66.6\overline{6}\%$$

Percent Problems

Now that we have an introduction to percents, we want to use them in problems. We have already discussed how to denote percents and convert decimals to percents, and how to find out what percent a number is of another number. Here we want to consider the other possibilities.

In the example below, we will see how to find a certain percent of a number and how to solve increase and decrease problems. A basic formula for percents is:

Amount = percent × beginning

In most percent problems this formula can be manipulated into a form that will help us.

Examples
Simplify the following percent problems.

(a) 16% of 30

Here we are given the percent and the beginning amount. We are asked to find the final amount. When working with problems involving words, *of* normally means multiplication. Also, recall that when working with percents, we need to convert them into decimals. Therefore, this problem becomes

16% of 30 or 0.16 × 30

We are then able to do the multiplication and simplify this to 4.8. Thus, 4.8 is 16% of 30.

(b) 248% of 500

Here we are given the percent and the beginning amount. We are asked to find the final amount. When working with problems involving words, *of* normally means multiplication. Also, recall that when working with percents, we need to convert them into decimals. Therefore, this problem becomes

248% of 500 or 2.48 × 500

We are then able to do the multiplication and simplify this to 1,240. Thus, 1,240 is 248% of 500.

(c) 51.9% of 6

Here we are given the percent and the beginning amount. We are asked to find the final amount. When working with problems involving words, *of* normally means multiplication. Also, recall that when working with percents, we need to convert them into decimals. Therefore, this problem becomes

51.9% of 6 or 0.519 × 6

We are then able to do the multiplication and simplify this to 3.114. Thus, 3.114 is 51.9% of 6. If we round our answer to one decimal place we get 3.1.

Examples
Find the numbers described below.

(a) 25% of what number is 12?

In this problem, we are given the percent and the final amount, but not the beginning amount. We also know that we must change the percent to a decimal in order to work with it. To find our answer, we must divide the final amount by the percent. Here we have

$$\frac{12}{25\%} \text{ or } \frac{12}{0.25}$$

When we divide, we get 48. This tells us that 25% of 48 is 12.

(b) 17% of what number is 51?

In this problem, we are given the percent and the final amount, but not the beginning amount. We also know that we must change the percent to a decimal in order to work with it. To find our answer, we must divide the final amount by the percent. Here we have

$$\frac{51}{17\%} \text{ or } \frac{51}{0.17}$$

When we divide, we get 300. This tells us that 17% of 300 is 51.

Drill: Percent problems
Simplify the following percent problems.

1. 31% of 50

2. 59% of 600

Find the numbers described below.

3. 12% of what number is 25?

4. 67% of what number is 46?

5. 89% of what number is 512?

Answers to drill questions

1. 15.5

    31% of 50 = 31% × 50 = .31 × 50 = 15.5

2. 354

    59% of 600 = 59% × 600 = .59 × 600 = 354

3. 208.3$\overline{3}$

    The required number is

    25 ÷ 12% = 25 ÷ .12 = 208.3$\overline{3}$

4. 68.656716

    The required number is

    46 ÷ 67% = 46 ÷ .67 = 68.656716

5. 575.2809

    The required number is

    512 ÷ 89% = 512 ÷ .89 = 575.2809

VI. Advanced Topics

Probability

Now that we have a good understanding of mathematics, we want to discuss some other topics that are a little bit more involved. The first of these topics is probability. Geometry and multi-step word problems will be covered later in this section.

In probability, we are studying the chance of something happening. This is called a **successful outcome**. In other words, we want to know what is the chance that a successful outcome will occur in a certain situation. Here we will be looking at results that are not under our control. That is, the outcome is random. We come across a lot of places where probability can be used. Two examples would be the state lottery and game shows.

The probability of an outcome is expressed between 0 and 1. Percents can also be used here. A probability of 0 (or 0%) denotes an impossibility. An event with 0% probability will never happen. A probability of 1 (or 100%) must happen. An event with 100% probability will always occur. All other probabilities lie somewhere between 0 and 1, that is, between 0% and 100% (if percentages are used). Below is the general formula that can be used to calculate the probability of an event occurring.

$$\text{Probability} = \frac{\text{Number of ways a successful outcome can occur}}{\text{Number of possible outcomes}}$$

Examples

Twenty marbles are placed in a can. Two are black, six white, five red, four blue, and three yellow. Without looking, one marble is drawn from the can. What is the probability of the following occurring?

(a) What is the probability of drawing a blue marble?

Since our can contains four blue marbles, there are four ways for a successful outcome to occur. We have a total of 20 marbles in the can, and each has an equal chance of being drawn. Hence, there are 20 possible outcomes. We can now put this information into our formula and calculate the probability.

$$\text{Probability} = \frac{\text{Number of ways a successful outcome can occur}}{\text{Number of possible outcomes}}$$

$$\text{Probability} = \frac{4}{20} = 0.20$$

Therefore, the probability of drawing a blue marble is 0.2 or 20%.

(b) What is the probability of drawing a black marble?

Since our can contains two black marbles, there are two ways for a successful outcome to occur. We have a total of 20 marbles in the can, and each has an equal chance of being drawn. Hence, there are 20 possible outcomes. We can now put this information into our formula and calculate the probability.

$$\text{Probability} = \frac{\text{Number of ways a successful outcome can occur}}{\text{Number of possible outcomes}}$$

$$\text{Probability} = \frac{2}{20} = 0.10$$

Therefore, the probability of drawing a black marble is 0.1 or 10%.

(c) What is the probability of drawing a white marble?

Since our can contains six white marbles, there are six ways for a successful outcome to occur. We have a total of 20 marbles in the can, and each has an equal chance of being drawn. Hence, there are 20 possible outcomes. We can now put this information into our formula and calculate the probability.

$$\text{Probability} = \frac{\text{Number of ways a successful outcome can occur}}{\text{Number of possible outcomes}}$$

$$\text{Probability} = \frac{6}{20} = 0.30$$

Therefore, the probability of drawing a white marble is 0.3 or 30%.

(d) What is the probability of drawing a red, white, or blue marble?

Since our can contains five red, six white, and four blue marbles, there are 15 ways for a successful outcome to occur. We have a total of 20 marbles in the can, and each has an equal chance of being drawn. Hence, there are 20 possible outcomes. We can now put this information into our formula and calculate the probability.

$$\text{Probability} = \frac{\text{Number of ways a successful outcome can occur}}{\text{Number of possible outcomes}}$$

$$\text{Probability} = \frac{15}{20} = 0.75$$

Therefore, the probability of drawing a red, white, or blue marble is 0.75 or 75%.

Drill: Probability

Fifteen marbles are placed in a can. Five are pink, six blue, two yellow, one orange, and one white. Without looking, one marble is drawn from the can. Find the probability of the following events occurring.

1. What is the probability of drawing an orange marble?

2. What is the probability of drawing a blue marble?

3. What is the probability of drawing a yellow or white marble?

4. What is the probability of drawing a pink marble?

5. What is the probability of drawing a pink, yellow, orange, or white marble?

Answers to drill questions

1. $6.6\bar{6}\%$

Probability of drawing orange

$$= \frac{1}{15} = 6.6\bar{6}\%$$

2. 0.4 or 40%

Probability of drawing blue

$$= \frac{6}{15} = 40\%$$

3. 0.2 or 20%

Probability of drawing yellow or white

$$= \frac{2+1}{15} = \frac{3}{15} = 20\%$$

4. $0.\bar{3}$ or $33.3\bar{3}\%$

Probability of drawing pink

$$= \frac{5}{15} = 33.3\bar{3}\%$$

5. 0.6 or 60%

Probability of drawing pink, yellow, orange, or white

$$= \frac{5+2+1+1}{15} = \frac{9}{15} = 60\%$$

Geometry

A **circle** is an object where every point on the curve is an equal distance from a center point. We now need to introduce some terminology that is particular to circles. If we draw a straight line from one side of the circle, through the center, and then continue to the other side, this line is called the **diameter**. The formula for the diameter is

Diameter = 2 × radius. The **radius** is half of the diameter. The formula for the radius is

Radius = $\frac{1}{2}$ × diameter.

Examples

Find the radii of the following circles.

(a) Circle with diameter of 16 inches.

Since we know the diameter of this circle, we can calculate the radius easily.

Radius = $\left(\frac{1}{2}\right)$ × (diameter)

Radius = $\left(\frac{1}{2}\right)$ × (16) = 8

Therefore, the radius is 8 inches.

(b) Circle with diameter of 2 feet.

Since we know the diameter of this circle, we can calculate the radius easily.

Radius = $\left(\frac{1}{2}\right)$ × (diameter)

Radius = $\left(\frac{1}{2}\right)$ × (2), Radius = 1 foot

Therefore, the radius is 1 foot.

Examples

Find the diameters of the following circles.

(a) Circle with radius of 3 inches.

Since we know the radius, we can plug its value into our formula and calculate the diameter.

Diameter = (2) × (radius)
Diameter = (2) × (3)
Diameter = 6 inches
Therefore, the diameter of this circle is 6 inches.

(b) Circle with radius of 1.6 feet.

Since we know the radius, we can plug its value into our formula and calculate the diameter.

Diameter = (2) × (radius)
Diameter = (2) × (1.6)
Diameter = 3.2 feet
Therefore, the diameter of this circle is 3.2 feet.

Drill: Geometry

Find the radii of the following circles. If needed, round your answers to the hundredths place.

1. Circle with diameter of 13 inches.
2. Circle with diameter of 5 centimeters.

   Find the diameters of the following circles. If needed, round your answer to the hundredths place.
3. Circle with radius of 7 feet.
4. Circle with radius of 12.6 inches.
5. Circle with radius of 2.25 centimeters.

Answers to drill questions

1. $6\frac{1}{2}$ or 6.5 inches

$$\text{Radius} = \left(\frac{1}{2}\right) \times (\text{diameter})$$

$$\text{Radius} = \left(\frac{1}{2}\right) \times (13)$$

$$\text{Radius} = 6\frac{13}{2} = 6\frac{1}{2} \text{ or } 6.5 \text{ inches}$$

2. $2\frac{1}{2}$ or 2.5 centimeters

$$\text{Radius} = \left(\frac{1}{2}\right) \times (\text{diameter})$$

$$\text{Radius} = \left(\frac{1}{2}\right) \times (5)$$

$$\text{Radius} = \frac{5}{2} = 2\frac{1}{2} \text{ or } 2.5 \text{ centimeters}$$

3. 14 feet

   Diameter = (2) × (radius)
   Diameter = (2) × (7)
   Diameter = 14 feet

4. 25.2 inches

   Diameter = (2) × (radius)
   Diameter = (2) × (12.6)
   Diameter = 25.2 inches

5. 4.5 centimeters

   Diameter = (2) × (radius)
   Diameter = (2) × (2.25)
   Diameter = 4.5 centimeters

Multistep word problems

Since we are now "experts" in mathematics, we want to discuss multistep word problems. Throughout this section, we will be building upon ideas that we have already covered. In these examples, it is best to break the problem into different steps and then solve each of them separately.

The biggest area where this can be seen is when we spend money. Sometimes this is called Consumer Mathematics. A common question is how much money will we have left? To answer this question, we must first know how much we have and how much we spent. The following examples will show this in more detail.

Examples
Solve the following problems.

(a) Kelli goes to the store to get a few groceries. She buys two loaves of bread for $2.19, some oranges for $1.99, a pound of ham for $3.99, and three candy bars for $1.70. If Kelli gives the clerk $10, how much change will she get back?

First, we must find out how much she spent. This can be done by adding everything together.

Spent = (Bread) + (Oranges) + (Ham) + (Candy)
Spent = (2.19) + (1.99) + (3.99) + (1.70)
Spent = $9.87

Now that we know that she spent $9.87, we can subtract this value from the amount she gave the clerk to find out how much change she will get back.

Change = (Total) − (Spent)
Change = $10.00 − $9.87
Change = $0.13

Therefore, she will have $0.13 (or 13 cents) left after her purchases.

(b) George is buying furniture for his new home. He buys a couch and chair for $599, a television for $279, a bed for $978, and a table with chairs for $1,200. If the sales tax is $155 and George gives the salesperson $3,500, how much change will he get back?

First, we must find out how much he spent. This can be done by adding everything together.

Spent = (Couch & Chair) + (Television) + (Bed) + (Table & Chairs) + (Tax)
Spent = (599) + (279) + (978) + (1,200) + (155)
Spent = $3,211

Now that we know that he spent $3,211, we can subtract this value from the amount he gave the salesperson to find out how much change he will get back.

Change = (Total) − (Spent)
Change = $3,500 − $3,211
Change = $289

Therefore, he will have $289 left after his purchases.

Solving increase and decrease problems is a good example of how we can split problems into pieces. In most cases, percents are involved. We are looking to see what the final amount will be if the beginning amount is increased (or decreased) by a certain percent. The examples below will show this in more detail.

Examples

In the following problems, find the amount of increase and the new amount.

(a) The price of a $30 book is increased by 10%. What will be the new price of the book?

In this problem, the increase will be 10% of the original price (or $30). By converting the percent into a decimal and multiplying, we can find the amount of the increase.

Increase = 10% of $30
Increase = 0.10 × 30 = $3

By combining the increase with the original price, we can find the new price of the book easily. Therefore, the new price will be

(New Price) = (Old Price) + (Increase)
(New Price) = $30 + $3 = $33

Therefore, the new price will be $33.

(b) The attendance at a football game increases by 37%. If 12,000 people normally attend, how many will be attending now?

In this problem, the increase will be 37% of the original attendance (or 12,000). By converting the percent into a decimal and multiplying, we can find the amount of the increase.

Increase = 37% of 12,000
Increase = 0.37 × 12,000 = 4,440 people

By combining the increase with the original attendance, we can find the new attendance at the football game easily. Therefore, the new attendance will be

(New Attendance) = (Old Attendance) + (Increase)
(New Attendance) = 12,000 + 4,440 = 16,440 people

Therefore, the new attendance will be 16,440 people.

(c) A magazine normally contains 25 pages. If the number of pages increases by 145%, how many pages does it now have?

In this problem, the increase will be 145% of the original number of pages (or 25). By converting the percent into a decimal and multiplying, we can find the amount of the increase.

Increase = 145% of 25
Increase = 1.45 × 25 = 36.25 pages

By combining the increase with the original number of pages, we can find the new number of pages in the magazine easily. Therefore, the new number of pages will be

(New Number of Pages) = (Old Number of Pages) + (Increase)
(New Number of Pages) = 25 + 36.25 = 61.25

Therefore, the magazine will now have approximately 62 pages.

Examples

In the following problems, find the amount of decrease and the new amount.

(a) A grocery store is having a sale on hot dogs (normally priced at $1.09). If, during the sale, the price is reduced by 83%, what is the sale price?

In this problem, the discount will be 83% of the original price (or $1.09). By converting the percent into a decimal and multiplying, we can find the amount of the discount.

Discount = 83% of $1.09
Discount = 0.83 × 1.09 = $0.9047

By combining the discount with the original price, we can find the new price of the hot dogs easily. Therefore, the new price will be

(New Price) = (Old Price) − (Discount)
(New Price) = $1.09 − $0.9047 = $0.1853

Therefore, during the sale, a package of hot dogs will sell for $0.19 (or 19 cents).

(b) The attendance at a high school basketball game decreased by 17%. If 125 people normally attend, how many people will attend now?

In this problem, the decrease will be 17% of the original attendance (or 125). By converting the percent into a decimal and multiplying, we can find the amount of the decrease.

Decrease = 17% of 125
Decrease = 0.17 × 125 = 21.25 people

By combining the decrease with the original attendance, we can find the new attendance easily. Therefore, the new attendance will be

(New Attendance) = (Old Attendance) − (Decrease)
(New Attendance) = 125 − 21.25 = 103.75

Therefore, the new attendance at the basketball game will be approximately 104 people.

(c) The weight of a package of cookies decreases by 26%. What is the weight of a new package if the old package weighed 16 ounces?

In this problem, the decrease will be 26% of the original weight (or 16). By converting the percent into a decimal and multiplying, we can find the amount of the decrease.

Decrease = 26% of 16
Decrease = 0.26 × 16 = 4.16 ounces

By combining the decrease with the original weight, we can find the new weight easily. Therefore, the weight will become

(New Weight) = (Old Weight) − (Decrease)
(New Weight) = 16 − 4.16 = 11.84
Therefore, the new weight of the cookie package will be approximately 12 ounces.

Drill: Multi-Step word problems

Solve the following problems.

1. Sam goes to the store for groceries. He buys a turkey for $19.75, bread for $1.99, and peaches for $0.36. If he gives the cashier $30, how much will he get back?

2. Nancy is shopping at a craft store. If she has $10 and purchases styrofoam for $2.99, yarn for $1.99, glue for $0.99, and the sales tax is $0.36, how much will she get back?

3. Edith needs to send some flower arrangements. If she has $400 to spend and sends six arrangements at $39.90 each, how much will she have left?

   In the following problems, find the amount of increase and the new amount.

4. The price of a newspaper increases by 7%. If it originally cost $1.25, what would be the new price?

5. The attendance at a hockey game increases by 58%. If the original attendance is 37,000, what would be the new attendance?

6. The population of a town increased by 201%. If the original population was 47,123, what would be the new population?

7. The number of books published by REA increases by 2.572%. If it originally published 150 books, how many books does it now publish?

   In the following problems, find the amount of decrease and the new amount.

8. The population of a city decreases by 42%. If the original population was 152,967, what would be the new population?

9. A cookie is now 92% fat free. If the regular cookie contains 6.2 grams of fat, how much fat does the "fat free" cookie have?

10. The number of pages in a magazine decreases by 78%. If the original magazine contained 99 pages, how many pages will the magazine now have?

Answers to drill questions

1. $7.90

   $19.75
     1.99
   + .36
   _____
   $22.10 total purchases $\longrightarrow$

   $30.00
   − 22.10
   _____
   $ 7.90 change

2. $3.67

   $2.99
     1.99
      .99
   + .36
   _____
   $6.33 total $\longrightarrow$

   $10.00
   − 6.33
   _____
   $3.67 change

3. $160.60

   6 arrangements × $39.90 = 239.40 total

   $400.00
   − 239.40
   _____
   $160.60 left

4. $1.34

New price = $1.25 + (.07 × $1.25) = $1.34

5. 58,460 people

New attendance = 37,000 + (.58 × 37,000) = 58,460 people

6. 141,840 people

New population = 47,123 + (2.01 × 47,123) = 141,840 people

7. 154 books

Number of books = 150 + (.02572 × 150) = 154 books

8. 88,721 people

New population = 152,967 − (.42 × 152,967) = 88,721 people

9. 0.496 grams

Amount of fat = 6.2 − (.92 × 6.2) = .496 grams

10. 22 pages

Number of pages = 99 − (.78 × 99) = 22 pages

HSPT/COOP/TACHS

CHAPTER 6
QUANTITATIVE SKILLS REVIEW

CHAPTER 6

Quantitative Skills Review

I. Number Relationships

These problems require you to use quantitative reasoning and analysis to solve the problems. These questions will call for you to determine the relationship between the two numbers expressed. Each question will vertically display three numerical expressions. There will be a first number followed by an arrow, a box, another arrow, and second number. These types of expressions are often referred to as "In/Out Boxes." To solve this type of problem you need to envision that the box in the middle is a machine that transforms the first number into the second number. You need to ask yourself, "What has happened to the first number to result in this change to the second number?" Or, "What mathematical operation is the box performing?"

Example

Look at the following problem and ask yourself the two questions: "What has happened to the first number to result in this change to the second number?" and "What mathematical operation is the box performing?"

1	3	**(A)** 2
5	7	**(B)** 9
7	?	**(C)** 8
		(D) 4

What happens to the 1 to make it a 3? The answer is that 2 is added to the 1 to turn it into or equal 3. Now, check if this is true to for the next expression. If you add 2 to 5 will it turn into or equal 7? Yes, now you can add 2 to the number in the last expression. 7 plus 2 equals 9, which is your answer (B).

II. Visual Problems

These problems require you to consider the visual provided and determine a proportion. You need to assess the section of the object that is shaded in relation to the object as a whole. Then you will need to confirm which of the answer choices matches the amount represented by the drawing. You need to ask yourself, "What portion of the boxes is shaded in relation to the total number of boxes?" and "What number represents that relationship?"

Example

Look at the following problem and ask yourself the two questions: "What portion of the boxes is shaded in relation to the total number of boxes?" and "What number represents that relationship?"

(A) $\frac{1}{8}$

(B) $\frac{1}{3}$

(C) $\frac{1}{4}$

(D) $\frac{1}{2}$

In this example one out of the four boxes is shaded. This proportion is represented by the fraction one-fourth $\left(\frac{1}{4}\right)$. This is a simple fraction. Some examples will require you to determine the shaded portion of the whole and then choose an equivalent fraction from the answer choices provided.

Take a look at the next example:

In this case two out of the four boxes are shaded. This could be represented by the fraction two-fourths $\left(\frac{2}{4}\right)$ or the fraction can be reduced to one-half $\left(\frac{1}{2}\right)$. In order to reduce, you would divide the denominator (bottom number of the fraction) by the numerator (top number of the fraction).

Additional problems that require visual analysis are those found in the Ability section of the TACHS. This section usually involves three types of logical-abstract problems. One requires you to observe a figure to notice how it changes in the example; then you will apply this change to a section figure given in order to select your answer. A second type of visual problem may show a progression of changes or additions to a figure, and you will need to identify the choice that shows the next part of that sequence.

PAPER FOLDING PROBLEMS

The following type of problem involves folding a square piece of paper. You must be able to recognize how the paper will look after it is folded either once or twice. In addition, you will be required to identify how the paper appears when it is unfolded.

Example 1:

Consider the following square piece of paper ABCD.

The horizontal line EF shows the crease in the paper when it is folded in half. The arrow starting at A and ending at D indicates that the paper will be folded down, from AB to DC. Here is the result of this fold.

Notice that AB, AE, and BF have become dotted lines. The reason is that they don't exist now. A lies on top of D, B lies on top of C, AE lies on top of ED, BF lies on top of FC, and AB lies on top of DC.

Example 2:

Consider the following square piece of paper GHJK.

The verical line LM indicates the crease where the fold will take place. The arrow indicates that the paper will be folded to the right. Here is the result of this fold.

As with Example 1, GL, GK, and KM no longer exist. G lies on top of H, K lies on top of J, GL lies on top of LH, KM lies on top of MJ, and GK lies on top of HJ.

Now suppose that a second fold is involved. Look at the following.

The above figure means that we are about to do a second fold of GHJK. The arrow indicates that the LHJM will be folded up from MJ to LH. Now the paper will appear as follows.

The result of this second fold is the square LHPQ. The dotted lines MQ, PJ, and MJ no longer exist. You should be able to recognize that point M is now on top of point L and that point J is on top of point H.

There will be some examples in which the paper is already folded with a hole punch. Your objective is to determine how the paper will appear when it is unfolded.

Example 3:

Consider the following piece of square paper in which RSTU has already been folded along its crease XW.

Notice that after folding upward, a hole is punched in the lower right corner above W. The objective is to determine how the original paper will appear when RSWX is unfolded. The answer is that the hole will appear in two places, namely just above W and just below W. The following figure illustrates how the original paper will appear.

III. Symbol Relationships

In these problems, symbols or drawings are used to represent numerical values or amounts. Solving the problems will require you to determine the value of the symbols, based on the relationship shown. You will be given problems that use two symbols in different amounts that are arranged in a way that demonstrates that they are equivalent. When you figure out the value relationship between the two symbols, you will be able to analyze the answer choices to find the one that also demonstrates that value. You need to ask yourself, "How many of the first symbol does it take to equal the second symbol?" and "Which of the answer choices also depicts this value relationship?"

Example

Look at the following problem, which depicts symbols on a balance scale and ask yourself, "How many of the first symbol does it take to equal the second symbol?"

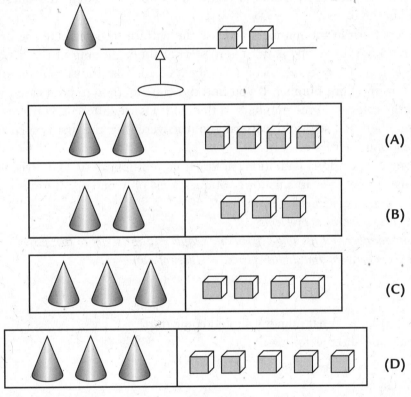

Because the scale is balanced, you know that one cone is equal to two cubes. Next, you need to analyze the answer choices provided by asking, "Which of the answer choices also depicts this value relationship?" You need to find the choice that also shows that one cone is equal to two cubes. In this case it would be choice A. Two cones would be equal to four cubes, based on the relationship shown in the initial problem.

Remember, there is no penalty for getting a wrong answer, so it is good test-taking practice to guess an answer if you cannot figure one out. While you are taking the test, guess the answers to questions you have trouble with, and check them on your question sheet. Then, if you have time at the end of the test, you can go back and look at them again. If you do skip questions, make sure you skip the corresponding spaces on the answer sheet. Check now and then during the test to be sure that the number on the answer sheet corresponds to the question you are answering.

In any case, there is a strong emphasis on questions that ask you to compare sizes, give sequences, and find numbers from word descriptions. If you had trouble with either the *Quantitative Skills* subtest of the HSPT or the *Sequences* test on the COOP, you'll need to take time and study one or more of the following areas:

- Sequences
- Geometric and nongeometric comparisons
- Number manipulations.

IV. Series Questions

Series questions begin with the words: "Look at this series," followed by a list of integers. This is followed by the question "What numeral should come next?" or, less often, the question "What numeral should fill in the blank?"

Your goal is to find a pattern in the numbers and use the pattern to determine the missing number. The best way to figure out the pattern is to start at the beginning of the list and see how to get from the first number to the second number. Then, take the second number and see how to get from it to the third number. If you find the same method in both cases, you have probably discovered the rule for all the numbers. If the methods are different, continue on to the next two pairs of numbers and see if the pattern you discovered for the first two pairs is repeated. If it is, you have found the rule.

The four basic arithmetic operations—addition, subtraction, multiplication, and division—are used to get from number to number. In a majority of questions, only one operation is used, but many questions involve two operations.

TIP: *Here is a good way to solve series problems.*

Write the operation and number you use to get from one number in the series to the next directly on the question sheet. Write them between and slightly above each pair of numbers.

Example

Look at the series: 2, 3, 7, 8, 12, . . . What numeral should come next?
To answer, write on the question sheet as follows:

$$+1 \quad +4 \quad +1 \quad +4 \quad +1 = 13$$
$$2, \quad 3, \quad 7, \quad 8, \quad 12, \ldots$$

The answer is the sum of 12 and 1, or 13.

Sometimes it is not clear what the rule is to get from one number to the next. Look at the next example.

Example

Look at the series: 2, 3, 6, 7, 14, 15, . . . What numeral should come next?
To answer, write on the question sheet as follows:

$$+1 \quad x2 \quad +1 \quad x2 \quad +1 \quad x2 = 30$$
$$+1 \quad +3 \quad +1 \quad +7 \quad +1 \quad +11?$$
$$2, \quad 3, \quad 6, \quad 7, \quad 14, \quad 15, \ldots$$

The answer is the product of 15 and 2, or 30. Note that the rule is not always clear, so keep all four arithmetic operations in mind while answering series questions.

Drill: Series

For questions 1 through 5, what numeral should come next?

1. 60, 68, 76, 84, 92, . . .
2. 96, 48, 24, 12, 6, . . .
3. 91, 87, 80, 76, 69, . . .
4. 4, 7, 11, 16, 22, . . .
5. 55, 50, 25, 20, 10, . . .

For question 6, what numeral should fill in the blank?

6. 14, 24, __, 41, 48, 54, . . .

Answers to drill questions

1. The correct answer is 100. To get from 60 to 68, add 8. To get from 68 to 76, add 8. The "add 8" rule applies to the next two numbers also. So, to get the last number, add 8 to 92, which yields 100.

$$\begin{array}{cccccc} +8 & +8 & +8 & +8 & +8 = 100 \\ 60, & 68, & 76, & 84, & 92, \ldots \end{array}$$

2. The correct answer is 3. To get from 96 to 48, you could subtract 48, divide by 2, or, what is the same thing, multiply by 1/2. To get from 48 to 24, you could subtract 24, or divide by 2. Since the rule "divide by 2" is repeated, we try it for the next two numbers. Since it works, the last number must be 6 divided by 2, which is 3.

$$\begin{array}{cccccc} \div 2 & \div 2 & \div 2 & \div 2 & \div 2 = 3 \\ & -48 & -24 \\ 96, & 48, & 24, & 12, & 6, \ldots \end{array}$$

3. The correct answer is 65. To get from 91 to 87, subtract 4. To get from 87 to 80, subtract 7. This is not a repeat of the "subtract 4" rule, so let's try the next two pairs of numbers. To get from 80 to 76, subtract 4, and from 76 to 69, subtract 7. Since the rules "subtract 4" and "subtract 7" repeat, we get the next number by subtracting 4, and 4 subtracted from 69 is 65.

$$\begin{array}{cccccc} -4 & -7 & -4 & -7 & -4 = 65 \\ 91, & 87, & 80, & 76, & 69, \ldots \end{array}$$

4. The correct answer is 29. To get from 4 to 7, add 3. To get from 7 to 11, add 4. This is not a repeat of the "add 3" rule, so let's try the next two pairs of numbers. To get from 11 to 16, add 5, and from 16 to 22, add 6. It appears that the number added goes up by one each time. So, to get the last number, we add 7 to 22 to get 29.

$$\begin{array}{cccccc} +3 & +4 & +5 & +6 & +7 = 29 \\ 4, & 7, & 11, & 16, & 22, \ldots \end{array}$$

5. The correct answer is 5. To get from 55 to 50, subtract 5. To get from 50 to 25, either subtract 25 or divide by 2. Let's try the next two pairs of numbers. To get from 25 to 20, subtract 5, and from 20 to 10, either subtract 10 or divide by 2. Since dividing by 2 is a repeat rule, we would use it if we had to. However, we get the next number using the "subtract 5" rule, and 5 subtracted from 10 is 5.

$$
\begin{array}{ccccc}
-5 & \div 2 & -5 & \div 2 & -5 = 5 \\
-5 & -25 & -5 & -10? & -5 \\
55, & 50, & 25, & 20, & 10, \ldots
\end{array}
$$

6. The answer is 33. This question is somewhat harder because the missing number is in the middle, not at the end. To get from 14 to 24, add 10. We can't do the next two pairs, but to get from 41 to 48, add 7, and to get from 48 to 54, add 6. The number being added seems to be decreasing by 1. Let's try adding 9 to 24 to get the following number, 33. If we then add 8 to 33 we get 41, so the rule—add a number that drops by 1 each time—works for all the numbers. Therefore, the missing number is 33.

$$
\begin{array}{ccccc}
+10 & +9 & +8 & +7 & +6 \\
14, & 24, & \_\_, & 41, & 48, & 54, \ldots
\end{array}
$$

TIP: *When you do series questions, first solve the problem, then look at the four choices. If you have done the problem correctly, you should find your answer on the list of choices. Then just mark it on the answer sheet. If you look at the choices first, you may confuse yourself and have trouble analyzing the series correctly.*

V. Comparison Questions

Comparison questions begin either with words similar to (1) "Examine (A), (B), and (C) and find the best answer," followed by three choices—(A), (B), and (C)—in picture form or numerical expression form, or the words (2) "Examine the figure (or circle, or graph, etc.) and find the best answer," followed by "a" geometric figure or graph. Most questions follow the "A, B, C" format, but a few follow the "examine the figure" format. All questions conclude with four statements comparing quantities in the pictures or expressions, and you must choose the statement that is true.

Pictures and Graphs

Pictures can represent any of the following: a number of items, a fraction or area, or a geometric figure. Graphs can be of different types, including picture graphs and bar graphs.

   TIP: *Here is a good way to solve comparison problems.*

   Write the quantity associated with each picture, graph, important part of the figure, or numerical expression directly on the question sheet. It will then be easier to choose the true statement at the end of the problem.

Drill: Pictures and graphs

DIRECTIONS: Choose the best answer.

Number of items

1. Examine (*A*), (*B*), and (*C*) and find the best answer.

(*A*)   (*B*)   (*C*)

                    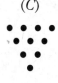

(A) *A* and *C* are equal.

(B) *B* is greater than *A*.

(C) *B* and *C* are equal.

(D) *A* is greater than *B*.

Fraction or area

2. Examine the equal rectangles (*A*), (*B*), and (*C*) and find the best answer regarding their shaded parts.

(*A*)   (*B*)   (*C*)

(A) *A* is greater than *B*.

(B) *A* is smaller than *C*.

(C) *B* is greater than both *A* and *C*.

(D) *A*, *B*, and *C* are equal.

Picture graph

3. Examine *A*, *B*, and *C* and find the best answer.

(A) *A* and *B* are equal.

(B) *A* plus *B* equals *C*.

(C) *C* is greater than *A* and *B* combined.

(D) *C* is less than *A* and *B* combined.

Geometric figure

4. Examine the circle with center *B* and find the best answer.

(A) *BC* is equal to *CD*.

(B) *AB* is equal to *CD*.

(C) *AC* is equal to *CD*.

(D) *BD* is equal to *AB*.

Bar graph

5.

(A) *A* plus *B* equals *C* plus *D*.

(B) *C* minus *D* equals *B* minus *A*.

(C) *C* minus *A* equals *B* minus *D*.

(D) *A* plus *D* equals *B* plus *C*.

Answers to drill questions

1. **(D)** The correct answer is **(D)**. Count the circles in each part and write the numbers on the picture. You should have $A = 12$, $B = 11$, and $C = 10$. Then it is obvious that the only correct answer is that *A* is greater than *B*.

2. **(D)** The correct answer is **(D)**. Write the fraction represented by each picture. You should have $A = \frac{1}{3}$, $B = \frac{1}{3}$, and $C = \frac{3}{9}$ which reduces to $\frac{1}{3}$. Since all three fractions are equal, **(D)** is the correct answer.

3. **(B)** The correct answer is **(B)**. Writing the number represented by the picture in each part, you should get $A = 10$ people, $B = 40 + 10 = 50$ people, and $C = 40 + (2 \times 10) = 40 + 20 = 60$ people. Since *A* (10 people) + *B* (50 people) = 60, **(B)** is the correct answer.

4. **(D)** The correct answer is **(D)**. *AB* is a radius of the circle, as is *BC* and *BD*. Since all radii are equal in length, **(D)** is the correct answer. Note that *CD* is longer than either *BD* or *BC* because it is the longest side in triangle *BCD*. On the other hand, *CD* cannot be as long as *AC* because *A* is the point on the circle that is farthest from *C*.

5. **(B)** The answer is **(B)**. Writing the height of each bar of the graph beside its label, you should get $A = 2$, $B = 4$, $C = 5$, and $D = 3$. Since $C - D = 2$, and $B - A = 2$, **(B)** is the correct answer.

Numerical Expressions

About half of the comparison questions involve numerical expressions. These are usually one of three kinds: grouping, numerals, or miscellaneous. The numerals may be in ratio, decimal, or percent form.

Remember: *Write the number or simplified version of each part on the question sheet beside the expression.*

Drill: Numerical expressions

DIRECTIONS: Choose the best answer.

Grouping

1. Examine (*A*), (*B*), and (*C*) and find the best answer.

(*A*) $(3 + 2) \times 4$

(*B*) $3 + (2 \times 4)$

(*C*) $(3 \times 4) + 2$

(A) *A* is greater than both *B* and *C*.

(B) *B* is greater than *C*.

(C) *C* is greater than *A*.

(D) *A*, *B*, and *C* are equal.

Numerals

2. Examine (*A*), (*B*), and (*C*) and find the best answer.

(*A*) 5%

(*B*) $\dfrac{1}{5}$

(*C*) .5

(A) *A* is the largest number.

(B) *B* is the largest number.

(C) *C* is the largest number.

(D) *A* and *C* are equal.

Miscellaneous

3. Examine (*A*), (*B*), and (*C*) and find the best answer.

(*A*) 2^3

(*B*) 3^2

(*C*) 3×2

(A) *A* is greater than *B*.

(B) *A* is equal to *B*.

(C) *A* and *C* are equal.

(D) *A* is greater than *C*.

Answers to drill questions

1. **(A)** Choice **(A)** is the correct answer. Evaluate each expression first, and write the answer on the question sheet beside the expression. Remember to do the expressions in parentheses first.

   For A, $(3 + 2) = 5$, and $5 \times 4 = 20$.

   For B, $(2 \times 4) = 8$, and $3 + 8 = 11$.

   For C, $(3 \times 4) = 12$, and $12 + 2 = 14$.

   Since 20 is greater than both 11 and 14, **(A)** is the correct answer.

2. **(C)** Choice **(C)** is the correct answer. Express each fraction in the same form. Let's try decimals.

   For **(A)**, $5\% = .05$.

   For **(B)**, $\frac{1}{5} = .20$.

   (C) is already expressed in decimal form, but let's write it to the same number of decimal places as **(A)** and **(B)**, or $.5 = .50$.

   Since .50 is greater than both .05 and .20, **(C)** is the correct answer.

3. **(D)** Choice **(D)** is the correct answer.

   For **(A)**, $2^3 = 2 \times 2 \times 2 = 8$.

   For **(B)**, $3^2 = 3 \times 3 = 9$.

   For **(C)**, $3 \times 2 = 6$.

   Since 8 is greater than 6, **(D)** is the correct answer.

TIP: *To do comparison questions, you have to consider the four choices you are given and choose the best one. You might find it helpful to cross off wrong answers as you reject them. This way, you won't get confused about which choices you have considered already and which you haven't. Also, if you correctly eliminate three answers, the fourth answer must be the right one.*

VI. Pre-Algebra Questions

Pre-algebra questions ask you to find a number from a word description. The questions begin with the words, "What number . . ." or an expression like, "$\frac{1}{2}$ of what number . . ." followed by information about the number or, in the second case, $\frac{1}{2}$ of the number. After you determine the number from the information you have been given, you choose the letter associated with it from the list of four choices that follows the question.

In order to answer the questions, you must know the mathematical meanings of certain words or expressions. Examine the following table:

Expression	Word Meaning	Mathematical Notation	Example
$\frac{1}{2}$ of	$\frac{1}{2}$ times	$\frac{1}{2} \times$	$\frac{1}{2}$ of $20 = \frac{1}{2} \times 20 = 10$
3 more than	add 3	$+ 3$	3 more than $12 = 12 + 3 = 15$

Expression	Word Meaning	Mathematical Notation	Example
3 less than	subtract 3	-3	3 less than 12 = 12 − 3 = 9
is, makes, leaves	equals	$=$	3 less than 12 makes = 12 − 3 = 9
4 squared	4 times itself	4^2 or 4×4	4 squared is $4^2 = 4 \times 4 = 16$
twice	2 times	$2 \times$	twice 7 = 2 × 7 = 14

There are two main ways to solve these questions. The first is to use algebra. If you have not studied algebra through simple linear equations, use the second method. The second is to do the calculation directly from the words of the question—the word method. Let's do an example using both methods. (*Note: We have called these questions "pre-algebra" questions because you do not need to know algebra to solve them.*)

Example

What number is 5 more than $\frac{1}{4}$ of 36?

A. Algebra method. Translate the sentence into algebra. Use x for "what number."

$$x = \left(\frac{1}{4} \times 36\right) + 5$$
$$x = 9 + 5$$
$$x = 14$$

B. Word method. First evaluate the expression after the word "equals," which is usually "is," "makes," or "leaves."

$$\frac{1}{4} \text{ of } 36 = \frac{1}{4} \times 36 = 9$$
$$5 \text{ more than } 9 = 9 + 5 = 14$$

Then determine the number from the remaining information. In this example, the number is 14.

Now let's do a more difficult example.

Example

What number subtracted from 35 leaves 6 less than $\frac{1}{3}$ of 42?

A. Algebra method. Translate into algebra.

$$35 - x = \left(\frac{1}{3} \times 42\right) - 6$$
$$35 - x = 14 - 6$$
$$35 - x = 8$$

Subtracting 35 from both sides of the equation gives
$$-x = 8 - 35$$
So, $-x = -27$, and multiplying both sides by -1 gives
$$x = 27$$

B. Word method. Evaluate the expression to the right of "leaves" in the question.

$$\frac{1}{3} \text{ of } 42 = \frac{1}{3} \times 42 = 14$$

6 less than $14 = 14 - 6 = 8$

If we subtract some number from 35 to get 8, the number must be 27 since $35 - 8 = 27$. So, the answer is 27.

TIP: *If you are using the word method, you might want to use the process of elimination once you have evaluated the expression to the right of the word "equals." That is, try each of the four choices you are given until you find the right one.*

For example, look at the problem we just did. It says, "What number subtracted from 35 leaves . . .," and you have figured out that it leaves 8. Assume that the question included the following four choices for answers: (A) 22; (B) 17; (C) 27; (D) 29. You could subtract each number from 35 until you get an answer of 8. Again, the obvious answer is (C) 27.

Try the following drill questions. Look at the table above if you are not sure what the words mean. Answers and explanations follow the questions. (Note that the four choices are not included here, but if you want to use the process of elimination method, you can practice it in the sample tests that follow this section.)

Drill: Pre-Algebra

DIRECTIONS: Solve the following problems using the algebra method or word method.

1. What number is 7 less than $\frac{2}{3}$ of 18?

2. What number divided by 6 leaves 8 more than 7?

3. What number added to 12 is twice the product of 3 and $\frac{1}{2}$ of 14?

4. $\frac{1}{4}$ of what number is 3 more than 2 squared?

5. What number multiplied by 4 makes 7 more than half of 26?

Answers to drill questions

1. The correct answer is 5.

   A. Algebra method. Translate the words into algebra.

   $$x = \left(\frac{2}{3} \times 18\right) - 7$$
   $$x = 12 - 7$$
   $$x = 5$$

   B. Word method. Evaluate the sentence after the word "is."

   $$\frac{2}{3} \text{ of } 18 = \frac{2}{3} \times 18 = 12$$

   7 less than $12 = 12 - 7 = 5$

2. The correct answer is 90.

   A. Algebra method.

   $$\frac{x}{6} = 7 + 8$$
   $$\frac{x}{6} = 15$$

Multiplying both sides of the equation by 6 yields
$x = 90$

B. Word method.

8 more than $7 = 7 + 8 = 15$

If a number divided by 6 equals 15, the number must be 6 times 15, which equals 90

3. The correct answer is 30.

A. Algebra method.

$$12 + x = 2 \times \left(3 \times \left(\frac{1}{2} \times 14 \right) \right)$$

Do parentheses from the inside out.

$12 + x = 2 \times (3 \times 7)$

$12 + x = 2 \times 21$

$12 + x = 42$

Subtract 12 from both sides.

$x = 30$

B. Word method.

$\frac{1}{2}$ of $14 = \frac{1}{2} \times 14 = 7$

the product of 3 and $7 = 3 \times 7 = 21$

twice $21 = 2 \times 21 = 42$

If a number is added to 12 to get 42, the number must be 42 minus 12, or 30.

4. The correct answer is 28.

A. Algebra method.

$$\frac{1}{4} \times x = (2 \times 2) + 3$$

$$\frac{1}{4} \times x = 4 + 3$$

$$\frac{1}{4} \times x = 7$$

Multiply both sides by 4, which gives
$x = 28$

B. Word method.

2 squared $= 2 \times 2 = 4$

3 more than $4 = 4 + 3 = 7$

$\frac{1}{4}$ of a number is 7, so the number must be 4 times 7, or 28.

5. The correct answer is 5.

A. Algebra method.

$$4x = \left(\frac{1}{2} \times 26\right) + 7$$

$$4x = 13 + 7$$

$$4x = 20$$

Divide both sides by 4.

$$x = 5$$

B. Word method.

$$\text{half of } 26 = \frac{1}{2} \times 26 = 13$$

$$7 \text{ more than } 13 = 13 + 7 = 20$$

If the number multiplied by 4 makes 20, the number must be 20 divided by 4, or 5.

Point to Remember: There are three types of questions. If you like doing one type more than the other two, do that type first. You will gain confidence as you do them and will be more likely to succeed with the harder questions later. Similarly, if there is one type of question you don't like to do, save questions of that type for the end.

HSPT

PRACTICE TEST 2

HSPT
SUBTEST 1

Verbal Skills

Time: 16 Minutes
60 Questions

DIRECTIONS: Select the best answer choice.

1. Microscope is to cell as telescope is to
   _____
   (A) far.
   (B) heat.
   (C) star.
   (D) astronomer.

2. Key is to door as combination is to
   _____
   (A) numbers.
   (B) safe.
   (C) open.
   (D) window.

3. Best is to good as worst is to _____
   (A) better.
   (B) worse.
   (C) bad.
   (D) well.

4. Usher is to aisle as actor is to _____
   (A) theater.
   (B) stage.
   (C) play.
   (D) role.

5. Flexible is to gymnast as eloquent is to
   _____
   (A) editor.
   (B) speech.
   (C) orator.
   (D) articulate.

6. Incite is to provoke as inception is to
   _____
   (A) stimulus.
   (B) beginning.
   (C) end.
   (D) celebrate.

GO TO NEXT PAGE ➡

7. Exhausted is to tired as ecstatic is to
   _____
   (A) relieved.
   (B) peaceful.
   (C) smile.
   (D) happy.

8. Bench is to park as sofa is to _____
   (A) living room.
   (B) church.
   (C) couch.
   (D) furniture.

9. Expand is to contract as reveal is to
   _____
   (A) conceal.
   (B) secret.
   (C) document.
   (D) disclose.

10. Impartial is to prejudiced as exploit is to
    _____
    (A) use.
    (B) protect.
    (C) expose.
    (D) prevent.

11. To loiter is to
    (A) litter.
    (B) relapse.
    (C) hasten.
    (D) linger.

12. Inflammable is
    (A) inflammation.
    (B) noncombustible.
    (C) similar.
    (D) flammable.

13. To vindicate is to
    (A) clear.
    (B) convict.
    (C) pose.
    (D) blame.

14. A premonition is a
    (A) promotion.
    (B) luxury.
    (C) dream.
    (D) forewarning.

15. Soothe means to
    (A) warn.
    (B) comfort.
    (C) blacken.
    (D) strengthen.

16. Fervent most nearly means
    (A) hesitant.
    (B) cool.
    (C) enthusiastic.
    (D) warm.

17. Crucial means
    (A) technical.
    (B) experimental.
    (C) fundamental.
    (D) advanced.

18. To reprimand is to
    (A) praise.
    (B) return.
    (C) correct.
    (D) threaten.

GO TO NEXT PAGE ➡

19. Chastity is
    (A) purity.
    (B) correction.
    (C) religious.
    (D) familiarity.

20. Disrespectful means
    (A) careless.
    (B) rude.
    (C) valuable.
    (D) safe.

21. Contempt is
    (A) temptation.
    (B) fear.
    (C) commend.
    (D) scorn.

22. Agile most nearly means
    (A) wool.
    (B) limber.
    (C) unpredictable.
    (D) difficult.

23. Redeem means to
    (A) recover.
    (B) locate.
    (C) destroy.
    (D) research.

24. To pulverize is to
    (A) grind.
    (B) attempt.
    (C) pervert.
    (D) preserve.

25. To presume is to
    (A) swindle.
    (B) predict.
    (C) prosper.
    (D) assume.

26. To prevaricate most nearly means to
    (A) endanger.
    (B) lie.
    (C) threaten.
    (D) prevent.

27. Postmortem most nearly means
    (A) after death.
    (B) celebration.
    (C) stockade.
    (D) position.

28. Patty is five years older than Stephanie. Stephanie is two years older than Kerri. Kerri is seven years younger than Patty. If the first two statements are true, the third is
    (A) true.
    (B) false.
    (C) uncertain.

29. Sue is two inches taller than Lynn. Lynn is three inches taller than Kate. Kate is five inches shorter than Sue. If the first two statements are true, the third is
    (A) true.
    (B) false.
    (C) uncertain.

30. Jarret earned more money over the summer vacation than his brothers. Matthew and Brian are his brothers. Matthew made less money than Jarret and Brian. If the first two statements are true, the third is
    (A) true.
    (B) false.
    (C) uncertain.

GO TO NEXT PAGE ➡

31. Phyllis read more books over the summer vacation than any of her friends. Betty and Lorraine are her friends. Betty read fewer books than Phyllis and Lorraine. If the first two statements are true, the third is
    (A) true.
    (B) false.
    (C) uncertain.

32. Main Street is wider than Ocean Avenue. Lake Avenue is wider than Willow Road and the same width as Ocean Avenue. Main Street is narrower than Willow Road. If the first two statements are true, the third is
    (A) true.
    (B) false.
    (C) uncertain.

33. Nicole can type faster than Michelle. Joanne can type faster than Nancy and the same speed as Michelle. Nicole types slower than Nancy. If the first two statements are true, the third is
    (A) true.
    (B) false.
    (C) uncertain.

34. Jennifer takes ballet lessons five days a week. Maryann takes ballet lessons three days a week. Jennifer and Maryann take ballet lessons on the same day at least once a week. If the first two statements are true, the third is
    (A) true.
    (B) false.
    (C) uncertain.

35. Joe plays basketball six days a week. Tony plays basketball four days a week. Joe and Tony play basketball on the same day at least three times a week. If the first two statements are true, the third is
    (A) true.
    (B) false.
    (C) uncertain.

36. Broccoli costs more than carrots. Onions cost less than broccoli and lettuce. Carrots cost more than lettuce. If the first two statements are true, the third is
    (A) true.
    (B) false.
    (C) uncertain.

37. Grapes cost more than plums. Peaches cost less than grapes and nectarines. Plums cost more than nectarines. If the first two statements are true, the third is
    (A) true.
    (B) false.
    (C) uncertain.

38. Which word does <u>not</u> belong with the others?
    (A) Irritate
    (B) Appease
    (C) Harass
    (D) Pester

39. Which word does <u>not</u> belong with the others?
    (A) Vacant
    (B) Empty
    (C) Spacious
    (D) Unoccupied

GO TO NEXT PAGE ➡

40. Which word does <u>not</u> belong with the others?
- **(A)** Placid
- **(B)** Chaotic
- **(C)** Calm
- **(D)** Peaceful

41. Which word does <u>not</u> belong with the others?
- **(A)** Artery
- **(B)** Capillary
- **(C)** Vein
- **(D)** Circulatory

42. Which word does <u>not</u> belong with the others?
- **(A)** Hobo
- **(B)** Ad
- **(C)** Exam
- **(D)** Memo

43. Which word does <u>not</u> belong with the others?
- **(A)** Fiscal
- **(B)** Annual
- **(C)** Perennial
- **(D)** Temporal

44. Which word does <u>not</u> belong with the others?
- **(A)** Hinder
- **(B)** Aid
- **(C)** Retard
- **(D)** Impede

45. Which word does <u>not</u> belong with the others?
- **(A)** Cheerful
- **(B)** Optimistic
- **(C)** Hopeful
- **(D)** Desperate

46. Which word does <u>not</u> belong with the others?
- **(A)** Recover
- **(B)** Relapse
- **(C)** Regress
- **(D)** Backslide

47. Which word does <u>not</u> belong with the others?
- **(A)** Gloomy
- **(B)** Dismal
- **(C)** Dreary
- **(D)** Bright

48. Which word does <u>not</u> belong with the others?
- **(A)** Defendant
- **(B)** Interrogate
- **(C)** Bailiff
- **(D)** Plaintiff

49. Which word does <u>not</u> belong with the others?
- **(A)** Period
- **(B)** Question mark
- **(C)** Comma
- **(D)** Exclamation point

50. Which word does <u>not</u> belong with the others?
- **(A)** Precise
- **(B)** Approximate
- **(C)** Exact
- **(D)** Accurate

51. Which word does <u>not</u> belong with the others?
- **(A)** Simple
- **(B)** Complex
- **(C)** Intricate
- **(D)** Complicated

52. Which word does <u>not</u> belong with the others?
- **(A)** Diverse
- **(B)** Heterogeneous
- **(C)** Uniform
- **(D)** Varied

GO TO NEXT PAGE →

53. Which word does <u>not</u> belong with the others?
    - (A) Dictionary
    - (B) Nonfiction
    - (C) Thesaurus
    - (D) Encyclopedia

54. Which word does <u>not</u> belong with the others?
    - (A) Itinerary
    - (B) Route
    - (C) Destination
    - (D) Portfolio

55. Which word does <u>not</u> belong with the others?
    - (A) Excrete
    - (B) Discharge
    - (C) Disburse
    - (D) Expel

56. Presume means the opposite of
    - (A) believe.
    - (B) disprove.
    - (C) suppose.
    - (D) conclude.

57. Disdainful does not mean
    - (A) arrogant.
    - (B) proud.
    - (C) aloof.
    - (D) humble.

58. Infamous is the opposite of
    - (A) notorious.
    - (B) wicked.
    - (C) prominent.
    - (D) dishonorable.

59. Perpetual does not mean
    - (A) constant.
    - (B) eternal.
    - (C) momentary.
    - (D) enduring.

60. Imminent does not mean
    - (A) proximate.
    - (B) impending.
    - (C) past.
    - (D) close.

STOP

HSPT
SUBTEST 2

Quantitative Skills

Time: 30 Minutes
52 Questions

DIRECTIONS: Select the best answer choice.

61. What number is 12 less than $\frac{1}{3}$ of 60?
    (A) 4
    (B) 13
    (C) 6
    (D) 8

62. Look at this series: 33, 25, 17, 9, . . .
    What numeral should come next?
    (A) 1
    (B) 3
    (C) 5
    (D) 7

63. Look at this series: 98, 82, 75, 59, 52, . . .
    What numeral should come next?
    (A) 43
    (B) 36
    (C) 39
    (D) 38

64. Examine (a), (b), and (c) and find the best answer.

(a)   (b)   (c)

    (A) (a) is equal to (b) which is equal to (c).
    (B) (a) is equal to (b) which is not equal to (c).
    (C) (b) is equal to (c) which is not equal to (a).
    (D) (a) is not equal to (b) which is not equal to (c).

GO TO NEXT PAGE ➡

65. Examine (a), (b), and (c) and find the best answer.
    (a) $(6 \times 1) + 2$
    (b) $(1 + 2) \times 6$
    (c) $(6 \times 2) + 1$
    (A) (a) is equal to (b) which is equal to (c).
    (B) (a) is greater than (b) and is greater than (c).
    (C) (b) is greater than (a) and is greater than (c).
    (D) (c) is greater than (a) and is greater than (b).

66. What number is 2 more than $\frac{3}{4}$ of 20?
    (A) 15
    (B) 7
    (C) 17
    (D) 11

67. What number is 9 less than $\frac{1}{2}$ of 32?
    (A) 9
    (B) 25
    (C) 13
    (D) 7

68. Look at this series: 52, 55, 60, 64, 70, . . . What numeral should come next?
    (A) 75
    (B) 76
    (C) 77
    (D) 78

69. Examine the equal squares (a), (b), and (c) and find the best answer regarding their shaded parts.

(a)   (b)   (c)

(A) (a) is equal to (b) which is equal to (c).
(B) (a) is greater than (b) which is equal to (c).
(C) (a) is equal to (b) which is greater than (c).
(D) (a) is equal to (b) which is less than (c).

70. What number added to 5 makes $\frac{5}{6}$ of 24?
    (A) 4
    (B) 5
    (C) 7
    (D) 15

71. Look at this series: 144, 140, 132, 120, 104, . . . What numeral should come next?
    (A) 96
    (B) 90
    (C) 84
    (D) 80

72. Look at this series: 72, 78, 83, 89, 94, . . . What numeral should come next?
    (A) 100
    (B) 96
    (C) 99
    (D) 97

73. What number is twice as much as 8 squared?
    (A) 32
    (B) 16
    (C) 96
    (D) 128

74. What number subtracted from 32 makes 6 more than 10?
    (A) 16
    (B) 4
    (C) 18
    (D) 12

GO TO NEXT PAGE ➡

75. Examine (a), (b), and (c) and find the best answer.

    (a) $\frac{2}{3}$ of 15

    (b) $\frac{2}{5}$ of 20

    (c) $\frac{3}{4}$ of 32

    (A) (c) is less than (a).

    (B) (b) is less than (a).

    (C) (c) is less than (b).

    (D) (a) is less than (b).

76. Examine the equal circles (a), (b), and (c) and find the best answer regarding their shaded parts.

    (a)   (b)   (c)

    (A) (a) is equal to (b) which is equal to (c).

    (B) (a) is equal to (b) which is not equal to (c).

    (C) (b) is equal to (c) which is not equal to (a).

    (D) (a) is not equal to (b) which is not equal to (c).

77. Look at this series: 1801, 1780, 1759, 1738, . . . What numeral should come next?

    (A) 1720

    (B) 1719

    (C) 1721

    (D) 1717

78. Look at this series: 42, 49, 56, __, 70, 77, . . . What numeral should fill in the blank?

    (A) 83

    (B) 84

    (C) 63

    (D) 35

79. What number added to 51 makes a number twice as large as 35?

    (A) 16

    (B) 21

    (C) 28

    (D) 19

80. Examine (a), (b), and (c) and find the best answer.

    (a) .08

    (b) 8%

    (c) $\frac{2}{25}$

    (A) (a) is equal to (b) which is equal to (c).

    (B) (b) is greater than (a).

    (C) (c) is greater than (a).

    (D) (c) is equal to (a) and not equal to (b).

81. What number subtracted from 96 makes 12 more than 11?

    (A) 84

    (B) 85

    (C) 23

    (D) 73

82. Examine the two connected squares and find the best answer.

    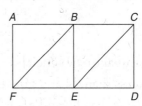

    (A) *AC* is equal to *CE*.

    (B) *FA* is equal to *FD*.

    (C) *FB* is equal to *EC*.

    (D) *BE* is equal to *BF*.

GO TO NEXT PAGE ➡

83. Look at this series: 250, 50, 10, 2, . . . What numeral should come next?
    (A) 1
    (B) .4
    (C) .5
    (D) .1

84. Look at this series: 100, 20, 25, 5, 10, . . . What numeral should come next?
    (A) 1
    (B) 2
    (C) 5
    (D) 10

85. What number added to 6 makes a number that is 8 less than 15?
    (A) 7
    (B) 2
    (C) 9
    (D) 1

86. Examine (a), (b), and (c) and find the best answer.
    (a) $\frac{3}{4}$

    (b) $\frac{2}{3}$

    (c) $\frac{19}{24}$

    (A) (a) is equal to (b) which is equal to (c).
    (B) (a) is less than (b) and greater than (c).
    (C) (b) is less than (c) and greater than (a).
    (D) (a) is less than (c) and greater than (b).

87. Look at this series: XX, XVI, XII, VIII, . . . What numeral should come next?
    (A) X
    (B) VI
    (C) IV
    (D) II

88. Look at this series: 84, 79, 68, 63, 52, . . . What numeral should come next?
    (A) 47
    (B) 42
    (C) 41
    (D) 40

89. One-half of what number is $\frac{2}{5}$ of 10?
    (A) 6
    (B) 4
    (C) 3
    (D) 8

90. Examine the circle with center E and find the best answer.

    (A) AD is equal to AE.
    (B) DC is equal to BD.
    (C) BC is equal to AD.
    (D) AC is equal to AB.

91. Look at this series: 18, 23, __, 37, 46, 51, 60, . . . What numeral should fill in the blank?
    (A) 69
    (B) 28
    (C) 35
    (D) 32

92. Look at this series: 5, 7, 14, 16, 32, . . . What numeral should come next?
    (A) 34
    (B) 64
    (C) 66
    (D) 40

GO TO NEXT PAGE ➡

93. Two-thirds of what number is 2 squared?
    (A) 12
    (B) 9
    (C) 6
    (D) 3

94. Examine (a), (b), and (c) and find the best answer.
    (a) $(12 \times 2) \div 3$
    (b) $(12 \times 3) \div 2$
    (c) $3 \times (12 \div 2)$
    (A) (a) is equal to (b) which is equal to (c).
    (B) (a) is equal to (b) which is not equal to (c).
    (C) (a) is equal to (c) which is not equal to (b).
    (D) (b) is equal to (c) which is not equal to (a).

95. What number multiplied by 5 is $\frac{3}{4}$ of 40?
    (A) 10
    (B) 5
    (C) 8
    (D) 6

96. Look at this series: 29, 35, 26, 32, 23, 29, . . . What two numerals should come next?
    (A) 35, 26
    (B) 35, 41
    (C) 20, 26
    (D) 20, 11

97. Examine the three regions of the circle with center E and find the best answer.

    (A) (x) is greater than (y) and equal to (2).
    (B) (y) is greater than (x) and equal to (2).
    (C) (2) is greater than (y) and equal to (x).
    (D) (2) is equal to (y) plus (x).

98. What number added to 5 leaves 7 less than $\frac{2}{5}$ of 80?
    (A) 16
    (B) 20
    (C) 25
    (D) 32

99. Examine (a), (b), and (c) and find the best answer.
    (a) $2(x + y)$
    (b) $2x + 2y$
    (c) $(x + y)2$
    (A) (a) is equal to (b) which is equal to (c).
    (B) (a) is equal to (b) but not equal to (c).
    (C) (a) is not equal to (b) but is equal to (c).
    (D) (a) is not equal to (b) and is not equal to (c).

100. What number subtracted from 50 leaves half the product of 10 and $\frac{2}{3}$ of 12?
    (A) 1
    (B) 4
    (C) 8
    (D) 10

101. Examine (a), (b), and (c) and find the best answer.

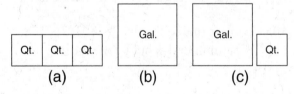

    (A) (a) equals (b) which equals (c).
    (B) (a) is greater than (b).
    (C) (c) is greater than (a).
    (D) (a) is equal to (b) but not equal to (c).

GO TO NEXT PAGE

102. Examine (a), (b), and (c) and find the best answer.

(a) 1^6

(b) 6^1

(c) 12^0

(A) (a) is equal to (b) but is not equal to (c).

(B) (b) is equal to (c) but is not equal to (a).

(C) (c) is equal to (a) but is not equal to (b).

(D) (a) is not equal to (b) and is not equal to (c).

103. What number divided by 4 leaves 2 times $\frac{1}{3}$ of 3?

(A) 16

(B) 12

(C) 4

(D) 8

104. Examine the graph and find the best answer.

(A) (a) minus (b) equals (d) minus (c).

(B) (d) minus (a) equals (a) minus (b).

(C) (c) plus (b) equals (a) plus (d).

(D) (d) minus (b) equals (c) minus (a).

105. Look at this series: 98, 28, 103, 26, 108, . . . What numeral should come next?

(A) 24

(B) 22

(C) 21

(D) 20

106. Examine (a), (b), and (c) and find the best answer.

(a) 60% of 50

(b) 50% of 60

(c) 40% of 70

(A) (a) is equal to (b) which is equal to (c).

(B) (a) is equal to (b) but is not equal to (c).

(C) (a) is equal to (c) but is not equal to (b).

(D) (b) is equal to (c) but is not equal to (a).

107. Examine the rectangle and find the best answer.

(A) The perimeter of the rectangle is 30.

(B) The perimeter of triangle ABC is 24.

(C) The area of triangle ABC is 48.

(D) The area of the rectangle is 60.

108. Look at this series: 60, 64, 16, 20, 5, . . . What numeral should come next?

(A) 1

(B) 2

(C) 9

(D) 10

109. Look at this series: 38, 34, 37, 31, 36, 28, 35, . . . What three numerals should come next?

(A) 26, 33, 24

(B) 27, 31, 23

(C) 25, 34, 22

(D) 23, 29, 20

GO TO NEXT PAGE ➡

110. What number subtracted from $\frac{1}{3}$ of 21 leaves $\frac{3}{8}$ of 16?

(A) 1

(B) 6

(C) 3

(D) 7

111. One-fifth of what number added to 5 makes 3 times $\frac{2}{3}$ of 18?

(A) 100

(B) 155

(C) 15

(D) 125

112. Look at this series: 32, 24, 27, 30, 22, 25, . . . What numeral should come next?

(A) 20

(B) 28

(C) 29

(D) 31

HSPT

STOP

HSPT
SUBTEST 3

Reading

Time: 25 Minutes
62 Questions

Comprehension

> **DIRECTIONS:** Read the following passages and then select the best answer choice.

Questions 113–117 are based on the following passage.

Forgery is a serious crime that can result in harsh prison sentences. In a recent case, a man was sent to jail for 15 years for committing forgery. He sold documents that he claimed were written by Abraham Lincoln. In fact, the man who sold them had written the documents himself. He was an antiques dealer and was very familiar with American history. He was able to make the documents look old, and he learned how to imitate Lincoln's handwriting based on real documents written by Lincoln that he had seen. He sold people letters, reports, and speeches that he claimed were Lincoln's.

He was caught when a woman who bought a letter from him took it to be analyzed in a laboratory. The people who examined it were experts on dating materials like paper and ink. It took them several weeks of careful investigation to discover that the paper the letter was written on was not more than 50 years old, so the letter could not possibly have been authentic. The woman alerted the police, who sent an undercover agent in to buy a document. When it too was shown to be a forgery, the antiques dealer was arrested.

At the sentencing, the judge told the man that he was "a liar who had betrayed the trust of his customers and distorted American history." In addition to jail time, the man must pay back all the money he earned from his fake documents.

GO TO NEXT PAGE

113. According to the passage, the antiques dealer was arrested for

(A) stealing from his employers.

(B) selling forged documents.

(C) attacking a woman in his store.

(D) cheating on his taxes.

114. The word <u>forgery</u> as underlined and used in the passage most nearly means

(A) stealing.

(B) breaking.

(C) insulting.

(D) faking.

115. Based on the passage, which of the following is TRUE?

(A) Forgery is not considered a serious crime.

(B) It is easy to detect when a document has been forged.

(C) The antiques dealer sold a forged document to an undercover police officer.

(D) The antiques dealer was discovered to be a forger when he was caught in the act of writing a fake letter.

116. According to the passage, the antiques dealer was caught based on what evidence?

(A) The kind of ink used on the letter had not existed when Lincoln was alive.

(B) The handwriting was different than Lincoln's.

(C) The letter contained many mistakes and errors.

(D) The paper was not old enough to have been written on by Abraham Lincoln.

117. The punishment of the antiques dealer

(A) includes only a 15-year prison sentence.

(B) is 15 hours of community service.

(C) was suspended by the judge.

(D) includes both a jail sentence and an order to pay back the money he earned with his false documents.

Questions 118–122 are based on the following passage.

The employee turnover rate is a growing concern in the restaurant industry. Most employees in this business are young and part-time workers who end up doing some of the most important work in the company. They tend to want flexibility, a feeling of purpose, recognition, and good wages. The future success of restaurants depends on maintaining a strong base of long-term employees. This is possible through <u>motivational</u> techniques that will ultimately save restaurant owners money and allow their businesses to grow and prosper.

The average employee turnover rate last year was 70 percent. This can be very expensive for restaurant owners. Every time an employee leaves and is replaced, the restaurant must invest time and energy in training the new employee, while all the time and energy that went into training the departing one is lost. Restaurant owners need to develop motivational techniques to create an environment in which workers will be content and productive.

GO TO NEXT PAGE

Such techniques could include regular pay raises; recognition programs, like selecting an "Employee of the Month;" and incentives such as movie passes or T-shirts for employees who demonstrate an excellent work record. Such programs will create a better atmosphere for workers and make them feel loyal to the company they work for, which will ultimately make the business more profitable.

118. The purpose of this passage is to
   (A) explain how employee turnover rates are calculated.
   (B) criticize employees for not remaining at one job for a long period of time.
   (C) warn restaurant owners that high employee turnover rates can be bad for their business and persuade them that motivational techniques will help keep employees happy with their jobs.
   (D) persuade restaurant owners to pay their employees less.

119. The word <u>motivational</u> as underlined and used in this passage, most nearly means
   (A) detrimental.
   (B) harsh.
   (C) encouraging.
   (D) discouraging.

120. According to the passage, high employee turnover rates are
   (A) beneficial to business owners.
   (B) harmful to business owners.
   (C) not a factor for business owners.
   (D) something that does not affect restaurants.

121. What is the tone of the author of this passage?
   (A) The author is impartial about employee turnover rates.
   (B) The author is mildly interested in trying to stop frequent turnover in restaurants.
   (C) The author feels that the danger of high employee turnover rates has been exaggerated.
   (D) The author strongly believes that high employee turnover rates is a matter that business owners should be concerned about.

122. Which of the following is NOT a motivational technique proposed in this passage?
   (A) Pay raises
   (B) Expense-paid vacations
   (C) Incentives
   (D) Recognition programs

Questions 123–127 are based on the following passage.

Cubism is an <u>abstract</u> form of painting that emphasizes fracture, wildness, and irrationality at the expense of unity, control, and logic. This type of painting is the opposite of art forms that strive to represent the world as it actually appears to us. Some people object to it because it appears nonsensical and because it fails to conform to traditionally accepted ideals of "beautiful" art.

GO TO NEXT PAGE ➡

For instance, in his painting *Three Musicians*, Pablo Picasso (1881–1971), a Spanish artist and one of the most famous Cubists, offers us a look at three figures playing musical instruments, a seemingly ordinary scene. And yet in this painting the three musicians are hardly distinguishable from each other. They are drawn in such a way that each blends into the next. Their features are distorted so that they do not look like "real" people, and their hands and limbs are not in proper proportion to their bodies. The instruments they play bear only a passing resemblance to actual musical instruments, and, despite the work's title, it is not clear exactly how many figures are in the painting.

Despite its radical nature, Cubism was one of the most important and powerful forms of artistic expression in the twentieth century. Cubism had a formative influence on the modern consciousness, and its effects can be seen in many forms of art, design, and architecture.

123. The purpose of this passage is to
   (A) give a brief summary of Cubism.
   (B) give a biography of Pablo Picasso.
   (C) explain why Cubism is better than other styles of painting.
   (D) criticize Cubist painters.

124. Cubist paintings are all of the following EXCEPT
   (A) abstract.
   (B) unconventional.
   (C) irrational.
   (D) realistic.

125. The passage about the painting *Three Musicians* is intended to
   (A) show that Picasso was really a poor painter.
   (B) show that Picasso was the greatest painter of the twentieth century.
   (C) provide an example of a Cubist painting.
   (D) criticize the painting for being Cubist.

126. The word <u>abstract</u> as underlined and used in this passage most nearly means
   (A) good.
   (B) colorful.
   (C) important.
   (D) difficult to understand.

127. The author contends that
   (A) Cubism is an important and influential style of painting.
   (B) Cubism has had little impact.
   (C) Cubism was very popular for a short time, but has since become unpopular.
   (D) Pablo Picasso was not really a Cubist.

GO TO NEXT PAGE ➡

Questions 128–132 are based on the following passage.

Millions of Americans do not have health insurance. This is a serious problem, but there is very little being done to address it. This is mostly due to a general feeling that any attempt to provide health care for people who don't have any would be too expensive. Lacking a plan to provide full health care costs to all Americans, we as a nation need at the very least to find a way to provide basic health care services.

Basic health care services would ensure that any American could visit a doctor of his or her choice for a diagnosis, medical counseling and advice, and preventative medicine, such as immunizations and screening for the early detection of illnesses. While this is not a full solution to the problem of rising health care costs, it is an immediate remedy for the millions of Americans who have nowhere to turn when they are feeling sick and have no access to medical advice when they have health questions. As a civilized and humane country, we need to continue to work toward finding a <u>comprehensive</u> solution, but for now we need to agree on providing basic health services for uninsured Americans.

128. The tone of this passage indicates that the author's purpose is to
   (A) convince readers that it is important to address the health needs of uninsured Americans.
   (B) give an impartial assessment of the problem.
   (C) teach readers about various diseases.
   (D) declare that he or she does not believe in providing health care to uninsured Americans.

129. According to the passage
   (A) there are many plans being put into effect to address health care problems.
   (B) health care reform is not very complicated.
   (C) not enough is being done to address health care problems.
   (D) Both A and B.

130. According to the author, providing basic health services
   (A) is a permanent solution to the problem of high medical costs.
   (B) is an idea that has been successfully tested in various cities.
   (C) would be too expensive.
   (D) is an important first step toward improving the health care system but not a permanent solution to its problems.

131. Which of the following would NOT be covered by the author's proposed basic health services?
   (A) Surgery
   (B) Medical advice
   (C) Immunizations
   (D) Health screenings

132. The word <u>comprehensive</u> as underlined and used in this passage most nearly means
   (A) incomplete.
   (B) complete.
   (C) unnecessary.
   (D) uninteresting.

GO TO NEXT PAGE ➡

Questions 133–137 are based on the following passage.

To the Shakers, perfection was found in the creation of an object that was both useful and simple. Their Society was founded in 1774 by Ann Lee, an Englishwoman from the working classes who brought eight followers to New York with her. "Mother Ann" established her religious community on the belief that worldly interests were evil.

To gain entrance into the Society, believers had to remain celibate, have no private possessions, and avoid contact with outsiders. The order came to be called "Shakers" because of the feverish dance the group performed. Another characteristic of the group was the desire to seek perfection in their work.

Shaker furniture was created to exemplify specific characteristics: simplicity of design, quality of craftsmanship, harmony of proportion, and usefulness. While Shakers did not create any innovations in furniture designs, they were known for their fine craftsmanship. The major emphasis was on function, and not on excessive or elaborate decorations that contributed nothing to the product's usefulness.

133. Based on the passage, how would you describe the lifestyle of the Shakers?
    (A) Decadent
    (B) Simple
    (C) Extravagant
    (D) Wasteful

134. According to the passage, the Shakers got their name from
    (A) a rival religious organization.
    (B) the town in which they built their community.
    (C) the dance they performed.
    (D) the Bible.

135. The Shakers were primarily
    (A) dancers.
    (B) furniture makers.
    (C) a religious community.
    (D) farmers.

136. Shaker furniture is characterized by
    (A) ornate designs.
    (B) its uselessness.
    (C) its functional simplicity.
    (D) its shoddy craftsmanship.

137. The purpose of this passage is
    (A) to provide a brief description of the Shakers.
    (B) to denounce the Shakers.
    (C) to advertise Shaker furniture.
    (D) to convert readers to the Shaker way of thinking.

GO TO NEXT PAGE ➡

Questions 138–142 are based on the following passage.

In 1975, Sinclair observed that it had often been supposed that the main factor in learning to talk is being able to imitate. Schlesinger (1975) noted that at certain stages of learning to speak, a child tends to imitate everything an adult says to him or her, and it therefore seems reasonable to accord to such imitation an important role in the acquisition of language.

Moreover, various investigators have attempted to explain the role of imitation in language. In his discussion of the development of imitation and cognition of adult speech sounds, Nakazema (1975) stated that although the parent's talking stimulates and accelerates the infant's articulatory activity, the parent's phonome system does not influence the child's articulatory mechanisms. Slobin and Welsh (1973) suggested that imitation is the reconstruction of the adult's utterance and that the child does so by employing the grammatical rules that he has developed at a specific time. Schlesinger proposed that by imitating the adult, the child practices new grammatical constructions. Brown and Bellugi (1964) noted that a child's imitations resemble spontaneous speech in that they drop inflections, most function words, and sometimes other words. However, the word order of imitated sentences usually was preserved. Brown and Bellugi assumed that imitation is a function of what the child attended to or remembered. Shipley et al. (1969) suggested that repeating an adult's utterance assists the child's comprehension. Ervin (1964) and Braine (1971) found that a child's imitations do not contain more advanced structures than his or her spontaneous utterances; thus, imitation can no longer be regarded as the simple behavioristic act that earlier scholars assumed it to be.

138. The main purpose of this passage is to
   (A) encourage parents to read to their children.
   (B) discourage parents from letting their children imitate them.
   (C) put a stop to studies of language acquisition.
   (D) relate the findings of several experts in the field of language acquisition.

139. The tone of the passage is
   (A) informal.
   (B) humorous.
   (C) academic.
   (D) sad.

140. The author of this passage would agree with which of the following statements?
   (A) Children only imitate other children.
   (B) Language acquisition is a traumatic experience for children.
   (C) Language skills are easier for girls to master than boys.
   (D) Imitation is not a simple behavioristic act.

GO TO NEXT PAGE →

141. All of the following are said to be asserted by Brown and Bellugi EXCEPT
    (A) children are sensitive to harsh words.
    (B) a child's imitations often sound like spontaneous sounds.
    (C) the word order of imitated sentences is usually preserved.
    (D) imitation is a function of what the child remembered.

142. Based on this passage, it is clear that
    (A) language acquisition is a neglected field of study.
    (B) there has been a great deal of research done on language acquisition.
    (C) language acquisition was only really studied in the nineteenth century.
    (D) language acquisition is not considered a serious field of study.

Questions 143–147 are based on the following passage.

The Indians of California had five varieties of acorns, which they used as their principal source of food. This was a noteworthy accomplishment in technology since they first had to make the acorn edible. A process had to be developed for leaching out the poisonous tannic acid. They ground the acorns into a meal and then filtered it many times with water. This had to be done through sand or through tightly woven baskets. Early Indian campsites reveal the evidence of the acorn-processing labor necessary to provide enough food for their <u>subsistence</u>. The women patiently ground acorns into meal with stone pestles. The result, a pinkish flour that was cooked into a mush or thin soup, formed the bulk of their diet.

143. The main point of this passage is to
    (A) encourage us to process food the way Indians did.
    (B) study more early food processing techniques.
    (C) convey information based on archaeological studies of Indians in California.
    (D) criticize European treatment of Native Americans.

144. According to the passage, the early California Indians were the first people to
    (A) weave baskets.
    (B) live in California.
    (C) irrigate crops.
    (D) make the acorn edible.

145. We know about early Indian food processing techniques from
    (A) drawings in caves.
    (B) written documents.
    (C) studies of tribes related to the early California Indians.
    (D) archaeological studies of campsites.

146. Based on the passage, we know all of the following EXCEPT
    (A) the early California Indians processed their food to make it edible.
    (B) the early California Indians fought with other Indian tribes.
    (C) acorns contain poisonous tannic acid.
    (D) acorns were the principal food source for the early California Indians.

147. The word <u>subsistence</u> as underlined and used in this passage most nearly means
    (A) survival.
    (B) digestion.
    (C) religious worship.
    (D) starvation.

GO TO NEXT PAGE ➡

Questions 148–152 are based on the following passage.

Results of a study released by the College Board and the Western Interstate Commission for Higher Education show that in a year, the majority of California's high school graduates will be non-white and in two years, one-third of all the nation's students will be from minority groups. It is also predicted that nationally the total non-white and Hispanic student population for all grade levels will increase from 10.4 million to 13.7 million in about a decade. These figures suggest that now, more than ever, equal educational opportunities for all students must be our nation's number one priority.

148. An inference that can be made from this passage is that
   (A) there are not enough teachers for California's high schools.
   (B) the United States is becoming increasingly diverse.
   (C) high schools are not providing an adequate education.
   (D) many high school graduates cannot read very well.

149. The author of this passage would agree that
   (A) schools should recruit more minority teachers.
   (B) more money needs to be spent on sports programs.
   (C) there are many unqualified teachers.
   (D) the dropout rate is too high.

150. This passage uses what to help make its point?
   (A) An anecdote
   (B) Emotional language
   (C) Threatening language
   (D) Statistics

151. The author of the passage argues that
   (A) American schools are substandard.
   (B) European schools are better than American schools.
   (C) equal opportunity in education is becoming increasingly important.
   (D) minority students are enrolling in colleges at a greater rate than they were 10 years ago.

152. Based on this passage, we can infer that
   (A) teaching high school is an excellent career.
   (B) statistical findings can be the basis for formulating policy ideas.
   (C) there is little evidence to suggest that there is discrimination against minority students.
   (D) minority students are concentrated in certain areas of California.

GO TO NEXT PAGE ➡

Vocabulary

DIRECTIONS: Choose the word that means the same or about the same as the underlined word.

153. the <u>apex</u> of his career
  (A) bottom
  (B) beginning
  (C) end
  (D) peak

154. <u>compulsory</u> education
  (A) required
  (B) limited
  (C) private
  (D) optional

155. feel the <u>acute</u> pain
  (A) slight
  (B) recurring
  (C) sharp
  (D) steady

156. the <u>ambiguous</u> message
  (A) understandable
  (B) puzzling
  (C) foreign
  (D) illegible

157. the <u>eminent</u> scholar
  (A) distinguished
  (B) intelligent
  (C) unknown
  (D) confident

158. <u>scrutinize</u> the document
  (A) forge
  (B) skim
  (C) copy
  (D) examine

159. <u>convene</u> a discussion
  (A) conclude
  (B) assemble
  (C) concentrate
  (D) counterbalance

160. a <u>judicious</u> decision
  (A) biased
  (B) reckless
  (C) sensible
  (D) sensitive

161. a <u>ferocious</u> animal
  (A) tame
  (B) stubborn
  (C) wild
  (D) humorous

162. <u>obliterate</u> the evidence
  (A) examine
  (B) conceal
  (C) create
  (D) destroy

163. a <u>pallid</u> complexion
  (A) rosy
  (B) pale
  (C) sad
  (D) healthy

164. his <u>impetuous</u> decision
  (A) planned
  (B) recent
  (C) impulsive
  (D) wise

GO TO NEXT PAGE ➡

165. <u>mutinous</u> crewmen
  (A) cooperative
  (B) quiet
  (C) changeable
  (D) rebellious

166. the <u>placid</u> sea
  (A) deep
  (B) calm
  (C) stormy
  (D) large

167. the <u>replica</u> of the ship
  (A) copy
  (B) forgery
  (C) original
  (D) wreckage

168. two <u>conspicuous</u> characteristics
  (A) hidden
  (B) shady
  (C) noticeable
  (D) significant

169. an <u>abridged</u> story
  (A) lengthened
  (B) true
  (C) shortened
  (D) false

170. the <u>plausible</u> excuse
  (A) unbelievable
  (B) praiseworthy
  (C) believable
  (D) unforgivable

171. <u>thwart</u> an attack
  (A) strengthen
  (B) repel
  (C) accelerate
  (D) wage

172. a <u>discreet</u> remark
  (A) hurtful
  (B) careful
  (C) insensitive
  (D) polite

173. a <u>frugal</u> meal
  (A) wasteful
  (B) thrifty
  (C) abundant
  (D) leftover

174. <u>meager</u> accommodations
  (A) lavish
  (B) large
  (C) inadequate
  (D) healthy

STOP

Mathematics

Time: 45 Minutes
64 Questions

Concepts

DIRECTIONS: Select the best answer choice.

175. Round off 6.874 to the nearest hundredth.

(A) 6.87

(B) 6.88

(C) 687

(D) 68700

176. Add together: $5x - 3y + 12$ and $3y + 3x - 10$.

(A) $8x + 2$

(B) $8x - 2$

(C) $8x + 6y$

(D) $15x - 9y - 120$

177. Which of the points in the graph represents $(6, -3)$?

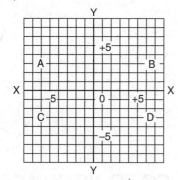

(A) A

(B) B

(C) C

(D) D

178. The sum of two consecutive even numbers is 74. What are the two numbers?

(A) 35, 39

(B) 36, 38

(C) 37, 37

(D) 34, 40

179. Simplify: $6\frac{2}{3} - 5\frac{1}{4}$.

(A) $\frac{5}{12}$

(B) $1\frac{5}{12}$

(C) $1\frac{11}{12}$

(D) $11\frac{11}{12}$

GO TO NEXT PAGE ➡

180. A perfect square number has 2 identical factors. Which of the following numbers is a perfect square?

(A) 12

(B) 14

(C) 16

(D) 18

181. In computing the area of a rectangle, Prince used the formula:

$$\text{Area} = \text{length} \times \text{width}.$$

After calculating the areas of four rectangles, including three squares, Prince misplaced his homework notebook from which he copied the measures of the sides of the rectangles. Which of the following numbers does <u>not</u> represent the area of the square? [Hint: Remember that the length and width of the square are equal.]

(A) 24

(B) 25

(C) 36

(D) 64

182. Simplify: $\frac{3}{5} \times \frac{5}{6} + 21$.

(A) $21\frac{1}{2}$

(B) $21\frac{8}{11}$

(C) $21\frac{5}{6}$

(D) $21\frac{18}{25}$

183. Simplify: $5\frac{1}{4} \div 2\frac{1}{3}$.

(A) $12\frac{1}{4}$

(B) $2\frac{1}{4}$

(C) $1\frac{1}{2}$

(D) $\frac{4}{9}$

184. What number subtracted from 14 leaves $\frac{1}{7}$ of 77?

(A) 3

(B) 7

(C) 11

(D) 14

185. What percent of 80 is 200?

(A) 25%

(B) 40%

(C) 120%

(D) 250%

186. Rewrite $2\frac{3}{5}$ as a percent.

(A) 260%

(B) 60%

(C) 26%

(D) 2.6%

187. $x(-y + z) =$

(A) $-xy - xz$

(B) $xy + z$

(C) $xz - xy$

(D) $x - y + z$

GO TO NEXT PAGE ➡

188. Albert worked for five days, earning $460. What was his average daily income?

(A) $92

(B) $94

(C) $120

(D) $125

189. A parallelogram has two pairs of equal sides. Which of the following sets of sticks can be arranged to form a parallelogram?

(A)
3
4
5
6

(B)
4
4
6
8

(C)
4
6
6
4

(D)
3
5
7
9

190. The sum of the measures of the four interior angles of a quadrilateral is always 360 degrees. Which of the following sets of numbers represents the measures of interior angles of a quadrilateral?

(A) 25, 30, 60, 65

(B) 80, 80, 90, 90

(C) 78, 85, 95, 102

(D) 75, 95, 95, 105

191. What number is 45% of 2,000?

(A) 1,955

(B) 1,945

(C) 1,100

(D) 900

The graph below shows the attendance in a middle-school class for one week. Use the information in the graph to answer question 192.

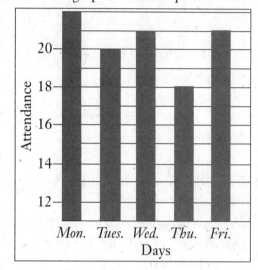

192. What was the average attendance from Wednesday to Friday?

(A) 18

(B) 19

(C) 20

(D) 22

GO TO NEXT PAGE ➡

The graph that follows is a record of the temperatures for each month of the year 1955 in Bluntsville, Kentucky. Use the information in this graph to answer questions 193–195.

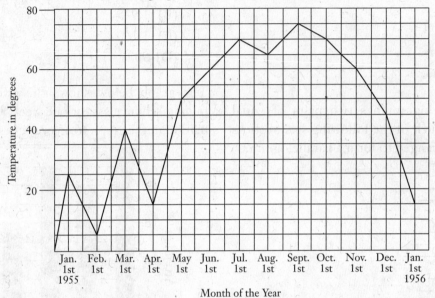

Month of the Year

193. In which two months did the temperature rise the most steeply?

(A) February to March and April to May

(B) March to April and August to September

(C) January to February and February to March

(D) October to November and November to December

194. In which single month did the temperature fall most sharply?

(A) February

(B) April

(C) August

(D) December

195. In which two months was the coldest temperature the same?

(A) February and April

(B) May and December

(C) June and November

(D) March and December

196. The "7" in 465.2671 is in the thousandths place. In what place is the "7" in 472.625?

(A) hundreds

(B) tens

(C) tenths

(D) hundredths

197. Which of the following is an obtuse triangle?

(A)

(B)

(C)

(D)

GO TO NEXT PAGE ➡

198. Find the value of x in the picture.

(A) 55°

(B) 125°

(C) 305°

(D) 360°

Problem-Solving

199. The simple interest, I, on d dollars for y years at the rate of r% per year is computed from the formula:

$$I = d \times y \times r.$$

Use this formula to compute the simple interest on $4,500 invested for 1 year at 6% per year.

(A) $27

(B) $270

(C) $2,700

(D) $27,000

200. A welder joins 12 pipes together to make a flag pole. If each pipe measures 8.5 ft, what is the length of the flag pole?

(A) 1,020 ft

(B) 205 ft

(C) 102 ft

(D) 1,120 ft

201. One rainy day attendance in a school dropped from 400 to 336. What was the percent decrease in attendance?

(A) 1.6%

(B) 1.9%

(C) 16%

(D) 19%

202. Sandra broke a rectangular bathroom mirror. The mirror costs $2.60 per square foot. If the mirror that Sandra broke measures 2.5 feet by 6.4 feet, how much will it cost to replace this mirror?

Hint: To find the area of a rectangle, you may use the formula:

Area = length × width.

(A) $6.50

(B) $16.64

(C) $23.14

(D) $41.60

203. An ice cream machine pumps out 9 pints of ice cream in 6 seconds. At this rate, how many pints of ice cream would this machine pump out in 3 minutes?

(A) 18 pts

(B) 27 pts

(C) 162 pts

(D) 270 pts

204. Michael, Jason, and Alan share a sum of money. Michael takes $\frac{2}{7}$ of the money, while Jason takes $\frac{2}{5}$ of it. What fraction of the money is left for Alan?

(A) $\frac{24}{35}$

(B) $\frac{11}{35}$

(C) $\frac{4}{11}$

(D) $\frac{7}{11}$

GO TO NEXT PAGE ➡

HSPT

205. The value of a computer decreases at the rate of 18% per year. If a new computer cost $1,500.00, what would be the value of this computer at the end of one year?

(A) $270

(B) $1,230

(C) $1,482

(D) $1,418

206. Damian won a television set in a raffle. But he decides to sell it for 22% less than its value of $375. How much does Damian sell the television set for?

(A) $457.50

(B) $353.00

(C) $292.50

(D) $82.50

207. To make a simple fence around her little rectangular flower garden, Jessica runs a rope around four pegs at the corners of the garden, as shown. What is the length of the rope?

(A) 14 ft

(B) 28 ft

(C) 24 ft

(D) 48 ft

208. The leatherback turtle is 8 feet long while the common mud turtle is 5 inches long. What fraction of the leatherback turtle's length is the common mud turtle's length?

(A) $\dfrac{96}{5}$

(B) $\dfrac{5}{96}$

(C) $\dfrac{8}{5}$

(D) $\dfrac{5}{8}$

209. If the Indian lizard is 10 ft long and the desertnight lizard is 5 in. long, what fraction of the Indian lizard's length is the desertnight lizard's length?

(A) $\dfrac{1}{2}$

(B) $\dfrac{1}{24}$

(C) $\dfrac{1}{4}$

(D) $\dfrac{5}{24}$

210. The anaconda may grow to 9 m long while an adult desert sidewinding viper measures only 25 cm. How many desert sidewinding vipers must be strung together, head to tail, to cover the length of one anaconda?

(A) 3.6

(B) 36

(C) 360

(D) 3,600

GO TO NEXT PAGE ➡

211. A few years ago Delaware had a population of 683,000 while Rhode Island had a population of 989,000. By how many people was the population of Rhode Island greater than that of Delaware?

(A) 36,000

(B) 206,000

(C) 306,000

(D) 316,000

212. There are 200 students in one small school. If 120 of these students are girls, what percent of them are boys?

(A) 80

(B) 70

(C) 60

(D) 40

213. Peter earned 84% by answering 63 questions correctly on a mathematics test. How many questions did he miss?

(A) 100

(B) 75

(C) 21

(D) 12

214. An ant can lift a weight up to 50 times its own body weight. If the weight-lifting power of a body builder is directly proportional to that of an ant, what weight should a man who weighs 175 lbs. be able to lift?

(A) 8,750 lb.

(B) 2,250 lb.

(C) 875 lb.

(D) 275 lb.

Use these diagrams to answer questions 215 and 216.

215. What fraction of this rectangle is shaded?

(A) $\dfrac{7}{15}$

(B) $\dfrac{8}{15}$

(C) $\dfrac{5}{9}$

(D) $\dfrac{4}{9}$

216. Approximately what percent of the rectangle is <u>not</u> shaded?

(A) 53%

(B) 15%

(C) 7%

(D) 17%

GO TO NEXT PAGE ➡

217. Observe that the attendance bar for Monday is "off the scale" (that is, the bar is too high to fit into the graph). If the average attendance for Monday and Tuesday was 23, what was the attendance on Monday?

(A) 30

(B) 26

(C) 23

(D) 20

218. Jeff's total score on 5 history tests was 395. When the teacher agreed to drop Jeff's lowest score, his total changed to 332. What was the test score that the teacher dropped?

(A) 63

(B) 79

(C) 82

(D) 85

219. The clear portions in this picture are half-circles. Find the area of the shaded region in the picture.

The area of a circle may be computed from the formula:

Area = $3.14 \times r^2$, where r = measure of radius of circle.

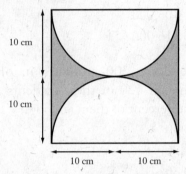

(A) 86 cm^2 (C) 157 cm^2

(B) 100 cm^2 (D) 243 cm^2

220. Mr. Stanley cuts off the top and bottom of a cylindrical milk can. Then he slices the can vertically into two halves. The picture below shows one of the two halves of the can. If the can is 10 cm high, find the area of the half shown below.

You may compute the circumference of a circle from the formula:

Circumference = $3.14 \times d$, where d = measure of diameter of circle.

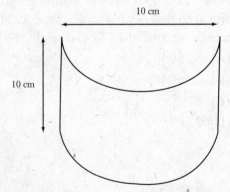

(A) 314 cm^2 (C) 31.4 cm^2

(B) 157 cm^2 (D) 15.7 cm^2

GO TO NEXT PAGE ➜

221. Find the area of the parallelogram below.
($a = b \times h$)

(A) 90 cm²

(B) 150 cm²

(C) 180 cm²

(D) 360 cm²

The circle graph shows how Simon spends the majority of his day, from 6:00 a.m. one morning to 6:00 a.m. the next morning. Use this information to answer questions 222 and 223 which follow.

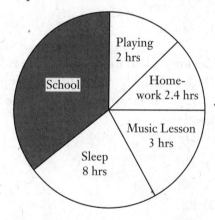

222. How much time does Simon spend at school?

(A) 15.4 hrs

(B) 4.6 hrs

(C) 8.6 hrs

(D) 6.8 hrs

223. What percent of Simon's time does he spend on his homework?

(A) 1%

(B) 10%

(C) 2.4%

(D) 24%

224. Mrs. Patterson's dinner pot consisted of 8 oz of black-eyed peas, $\frac{1}{2}$ lb of rice and 1 lb of red beans. What percent of the food in this pot is rice?

(A) 0.5%

(B) 18%

(C) 50%

(D) 25%

225. The ratio of midsized cars to big cars in a parking lot is 63 to 37. If there are spaces for 189 midsized cars in a parking lot, how many spaces are there for big cars?

(A) 100

(B) 37

(C) 111

(D) 126

226. Sharon bought a dress and a pair of shoes. The price of the dress was originally $60 but was being sold at a 20% discount. The pair of shoes originally cost $80 but was discounted 15%. What was her discount on the entire purchase? (approximately)

(A) 5%

(B) 17%

(C) 25%

(D) 32%

227. Ten apples and one orange cost $2.70, whereas ten oranges and one apple cost $3.24. What is the cost of one apple and one orange?

(A) .24

(B) .34

(C) .44

(D) .54

GO TO NEXT PAGE ➡

228. Amy, Brenda, and Carol go to a restaurant for lunch. They decide that Amy will pay $\frac{1}{3}$ of the food bill; Brenda will pay $\frac{1}{5}$ of the bill, and Carol will pay the remainder of the bill. If Amy ends up paying $10.70, how much does Carol pay?

(A) $19.26

(B) $17.12

(C) $14.98

(D) $12.84

229. A basketball team wins 70% of the first 30 games it plays. If the team wins only half of the remaining games, it will have won 62% of all its games. What is the total number of games the team will have played?

(A) 56

(B) 50

(C) 44

(D) 38

230. Brian rides his bike from home to school, a distance of 3 miles. If his speed is 10 miles per hour for the first 6 minutes, how fast should he go in order for his trip to take a total of 12 minutes?

(A) 20 mi/hr

(B) 16 mi/hr

(C) 12 mi/hr

(D) 10 mi/hr

231. The rate of vibration of a string varies inversely depending on its length. A string 40 inches long will vibrate 100 times per second. What is the length of a string which vibrates 250 times per second?

(A) 16

(B) 25

(C) 64

(D) 100

232. At a particular party of 60 people, every person is talking, dancing, or both; 35 people are talking. If 27 people are both talking and dancing, how many people are dancing?

(A) 25

(B) 33

(C) 44

(D) 52

233. A square has a side of 6 inches and a rectangle has a length of 18 inches. If the perimeter of the rectangle is two and one-half times the perimeter of the square, what is the width of the rectangle?

(A) 15 inches

(B) 12 inches

(C) 8 inches

(D) 5 inches

234. One angle of an isosceles triangle is known to be 80°. Which one of the following could not be the measure of another angle in this triangle?

(A) 10°

(B) 20°

(C) 50°

(D) 80°

235. In a family of three people, the mother weighs 45 pounds more than the child, and the father weighs 3 times as much as the child. If their total weight is 370 pounds, what is the difference in weight between the father and the mother?

(A) 120 pounds

(B) 110 pounds

(C) 85 pounds

(D) 65 pounds

GO TO NEXT PAGE ➡

236. Two trains leave a station at the same time, traveling in opposite directions. After 5 hours, they are 560 miles apart. If one train's rate is 6 miles per hour faster than that of the other train, how many miles will the faster train cover in 3 hours?

(A) 159

(B) 168

(C) 177

(D) 186

237. A quiz contains only five multiple-choice questions. The first three questions have 5 choices each, and the last two questions are true-false only. If a student randomly guesses on each question, what is his probability of getting all five questions right?

(A) $\dfrac{1}{30}$

(B) $\dfrac{1}{216}$

(C) $\dfrac{1}{500}$

(D) $\dfrac{1}{972}$

238. Nine people are in an elevator, four men and five women. The average weight of the women is 130 pounds. If the total weight of the people is 1,350 pounds, what is the average weight of the men?

(A) 140 pounds

(B) 162 pounds

(C) 170 pounds

(D) 175 pounds

HSPT

STOP

HSPT
SUBTEST 5

Language Skills

Time: 25 Minutes
60 Questions

Punctuation, Capitalization, and Usage

> **DIRECTIONS:** Look for errors of punctuation, capitalization, or usage in the following sentences. If there are no mistakes, mark "D."

239. **(A)** My older brother is on the football team
    (B) When it became warm, I opened the window.
    (C) I forgot where I left my hat.
    (D) No mistakes.

240. **(A)** His uncle took him to the ball game.
    (B) The baby gurgled.
    (C) The dog brought me his bone.
    (D) No mistakes.

241. **(A)** The window on the front door was broken.
    (B) We went behind the house for the barbecue.
    (C) The present a music box was wrapped in purple paper.
    (D) No mistakes.

242. **(A)** Could you turn off the radio?
    (B) Congratulations on such an excelent job.
    (C) We walked over to where he was standing.
    (D) No mistakes.

243. **(A)** My grandmother sent a letter to my brother and I.
    (B) A storm was predicted for Wednesday.
    (C) Josh did not like that lunch.
    (D) No mistakes.

244. **(A)** We plan to go ice skating in february.
    (B) The books were too heavy to bring home.
    (C) We had my favorite dessert.
    (D) No mistakes.

GO TO NEXT PAGE

245. (A) I tripped and hurt my knee.
    (B) He wandered in and said, "we wanted to do that."
    (C) Bowling can sometimes be fun.
    (D) No mistakes.

246. (A) We can't do that!
    (B) You doesn't have to help me.
    (C) Anne went home sick today.
    (D) No mistakes.

247. (A) Where did Marcia go?
    (B) My friends has a new baby sister.
    (C) Wait here for a minute.
    (D) No mistakes.

248. (A) I really can't help you.
    (B) I hope I have studied enough.
    (C) Isnt that your brother?
    (D) No mistakes.

249. (A) Mr Green wanted to hear me sing.
    (B) My neighbors started to laugh.
    (C) We walked in too soon.
    (D) No mistakes.

250. (A) We dove into the pool.
    (B) I hate shopping for new clothes.
    (C) We had a picnic outsides.
    (D) No mistakes.

251. (A) We carried the boxes out to the car.
    (B) Drawing are a fun course to take.
    (C) We met after school to discuss the election.
    (D) No mistakes.

252. (A) We ran, outside, quickly.
    (B) He doesn't understand the problem.
    (C) The car was unlocked, so we sat inside.
    (D) No mistakes.

253. (A) Could you please answer the telephone?
    (B) "Don't leave any lights on!" she said.
    (C) I waited for over an hour.
    (D) No mistakes.

254. (A) Are you sitting over there.
    (B) My favorite band is on the radio.
    (C) That is my favorite flavor.
    (D) No mistakes.

255. (A) That girl are making really funny faces.
    (B) "I'm going home now," she announced.
    (C) I have to help clean up.
    (D) No mistakes.

256. (A) We brought many cookie over to his house.
    (B) "You're standing on my foot!" I shrieked.
    (C) I had to start wearing glasses.
    (D) No mistakes.

257. (A) That book were very boring.
    (B) We were so tired that we slept until the afternoon.
    (C) I carried over the stereo, the books, and the chair.
    (D) No mistakes.

258. (A) I was looking for a large red car.
    (B) Patty is going to meet us later.
    (C) He had to mow the lawn before dinner.
    (D) No mistakes.

259. (A) We went swimming in the lake.
    (B) My friend moved to Arizona last year.
    (C) Scott hurt his head he went to the doctor.
    (D) No mistakes.

GO TO NEXT PAGE ➡

260. **(A)** The band sounded awful.
     (B) We almost danced until midnight.
     (C) I have to find a job.
     (D) No mistakes.

261. **(A)** We waited for the football game to begin.
     (B) John typed, read, and print out his report.
     (C) Pat wants to come over later.
     (D) No mistakes.

262. **(A)** Maxine is more better at math.
     (B) We are going to the Mexican restaurant later.
     (C) I fell asleep during the movie.
     (D) No mistakes.

263. **(A)** "What time is it?" she asked.
     (B) "Where are we going tonight" he wanted to know.
     (C) "Look at the old car!"
     (D) No mistakes.

264. **(A)** We see that television show last night.
     (B) Joy wants to do that tomorrow.
     (C) Our neighbor is building a pool in his backyard.
     (D) No mistakes.

265. **(A)** For days from now I will be on vacation.
     (B) He spent last year in England.
     (C) Joe wants to be a teacher.
     (D) No mistakes.

266. **(A)** "Jack went in that direction," she said.
     (B) The game starts after school.
     (C) We left at the begin of the match.
     (D) No mistakes.

267. **(A)** Ian asked us to visit him later.
     (B) She warned That isn't such a good idea.
     (C) My aunt cooks for us on the holidays.
     (D) No mistakes.

268. **(A)** There were too many bugs near our campground.
     (B) He is reading The Adventures of Huckleberry Finn.
     (C) We gave my grandmother a watch for her birthday.
     (D) No mistakes.

269. **(A)** We drove quickly over the bridge.
     (B) The cat ate the fish.
     (C) I can't find my wallet
     (D) No mistakes.

270. **(A)** My birthday was last month.
     (B) We had hot dogs, hamburgers, and corn at the barbecue.
     (C) Henry was late for the meeting.
     (D) No mistakes.

271. **(A)** Its time to go home now.
     (B) Laura is not feeling well this evening.
     (C) We waited for over an hour.
     (D) No mistakes.

272. **(A)** Martin is washing the dishes.
     (B) He was so tired that he fell asleep in the car.
     (C) The mysterious dark car.
     (D) No mistakes.

273. **(A)** I used to sell cookies when I was younger.
     (B) we brought cupcakes, plates, and napkins over to her house.
     (C) The balloons were rising in the air.
     (D) No mistakes.

GO TO NEXT PAGE

274. **(A)** My older brother carried the boxes out.
  (B) We walked quickly we thought someone was there.
  (C) Mike plays piano, guitar, and trumpet.
  (D) No mistakes.

275. **(A)** I don't think that I want to go.
  (B) What time does it start?
  (C) I through the ball at my sister.
  (D) No mistakes.

276. **(A)** Luke is afraid of planes.
  (B) I brought my lunch today.
  (C) My mom and dad likes to eat at restaurants.
  (D) No mistakes.

277. **(A)** The dogs jumped all over the couch.
  (B) I go to the store yesterday.
  (C) My cousin spends a lot of time using her computer.
  (D) No mistakes.

278. **(A)** I could not fall asleep last night.
  (B) Talking during the movie.
  (C) Sal has a lot of books to carry.
  (D) No mistakes.

Spelling

DIRECTIONS: Choose the sentence that contains a spelling error. If there are no errors, choose "D."

279. **(A)** The benefits outweigh the risks in his new business venture.
  (B) The speaker asked the group to complete a questionnaire.
  (C) Mrs. Blake's kindergarten class wore their Halloween costumes to school.
  (D) No mistakes.

280. **(A)** Boston is the capital of Massachusetts.
  (B) The newly married couple met with a financial advisor.
  (C) The atheletes are traveling to a basketball tournament.
  (D) No mistakes.

281. **(A)** The gardener was embarassed when he tripped over a hose.
  (B) The audience was fascinated when the tiger disappeared.
  (C) Nearly all of their possessions were destroyed in the hurricane.
  (D) No mistakes.

282. **(A)** Sharon's infection required immediate medical attention.
  (B) The desparate criminal hid in an abandoned factory.
  (C) The amateur photographer won first prize in the beach scene contest.
  (D) No mistakes.

GO TO NEXT PAGE ➡

283. **(A)** His physician urged him to eliminate sugar from his diet.

(B) First impressions are not always accurate or lasting.

(C) The child's frequent absenses are hindering her progress.

(D) No mistakes.

284. **(A)** They planned an expedition to the ancient ruins of Mexico.

(B) The maintainance crew was exhausted after the carnival.

(C) The mayor's commitment to help immigrants is evident.

(D) No mistakes.

285. **(A)** The scientist itemized the cost of new equipment for the laboratory.

(B) Congradulations on your successful completion of the program.

(C) I met my sisters-in-law in the theater lobby at intermission.

(D) No mistakes.

286. **(A)** Jim received many complements for his chocolate layer cake.

(B) The adolescent failed to consider the consequences of his actions.

(C) Katrina's interpersonal skills are a valuable asset on the job.

(D) No mistakes.

287. **(A)** Prioritizing tasks increases efficiency in the workplace.

(B) The yacht swerved off course in the turbulent waters.

(C) Studying a foreign language disciplines the mind.

(D) No mistakes.

288. **(A)** Whether to turn right or left at the intersection was a dilemma.

(B) Nearly all of their possessions were destroyed in the hurricane.

(C) The seniors were anxious to see their graduation date on the new school calender.

(D) No mistakes.

Composition

DIRECTIONS: Select the best answer choice.

289. Which of these best fits under the topic "Using Herbs to Season Food"?

(A) The flavor of herbs is most intense when they are fresh.

(B) Many kinds of herbs can grow easily from seed.

(C) Herbs should be protected from frost.

(D) None of these.

290. Which of these best fits under the topic "The Benefits of Vitamin C"?

(A) Vitamin C stays in the body for a short time and must be taken regularly.

(B) Strawberries and oranges are good sources of Vitamin C.

(C) Vitamin C helps the body resist infections.

(D) None of these.

GO TO NEXT PAGE ➡

291. Which of these best fits under the topic "Inventions of the 19th Century"?
    (A) Thomas Edison invented the phonograph in 1877.
    (B) In 1609, Galileo made a telescope and was the first to study the stars and planets.
    (C) Penicillin, the first antibiotic, was discovered by Alexander Fleming in 1928.
    (D) None of these.

292. Which of these best fits under the topic "Why Dinosaurs Became Extinct"?
    (A) The dodo and the mastodon are extinct.
    (B) Scientists learn about dinosaurs by studying fossils.
    (C) The Tyrannosaurus was a carnivore.
    (D) None of these.

293. Which topic is best for a one-paragraph theme?
    (A) Our Solar System
    (B) U. S. Presidents
    (C) Travel Safety Tips
    (D) None of these.

294. Which topic is best for a one-paragraph theme?
    (A) Telephone Etiquette
    (B) Trees of North America
    (C) Egyptian Art
    (D) None of these.

295. Where should the sentence "**To protect itself, the oyster encloses the irritant in a sac,**" be placed in the selection below?
    (1) A pearl forms in an oyster when a grain of sand, or another foreign substance, gets inside the oyster's shell. (2) The foreign substance irritates the oyster. (3) The oyster then secretes layers of mother-of-pearl, or nacre, around the sac to form a pearl.
    (A) The sentence does not fit in this paragraph.
    (B) after sentence 3
    (C) between sentences 1 and 2
    (D) between sentences 2 and 3

296. Where should the sentence "**For example, when you press the letter 'M' on the keyboard, the letter 'M' appears on the monitor screen,**" be placed in the selection below?
    (1) The step-by-step process of operating a computer is a series of causes and effects. (2) When a computer is turned on, electricity surges through its internal parts. (3) This begins a chain reaction of causes and effects.
    (A) The sentence does not fit in this paragraph.
    (B) After sentence 3
    (C) Between sentences 1 and 2
    (D) Between sentences 2 and 3

GO TO NEXT PAGE ➡

297. Which sentence does <u>not</u> belong in this paragraph?

(1) A computer system is made up of both hardware and software. (2) Hardware is the name for the parts of the system that you can see and touch. (3) Many students find the smaller laptop computers very convenient. (4) Software is the name for the instructions, or programs, that tell the hardware what to do.

(A) Sentence 1

(B) Sentence 2

(C) Sentence 3

(D) Sentence 4

298. Which sentence does <u>not</u> belong in this paragraph?

(1) Monticello was the home of Thomas Jefferson, the third president of the United States. (2) Jefferson designed the home himself and lived there until his death in 1826. (3) Many tourists visit Monticello, which is located in Charlottesville, Virginia. (4) Jefferson was the governor of Virginia from 1779 to 1781.

(A) Sentence 1

(B) Sentence 2

(C) Sentence 3

(D) Sentence 4

STOP

HSPT

Practice Test 2—Answer Key

Question Number	Correct Answer	If You Answered this Question Incorrectly, Refer to . . .
SUBTEST 1: VERBAL SKILLS		
1.	(C)	P. 231
2.	(B)	P. 231
3.	(C)	P. 231
4.	(B)	P. 231
5.	(C)	P. 231
6.	(B)	P. 231
7.	(D)	P. 227
8.	(A)	P. 231
9.	(A)	P. 227
10.	(B)	P. 227
11.	(D)	P. 233
12.	(D)	P. 233
13.	(A)	P. 233
14.	(D)	P. 233
15.	(B)	P. 233
16.	(C)	P. 233
17.	(C)	P. 233
18.	(C)	P. 233
19.	(A)	P. 233
20.	(B)	P. 233
21.	(D)	P. 233
22.	(B)	P. 233
23.	(A)	P. 233

Question Number	Correct Answer	If You Answered this Question Incorrectly, Refer to . . .
24.	(A)	P. 233
25.	(D)	P. 233
26.	(B)	P. 233
27.	(A)	P. 233
28.	(A)	P. 224
29.	(A)	P. 224
30.	(C)	P. 224
31.	(C)	P. 224
32.	(B)	P. 224
33.	(B)	P. 224
34.	(A)	P. 224
35.	(A)	P. 224
36.	(C)	P. 224
37.	(C)	P. 224
38.	(B)	P. 231
39.	(C)	P. 231
40.	(B)	P. 231
41.	(D)	P. 231
42.	(A)	P. 231
43.	(A)	P. 231
44.	(B)	P. 231
45.	(D)	P. 231
46.	(A)	P. 231
47.	(D)	P. 231
48.	(B)	P. 231
49.	(C)	P. 231
50.	(B)	P. 231
51.	(A)	P. 231
52.	(C)	P. 231
53.	(B)	P. 231
54.	(D)	P. 231
55.	(C)	P. 231
56.	(B)	P. 232
57.	(D)	P. 232

58.	(C)	P. 232
59.	(C)	P. 232
60.	(C)	P. 232

SUBTEST 2: QUANTITATIVE SKILLS

61.	(D)	P. 428
62.	(A)	P. 422
63.	(B)	P. 422
64.	(A)	P. 424
65.	(C)	P. 427
66.	(C)	P. 428
67.	(D)	P. 428
68.	(A)	P. 422
69.	(A)	P. 424
70.	(D)	P. 428
71.	(C)	P. 422
72.	(A)	P. 422
73.	(D)	P. 428
74.	(A)	P. 428
75.	(B)	P. 427
76.	(A)	P. 424
77.	(D)	P. 422
78.	(C)	P. 422
79.	(D)	P. 428
80.	(A)	P. 427
81.	(D)	P. 428
82.	(C)	P. 424
83.	(B)	P. 422
84.	(B)	P. 422
85.	(D)	P. 428
86.	(D)	P. 427
87.	(C)	P. 422
88.	(A)	P. 422
89.	(D)	P. 428
90.	(C)	P. 424
91.	(D)	P. 422
92.	(A)	P. 422
93.	(C)	P. 428

Question Number	Correct Answer	If You Answered this Question Incorrectly, Refer to . . .
94.	(D)	P. 427
95.	(D)	P. 428
96.	(C)	P. 422
97.	(D)	P. 424
98.	(B)	P. 428
99.	(A)	P. 427
100.	(D)	P. 428
101.	(C)	P. 424
102.	(C)	P. 427
103.	(D)	P. 428
104.	(B)	P. 424
105.	(A)	P. 422
106.	(B)	P. 427
107.	(B)	P. 424
108.	(C)	P. 422
109.	(C)	P. 422
110.	(A)	P. 428
111.	(B)	P. 428
112.	(B)	P. 422
SUBTEST 3: READING COMPREHENSION		
113.	(B)	P. 302
114.	(D)	P. 310
115.	(C)	P. 302
116.	(D)	P. 302
117.	(D)	P. 302
118.	(C)	P. 300
119.	(C)	P. 310
120.	(B)	P. 302
121.	(D)	P. 308
122.	(B)	P. 303
123.	(A)	P. 300
124.	(D)	P. 303
125.	(C)	P. 309
126.	(D)	P. 310
127.	(A)	P. 308

128.	(A)	P. 300
129.	(C)	P. 302
130.	(D)	P. 308
131.	(A)	P. 303
132.	(B)	P. 310
133.	(B)	P. 304
134.	(C)	P. 302
135.	(C)	P. 302
136.	(C)	P. 302
137.	(A)	P. 300
138.	(D)	P. 300
139.	(C)	P. 304
140.	(D)	P. 308
141.	(A)	P. 303
142.	(B)	P. 304
143.	(C)	P. 300
144.	(D)	P. 302
145.	(D)	P. 302
146.	(B)	P. 303
147.	(A)	P. 310
148.	(B)	P. 304
149.	(A)	P. 308
150.	(D)	P. 302
151.	(C)	P. 308
152.	(B)	P. 304

VOCABULARY

153.	(D)	P. 315
154.	(A)	P. 315
155.	(C)	P. 315
156.	(B)	P. 315
157.	(A)	P. 315
158.	(D)	P. 315
159.	(B)	P. 315
160.	(C)	P. 315
161.	(C)	P. 315
162.	(D)	P. 315
163.	(B)	P. 315

Question Number	Correct Answer	If You Answered this Question Incorrectly, Refer to . . .
164.	(C)	P. 315
165.	(D)	P. 315
166.	(B)	P. 315
167.	(A)	P. 315
168.	(C)	P. 315
169.	(C)	P. 315
170.	(C)	P. 315
171.	(B)	P. 315
172.	(B)	P. 315
173.	(B)	P. 315
174.	(C)	P. 315
SUBTEST 4: MATHEMATICS CONCEPTS		
175.	(A)	P. 373
176.	(A)	P. 427
177.	(D)	P. 424
178.	(B)	P. 337, 345
179.	(B)	P. 363
180.	(C)	P. 356
181.	(A)	P. 395
182.	(A)	P. 355, 365
183.	(B)	P. 352, 365, 370
184.	(A)	P. 362, 365
185.	(D)	P. 400
186.	(A)	P. 352, 399
187.	(C)	P. 427
188.	(A)	P. 390
189.	(C)	P. 395
190.	(C)	P. 337
191.	(D)	P. 401
192.	(C)	P. 390
193.	(A)	P. 424
194.	(D)	P. 424
195.	(D)	P. 424
196.	(B)	P. 373

197.	(A)	P. 408
198.	(C)	P. 408
PROBLEM-SOLVING		
199.	(B)	P. 402
200.	(C)	P. 395
201.	(C)	P. 410
202.	(D)	P. 395
203.	(D)	P. 341, 350
204.	(B)	P. 350
205.	(B)	P. 410
206.	(C)	P. 410
207.	(B)	P. 395
208.	(B)	P. 370
209.	(B)	P. 370
210.	(B)	P. 341, 345
211.	(C)	P. 339
212.	(D)	P. 399
213.	(D)	P. 410
214.	(A)	P. 341
215.	(A)	P. 350
216.	(A)	P. 350, 402
217.	(B)	P. 390
218.	(A)	P. 390
219.	(A)	P. 395, 407
220.	(B)	P. 407
221.	(C)	P. 395
222.	(C)	P. 350
223.	(B)	P. 350, 399
224.	(D)	P. 350, 399
225.	(C)	P. 365, 370
226.	(B)	P. 350, 399, 410
227.	(D)	P. 350, 373
228.	(C)	P. 362, 410
229.	(B)	P. 402, 410
230.	(A)	P. 341, 345
231.	(A)	P. 341, 345
232.	(D)	P. 337, 339

Question Number	Correct Answer	If You Answered this Question Incorrectly, Refer to . . .
233.	(B)	P. 395
234.	(A)	P. 407
235.	(C)	P. 337, 339, 341
236.	(C)	P. 337, 341
237.	(C)	P. 405
238.	(D)	P. 390
SUBTEST 5: LANGUAGE SKILLS PUNCTUATION, CAPITALIZATION, AND USAGE		
239.	(A)	P. 261
240.	(D)	P. 251
241.	(C)	P. 264
242.	(B)	P. 281
243.	(A)	P. 251
244.	(A)	P. 275
245.	(B)	P. 276
246.	(B)	P. 247
247.	(B)	P. 247
248.	(C)	P. 269
249.	(A)	P. 261
250.	(C)	P. 282
251.	(B)	P. 247
252.	(A)	P. 261
253.	(D)	P. 270
254.	(A)	P. 261
255.	(A)	P. 247
256.	(A)	P. 257
257.	(A)	P. 247
258.	(D)	P. 245, 251
259.	(C)	P. 242
260.	(B)	P. 240
261.	(B)	P. 246
262.	(A)	P. 258
263.	(B)	P. 261
264.	(A)	P. 246

HSPT

265.	(A)	P. 281
266.	(C)	P. 280
267.	(B)	P. 270
268.	(B)	P. 271, 276
269.	(C)	P. 261
270.	(D)	P. 246
271.	(A)	P. 269
272.	(C)	P. 241
273.	(B)	P. 275
274.	(B)	P. 242
275.	(C)	P. 246
276.	(C)	P. 247
277.	(B)	P. 246
278.	(B)	P. 241

SPELLING

279.	(D)	P. 279
280.	(C)	P. 280
281.	(A)	P. 281
282.	(B)	P. 281
283.	(C)	P. 279
284.	(B)	P. 282
285.	(B)	P. 280
286.	(A)	P. 280
287.	(D)	P. 279
288.	(C)	P. 280

COMPOSITION

289.	(A)	P. 300
290.	(C)	P. 300
291.	(A)	P. 300
292.	(D)	P. 300
293.	(C)	P. 300
294.	(A)	P. 300
295.	(D)	P. 300
296.	(B)	P. 300
297.	(C)	P. 303
298.	(D)	P. 303

Verbal Skills—Detailed Explanations of Answers

1. **(C)** A *telescope* is an instrument used to see things that are far away like *stars*; a *microscope* is an instrument used to make small things like *cells* appear larger. Both *telescope* and *microscope* are derived from the Greek root *scop*, which means *to look at*. The prefix *micro-* means *small*, while the prefix *tele-* means *far*.

2. **(B)** A *combination* unlocks a *safe* as a *key* unlocks a *door*.

3. **(C)** *Worst* is the superlative form of the adjective *bad* as *best* is the superlative form of the adjective *good*.

4. **(B)** An *actor* performs on a *stage* as an *usher* works in the *aisles* seating people.

5. **(C)** An *orator* can be described as *eloquent* as a *gymnast* can be described as *flexible*.

6. **(B)** *Inception* and *beginning* are synonyms, as are *incite* and *provoke*.

7. **(D)** *Ecstatic* means extremely *happy* as *exhausted* means extremely *tired*.

8. **(A)** A *sofa* is a seat for more than one person inside a house in a room such as a *living room*; a *bench* is a seat for more than one person in a *park*.

9. **(A)** *Reveal* and *conceal* are antonyms as are *expand* and *contract*.

10. **(B)** *Exploit* and *protect* are antonyms as are *impartial* and *prejudiced*.

11. **(D)** To *loiter* is to *pause, tarry, wait,* or *stay*. *Linger* **(D)** is the term which is closest to *loiter* in meaning. To *litter* **(A)** is to *scatter, strew,* or *disarrange*. Despite the similarity in spelling, the two words are not similar in meaning. Choice **(A)** is not appropriate. *Relapse* **(B)** means *deteriorate, regress,* or *decline*. The meaning of *relapse* is not related to the meaning of *loiter*. To *hasten* **(C)** is the opposite of to *loiter*; **(C)** is not the correct answer.

12. **(D)** *Inflammable* means *burnable, incendiary, combustible,* or *flammable* **(D)**. The best choice of a synonym is *flammable* **(D)**. The word *inflammation* **(A)** is similar in shape to *inflammable*, but it is not similar in meaning. An antonym of *inflammable* is *noncombustible* **(B)**; the directions do not indicate that the test-taker is to select an antonym. *Similar* **(C)** means

like, the same. These words are not synonymous with *inflammable*. The test-taker should choose **(D)**.

13. **(A)** To *vindicate* is to *acquit, absolve,* or *clear* **(A)**. The antonym of *vindicate* is *convict* **(B)** or *condemn*. The test-taker, however, is not to choose an antonym. To *pose* **(C)** is to *assert, state,* or *profess*. Neither choice **(B)** nor **(C)** is the synonym for *vindicate* that the test-taker should select. Choice **(D)**, or *blame*, is the opposite of *vindicate*.

14. **(D)** A *premonition* is a *forewarning* **(D)**. It is not a *promotion* **(A)**, or an *advancement*; neither is a *premonition* a *luxury* **(B)**, a *comfort*, or a *frill*. A *premonition* may come in the form of a *dream* **(C)**, but a *dream* is not synonymous with a *premonition*.

15. **(B)** *Soothe* means to *console* or to *comfort* **(B)**. *Soothe* is not synonymous with *warn* **(A)** or *blacken* **(C)**. *Warn* means to *advise* and *blacken* means to *darken*. The answer choice *strengthen* **(D)** is close to the meaning of *soothe* as in a kind of *encouragement*, but *comfort* **(B)** is the overall best answer.

16. **(C)** *Fervent* describes something of great *emotion* or *passion*; its best synonym would be the choice *enthusiastic* **(C)**. Choices *hesitant* **(A)** and *cool* **(B)** are antonyms for this word. The answer choice *warm* **(D)** does not reflect the same degree of emotion that is displayed in *enthusiastic* **(C)**.

17. **(C)** The word *crucial* means *of supreme importance*, and its best synonym would be the answer choice *fundamental* **(C)** which means *central* or *key*. The answer choice *technical* **(A)** means *pertaining to a process*; *experimental* **(B)** refers to something being *tried* or *tested*. Answer choice *advanced* **(D)** means *improved* or *promoted*. Therefore, *fundamental* **(C)** is the best answer.

18. **(C)** The word *reprimand* means to *scold* or *find fault with*. Its best synonym is *correct* **(C)** which means to *make right*. *Praise* **(A)** is the opposite of *reprimand*; it means to *speak highly of*. *Return* **(B)** means to *give back*, and *threaten* **(D)** means to *warn of danger or harm*. Therefore, the best answer choice is *correct* **(C)**.

19. **(A)** *Chastity* is *purity* **(A)**, *virtue*, or *honor*. *Correction* **(B)** is not the same as *chastity*. *Religious* **(C)** means *devout, pious,* and *holy*. *Religious* is not the best synonym for *chastity*. *Familiarity* **(D)**, or *informality*, is not synonymous with *chastity*. Choices **(B)**, **(C)**, and **(D)** are not appropriate choices. Choice **(A)** is the best answer.

20. **(B)** The synonym for the word *disrespectful*, which means *having no appreciation*, is *rude* **(B)**, which means *without manners or courtesy*. *Careless* **(A)** means *without thought or attention*. *Valuable* **(C)** means *having high worth or expensive qualities*. *Safe* **(D)** means *secure and without danger*. The best answer for a synonym for *disrespectful* is *rude* **(B)**.

21. **(D)** *Contempt* is *scorn* **(D)** or *disdain*. *Temptation* **(A)** means *inducement, enticement,* and *lure*; it does not relate to or serve as a synonym for the word *contempt*. *Fear* **(B)**, *horror*, and *dismay* are not words with meanings similar to *contempt*. *Commend* **(C)** is to *laud, compliment,* or *applaud*; it is not a synonym for *contempt*.

22. **(B)** *Agile* most nearly means *limber* **(B)**, *nimble*, or *spry*. *Agile* does not mean *wool* **(A)**. The test-taker who selects the word *wool* may have the word confused with *argyle*. *Unpredictable* **(C)**

means *random, irregular,* or *unexpected*; choice **(C)** is not related to *agile. Difficult* **(D)** is not synonymous with *agile*. It is readily apparent that **(A)**, **(C)**, and **(D)** are not appropriate synonyms for *agile*.

23. **(A)** *Redeem* means to *recover* **(A)**, to *reclaim*, and to *restore. Redeem* is not a synonym for *locate* **(B)**. *Locate* **(B)** means *find, search out,* or *discover*. There is no relationship between *redeem* and *destroy* **(C)**, which means *demolish* or *obliterate*. Choice **(D)**, *research*, means to *investigate* or *to study*. Choices **(B)**, **(C)**, and **(D)** are not the best choices for synonyms of *redeem*.

24. **(A)** To *pulverize* is to *grind* **(A)** or to *crush*. To *attempt* **(B)** is to *try*, to *strive*, or to *venture*; this verb is not a synonym for *pulverize*. To *pervert* **(C)** is to *corrupt, entice*, or *allure*; it is not a synonym for *pulverize*. To *preserve* **(D)** or to *save* has the same beginning sound as *pulverize*, but it does not have the same meaning as *pulverize*. Choice **(A)** is the best word to select as a synonym.

25. **(D)** To *presume* is to *assume*. The word *assume* **(D)** is the best synonym for *presume*. To *swindle* **(A)** means to *cheat* or to *take advantage of someone*. Choice **(A)** is not the best synonym for *presume*. To *predict* **(B)** is to *guess* or to *foresee*. Choice **(B)** is not an appropriate synonym. To *prosper* **(C)** is to *do well*, to *make advances*, or to *make gains*. Choice **(C)** is not the best term for a synonym of *presume*.

26. **(B)** To *prevaricate* means most nearly to *lie* **(B)**. Choice **(B)** is an acceptable substitute for *prevaricate*. Although it is sometimes *dangerous, unwise*, or *unsafe* to lie, to *endanger* **(A)**— to *put in danger*—is not the best choice as a synonym for *prevaricate*. To *threaten* **(C)** is to *torment* or to *scare*. To *prevent* **(D)** is to *impede*. This word (*prevent*) is not a synonym for *prevaricate*. It should be evident to the test-taker that **(B)** is the best answer.

27. **(A)** *Postmortem* means *after death* **(A)**. The prefix *post-* means *after*. The root word *mortem* refers to *death*. A *postmortem* is an autopsy performed after death. A *celebration* **(B)** is a gala or a joyful occasion. *Celebration* **(B)** is not a synonym for *postmortem*; choice **(B)** is therefore not an acceptable answer to this question. A *stockade* **(C)** is a *prison*; choice **(C)** is not an acceptable answer. *Position* **(D)** does not mean the same as *postmortem* since it refers to a place.

28. **(A)** **True** is correct. If Patty is five years older than Stephanie, and Stephanie is two years older than Kerri, then Kerri is 5 + 2 = 7 years younger than Patty.

29. **(A)** **True** is correct. If Sue is two inches taller than Lynn, and Lynn is three inches taller than Kate, then Kate is 2 + 3 = 5 inches shorter than Sue.

30. **(C)** **Uncertain** is correct. If Jarret earned more money than his brothers, Matthew and Brian, then we know for sure that Matthew made less money than Jarret, but we don't know if Matthew made more or less money than Brian.

31. **(C)** **Uncertain** is correct. If Phyllis read more books than any of her friends, and Betty and Lorraine are her friends, then we know for sure that Betty read fewer books than Phyllis, but we don't know if Betty read fewer or more books than Lorraine.

32. **(B)** **False** is correct. If the first two statements are true, then the opposite of the third statement is true: Main Street is *wider* than Willow Road.

33. (B) **False** is correct. If the first two statements are true, then the opposite of the third statement is true: Nicole types *faster* than Nancy.

34. (A) **True** is correct. Because there are seven days in a week, if Maryann takes ballet lessons five days a week, and Jennifer takes lessons three days a week, then they must take lessons on at least one of the same days. ($5 + 3 = 8 - 7 = 1$)

35. (A) **True** is correct. Because there are seven days in a week, if Joe plays basketball six days a week, and Tony plays basketball four days a week, then they must play basketball on at least three of the same days. ($6 + 4 = 10 - 7 = 3$)

36. (C) **Uncertain** is correct. We know that broccoli costs more than carrots and that onions cost less than broccoli and lettuce. However, the truth of the third statement is uncertain because we don't know the cost of carrots in relation to the cost of lettuce.

37. (C) **Uncertain** is correct. We know that grapes cost more than plums and that peaches cost less than plums and nectarines. However, the truth of the third statement is uncertain because we don't know the cost of plums in relation to the cost of nectarines.

38. (B) *Irritate*, *harass*, and *pester* have nearly the same meaning, while *appease* has the opposite meaning.

39. (C) *Vacant*, *empty*, and *unoccupied* have nearly the same meaning: *containing nothing*. Although *spacious* means a lot of space, the space is not necessarily empty.

40. (B) *Placid*, *calm*, and *peaceful* have nearly the same meaning, while *chaotic* has the opposite meaning.

41. (D) *Arteries*, *capillaries*, and *veins* are parts of the *circulatory* system.

42. (A) *Ad*, *exam*, and *memo* are "clipped words," words that have been shortened by common usage, while *hobo* is not. (*Ad: advertisement*; *exam: examination*; *memo: memorandum*)

43. (A) *Annual*, *perennial*, and *temporal* pertain to time; *fiscal* pertains to finances.

44. (B) *Hinder*, *retard*, and *impede* have nearly the same meaning, while *aid* has the opposite meaning.

45. (D) *Cheerful*, *optimistic*, and *hopeful* have nearly the same meaning, while *desperate* has the opposite meaning.

46. (A) *Relapse*, *regress*, and *backslide* have nearly the same meaning, while *recover* has the opposite meaning.

47. (D) *Gloomy*, *dismal*, and *dreary* have nearly the same meaning, while *bright* has the opposite meaning.

48. (B) A *defendant*, a *bailiff*, and a *plaintiff* are people in a courtroom, while *interrogate* is an action.

49. (C) A *period*, a *question mark*, and an *exclamation point* are end marks of punctuation; that is, they are used at the end of a sentence. A *comma* is not.

50. **(B)** *Precise, exact,* and *accurate* have nearly the same meaning, while *approximate* has a different meaning: *almost exact.*

51. **(A)** *Complex, intricate,* and *complicated* have nearly the same meaning, while *simple* has the opposite meaning.

52. **(C)** *Diverse, heterogeneous,* and *varied* have nearly the same meaning, while *uniform* has the opposite meaning.

53. **(B)** *Nonfiction* is a kind of prose, while a *dictionary,* a *thesaurus,* and an *encyclopedia* are reference books.

54. **(D)** Unlike *portfolio, itinerary, route,* and *destination* are words that relate primarily to travel.

55. **(C)** *Excrete, discharge,* and *expel* have nearly the same meaning, while *disburse* has a different meaning: *to pay out.*

56. **(B)** *Presume* means *believe* **(A)**, *assume,* or *suppose* **(C)**. *Presume* can also mean to *conclude* **(D)**. It does not mean *disprove* **(B)** or *refute.* The opposite of *presume* is **(B)**.

57. **(D)** *Disdainful* means *arrogant* **(A)**, *aloof* **(C)**, or *overconfident.* It can also mean *proud* **(B)** or *vain.* It does not mean *humble* **(D)**, *modest, meek,* or *lowly.* The opposite or the antonym of *disdainful* is *humble* **(D)**.

58. **(C)** *Infamous* means *notorious* **(A)**, *wicked* **(B)**, or *dishonorable* **(D)**. *Infamous* does not mean *great, distinguished,* or *prominent* **(C)**. The antonym of *infamous* is **(C)**.

59. **(C)** *Perpetual* means *eternal* **(B)** or *enduring* **(D)**. It also means *constant* **(A)** and *permanent.* *Perpetual* does not mean *fleeting* or *momentary* **(C)**. Therefore, *momentary* **(C)** is the best choice for an antonym of *perpetual.*

60. **(C)** *Imminent* means *close* **(D)** or *impending* **(B)**; it can mean *proximate* **(A)** or *soon.* It does not mean that which has already occurred or that which is *past* **(C)**. Because the antonym is the answer needed, *past* **(C)** is the best choice as an antonym of *imminent.*

Quantitative Skills—Detailed Explanations of Answers

For each problem, the answer will be given first. Then we will name the type of question—Series, Comparison, or Pre-algebra.

For Series questions, we will show the pattern on the list of numbers, state the rule, and get the answer.

For Comparison questions, we will give the quantities associated with (a), (b), and (c) or the picture, and, if necessary, explain how to get them. The correct choice of (A), (B), (C), or (D) will then be obvious.

For Pre-algebra questions, we will use the word method to arrive at the correct answer. Remember: you may want to use trial-and-error for some or all of the Pre-algebra questions.

61. (D) 8. Pre-algebra. $\frac{1}{3}$ of $60 = \frac{1}{3} \times 60 = 20$; 12 less than $20 = 20 - 12 = 8$.

62. (A) 1. Series.

$$
\begin{array}{ccccccccc}
& -8 & & -8 & & -8 & & -8 = \underline{1} \\
\diagup & \diagdown \diagup & \diagdown \diagup & \diagdown \diagup \\
33 & & 25 & & 17 & & 9
\end{array}
$$

Rule: Subtract 8. $9 - 8 = 1$.

63. (B) 36. Series.

$$
\begin{array}{ccccccccccc}
& -16 & & -7 & & -16 & & -7 & & 16 = \underline{36} \\
\diagup & \diagdown \diagup & \diagdown \diagup & \diagdown \diagup & \diagdown \diagup \\
98 & & 82 & & 75 & & 59 & & 52
\end{array}
$$

Rule: Subtract 16; subtract 7. $52 - 16 = 36$.

64. (A) (a) is equal to (b) which is equal to (c). Comparison. (a) = 12, (b) = 12, and (c) = 12. Count the circles.

65. (C) (b) is greater than (a) and is greater than (c). Comparison. (a) = 6 + 2 = 8, (b) = 3 × 6 = 18, and (c) = 12 + 1 = 13. Do parentheses first.

66. (C) 17. Pre-algebra. $\frac{3}{4}$ of 20 = $\frac{3}{4}$ × 20 = 15; 2 more than 15 = 15 + 2 = 17.

67. (D) 7. Pre-algebra. $\frac{1}{2}$ of 32 = $\frac{1}{2}$ × 32 = 16; 9 less than 16 = 16 − 9 = 7.

68. (A) 75. Series.

$$
\begin{array}{ccccccccccc}
& +3 & & +5 & & +4 & & +6 & & +5 = \underline{75} \\
\diagup & \diagdown & \diagup & \diagdown & \diagup & \diagdown & \diagup & \diagdown & \diagup \\
52 & & 55 & & 60 & & 64 & & 70
\end{array}
$$

Rule: Add each time. The amount added goes up by 2, then down by 1. 70 + 5 = 75.

69. (A) (a) is equal to (b) which is equal to (c). Comparison. The shaded portion of each square represents $\frac{1}{4}$ of the whole square. So (a), (b), and (c) are all equal.

70. (D) 15. Pre-algebra. $\frac{5}{6}$ of 24 = $\frac{5}{6}$ × 24 = 20. The number added to 5 to give 20 is 20 − 5, or 15.

71. (C) 84. Series.

$$
\begin{array}{ccccccccccc}
& -4 & & -8 & & -12 & & -16 & & -20 = \underline{84} \\
\diagup & \diagdown & \diagup & \diagdown & \diagup & \diagdown & \diagup & \diagdown & \diagup \\
144 & & 140 & & 132 & & 120 & & 104
\end{array}
$$

Rule: Subtract an amount that increases by 4 each time. 104 − 20 = 84.

72. (A) 100. Series.

$$
\begin{array}{ccccccccccc}
& +6 & & +5 & & +6 & & +5 & & +6 = \underline{100} \\
\diagup & \diagdown & \diagup & \diagdown & \diagup & \diagdown & \diagup & \diagdown & \diagup \\
72 & & 78 & & 83 & & 89 & & 94
\end{array}
$$

Rule: Add 6, add 5. 94 + 6 = 100.

73. (D) 128. Pre-algebra. 8 squared = 8 × 8 = 64; twice as much as 64 = 2 × 64 = 128.

74. (A) 16. Pre-algebra. 6 more than 10 = 10 + 6 = 16. The number subtracted from 32 that yields 16 is 32 − 16, or 16.

75. (B) (b) is less than (a). Comparison. (a) = $\frac{2}{3}$ of 15 = $\frac{2}{3}$ × 15 = 10, (b) = $\frac{2}{5}$ of 20 = $\frac{2}{5}$ × 20 = 8, and (c) = $\frac{3}{4}$ of 32 = $\frac{3}{4}$ × 32 = 24.

76. (A) (a) is equal to (b) which is equal to (c). Comparison. The shaded portion in each part represents half of the circle. (a) = $\frac{2}{4}$ = $\frac{1}{2}$, (b) = $\frac{3}{6}$ = $\frac{1}{2}$, and (c) = $\frac{4}{8}$ = $\frac{1}{2}$. So all three fractions, or areas, are equal.

77. **(D)** 1717. Series.

$$\overset{-21}{\diagup\diagdown} \quad \overset{-21}{\diagup\diagdown} \quad \overset{-21}{\diagup\diagdown} \quad \overset{-21\ =\ \underline{1717}}{\diagup\diagdown\diagup}$$
$$1801 \quad 1780 \quad 1759 \quad 1738$$

Rule: Subtract 21. $1738 - 21 = 1717$.

78. **(C)** 63. Series.

$$\overset{+7}{\diagup\diagdown} \quad \overset{+7}{\diagup\diagdown} \quad \overset{+7}{\diagup\diagdown} \quad \overset{+7}{\diagup\diagdown} \quad \overset{+7}{\diagup\diagdown}$$
$$42 \quad 49 \quad 56 \quad \underline{63} \quad 70 \quad 77$$

Rule: Add 7. $56 + 7 = 63$.

79. **(D)** 19. Pre-algebra. A number twice as large as $35 = 2 \times 35 = 70$. The number added to 51 to yield 70 is $70 - 51$, or 19.

80. **(A)** (a) is equal to (b) which is equal to (c). Comparison. (a) $= .08$, (b) $= 8\% = .08$, (c) $= \dfrac{2}{25} = \dfrac{8}{100}$. Convert all fractions to the same form, in this case, the decimal form. We could also use percent or ratio forms.

81. **(D)** 73. Pre-algebra. 12 more than $11 = 11 + 12 = 23$. The number subtracted from 96 to give 23 is $96 - 23$, or 73.

82. **(C)** *FB* is equal to *EC*. Comparison. In a square, the diagonal is longer than a side and shorter than twice a side. Here is what each answer means: **(A)** twice a side equals a diagonal; **(B)** a side equals twice a side; **(C)** a diagonal equals a diagonal; and **(D)** a side equals a diagonal. Only **(C)** is true.

83. **(B)** .4 Series.

$$\overset{\div 5}{\diagup\diagdown} \quad \overset{\div 5}{\diagup\diagdown} \quad \overset{\div 5}{\diagup\diagdown} \quad \overset{\div 5\ =\ \underline{.4}}{\diagup}$$
$$250 \quad 50 \quad 10 \quad 2$$

Rule: Divide by 5. $2 \div 5 = .4$.

84. **(B)** 2. Series.

$$\overset{\div 5}{\diagup\diagdown} \quad \overset{+5}{\diagup\diagdown} \quad \overset{\div 5}{\diagup\diagdown} \quad \overset{+5}{\diagup\diagdown} \quad \overset{\div 5\ =\ \underline{2}}{\diagup}$$
$$100 \quad 20 \quad 25 \quad 5 \quad 10$$

Rule: Divide by 5, add 5. $10 \div 5 = 2$.

85. **(D)** 1. Pre-algebra. 8 less than $15 = 15 - 8 = 7$. The number added to 6 to give 7 is $7 - 6$, or 1.

86. **(D)** (a) is less than (c) and greater than (b). Comparison. (a) $= \dfrac{3}{4} = \dfrac{18}{24}$, (b) $= \dfrac{2}{3} = \dfrac{16}{24}$, and (c) $= \dfrac{19}{24}$. Convert all fractions to fractions with the same denominator. In this case the smallest common denominator is 24.

87. **(C)** IV. Series.

Rule: Subtract 4. $8 - 4 = 4$. In Roman numerals, $X = 10$, $V = 5$, and $I = 1$. Smaller numbers that follow bigger numbers are added; smaller numbers that come before bigger numbers are subtracted. So, $XX = 20$, $XVI = 16$, $XII = 12$, and $VIII = 8$. In Roman numerals, 4 is IV, which means 5 minus 1.

88. **(A)** 47. Series.

$$
\begin{array}{ccccccccc}
& -5 & & -11 & & -5 & & -11 & & -5 = \underline{47} \\
\diagup & \diagdown & \diagup & \diagdown & \diagup & \diagdown & \diagup & \diagdown & \diagup \\
84 & & 79 & & 68 & & 63 & & 52
\end{array}
$$

Rule: Subtract 5, then subtract 11. $52 - 5 = 47$.

89. **(D)** 8. Pre-algebra. $\dfrac{2}{5}$ of $10 = \dfrac{2}{5} \times 10 = 4$. If $\dfrac{1}{2}$ of a number equals 4, the number is 2×4, or 8.

90. **(C)** *BC* is equal to *AD*. Comparison. The picture shows a square inside a circle. In a square, half of the diagonal is shorter than a side, which is shorter than the whole diagonal. Here is what the four answers mean: (A) a side equals half a diagonal; (B) a side equals a diagonal; (C) a side equals a side; (D) a diagonal equals a side. Clearly, (C) is the only choice that is true.

91. **(D)** 32. Series.

$$
\begin{array}{ccccccccccccc}
& +5 & & +9 & & +5 & & +9 & & +5 & & +9 \\
\diagup & \diagdown & \diagup & \diagdown & \diagup & \diagdown & \diagup & \diagdown & \diagup & \diagdown & \diagup & \diagdown \\
18 & & 23 & & \underline{32} & & 37 & & 46 & & 51 & & 60
\end{array}
$$

Rule: Add 5, then add 9. $23 + 9 = 32$.

92. **(A)** 34. Series.

$$
\begin{array}{ccccccccc}
& +2 & & \times 2 & & +2 & & \times 2 & & +2 = \underline{34} \\
\diagup & \diagdown & \diagup & \diagdown & \diagup & \diagdown & \diagup & \diagdown & \diagup \\
5 & & 7 & & 14 & & 16 & & 32
\end{array}
$$

Rule: Add 2, multiply by 2. $32 + 2 = 34$.

93. (C) 6. Pre-algebra. 2 squared = 2 × 2 = 4. If $\frac{2}{3}$ of a number is 4, $\frac{3}{2}$ of 4 must equal the number, or $\frac{3}{2}$ × 4 = 6.

94. (D) (b) is equal to (c) which is not equal to (a). Comparison. (a) = 24 ÷ 3 = 8, (b) = 36 ÷ 2 = 18, and (c) = 3 × 6 = 18. Do the parentheses first.

95. (D) 6. Pre-algebra. $\frac{3}{4}$ of 40 = $\frac{3}{4}$ × 40 = 30. If a number multiplied by 5 yields 30, the number is 30 ÷ 5, or 6.

96. (C) 20, 26. Series.

Rule: Add 6, then subtract 9. 29 − 9 = 20; 20 + 6 = 26.

97. (D) (2) is equal to (y) plus (x). Comparison. (2) takes up half of the circle, and (x) plus (y) takes up the other half. The two halves are equal.

98. (B) 20. Pre-algebra. $\frac{2}{5}$ of 80 = $\frac{2}{5}$ × 80 = 32. 7 less than 32 = 25. The number added to 5 that leaves 25 is 25 − 5, or 20.

99. (A) (a) is equal to (b) which is equal to (c). Comparison. This is a beginning algebra question. By the distributive property, (a) = 2(x + y) = 2x + 2y. This is the same as (b). By the commutative property, (c) = (x + y)2 = 2(x + y), which is the same as (a). So, all three expressions are equal.

100. (D) 10. Pre-algebra. $\frac{2}{3}$ of 12 = $\frac{2}{3}$ × 12 = 8. The product of 10 and 8 = 10 × 8 = 80, half of 80 = $\frac{1}{2}$ of 80 = $\frac{1}{2}$ × 80 = 40. The number subtracted from 50 that leaves 40 is 50 − 40, or 10.

101. (C) (c) is greater than (a). Comparison. There are 4 quarts in 1 gallon. So, in terms of quarts, the picture graphs represent the following amounts: (a) = 3 quarts, (b) = 4 quarts, and (c) = 5 quarts.

102. (C) (c) is equal to (a) but is not equal to (b). Comparison. The exponent tells the number of times you write the base number before multiplying. A zero exponent means the answer is 1 as long as the base number is not zero. (a) = 1^6 = 1 × 1 × 1 × 1 × 1 × 1 = 1, (b) = 6^1 = 6, and (c) = 12^0 = 1.

103. (D) 8. Pre-algebra. $\frac{1}{3}$ of 3 = $\frac{1}{3}$ × 3 = 1; 2 times 1 = 2 × 1 = 2. If the number divided by 4 leaves 2, the number is 4 × 2, or 8.

104. (B) (d) minus (a) equals (a) minus (b). Comparison. From the bar graph, (a) = 5, (b) = 2, (c) = 10, and (d) = 8. From these values, (B) is true and (A), (C), and (D) are false.

105. (A) 24. Series.

Rule: Starting with the first number, every other number increases by 5. Starting with the second number, every other number decreases by 2. 26 − 2 = 24.

It is possible to go from one number to the next, but it is more complicated. If you subtract an amount to go from one number to the next, you add 5 more than that amount to get the next number, then subtract 2 more than that new amount to get the next number. Using this approach, the number list looks like this:

$$-70 \quad +75 \quad -77 \quad +82 \quad -84 = \underline{24}$$
$$98 \qquad 28 \qquad 103 \quad 26 \qquad 108$$

The next number is still 24.

106. (B) (a) is equal to (b) but is not equal to (c). Comparison. (a) = 60% of 50 = .6 of 50 = .6 × 50 = 30, (b) = 50% of 60 = .5 of 60 = .5 × 60 = 30, and (c) = 40% of 70 = .4 of 70 = .4 × 70 = 28. To convert percents to decimals, move the decimal two places to the left. When multiplying, the number of decimal places in the answer is the sum of the decimal places in the numbers multiplied.

107. (B) The perimeter of triangle *ABC* is 24. Comparison. We can get the length of *AC* using the Pythagorean Theorem. $6^2 + 8^2 = 36 + 64 = 100$. $10^2 = 100$, so *AC* = 10. Look at our choices. (A) The perimeter of the rectangle is the sum of the sides = 6 + 8 + 6 + 8 = 28, not 30. (B) The perimeter of triangle *ABC* is 6 + 8 + 10 = 24, so (B) is true. For completeness, look at (C) and (D). (C) The area of triangle *ABC* is half the base times the height, or half of 8 times 6, which is half of 48, or 24. (D) The area of the rectangle is the base times the height, or 8 times 6, which is 48.

108. (C) 9. Series.

$$+4 \qquad \div 4 \qquad +4 \qquad \div 4 \qquad +4 = \underline{9}$$
$$60 \qquad 64 \qquad 16 \qquad 20 \qquad 5$$

Rule: Add 4, then divide by 4. 5 + 4 = 9.

109. (C) 25, 34, 22. Series.

Rule: Subtract, then add. The amount you subtract increases by 2 each time. The amount you add is 1 less than the amount you last subtracted. $35 - 10 = 25$, $25 + 9 = 34$, $34 - 12 = 22$. You could also do this by looking at every other number. Starting with the first number, you get the number after the next by subtracting 1. Starting with the second number, you get the one after the next by subtracting 3. The series of numbers would then look like this:

110. (A) 1. Pre-algebra. $\frac{3}{8}$ of $16 = \frac{3}{8} \times 16 = 6$; $\frac{1}{3}$ of $21 = \frac{1}{3} \times 21 = 7$. The number subtracted from 7 to leave $6 = 7 - 6$, or 1.

111. (B) 155. Pre-algebra. $\frac{2}{3}$ of $18 = \frac{2}{3} \times 18 = 12$; 3 times $12 = 3 \times 12 = 36$. A number added to 5 makes 36, so that number is $36 - 5$, or 31. But 31 is $\frac{1}{5}$ of another number, and that number must be 5 times $31 = 5 \times 31$, or 155.

112. (B) 28. Series.

$$\diagup -8 \diagdown \quad \diagup +3 \diagdown \quad \diagup +3 \diagdown \quad \diagup -8 \diagdown \quad \diagup +3 \diagdown \quad \diagup +3 = \underline{28}$$

32   24   27   30   22   25

Rule: Subtract 8, add 3, add 3: $25 + 3 = 28$.

Reading—Detailed Explanations of Answers

Comprehension

113. (B) The passage does not mention any employers **(A)**, an attack **(C)**, or taxes **(D)**. The crime of forgery **(B)** is mentioned specifically in the second sentence and elaborated on throughout the passage.

114. (D) The passage describes what the antiques dealer did: created documents that he claimed were written by someone else. Of the choices, "faking" **(D)** most closely expresses this.

115. (C) The passage specifically refutes choices **(A)** and **(B)**, while choice **(D)** represents a scenario not described at all. Choice **(C)** is supported explicitly.

116. (D) Although analysis of ink **(A)** is mentioned as one way to detect forgery, it is not said to be the reason that the antiques dealer was caught. The passage specifically says that the antiques dealer had studied Lincoln's handwriting and reproduced it effectively, so choice **(B)** must be incorrect. Choice **(C)** is never stated in the passage—only choice **(D)** is supported by the passage.

117. (D) The passage does say that the antiques dealer will get 15 years in jail, but it also gives additional information, so choice **(A)** is not the best answer. Choices **(B)** and **(C)** are clearly not supported by the passage, while choice **(D)** includes both the prisoner sentence and the order to make financial amends for his fraud.

118. (C) The tone of this passage is argumentative and persuasive. It is not just imparting information. It is trying to convince its reader to take action on something. Only choice **(C)** reflects this purpose.

119. (C) All the choices except **(C)** have a negative connotation. Choice **(C)** is in tune with the passage's message that workplaces need to be nicer atmospheres.

120. (B) Choice **(B)** is supported throughout the passage very explicitly. The other choices tend toward contradicting the main point of the passage.

121. **(D)** As with question 118, the answer is dependent on your ability to detect the author's interest in writing this passage. By the word choice and things that are specifically said it is clear that the author is very invested in persuading the reader of the importance of taking this information seriously, which is supported only by choice **(D)**.

122. **(B)** All the choices are explicitly mentioned except **(B)**.

123. **(A)** While Picasso **(B)** is used as an example of a Cubist painter, not enough is said about him to support calling this passage a biography of him. There is no attempt to compare Cubism **(C)** to other styles of painting or to critique Cubist painters **(D)**. The passage is mainly concerned with giving some facts about Cubism and offering an example, supported by choice **(A)**.

124. **(D)** The passage specifically mentions that Cubist paintings are NOT realistic **(D)**.

125. **(C)** The painting is discussed in such a way to demonstrate some of the Cubist principles that have been mentioned. None of the other choices are supported by the passage.

126. **(D)** The passage makes it clear that Cubism is important **(C)**, but choice **(D)** most accurately supports the usage of abstract here—particularly in the part about some objections to Cubism.

127. **(A)** The passage makes choice **(A)** explicit. The other choices are directly or indirectly refuted by the passage.

128. **(A)** The author is calling for specific action to be taken about a problem. The passage is clearly written to persuade rather than simply convey information. Therefore, choice **(A)** is best.

129. **(C)** The passage explicitly states that although the topic is under discussion, it is not being addressed **(C)**.

130. **(D)** The author is careful to emphasize that basic health services will not fix the problem of uninsured Americans. Choice **(D)** supports this.

131. **(A)** Surgery **(A)** is clearly not a basic health service; it is much more serious, time consuming, and expensive than the other proposals listed, and it is never mentioned in the passage.

132. **(B)** The context of the term indicates that its meaning most nearly means something wide-ranging or all-inclusive. The choice most like this is complete **(B)**.

133. **(B)** Choices **(A)**, **(C)**, and **(D)** all mean nearly the same thing, while choice **(B)** expresses a much different concept that is supported by the passage.

134. **(C)** There is specific mention of the origin of the Shaker name in their dance **(C)**.

135. **(C)** While the passage mentions dancing **(A)** and furniture making **(B)**, the passage makes clear that the Shakers were primarily a religious community **(C)**. There is no mention of farming **(D)**.

136. **(C)** The passage stresses that the Shakers believed in both simplicity and practicality. This is supported by choice **(C)**.

137. **(A)** The tone of the passage is descriptive rather than partial **(D)** or derogatory **(B)**. Choice **(A)** is the most accurate way to characterize the passage.

138. **(D)**   The passage follows a format wherein several studies are presented to the reader, making choice **(D)** most accurate.

139. **(C)**   The inclusion of academic studies and the scientific tone of the passage make it very much opposed to the suggestions of choices **(A)**, **(B)**, and **(D)**. Choice **(C)** is well supported by the passage.

140. **(D)**   Choice **(D)** is explicitly stated within the passage. None of the other choices are mentioned.

141. **(A)**   After Brown and Bellugi are mentioned, there is a listing of their findings, all of which appear in the choices except **(A)**.

142. **(B)**   The amount of scholarship mentioned in just this brief passage suggests that **(B)** is the best answer. The other choices are not implied or mentioned specifically.

143. **(C)**   The tone of this passage is reminiscent of a textbook. There is no strong language that would suggest **(D)** or persuasive rhetoric that would suggest **(A)**. While food processing is mentioned, the passage is about a specific kind of processing rather than about food processing in general **(B)**. Choice **(C)** is the best answer.

144. **(D)**   Choice **(D)** is directly supported by the passage.

145. **(D)**   There is no mention of cave drawings **(A)**, written documents **(B)**, or studies of any other tribes **(C)**. Choice **(D)** is supported by the passage.

146. **(B)**   There is no mention in the passage of any other Indian tribes or anything related to warfare **(B)**, while all the other choices are supported by instances in the passage.

147. **(A)**   The passage deals with strategies employed by Indians to find foods that would sustain them. This is best supported by choice **(A)**.

148. **(B)**   The statistics point toward an increasingly diverse nation **(B)** while none of the other choices are supported.

149. **(A)**   The author of this passage expresses a concern that schools may not at present be good atmospheres for minority students. Higher numbers of minority teachers **(A)** would no doubt make minority students feel more comfortable in California schools and be in line with the type of reform the author is advocating.

150. **(D)**   The author advances an argument based on numbers **(D)**. None of the other choices are represented.

151. **(C)**   The final point made in the passage is supported by the assessment offered in choice **(C)**.

152. **(B)**   One of the striking features of this passage is its use of statistics to advance an argument. This is clearly supported by choice **(B)** while the other choices are either inaccurate or not implied by the passage.

Vocabulary

153. **(D)**   The word *apex* means the *height* or *peak* **(D)**. Answer choice **(A)**, *bottom*, which means *lowest* or *base*, would be incorrect since it is the antonym of *apex*. Choice **(B)**, *beginning*, which means *start* or *inception*, and **(C)**, *end*, which means *conclusion* or *finale*, are opposites and have no connection with the word *apex*.

154. (A) An education is *compulsory* when it is necessary or *required* **(A)**. Answer choice **(B)**, *limited*, which means *inadequate*, and **(C)**, *private*, which means *restricted*, would both be incorrect. Answer choice **(D)**, *optional*, means *by choice* and would also be incorrect because it is an antonym of *compulsory*.

155. (C) The word *acute* means *sharp* **(C)** or *intense*. Answer choice **(A)**, *slight*, which means *small* or *insignificant*, would be incorrect since it is the antonym of *acute*. *Recurring* **(B)** would be incorrect since it means *frequent* or *repeated*. *Steady* **(D)** would also be incorrect since it means *constant* or *continuous*.

156. (B) A message would be *ambiguous* if it were *puzzling* **(B)**. Answer choice **(A)**, *understandable*, which means *comprehendible*, would be the wrong answer choice since it is an antonym of *ambiguous*. *Foreign* **(C)**, most commonly defined as *exotic*, might be chosen since it could mean *unknown*, but *puzzling* **(B)** is a better answer choice. Be careful not to select choice **(D)**, *illegible*, which means *unreadable*, as your answer choice—though it may appear correct; if something were *illegible* it could never be understood, yet if something were *ambiguous*, it could still be deciphered.

157. (A) When a scholar becomes *eminent*, he/she becomes *exalted* or *distinguished* **(A)**. Though intelligence would probably be necessary to become *eminent*, choice **(B)**, *intelligent*, which means *smart* or *keen*, would not be a proper answer choice. Choice **(C)**, *unknown*, which means *unrevealed* or *hidden*, would also be incorrect. Answer choice **(D)**, *confident*, a possible result of becoming *eminent*, means *assured* or *self-confident* and would not be a correct answer choice.

158. (D) When a person is told to *scrutinize* a document, he/she is to *inspect* and *examine* **(D)** it. He/she would not be asked to *forge* **(A)** it, which means *counterfeit* or *duplicate falsely*. Answer choice **(B)**, *skim*, which means to *browse* or *glance at*, would be the antonym of *scrutinize* and therefore wrong. Nor would it mean answer choice **(C)**, *copy*, which means to *replicate* or *reproduce*.

159. (B) In order to *convene* a discussion, it will need to be *assembled* **(B)** or *brought together*. Answer choice **(A)**, *conclude*, which means to *close* or *end*, would not be a correct answer choice. *Concentrate* **(C)**, which means *focus*, could be mistaken for the correct answer since it could mean to collect; however, in this question, choice **(B)** would be the most preferable answer choice. Answer choice **(D)**, *counterbalance*, means to *equalize* and would also not be the correct choice.

160. (C) A *judicious* decision is a *wise*, *rational*, or *sensible* **(C)** decision. A *judicious* decision would probably not be made with *biased* **(A)** information, which means *prejudiced* or *opinionated*. *Reckless* **(B)** means *rash* or *wild* and would most likely be an antonym of *judicious* and incorrect. *Sensitive* **(D)**, which means *tense* or *unstable*, would also not be a correct answer.

161. (C) The word *ferocious* means *savage*, *brutal*, or *wild* **(C)**. Choice **(A)**, *tame*, means *docile* and *gentle* and would be incorrect since it is an antonym of *ferocious*. Though a *ferocious* animal may be *stubborn* **(B)**, which means *inflexible* or *persistent*, it would be an incorrect answer choice. Choice **(D)**, *humorous*, which means *funny* or *amusing*, would also be an incorrect choice.

162. (D) To *obliterate* something means to *eliminate* or *destroy* **(D)** it. *Examine* **(A)**, which means to *study* or *analyze*, would not be a correct choice. Likewise, *conceal* **(B)**, which means to *hide* or *cover*, would also be incorrect. Choice **(C)**, *create*, which means to *produce* or *make*, would be incorrect because it is *obliterate's* antonym.

163. (B) A complexion that looks *pallid* is one that is *sickly* or *pale* **(B)**. Answer **(A)**, *rosy*, would be incorrect because it means *healthy* or *flush*, which is an antonym of *pallid*. A *pallid* complexion may look *gloomy* or *sad* **(C)**, but being gloomy and being pale are not synonymous. Choice **(D)**, *healthy*, means *hearty* or *robust* and would be incorrect since it is also an antonym.

164. (C) *Impetuous* decisions are made *hastily* or *impulsively* **(C)**. The antonym of this word, however, would have allowed the decision to have been *thought out* and *planned* **(A)**. The word *recent* **(B)** would not have been a correct choice since it means *modern* or *contemporary*. Choice **(D)**, *wise*, would not have been a correct choice either since it means *rational* or *intelligent*.

165. (D) *Mutinous* crewmen were known for their revolts and *rebellious* **(D)** deeds. This word's antonym, *cooperative* **(A)**, means *agreeing* and is not the correct answer. *Quiet* **(B)**, which means *silent* or *stillness*, would also be a wrong selection. Finally, if the crewmen had been *changeable* **(D)**, which means *adaptable* or *flexible*, they would not be *rebellious*, which makes **(D)** incorrect.

166. (B) A *placid* sea is *still* and *calm* **(B)**. A *calm* sea could be *deep* **(A)**, which means *low*, but *low* and *calm* are not synonymous words. Choice **(C)**, *stormy*, means *turbulent* or *wild* and is an incorrect choice since it is *placid's* antonym. Choice **(D)**, *large*, which means *huge* or *massive*, would be incorrect for the same reasons as choice **(A)**.

167. (A) A *replica* of something is a *reproduction* or *copy* **(A)**. Be careful not to choose answer choice **(B)**, *forgery*; even though it's a reproduction, **(B)** is an incorrect answer choice because it is done fraudulently. Answer choice **(C)**, *original*, which means *first* or *primary*, would be incorrect since it is the antonym of *replica*. Choice **(D)**, *wreckage*, means *debris* or *remains* and would also be an incorrect answer choice.

168. (C) Things are *conspicuous* if they are *seen* or *noticeable* **(C)**. Answer choice **(A)**, *hidden*, which means *concealed* or *unseen*, would be incorrect since it is an antonym of *conspicuous*. Answer choice **(B)**, *shady*, means *questionable* or *notorious* and would not be the correct answer choice. *Significant* **(D)** means *critical* or *serious* and would not be a correct answer choice.

169. (C) A story is *abridged* if it is *condensed* or *shortened* **(C)**. *Lengthened* **(A)**, which means *extended* or *made longer*, would be incorrect since it is an antonym of *abridged*. Answer choice **(B)**, *true*, which means *authentic* or *accurate*, would not be a correct answer choice. *False* **(D)**, which means *incorrect* or *wrong*, would also be an incorrect answer choice.

170. (C) An excuse is considered *plausible* if it is *convincing* or *believable* **(C)**. Answer choice **(A)**, *unbelievable*, would be incorrect since it is an antonym of *plausible*. *Praiseworthy* **(B)** means *reputable* or *commendable* and would not be a correct answer choice. *Unforgivable* **(D)** means *inexcusable* or *unallowable* and would be incorrect.

171. (B) In order to *thwart* an attack, you must *impede* or *repel* **(B)** it. Answer choice **(A)**, *strengthen*, which means *to intensify* or *fortify*, would not be a correct answer choice. *Accelerate* **(C)** means to *hasten* or *speed up* and is incorrect. *Wage* **(D)** which means to *undertake* or *carry on*, is also not a correct choice.

172. (B) A *discreet* remark is made *cautiously* and *carefully* **(B)**. If it were done with care, it would not be *hurtful* **(A)**, which means *insulting* or *offensive*. Answer choice **(C)**, *insensitive*, means *ruthless* or *unkind* and would not be correct. Choice **(D)**, *polite*, means *courteous* or *respectful* and would also be incorrect.

173. (B) A *frugal* meal is *economical* or *thrifty* **(B)**. *Wasteful* **(A)**, means *squandering* or *reckless* and would be incorrect. Answer choice **(C)**, *abundant*, means *fruitful* or *plentiful* and would also be incorrect. Answer choice **(D)**, *leftover*, means *remaining* or *extra* and would be incorrect.

174. (C) *Meager* means *inadequate* or *insufficient* **(C)**. *Large* **(B)** and *healthy* **(D)** are not correct. *Lavish* **(A)** means *luxurious* or *excessive*.

Mathematics—Detailed Explanations of Answers

Concepts

175. (A) The digit that comes immediately after the hundredths place is 4, which is less than 5. So we leave the 7 in the hundredths place as it is: $6.874 \cong 6.87$.

176. (A) Arrange like terms vertically and add:

$$
\begin{array}{r}
5x - 3y + 12 \\
3x + 3y - 10 \\
\hline
8x + 0 + 2
\end{array}
$$

Rearrange terms: $8x + 2$

177. (D) $(6, -3)$ is a point 6 spaces to the right of the Y-axis and 3 spaces below the X-axis. That is point D on the graph.

178. (B) Let n represent the smaller number, so the larger number must be $(n + 2)$. Then the sum of the two numbers must be: $n + (n + 2) = 2n + 2 = 74$. To solve this equation,

add -2 to both sides:

$$
\begin{array}{r}
2n + 2 = 74 \\
-2 \quad -2 \\
\hline
\end{array}
$$

divide both sides by 2: $\quad 2n = 72 \quad n = 36$.

The smaller number is $n = 36$ and the larger number is $n + 2 = 36 + 2 = 38$.

179. (B) $6\dfrac{2}{3} - 5\dfrac{1}{4} = \dfrac{20}{3} - \dfrac{21}{4} = \dfrac{(20 \times 4) - (21 \times 3)}{12} = \dfrac{80 - 63}{12} = \dfrac{17}{12} = 1\dfrac{5}{12}$.

180. (C) One easy way to answer this question is to list the pairs of factors of the given numbers and then select the one that has a pair of identical factors:

$12 = 1 \times 6 = 3 \times 4$. (no pair of identical factors)
$14 = 2 \times 7$. (no pair of identical factors)
$16 = 2 \times 8 = 4 \times 4$. (1 pair of identical factors)
$18 = 2 \times 9 = 3 \times 6$. (no pair of identical factors)
So the answer is 16 because 16 has exactly one pair of identical factors.

181. **(A)** Since width of square = length of square, the number representing the area of a square must be a perfect square number. That is, the number must have two identical factors. Here is one way to test for identical factors among the given numbers:

$24 = 2 \times 12 = 3 \times 8 = 4 \times 6.$ (no pair of identical factors)
$25 = 5 \times 5.$ (1 pair of identical factors)
$36 = 2 \times 18 = 3 \times 12 = 4 \times 9 = 6 \times 6.$ (1 pair of identical factors)
$64 = 2 \times 32 = 4 \times 16 = 8 \times 8.$ (1 pair of identical factors)

24 is the only number in the set that has no pair of identical factors. The answer must be 24.

182. **(A)** $\frac{3}{5} \times \frac{5}{6} + 21 = \left(\frac{3}{5} \times \frac{5}{6}\right) + 21 = \frac{1}{2} + 21 = 21\frac{1}{2}.$

183. **(B)** $5\frac{1}{4} \div 2\frac{1}{3} = \frac{21}{4} \div \frac{7}{3} = \frac{21}{4} \times \frac{3}{7} = \frac{9}{4} = 2\frac{1}{4}.$

184. **(A)** First find $\frac{1}{7}$ of 77.

$\frac{1}{7} \times \frac{77}{1} = \left[\frac{1}{1} \times \frac{77}{7}\right] = \frac{1}{1} \times \frac{11}{1} = 1.$ Then subtract eleven from fourteen to find the missing number. $14 - 11 = 3.$

185. **(D)** To express 200 as a percent of 80, write: $\frac{200}{80} \times \frac{100}{1} = 250\%$

186. **(A)** $2\frac{3}{5} = 2.6.$ So $2\frac{3}{5} = 2.6 \times 100 = 260\%$

187. **(C)** $x(-y + z) = -xy + xz = xz - xy.$

188. **(A)** Albert's average daily earnings for the five days must be: $\$460 \div 5 = \frac{\$460}{5} = \$92.$

189. **(C)** We need 2 pairs of equal measures to form the opposite sides of the parallelogram, which we find only in set (c), namely, 4 and 4; 6 and 6.

190. **(C)** If we add the four numbers in each set, in turn, we find that the only set that adds to exactly 360 is set (c), $[(78 + 85 + 95 + 102) = 360].$

191. **(D)** 45% of $2,000 = \frac{45}{100} \times \frac{2,000}{1} = 900.$

192. **(C)** When we examine the graph, we see that the attendance on Wednesday was 21; on Thursday it was 18; and on Friday the attendance was 21 again. So the total attendance for the three days was 60. The average attendance for the three days must be $60 \div 3 = 20.$

193. **(A)** First, observe that each space on the temperature scale represents 5 degrees. By comparing the temperatures in February and in March, we observe that the temperature rose by 35 degrees. Similarly, we notice that the temperature rose by 35 degrees from April to May. These are the steepest monthly rises.

194. **(D)** The temperature fell from 45° at the start of December to 15° at the end of the month. This was a drop of 30° and represents the steepest drop on the graph.

195. (D)   The lowest temperature was 15° at the end of March and December.

196. (B)   The "7" in 472.625 is in the tens position.

197. (A)   "Obtuse" in this context means having an angle greater than 90°. In the pictures, the triangle in (a) is the only one that has an obtuse angle.

198. (C)   The measure of the total angle in a circle is 360°. The measure of the unshaded angle in the picture is 55°. The measure of the shaded angle is $(360° - 55°) = 305°$.

Problem-Solving

199. (B)   Replace d with 4,500, y with 1, and r with 6:

$$I = \frac{4,500}{1} \times 1 \times \frac{6}{100} = \$270.$$

200. (C)   The length of the flagpole is the sum of the measures of the 12 pieces of pipe. Since the 12 pipes are equal in length, we could simply multiply the length of one piece by 12: $8.5 \times 12 = 102$ ft.

201. (C)   The decrease in attendance was $(400 - 336) = 64$. Express 64 to a percent of 400:

$$\frac{64}{400} \times \frac{100}{1} = 16\%.$$

202. (D)   First, find the area of the mirror, using the given formula: Area $= 2.5 \times 6.4 = 16$ ft². To find the cost of the new mirror, multiply the cost of 1 ft² by the area of the mirror: $\$2.60 \times 16 = \$41.60$.

203. (D)   First, convert 3 minutes to seconds, to make computation easier: 3 min $= 3 \times 60 = 180$ seconds. If in 6 seconds the pump pushes out 9 pts of ice cream, then in 1 second it must push out $9 \div 6 = \dfrac{9}{6}$ pts of ice cream. In 180 seconds, it must push out $\dfrac{9}{6} \times \dfrac{180}{1} = 270$ pts.

204. (B)   Michael and Jason together have $\dfrac{2}{7} + \dfrac{2}{5} = \dfrac{10 + 14}{35} = \dfrac{24}{35}$

$$\frac{35}{35} - \frac{24}{35} = \frac{11}{35}.$$

205. (B)   At the end of the year, the value of the computer decreases to $(100 - 18) = 82\%$. So we must find 82% of the value of a new computer: $\dfrac{82}{100} \times \dfrac{1,500}{1} = \$1,230$

206. (C)   With a deduction of 22%, Damian would have to accept only $(100 - 22) = 78\%$ of the marked price. 78% of $\$375 = \dfrac{78}{100} \times \dfrac{375}{1} = \$292.50$.

207. (B)   The task here is equivalent to finding the perimeter of the garden. In a rectangle the opposite sides are equal in measure. So there are two sides each measuring 8 ft and two sides each measuring 6 ft. The four sides of the rectangle must add up to $(8 + 8) + (6 + 6) = 28$ ft.

208. (B) First, convert 8 ft to inches: 8 ft = 8 × 12 = 96 in. Now we can express 5 in. as a fraction of 96 in.: $\frac{5}{96}$.

209. (B) Begin by converting 10 ft to inches: 10 ft = (10 × 12) = 120 in. Then express 5 in. as a fraction of 120 in: $\frac{5}{120} = \frac{1}{24}$.

210. (B) First, convert 9 m to cm: 9 m = (9 × 100) = 900 cm. To figure out how many desert sidewinding vipers must be strung together to obtain the length of an anaconda, divide 900 cm by 25 cm: 900 ÷ 25 = 36.

211. (C) The difference between the two populations is (989,000 − 683,000) = 306,000.

212. (D) Since 120 out of 200 students are girls, then there must be (200 − 120) = 80 boys in the school. To express 80 as a percent of 200, we write: $\frac{80}{200} \times \frac{100}{1} = 40\%$.

213. (D) 84% represents 63 questions. So 1% must represent $\frac{63}{84}$ questions and 100% must represent $\frac{63}{84} \times 100 = 75$. Then 75 − 63 = 12 missed questions.

214. (A) The task is simply to multiply 175 lb by 50: 175 × 50 = 8,750 lb.

215. (A) The rectangle has a total of 6 × 10 = 60 small squares, of which 28 are shaded. The fraction of the rectangle that is shaded is $\frac{28}{60} = \frac{7}{15}$.

216. (A) 32 of the 60 small squares are not shaded. This represents $\frac{32}{60} \times \frac{100}{1} = 53\%$.

217. (B) If the average attendance for Monday and Tuesday was 23, then the total attendance for those two days must be 23 × 2 = 46. From the graph, we see that the attendance on Tuesday alone was 20. So the attendance on Monday must be (46 − 20) = 26.

218. (A) Jeff's total dropped from 395 to 332. The difference is (395 − 332) = 63. This must be his score on the test that the teacher discarded.

219. (A) The rectangle in the picture is a square, since each side measures (10 + 10) = 20 cm. The area of the square must be 20 × 20 = 400 cm². The area of each clear region is one-half of a full circle with the same radius. The area of such a full circle is (3.14 × 10²) = 314 cm². The area of each clear region (half-circle) must be 314 ÷ 2 = 157 cm². The combined areas of the two quarter-circles must be 157 × 2 = 314 cm². The area of the unshaded region must be 400 − 314 = 86 cm².

220. (B) The half can is curved like a half-circle, so the length of the curved edge is half the circumference of a circle of the same diameter. The circumference of a full circle with the same diameter would be 3.14 × 10 = 31.4 cm, and half of that is 31.4 ÷ 2 = 15.7 cm. The area of the visible outer surface of the half can must be 15.7 × 10 = 157 cm².

221. (C) The height of the parallelogram is clearly shown as 12 cm. The base of the parallelogram is 15 cm. So the area of the parallelogram must be 12 × 15 = 180 cm².

222. (C) The total amount of time that Simon spends outside school is (2 hrs + 2.4 hrs + 3 hrs + 8 hrs) = 15.4 hr. So the time he spends in school is (24 − 15.4) = 8.6 hrs.

223. (B) Simon spends 2.4 hrs on his homework. Express this as a percent of 24 hrs: $\frac{2.4}{24} \times \frac{100}{1} = 10\%$.

224. (D) We first convert $\frac{1}{2}$ lb and 1 lb to ounces, to simplify computation: $\frac{1}{2}$ lb $= \frac{1}{2} \times \frac{16}{1} =$ 8 oz and 1 lb = 16 oz. Total amount of food in the pot = (8 oz + $\frac{1}{2}$ lb + 1 lb) = (8oz + 8 oz + 16oz) = 32 oz. Percent rice $= \frac{8}{32} \times \frac{100}{1} = 25\%$.

225. (C) The ratio of midsized cars to big cars may be written as 63:37 or as $\frac{63}{37}$. Let n represent the unknown number of big cars. Then we can write: $\frac{63}{37} = \frac{189}{n}$. So $63 \times n = 37 \times 189$ = 6,993 and $n = 111$.

226. (B) Sharon paid (.80)($60) = $48 for the dress and (.85)($80) = $68 for the shoes. Her total cost was $116 after the discounts. Without the discounts, her total cost would have been $60 + $80 = $140. Now, $140 − $116 = $24, and $24/$140 ≈ 17%.

227. (D) Let x = cost of one apple, y = cost of one orange. $10x + y = \$2.70$ and $x + 10y = \$3.24$. Multiply the first equation by 10 to get $100x + 10y = \$27.00$ and then subtract the original second equation ($x + 10y = \$3.24$) to get $99x = \$23.76$. So, $x = .24$. Substitute this value of x into the original first equation to get $(10)(.24) + y = \$2.70$. Then $y = .30$. Finally, $x + y = .54$.

228. (C) Carol's portion of the bill is $1 - \frac{1}{3} - \frac{1}{5} = \frac{7}{15}$. Since Amy paid $\frac{1}{3}$ of the bill, her payment of $10.70 means the bill totaled ($10.70)(3) = $32.10. Thus, Carol paid $\left(\frac{7}{15}\right)$ ($32.10) = $14.98.

229. (B) Let x = number of remaining games. The team has already won (.70)(30) = 21 games. If the team wins one-half of the remaining games, its total number of wins will be 21 + $\frac{1}{2}x$. The number of games played will be 30 + x. Then $\left(21 + \frac{1}{2}x\right) / (30 + x) = .62$. Simplifying, $21 + \frac{1}{2}x = .62(30 + x)$. Then, $2.4 = .12x$, and $x = 20$. Finally, the number of games played = 50.

230. (A) He has already traveled at 10 mi/hr for 6 minutes, which means he covered 1 mile. He must travel 2 more miles in 6 minutes. Since 60 ÷ 6 = 10, Brian must travel (10)(2) = 20 mi/hr for the remainder of the trip.

231. (A) In this inverse relationship, rate of vibration times length of the string must be a constant. (40)(100) = 4,000. Then, 4,000 ÷ 250 = 16.

232. (D) Let x = number of dancers only. Now 35 − 27 = 8 people who are talking only, so that 8 + 27 + x = 60. This leads to x = 25, which represents the number of dancing only. The total number of dancing must be 27 + 25 = 52.

233. (B) The perimeter of the square is (4)(6) = 24 inches. The rectangle's perimeter is $\left(2\frac{1}{2}\right)(24) =$ 60 inches. Since perimeter = (2)(length) + (2)(width), the length plus the width must be 30 inches for this rectangle. The width = 30 − 18 = 12.

234. (A) If the other base angle is 80°, the vertex angle = 180° − 80° − 80° = 20°. If the vertex angle = 80°, each base angle must be (180° − 80°)/2 = 50°. In either instance no angle of this triangle could be 10°.

235. (C) Let x = weight of the child; $x + 45$ = weight of the mother, and $3x$ = weight of the father. Then, $x + (x + 45) + 3x = 370$. Simplifying, $5x + 45 = 370$, so $x = 65$. The mother's weight = 65 + 45 = 110 pounds. The father's weight = (3)(65) = 195 pounds. Then 195 − 110 = 85 pounds.

236. (C) Let x and $x + 6$ be the rates of the two trains. Then $5x + 5(x + 6) = 560$. Solving, $x = 53$ and $x + 6 = 59$. The faster train goes (59)(3) = 177 miles.

237. (C) The student has a probability of $\frac{1}{5}$ to get any one of the first three questions correct. His probability of getting any one of the last two questions correct is $\frac{1}{2}$. The probability that he will correctly answer all 5 questions is $\left(\frac{1}{5}\right)\left(\frac{1}{5}\right)\left(\frac{1}{5}\right)\left(\frac{1}{2}\right)\left(\frac{1}{2}\right) = \frac{1}{500}$.

238. (D) The total weight of the women is (5)(130) = 650 pounds. The total weight of the men must be 1,350 − 650 = 700 pounds. Finally, the men's average weight = 700/4 = 175 pounds.

Language Skills—Detailed Explanations of Answers

Punctuation, Capitalization, and Usage

239. (A) This sentence needs end punctuation, which in this case should be a period.

240. (D) There are no mistakes.

241. (C) The phrase containing extra information, *a music box*, needs to be separated with a comma: "The present, a music box, was wrapped in purple paper."

242. (B) The word should be written *excellent*.

243. (A) The sentence should read "My grandmother sent a letter to my brother and me" since the subject of the sentence is "my grandmother" while "my brother and me" is the object.

244. (A) *February* is a proper noun and should be capitalized.

245. (B) Sentences that begin within quotation marks should begin with a capital letter: He wandered in and said, "We wanted to do that."

246. (B) For subject-verb agreement, the sentence should read "You don't have to help me."

247. (B) For subject-verb agreement, the sentence should read "My friend has a new baby sister" or "My friends have a new baby sister."

248. (C) The contraction for *isn't* needs an apostrophe.

249. (A) The abbreviation for *Mister* requires a period: "Mr. Green."

250. (C) The word is spelled *outside* and not *outsides*.

251. (B) For subject-verb agreement, the sentence should read "Drawing is a fun course to take."

252. (A) This sentence has too many commas. It should read "We ran outside quickly."

253. (D) There are no mistakes.

254. **(A)** This question needs to end in a question mark: "Are you sitting over there?"

255. **(A)** For subject-verb agreement, the sentence should read "That girl is making really funny faces."

256. **(A)** The word *many* means that there is more than one cookie; the sentence should read: "We brought many cookies over to his house."

257. **(A)** The verb should be in present tense.

258. **(D)** There are no mistakes.

259. **(C)** This is a run-on sentence that should be separated into two sentences: "Scott hurt his head. He went to the doctor." It could also be combined with a conjunction: "Scott hurt his head, so he went to the doctor."

260. **(B)** The modifier *almost* is misplaced. The sentence should read "We danced until almost midnight."

261. **(B)** The verbs should be in the same tense, such as "John typed, read, and printed out his report."

262. **(A)** Better should not be preceded by *more*; it is an irregular comparative adjective. The sentence should read "Maxine is better at math."

263. **(B)** Since the speaker is asking a question, the sentence should have a question mark: "Where are we going tonight?" he wanted to know.

264. **(A)** The wrong verb tense is used in this example. The sentence should read "We saw that television show last night."

265. **(A)** The word *four* should be used instead of *for*.

266. **(C)** The word should be *beginning*.

267. **(B)** The sentence is missing punctuation and quotation marks: She warned, "That isn't such a good idea."

268. **(B)** The first and main words of book titles are capitalized and the entire title is italicized. He is reading *The Adventures of Huckleberry Finn*.

269. **(C)** This sentence needs end punctuation, such as "I can't find my wallet!"

270. **(D)** There are no mistakes.

271. **(A)** *It's* should have an apostrophe to mean *it is*.

272. **(C)** This is a sentence fragment.

273. **(B)** The first word in a sentence should be capitalized.

274. **(B)** This is a run-on sentence that should be broken up: "We walked quickly. We thought someone was there." It could also be combined with a conjunction: "We walked quickly because we thought someone was there."

275. **(C)** The verb *threw* should be used instead of the word *through*.

276. **(C)** For subject-verb agreement, the sentence should read "My mom and dad like to eat at restaurants."

277. **(B)** The verb should be past tense since the action took place in the past: "I went to the store yesterday."

278. **(B)** This is a sentence fragment.

Spelling

279. **(D)** There are no mistakes.

280. **(C)** *The atheletes are traveling to a basketball tournament.* The correct spelling is **athletes**.

281. **(A)** *The gardener was embarassed when he tripped over the hose.* The correct spelling is **embarrassed**.

282. **(B)** *The desparate criminal hid in an abandoned factory.* The correct spelling is **desperate**.

283. **(C)** *The child's frequent absenses are hindering her progress.* The correct spelling is **absences**.

284. **(B)** *The maintainance crew was exhausted after the carnival.* The correct spelling is **maintenance**.

285. **(B)** *Congradulations on your successful completion of the program.* The correct spelling is **congratulations**.

286. **(A)** *Jim received many complements for his chocolate layer cake.* The correct spelling is **compliments**.

287. **(D)** There are no misspelled words.

288. **(C)** *The seniors were anxious to see the graduation date on the new school calender.* The correct spelling is **calendar**.

Composition

289. **(A)** Of the choices, *The flavor of herbs is most intense when they are fresh* is the only sentence that gives information about the topic.

290. **(C)** Of the choices, *Vitamin C helps the body resist infections* is the only sentence that states a benefit of vitamin C.

291. **(A)** Of the choices, *Thomas Edison invented the phonograph in 1877* is the only sentence that gives an example of a 19th-century invention.

292. **(D)** None of the choices gives information about the topic.

293. **(C)** *Travel Safety Tips* is the only topic that is narrow enough to be contained in one paragraph. The others are far too broad.

294. **(A)** *Telephone Etiquette* is the only topic that is narrow enough to be contained in one paragraph. The others are far too broad.

295. (D) The given sentence links sentences 2 and 3:

(2) The foreign substance irritates the oyster.

To protect itself, the oyster encloses the irritant in a sac.

(3) The oyster then secretes layers of mother-of-pearl, or nacre, around the sac to form a pearl.

296. (B) The given sentence follows sentence 3 because it gives an example of a cause and effect:

(3) This begins a chain reaction of causes and effects.

For example, when you press the letter "M" on the keyboard, the letter "M" appears on the monitor screen.

297. (C) To choose the sentence that does not belong in the paragraph, you must first identify the topic sentence. The topic sentence states the controlling idea of the paragraph. Sentence 1 is the topic sentence of the paragraph: *A computer system is made up of both hardware and software*. Sentences 2 and 4 both support the topic sentence by defining hardware and software. Although sentence 3, ***Many students find the smaller laptop computers very convenient***, does contain information about computers, it is not directly related to the topic sentence. Therefore, it does not belong in the paragraph.

298. (D) To choose the sentence that does not belong in the paragraph, you must first identify the topic sentence. The topic sentence states the controlling idea of the paragraph. Sentence 1 is the topic sentence of the paragraph: *Monticello was the home of Thomas Jefferson, the third president of the United States*. Sentences 2 and 3 both support the topic sentence by giving additional information about Monticello. Sentence 3, ***Jefferson was the governor of Virginia from 1779 to 1781***, is not directly related to the topic sentence.

COOP
PRACTICE TEST 2

COOP
SUBTEST 1

Sequences

Time: 15 Minutes
20 Questions

DIRECTIONS: Study the sequences and then choose the best answer from the choices given.

1. ○○○◎ | ○○○◎◎ | ○○◎○◎◎ | ──

  (A) ○○◎○○◎
  (B) ◎○◎◎○◎
  (C) ○○◎○
  (D) ◎○◎○◎○

2. ☒☒☒☒ | ☒☒☒☒ | ☒☒☒☒ | ____

  (F) ☒☒☒☒
  (G) ☒☒☒☒
  (H) ☒☒☒☒
  (J) ☒☒☒☒

3. ○△△ | △△○ | △○△ | ____

  (A) ○△△
  (B) △○△
  (C) △△○
  (D) ○△△

4. ☐☐☐☐ | ☐☐☐☐ | ☐☐☐☐ | ☐ __

  (F) ☐☐☐
  (G) ☐☐☐
  (H) ☐☐☐
  (J) ☐☐☐

5. ☐☐ | ☐☐ | ☐☐ | ____

  (A) ☐☐
  (B) ☐☐
  (C) ☐☐
  (D) ☐☐

6. ×× + × | × + ×× | ____ | ××× +

  (F) + × + ×
  (G) + + + ×
  (H) + × × ×
  (J) × × + ×

GO TO NEXT PAGE

7. $\triangle\,\bigcirc\,\square\mid\bigcirc\,\square\,\diamondsuit\mid\square\,\diamondsuit\,\bigcirc\mid\underline{\hspace{1cm}}\mid\bigcirc\,\triangle\,\square\mid$
   - (A) $\square\,\triangle\,\bigcirc$
   - (B) $\diamondsuit\,\bigcirc\,\triangle$
   - (C) $\square\,\bigcirc\,\diamondsuit$
   - (D) $\diamondsuit\,\triangle\,\bigcirc$

8. LPK │ PKG │ KGR │ _____ │ RSE
   - (F) GKP
   - (G) GRS
   - (H) GRE
   - (J) GKR

9. ADKX │ BELY │ _____ │ DGNA
   - (A) CGLZ
   - (B) CDKW
   - (C) CGMZ
   - (D) CFMZ

10. HLM │ PHL │ CPH │ _____ │ XNC
    - (F) PHN
    - (G) HXN
    - (H) NCP
    - (J) NPC

11. TIKI │ KIWI │ _____ │ LIPI
    - (A) TIPI
    - (B) KIPI
    - (C) WILI
    - (D) WIPI

12. $J_5\,K_5\,L_5$ │ $J_5\,K_5\,L_4$ │ $J_5\,K_4\,L_3$ │ _____
    - (F) $J_4\,K_3\,L_2$
    - (G) $J_5\,K_4\,L_4$
    - (H) $J_4\,K_4\,L_3$
    - (J) $J_4\,K_3\,L_3$

13. $E_1\,K_2\,H_3$ │ $E_2^1\,K_3\,H_2$ │ _____ │ $E_2^3\,K_1^2\,H_3^1$
    - (A) $E_2^1\,K_3^2\,H_2^1$
    - (B) $E_2^1\,K_3^2\,H_2$
    - (C) $E_3^1\,K_2^2\,H_1$
    - (D) $E_3^2\,K_2^1\,H_1$

14. $W_5\,X_5\,Y$ │ $W_4\,X_5\,Y$ │ $W_4\,X_4\,Y$ │ _____ │ $W_3\,X_3\,Y$
    - (F) $W_3\,X_5\,Y$
    - (G) $W_4\,X_3\,Y$
    - (H) $W_5\,X_4\,Y$
    - (J) $W_3\,X_4\,Y$

15. 3 12 18 │ 4 16 22 │ 6 24 __
    - (A) 28
    - (B) 30
    - (C) 32
    - (D) 36

16. 3 18 7 │ 5 30 19 │ 6 __ 25
    - (F) 36
    - (G) 40
    - (H) 30
    - (J) 42

17. 7 14 5 │ 10 20 11 │ 30 60 51 │ 60 __ __
    - (A) 120 91
    - (B) 120 111
    - (C) 90 81
    - (D) 90 91

GO TO NEXT PAGE ➡

18. $6\dfrac{3}{5}\dfrac{3}{10}\Big|8\dfrac{4}{5}\dfrac{4}{10}\Big|12\text{—}\Big|14\dfrac{7}{5}\dfrac{7}{10}$

   (F) $1\dfrac{1}{2}$

   (G) $\dfrac{5}{5}\dfrac{5}{10}$

   (H) $\dfrac{6}{5}\dfrac{6}{10}$

   (J) $\dfrac{12}{5}\dfrac{12}{10}$

19. 2 3 5 7 | 3 5 7 11 | 5 7 11 13 | _ _ _ _

   (A) 7 11 13 15

   (B) 7 11 13 19

   (C) 7 11 13 17

   (D) 7 11 13 21

20. 36 12 24 | 54 18 36 | 48 16 32 | 18 _ _

   (F) 6 12

   (G) 9 18

   (H) 4 16

   (J) 8 12

COOP

STOP

COOP
SUBTEST 2

Analogies

Time: 7 Minutes
20 Questions

DIRECTIONS: For numbers 1–20, choose the picture that would go in the empty box so that the bottom two pictures are related in the same way the top two are related.

GO TO NEXT PAGE

527

4)   (F)   (G)   (H)   (J)

5)   (A)   (B)   (C)   (D)

6)   (F)   (G)   (H)   (J)

7)   (A)   (B)   (C)   (D)

8)   (F)   (G)   (H)   (J)

9)   (A)   (B)   (C)   (D)

GO TO NEXT PAGE ➡

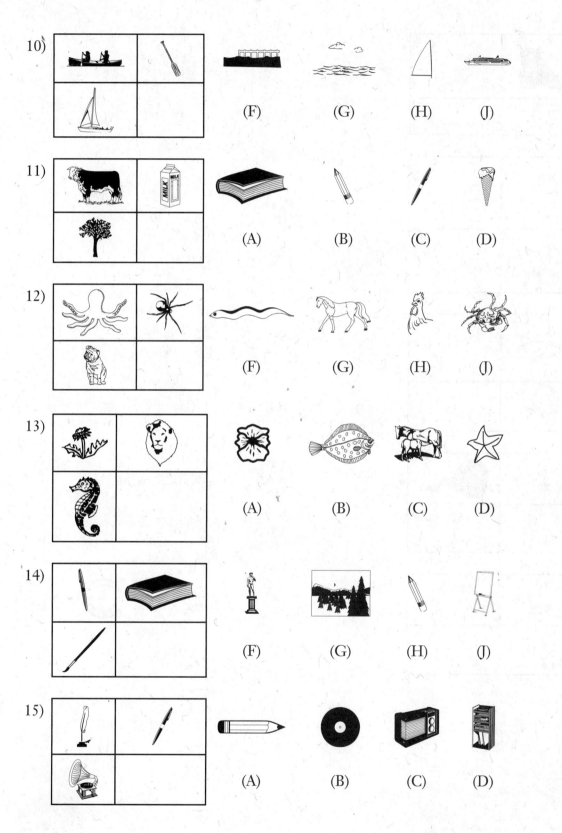

10) (F) (G) (H) (J)

11) (A) (B) (C) (D)

12) (F) (G) (H) (J)

13) (A) (B) (C) (D)

14) (F) (G) (H) (J)

15) (A) (B) (C) (D)

COOP

GO TO NEXT PAGE ➡

16)

(F)   (G)   (H)   (J)

17)

(A)   (B)   (C)   (D)

18)

(F)   (G)   (H)   (J)

19)

(A)   (B)   (C)   (D)

20)

(F)   (G)   (H)   (I)

STOP

COOP
SUBTEST 3

Quantitative Reasoning

Time: 15 Minutes
20 Questions

DIRECTIONS: For numbers 1–7, find the relationship of the numbers in one column to the numbers in the other column. Find the missing number.

1.

1 → ▢ → 7   (A) 5   (C) 6

4 → ▢ → 10   (B) 14   (D) 13

7 → ▢ → ?

2.

3 → ▢ → 14   (F) 13   (H) 15

6 → ▢ → 17   (G) 11   (J) 12

2 → ▢ → ?

3.

5 → ▢ → 0   (A) 4   (C) 2

9 → ▢ → 4   (B) 12   (D) 10

7 → ▢ → ?

4.

16 → ▢ → 7   (F) 0   (H) 6

13 → ▢ → 4   (G) 9   (J) 8

9 → ▢ → ?

5.

4 → ▢ → 8   (A) 10   (C) 8

6 → ▢ → 12   (B) 16   (D) 18

8 → ▢ → ?

6.

3 → ▢ → 12   (F) 18   (H) 36

6 → ▢ → 24   (G) 32   (J) 27

9 → ▢ → ?

7.

21 → ▢ → 7   (A) 5   (C) 3

36 → ▢ → 12   (B) 45   (D) 12

15 → ▢ → ?

COOP

GO TO NEXT PAGE →

DIRECTIONS: For numbers 8–14, find the fraction of the grid that is shaded black.

8.

(A) $\frac{2}{3}$ (B) $\frac{3}{4}$ (C) $\frac{1}{2}$ (D) $\frac{1}{4}$

9.

(F) $\frac{1}{6}$ (G) $\frac{1}{3}$ (H) $\frac{2}{4}$ (J) $\frac{12}{8}$

10.

(A) $\frac{1}{4}$ (B) $\frac{1}{2}$ (C) $\frac{2}{4}$ (D) $\frac{1}{5}$

11.

(F) $\frac{2}{3}$ (G) $\frac{1}{6}$ (H) $\frac{2}{6}$ (J) $\frac{1}{2}$

12.

(A) $\frac{1}{2}$ (B) $\frac{5}{8}$ (C) $\frac{3}{5}$ (D) $\frac{2}{8}$

13.

(F) $\frac{1}{2}$ (G) $\frac{3}{8}$ (H) $\frac{1}{4}$ (J) $\frac{4}{9}$

14.

(A) $\frac{1}{3}$ (B) $\frac{3}{9}$ (C) $\frac{5}{9}$ (D) $\frac{5}{8}$

DIRECTIONS: For numbers 15–20, the scale shows sets of shapes with equal weight. Find an equivalent pair of sets that would balance the scale as well.

15.

16.

(F)	△△△▢▢	△△△
(G)	▢▢△	△△▢▢
(H)	△▢△△	△▢▢
(J)	▢▢△△△	▢△

17.

(A)	△▢	▢▢▢
(B)	△△△	▢▢▢
(C)	△△△△	△▢▢
(D)	▢	△△

18.

(F)	▢△	△△
(G)	▢▢▢	△
(H)	△△△△	▢▢▢
(J)	▢▢	△△△△

19.

(A)	△△▢	△△△△△
(B)	△	▢▢
(C)	▢▢▢	△△△△△▢
(D)	▢△	▢▢▢

20.

(F)	▢▢	△▢△▢
(G)	△△△	▢
(H)	▢△△	△△△△△△
(J)	▢▢△△	△△△▢▢

COOP

STOP

COOP
SUBTEST 4

Verbal Reasoning–Words

Time: 15 Minutes
20 Questions

DIRECTIONS: For numbers 1–6, find the word that names a necessary part of the underlined word.

1. <u>pen</u>
   (A) paper
   (B) pencil
   (C) ink
   (D) crayon

2. <u>computer</u>
   (F) power
   (G) games
   (H) printer
   (J) CD-ROM

3. <u>ice</u>
   (A) snow
   (B) sleet
   (C) water
   (D) blue

4. <u>canine</u>
   (F) hound
   (G) cat
   (H) paws
   (J) collar

5. <u>coffee</u>
   (A) mug
   (B) tea
   (C) sugar
   (D) beans

6. <u>fork</u>
   (F) tine
   (G) spoon
   (H) metal
   (J) chopstick

GO TO NEXT PAGE

DIRECTIONS: For numbers 7–12, the words in the top row are related in some way. The words in the bottom row are related in the same way. For each item, find the word that completes the bottom row of words.

7. whisper   talk   shout

   whimper   cry

   (A) sob   **(C)** yell
   (B) howl   **(D)** tears

8. sandals   bathing suit   shorts

   boots   mittens

   (F) snow   **(H)** scarf
   (G) skis   **(J)** shirt

9. Empire State Building   Mount Rushmore   Golden Gate Bridge

   Colosseum   Leaning Tower of Pisa

   (A) the Vatican   **(C)** vacation
   (B) the Great Wall of China   **(D)** the Statue of Liberty

10. iris   retina   cornea

    lobe   drum

    (F) seeing   **(H)** body
    (G) canal   **(J)** hearing

11. patients   beds   medicine

    students   chalk

    (A) hospital   **(C)** study
    (B) doctors   **(D)** desks

12. man   worker   union

    boy   player

    (F) baseball   **(H)** team
    (G) batter   **(J)** catcher

COOP

GO TO NEXT PAGE

DIRECTIONS: For numbers 13 – 20, the underlined words are related in some way. Find the word that is most like the underlined words.

13. couch   table   bed

    (A) rug   **(C)** mirror
    (B) chair   **(D)** picture

14. watering can   hoe   rake

    (F) dirt   **(H)** wheelbarrow
    (G) garage   **(J)** gloves

15. sandals   pumps   loafers

    (A) towel   **(C)** gloves
    (B) socks   **(D)** sneakers

16. collie   poodle   beagle

    (F) Labrador   **(H)** tabby
    (G) dog   **(J)** shaggy

17. chicken noodle   split pea   vegetable

    (A) bowl   **(C)** spoon
    (B) rice   **(D)** tomato

18. lizard   snake   iguana

    (F) frog   **(H)** toad
    (G) turtle   **(J)** shark

19. mitt   base   dugout

    (A) bat   **(C)** club
    (B) puck   **(D)** volleyball

20. daffodil   carnation   rose

    (F) bouquet   **(H)** lily
    (G) vase   **(J)** petal

COOP

COOP
SUBTEST 5
Verbal Reasoning–Context

Time: 15 Minutes
20 Questions

DIRECTIONS: For numbers 1–20, find the statement that is true according to the given information.

1. Joey has 3 cats. He also has 2 dogs, but he doesn't have any birds.
   - **(A)** Joey doesn't like birds.
   - **(B)** Joey doesn't want any more pets.
   - **(C)** Joey has at least 5 pets.
   - **(D)** Joey's mother won't let him get any birds.

2. Bob's soccer team is in a special tournament. Once the team loses a game, they're out of the tournament. They had their first game today, and Bob is getting ready for tomorrow's game.
   - **(F)** Bob's team won the game today.
   - **(G)** Bob's team lost the game today.
   - **(H)** Bob will be happy when the tournament is over.
   - **(J)** Bob will play basketball when the soccer season is over.

3. In September, Jack went back to school and started 9th grade. The teacher asked all the students what book they had read last. Some students had read over the summer and some had not. Jack told the teacher the last book he had read was *Tom Sawyer* in 8th grade.
   - **(A)** Jack was too busy to read during the summer.
   - **(B)** Jack can't read.
   - **(C)** Jack doesn't like to read.
   - **(D)** Jack didn't read over the summer.

4. Jim, who had always been a little chubby, took his favorite pants out of the closet. He hadn't worn them since last fall because they were a little tight. He put them on and they were a little loose. This made Jim smile.
   - **(F)** Jim lost weight.
   - **(G)** Jim likes baggy pants.
   - **(H)** Jim recently bought several new pairs of pants.
   - **(J)** Jim gained weight over the winter.

GO TO NEXT PAGE

5. When the waiter brought the pizza to the table, the cheese was sizzling and bubbling. It smelled and looked so good that Mark couldn't wait to take a bite. As he bit into it, he yelled and spit out the pizza.

   (A) Mark will never eat pizza again.

   (B) Mark doesn't like pizza.

   (C) The waiter brought the wrong kind of pizza to Mark's table.

   (D) Mark burnt his mouth.

6. Jared went to his gymnastics class. He walked on the balance beam, hung from the bars, and did a tumble roll on the mat. He was disappointed not to get a turn on the trampoline before class ended.

   (F) Jared does not like the trampoline.

   (G) Jared is great on the balance beam.

   (H) Jared likes the trampoline.

   (J) Jared did at least four things at the class.

7. Kimberly went to the pet store. She wanted a friend for the hamster she has at home. The two teddybear hamsters at the store were so cute that she bought them both.

   (A) Kimberly did not plan to buy two hamsters.

   (B) Kimberly only likes hamsters.

   (C) Kimberly wants more hamsters.

   (D) Teddybear hamsters are the cutest type of hamster.

8. The pizza parlor had many toppings to choose from. There was sausage, pepperoni, mushrooms, peppers, and eggplant. Sal chose peppers and mushrooms for his pizza.

   (F) Sal is a vegetarian.

   (G) Sal does not like eggplant.

   (H) Sal likes at least two vegetables.

   (J) Sal often picks peppers and mushrooms.

9. The Empire State Building is in New York City. Many people visit this attraction each day. Carlos went to New York City last fall with his cousins.

   (A) Carlos's cousins live near the Empire State Building.

   (B) Carlos visited the Empire State Building.

   (C) Carlos has many cousins.

   (D) Carlos has been to New York City at least once.

10. Samantha was looking forward to going to the aquarium all week. When she got there she spent time looking at each tank, but especially enjoyed the jelly fish. She read all about them and told her dad much information about the jelly fish when she got home. Her dad was quite impressed.

    (F) Samantha remembered a lot about the jelly fish.

    (G) Samantha's dad did not know anything about jelly fish.

    (H) Samantha saw jelly fish at the beach.

    (J) Samantha did not see any sharks.

11. Eric put a quarter in a gumball machine. A big red gumball came out, so he put in another quarter. The second time a big green gumball came out. The next quarter got him a big yellow gumball. He crossed his fingers and put in his last quarter, but he got another red one.

    (A) Eric wanted many gumballs.

    (B) Eric did not get the color gumball he wanted.

    (C) Eric likes red gumballs the best.

    (D) Eric chews a lot of gum.

GO TO NEXT PAGE

12. Jillian stood on the lunch line and looked at all the choices. She wanted to put together the healthiest lunch. She saw chicken nuggets, baked chicken, French fries, fruit and salad. Jillian selected the baked chicken, salad, and an apple.

   (F) Jillian never eats food that is fried.

   (G) Jillian was not very hungry that day.

   (H) Jillian thinks the food in the cafeteria is not healthy.

   (J) Jillian thinks baked chicken is healthier than chicken nuggets.

13. Mei was playing volleyball at the beach with her friends. Since she was such a good player, everyone wanted her on their team. During the game, the ball came over the net and all the way back to Mei. She jumped and reached for it, but needed to shield her eyes and missed the ball.

   (A) Mei is short for a volleyball player.

   (B) The sun was in Mei's eyes.

   (C) Mei's team lost the game.

   (D) The other players were upset with Mei.

14. Jake was hoping to get three computer games for his birthday. One was a survival game, one was football, and the third was chess. He only got two of the games as presents, but he got a gift card to a gaming store as well. When Jake got to the store, unfortunately, they were out of the football game he wanted.

   (F) Jake bought a different football game.

   (G) Jake was happy with his presents.

   (H) Jake went back to the store a week later.

   (J) Jake did not get the football game as a present.

15. At the flower shop there were carnations, roses, and lilies. Suzanne wanted to buy some for her grandmother who really loves pink flowers. She left with some carnations and lilies.

   (A) The lilies were the prettiest.

   (B) The roses were not pink.

   (C) Her grandmother loved the flowers.

   (D) The roses were white.

16. Caroline likes a variety of music. She has CDs that are country, punk, rap, and pop. She listens to them in her car.

   (F) Caroline has a big CD collection.

   (G) Caroline likes at least four types of music.

   (H) Caroline does not listen to CDs at home.

   (J) Caroline does not like rock music.

17. Patrick was leaving soon to meet his friends at the mall. He knew what time to be there but did not know where to meet them. He checked to make sure he had his cell phone on him before he headed out.

   (A) Patrick planned to call his friends.

   (B) Patrick looked in the food court first.

   (C) Patrick's phone was ringing.

   (D) Patrick likes to talk on the phone.

18. Kyle was playing dodge ball, and he does not like to lose. There were really good players on both team. The game was tough. When the game was over, Kyle threw his sneakers into his locker and slammed the door shut.

   (F) Kyle was anxious to get home after the game.

   (G) The other team had better players.

   (H) Kyle's team lost the game.

   (J) Kyle does not like to play dodge ball.

COOP

GO TO NEXT PAGE ➡

COOP

19. There were several choices of toppings at the ice cream shop. Christina looked at the chocolate and the rainbow sprinkles, chopped peanuts, crushed cookies, and peanut butter cups. Then she saw that they had chocolate, strawberry, and caramel sauces. She ordered a cup of vanilla ice cream with crushed cookies, chocolate sauce, and chocolate sprinkles.

(A) Christina likes vanilla ice cream the most.

(B) Christina is allergic to peanuts.

(C) Christina does not like strawberry sauce.

(D) Christina likes chocolate.

20. The Space Needle is a very tall building in Seattle, Washington. Sam went to Seattle on vacation with his family. It took them eight hours to drive there from where they live. Sam thought the view from the top was worth the long drive.

(F) Sam visited the Space Needle.

(G) The Space Needle is Seattle's biggest attraction.

(H) Sam drove the car on their trip.

(J) Sam's family often takes long drives.

STOP

Reading and Language Arts

Time: 40 Minutes
40 Questions

> **DIRECTIONS:** Each passage is followed by questions based on its content. After reading the passage, choose the best answer to each question. Answer all questions based on what is indicated or implied in that passage.

Questions 1–4 are based on the following passage.

To the Shakers, perfection was found in the creation of an object that was both useful and simple. Their Society was founded in 1774 by Ann Lee, an Englishwoman from the working classes who brought eight followers to New York with her. "Mother Ann" established her religious community on the belief that worldly interests were evil.

To gain entrance into the Society, believers had to remain celibate, have no private possessions, and avoid contact with outsiders. The order came to be called "Shakers" because of the feverish dance the group performed. Another characteristic of the group was the desire to seek perfection in their work.

Shaker furniture was created to exemplify specific characteristics: simplicity of design, quality of craftsmanship, harmony of proportion, and usefulness. While Shakers did not create any innovations in furniture designs, they were known for fine craftsmanship. The major emphasis was on function and not on excessive or elaborate decorations that contributed nothing to the product's usefulness.

GO TO NEXT PAGE

1. The Shakers were
   (A) a religious community.
   (B) a furniture company.
   (C) a dance troupe.
   (D) an English family.

2. The group came to be called the Shakers because
   (F) they made Shaker furniture.
   (G) they were from the working class.
   (H) they did a shaking dance.
   (J) they avoided contact with outsiders.

3. Shaker furniture is known for its
   (A) elaborate decoration.
   (B) high quality and simplicity.
   (C) high cost.
   (D) low cost.

4. The main purpose of this passage is
   (F) to convince people to join the Shakers.
   (G) to explain why the Shakers no longer exist.
   (H) to talk about Shaker quilts and furniture.
   (J) to tell about the Shakers and their furniture.

Questions 5–8 are based on the following passage.

Teachers should be cognizant of the responsibility they have for the development of children's competencies in basic concepts and principles of free speech. Freedom of speech is not merely the utterance of sounds into the air; rather, it is couched in a set of values and legislative processes that have developed over time. These values and processes are a part of our political conscience as Americans. Teachers must provide ample opportunities for children to express themselves effectively in an environment where their opinions are valued. Children should have ownership in the decision-making process in the classroom and should be engaged in activities where alternative resolutions to problems can be explored. Because teachers have such tremendous power to influence in the classroom, they must be careful to refrain from presenting their own values and biases that could "color" their students' belief systems. If we want children to develop their own voices in a free society, then teachers must support participatory democratic experiences in the daily workings of the classroom.

5. This passage is most likely written for
   (A) students.
   (B) teachers.
   (C) parents.
   (D) substitute teachers.

6. The word *cognizant*, as used in the first line of the passage, means
   (F) proud.
   (H) fearful.
   (G) aware.
   (J) ignorant.

7. Which of the following is the main idea of the paragraph?
   (A) Teachers should let children make the classroom rules.
   (B) Teachers should have the children solve their own arguments.
   (C) Teachers should talk to children about voting.
   (D) Teachers must help children develop the ability to exercise free speech.

GO TO NEXT PAGE

8. From the passage, it can be inferred that free speech
   (F) is an idea that never changes.
   (G) is an idea that changes and develops over time.
   (H) exists only in the United States.
   (J) cannot be taught in the classroom.

Questions 9–12 are based on the following passage.

Experienced lawyers know that most lawsuits are won or lost before they are ever heard in court. Thus, successful lawyers prepare their cases carefully, undertaking exhaustive research and investigation prior to going to court. Interviews and statements allow one to ascertain those who are likely to be called as witnesses for the other side. This is the time for strategy planning in the building of the case: decisions to be made about expert witnesses to be called (such as doctors, chemists, or others who have special knowledge of the subject matter); books and articles to be read pertaining to the subject matter of the case; and meetings with witnesses to prepare them for possible questions by the opposing lawyers and to review the case. Finally, in preparing the case, a trial memorandum of law is handed to the judge at the outset of the trial. As a result of this thorough preparation, experienced lawyers know their strong and weak points and can serve their clients well.

9. Drawing an inference from the passage, why are most cases won or lost before they are heard in court?
   (A) It is easy to tell who is going to win most cases.
   (B) The judge gets the trial memorandum before hearing the case.
   (C) Research is the most important part of a case.
   (D) Lawyers have strong and weak points, and picking the best lawyer is the most important part of the trial.

10. The primary purpose of this passage is to illustrate
    (F) that the legal system is biased against women.
    (G) that the legal system is biased against the poor.
    (H) the work lawyers do before they go to court.
    (J) the work lawyers do to present their cases in court.

11. To build a case, lawyers do all of the following EXCEPT
    (A) read books and articles that relate to the case.
    (B) meet with witnesses.
    (C) meet with the judge.
    (D) consider calling expert witnesses.

12. This passage was probably intended for an audience
    (F) of lawyers.
    (G) of judges.
    (H) of people involved in a lawsuit.
    (J) of people without any specialized knowledge of lawsuits.

COOP

GO TO NEXT PAGE

COOP

Questions 13–16 are based on the following passage.

It is important to learn proper communication and the meaning in language. Yet the use of notions such as communication and meaning as the basic criteria for instruction, experiences, and materials in classrooms may misguide a child in several respects. Communication in the classroom is vital. The teacher should use communication to help students develop the capacity to make their private responses become public responses. Otherwise, one's use of language would be in danger of being what the younger generation refers to as mere words, mere thoughts, and mere feelings.

Learning theorists emphasize specific components of learning: behaviorists stress behavior in learning; humanists stress the affective domain in learning; and cognitivists stress cognition in learning. All three of these components occur simultaneously and cannot be separated from each other in the learning process. In 1957, Festinger referred to dissonance as the lack of harmony between what one does (behavior) and what one believes (attitude). Attempts to separate the components of learning either knowingly or unknowingly create dissonances wherein language, thought, feeling, and behavior become diminished of authenticity. As a result, ideas and concepts lose their content and vitality, and the manipulation and politics of communication assume prominence.

13. The word *dissonance* as used in the passage means
(A) happiness.
(B) anger.
(C) disagreement.
(D) agreement.

14. According to the passage, humanist learning theorists consider which of the following most important?
(F) The affective domain
(G) Behavior
(H) Cognition
(J) Dissonance

15. This passage is probably aimed toward
(A) learning theorists.
(B) language theorists.
(C) teachers.
(D) students.

16. From the tone of the passage, the author
(F) is not really interested in the topic.
(G) is confused about what teachers should do.
(H) feels strongly about the topic.
(J) does not have a strong opinion.

Questions 17–20 are based on the following passage.

In 1975, Sinclair observed that it had often been supposed that the main factor in learning to talk is being able to imitate. Schlesinger (1975) noted that at certain stages of learning to speak, a child tends to imitate everything an adult says to him or her, and it therefore seems reasonable to accord to such imitation an important role in the acquisition of language.

GO TO NEXT PAGE

Moreover, various investigators have attempted to explain the role of imitation in language. In his discussion of the development of imitation and cognition of adult speech sounds, Nakazema (1975) stated that although the parent's talking stimulates and accelerates the infant's articulatory activity, the parent's phoneme system does not influence the child's articulatory mechanisms. Slobin and Welsh (1973) suggested that imitation is the reconstruction of the adult's utterance and that the child does so by employing the grammatical rules that he has developed at a specific time. Schlesinger proposed that by imitating the adult, the child practices new grammatical constructions. Brown and Bellugi (1964) noted that a child's imitations resemble spontaneous speech in that they drop inflections, most function words, and sometimes other words. However, the word order of imitated sentences usually was preserved. Brown and Bellugi assumed that imitation is a function of what the child attended to or remembered. Shipley et al. (1969) suggested that repeating an adult's utterance assists the child's comprehension. Ervin (1964) and Braine (1971) found that a child's imitations do not contain more advanced structures than his or her spontaneous utterances; thus, imitation can no longer be regarded as the simple behavioristic act that earlier scholars assumed it to be.

17. The main topic of this passage is

(A) how children learn to talk.

(B) children's first words.

(C) the role imitation plays in learning to talk.

(D) how to teach a child to talk.

18. The author wrote this paragraph to

(F) tell parents how to teach their children to talk.

(G) tell teachers how to teach their classes to read.

(H) explain that children shouldn't imitate their parents.

(J) explain how imitation works for a child who is learning to talk.

19. Researchers have changed their minds about the importance of imitation because

(A) a child doesn't think about what he/she imitates.

(B) a child can only imitate grammar that he/she already knows.

(C) a child only imitates what he/she does not understand.

(D) a child's imitations are spontaneous.

20. Researchers included in the passage have found all of the following EXCEPT

(F) a child's imitation often adds new words to what the adult has said.

(G) a child's imitation is the reconstruction of an adult's speech.

(H) a child's imitations resemble spontaneous speech.

(J) a child's imitations help him or her understand what the adult has said.

COOP

GO TO NEXT PAGE ➡

DIRECTIONS: For numbers 21–26, choose the answer that best completes the sentence.

21. After Mrs. Howard returned from her shopping trip, she _____ to the kitchen to make herself a cup of tea.
    (A) have gone
    (B) had went
    (C) went
    (D) has gone

22. I really didn't enjoy that horror book I just finished. _____, I am never going to read another book by the same author.
    (F) Regardless
    (G) Because
    (H) As a result
    (J) However

23. Those roses are the _____ flowers I have ever seen.
    (A) most beautiful
    (B) more beautiful
    (C) as beautiful
    (D) less beautiful

24. _____ I am your father, it is my responsibility to take care of you and keep you safe.
    (F) Besides
    (G) However
    (H) Even though
    (J) Because

25. I want to compliment _____ new hairstyle. It looks lovely on you.
    (A) you're
    (B) you are
    (C) your
    (D) yore

26. _____ he had been given his allowance on Friday, Matt still didn't have enough money for the movie.
    (F) Although
    (G) Because
    (H) Since
    (J) If

DIRECTIONS: Choose the sentence that is complete and that is written correctly.

27. (A) The tornado approached slowly houses and trees were torn up in its path.
    (B) Tearing up houses and trees in its path, the tornado approached slowly.
    (C) Slowly approaching as it tore up houses and trees in its path.
    (D) The tornado slowly approaching tearing up houses and trees in its path.

28. (F) Giving me lots of energy in the morning, I enjoy a big breakfast.
    (G) Having a big breakfast in the morning gives me lots of energy.
    (H) A big breakfast in the morning giving me lots of energy.
    (J) I eat a big breakfast in the morning it gives me lots of energy.

GO TO NEXT PAGE

COOP

29. **(A)** For her birthday, a puppy will be given to Sandi because she is old enough now.

    (B) Sandi is getting a puppy for her birthday, she is old enough to take care of it now.

    (C) Getting a puppy because Sandi is old enough to take care of it now.

    (D) Now that she is old enough to take care of it, Sandi is getting a puppy for her birthday.

30. **(F)** When it is time for it to spawn and die, the salmon will swim against the current to the stream where it was born.

    (G) The salmon swimming upstream will spawn and die it was born in that stream.

    (H) Swimming against the current and spawning and dying in the stream where it was born.

    (J) Swimming against the current to spawn and die, the salmon.

31. **(A)** Every Memorial Day and Veterans' Day my grandmother puts up our flag my grandfather fought in World War II.

    (B) Since my grandfather fought in World War II and my grandmother puts out the flag every Veterans' Day and Memorial Day.

    (C) By putting out the flag every Veterans' Day and Memorial Day, my grandmother remembers my grandfather, who fought in World War II.

    (D) Putting out the flag on Veterans' Day and Memorial Day, and remembering my grandfather who fought in World War II.

32. **(F)** Street hockey is our favorite game in my neighborhood since we live on a dead-end street with a paved circle at the end.

    (G) Living on a dead-end street with a paved circle at the end and playing street hockey.

    (H) We play street hockey on our dead-end street we have a paved circle.

    (J) Since we live on a paved dead-end street and play our favorite game; street hockey.

COOP

DIRECTIONS: For numbers 33–37, choose the sentence that uses verbs correctly.

33. **(A)** Even though the television was still on, I can hear the radio clearly.

    (B) Hugh wanted his cat to come inside, so he puts cat food by the door.

    (C) Terry will be leaving this afternoon after she got back from the movies.

    (D) As a result of an error by the airline, his luggage will be arriving on a later plane.

34. **(F)** Angie plays tennis with Mark every Saturday, but this week he can't come.

    (G) The saxophone had a stuck key so Mr. Kady fixes it before the concert.

    (H) If we are going jogging this morning, you need to got dressed soon.

    (J) Eve says you shouldn't have took her new jeans from her closet yesterday.

GO TO NEXT PAGE

COOP

35. **(A)** I wish Gene and Val would have helped with the dishes and brang in the newspaper.
    (B) The Nelson's turtle often climbs on the rocks and knocks over its water dish.
    (C) You shouldn't of given her my phone number without my permission.
    (D) Jessie and I were going to meet the new boy at the museum, but he doesn't see us there.

36. **(F)** Dad picked up the new book from the library, and I taked it to school with me.
    (G) After Karen takes her brother to his music lesson, she stopped by the gym.
    (H) Lennie has been away on vacation since Friday and is expected home next Wednesday.
    (J) Before Nick gets back from wrestling, I returned his radio to his room.

37. **(A)** Mr. Post says you should of handed in your term paper yesterday.
    (B) My kitten loved to play with ribbon, but she gets tired easily and needs to sleep.
    (C) Bluefish can be broiled or baked, but it cooks fast and gets tough if you over-cook it.
    (D) For the last few weeks the weather has been terrible, and my mother's arthritis been bothering her.

DIRECTIONS: In numbers 38–40, choose the topic sentence that best fits the paragraph.

38. _____. The northern states wanted to extend the power of the federal government, while the southern states wanted to reserve as many rights as possible for the states. The North wanted federal money for projects such as railroads, canals, and roads, while the South had no need for these projects. The North favored the prohibition of slavery in the western states as they entered the union, while the South hoped to increase the number of slave states so as to ensure slavery's future.

(F) The Civil War was a result of many opposing points of view between the North and the South.

(G) The Civil War was the only war in which Americans fought themselves.

(H) Slavery was the main cause of the Civil War.

(J) The Civil War was a tragic and brutal war that caused misery for both the North and the South.

GO TO NEXT PAGE ➡

39. _____. Averaging 1.5 gallons in the typical adult, and comprising less than 10% of our total weight, blood carries all the nutrients and oxygen to the cells of our bodies through its vast circulatory system. It picks up oxygen from the lungs and nutrients from the digestive tract and carries them to the cell membranes, where it exchanges them for waste products that are then carried to the kidneys. In addition, blood carries heat produced by the muscles to all the other organs of the body.

(A) Blood is composed of water and red and white blood cells.

(B) Blood is important to our health.

(C) Blood is our body's internal transportation system.

(D) If we didn't have blood, we would die.

40. _____. Some poisonous plants such as bittersweet or nightshade can cause death or injury if leaves or berries are swallowed by animals. Other plants such as poison ivy and poison oak need only be touched to transfer their poisons. Still others, including some fungi, spread airborne toxins that are inhaled. Scientists believe that the purpose of all of these poisons, called biotoxins, is to defend plants against plant-eating animals.

(F) Plants have many ways to defend themselves.

(G) Poisonous plants use several different methods to ward off predators.

(H) Plants can be dangerous and should be handled carefully.

(J) Many botanists study poisonous plants.

COOP

STOP

COOP

SUBTEST 7

Mathematics

Time: 35 Minutes
40 Questions

DIRECTIONS: Select the best answer choice.

1. What is the value of q in the equation $4q + 8 = 16$?
   - (A) 24
   - (B) 8
   - (C) 6
   - (D) 2

2. Mr. Matthews worked for five days in a week. He earned $125 on Monday, $115 on Tuesday, $118 on Wednesday, and $123 on Thursday. If he earned a total of $591 for the week, how much was he paid on Friday?
   - (F) $125
   - (G) $120
   - (H) $110
   - (J) $100

3. Mary's average score on 5 tests was 88. If she scored 82 on test 1, 93 on test 2, 79 on test 3, and 90 on test 4, what was her score on test 5?
   - (A) 96
   - (B) 90
   - (C) 86
   - (D) 82

4. Rudy divided a certain number by 15 and the answer was 7.56. What is the value of the 6?
   - (F) 6 tens
   - (G) 6 singles
   - (H) 6 tenths
   - (J) 6 hundredths

GO TO NEXT PAGE ➡

5. Instead of dividing a certain number by 100, Martha multiplied it by 100. If Martha wrote 8.47265 as the answer, what should be the correct answer?

   (A) 84726.5

   (B) 847.265

   (C) 0.0847265

   (D) 0.000847265

6. Dwayne added 34 to a certain number when the teacher told him to subtract 34 from the number. Dwayne wrote the answer as 15. If he had done what the teacher said, what should have been the correct answer?

   (F) –53

   (G) 19

   (H) 49

   (J) 83

7. Arrange the following quantities in order, from <u>largest to smallest</u>: $\sqrt{36}$ 36   3.6

   (A) 36, 3.6, $\sqrt{36}$

   (B) $\sqrt{36}$, 3.6, 36

   (C) 36, $\sqrt{36}$, 3.6

   (D) 3.6, $\sqrt{36}$, 36

8. Tamara works for 20 hours at $4.75 an hour. How much does she earn for the 20 hours?

   (F) $950.00

   (G) $95.00

   (H) $24.75

   (J) $9.50

9. If $u = 5$ and $v = 3$, what is the value of $-2u + 3v$?

   (A) –19

   (B) –1

   (C) 1

   (D) 19

10. If $x = -3$ and $y = 2$, find the value of $(3xy)^2$.

    (F) 324

    (G) 36

    (H) –36

    (J) –324

11. Raymond's order of books arrived in 6 boxes of 9 books each and one box of 2 books. How many books did Raymond receive?

    (A) 63

    (B) 56

    (C) 54

    (D) 52

12. From the school's store room, Mrs. White collected 7 full boxes of marbles for her 12 students. If each full box holds 15 marbles, what is the minimum number of additional marbles that Mrs. White must collect in order to give her students exactly the same number of marbles?

    (F) 3

    (G) 9

    (H) 84

    (J) 105

13. The sum of two consecutive multiples of 7 is 1 less than the square of 6. Find the larger of the two multiples of 7.

    (A) 42

    (B) 35

    (C) 21

    (D) 14

GO TO NEXT PAGE ➡

14. In the figure, $\overline{AB}$ is a straight line. Find the value of x.

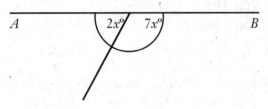

    (F) 20

    (G) 40

    (H) 45

    (J) 60

15. Find the value of v in the figure.

    (A) 32

    (B) 72

    (C) 108

    (D) 148

16. What is the value of y in the figure?

    (F) 42

    (G) 58

    (H) 52

    (J) 138

17. Two sets of straws are shown with the measures of their lengths. Which straw in set 2 would you combine with the two straws in set 1 so they can be joined end-to-end to form a triangle?

    _____ 26 cm   Set 1

    _____ 11 cm

    (A) _____14 cm

    (B) _____18 cm   Set 2

    (C) _____13 cm

    (D) _____37 cm

18. Two sets of sticks are shown with the measures of their lengths. Which stick in set 2 would you combine with the two sticks in set 1 so they can be joined end-to-end to form a right triangle?

    _____ 8 cm   Set 1

    ___ 6 cm

    (F) _____ 8 cm

    (G) _____ 10 cm Set 2

    (H) _____ 6 cm

    (J) _____ 37 cm

19. Sally says, "If you double a certain number, n, and then add 7 to the result, you obtain 35." Which one of the following equations accurately expresses Sally's original statement?

    (A) $2n + 7 = 35$

    (B) $2n - 7 = 35$

    (C) $n + 7 \times 2 = 35$

    (D) $2(n + 7) = 35$

20. There are 17 students in Mr. Anderson's class. 16 of these students are the same age and the 17th student is 9 years old. Let y represent the age of the 16 students. Which one of the following expressions best describes the total age of the students in Mr. Anderson's class?

    (F) $17y + 9$

    (G) $17(y - 9)$

    (H) $16(y + 9)$

    (J) $16y + 9$

GO TO NEXT PAGE ➡

21. What is the product of $4x - 1$ and $2x + 5$?
  (A) $8x^2 + 18x - 5$
  (B) $8x^2 + 22x - 5$
  (C) $8x^2 - 18x - 5$
  (D) $8x^2 - 20x - 5$

22. Simplify: $(3 + 5) \times 15 - 3$.
  (F) 120
  (G) 117
  (H) 78
  (J) 75

23. Multiply 35% of 140 by 16% of 50.
  (A) 560
  (B) 392
  (C) 39.2
  (D) 56

24. What is 135% of 80?
  (F) 10.8
  (G) 108
  (H) 1,080
  (J) 10,800

25. Pencils are sold in boxes of 24. Mrs. Archibald needs 6 pencils for each of her 22 students. What is the minimum number of boxes that Mrs. Archibald must buy?
  (A) 144
  (B) 132
  (C) 6
  (D) 5

Information for questions 26 to 29
Seven athletes took part in a broad jump. Each athlete competed in two rounds. Here are the distances they jumped in inches.

Athlete's name	Round 1	Round 2
Emelda	88	88
Frank	92	87
George	87	90
Linda	75	67
Maria	83	88
Tricia	79	82
Victor	91	93

26. Which one of the athletes improved the most, from the first to the second round?
  (F) George
  (G) Maria
  (H) Tricia
  (J) Victor

27. On the average, which one of the athletes jumped the longest distance?
  (A) Frank
  (B) George
  (C) Maria
  (D) Victor

GO TO NEXT PAGE ➡

28. What was the average score for the seven athletes in the first round?

(F) 90

(G) 87

(H) 85

(J) 82

29. If Linda's score in the second round were dropped, by how many inches would the average score for the remaining 6 athletes improve?

(A) 88

(B) 75

(C) 5

(D) 3

30. Brenda took 5 tests in the first semester, scoring an average of 64 points. During the second semester, she took 3 tests and scored an average of 55 points. During the third semester, Brenda took 4 tests, scoring an average of 59 points. Approximately what was Brenda's average score per test for the three semesters?

(F) 55

(G) 59

(H) 60

(J) 62

31. If 1 cm³ of loose snow weighs 0.125 gram, how many grams would 1,000,000 cm³ of loose snow weigh?

(A) 1,250,000

(B) 125,000

(C) 125

(D) 0.000000125

32. Solve for y: $5y + 6 = 51$.

(F) 8

(G) 9

(H) 45

(J) 57

33. Find the slope of the line in the graph.

(A) $\dfrac{3}{4}$

(B) $-\dfrac{3}{4}$

(C) $-\dfrac{4}{3}$

(D) $\dfrac{4}{3}$

34. *ABCDEF* in the figure is a regular hexagon (it has 6 congruent sides and 6 congruent angles). Find the sum of all the interior angles of hexagon *ABCDEO*, in thick lines. These angles are marked 1, 2, ... , 6. (*Hint: You may use the dotted lines as a clue.*)

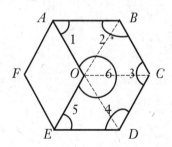

(F) 720°

(G) 540°

(H) 480°

(J) 360°

GO TO NEXT PAGE ➡

35. Find the total area of the 3 <u>visible faces</u> of the cube shown below.

8 cm   8 cm   8 cm

(A) 512 cm²

(B) 384 cm²

(C) 256 cm²

(D) 192 cm²

36. The formula for the area of a circle is πr^2, where r represents the radius of the circle. Find the area of the shaded region in the figure below, if $\pi = 3.14$.

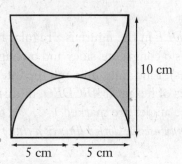

10 cm

5 cm   5 cm

(F) 78.5 cm²

(G) 60.75 cm²

(H) 39.25 cm²

(J) 21.5 cm²

37. One mile equals 1.6 kilometers. If a car travels for 400 miles, how many kilometers were traveled?

(A) 640

(B) 250

(C) 64

(D) 25

38. On a map 1.5 in. represent 45 miles. What is the actual road distance, in miles, between two cities represented by 30 in. on the same map?

(F) 20

(G) 900

(H) 1,350

(J) 9,000

GO TO NEXT PAGE ➡

Information for questions 39 and 40

Adrian participated in a weight exercise program for a period of time. The graph below shows how Adrian's weight changed between January and August of the same year.

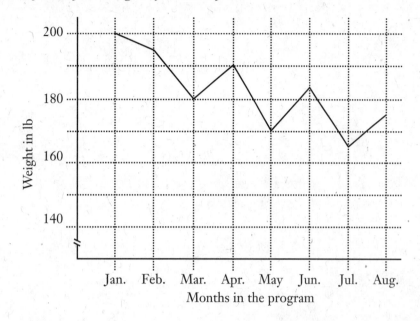

39. What was Adrian's overall weight loss between January and August?

  (A) 25 lbs

  (B) 35 lbs

  (C) 40 lbs

  (D) 60 lbs

40. What was Adrian's average weight loss between February and July?

  (F) 30 lbs

  (G) 25 lbs

  (H) 9 lbs

  (J) 6 lbs

COOP

STOP

COOP

Practice Test 2—Answer Key

Question Number	Correct Answer	If You Answered this Question Incorrectly, Refer to . . .
SUBTEST 1: SEQUENCES		
1.	(B)	P. 422
2.	(H)	P. 422
3.	(A)	P. 422
4.	(J)	P. 422
5.	(A)	P. 422
6.	(H)	P. 422
7.	(B)	P. 422
8.	(G)	P. 422
9.	(D)	P. 422
10.	(H)	P. 422
11.	(C)	P. 422
12.	(F)	P. 422
13.	(D)	P. 422
14.	(J)	P. 422
15.	(B)	P. 422
16.	(F)	P. 422
17.	(B)	P. 422
18.	(H)	P. 422
19.	(C)	P. 422
20.	(F)	P. 422

COOP

Question Number	Correct Answer	If You Answered this Question Incorrectly, Refer to . . .
SUBTEST 2: ANALOGIES		
1.	(D)	P. 227
2.	(H)	P. 227
3.	(C)	P. 227
4.	(H)	P. 227
5.	(A)	P. 227
6.	(H)	P. 227
7.	(C)	P. 227
8.	(F)	P. 227
9.	(B)	P. 227
10.	(H)	P. 227
11.	(A)	P. 227
12.	(G)	P. 227
13.	(C)	P. 227
14.	(G)	P. 227
15.	(D)	P. 227
16.	(F)	P. 227
17.	(C)	P. 227
18.	(G)	P. 227
19.	(C)	P. 227
20.	(G)	P. 227
SUBTEST 3: QUANTITATIVE REASONING		
1.	(D)	P. 417
2.	(F)	P. 417
3.	(C)	P. 417
4.	(F)	P. 417
5.	(B)	P. 417
6.	(H)	P. 417
7.	(A)	P. 417
8.	(C)	P. 418
9.	(G)	P. 418
10.	(A)	P. 418
11.	(J)	P. 418
12.	(B)	P. 418

13.	(H)	P. 418
14.	(C)	P. 418
15.	(D)	P. 421
16.	(F)	P. 421
17.	(B)	P. 421
18.	(J)	P. 421
19.	(C)	P. 421
20.	(H)	P. 421
SUBTEST 4: VERBAL REASONING–WORDS		
1.	(C)	P. 228
2.	(F)	P. 228
3.	(C)	P. 228
4.	(H)	P. 228
5.	(D)	P. 228
6.	(F)	P. 228
7.	(A)	P. 227
8.	(H)	P. 227
9.	(A)	P. 227
10.	(G)	P. 227
11.	(D)	P. 227
12.	(H)	P. 227
13.	(B)	P. 227
14.	(H)	P. 227
15.	(D)	P. 227
16.	(F)	P. 227
17.	(D)	P. 227
18.	(G)	P. 227
19.	(A)	P. 227
20.	(H)	P. 227
SUBTEST 5: VERBAL REASONING–CONTEXTS		
1.	(C)	P. 302
2.	(F)	P. 302
3.	(D)	P. 302
4.	(F)	P. 302
5.	(D)	P. 302
6.	(H)	P. 302
7.	(A)	P. 302

COOP

Question Number	Correct Answer	If You Answered this Question Incorrectly, Refer to . . .
8.	(H)	P. 302
9.	(D)	P. 302
10.	(F)	P. 302
11.	(B)	P. 302
12.	(J)	P. 302
13.	(B)	P. 302
14.	(J)	P. 302
15.	(B)	P. 302
16.	(G)	P. 302
17.	(A)	P. 302
18.	(H)	P. 302
19.	(D)	P. 302
20.	(F)	P. 302
SUBTEST 6: READING AND LANGUAGE ARTS		
1.	(A)	P. 302
2.	(H)	P. 302
3.	(B)	P. 302
4.	(J)	P. 300
5.	(B)	P. 304
6.	(G)	P. 310
7.	(D)	P. 300
8.	(G)	P. 304
9.	(C)	P. 304
10.	(H)	P. 300
11.	(C)	P. 303
12.	(J)	P. 304
13.	(C)	P. 310
14.	(F)	P. 302
15.	(C)	P. 304
16.	(H)	P. 308
17.	(C)	P. 300
18.	(J)	P. 300
19.	(B)	P. 302
20.	(F)	P. 303

COOP

21.	(C)	P. 246
22.	(H)	P. 261
23.	(A)	P. 258
24.	(J)	P. 261
25.	(C)	P. 269
26.	(F)	P. 266
27.	(B)	P. 262
28.	(G)	P. 262
29.	(D)	P. 262
30.	(F)	P. 262
31.	(C)	P. 262
32.	(F)	P. 266
33.	(D)	P. 246
34.	(F)	P. 246
35.	(B)	P. 246
36.	(H)	P. 246
37.	(C)	P. 246
38.	(F)	P. 300
39.	(C)	P. 300
40.	(G)	P. 300

SUBTEST 7: MATHEMATICS

1.	(D)	P. 428
2.	(H)	P. 337, 339
3.	(A)	P. 390
4.	(J)	P. 373, 428
5.	(D)	P. 381, 428
6.	(F)	P. 337, 339
7.	(C)	P. 373, 392
8.	(G)	P. 379
9.	(B)	P. 428
10.	(F)	P. 388, 428
11.	(B)	P. 337, 341
12.	(F)	P. 341, 345
13.	(C)	P. 341, 392
14.	(F)	P. 407
15.	(C)	P. 407
16.	(F)	P. 407

COOP

Question Number	Correct Answer	If You Answered this Question Incorrectly, Refer to . . .
17.	(B)	P. 395
18.	(G)	P. 395
19.	(A)	P. 428
20.	(J)	P. 428
21.	(A)	P. 428
22.	(G)	P. 388, 428
23.	(B)	P. 341, 402
24.	(G)	P. 402
25.	(C)	P. 341
26.	(G)	P. 339
27.	(D)	P. 390
28.	(H)	P. 390
29.	(D)	P. 390
30.	(H)	P. 390
31.	(B)	P. 379
32.	(G)	P. 428
33.	(B)	P. 428
34.	(F)	P. 407
35.	(D)	P. 395
36.	(J)	P. 395, 407
37.	(A)	P. 379
38.	(G)	P. 341
39.	(A)	P. 424
40.	(J)	P. 389

COOP

COOP
SUBTEST 1

Sequences—Detailed Explanations of Answers

1. **(B)** The number of double-rings increases from the right in each set.

2. **(H)** The figures in the first and third sets move clockwise from left to right. The second set figures move counterclockwise. The fourth set figures are counterclockwise.

3. **(A)** The first figure becomes the last; the other figures move one position to the left.

4. **(J)** The dots in each set move clockwise.

5. **(A)** The sets alternate between one dot outside a square and both dots inside the squares.

6. **(H)** The plus sign moves one position to the left, then starts on the far right.

7. **(B)** The first figure in each set is removed; the second and third figures move one position to the left; a new figure becomes the third.

8. **(G)** The first letter in each set is removed; the second and third letters move one position to the left; a new letter becomes the third.

9. **(D)** Each letter in a set becomes the next letter in the alphabet.

10. **(H)** The last letter in each set is removed; the first and second letters move one position to the right; a new letter becomes the first.

11. **(C)** The second and fourth letters are always I; the third letter becomes the first letter.

12. **(F)** The subscripts decrease by one, from right to left, one at a time.

13. **(D)** The subscripts move clockwise around the letters.

14. **(J)** The subscripts decrease by one, from left to right, one at a time.

15. **(B)** The second number in each set is 4 times the first number; the third number is 6 more than the second number.

16. **(F)** The second number in each set is 6 times the first number; the third number is 11 less than the second number.

17. **(B)** The second number in each set is 2 times the first number; the third number is 9 less than the second number.

18. **(H)** The second number in each set is the first number divided by 10; the third number is the second number divided by 2.

19. **(C)** Each set is made up of consecutive prime numbers. The first number of a set is the second number of the previous set.

20. **(F)** The second number in each set is the first number divided by 3; the third number is 2 times the second number.

COOP
SUBTEST 2

Analogies—Detailed Explanations of Answers

1. **(D)** A wing is part of an insect, just as an arm is part of a person **(D)**. Choices **(A)**, hand, and **(B)**, leg, are parts of a person, but the relationship is concerned with the part and then the whole entity. If **(A)** or **(B)** were selected, the analogy would be listing two parts, which does not match the first pair of pictures. Choice **(C)**, flower, may be associated with insects, but it has nothing to do with an "arm."

2. **(H)** Scissors are used to cut paper, just as a chainsaw is used to cut down trees **(H)**. Choice **(F)**, knife, and **(J)**, saw, are additional objects which may be used in cutting, but they are not the objects cut primarily by chainsaws. Choice **(G)**, barrel, is also an incorrect answer choice.

3. **(C)** A mailbox holds letters, just as a change purse holds coins **(C)**. Answer choices **(A)**, stamp, and **(B)**, envelope, are associated with the first pair of pictures, but they have nothing to do with change purse. Choice **(D)**, woman, may carry a change purse, but the relationship is carrier/contents, not carrier/user.

4. **(H)** A finger is where one wears a ring, just as a wrist is where one wears a watch, choice **(H)**. Choice **(F)**, hand, would be incorrect since the picture would need to be an object, what is being worn. Answer choice **(G)**, necklace, is not worn on the wrist; it is worn on the neck. Lastly, choice **(J)**, person, would be incorrect since the picture that is required should relate to ring (which, again, is an object).

5. **(A)** Both books and newspapers are read, just as both pens and pencils **(A)** are used for writing. Choice **(B)**, a paintbrush, is used for painting, not writing, and should not be paired with a pen. Choice **(C)**, a crayon, is generally used for drawing or coloring, also not writing. Lastly, a television, choice **(D)**, is watched, not used as a writing tool.

6. **(H)** An hour glass is an old-fashioned method of telling time, and a digital clock is a modern method of telling time, just as a horse and buggy is an old-fashioned method of transportation and an automobile **(H)** is a modern method. Choices **(F)**, bicycle, and **(J)**, horse, are both methods of transportation, but they are not modern methods—at least

not in comparison to the automobile. A train, choice **(G)**, is a relatively modern mode of transportation, yet notice the picture that it would be compared to—a horse and buggy. Automobile would be a better choice than train in this analogy since automobiles transport nearly the same number of people as horse and buggies did. Trains are for public transportation, and the selection would be incorrect since they carry a greater number of people.

7. **(C)** A baby is a newborn human being, just as a kitten is a cat which has recently been born. Answer choice **(A)**, the picture of the girl, is not how you would picture a grown kitten; this choice is incorrect. Choice **(B)**, dog, would only be correct if the first picture were a puppy, but since it is a kitten, this selection is wrong. Do not let choice **(D)**, lion, confuse you. Lions are cats, but a newborn lion would be pictured as a cub—not a kitten.

8. **(F)** A train conductor operates a train, just as a captain controls a ship **(F)**. Answer choice **(G)**, car, would not be a correct answer choice since the person who ordinarily operates a car is the driver. Answer choice **(H)**, airplane, would also be incorrect since the person who operates an airplane is the pilot. Lastly, motorcycles, answer choice **(J)**, are normally operated by drivers, not captains.

9. **(B)** A camel and a cactus are living things associated with a desert climate, just as a polar bear and a penguin **(B)** are living things associated with a polar climate. Answer choice **(A)**, snowflake, can be associated with the polar climate; however, snowflakes are inanimate objects. The picture that completes the analogy would need to be a living thing. Answer choices **(C)**, lizard, and **(D)**, palm tree, are both associated with warmer weather and would not relate with polar bear (which is of a polar climate).

10. **(H)** A canoe moves through the water by using paddles, just as a sailboat moves through the water by using a sail **(H)**. Answer choices **(F)**, dock, and **(G)**, water, are places that are associated with boats; these two answer choices take no part in the actual movement of the boat through the water. Answer choice **(J)**, yacht, would be incorrect since it is just another type of boat.

11. **(A)** Just as milk is made directly from cows, a book is made up of paper which is taken from a tree. **(D)**, a branch is part of a tree and **(B)** and **(C)** are not made directly from trees.

12. **(G)** An octopus has eight legs and a spider has eight legs just as a dog has four legs and a horse **(G)** has four legs. Answer choices **(F)**, eel, **(H)**, rooster, and **(J)**, crab, are all incorrect since none of these animals has four legs like a dog.

13. **(C)** Just as a lion is found in the name of the flower dandelion, horse is found within the name seahorse. Answer choice **(A)**, flower, would be incorrect since it is not found within the word seahorse. Though similar to the seahorse, answer choices **(B)**, fish, and **(D)**, starfish, would be incorrect since their names are not found in the word seahorse. Be careful not to think that any of these incorrect answers are correct simply because they might be closely associated with the words listed.

14. **(G)** An author uses a pen to write a book, just as an artist uses a paintbrush to create a painting. Answer choice **(F)**, sculpture, is not usually made with a paintbrush. Artists who make sculptures usually use chisels or other such tools. Answer choice **(H)**, pencil, could be

used by both an author and artist; however, the missing picture needs to be what the first picture (the tool) helps in creating. Answer choice (**J**), easel, would be incorrect for the same reason; it might also be a tool for an artist, but the picture needs to be the product.

15. (**D**) A feather pen is an old-fashioned writing implement and a pen is a modern writing implement just as a phonograph is an old-fashioned piece of equipment for playing music and a stereo (**D**) is a modern piece of equipment for playing music. Answer choice (**A**), pencil, is incorrect since the missing picture should be an updated version of the first picture. A record, answer choice (**B**), is an old way of recording music. This answer choice is incorrect since the missing picture needs to be both contemporary and an updated version of the first picture. An old radio, answer choice (**C**), would be incorrect since the missing second picture needs to be a more contemporary version of the first picture.

16. (**F**) A boot is placed on a foot just as glasses are placed on the eyes (**F**). Answer choice (**G**), hand, would be incorrect since the picture that would complete the analogy needs to be the corresponding place where people put their glasses. Answer choice (**H**), eye chart, is used to determine whether glasses are needed or not, but it is also not where a person places glasses. Answer choice (**J**), sock, is associated with boots and feet, but is again, not a location where people normally place their glasses.

17. (**C**) Just as a cowboy uses a lasso to do his job herding animals, so does a butcher use a cleaver (**C**) to cut meat and do his job. Answer choice (**A**), horse, is the usual animal a cowboy rides to herd animals but it is not used by butchers. Answer choice (**B**), sheep, are a kind of meat to be cut, but, they are not used by butchers as a tool. Lastly, answer choice (**D**), gun, is incorrect because butchers do not use guns.

18. (**G**) Glasses for the eyes sounds the same as glasses for drinking, just as the hair on top of a person's head sounds the same as the animal hare (rabbit). Answer choice (**F**), pony tail, is something someone can do with hair; it is not a homonym for hair. Answer choice (**H**), eyes, are what glasses are used for, but it is also not a homonym for hair. A pitcher, answer choice (**J**), is made of glass, but it also does not have anything to do with hair, nor is it a homonym of it.

19. (**C**) In the same way that a frog is an adult tadpole, a butterfly is an adult caterpillar. Answer choices (**A**), leaf, and (**B**), flower, are incorrect since they do not complete the analogy of the butterfly. The missing picture would need to be a young butterfly, or a caterpillar, answer choice (**C**). Answer choice (**D**), worm, is a different type of invertebrate.

20. (**G**) An easel and a paint pallet would be found in an artist's studio just as a test tube and a microscope (**G**) would be found in a scientist's lab. Answer choice (**F**), paintbrush, would be found in the art studio, but the picture that is needed to complete the analogy should be science-related. A scientist, answer choice (**H**), would be found in a laboratory, but the pictures listed in this analogy need to be objects found in the art studio and laboratory, not the people who work there. Answer choice (**J**), clock, is not the best answer choice because it is too vague of an object. A microscope is a more specific piece of equipment for a science lab, so it is the better choice.

Quantitative Reasoning— Detailed Explanations of Answers

1. **(D)** Here 6 is added to each number. 7 plus 6 equals 13, which is the correct answer.

2. **(F)** Here 11 is added to each number. 2 plus 11 equals 13, which is the correct answer.

3. **(C)** Here 5 is subtracted from each number. 7 minus 5 equals 2, which is the correct answer.

4. **(F)** Here 9 is subtracted from each number. 9 minus 9 equals 0, which is the correct answer.

5. **(B)** Here each number is multiplied by 2. 8 times 2 equals 16, which is the correct answer.

6. **(H)** Here each number is multiplied by 4. 9 times 4 equals 36, which is the correct answer.

7. **(A)** Here each number is divided by 3. 15 divided by 3 equals 5, which is the correct answer.

8. **(C)** In this example, 2 out of four boxes are shaded. The fraction $\frac{2}{4}$ can be reduced to $\frac{1}{2}$, which is the correct answer.

9. **(G)** In this example, 2 out of 6 boxes are shaded. The fraction $\frac{2}{6}$ can be reduced to $\frac{1}{3}$, which is the correct answer.

10. **(A)** In this example, 2 half boxes are shaded out of 4 boxes. Since 2 halves equal 1 whole, there is a total of 1 out of 4 boxes shaded. The correct answer is $\frac{1}{4}$.

11. **(J)** In this example, 2 full boxes and 2 half boxes are shaded. Since 2 halves equal 1 whole and 2 plus 1 equals 3, there is a total of 3 out of 6 boxes shaded. The fraction $\frac{3}{6}$ can be reduced to $\frac{1}{2}$, which is the correct answer.

12. **(B)** In this example, 5 out of 8 boxes are shaded. The correct answer is $\frac{5}{8}$.

13. **(H)** In this example, 4 half boxes are shaded. Since 2 halves equal 1 whole, 2 whole boxes out of 8 are shaded. The fraction $\frac{2}{8}$ can be reduced to $\frac{1}{4}$, which is the correct answer.

14. **(C)** In this example, 5 out of 9 boxes are shaded. The correct answer is $\frac{5}{9}$.

15. **(D)** 2 cones are equal to 4 cubes. In this example, the scale is balanced with 2 cubes on one side and 1 cone on the other. 2 cubes are equal to 1 cone.

16. **(F)** 3 cones and 2 cubes are equal to 3 cubes. In this example, the scale is balanced with 1 cube on one side and 3 cones on the other. 1 cube equals 3 cones.

17. **(B)** 3 cones are equal to 3 cubes. In this example, the scale is balanced with 2 cones and 1 cube on one side and 3 cubes on the other. 1 cube is equal to 1 cone.

18. **(J)** 2 cubes are equal to 4 cones. In this example, the scale is balanced with 2 cubes and 1 cone on one side and 5 cones on the other. 2 cones are equal to 1 cube.

19. **(C)** 3 cubes are equal to 4 cones and 1 cube. In this example, the scale is balanced with 2 cones and 3 cubes on one side and 2 cubes and 4 cones on the other. 2 cones are equal to 1 cube.

20. **(H)** 1 cube and 2 cones are equal to 6 cones. In this example, the scale is balanced with 5 cones on one side and 1 cube and 1 cone on the other. 4 cones are equal to 1 cube.

COOP
SUBTEST 4
Verbal Reasoning–Words—Detailed Explanations of Answers

1. **(C)** **Ink.** A pen is useless without ink; ink is a necessary part of a pen. Paper **(A)** is what a pen writes on, but it is not a necessary part of a pen. A pencil **(B)** and a crayon **(D)** are just other writing implements; they are not a part of a pen.

2. **(F)** **Power.** A person cannot use a computer without power; power is a necessary part of a computer. Some computers have game software **(G)** on them, others do not. Even though some people love computer games, they're not a necessary part of a computer. A computer is useful in many ways, even without a printer **(H)**. A CD-ROM **(J)** is a good thing to have, but not all computers have one.

3. **(C)** **Water.** Ice is frozen water. Without water there could be no ice; water is a necessary part of ice. Snow **(A)** and sleet **(B)** are different forms of precipitation. They are often associated with ice, but they are not a part of ice. Sometimes ice looks blue **(D)**, but it is not a necessary part of ice.

4. **(H)** **Paws.** Canines have paws; paws are a part of a canine. A hound **(F)** is a type of canine. They are the same thing, not parts. A cat **(G)** is just another type of animal; it is not a part of a canine. Some canines wear collars **(J)**, but some do not. There are canines without collars; a collar might be a part of a canine, but it is not a necessary part of a canine.

5. **(D)** **Beans.** Coffee is made from beans; without the beans there would be no coffee. A mug **(A)** is a coffee container. It is used to hold coffee, but it is not part of the coffee itself. Tea is just another type of beverage; it is not a part of coffee **(B)**. Some people put sugar in their coffee, but one can have coffee without sugar; it is not a necessary part of coffee **(C)**.

6. **(F)** **Tine.** A fork is composed of a few tines. Tines are a necessary part of a fork. A spoon **(G)** is another type of utensil. It is commonly associated with a fork, but it is not a part of a fork. Some forks are made of metal **(H)**, but not all are, so metal is not a necessary part of a fork. Like the spoon, a chopstick is just another type of utensil, not a part of a fork **(J)**.

7. **(A)** **Sob.** The relationship between whisper/talk/shout is that they show an increasing intensity of the same action. Talk is louder than whisper, and shout is louder than talk. Whimper/cry/sob

575

show the same increase in intensity. Howl **(B)** and yell, **(C)** are other types of actions that a person can do, but they are not the same as whimpering and crying, so they do not show an increase in intensity. Tears **(D)** are what one would shed when crying or sobbing. This analogy contains actions or verbs of increasing intensity, not nouns used or produced during the actions.

8. **(H)** **Scarf.** The relationship between sandals/bathing suit/shorts is that they are summer apparel. Boots/mittens/scarf are winter apparel. All of the items are connected based on their season of use. It may snow during the season one uses boots and mittens, but all of the items need to be clothing items **(F)**. Skis are equipment one uses in the winter; they are not apparel **(G)**. It's true that a shirt is an item of apparel that one wears in the winter, but one wears a shirt in the summer, spring, and fall also, so it is not the best choice for a winter apparel item **(J)**.

9. **(A)** **The Vatican.** The relationship between the Empire State Building/Mount Rushmore/the Golden Gate Bridge is that they are all famous landmarks in the United States. Likewise, the Colosseum, the Leaning Tower of Pisa, and the Vatican are all famous landmarks in Italy. The Great Wall of China **(B)** is a famous landmark, but it is not located in the same country as the other two items. The Empire State Building, Mount Rushmore, and the Golden Gate Bridge are all located in the same country, so the second set of words should also have the same relationship. One might take a vacation **(C)** to all of these places, but the location is a more specific connection. The Statue of Liberty **(D)** is located in the United States, making a good connection with the first three landmarks, but it is not a match with the Colosseum and the Leaning Tower of Pisa.

10. **(G)** **Canal.** The relationship between the iris/retina/cornea is that they are all parts of the eye. Lobe/drum/canal are all parts of the ear. All of these things are connected as parts of specific parts of the body. Seeing is what the eye does **(F)**, and hearing is what the ear does **(J)**, but they are not parts. In this analogy, one is looking for parts of the same whole, not the function of the parts. The parts of the eye and the parts of the ear are parts of the body **(H)**, but this is too broad. Canal, a specific part of the ear, like lobe and drum, is a much better answer.

11. **(D)** **Desks.** The relationship between patients/beds/medicine is that they are things found in a specific place—a hospital. Students/chalk/desks are all things found in a specific place—a school. A hospital **(A)** is the place where the first 3 items are found; it has nothing to do with the second set of words. Doctors **(B)** are found in a hospital (with the first set of words), not a school, like the second set of words. Study **(C)** is an action that students should do in school, but the words listed are items or nouns, not verbs.

12. **(H)** **Team.** The relationship between man/worker/union is of one's role. A man can become a worker and join a union. A boy can be a player and join a team. Baseball **(F)** might be one type of team, but the question is of what can the boy be a part? A boy can be part of a team just as the worker can be a part of a union. Batter **(G)** and catcher **(J)** are types of players, but again the answer needs to be what the player can join, not what type of player he might be.

13. **(B)** **Chair.** The relationship between couch/table/bed is that they are all furniture. A rug, mirror and picture may all be part of a room, but are not considered to be furniture.

14. **(H)** **Wheelbarrow.** The relationship between watering can/hoe/rake is that they are all tools used for gardening. Dirt, a garage, and gloves may all be used while gardening, however, they are not tools.

15. **(D)** **Sneakers.** The relationship between sandals/pumps/loafers is that they are types of shoes. The other items may be worn, but are not shoes.

16. **(F)** **Labrador.** The relationship between collie/poodle/beagle is that they are all types or breeds of dogs.

17. **(D)** **Tomato.** The relationship between chicken noodle/split pea/vegetable is that they are types of soups. Rice, spoon, and bowl are associated with soup, but are not varieties of soup.

18. **(G)** **Turtle.** The relationship between lizard/snake/iguana is that they are all reptiles. The other choices are not.

19. **(A)** **Bat.** The relationship between mitt/base/dugout is that they are associated with baseball. The other choices—puck, club, and volleyball—are related to other sports.

20. **(H)** **Lily.** The relationship between daffodil/carnation/rose is that they are all varieties of flowers. Bouquet, vase, and petal are associated with flowers, but are not types of flowers.

COOP

Verbal Reasoning–Context– Detailed Explanations of Answers

1. **(C)** Joey has at least 5 pets. If you add up the 3 cats and the 2 dogs, you see Joey has at least 5 pets. Even though he doesn't have any birds, he might have more pets, but we know he has at least those 5. The fact that he doesn't have any birds doesn't mean he doesn't like birds **(A)**. There is nothing indicating whether Joey wants more pets **(B)**. He may or may not. Joey's mom is not mentioned, and we have no idea why Joey doesn't have any birds **(D)**.

2. **(F)** Bob's team won the game today. If they hadn't won, they would be out of the tournament, and there would be no reason for Bob to get ready for another game. If they had lost, they would be out of the tournament, and there would be no game to get ready for the next day **(G)**. There is nothing indicating whether Bob enjoys playing **(H)**. We have no reason to suspect that he wants the tournament to end. Basketball is not mentioned, and we have no idea what Bob plans to do in the future, other than play tomorrow's game **(J)**.

3. **(D)** Jack didn't read over the summer. Jack hasn't read anything since 8th grade. It's now September, so he must not have read anything over the summer. We have no idea why Jack didn't read over the summer. We only know that he did not **(A)**. Nothing is mentioned to explain why **(B)**. Also, if he read *Tom Sawyer*, he is able to read **(C)**.

4. **(F)** Jim lost weight. Since the pants that were tight before are loose now and Jim is smiling, it seems likely that he lost some weight. Since Jim was always chubby, and he hadn't worn his favorite pants for a while and was trying them now, it would seem that he was trying them because he hoped they would fit better. He might not like pants that are too tight, but we don't know if he really likes baggy pants **(G)**. There is nothing indicating whether Jim bought any new pants. There is no mention of new pants at all **(H)**. If Jim last wore the pants in the fall because they were too tight, and now they are a little loose, we know he lost weight. We have no reason to suspect that he gained weight **(J)**. Although it is possible that he gained and then lost, there is nothing suggesting this, so it is not the best choice for an answer.

5. **(D)** Mark burnt his mouth. Since the pizza was sizzling and bubbling, we can guess by his reaction that it was too hot and Mark burnt his mouth. There is nothing indicating whether Mark will ever eat pizza again **(A)**. Although it is possible, we have no reason to suspect that he will not eat pizza again. Both **(B)** and **(C)** might be true, but the sizzling and bubbling cheese make **(D)** a stronger choice for an answer. Also, there isn't really anything suggesting the waiter made a mistake.

6. **(H)** Jared likes the trampoline. Since it states that he was disappointed not to get a turn on the trampoline, this is the best answer. Jared would not be disappointed if he did not like the trampoline **(F)**. We have no information that Jared is great on the balance beam **(G)**. The scenario describes three things that Jared did, so he may or may not have done four things at the class **(J)**.

7. **(A)** Kimberly did not plan to buy two hamsters. Since it states that she wanted *a* friend for the hamster she has at home, it implies that Kimberly planned on only buying one hamster. We do not know if Kimberly likes other animals **(B)** or if she wants more hamsters **(C)**. Just because she found the hamsters to be cute does not necessarily mean that teddy-bear hamsters are the cutest type of hamster **(D)**.

8. **(H)** Sal likes at least two vegetables. Since we know that Sal chose peppers and mushrooms for his pizza, this is the best answer. This does not necessarily mean that Sal is a vegetarian **(F)** or that he does not like eggplant **(G)**. The information does not tell us how often he picks peppers and mushrooms **(J)**.

9. **(D)** Carlos has been to New York City at least once. Since it states that Carlos went to New York City last fall with his cousins, this is the best answer. We do not know if Carlos's cousins live near the Empire State Building **(A)**. Just because he went to New York City, we do not know if Carlos visited the Empire State Building **(B)**. While we know that Carlos has more than one cousin, we do not know if he has many cousins **(C)**.

10. **(F)** Samantha remembered a lot about the jelly fish. The scenario tells us that Samantha told her dad much information about the jelly fish when she got home. Just because her dad was impressed, it does not necessarily mean that **(G)** Samantha's dad did not know anything about jelly fish. It states that she saw jelly fish at the aquarium, not at the beach **(H)**. Samantha may or may not have seen **(J)** any sharks.

11. **(B)** Eric did not get the color gumball he wanted. Since it states that a big red gumball came out so he put in another quarter, it implies that he did not want that color. This rules out Eric likes red gumballs the best **(C)**, as well. Because it also states that Eric crossed his fingers we know that he was hoping for something. He did not necessarily want many gumballs **(A)** or chew them all **(D)**.

12. **(J)** Jillian thinks baked chicken is healthier than chicken nuggets. Since it states that Jillian wanted to make the healthiest lunch, this is the best answer. Just because Jillian selected the baked chicken, salad, and an apple in this scenario it does not mean that Jillian never eats food that is fried **(F)**. We have no reason to think that Jillian was not very hungry that day **(G)**. Jillian likely thinks that **some** of the food in the cafeteria is unhealthy, but not **all** based on her choice to eat there **(H)**.

13. **(B)** The sun was in Mei's eyes. This is the best answer since it states that Mei needed to shield her eyes. We do not know if Mei is short for a volleyball player **(A)**. Mei's team may or may not have lost the game **(B)**. We do not know if the other players were upset **(D)**.

14. **(J)** Jake did not get the football game as a present. Since it states that when Jake got to the store, they were out of the football game he wanted we know that he did not receive that game. Jake may or may not have bought a different football game **(F)**. There is no information to tell us if Jake was happy with his presents **(G)** or if he went back to the store a week later **(H)**.

15. **(B)** The roses were not pink. Since it states that Suzanne left with some carnations and lilies and that her grandmother loves pink flowers, we can conclude that the roses were not pink. However, they may not have been white **(D)**. The lilies may or may not have been the prettiest **(A)**. There is no information to tell us if her grandmother loved the flowers **(C)**.

16. **(G)** Caroline likes at least four types of music. Since it states that she has CDs that are country, punk, rap, and pop, this represents four types of music. This does not necessarily mean that she has a big CD collection **(F)**. Simply because she listens to them in her car does not mean that Caroline does not listen to CDs at home **(H)**. We do not know if she does not like rock music **(J)**.

17. **(A)** Patrick planned to call his friends. Since it states that Patrick does not know where to meet his friends and he checked to make sure he had his cell phone on him before he headed out, this is the best answer. There is no information on where he looked first **(B)** or that tells us that Patrick's phone was ringing **(C)**. He may or may not like to talk on the phone **(D)**.

18. **(H)** Kyle's team lost the game. This is the best answer since it states that he does not like to lose and that Kyle threw his sneakers into his locker and slammed the door shut. This does not necessarily mean that Kyle was anxious to get home after the game **(F)**. It states that there were really good players on both team, which does not imply that the other team had better players **(G)**. We do not know if Kyle does not like to play dodge ball **(J)**.

19. **(D)** Christina likes chocolate. We know that this is true, because if she did not like chocolate she would not have ordered chocolate sauce and chocolate sprinkles. Just because she ordered vanilla ice cream, it does not mean that she likes this flavor the most **(A)**. There is no information to support that Christina is allergic to peanuts **(B)** or that Christina does not like strawberry sauce **(C)**.

20. **(F)** Sam visited the Space Needle. Since it states that the Space Needle is a very tall building and that Sam thought the view from the top was worth the long drive, this is the best answer. The Space Needle may or may not be Seattle's biggest attraction **(G)**. There is no information regarding who drove the car on their trip **(H)** or how often Sam's family takes long drives **(J)**.

Reading and Language Arts— Detailed Explanations of Answers

1. **(A)** The last sentence of the first paragraph says that the Shakers were a religious community. Although the Shakers made furniture they were not a furniture company **(B)**. They did a shaking dance but were not a dance troupe **(C)**. Although the founders came from England and called the leader "Mother Ann," they weren't a family **(D)**.

2. **(H)** The second paragraph explains that the group was called the Shakers because of the dance they did. Shaker funiture is called that because it was made by the Shakers **(F)**, not the other way around. **(G)** and **(H)** are true but are unrelated to the name Shakers.

3. **(B)** The last paragraph discusses Shaker furniture and its emphasis on quality and simplicity. The passage states that Shaker furniture wasnot elaborately decorated **(A)**. The passage does not mention cost **(C)** and **(D)**.

4. **(J)** The passage discusses the Shakers and their furniture. It doesn't try to recruit new members **(F)**, or explain why the Shakers no longer exist **(G)**. Although the passage talks about furniture, it does not mention quilts **(H)**.

5. **(B)** The author seems to have a strong interest in advising teachers; many sentences and clauses in the passage begin with "Teachers must. . ." and "Teachers should. . ." The passage does hot address students **(A)** or parents **(C)**. Because the passage is advising teachers on how to run their classrooms, the advice does not really apply to substitute teachers **(D)**, who don't have their own classes.

6. **(G)** "Cognizant" means aware. Ignorant **(J)** is the opposite of cognizant. Choices **(F)** and **(H)** are unrelated.

7. **(D)** In this passage the author is arguing that teachers should help their students develop their powers of free speech. The passage does say that children should be involved in the decisions

and problem solving of the classroom, but children making the classroom rules (A) and solving their own arguments (B) are not the main focus of the passage. The passage does not mention voting (C).

8. **(G)** In the second sentence of the passage the author states that free speech has developed over time, not the opposite (F). The author doesn't say that free speech only exists in the U.S. (H). The entire passage argues that free speech can be taught in the classroom (J).

9. **(C)** The first two sentences of the passage establish that research and investigation are the most important parts of a ease. There is no evidence for choice (A) in the passage. The judge does receive a trial memorandum (B), but this has nothing to do with the winning or losing of a case. The passage does mention strong and weak points (D), but this is not why cases are won or lost before court.

10. **(H)** This passage discusses the work done by lawyers before they present the case. It does not mention biases of the legal system (F) and (G), nor does it cover the work lawyers do once they are in court (J).

11. **(C)** The passage does not say that lawyers meet with the judge before the case is in court. The passage does describe reading books and articles (A), meeting with witnesses (B), and considering calling expert witnesses (D).

12. **(J)** This passage is for the average public because it explains, in non-technical language, what lawyers do to prepare a case. Lawyers (F) and judges (G) would not need this process explained to them. The passage does not give advice or instructions to the reader, making it unlikely that the passage is intended for those involved in lawsuits (H).

13. **(C)** "Dissonance" most nearly means disagreement. Agreement (D) is the opposite. Happiness (A) and anger (B) are unrelated to dissonance.

14. **(F)** The first sentence of the second paragraph lists learning theorists and what they stress: humanists stress the affective domain (F), behaviorists stress behavior (G), and cognitivists stress cognition (H). Dissonance (J), discussed a few lines later, is not a type of learning theorist.

15. **(C)** This passage is probably aimed at teachers because it explains different theories while assuming some knowledge of the subject. It also gives advice on what the teacher should do. Learning theorists (A) would not need the explanations in this paragraph. This passage would not be for language theorists (B) because it discusses learning theory, not language theory. The reading leve of this passage is too difficult for students (D), and it also describes what teachers should do to help students, not what the students themselves should do.

16. **(H)** The author seems to feel quite strongly about the ideas he or she is presenting in the passage. The first paragraph is about how important this topic is, and this importance is stressed in the second paragraph as well. The author of this paragraph is arguing for a certain kind of teaching; therefore, he or she is interested in the topic (F), has a strong opinion about it (J), and has definite ideas about how teachers should teach (G).

17. **(C)** The author gives the topic of the passage from the very first sentence. The passage is about the role of imitation in learning to talk, but does not describe how children learn to talk (A), first words (B), or how to teach a child to talk (D).

18. **(J)**   The author wrote this passage to explain how imitation works for a child learning to talk. The passage does not give directions to parents **(F)** or teachers **(G)**. We can infer from the passage that it is very important that children do imitate their parents; therefore **(H)** is incorrect.

19. **(B)**   The last sentence of the passage says that a child only imitates structures that he or she has already come up with on her or his own. Thus, imitation is not as simple a behavior as researchers had thought. It seems that a child must know or understand a structure to imitate it; therefore, **(A)** and **(C)** are false. In the last sentence, spontaneous speech is set up as the opposite of imitation **(D)**.

20. **(F)**   The passage does not say that a child adds to what an adult has said. Slobin and Welsh call the imitation a reconstruction **(G)**. Brown and Bellugi say that imitation resembles spontaneous speech **(H)**. Shipley says that imitation aids the child's comprehension **(J)**.

21. **(C)**   The verb must be past tense to agree with "returned."

22. **(H)**   The relationship is cause and effect.

23. **(A)**   The statement implies more than two flowers being compared.

24. **(J)**   The relationship is cause and effect.

25. **(C)**   The pronoun "your" is used for possession.

26. **(F)**   The sentence implies that the outcome was not to be expected, so "although" is the correct choice.

27. **(B)**   **(A)** is a run-on sentence; **(C)** and **(D)** are not sentences.

28. **(G)**   **(F)** is impossibly awkward, **(H)** is not a sentence, and **(J)** is a run-on sentence.

29. **(D)**   **(A)** is impossibly awkward, **(B)** is a comma splice, and **(C)** is not a sentence.

30. **(F)**   **(G)** is a run-on sentence; **(H)** and **(J)** are not sentences.

31. **(C)**   **(A)** is a run-on sentence; **(B)** and **(D)** are not sentences.

32. **(F)**   **(G)** and **(J)** are not sentences, and **(H)** is a run-on sentence.

33. **(D)**   **(A)**, **(B)**, and **(C)** have conflicting tenses within the sentence.

34. **(F)**   **(G)** has conflicting tenses; **(H)** contains "to got," and **(J)** contains "have took."

35. **(B)**   **(A)** contains "brang," **(C)** contains "shouldn't of," and **(D)** has conflicting tenses.

36. **(H)**   **(F)** contains "taked," and **(G)** and **(J)** have conflicting tenses.

37. **(C)**   **(A)** contains "should of," and **(B)** and **(D)** contain conflicting tenses.

38. **(F)**   The paragraph contrasts the concerns of the northern and southern states.

39. **(C)**   The paragraph stresses that the circulatory system carries things through the body.

40. **(G)**   The focus is only on poisonous plants, and it stresses self-defense.

COOP
SUBTEST 7

Mathematics—Detailed
Explanations of Answers

1. **(D)** Subtract 8 from both sides of the equation: $4q + 8 - 8 = 16 - 8$; so $4q = 8$. Divide both sides by 4: $\dfrac{4q}{4} = \dfrac{8}{4}$; so $q = 2$.

2. **(H)** Mr. Matthews' total earnings for the first 4 days was ($125 + $115 + $118 + $123) = $481. His earnings for Friday must be $591 − $481 = $110.

3. **(A)** Mary's total test score for the 5 tests is $88 \times 5 = 440$. The subtotal for the first 4 tests is (82 + 93 + 79 + 90) = 344. The missing score must be 440 − 344 = 96.

4. **(J)** The 6 is two places to the right of the decimal point. So it is in the hundredths position, that is, 6 hundredths.

5. **(D)** In order to recover the original number, we must undo the effect of multiplication, by dividing $8.47265 \div 100 = 0.0847265$. Now we must perform the division that Martha should have performed: $0.0847265 \div 100 = 0.000847265$.

6. **(F)** In order to recover the original number, let us undo the effect of addition: $15 - 34 = -19$. Now we can perform the subtraction, which Dwayne should have performed: $-19 - 34 = -53$.

7. **(C)** First, find $\sqrt{36}$: $\sqrt{36} = 6$. The correct order is 36, $\sqrt{36}$, 3.6.

8. **(G)** Tamara's total earnings for the 20 hours is $4.75 \times 20 = $95.

9. **(B)** $-2u + 3v = -2(5) + 3(3) = -10 + 9 = -1$.

10. **(F)** $(3xy)^2 = 3^2 x^2 y^2 = 9(-3)^2(2)^2 = 9 \times 9 \times 4 = 324$.

11. **(B)** The number of books in the 6 full boxes is $6 \times 9 = 54$. The total number of books that Raymond received is 54 + 2 = 56.

12. **(F)** The total number of marbles in the 7 full boxes is $7 \times 15 = 105$. Each of the 12 students would receive $105 \div 12 = 8$, remainder 9. The number of additional marbles that Mrs. White must collect is $12 - 9 = 3$.

13. **(C)** Let n represent the smaller of the two multiples of 7. Then the next larger multiple of 7 must be $n + 7$, and the sum of these two multiples of 7 is $n + (n + 7)$ or $2n + 7$. The square of 6 is $6 \times 6 = 36$. Since $2n + 7$ is 1 less than 36, then: $2n + 7 = 36 - 1$ or $2n + 7 = 35$. Let us add -7 to both sides of the equation: $2n + 7 - 7 = 35 - 7$, or $2n = 28$. Divide both sides by 2: $\frac{2n}{2} = \frac{28}{2}$. So the smaller multiple of 7 is $n = 14$ and the larger one is $n + 7 = 14 + 7 = 21$.

14. **(F)** The whole angle below $\overline{AB}$ measures $180°$. So $2x + 7x = 180$, or $9x = 180$. (We can safely ignore the degree sign.) Divide both sides of the equation by 9: $\frac{9x}{9} = \frac{180}{9}$, which shows that $x = 20$.

15. **(C)** The sum of the measures of the exterior angle ABE and the (unmarked) interior angle ABC is $180°$. (Angles ABE and ABC are supplementary.) So the measure of interior angle ABC is $180° - 148° = 32°$. The sum of interior angles BAC, ACB, and ABC is $40° + v° + 32° = 180°$. So $v + 72 = 180$ (we shall ignore the degree sign). Add -72 to both sides: $v + 72 - 72 = 180 - 72$, or $v = 108$.

16. **(F)** When two straight lines intersect at one point, the vertically opposite angles so formed are congruent. Hence, $y = 42$.

17. **(B)** Recall that the sum of the measures of any two sides of a triangle must be greater than the measure of the third side. The straw shown in **(B)** is the only one that can be combined with the two in set 1 to meet this requirement. **(D)** 37 cm would be too big for the triangle.

18. **(G)** Pythagoras' theorem states that the sum of the squares of the measures of the two shorter sides of a right triangle equals the square of the measure of the longest side. The stick in **(G)** is the only one that can be grouped with the two in set 1 to meet this requirement.

19. **(A)** If we doubled n and added 7 to the result, you would obtain $2n + 7$. So $2n + 7 = 35$.

20. **(J)** The total age of the first 16 students is $16 \times y = 16y$. The total age of the 17 students is $16y + 9$.

21. **(A)** Multiply each term in $4x - 1$ by each term in $2x + 5$, and collect terms: $(4x - 1)(2x + 5) = 8x^2 + 18x - 5$.

22. **(G)** $(3 + 5) \times 15 - 3 = 8 \times 15 - 3 = 120 - 3 = 117$.

23. **(B)** First calculate 35% of 140: $\frac{35 \times 140}{100} = 49$. Next, calculate 16% of 50: $\frac{16 \times 50}{100} = 8$. Finally, multiply 49 by 8: $49 \times 8 = 392$.

24. **(G)** 135% of 80 is $\frac{135 \times 80}{100} = 108$.

25. (C) The total number of pencils needed is $22 \times 6 = 132$. At 24 pencils per full box, the number of boxes that will hold 132 pencils must be $132 \div 24 = 5.5$. Since pencils are sold only in full boxes, Mrs. Archibald must buy 6 boxes.

26. (G) First, calculate the improvement for each athlete (all figures are in inches): George—$90 - 87 = 3$, Maria—$88 - 83 = 5$, Tricia—$82 - 79 = 3$, and Victor—$93 - 91 = 2$. From these figures, we see that Maria showed the most improvement.

27. (D) Begin by computing the athlete's total scores (all figures are in inches): Frank—$92 + 87 = 179$, George—$87 + 90 = 177$, Maria—$83 + 88 = 171$, and Victor—$91 + 93 = 184$. These figures indicate that Victor jumped the longest distance. (Notice that it was not necessary to compute the actual averages, since the ranking would remain unchanged if we divided all the totals by 2 to find the averages.)

28. (H) The average score for the 7 athletes in the first round is $(88 + 92 + 87 + 75 + 83 + 79 + 91) \div 7 = 595 \div 7 = 85$.

29. (D) First calculate the average score, with Linda's score included, for the second round: $(88 + 87 + 90 + 67 + 88 + 82 + 93) \div 7 = 595 \div 7 = 85$. Next, compute the average score, without Linda's score: $(88 + 87 + 90 + 88 + 82 + 93) \div 6 = 528 \div 6 = 88$. (Remember that, without Linda, there are only 6 athletes.) So the increase in the average score is $88 - 85 = 3$ in.

30. (H) Begin by computing the total score for each semester: total score for semester 1—$64 \times 5 = 320$, total score for semester 2—$55 \times 3 = 165$, and total score for semester 3—$59 \times 4 = 236$. The total score for semesters 1, 2, and 3 is $320 + 165 + 236 = 721$. Since Brenda took $5 + 3 + 4 = 12$ tests, her average score for the 3 semesters is $721 \div 12 = 60.083$, which can be rounded to 60.

31. (B) Multiply 0.125 by 1,000,000: $0.125 \times 1,000,000 = 125,000$.

32. (G) Add -6 to both sides of the equation: $5y + 6 - 6 = 51 - 6$, so $5y = 45$. Divide both sides by 6: $\frac{5y}{5} = \frac{45}{5}$, so $y = 9$.

33. (B) The graph intersects the y-axis at 3 points from the 0 position and the x-axis at 4 points from the 0 position. Observing that the line is left-inclined (running from upper left to lower right), we see that the slope of the line is $-\frac{3}{4}$. (The slope is negative because the line is left-inclined.)

34. (F) (The numbering of the angles only serves to indicate precisely which angles to focus on, and the information that $ABCDEF$ is a regular hexagon is irrelevant.) It would be wise, however, to make use of the hint, which reminds us that concave hexagon $ABCDEO$ consists of the 4 triangles AOB, BOC, COD, and DOE. The sum of the measures of the interior angles of hexagon $ABCDEO$ must equal the sum of the measures of the interior angles of triangles AOB, BOC, COD, and DOE. Remember that the sum of the measures of the three interior angles of any triangle is $180°$. So the sum of the interior angles of these 4 triangles is $180° \times 4 = 720°$.

COOP

35. **(D)** Since the 6 faces of any cube are congruent, their areas must also be congruent. So, to compute the area of the three visible faces of a cube, we need only to compute the area of one face and multiply it by 3: The area of 1 face is 8 cm × 8 cm = 64 cm². So the area of 3 faces is 3 × 64 cm² = 192 cm².

36. **(J)** The boundary of the composite picture is a square and the unshaded regions are semi-circles. Compute the area of the whole square: The total width of the square is 5 cm + 5 cm = 10 cm. So the area of the square is 10 cm × 10 cm = 100 cm². The radius of each semicircle is 5 cm. The combined areas of the two semicircles would be equal to the area of one full circle with the same radius. Thus, the combined areas of the semicircles is $\pi r^2 = 3.14 \times 5^2 = 3.14 \times 25 = 78.5$ cm². Hence, the area of the shaded region is 100 cm² − 78.5 cm² = 21.5 cm².

37. **(A)** If 1 mile equals 1.6 kilometers, then 400 miles = 1.6 × 400 = 640 kilometers.

38. **(G)** If 1.5 in. represents 45 miles, then 30 in. must represent $\dfrac{30 \times 45}{1.5}$ = 900 miles.

39. **(A)** The quickest way to compute Adrian's weight loss between January and August is to subtract his weight in August from his weight in January: 200 lbs − 175 lbs = 25 lbs (Of course, we could also find the overall weight loss by subtracting the intermediate losses and adding the intermediate gains. You can verify that this would yield the same result but waste time.)

40. **(J)** The fastest way to compute Adrian's average weight loss between February and July is to subtract his weight in July from his weight in February and divide by 5: (195 lbs − 165 lbs) ÷ 5 = 30 ÷ 5 = 6 lbs. To check this shortcut, do this (ignore the pound sign; make gains + and losses −):

Period	Weight Change
February to March	195 − 180 = −15
March to April	180 − 190 = +10
April to May	190 − 170 = −20
May to June	170 − 185 = +15
June to July	185 − 165 = −20
Total weight change	−30

So, the average weight loss = 30 lbs ÷ 5 = 6 lbs, as obtained by the shortcut method.

TACHS
PRACTICE TEST 2

TACHS
SUBTEST 1

Reading

Time: Unspecified
50 Questions

> **DIRECTIONS:** Questions 1–20 comprise the Vocabulary portion of the Reading test. Read each phrase or sentence to determine the word choice that most nearly means the same as that word.

1. <u>Infer</u> the meaning
   (A) define
   (B) suppose
   (C) include
   (D) complicate

2. He was <u>livid</u>
   (J) inconclusive
   (K) energetic
   (L) mournful
   (M) furious

3. An <u>incredulous</u> look
   (A) wonderful
   (B) understanding
   (C) unbelieving
   (D) truthful

4. <u>Verify</u> the answer
   (J) confirm
   (K) disprove
   (L) assume
   (M) dispute

5. A <u>lethargic</u> way of walking
   (A) angry
   (B) joyful
   (C) tired
   (D) loose

6. <u>Pounce</u> on the toy mouse
   (J) collapse
   (K) repel
   (L) slumber
   (M) leap

GO TO NEXT PAGE

TACHS

7. Vilify his opponent
   (A) compliment
   (B) anger
   (C) criticize
   (D) reduce

8. Proficient at guitar playing
   (J) carefree
   (K) expert
   (L) incompetent
   (M) confused

9. Probe for answers
   (A) rely on
   (B) officially state
   (C) liberate
   (D) investigate

10. Disintegrate the pieces
    (J) collapse
    (K) compress
    (L) grind
    (M) circulate

11. A permanent loss
    (A) exuberant
    (B) lasting
    (C) fleeting
    (D) obvious

12. Serene music
    (J) agitated
    (K) translucent
    (L) calm
    (M) chaotic

13. Relish these memories
    (A) appreciate
    (B) dislike
    (C) destroy
    (D) refurbish

14. A bashful child
    (J) joyous
    (K) anxious
    (L) waning
    (M) timid

15. Sway his opinion
    (A) counter
    (B) manipulate
    (C) dissolve
    (D) retract

16. Assertive personality
    (J) forceful
    (K) mournful
    (L) timid
    (M) static

17. Trivial information
    (A) enduring
    (B) current
    (C) essential
    (D) insignificant

18. Contrary opinions
    (J) similar
    (K) differing
    (L) quiet
    (M) superb

19. Resembles his brother
    (A) frightens
    (B) puts together
    (C) looks like
    (D) transfers

20. A tragic story
    (J) joyous
    (K) thrilling
    (L) humorous
    (M) unfortunate

GO TO NEXT PAGE ➡

TACHS

DIRECTIONS: Questions 21–50 comprise the Reading Comprehension portion of the Reading test. Each passage is followed by questions based on its content. After reading the passage, choose the best answer for each question.

Questions 21–25 are based on the following passage.

The first child labor laws were enacted in England through the efforts of those members of Parliament whose hearts were wrung by the condition of the little parish apprentices bound out to the early textile manufacturers of the north. Through the long years they were required to build up the code of child labor legislation which England now possesses. Knowledge of the labor conditions has always preceded effective legislation. The efforts of that small number in every community who believe in legislative control have always been reinforced by the efforts of trade unionists rather than by the efforts of employers. This is partly because the employment of workingmen in the factories brings them in contact with the children who tend to earn lower wages and demoralize their trades and partly because workingmen have no money or time to spend for alleviating philanthropy, and must seize upon agitation and legal enactment as the only channel of redress which is open to them.

We may illustrate by imagining a row of people seated in a moving streetcar into which darts a boy of eight, calling out the details of the last murder, in the hope of selling an evening newspaper. A comfortable-looking man buys a paper from him with no sense of moral shock; he may even be a trifle complacent that he has helped along the little fellow, who is making his way in the world. The philanthropic lady sitting next to him may perhaps reflect that it is a pity that such a bright boy is not in school. She may make up her mind in a moment of compunction to redouble her efforts for various newsboys' schools and homes, that this poor child may have better teaching. Next to her sits a workingman trained in trade union methods. He knows that the boy's natural development is arrested, and that the abnormal activity of his body and mind uses up the force which should go into growth, moreover, that this premature use of his powers has but a momentary and specious value. He is forced to those conclusions because he has seen many a man, entering the factory at eighteen and twenty, so worn out by premature work that he was "laid on the shelf" within ten or fifteen years. He knows very well that he can do nothing in the way of ameliorating the lot of this particular boy; his only possible chance is to agitate for proper child-labor laws, to regulate, and if possible prohibit, street-vending by children, in order that the child of the poorest may have his school time secured to him and may have at least his short chance for growth.

TACHS

GO TO NEXT PAGE

21. The primary purpose of the passage is to show
    (A) that the only way to end child labor is through law.
    (B) that children learn more by working than they would in school.
    (C) that children can work full time and study at night.
    (D) that schools should teach children job skills.

22. Trade unionists agitate for laws against child labor because
    (J) they work in factories and they see the harm factories do to children.
    (K) factory owners pay everyone less when they hire children.
    (L) they know that the only way to end child labor is with child labor laws.
    (M) All of the above.

23. The author of the passage is against child labor because
    (A) she believes children are not responsible enough to work.
    (B) she believes the United States should follow England's lead in making laws against child labor.
    (C) she believes children should have the chance to go to school.
    (D) All of the above.

24. The author makes all of the following arguments against child labor EXCEPT that
    (J) it stunts children's growth.
    (K) it demoralizes the trades.
    (L) it takes away jobs from adults.
    (M) England has already abolished child labor.

25. In the last sentence of the passage, the word "ameliorating" is used to mean
    (A) calling attention to.
    (B) improving.
    (C) showing.
    (D) understanding.

Questions 26–30 are based on the following passage.

The primary aim of comedy is to amuse us with a happy ending; although comedies can vary according to the attitudes they project, which can be broadly identified as either high or low, terms having nothing to do with an evaluation of the play's merit. Generally, the amusement found in comedy comes from an eventual victory over threats or ill fortune. Much of the dialogue and plot development might be laughable, yet a play need not be funny to be comic. In fact, some critics in the Renaissance era thought that the highest form of comedy should elicit no laughter at all from its audience. A comedy that forced its audience into laughter failed in the highest comic endeavor, whose purpose was to amuse as subtly as possible. Note that Shakespeare's comedies themselves were often under attack for their appeal to laughter.

GO TO NEXT PAGE

Farce is low comedy intended to make us laugh by means of a series of exaggerated, unlikely situations that depend less on plot and character than on gross absurdities, sight gags, and coarse dialogue. The "higher" a comedy goes, the more natural the characters seem and the less boisterous their behavior. The plots become more sustained, and the dialogue shows more weighty thought. As with all dramas, comedies are about things that go wrong. Accordingly, comedies create deviations from accepted normalcy, presenting problems which we might or might not see as harmless. If these problems make us judgmental about the involved characters and events, the play takes on the features of satire, a rather high comic form implying that humanity and human institutions are in need of reform. If the action triggers our sympathy for the characters, we feel even less protected from the incongruities as the play tilts more in the direction of tragicomedy. In other words, the action determines a figurative distance between the audience and the play. Such factors as characters' personalities and the plot's predictability influence this distance. The farther away we sit, the more protected we feel and usually the funnier the play becomes. Closer proximity to believability in the script draws us nearer to the conflict, making us feel more involved in the action and less safe in its presence.

26. According to the passage, a play is called a comedy if it
   (J) is funny.
   (K) has a happy ending.
   (L) is absurd.
   (M) has funny characters.

27. A comedy is called a farce if it
   (A) is exaggerated.
   (B) is high comedy.
   (C) makes people think.
   (D) is funny.

28. A comedy is called a satire if it
   (J) is high comedy.
   (K) is low comedy.
   (L) criticizes humanity and human institutions.
   (M) is predictable but funny.

29. According to the passage, the more believable a comedy is
   (A) the funnier it is.
   (B) the more involved and less safe the audience feels.
   (C) the more harmless it is to the audience.
   (D) the closer to Shakespeare's comedies it is.

30. The main purpose of this passage is
   (J) to explain the different types of comedies and how they work.
   (K) to argue that comedies are more enjoyable than tragedies.
   (L) to prove that Shakespeare' s comedies are the best ever written.
   (M) to explain figurative distance.

TACHS

GO TO NEXT PAGE ➡

Questions 31–35 are based on the following passage.

[1] The beautiful Painted Lady butterfly is one of the most *prevalent* butterflies on Earth. [2] They can be found on several continents, such as North America, Asia, Europe, and Africa. [3] The Painted Lady endures an amazing transformation from egg to butterfly. [4] This change is known as *metamorphosis*. [5] The life cycle of a butterfly is fascinating to study. [6] Each spring female butterflies lay their eggs on the leaves of plants such as thistles, hollyhocks, and nettle bushes. [7] A female butterfly chooses these host plants which will serve as food for the baby caterpillars that will emerge from her eggs. [8] The very hungry *larva* will use its powerful jaws to consume a great amount of food in a short amount of time. [9] As the caterpillar eats and grows, it will shed its skin several times, before it forms its *chrysalis*. [10] In this state, the creature hangs from a thin silky thread for approximately two weeks. [11] A few hours after emerging from its chrysalis wet and crumpled, the Painted Lady spreads its wings to take flight. [12] Soon the life cycle will begin again.

31. According to the passage, *prevalent* likely means which of the following?
    (A) limited
    (B) common
    (C) stunning
    (D) scarce

32. Which of the following statements expresses an opinion?
    (J) Sentence 5
    (K) Sentence 6
    (L) Sentence 8
    (M) Sentence 11

33. According to the passage, what is the purpose of the host plants?
    (A) To make an attractive garden
    (B) To provide food for the butterflies
    (C) To protect the caterpillars from predators
    (D) To serve as food for the caterpillars

34. Which of the following is a name for the young caterpillar?
    (J) larva
    (K) chrysalis
    (L) metamorphosis
    (M) consume

35. Which of these titles best fits this passage?
    (A) The Life Cycle of a Painted Lady
    (B) How to Attract Butterflies
    (C) How Caterpillars Grow
    (D) Butterflies Around the World

GO TO NEXT PAGE ➡

TACHS

Questions 36–40 are based on the following passage.

[1] George Washington took charge of the American army outside of Boston in June of 1775. [2] The thousands of soldiers he took command of had little formal military training, but yet had defeated the British troops in Boston at the battles of Bunker Hill and Lexington and Concord. [3] However, the British would prove to be a much tougher challenge in the years ahead.

[4] By the end of 1776, the American army under General George Washington was in trouble. [5] Defeats on Long Island and Manhattan and New Jersey had driven his small force southward across the temporary safety of the Delaware River. [6] Fortunately, the British army under Cornwallis *did not press its advantage*, instead retreating to winter quarters in New York City and leaving a smaller force of Hessian soldiers to guard the town of Trenton and watch the Americans across the river.

[7] Facing the end of many of his soldier's enlistments, Washington decided to attack the Hessian outpost while he still had an army to command. [8] At *dusk* on December 25, he gathered his army and crossed the Delaware River into New Jersey. [9] By *dawn*, the Americans were approaching the Hessian guards at Trenton. [10] Using cannons and bayonet charges, the Americans attacked directly into the town, forcing the Hessians to surrender in large numbers. [11] An American victory had been achieved.

[12] While the American army would face five more years of fighting against the British, they had survived a difficult year with two important victories. [13] Their *morale* was high and Washington's legacy as a military leader was much improved.

36. In the passage above, "the British army under Cornwallis *did not press its advantage*" refers to which of the following?
    (J) The British army could have maintained its command by keeping a larger force of soldiers.
    (K) The American army had the advantage, but lost it when it reached the Delaware.
    (L) Cornwallis and the British army held fast to their advantage over the American army.
    (M) The small force of Hessian soldiers was a sufficient group to face the Americans.

37. The words *dusk* and *dawn* are examples of which of the following?
    (A) homophones
    (B) synonyms
    (C) antonyms
    (D) homonyms

38. Based on this passage, with five years remaining in the war, General George Washington can be described as which of the following?
    (J) a highly successful leader
    (K) an unsuccessful leader
    (L) well-liked by his soldiers
    (M) a fairly successful leader

GO TO NEXT PAGE ➡

TACHS

39. In the passage above, *morale* most nearly means, which of the following?

(A) friendship

(B) confidence

(C) resentment

(D) anxiety

40. Who is likely to be the audience of this passage?

(J) soldiers

(K) teachers

(L) students

(M) generals

Questions 41–45 are based on the following poem by William Wordsworth.

I Wandered Lonely As a Cloud

I wandered lonely as a cloud
That floats on high o'er vales and hills,
When all at once I saw a crowd,
A host, of golden daffodils;
Beside the lake, beneath the trees,
Fluttering and dancing in the breeze.

Continuous as the stars that shine
And twinkle on the milky way,
They stretched in never-ending line
Along the margin of a bay:
Ten thousand saw I at a glance,
Tossing their heads in sprightly dance.

The waves beside them danced; but they
Out-did the sparkling waves in glee:
A poet could not but be gay,
In such a *jocund* company:
I gazed - and gazed - but little thought
What wealth the show to me had brought:

For oft, when on my couch I lie
In vacant or in pensive mood,
They flash upon that inward eye
Which is the bliss of solitude;
And then my heart with pleasure fills,
And dances with the daffodils.

41. What is the mood of the poem?

(A) angry

(B) joyful

(C) anxious

(D) mournful

42. What does *they* refer to in the line "They stretched in never-ending line?"

(J) clouds

(K) dancers

(L) stars

(M) daffodils

 GO TO NEXT PAGE

43. "Tossing their heads in sprightly dance" is an example of which of the following literary devices?

    (A) personification

    (B) metaphor

    (C) hyperbole

    (D) simile

44. Based on the passage, *jocund* most likely means which of the following?

    (J) miserable

    (K) quiet

    (L) cheerful

    (M) repulsive

45. When the poet lies on the couch lost in thought, what does he think about?

    (A) The vision of the dancing daffodils.

    (B) The shapes that the clouds make in the sky.

    (C) Dancing with the one he loves.

    (D) Sparkling waves on the seashore.

Questions 46–50 are based on the following passage.

The First Amendment to the Constitution of the United States guarantees that Congress shall not make a law prohibiting the free exercise of religion or respecting an establishment of religion. Many voices in the country offer conflicting ideas. A Chief Justice of the Supreme Court of the United States described the *separation* of church and state as a wall based on bad history, a guide which is useless to judging, and a metaphor which should be discarded. A contemporary, prominent church pastor viewed this enforced separation of civil and religious authority as the result of the work of an infidel. A religious leader of the colonial period **reaffirmed** this amendment by asking that government continue to let people speak as they please and worship freely whether it be none, one, or 20 gods. In the modern context, then, it seems that threats to religious freedom still exist. Separation of church and state is not universally accepted.

46. Congress is required by the First Amendment to

    (J) guarantee the free exercise or establishment of religion.

    (K) laws which prohibit freedom of religion.

    (L) free speech.

    (M) the free exercise or establishment of organizations.

47. According to the passage, one critic of the First Amendment

    (A) believes the Constitution is a guide which is useless to judging.

    (B) believes it is the work of a British Loyalist.

    (C) believes that religious leaders should rewrite the Constitution.

    (D) believes that churches have the final authority over the United States government.

GO TO NEXT PAGE

48. In the passage, the word *separation* means

    (J) keep apart.

    (K) to leave.

    (L) break into pieces.

    (M) ignored.

49. According to the passage, a religious leader believes people should

    (A) worship one God.

    (B) worship 20 Gods.

    (C) worship freely.

    (D) worship no Gods.

50. The author's intention is to

    (J) show that the separation of church and state is under attack.

    (K) show that everyone believes in the separation of church and state.

    (L) show that no one pays attention to the separation of church and state anymore.

    (M) prove that the government should control religion.

TACHS

STOP

TACHS
SUBTEST 2

Language

Time: Unspecified
40 Questions

DIRECTIONS: Questions 1–10 comprise the Spelling portion of the Language Test. Look at the four words carefully to determine if there are any errors in <u>spelling.</u> Choose the word that is misspelled or choose "no mistakes."

1. **(A)** trofhy
   (B) fortune
   (C) invention
   (D) sorrow
   (E) No mistakes

2. **(J)** calendar
   (K) explosion
   (L) adventur
   (M) present
   (N) No mistakes

3. **(A)** reversal
   (B) situation
   (C) author
   (D) explaination
   (E) No mistakes

4. **(J)** autumn
   (K) treasure
   (L) exception
   (M) always
   (N) No mistakes

5. **(A)** balanced
   (B) superb
   (C) beautys
   (D) frequent
   (E) No mistakes

6. **(J)** hopefull
   (K) superior
   (L) extinct
   (M) creative
   (N) No mistakes

GO TO NEXT PAGE

TACHS

7. (A) excellent
(B) qantity
(C) fortunate
(D) silence
(E) No mistakes

8. (J) computation
(K) personal
(L) ambitious
(M) guilty
(N) No mistakes

9. (A) painting
(B) climbing
(C) swiming
(D) steering
(E) No mistakes

10. (J) hexagon
(K) recieve
(L) accept
(M) musical
(N) No mistakes

DIRECTIONS: Questions 11–20 comprise the Capitalization portion of the Language Test. Look at the sentences carefully to determine if there are any errors in <u>capitalization</u>. Choose the section that contains the error or choose "no mistakes."

11. (A) On saturday, his baseball
(B) championship game was
(C) rained out.
(D) No mistakes

12. (J) Did you know that Italy
(K) is a country on the
(L) continent of europe?
(M) No mistakes

13. (A) Whenever we go to the
(B) movies, my friend mike
(C) expects me to pay.
(D) No mistakes

14. (J) November is one of
(K) my favorite months of
(L) the year.
(M) No mistakes

15. (A) In English class, we read
(B) *To kill a mockingbird* and now
(C) it's one of my favorite books.
(D) No mistakes

16. (J) Joey worked hard to be
(K) able to buy his first car, which
(L) is a mustang.
(M) No mistakes

17. (A) We planted a lot of
(B) vegetables in our garden, including
(C) zucchini, carrots, and peas.
(D) No mistakes

18. (J) On my last test, my
(K) math Teacher found no
(L) mistakes at all.
(M) No mistakes

19. (A) Sarah got the leading
(B) role in *guys and dolls*, this
(C) year's eighth grade play.
(D) No mistakes

20. (J) I can never remember if
(K) Father's Day comes before or
(L) after the fourth of july.
(M) No mistakes

GO TO NEXT PAGE ➡

DIRECTIONS: Questions 21–30 comprise the Punctuation portion of the Language Test. Look at the sentences carefully to determine if there are any errors in <u>punctuation</u>. Choose the section that contains the error or choose "no mistakes."

21. **(A)** When you hold the meeting
    (B) at your house, its your job to
    (C) provide the refreshments.
    (D) No mistakes

22. **(J)** Some people say theres'
    (K) a home team advantage
    (L) at sporting events.
    (M) No mistakes

23. **(A)** When you consider how many people
    (B) tried out for the squad, you must
    (C) be really good to have made the team.
    (D) No mistakes

24. **(J)** Ham, and cheese is the
    (K) only kind of sandwich
    (L) he will eat.
    (M) No mistakes

25. **(A)** It's right around
    (B) the corner from
    (C) your friends house.
    (D) No mistakes

26. **(J)** I have big assignments
    (K) in all my classes including
    (L) Science, Social Studies, and Math.
    (M) No mistakes

27. **(A)** Sometimes she doesnt want
    (B) to have activities after school, just
    (C) time to hang out with her friends.
    (D) No mistakes

28. **(J)** There's a really good
    (K) band that's playing at our
    (L) block party this summer.
    (M) No mistakes

29. **(A)** "I really want a dog,"
    (B) Max said. "I promise I will
    (C) take good care of it.
    (D) No mistakes

30. **(J)** This Saturday is our class
    (K) field day. Do you really think
    (L) that it's going to rain.
    (M) No mistakes

DIRECTIONS: Questions 31–40 comprise the Usage and Expression portion of the Language Test. Look at the sentences carefully to determine if there are any errors in word <u>usage and expression</u>. Choose the section that contains the error or choose "no mistakes."

31. **(A)** The orchard had many apple trees.
    (B) When fall came the apples were red.
    (C) They were finally ready to be picked.
    (D) No mistakes

32. **(J)** It was time for the annual school picnic.
    (K) Sam brung his football with him.
    (L) He hoped to play a game with his friends.
    (M) No mistakes

GO TO NEXT PAGE

33. **(A)** My little brother growed so
    (B) quickly, that now he is taller
    (C) than our mother.
    (D) No mistakes

34. **(J)** Just when I thought winter
    (K) had ended, we had one
    (L) more bigger storm.
    (M) No mistakes

35. **(A)** She had studied so hard for
    (B) the test, that when the day finally
    (C) came she thought it was easy.
    (D) No mistakes

36. **(J)** He didn't have nothing to
    (K) do with the broken instruments.
    (L) He was not even at band practice.
    (M) No mistakes

For Questions 37 and 38, choose the best way of <u>expressing</u> an idea.

37. **(A)** Before applying the new paint color, it is necessary to scrape off the old paint, sand the entire item, and paint a base coat.
    (B) Scrape off the old paint, sand the entire item and paint a base coat, it is necessary before applying the new paint color.
    (C) Before applying the new paint color, scrape off the old paint, sand the entire item, it is necessary and paint a base coat
    (D) It is necessary to scrape off the old paint, paint a base coat and sand the entire item before applying the new paint color.

38. **(J)** Brush your teeth carefully after every meal and dentists recommend that you floss regularly.
    (K) Dentists recommend that you brush your teeth carefully after every meal and use floss regularly.
    (L) Dentists recommend that you brush your teeth and use floss regularly carefully after every meal.
    (M) Use floss regularly and that you brush your teeth carefully after every meal dentists recommend.

TACHS

GO TO NEXT PAGE ➡

For Questions 39 and 40, choose the best answers based on the following passage.

[1] Learning how to drive is an exciting experience. [2] However, it is important that you consider driving to be both a privilege and a responsibility. [3] In order to earn your driver's license you will need to pass both a written and a field or driving test. [4] There is a manual of rules and regulations that you will need to study for the written portion. [5] Many people take a driver's education course, while others learn <u>by</u> a parent or other adult. [6] Some argue that older adults should be required to be retested from time to time. [7] Learning how to be a good driver takes time, practice, and concentration.

39. **Which sentence should be left out of this paragraph?**
    (A) Sentence 2
    (B) Sentence 3
    (C) Sentence 5
    (D) Sentence 6

40. **What is the <u>best</u> way to write the underlined part of sentence 5?**
    (J) with
    (K) among
    (L) from
    (M) No change

STOP

TACHS

Mathematics

Time: 40 Minutes
40 Questions

1. Which of the following is a multiple of 7?
   (A) 24
   (B) 56
   (C) 71
   (D) 18

2. What is the value of x, if $36 \div x = 9$ is a true statement?
   (J) 6
   (K) 3
   (L) 5
   (M) 4

3. Joey is riding his bike to raise money for charity. He asked each sponsor to donate $3.00 for every mile he rides. If Joey rides a total of 63 miles, how much money total will he receive from 7 sponsors?
   (A) $1,323
   (B) $441
   (C) $1,732
   (D) $859

4. Which of the following is **not** a factor of 32?
   (J) 4
   (K) 8
   (L) 12
   (M) 16

5. Tory wants to buy a new gaming system that costs $255.99. He has $186.53. How much more does he need?
   (A) $131.46
   (B) $69.46
   (C) $58.64
   (D) $442.52

6. Which of the following is **not** a prime number?
   (J) 7
   (K) 11
   (L) 13
   (M) 15

7. Find the product of $\frac{3}{5}$ and $\frac{4}{6}$. Then reduce to lowest terms.

   (A) $\frac{4}{10}$

   (B) $\frac{12}{30}$

   (C) $\frac{2}{5}$

   (D) $\frac{5}{12}$

GO TO NEXT PAGE ➡

TACHS

DIRECTIONS: Use the chart below to answer questions 8–10.

Five student athletes participated in a 5K competition. They each ran two 5K races. Here are their finishing times for each race.

Runner's Name	Race 1	Race 2
Stacey	27.4	25.9
Kenny	22.6	22.3
Emily	22.1	23.8
Lydia	29.4	27.7
Jerome	24.2	22.7

8. Which of the athletes improved the most from the first to the second race?

(J) Stacey

(K) Kenny

(L) Emily

(M) Lydia

9. What was the average time for the runners in the first race? Round to the nearest whole number.

(A) 26

(B) 24

(C) 25

(D) 30

10. Which runner has the fastest average time for the two races?

(J) Stacey

(K) Kenny

(L) Emily

(M) Jerome

11. What is the equivalent of $(4 + 5) \times 18 - 7$?

(A) 162

(B) 155

(C) 152

(D) 99

12. What is 140% of 70?

(J) 20

(K) 980

(L) 98

(M) 78

13. In the figure below, ABC is a right triangle.

What is the value of x?

(A) 28

(B) 44

(C) 56

(D) 62

14. In the figure below, DEFG is a rectangle.

If the perimeter of DEFG is 80, what is the value of y?

(J) 24

(K) 32

(L) 40

(M) 48

GO TO NEXT PAGE ➡

DIRECTIONS: Use the chart below to answer questions 15–16.

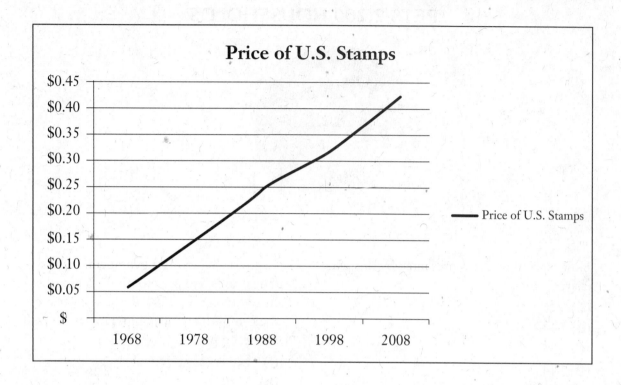

Price of U.S. Stamps

15. What is the approximate difference between the price of stamps in 1978 and 2008?
   (A) $0.57
   (B) $0.20
   (C) $0.27
   (D) $0.36

16. Which decade showed the lowest increase in the price of stamps?
   (J) 1998 to 2008
   (K) 1988 to 1998
   (L) 1978 to 1988
   (M) 1968 to 1978

17. What is 2,860 divided by 44?
   (A) 65
   (B) 72
   (C) 68
   (D) 75

18. Kiren took a job as a camp counselor. Her contract stated that she would be paid $1,800 for the 8 weeks of camp. Kiren was to receive $\frac{1}{3}$ of the salary at the end of the first week of camp and $\frac{1}{2}$ of the remaining salary after the fourth week of camp. How much had Kiren received at the beginning of week 5?
   (J) $600
   (K) $900
   (L) $1,200
   (M) $1,400

GO TO NEXT PAGE

TACHS

DIRECTIONS: Use the chart below to answer questions 19–20.

PETS 2,200 HOUSEHOLDS

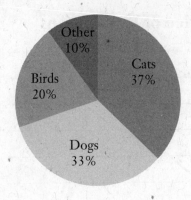

19. How many dogs are represented by this pie chart?

    (A) 726

    (B) 814

    (C) 826

    (D) 914

20. How many less birds than cats are represented by this pie chart?

    (J) 334

    (K) 286

    (L) 374

    (M) 220

21. What is $5^4 + 12^2$?

    (A) 625

    (B) 769

    (C) 649

    (D) 269

22. Cameron is getting a gym membership. The deal is $40 per month for 6 months. In addition, take 15% off the total cost of the 6-month membership. How much will Cameron pay?

    (J) $204

    (K) $240

    (L) $276

    (M) $256

23. Zack set a goal to ride his bike 1,000 miles this spring. He has ridden 375 miles so far. If he rides 60 miles a week, what is the least number of weeks it will take for Zack to reach his goal?

    (A) 12 weeks

    (B) 10 weeks

    (C) 11 weeks

    (D) 13 weeks

GO TO NEXT PAGE ➡

24. Which of the following is a factor of 48?

(J) 9

(K) 5

(L) 7

(M) 6

25. Convert 6.25 to a mixed numeral and reduce to lowest terms.

(A) $6\dfrac{12}{50}$

(B) $6\dfrac{1}{4}$

(C) $6\dfrac{1}{25}$

(D) $6\dfrac{25}{100}$

26. The local bookstore manager was keeping track of the number of books sold each week. The following numbers represent the books sold during a 6-week period: 117, 89, 97, 165, 124, 79. What is the average amount of books sold weekly?

(J) 107

(K) 110

(L) 103

(M) 112

27. A group of students held a fundraiser to donate money to different charities. They collected a total of $1,400, which they shared equally among the charities. How many charities shared the money?

(A) 6

(B) 11

(C) 8

(D) 9

28. The high school choir went to a singing competition 162 miles away. The bus left the school at 7:30 a.m. and arrived at 10:30 a.m. They made no stops along the way. What was their average rate of speed?

(J) 48 mph

(K) 54 mph

(L) 57 mph

(M) 60 mph

29. Find the product of 671 and 405.

(A) 271,755

(B) 278,465

(C) 267,705

(D) 281,765

30. The weight of a ceramic floor tile is 3.7 pounds per square foot. What is the total weight of floor tiles that cover a 14-foot by 11-foot room?

(J) 559.6 pounds

(K) 570.1 pounds

(L) 569.8 pounds

(M) 571.8 pounds

GO TO NEXT PAGE ➡

TACHS

Estimation

DIRECTIONS: For questions 31–40, <u>estimate</u> the answer in your head. No scratch work is allowed. Do <u>not</u> to try to compute the exact answers. Choose the best answer.

31. The closest estimate of $(59 \times 3) + (37 \times 2)$
- **(A)** 340
- **(C)** 290
- **(B)** 350
- **(D)** 260

32. The closest estimate of $6,422 \div 84$ is
- **(J)** 70
- **(L)** 60
- **(K)** 80
- **(M)** 90

33. On an average summer day the local pool gets 785 visitors. What is the closest estimate of the number of visitors that go to the pool over 18 days?
- **(A)** 8,000
- **(C)** 1,600
- **(B)** 17,000
- **(D)** 15,000

34. Depal offered to bring soda for the freshmen class picnic. There are 276 students attending. If 2-liter bottles serve about 7 people, what is the closest estimate of how many liters are needed?
- **(J)** 40 liters
- **(K)** 60 liters
- **(L)** 80 liters
- **(M)** 90 liters

35. The closest estimate of 287×19 is _____.
- **(A)** 5000
- **(B)** 5,600
- **(C)** 4,800
- **(D)** 4,600

36. The closest estimate of $7,204 - 3,965$ is _____.
- **(J)** 4,000
- **(K)** 2,000
- **(L)** 10,000
- **(M)** 3,000

37. The closest estimate of $4\frac{1}{18} + 2\frac{3}{4} + 5\frac{2}{8}$ is _____.
- **(A)** 10
- **(B)** $11\frac{1}{2}$
- **(C)** 12
- **(D)** $12\frac{5}{8}$

38. The closest estimate of $(3.9)^3$ is _____.
- **(J)** 27
- **(K)** 64
- **(L)** 12
- **(M)** 56

39. Brian and Steven are working to save up some money. Brian makes $7.25 an hour working at a pizza shop. Steven makes $10.16 an hour working at an after-school program. In one 12-hour work week, what is the closest estimate of how much more Steven will earn?
- **(A)** $36
- **(B)** $48
- **(C)** $84
- **(D)** $26

40. Kristen drove 178 miles to visit a college. If she drove an average of approximately 62 miles per hour, what is the closest estimate of how long the drive will take?
- **(J)** 3 hours
- **(K)** 2 hours
- **(L)** 4 hours
- **(M)** 5 hours

TACHS

TACHS
SUBTEST 4

Ability

1

A B C D E

2

J K L M N

3

A B C D E

4

J K L M N

5

△ □ ⧁ | **A** ○ **B** ▽ **C** ▢ **D** ⬡ **E** ⏢

6

◎ ◎ ◎ | **J** ◉ **K** ⊙ **L** ○ **M** ◎ **N** ●

7

▨ ▨ ▨ | **A** ▨ **B** ▨ **C** ▨ **D** ▨ **E** ◪

8

PQRS is a square piece of paper that is folded along the crease TU. The arrow from P to Q indicates the direction of the fold. Which of the following is the result of this fold?

(J)

(L)

(K)

(M)

9

A square piece of paper ACEG is folded along a crease HJ, as shown by the arrow from G to J. A hole is punched in the folded paper. If the paper is then unfolded, what is the result?

(A)

(C)

(B)

(D)

10

A square piece of paper BDFH is folded along a crease MP, as shown by the arrow from D to B. Two holes are punched in the folded paper. If the paper is then unfolded, what is the result?

(J)

(L)

(K)

(M)

TACHS

Practice Test 2—Answer Key

Question Number	Correct Answer	If You Answered this Question Incorrectly, Refer to . . .
SUBTEST 1: READING		
1.	(B)	P. 313
2.	(M)	P. 313
3.	(C)	P. 313
4.	(J)	P. 313
5.	(C)	P. 313
6.	(M)	P. 313
7.	(C)	P. 313
8.	(K)	P. 313
9.	(D)	P. 313
10.	(J)	P. 313
11.	(B)	P. 313
12.	(L)	P. 313
13.	(A)	P. 313
14.	(M)	P. 313
15.	(B)	P. 313
16.	(J)	P. 313
17.	(D)	P. 313
18.	(K)	P. 313
19.	(C)	P. 313
20.	(M)	P. 313

Question Number	Correct Answer	If You Answered this Question Incorrectly, Refer to . . .
21.	(A)	P. 300
22.	(M)	P. 302
23.	(C)	P. 302
24.	(L)	P. 303
25.	(B)	P. 310
26.	(K)	P. 302
27.	(A)	P. 302
28.	(L)	P. 302
29.	(B)	P. 302
30.	(J)	P. 300
31.	(B)	P. 310
32.	(J)	P. 308
33.	(D)	P. 302
34.	(J)	P. 302
35.	(A)	P. 300
36.	(J)	P. 302
37.	(C)	P. 310
38.	(M)	P. 302
39.	(B)	P. 310
40.	(L)	P. 300
41.	(B)	P. 308
42.	(M)	P. 302
43.	(A)	P. 297
44.	(L)	P. 310
45.	(A)	P. 302
46.	(J)	P. 302
47.	(B)	P. 302
48.	(J)	P. 310
49.	(C)	P. 303
50.	(F)	P. 300
SUBTEST 2: LANGUAGE		
1.	(A)	P. 283
2.	(L)	P. 279
3.	(D)	P. 281

TACHS

4.	(N)	P. 279
5.	(C)	P. 280
6.	(J)	P. 281
7.	(B)	P. 283
8.	(N)	P. 279
9.	(C)	P. 283
10.	(K)	P. 283
11.	(A)	P. 275
12.	(L)	P. 275
13.	(B)	P. 275
14.	(M)	P. 275
15.	(B)	P. 276
16.	(L)	P. 275
17.	(D)	P. 275
18.	(K)	P. 275
19.	(B)	P. 276
20.	(L)	P. 275
21.	(B)	P. 269
22.	(J)	P. 269
23.	(D)	P. 267
24.	(J)	P. 267
25.	(C)	P. 269
26.	(K)	P. 262
27.	(A)	P. 269
28.	(M)	P. 261
29.	(C)	P. 270
30.	(L)	P. 261
31.	(D)	P. 239
32.	(K)	P. 246
33.	(A)	P. 246
34.	(L)	P. 258
35.	(D)	P. 239
36.	(J)	P. 239
37.	(A)	P. 239
38.	(K)	P. 239
39.	(D)	P. 239
40.	(L)	P. 239

Question Number	Correct Answer	If You Answered this Question Incorrectly, Refer to . . .
SUBTEST 3: MATHEMATICS		
1.	(B)	P. 341
2.	(M)	P. 345
3.	(A)	P. 379
4.	(L)	P. 341
5.	(B)	P. 377
6.	(M)	P. 341
7.	(C)	P. 350
8.	(M)	P. 377
9.	(C)	P. 390
10.	(K)	P. 390
11.	(B)	P. 389
12.	(L)	P. 389
13.	(D)	P. 407
14.	(J)	P. 395
15.	(C)	P. 424
16.	(K)	P. 424
17.	(A)	P. 345
18.	(L)	P. 410
19.	(A)	P. 410
20.	(L)	P. 410
21.	(B)	P. 392
22.	(J)	P. 410
23.	(C)	P. 410
24.	(M)	P. 341
25.	(B)	P. 350
26.	(M)	P. 410
27.	(C)	P. 345
28.	(K)	P. 390
29.	(A)	P. 341
30.	(L)	P. 410
31.	(D)	P. 337, 341
32.	(K)	P. 345
33.	(D)	P. 341

34.	**(L)**	P. 341, 345
35.	**(B)**	P. 341
36.	**(M)**	P. 339
37.	**(C)**	P. 355
38.	**(K)**	P. 392
39.	**(A)**	P. 334, 379
40.	**(J)**	P. 345
SUBTEST 4: ABILITY		
1.	**(D)**	P. 422
2.	**(N)**	P. 422
3.	**(D)**	P. 422
4.	**(L)**	P. 422
5.	**(D)**	P. 422
6.	**(L)**	P. 422
7.	**(B)**	P. 422
8.	**(K)**	P. 419
9.	**(B)**	P. 419
10.	**(M)**	P. 419

Reading—Detailed Explanations of Answers

Vocabulary 1–20

1. **(B)** **Suppose.** *Infer* means to *assume, conclude,* or *suppose.*

2. **(M)** **Furious.** *Livid* means *enraged, fuming, up in arms,* or *furious.*

3. **(C)** **Unbelieving.** *Incredulous* means *doubtful, skeptical,* or *unbelieving.*

4. **(J)** **Confirm.** *Verify* means to *validate, prove, make sure,* or *confirm.*

5. **(C)** **Tired.** *Lethargic* means *sluggish, weary, exhausted,* or *tired.*

6. **(M)** **Leap.** *Pounce* means to *swoop, bound,* or *leap.*

7. **(C)** **Criticize.** *Vilify* means to *speak ill of, belittle,* or *criticize.* The opposite would be *compliment.*

8. **(K)** **Expert.** *Proficient* means *capable, talented, skillful,* or *expert.*

9. **(D)** **Investigate.** *Probe* means to *search, look into, survey,* or *investigate.*

10. **(J)** **Collapse.** *Disintegrate* means to *crumble, break up, fragment,* or *collapse.*

11. **(B)** **Lasting.** *Permanent* means *enduring, stable, unending,* or *lasting.*

12. **(L)** **Calm.** *Serene* means *peaceful, still, quiet.*

13. **(A)** **Appreciate.** *Relish* means to *enjoy, delight,* or *appreciate.* The opposite would be *dislike.*

14. **(M)** **Timid.** *Bashful* means *reserved, shy, withdrawn,* or *timid.*

15. **(B)** **Manipulate.** *Sway* means to *convince, persuade, control,* or *manipulate.*

16. **(J)** **Forceful.** *Assertive* means *forward, confident,* or *forceful.* The opposite would be *timid.*

17. **(D)** **Insignificant.** *Trivial* means *minor, unimportant, slight,* or *insignificant.*

18. **(K)** **Differing.** *Contrary* means *dissimilar, opposing,* or *differing.*

19. **(C)** **Looks like.** *Resembles* means to *be like, reminds you of,* or *looks like.*

20. **(M)** **Unfortunate.** *Tragic* means *disastrous, awful,* or *unfortunate.* The opposite would be *joyous.*

Reading Comprehension 21–50

21. **(A)** The passage concentrates on showing that child labor will only be ended through protest and legal enactment, not by employers or philanthropists. The passage argues that children should be given the chance to go to school **(B)**. The passage does not mention night school **(C)** or what schools should teach children **(D)**.

22. **(M)** All of the statements about why trade unionists agitate for child labor laws are in the passage **(J)**, **(K)**, and **(L)**.

23. **(C)** The passage mentions several times that children should be in school, and it is clearly stated in the last sentence of the passage. The passage does not say that children are irresponsible **(A)**. Although one of the arguments the author uses in her case against child labor in America is that England has already abolished it, this is not her reason for trying to end child labor **(B)**.

24. **(L)** The author does not say that child laborers take jobs away from adults, but she does say that it demoralizes the trades that employ children **(K)**. She says that it takes energy away from growth **(J)** and that England has abolished child labor **(M)**.

25. **(B)** *Ameliorating* means *improving* or *bettering*. Choices **(A)**, **(C)**, and **(D)** are unrelated.

26. **(K)** The first sentence of the passage defines comedy as having a happy ending. A comedy may be funny **(J)**, absurd **(L)**, or have funny characters **(M)**, but it doesn't have to in order to be a comedy.

27. **(A)** The first sentence of the second paragraph says a farce is a low comedy **(B)** that depends upon exaggeration **(A)**. A farce does not have to make people think **(C)** or be funny **(D)**.

28. **(L)** Satire is defined in the second paragraph of the passage as implying that humanity and human institutions need to be reformed. Although a satire is a form of high comedy, a high comedy is not necessarily a satire **(J)**. Low comedies **(K)** and predictable comedies **(M)** are not called satires.

29. **(B)** The last few sentences of the passage explain that the more believable a comedy is, the less distanced from it an audience feels. Therefore, the audience feels more involved in the action and less protected from the conflicts on stage. The more an audience cares about what happens to the characters, the less funny **(A)** and less harmless **(C)** the play seems to the audience. The passage does not discuss the "believability" of Shakespeare's comedies **(D)**.

30. **(J)** This passage names different types of comedies and explains what defines them and how they function for the audience. The passage does not measure the enjoyability of comedies and tragedies **(K)**. The passage points out that Shakespeare's comedies have been criticized for their appeal to laughter **(L)**. Although the passage explains the concept of figurative distance **(M)**, this is not the passage's main purpose.

31. **(B)** *Prevalent* most nearly means *common* or *widespread*. *Limited* **(A)** and *scarce* **(D)** both mean the opposite of prevalent, and *stunning* **(C)** is unrelated.

32. **(J)** Sentence 5: "The life cycle of a butterfly is fascinating to study" expresses an opinion. Some people may agree with this sentiment, while others may not. The other choices **(K)**, **(L)**, and **(M)** are more closely based on scientific facts or observations.

33. **(D)** According to the passage, the purpose of the host plants is to serve as food for the caterpillars. While the plants may make an attractive garden **(A)**, this is not the purpose of the host plants, nor is it specifically to provide food for the butterflies **(B)**. There is no mention that the plants are chosen to protect the caterpillars from predators **(C)**.

34. **(J)** *Larva* is another name for the young caterpillars. The passage uses the term *caterpillars* in sentences 7 and 9, and the term *larva* in sentence 8. This implies that the terms are synonymous in this example. *Chrysalis* **(K)** refers to a stage of the butterfly's life cycle. *Metamorphosis* **(L)** refers to the transformation from egg to caterpillar to butterfly. *Consume* most nearly means to eat.

35. **(A)** The passage discusses the life of the Painted Lady variety of butterfly, which makes **(A)** "The Life Cycle of a Painted Lady" the best title. It does not address "How to Attract Butterflies" **(B)** or the specifics regarding **(C)** "How Caterpillars Grow." While it mentions where the Painted Lady lives around the world, the passage is not focused on "Butterflies Around the World" **(D)**.

36. **(J)** The passage explains "The British army under Cornwallis ***did not press its advantage***," instead it left behind a smaller force of Hessian soldiers to guard the town of Trenton. Since the Americans were victorious, one can conclude that the British army could have maintained its command by keeping a larger force of soldiers **(J)**. The passage states that the American army was in trouble, which means it did not have the advantage **(K)**. Since the Americans won the battle, we know that Cornwallis and the British army did not hold their advantage **(L)**, and that the small force of Hessian soldiers was not enough to face their army **(M)**.

37. **(C)** The words *dusk* and *dawn* are examples of antonyms or opposites (C). *Dusk* refers to early evening, while *dawn* refers to early morning. Homophones **(A)** and homonyms **(D)** are words that sound the same, but have different meanings. Synonyms are words that share the same meaning **(B)**.

38. **(M)** At the timeframe the passage was written about, General George Washington can be described as a fairly successful leader **(M)**. He and his army had faced several defeats and were in trouble, before rallying to victory. Washington was not a "highly successful leader" **(J)** at this point, or an "unsuccessful leader" **(K)**. There is no information regarding if he was well-liked by his soldiers **(L)**.

39. **(B)** *Morale* means *spirits, drive, self-esteem,* or *confidence* **(B)**. *Friendship* is unrelated to the word *morale* and the passage **(A)**. *Resentment* **(C)** means *bitterness, hatred,* or *dislike*. *Anxiety* **(D)** is another word for *worry, concern,* or *unease*.

40. **(L)** Students are the most likely to be the audience of this passage. It has the tone of a history textbook. It is less likely to be specifically directed to soldiers **(J)**, teachers **(K)**, or generals **(M)**.

41. **(B)** The mood of the poem is joyful **(B)**. This is apparent through the imagery and the use of words such as "fluttering," "dancing," "gay," and "pleasure." The tone or mood does not imply that the poet is **(A)** angry, **(C)** anxious, or **(D)** mournful.

42. **(M)** "A host, of golden daffodils" is the main subject of the entire poem. While there is reference to clouds **(J)**, they are not described "stretched in never-ending line." The daffodils are described as dancers **(K)**, but this is not the noun the line refers to. The daffodils are being compared to **(L)** stars in the poem.

43. **(A)** "Tossing their heads in sprightly dance" is an example of personification **(A)**. This device gives human attributes (heads) and movements (tossing), to nonhuman objects (daffodils). Metaphors **(B)** use one thing to mean another and makes a comparison between the two, and similes compare two different things in order to create a new meaning **(D)**. A hyperbole is an exaggeration.

44. **(L)** Looking at the word *jocund* in context—"A poet could not but be gay, In such a **jocund** company"—one can determine that it means *cheerful*. *Gay* and *cheerful* are synonyms of *happy*. *Miserable* **(J)** and *repulsive* **(M)** mean the opposite. *Quiet* **(K)** is an unrelated word.

45. **(A)** When the poet lies on the couch lost in thought, what he remembers is the vision of the dancing daffodils. They are the main topic of the poem. While the other choices **(B)**, **(C)**, and **(D)** relate to the poem in some way, they are not the focus of the poet's thoughts.

46. **(J)** The answer to this question is found in the very first sentence of the passage: the First Amendment outlaws Congress passing any laws which prohibit freedom of religion. Outlawing freedom of religion is the opposite **(K)**. Choices **(L)** and **(M)** are wrong because they are about free speech, not freedom of religion.

47. **(B)** The passage states that one critic of the First Amendment has called it a guide which is useless to judging. The statements in choices **(A)**, **(C)**, and **(D)** are not included in the passage.

48. **(J)** *Separation* most nearly means to keep apart. *To Leave* is not relevant to the context and *break into pieces* and *ignored* and unrelated.

49. **(C)** The religious leader believes people should worship freely nomatter now they worship

50. **(J)** The second to last sentence states that threats to religious freedom still exist **(J)**. Choice **(K)** is disproved in the last sentence, which says that not everyone accepts the separation of church and state. This passage shows that there is still interest in the separation of church and state **(L)** and it is against government control of religion **(M)**.

TACHS
SUBTEST 2

Language—Detailed Explanations of Answers

1. **(A)** *She won a **trofhy** at the tournament.* The correct spelling is **trophy**.

2. **(L)** *The book described a great **adventur**.* The correct spelling is **adventure**.

3. **(D)** *You had better have a good **explaination**.* The correct spelling is **explanation**.

4. **(N)** There are no misspelled words.

5. **(C)** *Those roses are real **beautys**.* The correct spelling is **beauties**.

6. **(J)** *We were **hopefull** that he'd like the gift.* The correct spelling is **hopeful**.

7. **(B)** *You will need a large **qantity** of snacks.* The correct spelling is **quantity**.

8. **(N)** There are no misspelled words.

9. **(C)** *Ducks were **swiming** in the pond.* The correct spelling is **swimming**.

10. **(K)** *Did you **recieve** my e-mail?* The correct spelling is **receive**.

11. **(A)** The proper noun *Saturday* needs to be capitalized.

12. **(L)** Since the names of continents are proper nouns, *Europe* needs to be capitalized.

13. **(B)** The proper noun *Mike* needs to be capitalized.

14. **(M)** There are no errors in capitalization.

15. **(B)** The title of the book *To Kill a Mockingbird* needs to be capitalized as such.

16. **(L)** The proper noun *Mustang* needs to be capitalized.

17. **(D)** There are no errors in capitalization.

18. **(K)** *Teacher* is not a proper noun and does not need to be capitalized.

19. **(B)** The title of the play *Guys and Dolls* needs to be capitalized as such.

20. **(L)** Since holidays are proper nouns, *Fourth of July* needs to be capitalized.

21. **(B)** In this example, *its* is the shortened form of *it is*. The contraction should be written as *it's*.

22. **(J)** In this example, *theres* is the shortened form of *there is*. The contraction should be written as *there's*.

23. **(D)** There are no errors in punctuation.

24. **(J)** A comma is not needed before *and*. It should read "ham and cheese."

25. **(C)** An apostrophe should be added to show possession: "friend's house" or if referring to more than one friend: "friends' house."

26. **(K)** Introductory clauses should be separated with a comma: "I have big assignments in all my classes, including Science, Social Studies, and Math."

27. **(A)** In this example, *doesnt* is the shortened form of *does not*. The contraction should be written as *doesn't*.

28. **(M)** There are no errors in punctuation.

29. **(C)** The closing quotation mark is missing. The sentence should read "I promise I will take good care of it."

30. **(L)** Sentences that are questions need to end with a question mark: "Do you really think that it's going to rain?"

31. **(D)** There are no errors in this sentence.

32. **(K)** The correct form of the verb *bring* in this example is *brought*. This is the correct word to express past tense.

33. **(A)** The correct form of the verb *grow* in this example is *grew*. This is the correct word to express past tense.

34. **(L)** Instead of *more bigger*, which is redundant, *bigger* is the correct wording.

35. **(D)** There are no errors in this sentence.

36. **(J)** *Didn't* and *nothing* are both negatives. A double-negative becomes a positive, thus if you did not have nothing, you would have something. The sentence should read "He didn't have anything to do with the broken instruments."

37. **(A)** The sentence is best written this way: "Before applying the new paint color, it is necessary to scrape off the old paint, sand the entire item, and paint a base coat."

38. **(K)** The sentence is best written this way: "Dentists recommend that you brush your teeth carefully after every meal and use floss regularly."

39. **(D)** Sentence 6: "Some argue that older adults should be required to be retested from time to time" is unnecessary to the passage.

40. **(L)** The correct preposition should be *from* rather than *by*.

Mathematics—Detailed Explanations of Answers

1. **(B)** 56 is the only multiple of 7 listed in the choices. $7 \times 8 = 56$.

2. **(M)** To find the value of x, divide 36 by 9. $36 \div 9 = 4$. $x = 4$.

3. **(A)** First multiply 3 ($3.00 per mile) by 63 (miles) to get 189 or $189.00. Then multiply $189.00 by 7 (number of sponsors). $189.00 \times 7 = \$1,323.00$

4. **(L)** 4, 8, and 16 are all factors of 32. 12 is the only choice that does not divide into 32 without a remainder.

5. **(B)** Find the difference between what Tory needs ($255.99) and what he has ($186.53). $\$255.99 - \$186.53 = \$69.46$.

6. **(M)** 7, 11, and 13 are all prime numbers. 15 is the only choice that has factors other than one and itself.

7. **(C)** First multiply the numerators and denominators. Then reduce the fraction to lowest terms. $\frac{3}{5} \times \frac{4}{6} = \frac{12}{30} = \frac{2}{5}$.

8. **(M)** To find out who improved the most, find the difference between each runner's two race times by subtracting. Lydia shows the most improvement: $29.4 - 27.7 = 1.7$.

9. **(C)** To find out the average time for the first race, start by adding all of the times. Then divide that sum (125.7) by 5 (the number of racers). Since it says to round to the nearest whole number, find the quotient of $125 \div 5 = 25$.

10. **(K)** To find the runner with the fastest average time. Find the average of the two race times for each runner. Add each athlete's times and divide by 2 (the number of races). Kenny had the fastest average time. $22.6 + 22.3 = 44.9$. Then $44.9 \div 2 = 22.45$ minutes.

11. **(B)** Follow the order of operations to solve this equation. $(4 + 5) \times 18 - 7 =$

    $(4 + 5) = 9 \qquad 9 \times 18 = 162 \qquad 162 - 7 = 155$

12. **(L)** "140% of 70" means "140% times 70." Change 140% to 1.4. Then (1.4) (70) = 98.

13. **(D)** The sum of the three angles of any triangle is 180°. Then 90 + 28 + X = 180. This equation simplifies to 118 + X = 180. Thus, X = 180 − 118 = 62.

14. **(J)** GF can also be represented by y, since opposite sides of a rectangle have the same length. Sinmilarly, DG has a value of 16. Then y + 16 + 16 = 80. This equation simplifies to 2y + 32 = 80. Then 2y = 80 − 32 = 48. Thus, $y = \frac{48}{2} = 24$.

15. **(C)** Read the line graph to determine the price of stamps in 1978 ($0.15) and 2008 ($0.42). Then find the difference. .42 − .15 = .27 cents.

16. **(K)** To find the decade with the lowest increase in the price of stamps, first find the difference in price during each ten-year period. The graph shows the lowest increase (about 10 cents) from 1988 to 1998.

17. **(A)** To find the quotient, you must divide 2,860 by 44.

$$44\overline{)2,860}$$ with quotient 65

18. **(L)** First find $\frac{1}{3}$ of 1,800 by dividing: 1800 ÷ 3 = 600 (salary received after week one). Then subtract that from the total. 1800 − 600 = 1200 (remaining salary). Next find $\frac{1}{2}$ of 1200 by dividing: 1200 ÷ 2 = 600 (salary received after week 4). Add to find salary received by week 5: 600 + 600 = $1,200.

19. **(A)** To find the number of dogs, calculate 33% of 2,200 (total). Change 33% to 0.33 and multiply by 2,200. Thus, (0.33) (2,200) = 726.

20. **(L)** First calculate the number of birds: 20% of 2,200 = 440. Then find the number of cats: 37% of 2,200 = 814. Find the difference by subtracting: 814 − 440 = 374.

21. **(B)** Multiply each number noted by the exponent, and then add: 5 × 5 × 5 × 5 = 625

               12 × 12 = 144   625 + 144 = 769

22. **(J)** First multiply $40 (the cost per month) by 6 (the number of months): $40 × 6 = $240. Next find 15% of $240 = $36 (discount). $240 − $36 = $204.

23. **(C)** First find the difference between the number of miles Zack wants to ride (1,000) and the number he has ridden (375): 1,000 − 375 = 625. Next, since Zach rides 60 miles a week, figure it will take 10 weeks to ride 600 miles, and 11 weeks to reach 625.

24. **(M)** 6 is the only choice that is a factor of 48. 6 × 8 = 48.

25. **(B)** First write 6.25 as a mixed number. Then reduce this fraction to its lowest term. $6.25 = 6\frac{25}{100}$ (Divide the numerator into the denominator by 25) $= 6\frac{1}{4}$.

26. **(M)** First add the weekly sales to find the sum.

    117 + 89 + 97 + 165 + 124 + 79 = 671. Then divide 671 by the number of weeks (6).

$$6\overline{)671}$$ with quotient $111.83, which rounds to $112.

27. **(C)** In order to find out how many charities received donations, divide each of the answer choices into 1,400 (the amount of dollars collected). The number that divides evenly with no remainders is the correct answer: $\dfrac{175}{8\overline{\smash{\big)}1400}}$.

28. **(K)** First find how much time elapsed between 7:30 a.m. and 10:30 a.m. Then divide the distance traveled (162 miles) by the time passed (3 hours). $162 \div 3 = 54$ miles per hour.

29. **(A)** To find the product of 671 and 405, you must multiply.

$$\begin{array}{r} 671 \\ \times\, 405 \\ \hline 271{,}755 \end{array}$$

30. **(L)** First multiply 14×11 to find the area of the room. $14 \times 11 = 154$. Then multiply the area (154 square feet) by the weight of each tile (3.7 pounds). $154 \times 3.7 = 569.8$ pounds.

31. **(D)** First solve the problems in the parentheses by rounding to easier terms.

$(59 \times 3) + (37 \times 2)$ becomes $(60 \times 3) = 180 + (40 \times 2) = 80 \qquad 180 + 80 = 260$

32. **(K)** Round 6,422 to 6,400 and round 84 to 80. Since $64 \div 8 = 8$, then $6{,}400 \div 80 = 80$.

33. **(D)** First round 785 to 800 (number of visitors per day) and round 18 to 20 (number of days). Then multiply the easier terms: $800 \times 20 = 16{,}000$. Look at your choices, since you rounded the numbers up you know that the closest estimate is less than 16,000. The closest estimate is 15,000.

34. **(L)** Since one 2-liter bottle of soda serves 7 people, you want to find out how many groups of seven are in the total number of students (276). Round to a number that is a multiple of 7 and divide: $280 \div 7 = 40$ bottles. Since each bottle is 2 liters, multiply $40 \times 2 = 80$ liters.

35. **(B)** Round 287×19 to 280×20. $28 \times 2 = 56$, so $280 \times 20 = 5{,}600$.

36. **(M)** Round the numbers to easier terms, and then find the difference.

$7{,}204 - 3{,}965 \qquad 7{,}000 - 4{,}000 = 3{,}000$

37. **(C)** To estimate the sum of $4\frac{1}{18}, 2\frac{3}{4}$, and $5\frac{2}{8}$, first add the whole numbers, then the larger fractions. You can drop $\frac{1}{18}$ because it is so small.

$4 + 2 + 5 = 11 \qquad \frac{2}{8} = \frac{1}{4} \qquad \frac{1}{4} + \frac{3}{4} = \frac{4}{4}$ or $1 \qquad 11 + 1 = 12$

38. **(K)** To estimate $(3.9)^3$, round 3.9 to 4, then multiply as follows: $4 \times 4 = 16 \times 4 = 64$.

39. **(A)** First round the hourly salaries to the nearest dollar. $7.25 rounds to $7.00 (Brian) and $10.16 rounds to $10.00 (Steven). Multiply each by 12 (hours of work). $7.00 \times 12 = $84.00 (Brian) and $10.00 \times 12 = $120 (Steven). Find the difference: $120 - $84 = $36.

40. **(J)** To estimate the speed, first round the number of miles traveled. 178 rounds to 180 miles. Next, round the speed of 62 miles per hour to 60. Divide the miles by the speed to find the length of the trip. 180 miles $\div$ 60 mph = 3 hours.

TACHS

TACHS
SUBTEST 4

Ability—Answers

1. **(D)** In the example, the diagonal stripes are only on the outer triangle and then they move to the inside triangle only. Choice D shows this same change for the square.

2. **(N)** In the example, a large white "A" becomes a solid upside-down "A." Choice N shows this same change for the large "T."

3. **(D)** In this example, the triangle is divided into three segments. At first the triangle has one shaded section, next it has two. Choice D shows this same change for the circle.

4. **(L)** In this example, a plain trapezoid turns upward and becomes a spotted trapezoid. Choice L shows this same change made to the rectangle.

5. **(D)** The progression shows a 3-sided figure, followed by a 4-sided figure, and then a 5-sided figure. Choice D shows a 6-sided figure, which would be next in the progression.

6. **(L)** This progression shows a circle with inner rings. Each ring is removed until the last circle is empty, as seen in choice L.

7. **(B)** In this progression, only the left section of the inside of the square is striped, then the top and bottom sections are striped. The remaining part of the sequence is shown in choice B.

8. **(K)** The paper is being folded using a vertical crease, from left to right. P lies on top of Q and S lies on top of R.

9. **(B)** The paper is folded upward along the horizontal crease HJ. When the paper is unfolded, the original hole must still appear in the same place. A second hole must appear on the right side below the crease.

10. **(M)** The paper is folded from right to left along the vertical crease MP. When the paper is unfolded, the hole along side BH will appear again, as will its image along side DF. Similarly, the hole nearest the crease just above HF will appear again. Also, another hole will appear on the opposite side of the crease and above HF.

HSPT/COOP/TACHS PRACTICE TEST

ANSWER SHEET

HSPT
PRACTICE TEST

Answer Sheet

Photocopy this answer sheet and use it to complete the practice tests.

Verbal Skills

1. Ⓐ Ⓑ Ⓒ Ⓓ	13. Ⓐ Ⓑ Ⓒ Ⓓ	25. Ⓐ Ⓑ Ⓒ Ⓓ	37. Ⓐ Ⓑ Ⓒ Ⓓ	49. Ⓐ Ⓑ Ⓒ Ⓓ
2. Ⓐ Ⓑ Ⓒ Ⓓ	14. Ⓐ Ⓑ Ⓒ Ⓓ	26. Ⓐ Ⓑ Ⓒ Ⓓ	38. Ⓐ Ⓑ Ⓒ Ⓓ	50. Ⓐ Ⓑ Ⓒ Ⓓ
3. Ⓐ Ⓑ Ⓒ Ⓓ	15. Ⓐ Ⓑ Ⓒ Ⓓ	27. Ⓐ Ⓑ Ⓒ Ⓓ	39. Ⓐ Ⓑ Ⓒ Ⓓ	51. Ⓐ Ⓑ Ⓒ Ⓓ
4. Ⓐ Ⓑ Ⓒ Ⓓ	16. Ⓐ Ⓑ Ⓒ Ⓓ	28. Ⓐ Ⓑ Ⓒ Ⓓ	40. Ⓐ Ⓑ Ⓒ Ⓓ	52. Ⓐ Ⓑ Ⓒ Ⓓ
5. Ⓐ Ⓑ Ⓒ Ⓓ	17. Ⓐ Ⓑ Ⓒ Ⓓ	29. Ⓐ Ⓑ Ⓒ Ⓓ	41. Ⓐ Ⓑ Ⓒ Ⓓ	53. Ⓐ Ⓑ Ⓒ Ⓓ
6. Ⓐ Ⓑ Ⓒ Ⓓ	18. Ⓐ Ⓑ Ⓒ Ⓓ	30. Ⓐ Ⓑ Ⓒ Ⓓ	42. Ⓐ Ⓑ Ⓒ Ⓓ	54. Ⓐ Ⓑ Ⓒ Ⓓ
7. Ⓐ Ⓑ Ⓒ Ⓓ	19. Ⓐ Ⓑ Ⓒ Ⓓ	31. Ⓐ Ⓑ Ⓒ Ⓓ	43. Ⓐ Ⓑ Ⓒ Ⓓ	55. Ⓐ Ⓑ Ⓒ Ⓓ
8. Ⓐ Ⓑ Ⓒ Ⓓ	20. Ⓐ Ⓑ Ⓒ Ⓓ	32. Ⓐ Ⓑ Ⓒ Ⓓ	44. Ⓐ Ⓑ Ⓒ Ⓓ	56. Ⓐ Ⓑ Ⓒ Ⓓ
9. Ⓐ Ⓑ Ⓒ Ⓓ	21. Ⓐ Ⓑ Ⓒ Ⓓ	33. Ⓐ Ⓑ Ⓒ Ⓓ	45. Ⓐ Ⓑ Ⓒ Ⓓ	57. Ⓐ Ⓑ Ⓒ Ⓓ
10. Ⓐ Ⓑ Ⓒ Ⓓ	22. Ⓐ Ⓑ Ⓒ Ⓓ	34. Ⓐ Ⓑ Ⓒ Ⓓ	46. Ⓐ Ⓑ Ⓒ Ⓓ	58. Ⓐ Ⓑ Ⓒ Ⓓ
11. Ⓐ Ⓑ Ⓒ Ⓓ	23. Ⓐ Ⓑ Ⓒ Ⓓ	35. Ⓐ Ⓑ Ⓒ Ⓓ	47. Ⓐ Ⓑ Ⓒ Ⓓ	59. Ⓐ Ⓑ Ⓒ Ⓓ
12. Ⓐ Ⓑ Ⓒ Ⓓ	24. Ⓐ Ⓑ Ⓒ Ⓓ	36. Ⓐ Ⓑ Ⓒ Ⓓ	48. Ⓐ Ⓑ Ⓒ Ⓓ	60. Ⓐ Ⓑ Ⓒ Ⓓ

Quantitative Skills

61. Ⓐ Ⓑ Ⓒ Ⓓ	72. Ⓐ Ⓑ Ⓒ Ⓓ	83. Ⓐ Ⓑ Ⓒ Ⓓ	93. Ⓐ Ⓑ Ⓒ Ⓓ	103. Ⓐ Ⓑ Ⓒ Ⓓ
62. Ⓐ Ⓑ Ⓒ Ⓓ	73. Ⓐ Ⓑ Ⓒ Ⓓ	84. Ⓐ Ⓑ Ⓒ Ⓓ	94. Ⓐ Ⓑ Ⓒ Ⓓ	104. Ⓐ Ⓑ Ⓒ Ⓓ
63. Ⓐ Ⓑ Ⓒ Ⓓ	74. Ⓐ Ⓑ Ⓒ Ⓓ	85. Ⓐ Ⓑ Ⓒ Ⓓ	95. Ⓐ Ⓑ Ⓒ Ⓓ	105. Ⓐ Ⓑ Ⓒ Ⓓ
64. Ⓐ Ⓑ Ⓒ Ⓓ	75. Ⓐ Ⓑ Ⓒ Ⓓ	86. Ⓐ Ⓑ Ⓒ Ⓓ	96. Ⓐ Ⓑ Ⓒ Ⓓ	106. Ⓐ Ⓑ Ⓒ Ⓓ
65. Ⓐ Ⓑ Ⓒ Ⓓ	76. Ⓐ Ⓑ Ⓒ Ⓓ	87. Ⓐ Ⓑ Ⓒ Ⓓ	97. Ⓐ Ⓑ Ⓒ Ⓓ	107. Ⓐ Ⓑ Ⓒ Ⓓ
66. Ⓐ Ⓑ Ⓒ Ⓓ	77. Ⓐ Ⓑ Ⓒ Ⓓ	88. Ⓐ Ⓑ Ⓒ Ⓓ	98. Ⓐ Ⓑ Ⓒ Ⓓ	108. Ⓐ Ⓑ Ⓒ Ⓓ
67. Ⓐ Ⓑ Ⓒ Ⓓ	78. Ⓐ Ⓑ Ⓒ Ⓓ	89. Ⓐ Ⓑ Ⓒ Ⓓ	99. Ⓐ Ⓑ Ⓒ Ⓓ	109. Ⓐ Ⓑ Ⓒ Ⓓ
68. Ⓐ Ⓑ Ⓒ Ⓓ	79. Ⓐ Ⓑ Ⓒ Ⓓ	90. Ⓐ Ⓑ Ⓒ Ⓓ	100. Ⓐ Ⓑ Ⓒ Ⓓ	110. Ⓐ Ⓑ Ⓒ Ⓓ
69. Ⓐ Ⓑ Ⓒ Ⓓ	80. Ⓐ Ⓑ Ⓒ Ⓓ	91. Ⓐ Ⓑ Ⓒ Ⓓ	101. Ⓐ Ⓑ Ⓒ Ⓓ	111. Ⓐ Ⓑ Ⓒ Ⓓ
70. Ⓐ Ⓑ Ⓒ Ⓓ	81. Ⓐ Ⓑ Ⓒ Ⓓ	92. Ⓐ Ⓑ Ⓒ Ⓓ	102. Ⓐ Ⓑ Ⓒ Ⓓ	112. Ⓐ Ⓑ Ⓒ Ⓓ
71. Ⓐ Ⓑ Ⓒ Ⓓ	82. Ⓐ Ⓑ Ⓒ Ⓓ			

Reading

113. Ⓐ Ⓑ Ⓒ Ⓓ	126. Ⓐ Ⓑ Ⓒ Ⓓ	139. Ⓐ Ⓑ Ⓒ Ⓓ	152. Ⓐ Ⓑ Ⓒ Ⓓ	165. Ⓐ Ⓑ Ⓒ Ⓓ
114. Ⓐ Ⓑ Ⓒ Ⓓ	127. Ⓐ Ⓑ Ⓒ Ⓓ	140. Ⓐ Ⓑ Ⓒ Ⓓ	153. Ⓐ Ⓑ Ⓒ Ⓓ	166. Ⓐ Ⓑ Ⓒ Ⓓ
115. Ⓐ Ⓑ Ⓒ Ⓓ	128. Ⓐ Ⓑ Ⓒ Ⓓ	141. Ⓐ Ⓑ Ⓒ Ⓓ	154. Ⓐ Ⓑ Ⓒ Ⓓ	167. Ⓐ Ⓑ Ⓒ Ⓓ
116. Ⓐ Ⓑ Ⓒ Ⓓ	129. Ⓐ Ⓑ Ⓒ Ⓓ	142. Ⓐ Ⓑ Ⓒ Ⓓ	155. Ⓐ Ⓑ Ⓒ Ⓓ	168. Ⓐ Ⓑ Ⓒ Ⓓ
117. Ⓐ Ⓑ Ⓒ Ⓓ	130. Ⓐ Ⓑ Ⓒ Ⓓ	143. Ⓐ Ⓑ Ⓒ Ⓓ	156. Ⓐ Ⓑ Ⓒ Ⓓ	169. Ⓐ Ⓑ Ⓒ Ⓓ
118. Ⓐ Ⓑ Ⓒ Ⓓ	131. Ⓐ Ⓑ Ⓒ Ⓓ	144. Ⓐ Ⓑ Ⓒ Ⓓ	157. Ⓐ Ⓑ Ⓒ Ⓓ	170. Ⓐ Ⓑ Ⓒ Ⓓ
119. Ⓐ Ⓑ Ⓒ Ⓓ	132. Ⓐ Ⓑ Ⓒ Ⓓ	145. Ⓐ Ⓑ Ⓒ Ⓓ	158. Ⓐ Ⓑ Ⓒ Ⓓ	171. Ⓐ Ⓑ Ⓒ Ⓓ
120. Ⓐ Ⓑ Ⓒ Ⓓ	133. Ⓐ Ⓑ Ⓒ Ⓓ	146. Ⓐ Ⓑ Ⓒ Ⓓ	159. Ⓐ Ⓑ Ⓒ Ⓓ	172. Ⓐ Ⓑ Ⓒ Ⓓ
121. Ⓐ Ⓑ Ⓒ Ⓓ	134. Ⓐ Ⓑ Ⓒ Ⓓ	147. Ⓐ Ⓑ Ⓒ Ⓓ	160. Ⓐ Ⓑ Ⓒ Ⓓ	173. Ⓐ Ⓑ Ⓒ Ⓓ
122. Ⓐ Ⓑ Ⓒ Ⓓ	135. Ⓐ Ⓑ Ⓒ Ⓓ	148. Ⓐ Ⓑ Ⓒ Ⓓ	161. Ⓐ Ⓑ Ⓒ Ⓓ	174. Ⓐ Ⓑ Ⓒ Ⓓ
123. Ⓐ Ⓑ Ⓒ Ⓓ	136. Ⓐ Ⓑ Ⓒ Ⓓ	149. Ⓐ Ⓑ Ⓒ Ⓓ	162. Ⓐ Ⓑ Ⓒ Ⓓ	
124. Ⓐ Ⓑ Ⓒ Ⓓ	137. Ⓐ Ⓑ Ⓒ Ⓓ	150. Ⓐ Ⓑ Ⓒ Ⓓ	163. Ⓐ Ⓑ Ⓒ Ⓓ	
125. Ⓐ Ⓑ Ⓒ Ⓓ	138. Ⓐ Ⓑ Ⓒ Ⓓ	151. Ⓐ Ⓑ Ⓒ Ⓓ	164. Ⓐ Ⓑ Ⓒ Ⓓ	

Mathematics

175. Ⓐ Ⓑ Ⓒ Ⓓ	188. Ⓐ Ⓑ Ⓒ Ⓓ	201. Ⓐ Ⓑ Ⓒ Ⓓ	214. Ⓐ Ⓑ Ⓒ Ⓓ	227. Ⓐ Ⓑ Ⓒ Ⓓ
176. Ⓐ Ⓑ Ⓒ Ⓓ	189. Ⓐ Ⓑ Ⓒ Ⓓ	202. Ⓐ Ⓑ Ⓒ Ⓓ	215. Ⓐ Ⓑ Ⓒ Ⓓ	228. Ⓐ Ⓑ Ⓒ Ⓓ
177. Ⓐ Ⓑ Ⓒ Ⓓ	190. Ⓐ Ⓑ Ⓒ Ⓓ	203. Ⓐ Ⓑ Ⓒ Ⓓ	216. Ⓐ Ⓑ Ⓒ Ⓓ	229. Ⓐ Ⓑ Ⓒ Ⓓ
178. Ⓐ Ⓑ Ⓒ Ⓓ	191. Ⓐ Ⓑ Ⓒ Ⓓ	204. Ⓐ Ⓑ Ⓒ Ⓓ	217. Ⓐ Ⓑ Ⓒ Ⓓ	230. Ⓐ Ⓑ Ⓒ Ⓓ
179. Ⓐ Ⓑ Ⓒ Ⓓ	192. Ⓐ Ⓑ Ⓒ Ⓓ	205. Ⓐ Ⓑ Ⓒ Ⓓ	218. Ⓐ Ⓑ Ⓒ Ⓓ	231. Ⓐ Ⓑ Ⓒ Ⓓ
180. Ⓐ Ⓑ Ⓒ Ⓓ	193. Ⓐ Ⓑ Ⓒ Ⓓ	206. Ⓐ Ⓑ Ⓒ Ⓓ	219. Ⓐ Ⓑ Ⓒ Ⓓ	232. Ⓐ Ⓑ Ⓒ Ⓓ
181. Ⓐ Ⓑ Ⓒ Ⓓ	194. Ⓐ Ⓑ Ⓒ Ⓓ	207. Ⓐ Ⓑ Ⓒ Ⓓ	220. Ⓐ Ⓑ Ⓒ Ⓓ	233. Ⓐ Ⓑ Ⓒ Ⓓ
182. Ⓐ Ⓑ Ⓒ Ⓓ	195. Ⓐ Ⓑ Ⓒ Ⓓ	208. Ⓐ Ⓑ Ⓒ Ⓓ	221. Ⓐ Ⓑ Ⓒ Ⓓ	234. Ⓐ Ⓑ Ⓒ Ⓓ
183. Ⓐ Ⓑ Ⓒ Ⓓ	196. Ⓐ Ⓑ Ⓒ Ⓓ	209. Ⓐ Ⓑ Ⓒ Ⓓ	222. Ⓐ Ⓑ Ⓒ Ⓓ	235. Ⓐ Ⓑ Ⓒ Ⓓ
184. Ⓐ Ⓑ Ⓒ Ⓓ	197. Ⓐ Ⓑ Ⓒ Ⓓ	210. Ⓐ Ⓑ Ⓒ Ⓓ	223. Ⓐ Ⓑ Ⓒ Ⓓ	236. Ⓐ Ⓑ Ⓒ Ⓓ
185. Ⓐ Ⓑ Ⓒ Ⓓ	198. Ⓐ Ⓑ Ⓒ Ⓓ	211. Ⓐ Ⓑ Ⓒ Ⓓ	224. Ⓐ Ⓑ Ⓒ Ⓓ	237. Ⓐ Ⓑ Ⓒ Ⓓ
186. Ⓐ Ⓑ Ⓒ Ⓓ	199. Ⓐ Ⓑ Ⓒ Ⓓ	212. Ⓐ Ⓑ Ⓒ Ⓓ	225. Ⓐ Ⓑ Ⓒ Ⓓ	238. Ⓐ Ⓑ Ⓒ Ⓓ
187. Ⓐ Ⓑ Ⓒ Ⓓ	200. Ⓐ Ⓑ Ⓒ Ⓓ	213. Ⓐ Ⓑ Ⓒ Ⓓ	226. Ⓐ Ⓑ Ⓒ Ⓓ	

Language

239. Ⓐ Ⓑ Ⓒ Ⓓ	251. Ⓐ Ⓑ Ⓒ Ⓓ	263. Ⓐ Ⓑ Ⓒ Ⓓ	275. Ⓐ Ⓑ Ⓒ Ⓓ	287. Ⓐ Ⓑ Ⓒ Ⓓ
240. Ⓐ Ⓑ Ⓒ Ⓓ	252. Ⓐ Ⓑ Ⓒ Ⓓ	264. Ⓐ Ⓑ Ⓒ Ⓓ	276. Ⓐ Ⓑ Ⓒ Ⓓ	288. Ⓐ Ⓑ Ⓒ Ⓓ
241. Ⓐ Ⓑ Ⓒ Ⓓ	253. Ⓐ Ⓑ Ⓒ Ⓓ	265. Ⓐ Ⓑ Ⓒ Ⓓ	277. Ⓐ Ⓑ Ⓒ Ⓓ	289. Ⓐ Ⓑ Ⓒ Ⓓ
242. Ⓐ Ⓑ Ⓒ Ⓓ	254. Ⓐ Ⓑ Ⓒ Ⓓ	266. Ⓐ Ⓑ Ⓒ Ⓓ	278. Ⓐ Ⓑ Ⓒ Ⓓ	290. Ⓐ Ⓑ Ⓒ Ⓓ
243. Ⓐ Ⓑ Ⓒ Ⓓ	255. Ⓐ Ⓑ Ⓒ Ⓓ	267. Ⓐ Ⓑ Ⓒ Ⓓ	279. Ⓐ Ⓑ Ⓒ Ⓓ	291. Ⓐ Ⓑ Ⓒ Ⓓ
244. Ⓐ Ⓑ Ⓒ Ⓓ	256. Ⓐ Ⓑ Ⓒ Ⓓ	268. Ⓐ Ⓑ Ⓒ Ⓓ	280. Ⓐ Ⓑ Ⓒ Ⓓ	292. Ⓐ Ⓑ Ⓒ Ⓓ
245. Ⓐ Ⓑ Ⓒ Ⓓ	257. Ⓐ Ⓑ Ⓒ Ⓓ	269. Ⓐ Ⓑ Ⓒ Ⓓ	281. Ⓐ Ⓑ Ⓒ Ⓓ	293. Ⓐ Ⓑ Ⓒ Ⓓ
246. Ⓐ Ⓑ Ⓒ Ⓓ	258. Ⓐ Ⓑ Ⓒ Ⓓ	270. Ⓐ Ⓑ Ⓒ Ⓓ	282. Ⓐ Ⓑ Ⓒ Ⓓ	294. Ⓐ Ⓑ Ⓒ Ⓓ
247. Ⓐ Ⓑ Ⓒ Ⓓ	259. Ⓐ Ⓑ Ⓒ Ⓓ	271. Ⓐ Ⓑ Ⓒ Ⓓ	283. Ⓐ Ⓑ Ⓒ Ⓓ	295. Ⓐ Ⓑ Ⓒ Ⓓ
248. Ⓐ Ⓑ Ⓒ Ⓓ	260. Ⓐ Ⓑ Ⓒ Ⓓ	272. Ⓐ Ⓑ Ⓒ Ⓓ	284. Ⓐ Ⓑ Ⓒ Ⓓ	296. Ⓐ Ⓑ Ⓒ Ⓓ
249. Ⓐ Ⓑ Ⓒ Ⓓ	261. Ⓐ Ⓑ Ⓒ Ⓓ	273. Ⓐ Ⓑ Ⓒ Ⓓ	285. Ⓐ Ⓑ Ⓒ Ⓓ	297. Ⓐ Ⓑ Ⓒ Ⓓ
250. Ⓐ Ⓑ Ⓒ Ⓓ	262. Ⓐ Ⓑ Ⓒ Ⓓ	274. Ⓐ Ⓑ Ⓒ Ⓓ	286. Ⓐ Ⓑ Ⓒ Ⓓ	298. Ⓐ Ⓑ Ⓒ Ⓓ

COOP
PRACTICE TEST

Answer Sheet

Photocopy this answer sheet and use it to complete the practice tests.

Sequences

1. Ⓐ Ⓑ Ⓒ Ⓓ	5. Ⓐ Ⓑ Ⓒ Ⓓ	9. Ⓐ Ⓑ Ⓒ Ⓓ	13. Ⓐ Ⓑ Ⓒ Ⓓ	17. Ⓐ Ⓑ Ⓒ Ⓓ
2. Ⓕ Ⓖ Ⓗ Ⓙ	6. Ⓕ Ⓖ Ⓗ Ⓙ	10. Ⓕ Ⓖ Ⓗ Ⓙ	14. Ⓕ Ⓖ Ⓗ Ⓙ	18. Ⓕ Ⓖ Ⓗ Ⓙ
3. Ⓐ Ⓑ Ⓒ Ⓓ	7. Ⓐ Ⓑ Ⓒ Ⓓ	11. Ⓐ Ⓑ Ⓒ Ⓓ	15. Ⓐ Ⓑ Ⓒ Ⓓ	19. Ⓐ Ⓑ Ⓒ Ⓓ
4. Ⓕ Ⓖ Ⓗ Ⓙ	8. Ⓕ Ⓖ Ⓗ Ⓙ	12. Ⓕ Ⓖ Ⓗ Ⓙ	16. Ⓕ Ⓖ Ⓗ Ⓙ	20. Ⓕ Ⓖ Ⓗ Ⓙ

Analogies

1. Ⓐ Ⓑ Ⓒ Ⓓ	5. Ⓐ Ⓑ Ⓒ Ⓓ	9. Ⓐ Ⓑ Ⓒ Ⓓ	13. Ⓐ Ⓑ Ⓒ Ⓓ	17. Ⓐ Ⓑ Ⓒ Ⓓ
2. Ⓕ Ⓖ Ⓗ Ⓙ	6. Ⓕ Ⓖ Ⓗ Ⓙ	10. Ⓕ Ⓖ Ⓗ Ⓙ	14. Ⓕ Ⓖ Ⓗ Ⓙ	18. Ⓕ Ⓖ Ⓗ Ⓙ
3. Ⓐ Ⓑ Ⓒ Ⓓ	7. Ⓐ Ⓑ Ⓒ Ⓓ	11. Ⓐ Ⓑ Ⓒ Ⓓ	15. Ⓐ Ⓑ Ⓒ Ⓓ	19. Ⓐ Ⓑ Ⓒ Ⓓ
4. Ⓕ Ⓖ Ⓗ Ⓙ	8. Ⓕ Ⓖ Ⓗ Ⓙ	12. Ⓕ Ⓖ Ⓗ Ⓙ	16. Ⓕ Ⓖ Ⓗ Ⓙ	20. Ⓕ Ⓖ Ⓗ Ⓙ

Quantitative Reasoning

1. Ⓐ Ⓑ Ⓒ Ⓓ	5. Ⓐ Ⓑ Ⓒ Ⓓ	9. Ⓐ Ⓑ Ⓒ Ⓓ	13. Ⓐ Ⓑ Ⓒ Ⓓ	17. Ⓐ Ⓑ Ⓒ Ⓓ
2. Ⓕ Ⓖ Ⓗ Ⓙ	6. Ⓕ Ⓖ Ⓗ Ⓙ	10. Ⓕ Ⓖ Ⓗ Ⓙ	14. Ⓕ Ⓖ Ⓗ Ⓙ	18. Ⓕ Ⓖ Ⓗ Ⓙ
3. Ⓐ Ⓑ Ⓒ Ⓓ	7. Ⓐ Ⓑ Ⓒ Ⓓ	11. Ⓐ Ⓑ Ⓒ Ⓓ	15. Ⓐ Ⓑ Ⓒ Ⓓ	19. Ⓐ Ⓑ Ⓒ Ⓓ
4. Ⓕ Ⓖ Ⓗ Ⓙ	8. Ⓕ Ⓖ Ⓗ Ⓙ	12. Ⓕ Ⓖ Ⓗ Ⓙ	16. Ⓕ Ⓖ Ⓗ Ⓙ	20. Ⓕ Ⓖ Ⓗ Ⓙ

Verbal Reasoning—Words

1. Ⓐ Ⓑ Ⓒ Ⓓ	5. Ⓐ Ⓑ Ⓒ Ⓓ	9. Ⓐ Ⓑ Ⓒ Ⓓ	13. Ⓐ Ⓑ Ⓒ Ⓓ	17. Ⓐ Ⓑ Ⓒ Ⓓ
2. Ⓕ Ⓖ Ⓗ Ⓙ	6. Ⓕ Ⓖ Ⓗ Ⓙ	10. Ⓕ Ⓖ Ⓗ Ⓙ	14. Ⓕ Ⓖ Ⓗ Ⓙ	18. Ⓕ Ⓖ Ⓗ Ⓙ
3. Ⓐ Ⓑ Ⓒ Ⓓ	7. Ⓐ Ⓑ Ⓒ Ⓓ	11. Ⓐ Ⓑ Ⓒ Ⓓ	15. Ⓐ Ⓑ Ⓒ Ⓓ	19. Ⓐ Ⓑ Ⓒ Ⓓ
4. Ⓕ Ⓖ Ⓗ Ⓙ	8. Ⓕ Ⓖ Ⓗ Ⓙ	12. Ⓕ Ⓖ Ⓗ Ⓙ	16. Ⓕ Ⓖ Ⓗ Ⓙ	20. Ⓕ Ⓖ Ⓗ Ⓙ

Verbal Reasoning—Context

1. Ⓐ Ⓑ Ⓒ Ⓓ	5. Ⓐ Ⓑ Ⓒ Ⓓ	9. Ⓐ Ⓑ Ⓒ Ⓓ	13. Ⓐ Ⓑ Ⓒ Ⓓ	17. Ⓐ Ⓑ Ⓒ Ⓓ
2. Ⓕ Ⓖ Ⓗ Ⓙ	6. Ⓕ Ⓖ Ⓗ Ⓙ	10. Ⓕ Ⓖ Ⓗ Ⓙ	14. Ⓕ Ⓖ Ⓗ Ⓙ	18. Ⓕ Ⓖ Ⓗ Ⓙ
3. Ⓐ Ⓑ Ⓒ Ⓓ	7. Ⓐ Ⓑ Ⓒ Ⓓ	11. Ⓐ Ⓑ Ⓒ Ⓓ	15. Ⓐ Ⓑ Ⓒ Ⓓ	19. Ⓐ Ⓑ Ⓒ Ⓓ
4. Ⓕ Ⓖ Ⓗ Ⓙ	8. Ⓕ Ⓖ Ⓗ Ⓙ	12. Ⓕ Ⓖ Ⓗ Ⓙ	16. Ⓕ Ⓖ Ⓗ Ⓙ	20. Ⓕ Ⓖ Ⓗ Ⓙ

Reading and Language Arts

1. Ⓐ Ⓑ Ⓒ Ⓓ	9. Ⓐ Ⓑ Ⓒ Ⓓ	17. Ⓐ Ⓑ Ⓒ Ⓓ	25. Ⓐ Ⓑ Ⓒ Ⓓ	33. Ⓐ Ⓑ Ⓒ Ⓓ
2. Ⓕ Ⓖ Ⓗ Ⓙ	10. Ⓕ Ⓖ Ⓗ Ⓙ	18. Ⓕ Ⓖ Ⓗ Ⓙ	26. Ⓕ Ⓖ Ⓗ Ⓙ	34. Ⓕ Ⓖ Ⓗ Ⓙ
3. Ⓐ Ⓑ Ⓒ Ⓓ	11. Ⓐ Ⓑ Ⓒ Ⓓ	19. Ⓐ Ⓑ Ⓒ Ⓓ	27. Ⓐ Ⓑ Ⓒ Ⓓ	35. Ⓐ Ⓑ Ⓒ Ⓓ
4. Ⓕ Ⓖ Ⓗ Ⓙ	12. Ⓕ Ⓖ Ⓗ Ⓙ	20. Ⓕ Ⓖ Ⓗ Ⓙ	28. Ⓕ Ⓖ Ⓗ Ⓙ	36. Ⓕ Ⓖ Ⓗ Ⓙ
5. Ⓐ Ⓑ Ⓒ Ⓓ	13. Ⓐ Ⓑ Ⓒ Ⓓ	21. Ⓐ Ⓑ Ⓒ Ⓓ	29. Ⓐ Ⓑ Ⓒ Ⓓ	37. Ⓐ Ⓑ Ⓒ Ⓓ
6. Ⓕ Ⓖ Ⓗ Ⓙ	14. Ⓕ Ⓖ Ⓗ Ⓙ	22. Ⓕ Ⓖ Ⓗ Ⓙ	30. Ⓕ Ⓖ Ⓗ Ⓙ	38. Ⓕ Ⓖ Ⓗ Ⓙ
7. Ⓐ Ⓑ Ⓒ Ⓓ	15. Ⓐ Ⓑ Ⓒ Ⓓ	23. Ⓐ Ⓑ Ⓒ Ⓓ	31. Ⓐ Ⓑ Ⓒ Ⓓ	39. Ⓐ Ⓑ Ⓒ Ⓓ
8. Ⓕ Ⓖ Ⓗ Ⓙ	16. Ⓕ Ⓖ Ⓗ Ⓙ	24. Ⓕ Ⓖ Ⓗ Ⓙ	32. Ⓕ Ⓖ Ⓗ Ⓙ	40. Ⓕ Ⓖ Ⓗ Ⓙ

Mathematics

1. Ⓐ Ⓑ Ⓒ Ⓓ	9. Ⓐ Ⓑ Ⓒ Ⓓ	17. Ⓐ Ⓑ Ⓒ Ⓓ	25. Ⓐ Ⓑ Ⓒ Ⓓ	33. Ⓐ Ⓑ Ⓒ Ⓓ
2. Ⓕ Ⓖ Ⓗ Ⓙ	10. Ⓕ Ⓖ Ⓗ Ⓙ	18. Ⓕ Ⓖ Ⓗ Ⓙ	26. Ⓕ Ⓖ Ⓗ Ⓙ	34. Ⓕ Ⓖ Ⓗ Ⓙ
3. Ⓐ Ⓑ Ⓒ Ⓓ	11. Ⓐ Ⓑ Ⓒ Ⓓ	19. Ⓐ Ⓑ Ⓒ Ⓓ	27. Ⓐ Ⓑ Ⓒ Ⓓ	35. Ⓐ Ⓑ Ⓒ Ⓓ
4. Ⓕ Ⓖ Ⓗ Ⓙ	12. Ⓕ Ⓖ Ⓗ Ⓙ	20. Ⓕ Ⓖ Ⓗ Ⓙ	28. Ⓕ Ⓖ Ⓗ Ⓙ	36. Ⓕ Ⓖ Ⓗ Ⓙ
5. Ⓐ Ⓑ Ⓒ Ⓓ	13. Ⓐ Ⓑ Ⓒ Ⓓ	21. Ⓐ Ⓑ Ⓒ Ⓓ	29. Ⓐ Ⓑ Ⓒ Ⓓ	37. Ⓐ Ⓑ Ⓒ Ⓓ
6. Ⓕ Ⓖ Ⓗ Ⓙ	14. Ⓕ Ⓖ Ⓗ Ⓙ	22. Ⓕ Ⓖ Ⓗ Ⓙ	30. Ⓕ Ⓖ Ⓗ Ⓙ	38. Ⓕ Ⓖ Ⓗ Ⓙ
7. Ⓐ Ⓑ Ⓒ Ⓓ	15. Ⓐ Ⓑ Ⓒ Ⓓ	23. Ⓐ Ⓑ Ⓒ Ⓓ	31. Ⓐ Ⓑ Ⓒ Ⓓ	39. Ⓐ Ⓑ Ⓒ Ⓓ
8. Ⓕ Ⓖ Ⓗ Ⓙ	16. Ⓕ Ⓖ Ⓗ Ⓙ	24. Ⓕ Ⓖ Ⓗ Ⓙ	32. Ⓕ Ⓖ Ⓗ Ⓙ	40. Ⓕ Ⓖ Ⓗ Ⓙ

TACHS
PRACTICE TEST

Answer Sheet

Photocopy this answer sheet and use it to complete the practice tests.

Reading

1. Ⓐ Ⓑ Ⓒ Ⓓ	11. Ⓐ Ⓑ Ⓒ Ⓓ	21. Ⓐ Ⓑ Ⓒ Ⓓ	31. Ⓐ Ⓑ Ⓒ Ⓓ	41. Ⓐ Ⓑ Ⓒ Ⓓ
2. Ⓙ Ⓚ Ⓛ Ⓜ	12. Ⓙ Ⓚ Ⓛ Ⓜ	22. Ⓙ Ⓚ Ⓛ Ⓜ	32. Ⓙ Ⓚ Ⓛ Ⓜ	42. Ⓙ Ⓚ Ⓛ Ⓜ
3. Ⓐ Ⓑ Ⓒ Ⓓ	13. Ⓐ Ⓑ Ⓒ Ⓓ	23. Ⓐ Ⓑ Ⓒ Ⓓ	33. Ⓐ Ⓑ Ⓒ Ⓓ	43. Ⓐ Ⓑ Ⓒ Ⓓ
4. Ⓙ Ⓚ Ⓛ Ⓜ	14. Ⓙ Ⓚ Ⓛ Ⓜ	24. Ⓙ Ⓚ Ⓛ Ⓜ	34. Ⓙ Ⓚ Ⓛ Ⓜ	44. Ⓙ Ⓚ Ⓛ Ⓜ
5. Ⓐ Ⓑ Ⓒ Ⓓ	15. Ⓐ Ⓑ Ⓒ Ⓓ	25. Ⓐ Ⓑ Ⓒ Ⓓ	35. Ⓐ Ⓑ Ⓒ Ⓓ	45. Ⓐ Ⓑ Ⓒ Ⓓ
6. Ⓙ Ⓚ Ⓛ Ⓜ	16. Ⓙ Ⓚ Ⓛ Ⓜ	26. Ⓙ Ⓚ Ⓛ Ⓜ	36. Ⓙ Ⓚ Ⓛ Ⓜ	46. Ⓙ Ⓚ Ⓛ Ⓜ
7. Ⓐ Ⓑ Ⓒ Ⓓ	17. Ⓐ Ⓑ Ⓒ Ⓓ	27. Ⓐ Ⓑ Ⓒ Ⓓ	37. Ⓐ Ⓑ Ⓒ Ⓓ	47. Ⓐ Ⓑ Ⓒ Ⓓ
8. Ⓙ Ⓚ Ⓛ Ⓜ	18. Ⓙ Ⓚ Ⓛ Ⓜ	28. Ⓙ Ⓚ Ⓛ Ⓜ	38. Ⓙ Ⓚ Ⓛ Ⓜ	48. Ⓙ Ⓚ Ⓛ Ⓜ
9. Ⓐ Ⓑ Ⓒ Ⓓ	19. Ⓐ Ⓑ Ⓒ Ⓓ	29. Ⓐ Ⓑ Ⓒ Ⓓ	39. Ⓐ Ⓑ Ⓒ Ⓓ	49. Ⓐ Ⓑ Ⓒ Ⓓ
10. Ⓙ Ⓚ Ⓛ Ⓜ	20. Ⓙ Ⓚ Ⓛ Ⓜ	30. Ⓙ Ⓚ Ⓛ Ⓜ	40. Ⓙ Ⓚ Ⓛ Ⓜ	50. Ⓙ Ⓚ Ⓛ Ⓜ

Language

1. Ⓐ Ⓑ Ⓒ Ⓓ	9. Ⓐ Ⓑ Ⓒ Ⓓ	17. Ⓐ Ⓑ Ⓒ Ⓓ	25. Ⓐ Ⓑ Ⓒ Ⓓ	33. Ⓐ Ⓑ Ⓒ Ⓓ
2. Ⓙ Ⓚ Ⓛ Ⓜ	10. Ⓙ Ⓚ Ⓛ Ⓜ	18. Ⓙ Ⓚ Ⓛ Ⓜ	26. Ⓙ Ⓚ Ⓛ Ⓜ	34. Ⓙ Ⓚ Ⓛ Ⓜ
3. Ⓐ Ⓑ Ⓒ Ⓓ	11. Ⓐ Ⓑ Ⓒ Ⓓ	19. Ⓐ Ⓑ Ⓒ Ⓓ	27. Ⓐ Ⓑ Ⓒ Ⓓ	35. Ⓐ Ⓑ Ⓒ Ⓓ
4. Ⓙ Ⓚ Ⓛ Ⓜ	12. Ⓙ Ⓚ Ⓛ Ⓜ	20. Ⓙ Ⓚ Ⓛ Ⓜ	28. Ⓙ Ⓚ Ⓛ Ⓜ	36. Ⓙ Ⓚ Ⓛ Ⓜ
5. Ⓐ Ⓑ Ⓒ Ⓓ	13. Ⓐ Ⓑ Ⓒ Ⓓ	21. Ⓐ Ⓑ Ⓒ Ⓓ	29. Ⓐ Ⓑ Ⓒ Ⓓ	37. Ⓐ Ⓑ Ⓒ Ⓓ
6. Ⓙ Ⓚ Ⓛ Ⓜ	14. Ⓙ Ⓚ Ⓛ Ⓜ	22. Ⓙ Ⓚ Ⓛ Ⓜ	30. Ⓙ Ⓚ Ⓛ Ⓜ	38. Ⓙ Ⓚ Ⓛ Ⓜ
7. Ⓐ Ⓑ Ⓒ Ⓓ	15. Ⓐ Ⓑ Ⓒ Ⓓ	23. Ⓐ Ⓑ Ⓒ Ⓓ	31. Ⓐ Ⓑ Ⓒ Ⓓ	39. Ⓐ Ⓑ Ⓒ Ⓓ
8. Ⓙ Ⓚ Ⓛ Ⓜ	16. Ⓙ Ⓚ Ⓛ Ⓜ	24. Ⓙ Ⓚ Ⓛ Ⓜ	32. Ⓙ Ⓚ Ⓛ Ⓜ	40. Ⓙ Ⓚ Ⓛ Ⓜ

Math

1. Ⓐ Ⓑ Ⓒ Ⓓ	9. Ⓐ Ⓑ Ⓒ Ⓓ	17. Ⓐ Ⓑ Ⓒ Ⓓ	25. Ⓐ Ⓑ Ⓒ Ⓓ	33. Ⓐ Ⓑ Ⓒ Ⓓ
2. Ⓙ Ⓚ Ⓛ Ⓜ	10. Ⓙ Ⓚ Ⓛ Ⓜ	18. Ⓙ Ⓚ Ⓛ Ⓜ	26. Ⓙ Ⓚ Ⓛ Ⓜ	34. Ⓙ Ⓚ Ⓛ Ⓜ
3. Ⓐ Ⓑ Ⓒ Ⓓ	11. Ⓐ Ⓑ Ⓒ Ⓓ	19. Ⓐ Ⓑ Ⓒ Ⓓ	27. Ⓐ Ⓑ Ⓒ Ⓓ	35. Ⓐ Ⓑ Ⓒ Ⓓ
4. Ⓙ Ⓚ Ⓛ Ⓜ	12. Ⓙ Ⓚ Ⓛ Ⓜ	20. Ⓙ Ⓚ Ⓛ Ⓜ	28. Ⓙ Ⓚ Ⓛ Ⓜ	36. Ⓙ Ⓚ Ⓛ Ⓜ
5. Ⓐ Ⓑ Ⓒ Ⓓ	13. Ⓐ Ⓑ Ⓒ Ⓓ	21. Ⓐ Ⓑ Ⓒ Ⓓ	29. Ⓐ Ⓑ Ⓒ Ⓓ	37. Ⓐ Ⓑ Ⓒ Ⓓ
6. Ⓙ Ⓚ Ⓛ Ⓜ	14. Ⓙ Ⓚ Ⓛ Ⓜ	22. Ⓙ Ⓚ Ⓛ Ⓜ	30. Ⓙ Ⓚ Ⓛ Ⓜ	38. Ⓙ Ⓚ Ⓛ Ⓜ
7. Ⓐ Ⓑ Ⓒ Ⓓ	15. Ⓐ Ⓑ Ⓒ Ⓓ	23. Ⓐ Ⓑ Ⓒ Ⓓ	31. Ⓐ Ⓑ Ⓒ Ⓓ	39. Ⓐ Ⓑ Ⓒ Ⓓ
8. Ⓙ Ⓚ Ⓛ Ⓜ	16. Ⓙ Ⓚ Ⓛ Ⓜ	24. Ⓙ Ⓚ Ⓛ Ⓜ	32. Ⓙ Ⓚ Ⓛ Ⓜ	40. Ⓙ Ⓚ Ⓛ Ⓜ

Ability

1. Ⓐ Ⓑ Ⓒ Ⓓ	3. Ⓐ Ⓑ Ⓒ Ⓓ	5. Ⓐ Ⓑ Ⓒ Ⓓ	7. Ⓐ Ⓑ Ⓒ Ⓓ	9. Ⓐ Ⓑ Ⓒ Ⓓ
2. Ⓙ Ⓚ Ⓛ Ⓜ	4. Ⓙ Ⓚ Ⓛ Ⓜ	6. Ⓙ Ⓚ Ⓛ Ⓜ	8. Ⓙ Ⓚ Ⓛ Ⓜ	10. Ⓙ Ⓚ Ⓛ Ⓜ

REA's Test Preps
The Best in Test Preparation

- REA "Test Preps" are **far more** comprehensive than any other test preparation series
- Each book contains full-length practice tests based on the most recent exams
- **Every** type of question likely to be given on the exams is included
- Answers are accompanied by **full** and **detailed** explanations

REA publishes hundreds of test prep books. Some of our titles include:

Advanced Placement Exams (APs)
Art History
Biology
Calculus AB & BC
Chemistry
Economics
English Language & Composition
English Literature & Composition
European History
French Language
Government & Politics
Latin
Physics B & C
Psychology
Spanish Language
Statistics
United States History
World History

College-Level Examination Program (CLEP)
Analyzing and Interpreting Literature
College Algebra
Freshman College Composition
General Examinations
History of the United States I
History of the United States II
Introduction to Educational Psychology
Human Growth and Development
Introductory Psychology
Introductory Sociology
Principles of Management
Principles of Marketing
Spanish
Western Civilization I
Western Civilization II

SAT Subject Tests
Biology E/M
Chemistry
French
German
Literature
Mathematics Level 1, 2
Physics
Spanish
United States History

Graduate Record Exams (GREs)
Biology
Chemistry
Computer Science
General
Literature in English
Mathematics
Physics
Psychology

ACT - ACT Assessment

ASVAB - Armed Services Vocational Aptitude Battery

CBEST - California Basic Educational Skills Test

CDL - Commercial Driver License Exam

CLAST - College Level Academic Skills Test

COOP, HSPT & TACHS - Catholic High School Admission Tests

FE (EIT) - Fundamentals of Engineering Exams

FTCE - Florida Teacher Certification Examinations

GED

GMAT - Graduate Management Admission Test

LSAT - Law School Admission Test

MAT - Miller Analogies Test

MCAT - Medical College Admission Test

MTEL - Massachusetts Tests for Educator Licensure

NJ HSPA - New Jersey High School Proficiency Assessment

NYSTCE - New York State Teacher Certification Examinations

PRAXIS PLT - Principles of Learning & Teaching Tests

PRAXIS PPST - Pre-Professional Skills Tests

PSAT/NMSQT

SAT

TExES - Texas Examinations of Educator Standards

THEA - Texas Higher Education Assessment

TOEFL - Test of English as a Foreign Language

USMLE Steps 1,2,3 - U.S. Medical Licensing Exams

For information about any of REA's books, visit www.rea.com

Research & Education Association
61 Ethel Road W., Piscataway, NJ 08854
Phone: (732) 819-8880

Installing REA's TestWare®

System Requirements

Pentium 75 MHz (300 MHz recommended), or a higher or compatible processor; Microsoft Windows 98 or later; 64 MB available RAM; Internet Explorer 5.5 or higher.

Installation

1. Insert the Catholic High School Entrance Exams (CHSEE) TestWare® CD-ROM into the CD-ROM drive.
2. If the installation doesn't begin automatically, from the Start Menu choose the RUN command. When the RUN dialog box appears, type d:\setup (where d is the letter of your CD-ROM drive) at the prompt and click OK.
3. The installation process will begin. A dialog box proposing the directory "C:\Program Files\REA\CHSEE" will appear. If the name and location are suitable, click OK. If you wish to specify a different name or location, type it in and click OK.
4. Start the CHSEE TestWare® application by double-clicking on the icon.

REA's CHSEE TestWare® is **EASY** to **LEARN AND USE**. To archieve maximum benefits, we recommend that you take a few minutes to go through the on-screen tutorial on your computer.

Technical Support

REA's TestWare® is backed by customer and technical support. For questions about **installation or operation of your software,** contact us at:

Research & Education Association
Phone: (732) 819-8808 (9 a.m. to 5 p.m. ET, Monday–Friday)
Fax: (732) 819-8808
Website: www.rea.com
E-mail: info@rea.com

Note to Windows XP Users: In order for the TestWare® to function properly, please install and run the application under the same computer administrator-level user account. Installing the TestWare® as one user and running it as another could cause file-access path conflicts.